DATE DUE

ESCAPE FROM THE FUTURE

VLADIMIR PETROV

Escape from the Future

The Incredible Adventures
of a Young Russian

INDIANA UNIVERSITY PRESS   •   BLOOMINGTON & LONDON

Publishd in Canada by Fitzhenry & Whiteside Limited, Don Mills, Ontario
Library of Congress catalog card number: 73-80380
ISBN: 0-253-12360-7 cl; 0-253-20172-1 pa
Manufactured in the United States of America

In memory of those who never came back

"Out of this nettle, danger,
we pluck this flower, safety."

Henry IV, Pt. I, Act II, Sc. iii, ll. 11-12.

CONTENTS

Chapter   Page

Book One. SOVIET GOLD

PREFACE   ix

Part I. The Making of a Prisoner

1. THE BIG HOUSE   17
2. PRISONS OF THE CITY OF LENIN   48
3. IN THE TRAIN   97

Part II. The Mines of Kolyma

4. MAGADAN – CAPITAL OF THE KOLYMA   119
5. MY FIRST ACQUAINTANCE WITH THE MINES   138
6. IN CAMP KHATTYNAKH   157

Part III. Black Times in the Gold Fields

7. BLACK TIMES   175
8. A HARD WINTER   202
9. AT THE BOTTOM   225

Part IV. The Way to Freedom

10. ON THE WAY TO FREEDOM   255

Book Two. ESCAPE

Part I. Through Fighting Russia

1. EXTRAORDINARY BULLETIN   275
2. MAGADAN   279
3. THE OPEN SEA   283
4. THE FAR EAST AT WAR   287
5. LIFE ON THE RAILWAY   295
6. INTERLUDE IN ALMA ATA   302
7. ACROSS THE CASPIAN SEA   312
8. HOME   324
9. A 'WOLF'S TICKET'   327

Part II. Under German Occupation

Chapter   *Page*

10. THE FIRST DAYS   337

11. THE SLIPPERY WAY   345

12. CITY FATHERS   354

13. FLIGHT   373

14. A FREE ENTERPRISE   381

15. IN TRANSNISTRIA   396

Part III. Europe

16. RUMANIA, VANISHING EDEN   407

17. EXCELLENCIES AND GENERALS   412

18. INTRODUCTION TO VIENNA   418

19. AMERICAN BOMBS   429

20. UNDER ST. ANDREW'S FLAG   434

21. THE CRASH   447

22. WESTWARD   456

    EPILOGUE   469

    MAP   xii-xiii

PREFACE

MEMOIRS ARE COMMONLY WRITTEN at the end of active life as the author
records for the benefit of posterity what appears in retrospect to have
been the most significant and colorful of his experiences. Occasionally
the story is told at an earlier stage, especially if the author has an
important message to convey.

My reminiscences seem to be somewhat different. When I began
putting them on paper twenty-five years ago, my major concern was to
record what I had witnessed while the memory of detail was still fresh.
I did not feel that my story was exceptional in itself, for there was
little that had set me apart from hundreds and thousands of people I
had encountered during the years I wanted to describe. I knew there
was little heroic in what I did; my own role in the events was important
only infrequently; more often than not I was closer to the bottom of
the pile than the top. I would have probably eliminated the first person
pronoun altogether except that this would have converted my story
into a work of fiction.

As to the message, initially I didn't think about it. Although I
wanted the reader to know how bad the conditions were in Stalin's
concentration camps, my instinct was to understate the case; some of
the more depressing episodes I witnessed, I deliberately left out. It was
not my intent to shock the reader. In fact, my tale is much more
optimistic in tone than Solzhenitsyn's *One Day in the Life of Ivan Deniso-
vich*, published in Russia a decade later.

This optimism notwithstanding, when my *Soviet Gold* appeared in
1949, two years after my arrival in this country, it was received by
many reviewers and readers as a contribution to America's cold war
effort. The follow-up volume, *My Retreat From Russia*, published in 1950,
evoked a more mixed reaction. While already struggling against communism, the United States was still emotionally fighting Nazi Germany
and anyone who admitted any kind of collaboration with the Germans
was (and in places still is) regarded distinctly less than a hero. I now
suspect that it was for this reason that the combined and somewhat
abridged volume, initially published in London in 1951 and now re-
produced here, contained a much fuller version of *Soviet Gold* than of
My Retreat From Russia.

Such a disparate treatment appeared to me unjustifiable, for there

was in fact an organic unity to the whole story, a completed chapter of
one's lifetime. In the present publication, I am leaving the British
edition intact, save for the elimination of two paragraphs (inserted in
the original text on the advice of the publishers) in which I declare my
undying hatred for communism. This does not mean that I have made
my peace with communism. It only means that my political feelings
have never been terribly intense. I am simply not, and have never been,
a crusader.

Today, from a distance of a quarter of a century, I view my past
with detachment, feeling neither pride nor remorse for my deeds. For
all intents and purposes everything described in my book is a closed
page. Unlike so many first generation Americans, I broke away early
from immigrants' life and interests, and no one can undergo integration
in the American society (and acquire, as I did, nine children born to
him in this country) and hope to preserve the continuity of his total life
experience. Much as my outlook remains colored by my origin and the
fact that the first half of my life I lived elsewhere, Mother Russia does
not provide a sentimental framework for my present. It never did.

In this estrangement, I am not unique in my generation. To a
different degree and in different ways, this feeling is common even
among the Soviet survivors of the cataclysmic years of Stalin's terror
and the butchery of the war. For better or worse, today's Russia is not
the country of their youth.

Thus my memoirs, having lost the significance of a political document, remain a chronicle, a narrative of a young man, with taste for
adventure and acute interest in fellow human beings, uprooted early
in life and drawn into the maelstrom of great events of the period. He
tried to stay alive, naturally, but also, whenever possible, be on top
rather than drift helplessly with the current. His skepticism and sense
of humor were of help but his proclivity for challenging the high and
the mighty—and mischief for mischief's sake—recurrently got him into
trouble. In the end he did well but probably more because of sheer luck
(or thanks to Divine Providence) than because of his resourcefulness.
Others may conclude differently, but this is the way I read this man's
story today.

Washington, D. C.   VLADIMIR PETROV

May 1973

Berlin
Leningrad
Moscow
Milan Salzburg Karlsbad
Vienna Prague Warsaw
Lienz Krakow
Lvov Kiev
Stryj
Belgrade Timişoara Złoczynka
Bucharest Zaporozhe
Odessa
Black Sea
"My City"
Makhachkala
Krasnovodsk
Tashkent
Ashkhabad

U. S.

Caspian Sea

Sea

---- My journey east to camp

—— My journey west through the U.S.S.R.

········ My journey through Europe

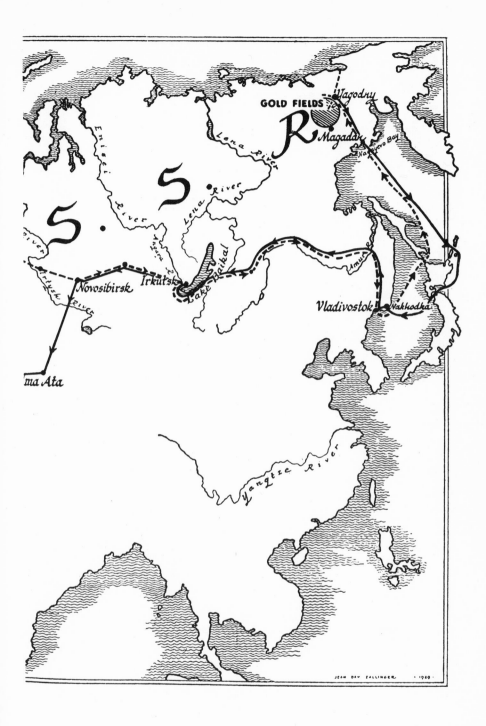

Book One

SOVIET GOLD

Part I. The Making of a Prisoner

1. THE BIG HOUSE

FOR many years there had been a tense feeling in the air, but the winter of 1934–35 found the residents of Leningrad under more than ordinary strain. On December 1, 1934, Sergei Kirov, the all-powerful head of the Leningrad province, and personal appointee of Stalin, was murdered. The assassin was a young man named Nikolayev.

The political purpose behind this assassination is a mystery. But there was nothing mysterious about the wave of government-prompted terror which followed Kirov's death. It rolled over all Russia, and crashed upon the inhabitants of the City of Lenin.

There is a saying in Soviet Russia: 'Thieves, prostitutes, and the N.K.V.D. work mostly at night.' As night fell over the city, passers-by hugged the dark entrances of the houses when they saw the peculiarly shaped ghostlike automobiles known as Black Ravens. Such a car would stop outside a chosen house. Several men wearing the dreaded blue peaked caps with red bands would jump off and step quickly into the darkened house where the residents pretended to be asleep. The men of the family would be roused from their beds, taken out of the house and shoved into the already packed windowless automobile. The Black Raven would speed off leaving behind a sobbing mother, wife, and children, and a home turned topsy-turvy.

Or, the deft agents of the N.K.V.D. would set a mousetrap in a suspect apartment. Anybody could go in, but nobody could come out. The agents would wait patiently for two or three days, if need be, until the apartment or room was filled with friends and acquaintances of the occupant. Then up would roll the Black Raven and drive away with those captured in the trap.

I was arrested on the night of February 17, 1935. Like all others caught in that wave of reprisals, during my entire stay in N.K.V.D. prisons and concentration camps I was given the honorary title of a 'Kirov man'. Actually, I had no connection in any conceivable way with Kirov's murder.

Just nineteen at the time of my arrest, I was a student in one of the technical institutes in Leningrad. I was diligent and quite proficient in my studies, and as for politics, my interest was strictly confined within the limits graciously set down from on high for us Soviet citizens. I did not regard the Soviet regime as the best in the world, but neither did I think of it as exceptionally bad.

All I knew of political terror in the country was based upon vague rumours, and it never seemed as widespread and terrible as it was. What appeared at that time to be the errors of the Soviet government, such as forcible collectivization of peasant holdings and the famine of the early thirties, I blamed partly on the wrecking activities of counter-revolutionary elements in the ruling circles and partly on forgivable slips in Soviet domestic policies. As a matter of fact, I viewed the Soviet government in an optimistic light and felt sure that in due time everything would be straightened out. There was no justifiable legal reason for my arrest that February night.

This most important event in my life was the final link in a long chain of circumstances which had seemed too insignificant to me to deserve much attention.

It all began with a conversation which in itself was an unavoidable part of a student's existence. Soon after I had joined one of the technical institutes in Leningrad, I was summoned to the so-called *Spetsotdel* (Special Section) of the institute, an office of odious reputation which exists in every Soviet institution. Everyone knew that in addition to its official function which was the registration of students for universal military training, the Special Section also performed unofficial duties in reporting on political attitudes of students, and in gathering information about them in ways both open and secret. I was conscious of my complete loyalty to the Soviet regime, but aware of the extreme suspiciousness of the functionaries who acted as local representatives of the all-powerful N.K.V.D., I went to that office with no feeling of joy.

When I entered the small room of the Special Section which was lined with filing cases containing students' records, I was somewhat disappointed to find, sitting at the table, a cheerful round-faced girl of about twenty-six. She invited me to take a seat, and with a broad smile began to ask routine questions, entering my answers in a bulky questionnaire. This work over, we talked for a while about various things, then parted, both obviously pleased with each other. Before I left, the girl told me her name was Nadya and that she would be glad to see me as often as I might wish to call.

This acquaintanceship was not followed up for some time. Not that I felt any antipathy for Nadya – as a matter of fact I did not – but rather the knowledge that she was an agent of the N.K.V.D. acted as a deterrent, keeping me away from calling at the Special Section unless obliged to do so. Moreover, although I was already nineteen, I did not believe as other students did in carrying on indiscriminately with various girls; for another girl, of whom no one in the institute knew anything, already held a firm place in my heart.

The next link in the chain of circumstances which ended in my arrest I forged myself at one of the dancing parties regularly held at my institute. I was in a happy mood, and although I could not dance, kept joining in the dances. It so happened that on several occasions Nadya, who wore a lownecked dress, was my partner. I was in fine fettle, regaled her with talk which made her laugh incessantly, trod on her toes while waltzing, and showered her with compliments until her eyes sparkled. When the party was over she demanded that I see her home. I fell in readily, but when we reached her house, I declined her invitation to go in, excusing myself by the lateness of the hour.

A few days later I was summoned to the Special Section. Nadya was amiable but serious. We talked about one thing and another, and I spoke on the subject which interested me most at that time – my studies in history. Nadya expressed a desire to extend her education and asked me to bring her books I would recommend for her reading. I responded promptly, and the next day brought her a couple of books of a historico-philosophical nature.

Then an event took place which, little as it had to do with the life in my institute, nevertheless supplied a new link in my progress toward jail. It was the assassination of Kirov. At that time I was not particularly interested in who killed him or why. To be sure, there was a meeting in the great hall of the institute at which we unanimously passed a resolution, submitted by the secretary of our Communist party unit, which demanded stern punishment for the murderers. But with this, it seemed, the whole matter was over. There were rumours soon after that a number of students and one or two professors were put under arrest, but nobody paid much attention to that, since arrests were a pretty common thing in Soviet life, and besides we believed that if people were arrested they were certainly implicated in anti-Soviet or criminal activities. Then, rumours spread that arrests on a mass scale were being made all over the city. When anyone mentioned this to me I only shrugged my shoulders, refraining from any discussion of what was unquestionably a delicate subject. And when asked point blank what I thought of the matter I answered, aware of great numbers of informers among the students, that if people were arrested it was probably for good reason.

One day I stopped in at Nadya's office to give her one more book and a couple of illustrated foreign magazines I had received from a friend who had permission to subscribe for them. Nadya was very busy, but was pleased to see me and said she had made a resolution to teach me how to dance. She made me promise her that I would come to her room especially for that purpose a few days later.

The evening I agreed to meet Nadya I had nothing else to do, and so arrived early, at about eight o'clock. She occupied a little room in a large house. She lived modestly, but was able to treat me to an excellent supper with an accompaniment of foreign dance music, of which she had records in considerable number. After supper Nadya spoke to me about her life; how badly it had turned out, how she had to break up with her husband, how lonely she was, and how she detested the secret work she had to do. I was a sympathetic listener, although something in her manner, in the significance of her glances, made me feel ill at ease. This feeling became still more intense when Nadya locked her door, and putting her arm on my shoulder said, 'Now, let's dance.'

The dancing lesson was a failure. Either because the room with its large bed was too small, or because Nadya clung to me much too tightly, I proved to be a dullard in picking up the steps of foxtrot and tango. Finally Nadya's eyes began to glow with such fire that I abruptly broke off our dance and stated categorically that I had to go home.

'What's the hurry?' Nadya asked in a tone of reproach.

'It's late. I have to be at the institute at eight in the morning, and it's a long way to my home,' I answered.

'Nonsense. It's only twelve o'clock. If the worst comes to the worst, you can stay here – we'll manage some way. And the institute is only a short distance from here.'

Nadya's suggestion that I spend the night with her enhanced my desire to leave. By now I regretted I had come at all. Adamantly I bade her goodnight.

'You're making a mistake, Vladimir,' she said, underscoring the word 'mistake'. 'It would be better in every way if you stayed.'

I left. On the way to my hostelry I could not shake off the unpleasant sensation that I had done something I should not have done.

A week passed, and Nadya again called me to the Special Section. She looked worn out, and was blue under the eyes. Locking the door and continuing to stand, she asked, 'Well, how did you like the dancing lesson?'

I muttered something inarticulate.

'Shall we repeat it tonight?'

'No, Nadya. I'm busy tonight. I have to go to work.'

'I don't believe you. Come, we'll have a fine time. Please, Vladimir.'

'No, Nadya. It would be better if I don't come.'

'Why? Am I so distasteful to you?'

'Not at all. But this may lead us too far – these dancing lessons, I mean.'

'Are you afraid of that?' Nadya asked in a low voice, staring at me. 'What's disturbing you? Is it the fact that I'm six years older than you?'

'How ridiculous!' I exclaimed. 'I've never given that a moment's thought. But I give you my word of honour that for the present I'm interested in nothing except my studies. Some time later, perhaps . . .'

Nadya took my hands into her own, and looking at me with almost tragic eyes, said, 'This cannot be. I'll be frank with you. I want us to live together. I earn a good living, and you will have everything you need, so you'll be able to go on with your studies without any worries. But you must move over to my place. If you think my room is too small, I'll find another one. Think it over.'

I shook my head. For various reasons I could not possibly accept Nadya's offer. I got up.

'Thank you, Nadya. I'm sure your intentions are of the best. I like you very much, but not enough to make me venture on such a step.' I paused. 'At least, not now,' I added hastily noticing Nadya's frown.

She sat down, and without looking at me asked:

'You have another girl? I've made inquiries, and as far as I know you have no friends outside the institute, except for two artists.'

'Oho!' I thought. 'Things must have gone pretty far if Nadya is conducting inquiries among my friends.' Aloud I told a lie:

'You're quite right. I have no friends in Leningrad outside the institute – I haven't been here long. But this doesn't change the situation, Nadya dear, and I can give no other answer to your suggestion than the one I've already given.'

'All right, you can go,' she said, opening the door. 'Go and think it over. I give you three days, then I'll expect your answer. Consider all the circumstances and bear in mind everything I can do.'

Her last words sounded as if they carried special significance, and I thought I detected a threatening note in them. But unpleasant as my impression of the conversation was, I failed to see its true significance. I was too naïve at that time. I regarded myself as an impeccable Soviet citizen who could have no fears of the N.K.V.D. for which Nadya worked. That's why, when three days later she spotted me in a hall and leading me aside asked:

'Well, what's your answer?'

I replied with a single word: 'No.'

Her face turned dark as she looked at me and forebodingly said: 'You may be sorry for this one day.'

And so we parted.

Events rapidly fulfilled her prophecy. In fact, they did that same day. At that time, after lecture hours, except when I went to my job of unloading freight cars which I did to earn enough money for food, I slept in a students' hostelry. When I returned to the hostelry in the evening after breaking off with Nadya, I found a package of books lying on my bed. My room mates told me the package had been brought by a young man who said Nadya was returning some books I had loaned her. I looked at the titles and was surprised to discover that, with the exception of a couple of volumes that were actually mine, the rest were unfamiliar works that I did not own and had never read. What's more, they were all by authors with politically damaging reputations such as

Trotsky, Bukharin, Zinoviev and others – all leaders of the anti-Stalin opposition in the Communist party.

I concluded that there had been a misunderstanding, tossed the bundle on a shelf, and went to bed, deciding to clear up the matter next day. I was awakened in the middle of the night by a loud knocking on the door. A drunken student trying to get into the wrong room, I thought – and told the late visitor to go to hell. Then came a loud rattling, the door hook gave way, the light was switched on, and there stood three armed men in the familiar blue peaked caps, accompanied by the manager of the hostelry.

'Hands up!' The leader of the group had a quiet but authoritative voice. 'Which one here is Petrov?'

Obediently I drew my hands from under the blanket, and raised them.

'Get up!' came the sharp command. With my hands still raised I got out of bed and stood against the wall, shivering with fear and cold. From the other beds three pairs of eyes gazed in horror and sympathy. Their owners lay with absurdly lifted arms.

The senior member of the police group who had two bars on the collar of his uniform, barked, 'Which are your things?' His gun pointed in my direction.

Silently I indicated with my foot a couple of suitcases under the bed. My belongings, the entire worldly possessions of a poor Soviet student, were instantly emptied on the floor, and the armed men began sorting them. Letters and photographs were put aside in one heap. A volume of Shakespeare in English, which my visitors were evidently unable to identify, was added; also a folder with a collection of stamps, the fruit of many years loving effort, and, after some hesitation, a Waterman fountain pen, a gift from my father which I never saw again.

Then the chief looked in his notebook and asked where I kept my books. I nodded toward the bookshelf, and confirming my suspicions, he unhesitatingly picked the bundle which had been sent by Nadya a few hours before. The search was ended.

'Get dressed!'

I obeyed with dispatch.

'Walk down the stairs!'

The commiserating glances of my room mates followed through the doorway. Behind me walked the chief with a gun in his hand and two N.K.V.D. soldiers with rifles on their shoulders, carrying what they had selected of my belongings.

A windowless automobile – a Black Raven – was waiting at the kerb. I was ordered into the back seat along with two soldiers. The head man sat beside the driver, and the car started to move.

We stopped some twenty minutes later. The front door slammed, and apparently the head man got out – he was blocked from my view. But he was back shortly for I heard his voice. 'It's full up,' he said, adding a few choice swear words. 'Drive to the Nizhegorodsky and be quick about it!'

We were off again, and when we stopped the next time, the driver tooted his horn. I heard the creak of an opening gate, and we drove in. The door of my prison on wheels was opened. I was told to get out.

We crossed the eerie prison courtyard and entered a building. After walking down a hall we came to a well-lighted barren room with a single occupant – an official with eyes inflamed from lack of sleep, who sat behind a table in one corner. My blue-capped escort walked over to him and presented a slip of paper. The man signed the paper, Blue-cap picked it up and walked out. The official and I were left alone.

He looked at me sullenly, rummaged through the table drawer and tore out a sheet of paper. My first cross-examination in prison began. Soviet citizens are accustomed to filling in questionnaires, and the one I had to answer now was very much like those I had filled in on in-numerable past occasions. As I began, I risked seating myself on a chair. My interrogator was on the point of stopping me, but changed his mind.

The questions which followed one after another were so familiar that I soon recovered my composure. I signed the questionnaire.

'Take your clothes off,' he commanded.

I looked at him in surprise.

'You heard me. Do as you're told!'

I began pulling off my clothes as quickly as I could, until I was totally naked.

The man picked up my things, put them on his table, and examined them with professional thoroughness. He felt every seam, ripped the lining of both jacket and overcoat, searched every pocket, and carefully raked out the contents. Contemptuously he counted my money, found only forty-six kopecks, wrote out a receipt for the sum and shoved it into a pocket of my jacket, and tossed the clothes into my arms. Blue with cold, I hastened to put them on. My belt was not returned, and the laces were removed from my boots. My pockets were empty.

The official opened the door opposite the one through which I had come in, and signalled me to walk ahead. We walked down several long corridors without meeting a soul. Only once, as we were passing a door, I heard a blood-chilling scream and involuntarily slowed down my steps. A forceful push in the back was enough to make me move faster. We came to an iron-latticed door, where another guard, who was sitting on a stool, unlocked it and we entered a spacious T-shaped hall of the Nizhegorodsky prison. Right and left, rising in three tiers, there stretched even rows of doors which obviously led to small cells. Narrow iron balconies ran in front of them and down the length of the hall. From the top of the first floor a huge rope net was suspended over the hall. I afterward learned its purpose was to frustrate attempts at suicide by prisoners jumping from the balconies.

I was stopped at the door numbered 81. The warder opened it with a large key, let me in, and slammed the door behind me. The lock caught with a loud jangle.

The first thing that struck me inside the cell was the heavy, suffocating smell which came from the thin straw mattress covering a wall bed. For a few seconds I could hardly breathe.

I looked around. The cell was six feet by twelve, had a vaulted ceiling, and after the dog-hole I had just left, seemed very roomy. A lighted bulb, covered by a wire net, was fastened to the ceiling. On my left was a folding iron table anchored to the wall, and a stool. In the corner, a sink with running water – to complete the comforts, a primitive toilet arrangement. The window was high on the wall and had iron bars inside and an awning outside so I could see only a small bit of the dark, starlit winter sky.

Without undressing, I stretched out on the loathsome, stinking bed, devoid of any linen, laid my head on the prickly straw pillow, drew over myself an incredibly dirty and tattered blanket, and, exhausted by the new impressions, fell asleep.

I was awakened by a knock on the door and the call, 'Rising time!' in the sepulchral tones of a prison warder. I got up and washed although the lining of my overcoat was the only thing usable as a towel. I examined the door. It was heavy, lined with steel, with a peephole at the top, covered from the outside by a hinged iron plate, and lower down a rectangular opening, locked from the outside, for handing in food. Even more than the barred window, this door was the symbol of prison.

Suddenly there was a noise in the hall. The small rectangle in the door opened, something crashed to the floor, and the rectangle closed with a bang. Picking up what was thrown in, I recognized two dirty brushes. While wondering what to do with them, a command came from the hall: 'Polish the floor!' and simultaneously I saw a bulging eye at the peephole. I got down on my knees and now with one brush, then the other, began to scrub the cement floor.

Later on, the rectangle opened once more, the invisible person demanded the return of the brushes, and in exchange shoved in a mug of hot water and a chunk of bread weighing about a pound.

The pleasant task of crawling over dirty prison floors to make them shine like parquet became my daily occupation for the next five months. After a short time I learned a trick: I gave a mirror-like shine to only the spot on the floor which, according to my precise calculations, would show a reflection of light when seen through the opening. The rest of the floor I merely dusted.

After receiving the hot water and bread I hungrily consumed both since I had eaten no food for a day and a half. I didn't realize that that portion of bread was my whole day's ration. Nobody disturbed me again, and I took time to study the walls on which were still left a few inscriptions made by my predecessors. One message pencilled on the wall appealed to me a great deal. It read:

Here dwelt seven courageous tourists who are, for the sins of their fathers, being sent to develop the natural resources of Karaganda. Thou who wilt come after us, do not lose heart! Remember, thy fate was pre-ordained before thy birth, but it is not given to man to know his future. Believe in thy stars and look boldly ahead!

After pacing up and down the cell for a couple of hours, I lay down on the bed, but was immediately roused by a rattling of the door and the admonition: 'No lying on the bed in the daytime!' I had to resume my walking until the little window in the door opened again and I was handed my dinner: a bowl of questionable-looking soup which I emptied into the toilet. A little later my bowl was filled with the second course – an oatmeal porridge made with water and without salt, which I swallowed with difficulty. Afterward I often recalled that emptied soup with much regret. Only a few days later my appetite far exceeded anything the prison had to offer. About seven in the evening I was given supper – a bowl of the same porridge. About two hours later I heard the command: 'Go to bed,' which I was only too glad to obey.

Six days passed in this wearisome monotony.

On the seventh day of my stay in the Nizhegorodsky prison, just before suppertime two uniformed men entered my cell. One of them, holding a paper in his hand, asked my name. I gave it to him.

'Get your things together,' he said. I looked around. Beside a mug and a bowl there were no other portable articles in the cell. The man understood me, said 'Let's go,' and we walked through familiar passageways to the yard where a Black Raven was waiting. I got in, the door slammed, and we drove off.

A quarter of an hour later I was ordered to get out. It was easy to guess that I was in the central investigation section of the prison in Shpalerny Street.

Again came the inevitable filling in of a questionnaire, again I was searched as thoroughly and with no more results than before, except this time my spectacles were taken away from me, and I found myself in cell No. 169 on the third floor of the second building. The cell was an exact replica of the one I had come from, but a little cleaner. The corridors, too, looked cleaner with their soft small rugs which deadened the sound of footsteps.

At the usual prison time I heard the command to go to bed. I fell asleep in spite of the bright glare of an electric light bulb, but was awakened in the middle of the night by a guard who had entered the cell without my hearing him.

'Get dressed. You're to be questioned!'

'At last,' I thought. 'Everything will be cleared up and I'll go home a free man.' I was seriously worried about the studying which had to be done for the spring term examinations at my institute.

I got dressed quickly. In the austere quiet of the night we walked down the prison corridors, crossed a small enclosed bridge with a barred gate at each end, entered the Big House, ascended a carpeted staircase, continued down a few more hallways and finally stopped outside a heavy polished oak door. My escort ordered me to sit in one of the chairs in the hall, and entered a door facing me.

The hall was bright and quiet. Men in the uniform of the N.K.V.D. Army Corps walked past from time to time, stepping noiselessly on the covered floor. Somewhere a typewriter was clicking. A sudden burst of muffled swearing and the sound of something heavy falling came from somewhere else.

The door facing me opened and I was called in. A spacious, luxuriously furnished private office was dimly lighted by a green-shaded lamp that stood on a big desk. In front of the desk was a little table with an armchair on each side of it. The rest of the room was in semi-darkness.

Two men were in the room. One, with three diamond-shaped bars on his uniform jacket, sat behind the desk in a chair with a tall back. The other, sitting in a chair opposite, was somebody I had met before – the man who placed me under arrest.

The man behind the desk silently motioned me to the unoccupied chair. I sat down, waiting for what was to follow. My heart thumped as if about to burst.

Putting his elbows on the desk and resting his head on his hands, the man in the high-backed chair looked searchingly into my eyes and said in a sinister voice:

'We know everything.'

I made no answer. Then I noticed lying on the desk a pile of my letters and photographs and a bundle of books – sent as a farewell.

'Why do you keep silent? Speak.'

'What can I say to you if you know everything?' I answered.

'We're giving you the last chance to make your lot easier, provided you honestly confess all your crimes. How do you regard the Soviet government?'

'Most favourably.'

'Then prove you are sincere. Confess everything and name your associates.'

'I have nothing to confess. I don't consider myself guilty of anything. I believe the whole thing is a misunderstanding.'

'A misunderstanding . . .' My interrogator burst into laughter.

'And what's this?' he asked, pointing to the letters and books.

'The books are not mine. You know this as well as I do,' I replied, leaning on the table and staring back at him.

'Oh, they're not yours? And these letters? Aren't they addressed to you? Your letters of espionage . . .' he continued with an oath.

'The letters are addressed to me. I collected stamps, but neither I nor those writing to me ever mentioned anything not connected with the trading of stamps.'

'You lie. It's plain from these letters that you regularly sent secret intelligence abroad. Who are these correspondents of yours?'

'One is a young Russian technician in Yugoslavia . . .'

'A White bandit?'

'A son of White Russian émigrés. The other is an American in San Francisco. I got the addresses of both of them by accident.'

'So you've decided not to tell. Very well, we'll write it down that way. But remember, I've forewarned you of your only chance to save yourself – that is by openly confessing everything,' he said, picking up a form for the record of interrogation.

Silence set in. The interrogator wrote:

'. . . I, chief of the Secret Political Section of the Leningrad N.K.V.D. head office, Korkin, this 24th day of February, 1935, interrogated——'

Further on came questions and answers. Having written everything, he held out the paper.

'Sign your name.'

'May I read it?' I inquired.

'Read it,' answered Korkin with a shrug.

My interest in what he wrote proved to be fully warranted since my answers were distorted out of all recognition, and everything appeared as if, in substance, I admitted being guilty of espionage and of keeping forbidden anti-Soviet literature.

'I can't sign this examination record,' I said.

'Why not?' asked Korkin, knitting his brows.

'You know I said nothing of the kind,' I said as softly as I could. 'This is something entirely different.'

There was a pause. Evidently Korkin was considering his next step. Then he said:

'Very well. Write in your corrections at the bottom of the record.'

I took a pen, read the record carefully again, and numbering each item wrote down my answers. After signing the paper I handed it to Korkin. He ran his eyes over my corrections and rose. I got up, too.

'You refuse to confess. All right. You'll be the one to suffer. Further investigation of your case will be conducted by' – here he pointed at the silent witness of our conversation – 'Comrade Zakharov, authorized representative of the N.K.V.D. from the Moscow district of Leningrad.

You may go.' With this he rang a bell. A guard entered and escorted me through the same corridors and stairways to my cell.

I had just fallen asleep when I was awakened by the call: 'Get up!' Deciding this did not apply to me, I turned over and went to sleep again. A deafening rattling of the door awoke me a couple of minutes later. A fiercely bulging eye was looking through the peephole.

'Weren't you told to get up?'

'I've just come back from an interrogation, and haven't slept the whole night.'

'Are you talking back? I'll give you one second to get up!' yelled the guard in the corridor. I had no choice but to obey.

Two days passed in complete idleness. I spent the time thinking about my situation. In all honesty I did not consider myself guilty, nor was I in fact, and my faith in the misunderstanding being cleared up sooner or later remained unshakable.

On the third night I was called for another interrogation. As on the previous occasion I was led through corridors by a guard who ordered me: 'Stand face to the wall', every time anyone else came along. On one occasion, squinting my eyes, I saw guards dragging some old man in a torn jacket, his eyes closed and his mouth wide open, with a trickle of blood running from his mouth and leaving a trail on the carpet. The experienced guard noticed my movement and gripping me silently by the scruff of the neck, knocked my head painfully against the wall.

We arrived at our destination.

'Wait,' said my escort entering an unfamiliar door and emerging immediately with the words: 'Turn away!' Before I had time to obey the order I saw a man coming out of the same door. Despite his over-grown beard and shabby clothes I recognized him as my old friend, Boris K., an artist by profession and my senior by some fifteen years, whom I had frequently met in the home of my other artist friend, Vladimir S. The three of us had often worked together to earn extra money by getting occasional orders to paint slogans, posters, portraits of Stakhanovites and such like.

'Oho!' I said to myself as I turned my face to the wall, pretending not to have recognized Boris, 'so I have an accomplice in my crimes!'

Boris was immediately led away and I entered a private office which I had not been in before. I may mention that throughout the six months of investigation, I was never interrogated twice in the same office. I don't know exactly how many such private offices there are in the Big House, but I believe they must number nearly a thousand. At all events, the distribution of office rooms among innumerable investigators must have been a very complicated business.

Inside the room I found the man who was present at my interroga-tion by Korkin – the investigator Zakharov. He sat behind a desk, his blouse unbuttoned and his hair dishevelled. The room was filled with tobacco smoke and cigarette butts were strewn all around.

'Sit down.'

I sat.

'New facts of your criminal activity have been brought to light,' Zakharov said, looking at me with a frown. 'Do you know what this is?' He pointed his finger at three thin copybooks inscribed on the covers in my handwriting. I knew at once what copybooks they were, and stretched out my hand for them, but Zakharov quickly moved them away from me.

'You don't have to look at them. You must remember. You wrote them – your Moscow diaries.'

I started inwardly. These were my diaries, written three years earlier, which contained some of my opinions on political matters. I don't know why I had been saving these diaries. After arriving in Leningrad I had put them in the safekeeping of the artist, Vladimir S., the mutual friend of Boris's and mine.

I was aware that the investigator could find comments in my diaries which could be held against me, and trying to speak calmly said:

'I know. These are diaries of my school days.'

'And I hold they are the most shameless counter-revolution!'

'Shameless or not, it's for you to judge. But you will agree that I can't be held responsible now for what I wrote when I was fifteen or sixteen. My views about many things have changed since then.'

'Oh, they've changed? I'm pleased to hear it. But don't you know that these writings are criminal in themselves, and that Soviet law has no such thing as a statute of limitation?'

I was stuck there – I didn't know the Soviet laws. However, I tried to argue.

'But these are diaries. I wrote them only for myself. They are just thoughts on paper.'

'Criminal thoughts,' said the investigator impressively. 'And why did you disseminate these thoughts among your friends by giving them counter-revolutionary literature to read which you call diaries?'

'That is not true. I never gave them to anybody to read. They were put in the safekeeping of Vladimir S. because I didn't want them to be read, even by accident, by fellow students in my hostelry.'

'And now you assert you no longer have such thoughts?'

'That's right.'

'In that case, why did you so carefully preserve these factual proofs of your former counter-revolutionary activity?'

This was difficult to answer. Lord knows why I had preserved these damn diaries. Zakharov laughed triumphantly and began to fill the interrogation form.

'This is not all,' he said, pausing in his writing. 'We know much more. We'll talk it over later.'

The remark was not comforting!

Zakharov went on completing the record, and when it was finished handed it to me for signature, adding:

'If you wish you can make your corrections, but you may just as well know, it won't help you.'

Nevertheless, I read the record and made a number of corrections, since in Zakharov's wording my answers were considerably distorted.

On returning to my cell I began to mull over my situation. As before, I did not consider myself guilty of any crime, but it was now plain that my case was getting more involved. At least two more people, Boris K. and Vladimir S., had been dragged by the investigators into the same mess in which I found myself. Equally evident was the fact that the appearance of my diaries created a positive basis for formulating charges against me, and that from now on I had to dismiss all hopes for an early return to my studies at the institute.

It was unpleasant to have to go without smoking. I lay on my bed, but could not fall asleep for a long time, my thoughts constantly returning to my sorry state.

All the following day I spent pacing almost without a stop, from one corner of my cell to the other, absorbed in attempts to guess what other surprises were being prepared for me by Zakharov. For some reason I did not particularly fear any physical methods of persuasion, or, more plainly, beatings, although I had no doubts that beatings were practised, and thorough beatings at that. But despite the absence of fear in the strict sense, I was seized even at that early stage of prison experience by a feeling of depression resulting from the realization of absolute helplessness and defencelessness. I could be beaten up, maimed, strangled, treated in any imaginable way, but I knew nobody would come to my aid, and nowhere could I find protection or justice. This realization of utter helplessness has to this day remained with me as one of the most painful memories associated with that period of my life.

Engrossed in my thoughts, I must have been making a diagonal crossing of the cell for the thousandth time when my attention was suddenly attracted by an even tapping on the wall at my left. I listened. Quiet and persistent this tapping resembled the clicking of a telegraph key. I knew of the existence of a prison Morse code, but was ignorant both of the code and the rules of tapping.

Seating myself at the iron table which was permanently fixed to the cell's lefthand wall and apparently connected by bolts with a similar table in my neighbour's cell, I tapped the top of the table a few times. My neighbour's tapping broke off for a minute, but started again with the same persistence. The intervals between the taps were different: short, long, and very long: dot-dot-dash, dot-dash-dot, dash-dot, dot-dash.

I did not answer. Instead, arming myself with a spoon which had a broken sharp end, I waited. My neighbour broke off. Seizing the pause, I tapped the table three times. There was silence. Then I heard four clear taps with different intervals. I scratched them on the table graphically as dots and dashes and named it A. This I tapped back carefully. Two strong encouraging knocks answered me, after which there was a pause and then four taps in a new combination of intervals. I wrote down the new sounds and marked them B.

I heard the footsteps of the guard who was walking down the corridor and peeping into every cell. This peeping inspection was repeated with almost mathematic precision every three to four minutes all the twenty-four hours of the day. With my hearing already sharpened by staying in prison I discerned the nearing soft footsteps, and sprang off the table to resume pacing the cell. The guard peeped in and went on his way. I rushed back to the table to repeat the last four taps. Two strong knocks, apparently signifying encouragement, came as an answer, and were followed by four taps in a new combination, which I took down and marked as the next letter.

The lesson continued for two hours during which I noted down about half the alphabet. Then there was a slight noise in the corridor and a clicking of the doorlock in the adjoining cell. The tapping stopped and everything was still: my neighbour had obviously been led away.

I attempted to get in touch with him next morning after breakfast, but could get no answer from him throughout the day. But on the third day my lessons were resumed. My instructor seemed to be in a hurry, and during the next two days I learned the alphabet so well that I was able to receive messages by ear.

'W-h-o a-r-e y-o-u?' my neighbour tapped out.

I answered, and addressed the same question to him.

'I am Kotolynov,' my neighbour introduced himself.

I was astonished to hear the name. Even before I was imprisoned I had read in the newspapers that a man named Kotolynov had been executed together with Nikolayev, the assassin of Kirov. I immediately tapped out my perplexity. The answer was brief:

'Not shot dead yet, but will be soon.'

'Do they beat you?' I put an important question.

'More than that,' came the answer.

'Do you want to say anything?' I asked. There was silence, then a brief:

'N-o!'

I stopped. Obviously my neighbour was afraid he might be talking to a stool pigeon. But my interest was much aroused by the conversation, and after waiting for the guard to go by I was about to resume tapping when I heard:

'What do you want to know?'

'Who killed Kirov?' I asked a stupid question, unexpectedly even to myself, for I knew from the newspapers that the assassin was a certain Nikolayev, a Trotskyite. But the answer was even more unexpected.

'S-t-a-l-i-n.'

'Go to bed!' sounded in the corridor. The conversation had to end. I immediately went to bed since I knew that was my night to be called for interrogation. This took place in due time, but my attempts to re-new conversation with Kotolynov the next day and the following days brought no results.

Toward the morning of the night after that I was just about to go to bed, after returning from an interrogation, when I heard sounds in the corridor. Somebody was being dragged.

'Let go!' a voice cried. Then the lock clicked in the door of the cell to my left, there were muffled blows, and something crashed heavily to the floor. The door slammed. With my heart thumping I listened.

Half an hour went by, and I was falling off to sleep when noise broke out in my neighbour's cell – he was knocking on the door. I could hear the guard come up and open the little door-window. In-stantly there was a piercing cry: 'Put Stalin in my cell!' And again and again, almost without pause: 'Put Stalin in my cell!'

Guards began to run about in their almost soundless manner. I could hear the iron door-shutter hit the jutting head time and again, and the same eerie voice shouting the same meaningless phrase:

'Put Stalin in my cell!'

Keys rattled, the lock in the next door clicked, and there was a shuffling noise, muted swearing. Through the three-foot thick walls I heard the muffled sound of blows. A wild cry broke out: 'Free my sister!' And there came again: 'Put Stalin in my cell!'

The entire building was filled with cries and racket. On every floor prisoners were knocking on their cell doors and shouting: 'Stop it!'

Kotolynov's voice now appeared stifled, as if his head had been covered with a pillow. The shuffling continued for a few minutes and then everything grew still. A few pairs of feet went past my cell.

For two days there was no sign of Kotolynov. On the third day I heard the approaching footsteps of several men and the familiar but now weak and expressionless voice which kept repeating:

'I'm vacating my cell for Stalin.'

Two days later the cell next door was empty: Kotolynov was taken away, and he never came back.

During all these happenings the investigation of my case continued. Every third night before midnight my door opened and a guard entered. After asking my name he would order me to dress and would lead me for an interrogation to one of the offices of the Big House.

The examinations followed the same pattern. My investigator,

Zakharov, devoted each session to some newly formulated charge which as a rule was so absurd I am firmly convinced he himself never regarded them seriously.

I recall that one questioning dealt with the subject of my espionage activities. In front of Zakharov lay a neatly bound collection of letters in English which I had received from a stamp collector in San Francisco. With it lay a typewritten Russian translation of the letters. By the side of this was a bundle of letters from an *émigré* in Yugoslavia.

We spent hours over those letters, with Zakharov 'reading between the lines' and trying to prove they were coded espionage instructions and not at all stamp numbers according to Ivert's catalogue. He had even obtained the catalogue in an attempt to decode the letters. I heatedly argued against the accusation, advancing proofs that all his suspicions were nonsense. He listened to me smilingly, then wrote down the record of the examination and passed it on to me. I entered my corrections at the bottom, signed the document, and we parted amicably.

On one occasion at an early stage of the investigation I asked Zakharov what was going to happen to me.

'Probably five or six years in a concentration camp,' he answered, shoving the interrogation record into the ever accumulating folder. I chuckled sceptically at the time. I was convinced he did not mean it.

One session of the interrogation dealt with the charge that I had tried to organize Cossack uprisings in the Kuban region during the time peasant farms were being collectivized. The only truth in this charge was the fact that during the summer of 1933 I had spent two months with my mother who lived in that region. The charge rested on the evidence of my friend Boris K. who stated, allegedly on the basis of what I had told him, that during my stay in the region I had visited one of the Cossack settlements and urged the Cossacks to rise up in arms against the Soviet government. I flatly denied the accusation and demanded to be confronted with the witness.

'You want to confront your accuser?' asked Zakharov in a mocking tone. 'Well, I may arrange it for you. Later.'

He kept his word. Three days later when I arrived at the office where the questioning was to be held, I saw my friend Boris sitting on a chair outside the door.

When I came into the room, Zakharov seated me on one side of his desk, then ordered Boris to be brought in and seated him on the other side.

'You mustn't talk to each other,' warned Zakharov. 'You will only answer the questions which I will put to you.'

Boris sat gloomy and frowning, his myopic eyes narrowed behind thick spectacles. He was dirty, with an overgrown beard, as was I, and intent. Turning to him Zakharov asked:

'On such-and-such a date you testified at the interrogation that he,' pointing his finger at me, 'had told you so-and-so. Do you confirm your testimony?'

"I do," said Boris gazing into space.

'And you deny this, of course?' asked Zakharov turning to me.

'I do,' I answered.

The entire proceeding went on in this manner.

After we both signed the record of examination, I turned to Boris, ignoring Zakharov's warning and protesting gestures, and asked:

'Have you gone utterly mad? Do you realize what you have been saying, and what consequences it will have for both you and me?'

Boris looked at the investigator and made no answer.

Another session.

'What anti-Soviet anecdotes do you know?' Zakharov asked me.

'None,' I answered. I had heard that for telling and listening to anti-Soviet anecdotes people were handed up to five years imprisonment.

'You're telling a lie, my good man. There isn't a person in the Soviet Union who doesn't know any anti-Soviet anecdotes.'

'Then I'm the exception,' I continued stubbornly.

'Don't be obstinate. Believe me, there's more than enough evidence against you, and an extra couple of anecdotes won't make it any harder for you,' he persisted.

'Then why do you ask, if it won't affect my case?'

'So you do know some?' Zakharov tried to trip me.

'I've heard a few, but I've forgotten them,' I replied. The argument went on for some time until I gave in and told him some vapid and rather innocuous story.

'Are you making fun of me? My grandfather told that story to my grandmother on his death bed!' exclaimed Zakharov with genuine indignation. 'Stop playing the fool!'

So I told him another story. Noticing the expression of bored indifference on his face I had to break this off too, and begin a new anecdote. This one was non-political but pretty salty. Zakharov's face lighted up, he yanked a notebook from his pocket, and began to jot it down.

'Go on,' he ordered, 'something about Stalin.'

Here I flatly refused since the subject was absolutely outlawed.

'Have you heard this one?' Zakharov asked, and went on to tell me a funny story which I had known, but had forgotten.

The interrogation proceeded in this manner until the small hours. At the end I let myself go and ignoring all consequences told a story from the life in the Kremlin which was so racy that Zakharov simply screamed with delight and hurried to write it down in his notebook.

As I expected, no record of this interrogation was made.

Another session.

'Tell me how you planned to remove gold from the dome of St. Isaac's Cathedral in order to obtain means for your criminal activity,' Zakharov said, trying hard to look serious.

'Did Boris K. tell you that?'

'Yes, he did.'

'Then you'd better ask him. I only suggested the idea. Working out the technical methods was his concern,' I answered.

More interrogation.

'Tell me how you worked out plans for robbing agricultural co-operatives and savings banks.'

'But this, it seems to me, belongs to ordinary criminal activity, not political.'

'Everything we deal with belongs to ordinary criminal activity. The Soviet law does not recognize political crimes as such – that is in the first place. But in the second place, you planned your robberies for the same counter-revolutionary objectives.'

'Did Boris K. tell you that, too?' I asked.

'Here I ask questions, not you. Answer!' the investigator retorted, raising his voice.

'I'm sorry, I can tell you nothing about this matter. I was not let in on it,' I answered.

Throughout the period of solitary confinement I was perpetually tormented by the sensation of hunger. The quantity and quality of prison food was portioned out so that prisoners were not permitted to feel satisfied, and the ever-present emptiness in the stomach made me feel constantly depressed. I complained about this to Zakharov at one of the interrogations. 'We have two rations,' he said. 'One is the general kind which you're getting, and the other is a special kind given to those who regard themselves as political opponents of the Soviet government. Write me a statement that you want to be given the political ration, and I'll fill in an order for it right away.'

'What should I say?' I asked as I took the paper that Zakharov obligingly handed me.

'I'll dictate to you. Write: "Regarding myself as a political enemy of the Soviet regime I demand the ration established for this category." . . . Why have you stopped?'

I lifted my head and looked at him. Then I put down the pen and tore up the paper.

'What's the matter? Have you lost your appetite?' asked Zakharov with a chuckle.

'I'm not such a fool,' I answered.

However, I outsmarted him. About two months before leaving this prison I demanded to see the deputy commander of the building and complained to him of acute stomach pains. Soon after he left, a nurse from the prison dispensary, a very nice young woman, came to my cell.

I told her frankly about my incessant hunger. She sympathetically heard me out, and paused in thought.

'All right. I'll see that you get additional food. But promise, not a word about it to the investigator.' Of course, I gave her my promise.

It was a delightful surprise next morning when an hour after the usual portion of hot water I was given a mug of hot milk and a loaf of white bread weighing as much as a pound. Naturally, I never mentioned the unexpected increase in my daily ration to Zakharov.

Another great hardship to bear was insufficient sleep. Although I had no sleep every third night when I was called for interrogation, I was barred even from sitting on the bed in the daytime. I tried to disregard orders, but this only led to a clash with the guard and the commander of the building, which resulted in my hinged bed being lifted and locked flat against the wall. My punishment came when for a week's time I had to sleep on the cold cement floor.

Interrogations, interrogations, interrogations. . . .

Zakharov's patience was inexhaustible. Although toward the end of the investigation he showed little evidence of honestly believing in my criminal activities, he tried his best to buttress the case with the necessary material. In a sense he did not have to worry on this point since he had in his hands some material evidence, such as the letters from abroad, my diaries and the testimony of witnesses. With this it was not difficult to prepare my case for a court trial. It was different with the overwhelming majority of people thrown into prisons or concentration camps after the murder of Kirov. The charges against them were so unsupported by evidence that as a rule they were tried in absentia by the N.K.V.D. or by the Special Council attached to the People's Commissar, Yagoda, head of the N.K.V.D. Trial in absentia, however, presented no obstacle to sentencing people to death by shooting, or long term sentences in concentration camps, even if their guilt could not be proved. There were even cases in which a man was informed that he was sentenced to death without being called for interrogation a *single time*.

My interrogations, which had been held with the utmost regularity, suddenly stopped. One week then another passed. I kept count of the time by marking each day with a deep scratch on the wall, but I was not called. At times I even longed to see the dull, expressionless face of the guard whose footsteps I could hear in the corridor.

I waited impatiently for what was to come next. At length, one day before dinner my door opened and I was called to go to the baths, for the first time in many months. I walked along deserted corridors accompanied by the inevitable guard. By now I knew them all. There were three guards, each remaining on duty for twelve hours and resting for the next twenty-four. Through some unfamiliar passages we reached the baths which was simply a room with stall showers. I quickly undressed and had a glorious time washing myself. The guard kept urging me to hurry. Putting on my clothes I came out into the ante-room. The guard told me to sit on a chair and then, with a dull razor, he scraped off my beard.

Then we again marched off somewhere – high up a staircase where we entered a bright room. In the centre of the room stood photographic equipment, and next to than an elderly photographer. Two pictures were taken of me – full face and profile. After this I was escorted home, to my cell. A cold dinner was waiting on the table for me.

Days and days dragged by.

At last I was awakened in the night.

'Interrogation!' said the guard, and we were off. I was led into an investigator's office. Sitting at the desk was a uniformed man whom I had never seen before.

I sat down, but a savage shout 'Get up!' followed by swearing made me jump to my feet. I stood waiting for what would follow.

'So, that's the kind of rat you are!' said the investigator with hatred in his eyes. 'Well, go on, tell us about your little affairs!'

'I don't know what you're referring to.'

'Oh, you don't know?' uttered the investigator with a menacing look as he rose from his chair. 'Well, see to it that you find out.'

My morale dropped to low ebb. Coming out from behind his desk and walking right up to me, his hands in his pockets, my interlocutor roared out:

'Are you going to talk or not?'

'But tell me what I have to say,' I murmured. Before I finished the sentence, a strong blow on my left temple knocked me off my feet. Everything began to float before my eyes and falling to the floor I knocked against a chair near by. Lying in the corner of the room I tried to rise, but a new strong blow, this time with a man's boot, sent me crashing back to the floor. I lay waiting for what would come next.

The investigator gave a disgusted look, swore obscenely and returned to his seat.

'Get up!' he ordered. 'Stand against that wall.'

I did as I was told. The investigator opened his holster, drew a revolver and placed it in front of himself on the desk.

'Don't move! I'll kill you like a dog!' he announced.

I stood motionless.

'Will you answer or not?' There was more swearing.

'I will,' I said weakly.

Taking an interrogation form he began to fill it in. A minute later he asked:

'When did you start working at the plant?'

'I didn't work at a plant in Leningrad,' I said incautiously.

With a wild roar the investigator rushed from behind the desk, flew toward me, gripped me by the throat and with great force banged my head against the wall several times. I could feel myself losing consciousness and sliding to the floor. Blows followed blows, but I soon ceased to feel them.

I came to with a sharp pain in my side. When I opened my eyes I saw the investigator standing in front and found myself sprawled in an armchair. His hand, smeared with blood, was holding a short awl with which he had been bringing me to consciousness.

'Well, now will you stop lying?' he asked.

'I will,' I said diffidently.

'Answer then. When did you start working at the Putilovsky?'

I acted as if trying to recall. For the life of me I did not know what to say. I had never set foot in the Putilovsky plant. I had already told that to the investigator, and my whole body was reacting painfully to the result. What was I to tell him now? Give him some arbitrary date? But new questions would inevitably follow, I would certainly get mixed up, and the whole thing would be repeated. However, I had to answer.

'In May, last year,' I said.

'In what section?'

'The smelting section,' I said in desperation.

Suddenly the door opened and in came a guard I hadn't met before. One recognized a guard not so much by his uniform as by the fact that unlike the investigators he carried no gun. The man walked up to the investigator and whispered something in his ear. The investigator listened and turning to me threateningly asked my name.

I told him.

'Why didn't you say so before, you bastard?' he roared, and bending over the desk he hit me on the chest with the butt of his gun. I cried with pain.

'Take him away and bring in the next one,' the bandit ordered. 'I'll teach them how to love freedom, these so-and-so and so-and-so's!'

It turned out there had been a misunderstanding: the guard made a mistake in the number of the cell and brought the wrong prisoner.

It took me several days to recover from this violent interrogation. In comparison with this butcher my Zakharov was an angel incarnate.

There were no further interrogations. As time went on, despair began to take possession of me. Several times I was near committing suicide. It required great effort to get one's mind in proper order, but I finally pulled myself together – so much so, indeed that, to distract my mind, I decided to recall all the songs, arias, and tunes I had ever heard.

So it came about that one morning after breakfast I began, in a fairly quiet voice, to sing a song.

The staring, inquisitive eye of a guard appeared in the peephole. There was a knock, and the admonition:

'No singing allowed!'

Ignoring the order I went on singing. The peephole closed, but a minute later the commander of the building was in my cell. Two guards were behind him.

'Haven't you been told singing is not allowed here?' he asked.

'I have.'

'Stop it at once. This is no opera house, it's a prison.'

'Is that so? It's rather strange. I think it's a theatre, and not a very good one at that,' I answered impertinently.

'Are you going to stop singing, or not?' the commander asked, drawing his eyebrows together.

'No.'

'Take him downstairs,' he ordered the guards.

The men dashed towards me as if they had been waiting for the opportunity. I dodged them successfully. Snatching a bowl with the remains of dinner porridge I emptied it on the head of one of my pursuers. Then, with the same bowl smashed the window pane. Tinkling, broken glass flew in all directions. 'Help! Help!' I shouted, although I knew nobody could help me. But I was completely seized by a nervous onrush of gaiety. I threw myself under the feet of one of the guards and brought him crashing down on top of me. However, at the same moment I felt two other guards bear down on me breathing heavily, grabbing my arms and twisting them behind my back, and kicking me with their heavy boots. This combination of pain somewhat sobered me up. Nevertheless, I kept up resistance and drew up my legs as gripping me under my arms they tried to drag me out of the cell. Balked, they pushed me on the bed, pressed painfully behind my ears, forced me to open my mouth, shoved in a stinking gag, tied my hands and feet with thin wire, lifted me, then deliberately dropped me on the cement floor, lifted me again and carried me out.

Down——down——down——

Stunned by the fall, I was unconscious for a while. I came to from a new fall – on the floor of a damp cellar with a vaulted ceiling. The place was brilliantly lighted. The men now untied my hands and feet. But at the first attempt to rise I dropped again, sent down by a strong blow to my abdomen. Then, spurred on with boot kicks, I was pushed over the threshold of an open door which slammed behind me.

Fortunately, my fall was short. One, two, three steps, and I fell with my face plastered into stinking mud. I rose with difficulty and pulled the dirty rag out of my mouth. My whole body was aching.

I found myself in a disgusting looking place. It was a narrow, tall and windowless stone well. The floor was covered with muck six inches deep, and the air was so fetid it was difficult to breathe. The furnishings consisted of a battered rusty mug and a straw mattress floating in the mud. High up under the ceiling an electric lamp gave out a dim light. It was cold. The walls were moist, and it is possible the cell was below the level of the river Neva.

I stood leaning against the wall, and began to be assailed by contrition for my senseless conduct.

Hours followed hours, hunger was tightening my stomach, my whole body craved sleep. At length, completely exhausted, I lay down on the dirty mattress and fell into deep slumber.

I don't know how long I slept. When I awoke I was shivering with cold and dampness. To warm myself I began pacing up and down and did some physical exercises. I felt a little warmer, but the sensation of hunger became more acute. Grown wise by former experience, I refrained from knocking on the door.

The door-window opened and a hoarse voice asked for the mug. I held it out and it was filled with hot water, after which I was handed a half-pound chunk of bread. I gobbled up the bread and washed it down with the hot water.

Again hours dragged by. I could not tell whether it was day or night. Once more I fell asleep. Suddenly I was awakened by a sharp bite. Some small animals were running over me, and I leaped to my feet like fury. In the semi-darkness of the cell I saw two huge rats rush about and then suddenly disappear. I stood leaning against the wall, trembling, and the cold sweat began to run down my body.

I did not have the courage to lie down again, and I dozed off standing, now sliding down, now getting up. More time went by. There was no more food – apparently bread and hot water were furnished only once a day.

Forced by general weakness I eventually lay down on the mattress, and in my fitful sleep woke up several times to drive away the rats that came from I know not where. Huge and fat, with revoltingly thick tails, their little black eyes glittered and watched my every movement. Soon they no longer feared me, and time and again I felt their sharp teeth driving into my leg or arm.

Soon afterward I fainted once more.

I came to after a heavy push.

'Get up and come out,' ordered a tall-looking guard.

With an effort I rose and crawled out of the cell. The bright light hurt my eyes. I was shoved through some door into a dark and tiny closet-like room. I was utterly perplexed. Suddenly a shower of water burst from above and soaked me from head to foot. In a few seconds I was drenched right through. This was washing oneself and cleaning the clothes all at the same time. The water temperature fell rapidly from near boiling to almost icy. Then the shower stopped. I shook as if with ague. Suddenly I felt the temperature in the closet was rising. Steam began to rise from the floor and heat came through the soles of my boots, scorching my feet. A few minutes of this, and I could hardly breathe. I stripped myself to the skin, but this brought little relief. Blood was pounding in my temples. With perspiration streaming over me, I began knocking on the door and shouted:

'That's enough!'

There was laughter outside, and a minute later the temperature began to fall off. I dressed, the door opened, and hardly able to stay on my feet I entered the bright room.

I must have looked pretty funny, for the moment they saw me two guards burst into fits of laughter.

'Washed you and dried you, didn't we? How do you like our system?'

I didn't answer.

'Well, come on,' said one of the happy guards, and escorted me to my old cell. I had the feeling of coming back to my native home.

The night sky of Leningrad was visible through the slit at the top of the window. Without undressing I dropped on the bed and was instantly dead to the world.

A few days passed.

One morning – by that time I had lost count of the days I had spent in prison – a guard entered my cell.

'Interrogation!'

I dressed quickly and we went off. There were the same silent corridors, stairways, and identical-looking doors. When we reached the right office, the guard told me to sit outside and he walked in. Presently he was back and, ordering me to wait, strode away.

The door next to which I was sitting opened and Zakharov popped his head out. He called me in and busied himself with the papers which lay in front of him.

I sat silent, showing the effectiveness of prison education.

Zakharov raised his head, and as if answering my thoughts said:

'You went on a rampage during my absence, didn't you? That was a mistake. You must remember once and for all that if you want to get out alive, every protest, no matter how light, will make your position unquestionably worse. This is the case in ordinary free life, and all the more so within the system of the N.K.V.D. You cannot help anything or anyone. So have a cigarette and stop thinking of anything except your own case.'

Without speaking I lit a cigarette. My hands were still shaking.

'This is our last meeting,' continued Zakharov. 'I'm writing the record of the conclusion of the investigation. If you wish you can go over the material in your case while I'm writing. This is against the rules, but never mind——' With this he pushed a bound folder toward me, and began writing.

I leafed quickly through the records of my own interrogations. I remembered them well, knew I had not tripped, and was not interested in them. Further, further, I said to myself. Here, at last, were the records of Boris's interrogations. I read them carefully, but could make no head or tail of them – utter nonsense from beginning to end. What had made Boris, who was far from being a fool, talk such tommyrot? He confessed to having committed all sorts of crimes, and heaped the most grotesque charges on me. His records were followed by just a single record of the interrogation of Vladimir S., our mutual friend. As usual the investigator's questions were tricky, but Vladimir had answered them tersely, with much reserve, and without a single slip from the truth. Yet he and Boris lived together and I knew them both equally well. I was completely at a loss.

Finally, at the end of the volume, following the record was an envelope sealed with wax. I don't know what was in it, but I believe it contained reports of the N.K.V.D. and its secret informants, plus the investigator's conclusion.

'Have you looked it over?' Zakharov inquired.

'Yes, except this envelope,' I answered.

'Oh, that's not for you. Now sign your name.' He handed me a sheet on which I put my name under a statement saying I was informed of the conclusion of the investigation of my case. 'Now wait for your turn,' continued Zakharov. 'Your case will be tried in court.'

'What do you think they'll hand me?' I asked.

'I've already told you – not less than five years of prison or concentration camp. Now let's go.'

'Goodbye,' I said.

'Till we meet again,' Zakharov answered as each of us went his way. But Zakharov's last words proved more true than he suspected. We did meet again, although several years later and in entirely different circumstances.

I walked on, escorted by the guard who, as usual, indicated the direction at turnings. Suddenly I noticed we were following an unfamiliar route. One more turn and we ascended a stairway I had never set foot on before. Then there was a crossbridge gallery from the Big House into the prison, which was also new to me, and next a waiting-room filled with guards.

A big door opened and my ears were assailed by unaccustomed noise. We entered a wide hallway in which, instead of walls, there were some kind of grilles like those seen in a zoo rising high up to the ceiling.

Behind the grillework were human-looking animals clinging tightly to the bars, shouting, asking questions. Far in the back one could discern figures more like human beings. As we reached the end of the corridor I was pushed into one of these cages, cell No. 11.

I was immediately surrounded by a crowd of people. My first thought was: 'Is it possible I look like them?' Shaggy-haired, long-bearded, stripped to the waist, they showered questions on me. After the solitary cell I felt odd, and didn't know what to do.

One of the prisoners came to my rescue.

'Let the man recover his senses. Are you just out of solitary confinement?' he asked me. I nodded. Instantly he pushed the crowd away, and cleared a place for me at the table. As I sat down he sat next to me and introduced himself.

'I am the elected headman of this club,' he began. 'Formerly a battalion commander. I'm charged with having plotted a terrorist act. During the checking before the May Day parade a live cartridge was found in my revolver. It was there by accident. They threaten to put me before a firing squad, but I hope it will work out all right. My advice to you is not to talk to anyone about your case since there are about a dozen stool pigeons in the cell who have been forced to supply information to the investigators.'

'How many of you are in this cell?' I inquired.

'Not of you, but of us,' he corrected. 'This morning there were 125.'

I looked around the cell. The room was about twelve yards by eight with two big grilled windows screened from the outside. In the centre stood a long table, straw mattresses were piled up along the walls, and there were two benches. It was just an ordinary sized cell, to hold from twenty to thirty men. But it was so packed with people that one could hardly move. They were everywhere – sitting, standing or moving about. In one corner men were playing chess with pieces made of bread. At the table somebody was fashioning playing cards with the help of newspapers, soap, and coloured pencils, but taking care not to be noticed by the guards by hiding their hands behind a huge copper teapot. Here and there men were reading books and newspapers. A short permanent screen cut off one corner where there was a toilet and washstand.

'What sort of people have – we in the cell?' I asked the headman.

'Rather a motley crowd. Just now the majority are students and engineers, but a month ago there were more workers. We have some fairly prominent people now – about a dozen professors, some with big names, a number of doctors. There's a large group of engineers from the Higher Technical School plant of the name of Stalin, but you'll find them in many cells. The workers are mostly from the Putilovsky and the Baltiysky plants – predominantly old men.'

'What have they been jailed for?' I inquired.

'It's impossible to tell. Nearly everybody is afraid to talk about his case. After all, how is one to know what is a crime and what is not? That's why they keep mum. As far as I can figure out, their offences are trivial. Serious offenders are not placed in common cells. Those are mostly in solitary confinement.'

'A fine state of affairs,' I reflected. 'I've spent five months in solitary confinement, therefore I must be a true criminal. Then what have all these others done?' Turning to the headman I asked: 'How long have you been here?'

'Practically no time at all. Only three months. But those five there,' he went on, pointing to a group of middle-aged men, 'are doing their seventh month, and haven't been called for interrogation once. Either they've been arrested through some mistake, or the investigator has lost the folder with their case – the devil only knows which. They write complaints to the public prosecutor every day, but it helps them as much as a good meal helps those who are dead. They tried to go on a hunger strike, but couldn't stand it – gave up on the third day. They can't make it out at all – have no idea why they've been jailed.'

'Where are we?' I asked.

'In the Shpalerny prison, the third building; in other words, in Tairov Lane.'

'What does that mean, in Tairov Lane?'

'Be damned if I know. It was named before the revolution. But by whom and just why, nobody knows. The name has stuck ever since. Men come and go and pass the name one to the other. The origin of the name is lost, but the words remain.'

I felt somewhat discomfited by this lengthy succession. Probably for thirty or forty years people had been passing through this cell in an unbroken stream. Some were released, others were sent to concentration camps, to hard penal labour, or to other prisons, still others were hanged or shot, but the odd name, Tairov Lane, is still alive.

Suddenly there was noise in the corridor. Everybody in the cell began to dress. My headman rose too. A crowd of people were walking past us in the hallway.

'What's the matter?' I asked.

'Going for a walk,' someone explained. 'Soon it'll be our turn.'

In some ten minutes, indeed, a guard announced: 'Time for a walk!' and opened our door. Everybody rushed out. To the right, close to our cell, was an exit to a staircase which led straight into a prison yard. We were on the fourth floor. When we reached the ground a strange feeling came over me. For the first time in many months I saw a big piece of blue summer sky, rays of the setting sun lighting the huge yard, and breathing deeply I filled my chest with the fresh air free of prison odours.

In the middle of the yard stood a toilet. Above the toilet rose a railed platform on which a guard kept a sharp eye on the prisoners who moved in a circle.

'Walk in twos! Keep a two-step distance between the pairs! No talking!' One kept hearing his shouts.

The yard was paved with asphalt. There was only one exit – the door through which we came out. Close to that door, and in the corners of the yard, stood N.K.V.D. soldiers trailing automatic rifles.

We walked like a herd, in uneven order, straining our ears to catch the shouts of the man on the platform.

'How many minutes do we have for walking?' I whispered to the man by my side. An expression of fear came over his face, and there was no answer.

'Double-quick time!' came a sudden command, and we began running around the circle. Some, particularly the old men, were panting, but kept running. This lasted a couple of minutes.

'Enough! Slow down! March to your cell!' the order sounded, and in a solid mass we began climbing up the stairs. We ran into another party of prisoners coming down. There was a general mix-up during which some men exchanged quick whispers. It was explained to me later that these men were involved in this or that case as accomplices.

At length we all returned to our cell. Supper was already waiting for us – a big kettle with porridge standing close by the door. Taking their turn men came holding out bowls, and the headman, using a big ladle, gave each one his portion. Some did not take their supper. They belonged to the lucky category of prisoners permitted by their investigators to receive packages from relatives on the outside. I, too, got my bowl of porridge. Somebody shared his bread with me, another gave me some salt, someone else a tiny piece of butter. These were gifts from the lucky prisoners.

There were quite a few foreigners in the cell: three Germans, one Italian, a few Lithuanians, Estonians, and Latvians. All, without exception, were Communists and were sincerely indignant at having been thrown in jail. Even now they kept aloof from the rest of the prisoners, regarding them as out-and-out counter-revolutionists.

I must say the impression I received from the men I met during the five days I spent in Tairov Lane was invariably that *every one* of them was an ardent supporter of the Soviet regime. Before my prison days I had never encountered loyal Soviet citizens in such strong concentration. The farther I moved toward a concentration camp the paler was the redness of the prisoners. It gradually gave way to disillusionment and bitterness.

Eventually came the hour when the guard on duty in the corridor ordered 'Go to bed!' and complicated preparations for sleep began in the cell. As I learned, only eighty men, or two-thirds of the whole number, could lie down at the same time. About one-half of these could lie 'on the rib', or on one side, on the available straw mattresses which were spread carpet-like along the walls. Four other men could find space on the long table, and four more on two one-foot wide benches. The rest stretched themselves on the floor.

In the morning we all got up at the signal and stacked the mattresses since sitting in the daytime was also done by turn. We began to wash up, constantly urged on by the headman: the entire complement of 125 men would manage to get through washing only by dinner time. I kept recalling my old solitary confinement cell with a kind of longing.

About eight o'clock bread and hot water were brought in, and men, making themselves as comfortable as they could, began their breakfast. Soon afterward three guards came in. One of them ordered us to line up for roll call. We all formed up in several rows. Then there was the command 'Attention!' and the deputy commander of the prison entered and began the roll call. As he called out names those answering walked over to the opposite side of the cell. When everybody was on the other side, those absent for interrogation were noted, and we were again called out to walk back where we started. This was to check the total number. But somehow the deputy commander's figures failed to tally, and we went through the same procedure for the third time. I was told that this business sometimes took as long as two hours.

After roll call the guards in the corridor dragged a board up to the grille carrying packages from outside for some men in our cell. The men called out in turn took small bundles containing their soiled linen, handed these over to the guards to be returned to their relatives, and received new packages of food, tobacco, or cigarettes. But in what condition it all came! Cigarettes were broken, tobacco loose, bread crumbled into tiny bits, sugar mixed with tobacco, cleaned herrings, and everything else. In spite of all this I envied those men: I had no one to send me parcels, since none of my close friends knew where I was.

Gradually I got to know the inmates in our cell. I felt especially attracted to three schoolboys fifteen to sixteen years old. They were typical Leningrad children of educated parents – clever, well-read, lively. One of them had an old bulldog revolver, and the boys had practised shooting in a suburb called Pargolovo. A militiaman arrested them, and now for six months they were kept in the Shpalerny prison on a charge of plotting to murder Stalin. I met one of them after leaving Tairov Lane. He told me they had been tried in absentia and the owner of the pistol had been given ten years, the other two five years of concentration camp.

No one disturbed me any more. As far as was possible, I grew accustomed to the new surroundings, got much pleasure from reading books which my cellmates loaned me out of respect for my previous solitary confinement, read newspapers, talked to fellow inmates, and observed a side of life which I had not known before. From time to time new men were brought in, and the old ones were taken away along with their belongings. There was no lack of material for observation.

However, on the morning of my sixth day in Tairov Lane, the guard in the corridor called my name. When I answered and came up to the grille, thinking that by some miracle there was a parcel for me, all the guard said was:

'Get ready with your belongings!'

I said hurried 'goodbyes' to my new comrades, received the inevitable commissions in case I was released – I entertained very little hope of that – and left Tairov Lane and the Shpalerny prison. My long road was only beginning.

I was taken to the prison office. In two minutes all the formalities were over, my escort was handed a thin grey envelope with my name in red pencil on its cover, and we walked into the prison yard. Waiting there was my old friend, a Black Raven, crammed with prisoners.

For the last time I glanced over the inner walls of the Shpalerny prison, the rows of barred windows partly covered with red screens, and got inside the car. The door slammed, the opening gate squeaked, and we drove off.

2. PRISONS OF THE CITY OF LENIN

AFTER a half-hour drive through the Leningrad streets in another crowded Black Raven, my companions and I were let out in a wide prison courtyard. The day was bright, and the sunshine was glaring after the dark car. Two stately brick buildings, each in the form of a cross, rose splendidly before our eyes. They were the famous Kresti – which means 'Crosses' in Russian – the prison where, in the old days, the occupants included great numbers of fighters against the Czarist autocracy, many of them leaders or participants in the two revolutions of 1917.

The necessary formalities of checking our arrivals were quickly over and, forming up in single file, we were led by two guards to the building on the left. The whole atmosphere of the Kresti was in sharp contrast to that of the Shpalerny prison – no longer the strict discipline, order, and cleanliness. Prisoners without escort were walking about the yard. As I learned later, they had already been given sentences, but were kept in the prison for work duties. They all had the look of hardened criminals.

Inside the Kresti we were ordered to line up. A prison official called out our names, and guards conducted us to cells. The interior of the building closely resembled the Nizhegorodsky prison. Each of the two Kresti buildings contained 999 cells. Why not the round number 1,000 is a mystery. The old-timers among the prison inhabitants told a story that the buildings had been designed to hold 1,000 cells, but through some error in construction one cell in each was left out. The architect, it was added, was so upset by the accident that he kept walking through the buildings looking for the lost cells, until he went out of his mind.

Another story claimed the number of cells in our building was actually 1,000 but by order of the Czar, while the prison was under construction, a guards officer, who had seduced one of the Czar's daughters, was immured in one of the cells and soon died of suffocation. I don't think this legend is true, but I met men who were thoroughly convinced that the ghost of the guardsman sometimes walked about the prison, especially on nights when the secret police came for their victims on the first floor of the southern wing – where doomed men were kept. There were about thirty such cells, used for criminals sentenced to death by the Leningrad courts but waiting the final decision of Moscow as to whether they were to be shot or were to have their sentences commuted to ten years' hard labour. Although these cells were always full, they held few political prisoners; the latter, after their cases were closed, were kept in the Shpalerny prison.

I was conducted to cell No. 369, on the top floor of the eastern wing, My first impression was pretty dismal. It was a hot summer day, and in

the cells on our floor, which faced south, the heat was terrific. The room, which under the Czars was used for a single prisoner, now held sixteen men. How so many people could move about and sleep in an area measuring three yards by four yards and provided with a single bed, is really baffling. Somehow they did. The cell was bright with sunshine, since no metal screen cut off the sky behind the barred window, and we were able to enjoy a broad vista of Leningrad including the Arsenal Embankment of the Neva, and the houses, factories, and tall smoke-stacks of the city's industrial suburbs.

I began to get acquainted with my cellmates through the inevitable questions: who are you, where do you come from, what are you charged with? Before long, I had a fairly clear impression of my companions. Approximately half of them were peasants from the former Pskov province – known in Leningrad as *Skobari* – illiterate, primitive people from solitary villages far removed from cities and railroads. They were all accused of counter-revolutionary activities.

One of them, a carroty young fellow named Petka, had got drunk and beat up the chairman of his collective farm. The charge against him was terrorism, and his case, still under investigation, was pretty bad. It looked as if he would have to face the firing squad.

Another peasant, Ivan, was arrested at one of the Leningrad open markets where he was selling potatoes that he had brought from his home. A stranger walked up to him and asked:

'Have you heard that Kirov has been killed?'

'It's all the same to me,' answered Ivan, who had no idea who Kirov was. 'Every day somebody gets killed. Today it's your Kirov, tomorrow it's somebody else.'

The stranger immediately called a militiaman, and an hour later Ivan found himself in the Kresti. His case had taken a bad turn since he was informed by the government investigator that he was charged with inciting to murder Stalin. A few days after I met him, Ivan was handed ten years' hard labour by a judgment in absentia of the Special Council.

There were two other Kirov men in the cell. They were workers from the Marti shipyard, jailed for running away from the solemn official procession which accompanied Kirov's body to the train – and also for trying to induce others to do likewise. These two were accused of anti-Soviet propaganda, and shortly afterward received three years in a concentration camp. Their sentences, too, were passed in absentia. The poor fellows were pleased: they had feared something much worse.

One prisoner, an old book-keeper – a jolly fellow who enjoyed a drink now and then – was in jail because, having had one too many in his own room, he sang the old national hymn 'God Save the Czar'. The book-keeper got five years, also in absentia.

There was also a former battalion commander who maintained

almost complete silence on the reason for his arrest. He had been imprisoned a long time, nearly a year, and had lodged in all the Leningrad jails. Every week he was called up for questioning. From the brief phrases which at times escaped his lips, it was possible to form some idea of his case. Apparently he was involved together with a whole group of artillery officers, most of whom were held in the Shpalerny prison. The investigator demanded that he give false evidence against his friends, threatening to punish his family – he had three children, a wife, and mother – if he refused. Though the man never admitted it, I believe he yielded to those demands, since, on the investigator's orders, he was permitted to receive parcels from outside.

I remember three other prisoners, two Estonians and one Latvian. They were naïve young peasants, not too bright, who had swallowed up Communist propaganda in their own countries and, without bothering about visas, had crossed the Soviet border in search of a better life. Charged with espionage, and called up for questioning only once, they were later sentenced in absentia to ten years in a concentration camp. They were much surprised.

Life in my cell was difficult. Only one-half of the inmates were able to sleep at night, and they did so in the most uncomfortable positions. Sleeping during the day was not forbidden, but with the close air, the heat, and the stench that filled the cell, only the insensitive Pskov *Skobari* could take advantage of this privilege. There was no regular toilet in the cell. Instead, there was a fetid bucket by the door which quickly filled up, and was emptied only once a day, during the time we were conducted to the men's room which was provided on each floor. We took turns as to who would sleep in the daytime, who at night, and who got the spot close to the bucket.

We received food three times a day, but what we were given was much worse than that in the Shpalerny prison. Skilly, made of rotten cabbage, alternated with soup made of spoiled millet. Both were so foul that even in extreme hunger I could never finish my portion, and used to give what was left to the undernourished peasants from Pskov who gobbled it up greedily.

With every passing day I grew more and more oppressed. I spent hours at the window trying to swallow a little fresh air, gazing at the Leningrad streets which I loved more than any other city in Russia, and thinking my own gloomy thoughts.

I slept every second night when it was my turn. But even nights did not bring coolness and rest. The thick brick walls, heated like an oven during the day, cooled off very slowly, and although we stripped to the skin the suffering was unbearable. The terribly overcrowded cell, the stench, and the uncertainty of the future finally brought me to a state where, unable to stand it any longer, I decided to declare a hunger strike.

One morning I approached the corridor guard and demanded a sheet of paper and a pencil. After three reminders he finally brought a small piece of paper and a pencil stub. Almost verbatim, this is what I wrote:

'. . . considering myself innocent of all charges that have been brought against me, or of any other crimes, I, this day, declare a protest hunger strike, and demand an immediate interview with a Public Prosecutor from the Control Organization over the N.K.V.D.,* a revision of my entire case, and humane conditions of confinement.'

I handed this over, together with my bread ration which had been brought in the morning, to the guard who was waiting at the door. He went off, and I began to wait for developments.

Half an hour later the door opened. The guard called me out and led me downstairs to the central hall which was surrounded by the offices of the commander of the building and the investigators. The building commander met me with a stern question:

'What's the big idea? What's all this about?'

'I wrote everything down in my statement,' I answered. 'I've done nothing wrong, and I don't belong in prison.'

'Don't you know that the declaration of a hunger strike is in itself a counter-revolutionary action which puts you on the same basis as the worst enemies of the Soviet regime?'

I didn't know that, but I was in such a state of mind that this piece of news didn't even stir my interest.

'That's my business,' I replied firmly. 'The Public Prosecutor will find out who's right and who's wrong.'

At that time and for a long time afterward, I believed unswervingly in the higher justice, and viewed my own misadventure as brought about by the wicked will of some one or more individuals. Observation of other prisoners had gradually led me to the conclusion that the Leningrad N.K.V.D. included a group of 'wreckers' who jailed innocent people with the deliberate purpose of arousing dissatisfaction with the Soviet government. I did not expect justice from the N.K.V.D., but I still believed then in the salutary role of the panel of public prosecutors set up to supervise the N.K.V.D.

'Well, as you please. Take him to 45,' the commander said, concluding my interview and turning to the guard.

We left the office, crossed the central hall and proceeded toward the wing on the ground floor where, behind a special railing, were cells of those condemned to death.

My new habitation turned out to be an empty and dirty cell, placed

* There exists a farcical organization of this name in Soviet Russia which is supposed to supervise the N.K.V.D. to prevent the miscarriage of justice.

next to those occupied by the doomed men. The guard locked me in, and with a feeling of delight at once again being away from other people I stretched on the bed, which had neither linen nor blanket, and gave myself to my thoughts.

I had only a vague idea of what a hunger strike meant except that it meant a refusal to eat, and sometimes to drink; the last being known as a 'dry hunger strike'. I had undergone a long experience as a semi-famished student, and while in prison, too, was never free of a sensation of hunger. Although I guessed semi-starvation in some way differed from complete hunger, I could not evaluate my own powers in this respect. However, the very fact of being transferred to a room for hunger strikers was a decided gain, a relief from the feeling of being jammed in with a crowd. The cell was cool, and I was able to spend hours on the bed without continually seeing or hearing the same human beings, my room-mates by the will of the N.K.V.D.

The day was nearing its end, but I felt no special pangs of hunger. However, I missed smoking more than usual. In the Kresti, it must be said, the shortage of tobacco and cigarettes was a hardship that for smokers was particularly painful to bear. Prisoners were not given tobacco; it could come only from outside. In our cell, with sixteen men, only two received parcels, and it was impossible for them to share their cigarettes with the others since their own supply was never allowed to exceed a certain very small quanity. When one of the lucky fellows smoked a cigarette, the rest of us kept staring like so many dogs watching their masters eat. So he would let one or two of us have a couple of drags from his stub. But could that satisfy a man? And some prisoners were such inveterate smokers nothing could ever satisfy them.

Eventually, one of the men invented a mixture made of local raw materials. He pulled some straw from the mattress, crushed it into fine bits and added bread crumbs and cotton from the lining of somebody's overcoat. Still there remained the problem of paper. No newspapers were allowed in the Kresti, and we all had to look for a substitute. Finally we tore the peaks from the pointed caps that some prisoners had, stripped the covering cloth, and so obtained cardboard which we split into thin pieces of paper. The most precious thing was matches. Each wooden match was carefully split lengthwise into four parts. Then we smoked, and with what delight! One shudders at the thought of it.

But in my new cell, where I was carrying on my hunger strike, there was nothing to smoke. That was much worse than having no food or water.

Sometimes there was savage swearing, and a noisy struggle in a nearby cell. Apparently some bandit was being taken away. One can always tell men of this class by the manner of their swearing and the tone of their shrieking voices. But there were few of them in those cells.

In a night, five, seven, ten people were taken off to be shot. The doomed men's cells held four or five persons each. This, I was told, was a precaution against prisoners committing suicide, or going insane.

During those terrible nights I was seized with a sort of morbid curiosity. As soon as I heard the guards starting on their round of cells, I jumped off my bed and, pressing my ear to the door – in the Kresti the doors are of wood and not very thick – listened to every sound. I was shaking as if with the ague, my teeth chattered, but I couldn't tear myself from the door, and I listened, listened. . . .

It is a strange fact, but I never heard any voices except those of the doomed victims, although by my calculations there were at least one hundred prisoners in doomed man's row. The rest kept silent, taking no part in the drama. Evidently each one hoped that his sentence of death would be commuted to imprisonment in a concentration camp. From one-third to one-half of the doomed men did get such commutations. There were few women in those cells.

By three o'clock in the morning everything was quiet. The prison pretended to be asleep. But my heart was thumping violently, cold sweat covered my whole body, and I felt that all the other inhabitants of that accursed floor were also going through the same experience, perhaps in an even worse form.

I slept only in the daytime. This possibly was the reason why I did not suffer much from hunger. I only felt a growing weakness and an unpleasant taste in the mouth. The sensation of hunger proper, as well as the tugging sensation in the stomach, ceased by the end of the third day. I know it wouldn't have been difficult for me to die in that stone trap, but this did not enter my plans. The hunger strike was not a goal in itself, merely a means to drive my legal case from deadlock.

I was aware that before the actual trial my case was in the hands of the investigator Zakharov whose interest it was to see that it was brought to a formal conclusion. I was also sure that he was informed of my hunger strike. Therefore, I patiently waited, continuing to refuse the food offered me once each day. More than the consequences of hunger, I feared, as did many other prisoners, that the uncertainty of being under investigation might drag on for a year or longer.

The fourth day passed as had the others, with my flat refusal of the guard's offer of meal or water. Toward the end of the day I well knew that my strength was markedly impaired. My head swam when I tried to get up, and I stayed in bed. My thoughts were concentrated on estimating my powers of resistance – on how much longer I could stand this self-imposed ordeal of hunger. It may be a day, or two, or three, I thought. I had heard that some prisoners went on with a dry hunger strike for eight days, but I think only healthy, strong men, and especially those fresh from the free world, could abstain that long.

The night of my fourth day in the cell was more than ordinarily disturbing. The executioners worked until dawn, carrying away their victims into the unknown. I did not keep count, but I believe about twenty of my neighbours met death that particular night. I never learned where these men were taken to be shot. The place and procedure of execution is one of the most jealously guarded secrets of the N.K.V.D.

At all events, the killings did not take place in the Kresti, since I heard no shots. Moreover, the Kresti was too populated a place for such a purpose. Rumour had it that a special soundproof hall was built deep in the earth under the Big House on Shpalerny Street, and that through a tunnel dug from that hall to the nearby Neva the victims' bodies, with weights tied to their legs, were dumped into the river. How much truth there is in this I cannot say.

The fifth day of my hunger strike came. About ten o'clock in the morning the door opened and the commander of the building walked in. He called out my name, but I made no answer, pretending that I was more weak than I actually was. He spoke to me again.

'The regional Public Prosecutor Lipatov has arrived,' he said. 'He wants to speak to you. Can you go?'

'I'll try,' I answered, rising from the bed with some difficulty. Holding on to the walls from time to time, I followed the commander, reached the central hall, and entered one of the offices for investigators.

An unfamiliar pimply-faced young man was there, sitting at a table with my old friend Zakharov by his side. In his hands the young man held my statement announcing my hunger strike.

'Sit down. Here's your statement. Now what's your complaint?' asked the pimply one.

'First of all, who are you?' I answered with my own question, taking no notice of Zakharov.

'I'm the regional Public Prosecutor acting as supervisor of the N.K.V.D.,' declared the young man with a show of self-assurance. He inspired little confidence. 'What do you want?' he demanded.

'I want the court to try my case without further delay. I've committed no crimes, and don't understand why I'm in prison.'

'As I have been informed by Comrade Zakharov, your case is in line for trial. The court cannot consider all cases in one day. You must have patience.'

'Let criminals be patient, I don't have to be,' I insisted.

'Comrade Zakharov, how soon can his case be tried?' the Public Prosecutor queried my investigator.

'I think during the next two weeks. He'll receive the indictment in a couple of days,' answered Zakharov.

This was important. I knew from the experience of others that court trial came soon after the serving of indictment, except, of course, where the case was tried in absentia by the Special Council of the N.K.V.D. It was the latter possibility which I feared most, for I was convinced that if I appeared at the trial I would be able to prove my innocence.

'Are you aware that your hunger strike will seriously impair your position at the trial? Don't you know that only enemies of the Soviet government do this sort of thing?' the Public Prosecutor asked me.

'I'm not afraid of that. I've done no harm to anybody in the world, least of all to the Soviet government. My hunger strike has nothing to do with my case. And now that you and Zakharov promise an early trial I shall discontinue my hunger strike.'

Zakharov nodded approvingly.

'Make a written statement that you end your hunger strike,' said the Public Prosecutor pushing a piece of paper toward me.

I wrote the statement and got up. The two officials also rose. We said goodbye to each other and parted. They went toward the exit, I, escorted by a guard, climbed the staircase – panting all the way – to return to my original cell with my old companions.

As soon as I got there I was offered the bed on which to lie down, and became the object of everybody's friendly attention: one offered bread, another what was left of his dinner gruel, the officer and book-keeper gave some delicacies from their parcels, cigarettes, tobacco. I was deeply moved – ate some of their food, and with great joy drew on a lighted cigarette.

During my absence an important event had taken place: prisoners were being taken out for walks in the prison yard – the section that lay in the north-western part. The inhabitants of the entire floor, sometimes of two floors, were taken out at the same time, and if one was nimble enough it was possible to mingle with the inmates of other cells and talk things over with them. This news aroused my greatest interest. I had reason to believe that my accomplices in the case – Boris and Vladimir – were also detained in the Kresti, and I wanted to meet them.

My hopes were realized the next morning. Soon after breakfast at which I ate little and cautiously – knowing of cases of death resulting from overeating after a hunger strike – the cell door opened and all of us together went out, and down the various corridors into the prison yard. There among the strollers I quickly spotted Boris and Vladimir, although they were almost unrecognizable under their prison-grown whiskers and beards. Cautiously manoeuvring in the mass of prisoners who walked around in a circle – gradually falling farther and farther behind – I got into line with my two friends. They didn't recognize me at first, worn-out bearded character that I was. When they did, they were shocked at my appearance. After a brief exchange of greetings I immediately went to work on Boris:

'Now that Zakharov isn't here, please explain your conduct at the interrogation. Why on earth did you give out all that tripe?'

'I keep asking him the same question, but he never answers me,' Vladimir joined in. 'He only grunts inarticulately.'

'But the evidence I gave is perfectly true,' Boris mumbled, screwing up his myopic eyes and smiling stupidly.

'This is no joking matter,' I said sternly. 'If you want to stay behind bars for five years, it's your affair. But you've acted like a skunk toward me and Vladimir. Remember, it won't end well for *you* either.'

'Don't you try to scare me,' burst out Boris half-threateningly. 'The investigator has tried to scare me, so has Vladimir, and now you're trying. I've had enough!'

Rage was choking me – but what could I do? Punch him in the face? I wasn't strong enough for that, and it wouldn't have helped any. Boris calmed down somewhat.

'Someday I'll tell you all about it,' he said. 'After the trial.' Then he reverted to complete silence. We couldn't get anything out of him during the rest of our walk.

Returning to the cell I began to mull it over in my head, trying hard to understand what could have forced Boris to assume the part of a false witness. After all, he was a decent fellow – I was certain of that. There could have been no other reason but some sort of blackmail on the part of the investigator. The problem was how to make him retract his former evidence at the trial. As I saw it, this was very important.

Despite my general weakness I continued to join in the walks in the prison yard. But I had only three more chances to speak to Boris since every day there was a new combination of floors and cells from which the prisoners were taken out for a walk. However, it was plain that all attempts to influence Boris were utterly futile. He obviously had weighty reasons for behaving the way he did – reasons which doubtless included a promise by the investigator that he would be set free after the trial. Vladimir was entirely on my side, and assured me he would say nothing at the trial to affect us adversely.

About six days after my conversation with the pimply Public Prosecutor – I was convinced he was not a Public Prosecutor, but an official of the N.K.V.D. – I was called downstairs and was handed the indictment drawn up by Zakharov and approved by Korkin, chief of the Secret Political Section. I signed a receipt for the indictment and returned to my cell to plunge into a study of this remarkable document.

It was clear that Zakharov had spared himself no pains in preparing the indictment. It covered eighteen pages and was written in the characteristic style of the N.K.V.D. with a touch of Nat Pinkerton. From the somewhat tragically comic document I learned for the first time some interesting details of Zakharov's activities in connection with my case. He seemed to have visited Moscow to obtain information about my father. I had told him nothing about my parents that would be politically compromising, yet the indictment stated I was the son of a 'well-known counter-revolutionary, formerly a member of the Socialist-Revolutionist party, against whom the Soviet government had, on several occasions, taken repressive measures'. Moreover – and this I learned much later – a search had been made by Zakharov's orders, in the apartment of my mother who lived 1,200 miles away from Leningrad, deep in the distant south. That search, I must add, yielded no incriminating data of any kind.

The detailed introductory part of the indictment dealt with my activities before I settled in Leningrad, and with my so-called counter-revolutionary activities since that time. It ended with a summing up in which Zakharov formulated the following charges against me. I quote them in brief:

1. Writing of anti-Soviet character (my diaries).
2. Possession of counter-revolutionary literature (the diaries and Nadya's books).
3. Espionage (correspondence with philatelists in the United States of America and Yugoslavia).
4. Anti-Soviet propaganda abroad (ditto).
5. Fomenting an armed uprising among the Cossacks (evidence given by Boris).
6. Preparations for robbing savings banks and co-operatives (ditto).
7. Organization of counter-revolutionary groups among the students of my institute (reports of the N.K.V.D. agents, or Nadya's contribution).
8. Anti-Soviet propaganda among the population (Boris's evidence).

All this, I learned, came under the definition of 'crime' in the Criminal Code of the Russian Soviet Federative Socialist Republic covered by paragraphs 2, 4, 6, 10 and 11 of Article 58, and paragraph 3 of Article 59 (banditry). Boris and Vladimir were charged with failure, while knowing of my criminal activities, to report them to the N.K.V.D., a crime covered by paragraph 12 of Article 59.

The concluding part of the indictment, in the section referring to me, stated:

'. . . has refused to admit guilt, but is fully shown to be guilty by the material evidence and the evidence of the witnesses.'

When I finished reading this legalistic composition, my spirits drooped. I knew how simple it was to throw people in concentration camps for ten years without any material evidence or evidence of witnesses. With the indictment so thoroughly prepared I felt sure a sentence to be shot was the least I could expect. My cellmates were much interested in the document, but I did not show it to anybody that day, fearing it would would make too bad an impression. Nor was I wrong. When on the next day I did show it to a few old-timers whom I wanted to consult, it was clear they felt that I was a doomed man. The officer even whistled and immediately cut me a big chunk of the sausage he had received, and gave me a packet of cigarettes. Then he began advancing arguments to prove that shooting was now frequently commuted to ten years of hard labour, and that I must not lose hope. Others seconded him.

But this unanimous moral support in no way helped cheer me up. I pictured myself appearing before the judges dirty, emaciated, heavily bearded, with all those charges to answer, and I felt that if I were placed in the judges' position I would sentence the villain to be shot.

The next day, when I met my two friends during the walk, I got some malicious satisfaction at the sight of their long faces. They had not expected such a remarkable flight of fancy from Zakharov, and Boris, who had clearly underrated the literary gifts of the investigator, was now doubtful about getting out of his scrape unharmed.

However, fate was kind to me. In the first place, all my cellmates were eager to fatten me up, at the sacrifice of their own meagre rations. And in the second place, two or three days after these events, all of us in the cell were taken to the bath-house in the prison yard. It was a disgustingly dirty place, but it had water, hot water, in sufficient quantity for one's needs, and it had soap which I had not held in my hands for many months. I had a wonderful time washing myself, and also washed my shirt, turned dark grey with dirt and time. To top it all, some prisoner of the ordinary criminal type gave me a shave in the dressing-room using a piece of broken glass for a razor. Painful as the operation was I bore it stoically, and the result was excellent.

This was all decidedly in my favour for, on the morning of the second day after visiting the baths, the deputy commander of the building opened the door of our cell, called out my name and told me to make ready to go to trial. I looked my natural self – a boy of nineteen whose thinness was further set off by the low white collar of the shirt. In fact, I didn't look even nineteen. I said goodbye to everybody, thanked them for their friendliness, and went out escorted by the deputy commander. Reaching the ground floor we turned into the prison office where I found Boris and Vladimir already waiting for me behind the bars, and to my great joy, looking dirty and wearing their beards – their cell had not been taken to the baths.

A quarter of an hour later, after we had been written off the prisoners' list of the Kresti, we were led to the yard and thrown into a Black Raven.

We drove a fairly long time, long enough indeed to be thoroughly depressed by the endless lamentations of Boris who by now had completely succumbed to his fears. Nevertheless, when we reached the court I stepped out of the Black Raven in a highly optimistic mood. Being familiar with Leningrad it was easy for me to identify the building which surrounded the courtyard as that of the Czarist General Staff.

As a matter of fact, there were only two courts which could try me – the Special Collegium of the Regional Court located on the Fontanka Embankment, or the Tribunal of the Military District which convened in the General Staff building. The Military Tribunal could have jurisdiction in my case because it often considered cases involving charges of espionage regardless of whether the defendants were military or civilian. The Tribunal was regarded as being more stern in its verdicts, though the Special Collegium, too, frequently passed death sentences. My arrival at the General Staff building was therefore quite a bad omen. But probably because of the sunny day and the new surroundings, or because of some subconscious hope, I was in excellent spirits, if a bit nervously excited.

We were quickly escorted into the building and, after a short peregrination in and out of corridors, were placed behind the grille which divided a fairly large and bright room into two sections. In the other section, shouldering arms, stood two sturdy young men wearing the uniform of the N.K.V.D.

Boris looked like a storm cloud, and kept muttering something in a lugubrious tone. He snapped back angrily whenever anyone spoke to him. Vladimir assumed an absurdly unnatural air of gaiety, and sang in his unpleasant voice, or whistled some popular tune.

We waited quite a long time. A soldier brought us a tray with some sort of breakfast: a couple of sausage sandwiches, an apple, and a glass of tea for each of us. Since Boris was in a state of jitters and Vladimir pretended he had just come from a gala dinner, I calmly helped myself to all three portions.

Before I had time to finish my last apple, the door opened and in came two young officers and three soldiers. One of the officers unlocked our grilled door, and after taking our copies of the indictment, he ordered us to walk out. We formed in single file. I went first, with a soldier carrying a rifle behind me. Next Boris, then another soldier; after him Vladimir who nonchalantly kept his hands in his pockets, and, finally, another soldier. Then one officer drew a revolver and warned us in a loud voice that if any of us attempted an escape he would be shot on the spot. With this officer at the head of the column and the other bringing up the rear we marched off.

I suppose our procession looked very impressive as we made our way down the long and devious corridors filled with a mixed crowd of military men and civilians. Everybody looked at us with an expression of fear. But they were furtive glances, not steady gazes.

Five minutes later we entered a large, barren room with its window-panes painted over. On one side of the room rose a platform on which was a table covered with red cloth. Below, facing the table, stood three chairs on which we were told to sit. I sat in the centre, Boris on my right, Vladimir on my left. The three soldiers placed themselves behind us, erect and motionless, shouldering arms. The first officer, with the revolver still in his hand, fussed around a little and then, obviously deciding that all preparations for the performance were completed, ran off somewhere. The other officer remained on guard outside the door. We sat waiting for what might come next.

After a short time the door was flung open and the same first officer burst into the room shouting in an unnaturally loud voice: 'Rise! The Tribunal is coming!' We instantly jumped to our feet, turning our heads toward the door. The Tribunal entered – three high-ranking officers and another military man who turned out to be a secretary and who at once proceeded toward a small table in the corner which I had not noticed before.

The Tribunal seated themselves at the red-topped table, while the young officer of the guard drew himself up near the door with his revolver held tensely in his hand. Hesitantly we sat down. The judges began rustling papers which they had brought with them, and whispered among themselves as they glanced at us from time to time. Then the one in the centre turned to the officer at the door.

'Why are there only three of them?' he asked, pointing at us.

The officer rushed over and started whispering in the ear of the chairman of the Tribunal. The secretary, too, hurried to the platform, and they all began to search among the contents of bulky briefcases packed with papers. Finally, they picked out a few folders and replaced those removed before. This done, the chairman turned to us and said:

'Rise.'

We rose, and he went on:

'You are present at the special sitting of the Military Tribunal of the Leningrad Military District, whose members are. . . .' He mentioned three names. 'Have you any objections to the membership of the court?' We had no objections, so he continued. Quoting some articles and paragraphs rapidly and indistinctly, he told us that, on pain of certain penalties, we were forbidden to lie. Then he inquired if we had received the indictment, and without waiting for our answer, began to read the piece in a loud voice. I had the impression he had never seen it before. I even believed he was reading the same copy which the young officer took away from me a quarter of an hour earlier – mine had its margins torn off (for cigarettes) and so had the one in his hands. The reading of the indictment took nearly half an hour. When he finished, he permitted us to resume our seats, but immediately called out my name, and I had to get up again.

After asking my first name, my father's, my family name, and when I was born, he questioned me about my parents.

'Who is your father?'

'My father is employed at the People's Commissariat – in Moscow.'

'Has he retained his connections with the Socialist-Revolutionists?'

'I don't know. He never told me he was a Socialist-Revolutionist.' (This was the truth.)

'Who used to visit your house?'

I mentioned two or three names which he wrote down.

'What persons did your father correspond with?'

'I don't know.'

'Do you know why your father was twice put in prison?'

'I don't. During those years between 1922 and 1929 I didn't live with him.'

'And he never told you?'

'No, never.' (This, too, was the truth.)

'Who is your mother?'

'She's a teacher – has been since 1912.'

'Why didn't she live with your father?'

'I don't know.'

After further detailed questioning about my life in Moscow, he took up the charges in the indictment. Showing me my ill-fated diaries, he asked:

'Were these written by you?'

'Yes – three years ago.'

'The Tribunal is not interested in that. We have no statute of limitation,' the judge said, passing my diaries to his colleagues who immediately began to study the places marked with a red pencil by Zakharov.

'Are these books yours?' asked the judge shaking Nadya's gift bundle.

'No, I never saw them. They were left at my place by somebody on the eve of my arrest. I think those books belong to the Special Section of our institute.'

The judge whispered and looked at some papers.

'Did you engage in espionage?'

'No. I was only a philatelist.'

'I'm a philatelist, too,' the judge said, 'but I don't combine collecting stamps with spy activities.'

'Neither do I,' I answered.

We talked a while on how espionage can be combined with philately, and passed on to the question of how I had engaged in anti-Soviet propaganda in my foreign correspondence.

'It is evident from the letters of your American correspondent in San Francisco that you had denounced the Soviet government.'

'This can't possibly be evident. The American, though not a Communist, is certainly in sympathy with the Soviets. I was sending him the magazine *The Bolshevik* and some Moscow newspapers. He's studying Russian.'

'Are you sure of that?' the judge asked, as if he was beginning to doubt his previous assertion.

'Absolutely. You can find this out yourself by reading his letters.'

The judges plunged into their papers again. There was silence, interrupted only by the rustling of paper. Meantime, I resumed my seat. Soon the chief judge began the cross-examination of Boris. After questioning him on routine biographical data the judge suddenly asked:

'Why were you ordered to leave Leningrad two years ago?'

'Oh, that's what it is!' I thought to myself. Boris had never mentioned this expulsion order, and it was clear that in this lay the secret of the investigator's power over Boris. His confusion confirmed this.

'Yes, I was ordered to leave, but Citizen Zakharov promised me . . .' he said.

'Yes, I know – that will do,' the judge interrupted, having meanwhile looked up some paper. 'Tell the Tribunal what you know about his activities.' He nodded in my direction.

In a dull voice Boris repeated all the cock and bull stories he had told at the interrogation. When he had finished, the judge asked me:

'Is all this true?'

'It's all lies, from beginning to end, and you know it is as well as Boris does – and as the investigator did,' I said with some temper. Again there was whispering among the judges behind the red table. The chief judge rang his little bell sternly as if calling me to order, then applied himself to Vladimir.

After the routine questions, he suddenly asked:

'You belong to the impressionist school as an artist, don't you?'

'I do,' answered Vladimir, holding on to the back of his chair with an air of defiance. Vladimir was a passionate believer in impressionistic painting, a cause of constant clashes between him and Boris.

'Don't you know this is a typically bourgeois movement that is unhealthy and decadent?' asked the judge, having apparently just read this definition in one of his papers.

At this point Vladimir, taking up a stupid pose, and speaking in a squeaky voice. launched into a speech intended to convince the Tribunal that impressionism is one of the highest achievements of the art of painting – that we must accept and utilize the best results of the bourgeois culture for the building of socialism, and such gibberish. The judge listened patiently for some time, but finally interrupted Vladimir by turning to his silent colleagues and saying:

'Well, everything seems clear. Have you any questions to ask the defendants?'

The two other judges, first one, then the other, took up the cross-examination, constantly consulting their notes. The one on the right questioned me with an obvious desire to drown me, speaking in a hostile voice tinged with mocking distrust of everything I was saying, while the one on the left put questions that showed a desire to help me out of my plight. I gave my answers in a tone of unshakable conviction of my innocence. One question from the lefthand judge put Boris in an awkward position.

'What do you think your sentence will be?' asked the judge.

'I think you'll acquit me,' answered Boris somewhat diffidently. 'The investigator told me . . .'

'Don't be so certain. This is not an investigation – it's a Tribunal. The bigger his crime,' he pointed at me, 'the bigger is yours for not reporting it in proper time.'

At last the chief judge rose and once more looked over the indictment. Then suddenly he sat down again.

'There is one other charge in the indictment,' he said, turning to me. 'You organized anti-Soviet groups among the students in your institute.'

'No, I did not,' I answered. 'I never engaged in anti-Soviet activities of any kind whatever, and I think it's already obvious to you.'

'All right. Now you can make your final statement of defence.'

I rose. What could I tell them? It seemed unnecessary for me to try to disprove the indictment. The utter hollowness of the entire case was too apparent, and they couldn't possibly regard the charges as seriously substantiated. However, I repeated my entire story as it actually was, to convince them I was completely innocent. I was followed by Boris who made an exceptionally stupid and confused speech in which he spoke of his repentance and the complete realization of having made the mistake of not informing on me earlier, and pleaded for forgiveness and leniency.

Lastly, Vladimir, apparently persuaded that the main charge against him was his faith in impressionism, made a long speech full of technical references in defence, not of himself, but of impressionism. The judges looked weary, but heard him out.

The chief judge stood up again.

'The court examination is concluded. Go to the adjoining room,' he said, signalling to the soldiers who stood motionless behind our chairs. We got up, and the soldiers turned around clicking their heels. The young officer with a revolver in his hand rushed up to take over command of our column, and we filed into the next room.

The deliberation of the judges did not last very long. We had been in the room about twenty minutes when the same young officer came in and escorted us back to the courtroom. We stood lined up before the judges' table. The judges rose, and the chief magistrate, in a tired and fairly indistinct voice read the verdict, beginning with: 'In the name of the Union of Soviet Socialist Republics . . .'

It went on to state the charges briefly; continued with the statement: 'Having considered the entire case in a court trial, the Tribunal has found so-and-so guilty of the following crimes' . . .

These were listed as:

1. Writing and keeping of anti-Soviet literature (my diaries).
2. An attempt to form an anti-Soviet organization (not stated with whom, when, and where).
3. Intention to rob savings banks and co-operatives.

Then the judge concluded: '. . . which is provided for in paragraphs 10 and 11 of Article 58. Accordingly he is sentenced to be deprived of freedom for a term of six years.'

My two friends, found guilty of non-informing, a crime provided for in paragraph 12 of Article 58, were each sentenced to three years in prison.

The sentences could be appealed against during the next seventy-two hours at the Military Collegium of the Supreme Court of the U.S.S.R.

We barely had time to hear the judge's last words, as the officer ordered us to follow him. Without saying goodbye we left the court-room, lined up next door in a column, and marched off to our old place – behind the grille in the room at the other end of the building. Other men were present, now waiting their turn to be tried. I was told that three Tribunal courts were in session at the same time in different rooms.

We sat on a bench in silence, each thinking his thoughts and reliving his experiences of the day.

Several hours went by. During those hours there was ceaseless move-ment in our cage. Escorted prisoners kept coming in from various prisons where they were detained while their cases were under investi-gation. After a short wait, excited by their forthcoming trials, they were taken to one of the rooms in which the courts of the Tribunal were sit-ting incessantly for ten hours a day, and an hour or two later were brought back struggling under the weight of the sentences they had received. That day more than twenty men were sentenced to death. By the end of the day our cage was packed with people.

About eight o'clock the young officer who headed our escort came in and handed everybody typewritten copies of their sentences. Then the other half of the room became filled with soldiers, and names were called out from a list of those sentenced to death. These were led away. Twenty minutes later those of us who remained were also taken out and loaded into a big open truck. We were joined by some eight soldiers armed with automatic rifles, and drove into the evening streets of Leningrad – streets where I had not walked for more than seven months.

It is difficult to convey the emotions of a man who had spent over half a year in jail and was to spend many more years in similar confinement when, for a brief hour, he finds himself among surroundings which were customary to him in former days. That evening when our open truck rolled down the brightly lighted streets of my beloved Leningrad, where I had walked innumerable times, and when I again saw the familiar buildings, movie houses, stores, and that endless stream of people on the pavements – that evening I realized for the first time how unbridgeable was the gulf that would separate me from the rest of the world for many years to come. I read the illuminated billboards, the advertising signs, peered into the faces of people who were casting frightened glances at our truck, and felt that an entirely different life was beginning for me – a life unlike that of the rest of the country's population. As we drove on I was inwardly saying farewell to everything that had been close and dear to my heart.

After driving along Liteyny, Nevsky and Old-Nevsky avenues, our car plunged into the streets of the eastern outskirts of Leningrad – a district unfamiliar to me – and soon stopped in front of a thick gate beyond which one could see dimly a tall, massive building that was to become my home for some months. The gate opened and we entered the yard of Leningrad's Transfer prison.

There some new people received us from the convoy, checked us on the list and told us to line up in pairs, then led us downstairs.

We entered a small hall below street level, and were literally shoved into one of the three big cells on that floor, already jammed with people. My recollections of the crowded conditions on Tairov Lane paled at once when I saw the state of things in this basement. It was physically impossible to lie down. At best, men sat on tables or on their bundles and travelling cases. Others simply remained on their feet.

A half hour later the new arrivals were called by name out to the hall where some prison official, sitting at a little table in the corner, filled in new prison cards and took fingerprints. Never having had my fingerprints taken, I looked disgustedly at my ink-soiled hands and realized that I was a true convict, sentenced to a long term of heavy penal labour. It had been different during the preceding investigation. Then it was only an examination of the case – the trial was still ahead – so I was able to think whatever I pleased: to hope for acquittal, for early liberation. Now, prison was revealed to me as a frightening reality.

I did not believe, I did not want to believe that my conviction was the work of the Soviet government – of that political regime under which I grew up to be a man. I could not, and at that time dared not think it was anything but a fortuitous, if unfortunate chain of circumstances, not a whole huge system that flung me, as well as many others, into this dungeon. Before I found myself in prison I had been firmly convinced that the N.K.V.D. jailed people for real crime – that those in prisons and concentration camps were actual criminals who were dangerous to society. This certain conviction was considerably shaken when I met the men who were imprisoned. I learned for what 'crimes' these people filled the jails. But even then I had some doubts. It was possible, I believed, that everyone concealed and knowingly denied his criminal activities for fear of being informed on by other prisoners.

Now I did not have even this comfort. I knew I was innocent of any crimes against the Soviet government; that I had done nothing wrong; that the investigator, as well as the judges, not only did not believe in my guilt, but did not even take the trouble to hide this fact.

And here I was in this dirty and stuffy cellar, from now on a political criminal, a branded enemy of the Soviet government, with six years of penal labour before me. And nearly all the men around me, too, were political criminals of the same kind – just ordinary, simple people.

I had thought that those imprisoned for counter-revolutionary activities were former capitalists, aristocrats, speculators, rich farmers familiarly known as kulaks, and perhaps a sprinkling of workers, peasants and white-collar employees fallen under the influence of elements hostile to the Soviets. The actual facts were the exact opposite. There were few of the types I have just mentioned – the overwhelming majority of prisoners were workers, white-collar men, and members of the intelligentsia.

My mind strained for an explanation of this phenomenon. I still believed in the infallibility of the higher organs of the state. I recalled vague rumours that had circulated in Leningrad, according to which Kirov's assassination was the work of the N.K.V.D., whose secret object was to let loose crushing reprisals on the heads of innocent people in order to arouse bitter anti-Soviet feelings among the population. That would have been a kind of counter-revolutionary political wrecking activity within the organization set up for state security. But it was difficult to reconcile this theory with the official statements I had read in the newspapers which told of the arrest and exile of the entire person-nel of the Leningrad N.K.V.D. staff – men like Medved, Zaporozhetz, Fomin, Yanishevsky and others who after the Kirov murder were removed from their high posts and flung into jail.

In short, I didn't know what to think.

The night passed amid these doubts. Next morning prison life resumed its usual course. We were given bread and hot water and the basement was filled with the endless grumbling of two hundred voices. Before midday dinner, to my great surprise, I heard my name called by the guard who brought the prisoner's mail. I instantly recognized my father's handwriting on the envelope. He wrote from Moscow without mentioning how he learned of my misadventure. He urged me not to lose heart for, he pointed out, one could learn much in prison which was a good training school for subsequent life, and, besides, it was possible that I might be released before the expiration date of my term. He added that I was to discount *everything* I might hear about him, and asked me to destroy his letter. Frankly, I did not understand his last request, but I tore it up and threw it away.

I did not speak to Boris or Vladimir who were in the same cell with me. There were too many things that bound us together, but also repelled us from one another. Besides, they were too engrossed in the letters they received – they had relatives in Leningrad – and in sorting out the parcels which were delivered to them soon after dinner. I began to take notice of those who were near me. A young stocky fellow who looked very strong physically and who wore a white peaked cap of military style attracted my attention. He was arguing heatedly with two other young men. There was nothing out of the ordinary in such arguments. Men arriving in prison after their trials as a rule relived their cases over and over again, painfully trying to recall what exactly they had said or done, for which they were sentenced to three, five, or ten years of penal labour. It should be noted that in Leningrad only men tried by the Regional Special Collegium, or the Tribunal, were sent to the Transfer prison. Those who were not called up for trial but were sentenced in absentia were detained before they proceeded to concentration camps or execution, in the second building (occasionally the first building) of the Kresti, in the Nizhegorodsky prison and even in the Central Isolator.

Returning to the three young men who were engaged in an argument, I began to listen to their conversation. Apparently they were unable to agree on the points at issue, and soon separated. I turned to the one who had impressed me favourably at first sight, and inquired about his case. He readily told me his very interesting story.

His name was Mikhail B. He came of peasant stock in Yaroslav province, and was a flyer by profession. After six years' service as an army flyer, he resigned and got a job as an instructor in civil aviation. One could instantly sense his fanatic faith in the Soviet regime. This was to be expected since in the U.S.S.R. flyers are a privileged class in the matter of living conditions, and to Mikhail, raised in a poor peasant family, his own position appeared exceptionally fine. He loved his work which, it seemed, he knew to perfection. His job was in Leningrad.

One day he chanced to meet two of his fellow villagers who were studying in the Higher Artillery School. They visited one another a few times – Mikhail had been recently married and lived in a good apartment in the central part of the city – but no great friendship developed between them. Mikhail was too fanatical in his faith in the Soviet system, while the other two were more critical toward it. Nevertheless, Mikhail talked to them about his work and showed them special maps of various airfields. Later another fellow-Yaroslavian turned up, and now and again they all got together. This man was close to the other two. He was an officer of the Red Army, but he seemed also to have something to do with the N.K.V.D.

Some two months after Mikhail first met these people, the two Artillery School students were arrested by a militiaman in the street as they were leaving the German Consulate in Senate Square. They were first taken to the militia station, and from there, on demand of the Military Public Prosecutor, to the Shpalerny prison where their case was taken up by the Special Section of the N.K.V.D. on charges of espionage. A number of arrests followed, and among the first to be seized was Mikhail and the Red Army Officer. Although he wasn't given much information by his investigator, Mikhail formed the opinion that their case was tied up with another case – the complicated and tangled affair of the so-called Novgorod Insurrectionists, which later resulted in the shooting of several hundred men. Furthermore, an underground organization was brought to light – one which had representatives in Moscow, Rostov-on-Don, and elsewhere, and in which Mikhail's new friend, the Red Army officer, seemed to have played an important role. The investigation had been dragging on for three months when suddenly all three of Mikhail's friends were released from prison by Volkov, the investigator of the Special Section, while broad hints were made to Mikhail of the possibility that the whole case might be dropped.

At this stage, the Military Public Prosecutor made another intervention, and on his demand, the two Artillery School visitors to the German Consulate were rearrested. The Red Army officer had disappeared from Leningrad, but on his return a month later, he, too, was apprehended. Meanwhile, investigation conducted by Volkov was deliberately made more involved and confusing. Now the connection with the Novgorod Insurrectionists was no longer mentioned; the officer, who had time to warn his friends during his absence from Leningrad, was allowed to have two visits from his wife – something unheard of in the Shpalerny prison; persons completely unrelated to the case were somehow dragged into it; and in the end, the Military Tribunal put on a stupid display in which none of the persons heading this, by all signs, real anti-Soviet organization, appeared. However, the two Artillery School students were sentenced to death by a firing squad; Mikhail, charged with treason to his country (Article 58 paragraph 1A) received ten years of penal labour, and the rest of the accomplices were given terms of imprisonment varying from three to eight years. No actual shooting of the sentenced men took place, for ten days later they were informed that their sentences had been commuted to ten years of penal labour.

In telling me all this Mikhail was full of sincere indignation. He felt particularly bitter about the fact that the investigator Volkov, some time after the trial, called the officer who had played such a suspicious part in this affair, to his office and promised him that he would be freed in a few months although his sentence was for six years. The officer did not even think it necessary to keep this promise secret, yet he and Mikhail were on the same prison floor.

After listening to Mikhail's rather confused story I asked him how he explained it all. Unhesitatingly he answered:

'Counter-revolutionists have found their way into N.K.V.D. headquarters in Leningrad. I'm convinced both Volkov and his superiors are German agents who cover up the underground organizations to save them from destruction.'

This fully tallied with my own thoughts, and Mikhail instantly aroused my confidence. If there is counter-revolution in the N.K.V.D., I thought, it must be everywhere else. Why then punish these men? I received the answer much later.

On the following day we were all busy writing appeals to the Supreme Court of the U.S.S.R. I wrote an appeal for Mikhail too, since he, like all young officers of the Red Army, was rather poor at grammar.

Somehow I ceased to notice my surroundings. At any rate, they no longer depressed me as much as they used to. To a certain extent I found comfort in the thought that I bore suffering without guilt, and that sooner or later justice would prevail. Days passed in endless conversation as we all waited for a change – for something new to happen.

One day, at last, those who had stayed in the basement two weeks – this, it turned out, was a quarantine period – were transferred to the higher floors. Before this change the prison commander Kazakov came down to the basement and asked which of us wished to work in the prison. He explained that the Transfer prison had two workshops, a mechanical shop in which spring-carts and couplings for truck-trailers were made, and a chemical shop in which rags and paper pulp were turned into a special kind of cellulose used for military purposes. He immediately picked out from among the volunteers a number of smiths, fitters and carpenters for the mechanical workshop. Some twenty men, I among them, offered to try their skills in the chemical workshop.

When, following this visit, we were taken upstairs, the volunteer workers were installed on the second floor, and those who preferred not to work, on the first. Three other men and I were put in cell No. 16, a large, fairly bright room with barred windows and a view of the Alexander Nevsky monastery. The cement floor was brilliantly polished. A table with a big copper teapot, and benches around it, occupied the

centre of the room. There were thirty beds for as many inmates who at
that moment were off at their jobs. The beds had grey blankets, and
everywhere there was scrupulous cleanliness and order. Only one man
was present, released from work for two days because of poor health.
He was busy tidying up the place.

We became acquainted at once. He was an old worker from the
Svetlana plant, sentenced, like me, under Article 58 (paragraph 10)
which dealt with anti-Soviet propaganda and the one most used in
jailing N.K.V.D. victims. He explained to me that paragraph 10 of that
article was regarded almost as if it were not counter-revolutionary –
in fact, so much so that the prison administration quite often used
prisoners convicted under '58-10' for such responsible work as that of
mechanics, blacksmiths, fitters, electricians, in ordinary life the most
privileged trades for workers. From this and many other talks I found
out the general make-up of the convict society.

At the top of the social ladder were those convicted of swindling,
speculation, forgery, non-payment of alimony, rape, and various so-
called criminal breaches of trust. Everywhere and at all times these
convicts enjoyed almost unlimited confidence of the prison and camp
administration, and were appointed to such soft jobs as working in
offices, prison stores, canteens, bath-houses, barber shops, and so on.

The next rung was occupied by thieves of every description, from
burglars to pickpockets. After them came the murderers and the gunmen, who completed the three upper strata forming one general class
of privileged prisoners. All these 'socially elect' prisoners, provided
they were in any way capable of work, were supported by the administration who tried to make them feel they were not actually criminals
and were capable of reforming, in contrast to the counter-revolutionists
who were 'irreconcilable enemies of the Soviet regime'.

This class of prisoners provided the social base upon which rested the
administration of prisons and concentration camps, and served as an
aid in applying stricter rules or repressive measures when there was
danger of mutiny. Especially for them the penal institutions ran the so-
called Cultural-Educational sections engaged in re-educating criminals
into sound citizens of the U.S.S.R. In my time this privileged class
comprised from ten to twenty per cent of the population of concentration camps. Their terms of punishment were sometimes cut in half. In
addition, members of the first group, swindlers, speculators, and so
forth, were as a rule spared from being sent to 'bad' camps, and if by
any chance they did get there, they were at once appointed to higher
posts on the administrative ladder.

Immediately below the 'socially elect' was the well-filled category
of the '58-10' – agitators against the Soviet regime – people who were
in prison by mere accident and whose crime (at most) consisted of an
incautious conversation on a political subject, telling a political anec-

dote, being of disapproved social origin – parents aristocrats, merchants, priests, kulaks – or the inability to get along with the local representatives of the Soviet government, such as the administrative officers of plants and collective farms, militiamen, Communists, and so forth.

Approximately the same social status was accorded the prisoners convicted of plunder of socialist property, under the law of August 7, 1934, mostly workers or peasants who stole something at a factory or collective farm, even when the value of the stolen article did not exceed ten rubles – and I knew of such ludicrous crimes as the theft of a few pounds of potatoes from collective farms. These offenders were always handed a ten-year sentence in a concentration camp.

Lastly, at the lowest rung of the social ladder, were the prisoners convicted not only under paragraph 10, Article 58, but also under other paragraphs of the same article, namely paragraph 6 (espionage), 7 (wrecking activities), 8 (terrorism), 9 (diversionary acts), 11 (belonging to a counter-revolutionary group), 12 (non-informing) and 13 (concealment of the prerevolutionary past). But even in this group of outcasts there were some whom everybody shunned. They were the prisoners convicted under these paragraphs of Article 58: 1A (treason), 2 (preparation of an insurrection) and 3, 4 and 5 (ties with foreign countries). During my many years of prison life I met hundreds of such counter-revolutionists, but I can say with almost complete assurance that not one of them was a serious threat to the Soviet state.

I must admit, though, the *real* political criminals, people of genuine importance, were never kept in ordinary concentration camps and prisons. They were confined to special isolators in Yaroslav, Sizran, Tomsk, Oryol, and other cities and to special concentration camps such as in Solovki on the White Sea, and in some of the wild regions of north-eastern Siberia, entirely cut off from the rest of the world.

On the morning following my arrival in 'the workers' cell' I was awakened by my new companions at six. After a quick breakfast of a chunk of bread, I lined up in a column with the others, and escorted by a special guard we walked out into the prison yard, turned around the main building, passed through two other yards, and finally reached a two-story brick building from which emanated a heavy, unpleasant odour. This was the chemical workshop of the prison where production covered the whole cost of the upkeep for the prisoners, and brought the N.K.V.D. a considerable income besides.

I was given the job of carting in a small barrow the ill-smelling rags, collected from the dustbins of the city, from the warehouse, where they were received, to the workshop. There, in a large room, huge wooden vats, each about four yards in diameter and about five yards deep, had been dug into the ground; and in them filthy rags, after being sorted out, were successively boiled in various chemical solutions. Prisoners stirred the rags with long hooked poles and carried them from one vat to another, gasping from the poisonous fumes which came from the chemicals. Taken out of the last vat the shapeless but still suffocating mass was transferred to another room where it was squeezed, dried and pressed. In still another room the finished product was packed in boxes ready for shipment to one of the plants manufacturing explosives.

Favourable as my general surroundings were, I could not hold out at my work for more than two weeks. The chemical fumes I had to inhale resulted in severe headaches, and I stopped going to the work-shop. Two days later I was transferred to the 'non-working' floor.

Conditions on that floor were somewhat worse, but I was fortunate in getting there the day after a huge group of prisoners, comprising almost half the population of the prison, had been sent to a concentra-tion camp, and was therefore able to get a bed right away.

Cell No. 8 was a little larger than the one I was in before. Its normal complement was about forty men although it often housed as many as 150, when men had to sleep on the floor and under the beds. How-ever, those who got in first retained the right to their beds, and over-crowding did not affect me personally.

It was much more gay in cell No. 8 than on the floor above. The occupants were very interesting people, and since we had absolutely nothing to do, our days were filled with playing chess and dominoes, reading books and newspapers, and talking on a wide range of subjects.

My neighbour on one side was George Dax, a chemical engineer of late middle age who, before the revolution, had travelled widely over Europe and Asia and I listened to his stories with an open mouth.

His occupation under the Soviets was scientific research in the photographic industry, and he was considered a valuable worker. To his misfortune, Dax possessed a sharp and observant mind, and a tongue that was not sufficiently restrained. The moment arrived when, in the eyes of the N.K.V.D., the trouble caused by Dax's tongue exceeded the recognized usefulness of his work. He was kept in solitary confinement for a year – that was before the Kirov incident– and was sentenced under a series of paragraphs of Article 58 to eight years of imprisonment. Dax tried to be cheerful, but at times he felt greatly depressed. Shortly before his arrest, at the age of fifty, he married a young and beautiful laboratory assistant in his institute. He was terribly affected by this enforced separation, and feared that once sent to a concentration camp he would never see his wife again. She visited him and brought him parcels every week.

Nearly everybody, I may add, received parcels, since the majority of the prisoners were from Leningrad, and Kazakov permitted every prisoner to receive one parcel a week, the delivery days being arranged in the alphabetical order of names.

There were two delightful old men who resembled each other amazingly. They had worked side by side in the same shoe factory, the *Skorokhod*, for thirty years. In them one met typical representatives of the regular workers of Leningrad – quick-witted, active, fairly well educated though they had no schooling, definite in their ideas on a variety of subjects. They never dissembled when they spoke about Soviet life, saying openly that the proletariat was brazenly deceived by the Bolsheviks and had lost not gained by the revolution. Workers of this type were often too free with their tongues even in ordinary life, and highly disapproving of such talk, I used to avoid them. Now, in prison, I felt differently about their simple, human and lucid philosophy, and spent many hours in conversation with them.

Innumerable people passed before my eyes during my stay in cell No. 8 of the Transfer prison. The composite of inmates in that cell was determined by Kazakov himself, on the basis of intelligence and culture. What put this idea into his head, no one could tell. But the men brought to the cell were usually interesting. There were very few crude peasants or city youths. From time to time the entire group was mercilessly broken up by the removal of men for transfer to concentration camps. But this was inevitable, for without taking some men away the prison would have burst. As a rule, we learned the time and destination of the next transfer from the 'socially elect' who worked in the prison office. The men managed to inform their relatives, and were thus able to get the things necessary for their long journey. Prisoners were permitted to write as many letters as they chose. The letters were censored, of course, but they usually reached their destination.

A week after my arrival in cell No. 8, Mikhail, who had been relieved of his duties in the chemical workshop as a man sentenced for too terrible a crime, was brought to my cell and became a neighbour. After much cogitation we decided to find out the truth in his tangled case. I wrote two letters, one to Akulov, Secretary of the Central Executive Committee, the other to A. A. Soltz, member of the Soviet Control Commission, who was popular among the prisoners. These letters began with the general picture of the situation as we saw it, stating that the N.K.V.D. was carrying out a policy of reprisals on a wide scale by jailing entirely innocent people, which planted anti-Soviet sentiments among the masses of the Leningrad population. A number of examples followed. Then I gave a detailed account of Mikhail's case, mentioning by name all the agents of the N.K.V.D. whose role in the case appeared suspicious to us. Needless to say, the letters were couched in the most loyal tone.

Mikhail was able to pass these letters to his wife when she came to visit, and she immediately proceeded to Moscow to deliver them in person.

At the same time we sent complaints against the unjustified verdicts

in our cases to Andrey Y. Vishinsky, then the Supreme Public Prosecutor of the U.S.S.R., and to Mikhail I. Kalinin, the President of the
Soviet Union.

Day followed day, but nothing was heard from Moscow. Meanwhile life in prison went on in its accustomed way.

Soon there was another extraordinary event. I was lying on my bed
reading a book. The cell was filled with the noise which usually
marked visiting hours. A guard kept calling out one name after
another. Suddenly I heard my name. I couldn't believe my ears, but
he repeated it, and when I walked up to him he handed me a notice for
a meeting with an unnamed visitor. Waiting to be taken down I tried
to figure out who it could be. I had not informed my Leningrad friends
of my misfortunes so as not to bring them to the attention of the
N.K.V.D. My mother couldn't have come because she couldn't
possibly afford the trip. And it could not have been my father.

At last there were enough of us to be taken down, and accompanied
by a guard we walked to a separate building, the other side of which
fronted the street. Ten of us were admitted to a big room divided into
two parts by two parallel railings which were about four feet high. A
soldier was pacing up and down between the railings. When we lined
up along one of the railings, the guards took their appointed places,
the door in the other half of the room opened, and the visitors began to
file in. They quickly spotted their relatives among the prisoners, and
gave awkward embraces and kisses across the two barriers. 'There must
be some misunderstanding,' I thought to myself, wondering why I
was there. Suddenly the short figure of a woman appeared in front of
me. I was taken by surprise as I recognized Nadya. She stood with a
big bundle in her arms and stared at me with tears streaming down her
cheeks. I felt embarrassed – not so much for myself as for her. What did
she think when she set out to see me?

'Do you recognize me?' Nadya asked diffidently, moving up to the
barrier.

'I do.'

'Can you forgive me?' her voice caught with tears again. She
dropped her bundle, and clawed at the barrier.

'What sense is there in your visit?' I answered with a question.

'I can't stand it any more. These past months have been torture. I
never imagined . . .' She didn't complete the sentence. I did it for her.

'That your informing on me would result in my being locked behind
bars for six years, is that it?' I asked.

Covering her face with her hands she nodded in silence. Then she
raised her wet face and said:

'Tell me what I can do for you. I'm willing to do anything.'

'Oh, I don't need anything. Other people are taking care of me now.

There's nothing else to be done. Besides, what could *you* do? All I can ask is that you stop doing that work – you know what I mean.'

'I will. I will. I've already decided to do that. But what can I do for *you?*' persisted Nadya sobbing.

'Absolutely nothing. And it will be better if you don't come back here.'

'Take this.' She bent down quickly, picked up her bundle, and held it out, entreaty and expectation in her eyes. I shook my head.

'Why can't you? You don't . . . You can't forgive me?'

I shrugged.

'Why these meaningless words? Forgiveness? Thanks to you I've been shut off from life for six years. I may not even live through it for all I know. You must understand that I can't be particularly grateful to you for your good turn. But I don't wish you any misfortune either. Live on in peace. If my words can make it easier for you, all right, I forgive you – but on one condition – that you never come here again.'

'But you'll take this, won't you?' She held out the bundle once again.

'No. You're asking too much. Goodbye.'

She cast a hasty glance at the clock.

'Five minutes more. Then we'll part – forever!' she sobbed, as the bundle fell from her hands between the barriers.

'Listen, you must permit me . . . When you're sent to a concentration camp, I'll go and live somewhere near by. I'll be able to make things easier for you.'

'By using your influence with a certain institution? No, thank you.'

Nadya was getting hysterical, and I began to feel sorry for her. After all, nothing could be changed in my position. My imprisonment was an inexorable fact, whereas this woman seemed to be sincerely repentant for what she had done.

'Listen, Nadya, stop crying,' I said. 'You can't help matters now. Better forget everything. Shake hands.'

She threw her arms around me, hanging over the barrier.

Fortunately, just then the supervising officer shouted: 'Time!' The visitors began taking leave of the prisoners with hurried embraces. I broke away from Nadya, and was the first of the prisoners to leave the room.

Returning to my cell I thought over the events of the day. How strange, indeed, is fate! What unaccountable accidents determine the present and future of a man! Had I, ten months before, consented to Nadya's proposition, I should now have been safely working on my diploma project, and would soon be graduating from the institute. Nadya's influence would have been enough to keep me out of trouble. Regret began to stir within me. I came to feel that life with a stranger might be better, after all, than prison.

Time passed quickly. Life was not too unbearable. Days were filled with talks. There was never a lack of interesting people. Study, books, daily half-hour walks in the prison yard, once or twice a week seeing the movies which those of us who didn't work could see over and over again, and mad chess playing. Sometimes, for instance, we held what we called 'blitz contests' – continuous playing until one of the players pleaded mercy. On one occasion, I remember, I played 118 games with Grinevich, without leaving the table. Grinevich finally gave up, crying uncle, although he was a better player. Every month a tournament was held, first in each cell, then on each floor, and, finally, for the entire prison. Our cell invariably led the rest. We had such excellent players as my friend Feofilov who would play blind six or seven opponents at the same time.

One day a group of upper-grade schoolboys were brought in from one of the best high schools in Leningrad. There were seven of them, all between sixteen and seventeen years old – quite intelligent boys from well-educated families. They were accused of holding gatherings out-side the school, at which they read anti-Soviet literature. The anti-Soviet literature included *The Decline of the West* by O. Spengler, works by Nietzsche, works by the Russian *émigré* writers Averchenko and Shulgin, and unpublished poems of Yesenin which circulated in hand-written copies. The boys were sentenced to from three to eight years of hard labour, and although they put on a brave front, one could see they were hard hit by their misfortune.

Generally speaking, those who passed through cell No. 8 varied greatly in age, but the majority were comparatively young – students, high-school boys, workers, engineers.

One evening a man from the prison office came to our cell and asked if there were anybody willing to do a couple of weeks' work wiring the building for fire alarms. I volunteered, having had a little experience as an electrician, and next morning set out on my task. The work was quite simple, there was nobody to egg me on, and I was glad to move about the building making holes in the walls, sticking in rollers, stretching wires, and fixing alarm buttons. Another man, an old mechanic from the Nevsky plant, worked with me.

One day, when I was fixing an alarm button, the prison commander Kazakov paused to watch me and asked how I got into prison. I told him my story briefly, and after a few more questions he walked away.

The following day one of the office messengers found me working in the loft, and took me to the commander's office. When he saw me, Kazakov broke off his conversation with somebody there and turned to me with the question:

'Can you do wiring for electric lights?'

'I can, though not very well,' I answered.

'Well then, you'll be taken to my house now, and my wife will tell you what has to be done.'

'But Citizen Commander, I can't guarantee good workmanship.'

'Never mind about that. So long as the lights go on, it's all right. Call in Karasev,' he said to one of his subordinates. A minute later a soldier stepped up before him.

'Take this man to my house.'

'Do you want me to wait for him there, Comrade Commander?'

'It's not necessary. My wife will keep the doors locked so that he doesn't run away.'

I rushed up to my cell, put on my old threadbare overcoat, came down to the soldier who was waiting, and we walked out of the prison.

Snow covered the Leningrad streets, as it had on the night of my arrest. It was not very cold, but it was rather damp. An extraordinary feeling came over me when the prison was left behind and we began to pass free men and women who did not even suspect that I was a man with more than five years of prison life still ahead of him. The soldier walked by my side. He carried no rifle, although he had a revolver swinging from the belt of his short winter coat. But I had no thought of running away. Such a thing seemed incompatible with my innocence.

It took no time to get to the commander's house, which was close to the prison. The soldier rang the doorbell, and a young, pleasant-looking woman opened the door.

'I know, I know, my husband has told me,' she said, interrupting my escort's explanation. 'You may go. I'll keep watch over him.'

The soldier left, and we entered the house. I took off my overcoat in the hall, and holding a small box of tools under my arm, I followed the lady of the house into Kazakov's study. She explained that I was to make a connection and fix a light over the couch on which her husband read in the evening. The job was a very small one – it wouldn't take longer than a couple of hours. I was about to start, but the lady led me to an adjoining room where breakfast was laid on the table.

'Please sit down and have something to eat,' she said. I sat down and gratefully gobbled up everything she offered me. Then I began my work while she sat on the couch and talked to me the entire time.

I soon noticed with sorrow that my work was almost finished. Just then the door opened and in walked Kazakov who came for his midday dinner.

'What, all finished? Quick work!'

'Yes, very nearly, Citizen Commander.' He sat beside his wife and began whispering to her while I finished up on the lamp.

'It's ready. I did the best I could,' I announced.

'And now back to prison?' he asked me. I didn't know what to answer.

'Look here,' he continued, 'it's one o'clock now. The roll call in your cell is at nine o'clock. I can let you go to town for eight hours, but'

– he looked me straight in the eye – 'you must give me your word of honour that you'll be back at your place for the roll call, and that not a soul in the prison will know of your outing. Remember, too,' he went on, 'that if you fail to be back in time, I'll be in for a lot of trouble.' He underscored the last words.

'Well, you promise?'

In my excitement I could only nod.

'Have you any money?' asked Kazakov.

'Yes, five rubles,' I said with a gasp.

'Take some more.' He rummaged through his pocketbook and handed me two *chervonetzs* (twenty rubles).

When he let me out of the house I must have looked half crazy. I walked as far as the first corner, and slowed down my steps, trying to figure out how to make the best use of my eight hours' freedom. Running away never entered my head.

As soon as I came to a decision, I crossed the road, and hurried into the section of numbered 'Soviet streets' (formerly Rozhdestvensky streets). A few minutes later I was ringing the bell at a familiar entrance. The door was opened by the wife of an old friend, Zina.

'Who do you want?' she asked. Then she exclaimed, 'Is that you, Vladimir? Where have you come from? Come in.'

I walked in, and she followed me. She looked me over with an expression of fear in her eyes.

'Have you – run away?' she asked. 'We know everything. We have known since the second day after your arrest. A room-mate of yours telephoned us. Where have you come from now?'

'Don't get excited, Zinochka,' I answered. 'Everything is perfectly all right. I was handed six years, and if the powers that be will it, I'll go through with the sentence. But at this moment I'm free – you understand? I'm free – for exactly eight hours.' And I told her briefly what had happened.

'And you think of going back? But this is – forgive my saying so – sheer idiocy. Listen to me. In an hour I'll get you some money and you'll take an express train at once to Moscow. Or, if you prefer, stay for awhile with us. Nobody will suspect anything – we have fine neighbours. And later, in a week or two, when they have given up looking for you, you'll go away in peace anywhere you want to. Vasya will arrange everything for you.'

Vasya was her husband and he held an important post in one of the government trusts in Leningrad.

Zina would have gone on trying to persuade me, but I cut her short.

'No, Zinochka, I'm going back. I don't want to live like a hunted hare. And furthermore, I won't let Kazakov down. That's settled. But if you wish, part of the time I have, we'll spend together.'

Zina shrugged.

'You're incorrigible. You always lived in a dream world, and you still do. I'm afraid even prison won't cure you. Well, tell me what you want to do.'

'First, I want to wash up. You'll heat me a bath. Next, you'll call the people whose names I'm going to give you. Then, you'll ask Valya [a friend of ours who worked in a theatre box office] to get me two tickets to the Alexandrinsky Theatre.'

'All right There's quite a lot to do, it seems. Here are cigarettes – smoke. I have to . . .'

She disappeared behind a door. She returned right away, but disappeared once more.

'There. Water's heating,' she said, emerging again. 'I phoned Galya and told her to come here at once. When you go to have your bath I'll run out to do some shopping. Meantime, tell me about yourself.' She sat by my side.

Galya! My heart suddenly sank. Galya was my principal reason for deciding nearly a year before to answer Nadya with a positive 'No'. Zina understood me without words.

'Galya often speaks of you,' she went on. 'She cried a great deal when you were taken, and didn't believe you were a counter-revolutionary. I heard they held a general meeting in your institute about the arrested students. You were mentioned as one of the leaders, but nobody believed it. If you only knew how many people were arrested. Everywhere it was terrible. Tell me, whom do you want me to call?'

I gave her the names of two good friends, a student and a young engineer, and also of a girl I knew. Alas, of all the hundreds of acquaintances I had in Leningrad, Zina and her husband, Galya and the other three were the only people I could trust unreservedly.

'All right. I'll get them. Go on with your story,' she broke in impatiently. 'You don't realize how anxious I am to know everything. Why didn't you write a single word? We could have taken you parcels, and it would have made your life a little easier.'

'I'll tell my story when everyone is here. Now I shall ask questions. Don't dare to think of parcels. Not a person, you hear, not a single person must know that we are friends. Don't you ever set foot in the prison or the N.K.V.D.!'

We began to talk. I asked questions about everything I had been torn away from for nearly a year – people, life, events. Zina jumped to her feet.

'We've forgotten all about the bath. Go in quick and bathe while I go shopping.'

I went into the bathroom, undressed and lowered myself with great pleasure into the warm water. I had just begun to soap my head when Zina knocked.

'It's I. Don't be embarrassed, I'm not looking,' she said, coming in.

'Here's underwear for you, also one of Vasya's suits, and a pair of boots. Put them on and throw your old clothes in the corner. Well, I'm off.'

It may have been from the soap, but the tears came to my eyes. Friends – real ones! My little world which I kept secret from all. Nobody in my institute knew of these friends, not even Boris and Vladimir. And here, this little world still survived. I wondered, for how much longer.

Finishing my bath, I dressed, tidied myself up, and returned to the living-room. Suddenly the bell rang in the community apartment, and a minute later there was a knock on the door.

'May I come in? Are you there, Zina?' asked a familiar voice.

'Come in, please.' I could hardly speak, as I stood by the window.

The door opened and Galya, her cheeks flushed, stood on the threshold.

'Where's Zina? Who are you?' She stared at me nearsightedly, then came closer: 'Vladimir! You?' And she rushed to me with outstretched arms.

Soon Zina returned, with a heap of packages.

'Oh, you're already here, Galya! I've bought everything, I could hardly carry it home. Heavens! It's three o'clock. Vasya will be back soon, and dinner isn't ready. Well, never mind, go on talking. Nina will be here in a minute – I called on her – and she'll give me a hand.'

Three o'clock! Six more hours of freedom! How much, and how little!

Zina kept running to and from the living-room and the kitchen, called somebody on the telephone, set bottles, plates, food on the table while Galya and I sat on the couch, holding hands and talking.

The doorbell rang again. Like a bullet in flew Nina; cold, and covered with snow. She threw her arms around me; a crazy sort of girl of whom we were very fond. Pretending to be cross, Zina dragged her to the hall to remove her coat. Nina resisted, but threw off her coat and galoshes and dashed back to me on the couch.

'Loafers! Who's going to help me? Come on. Get into action, all of you! You, too, Vladimir, or I won't be able to tear them away from you,' Zina shouted.

That extremely pleasant holiday bustle which always accompanied our little parties in the past was under way – and that day was really a holiday. Galya wound up the phonograph, and began to play one of my favourite songs. Glasses, decanters and all the other necessary paraphernalia were put on the table. The girls swirled around the apartment. Vasya and Zina had a large room, fairly well furnished, which served as a bedroom, dining-room, and living-room all in one. It was very cosy there. Vasya – or Vassily, to give him his full name – had a good salary, and enjoyed having our little parties at his place. Beside

Vasya, only Sasha, one of our friends, and myself, earned an adequate amount of money.

As for the girls, they never had any money. So, when our small parties were organized, expenses were divided among us three, although Vasya, always generous, took the lion's share.

Preparations for dinner were coming along nicely. At last we all sat down side by side on the couch waiting for Vasya. Zina had already telephoned him and asked him to tell Nikolay and Sasha.

Daylight was waning as we sat close together and talked in low voices. Suddenly Galya burst out crying. Nina followed suit, while Zina had been wiping her eyes even before that. I couldn't control myself either.

Voices and noise were heard in the entrance hall, and in burst my dear friends Vassily, Nikolay and Sasha. Zina lit the chandelier over the table. Again there were embraces, kisses, and questions.

'I took a taxi especially to pick up these fellows from all over town,' announced Vassily.

'I see you haven't been wasting time here,' he exclaimed. 'That's great! Well, friends, let's come to the table as in the good old days,' he said, his eyes wet with tears.

It was hard to be gay. I walked over to Galya who was still in one corner of the couch, sobbing.

'Don't, Galya, dear. We have only five more hours together. Stop crying, or we'll all be blubbering. What fun is that?'

Finally my words took effect and we both ran off to wash our faces. When we returned, the others all felt a little more cheerful. With her face still wet, Nina was chattering gaily. Nikolay was questioning her about me. Others tackled Zina as the one who knew most. Sasha was tuning his violin. He was quite a good engineer, but hated his work and dreamed of the music for which he had great talent.

Noisily we all sat around the table. As in the old days, the cork popped from the champagne bottle which Vassily had bought on his way home. Glasses were filled.

'To our Vladimir!' everybody declared in a chorus. Again embraces and kisses, again tears.

The conversation didn't cease for a moment. I told them all my adventures. Questions were thrown at me one after another, and I scarcely had time to answer them. Simultaneously I was asking them about events during the preceding ten months. Their answers painted a terrible picture of sweeping reprisals in Leningrad. People had been disappearing one after another, and never returned. They were taken from government departments, from plants, from educational institutions, everywhere. We spoke in half-whispers bending over the table.

Dinner was over and we moved to the couch. Those who couldn't find room brought up chairs. Zina closed the window shutters. Only one light bulb was left burning. In the semi-darkness of the room I sat with my friends and told them what I had learned during my absence. I said that I had faith in the possibility of an eventual happy ending, and that we had to muster all our strength and self-control to go through this terrible period, which certainly could not last very long. Vassily shook his head:

'You still hope for something, you still believe in some higher justice. It's futile. There's no way out for us but to forget completely that we are human beings. Only so can we survive. And that's how we dissemble, play the hypocrite, shout "Hurrah" in the common chorus. Here you have left us. Who'll be next?'

Sasha quietly rose from his chair.

'You're right, Vasya. Our only way out is to forget, to remove ourselves from reality,' he said, picking up his violin and beginning to play. We sat silent. Galya's hand was firmly pressed against mine. The music stopped.

'You haven't changed your mind about the theatre?' Zina broke in. 'The tickets are reserved, but you'll hardly have time to see even the first act. It starts at seven, and at nine you have to be back – at home.'

'No, I'll go. I want to gulp as much life as I can, to remember it later.'

'In that case you'll have to leave soon. Oh . . . Vladimir . . .' She started to break down again.

'Think it over,' Vassily said, 'if it's worth going back. I have money just now, somehow we'll get you the necessary documents. Of course, I understand your reasons, but consider well: your term has more than five years to go, and that's a long time. Will you hold out? I'm afraid you're in for a very hard pull.'

'No, don't try to change my mind. It's settled,' I said firmly.

'I understand him,' Nikolay chimed in. 'To live the life of a fugitive, to fear one's own shadow, to tremble day and night, and sooner or later to be caught – no! Prison is better.'

Galya, too, came to my support.

'Vladimir will not deceive the man to whom he gave his word of honour. No, it's better that way.'

Getting up, I said, 'Goodbye, my dear friends. Remember me kindly. With God's help I'll stay alive, though I can't say whether or not we'll meet again. Let's hope we will. Don't write to me or try to help with anything. I'll get along somehow, and you'd only get yourself into great trouble. Thank you for your friendship – for not forgetting me.'

'Shame on you for talking like that,' Zina exclaimed reprovingly as she embraced me. Vassily, Sasha, Nina – all dashed toward me. At last we got into the hall. Suddenly I remembered:

'Why, I'm wearing Vasya's suit. Quick, I must change!'

'Don't be foolish, my friend. The suit stays on you. And hide this away – please, no arguments – it'll come in handy,' Vassily was pushing some money into my pocket. I squeezed his hand.

Finally, we were in the street – Galya and I. Clinging to each other we sped in the direction of Nevsky Avenue. The snow which was falling slowly from the dark sky crunched pleasantly underfoot. The familiar, heart-warming picture of my beloved town! My Leningrad.

At Znamensky Square we took a taxi – I had money! – and some ten minutes later we were pushing through the crowd at the entrance to the Alexandrinsky Theatre. Leaving Galya for a moment, I elbowed my way to the manager's window, said a few words which served as a password for such occasions, and received two tickets for a box in the dress circle, the object of envy for many. Theatres in the Soviet Union are always packed since they are one of the few places left where people can escape from their hateful daily existence.

Only after we had taken our seats and opened the programme which I had bought on the way, did we learn that we were to see *Boris Godounoff* with Simonov in the leading role. This did not matter to me, though. All I wanted was to immerse myself in the familiar atmosphere of good theatre, which I loved so much, since my leave was nearing its end, and I was already casting glances at Galya's watch.

When the curtain rose, we watched the action on the stage for five minutes and then went out into the anteroom, sat on the small couch covered with red plush, and spent nearly an hour talking about the things that only a boy of twenty and a girl of eighteen might talk about under such peculiar circumstances. When the time came to leave I held tightly to Galya's hands, looked into her blue eyes, and said:

'You must promise me one thing. Forget me until the day I come back. You're not tied down to anything. Remain absolutely free, and act as if I did not exist. To do otherwise will poison all the rest of your life. Do you promise me?'

'I'll try – I understand,' whispered Galya, her eyes full of tears.

We walked into the foyer, put on our coats, and running downstairs jumped into a taxi.

'Six Konstaninogradsky Street,' I said to the driver. We went off. Lighted streets, store windows, crowds of people on the snow-covered pavements flickered before the eyes, then the cab turned into the dark side streets and finally stopped before the familiar iron gate. I gave the driver Galya's address, paid him in advance, embraced my dearest for the last time, and sprang out, banging the door. The taxi window came down suddenly.

'You go. I'll wait until you get in, and leave last,' said Galya. 'Goodbye, maybe forever.'

'Goodbye!' I answered and turned toward the small gate for

pedestrians. I rang the bell. The little window opened, and a helmeted head was thrust out at me.

'Who's there?'

'Friend, Karasyev, open the gate,' I answered, recognizing my soldier escort of the morning.

'Brother, you're a smart boy. I was getting jittery not knowing what to do. Get in, fast. Roll call will start any minute,' he said, opening the gate.

As I stepped in I turned around for the last time and waved to Galya. The taxi started off, and the gate slammed behind me.

I ran to my cell. All the doors opened before me. I barely had time to throw off my coat as I heard the command:

'Form up for roll call!'

We all formed up in lines as Kazakov and the deputy commander entered our cell. Kazakov's eyes roved rapidly over the prisoners' faces until they spotted me. Noting that I was back in my place he nodded with satisfaction, gave me a friendly smile, and walked out.

The direct result of this whole episode was complete freedom within the walls of the prison. No order from Kazakov was needed for that. The law of servility made all the functionaries of the 'socially preferred' feel bound to show me every attention as a man whom the prison commander graced with his favour. I also had plenty of money, by prison standards, for Vassily had given me over 200 rubles. My fellow prisoners were good comrades. There was a frequent change of personnel. There were interesting books, movies, and newspapers. I was almost content. One of the prisoners, a university professor of mathematics – an old man sentenced to ten years for corresponding with men in other countries – gave me lessons in higher mathematics. With another, an entertaining railroad engineer who was short and fat, I studied photography. At one time I took lessons in German from a Protestant parson convicted on a charge of espionage, and studied automobile driving – in theory at least – under the guidance of a mechanic, a fine young fellow. He said that in another month of study he would give me a licence for driving a bus.

In short, my time was not wasted. Thanks to extensive practice I took a place among the best chess players in the prison, and on one occasion even received a prize – a box of good cigarettes.

The only letters I received were from my mother. I deliberately refused to keep up connections with old friends, knowing the enormous risk involved in such correspondence for those who were not in prison.

In the midst of these preoccupations I entered upon a new year, 1936.

On the second day of the new year, a guard came to the cell of the privileged prisoners on the upper floor where I was playing chess, interrupted the game and took me to the office downstairs. There I found

Kazakov and a man in the uniform of the N.K.V.D. The stranger glanced at me and said:

'Is this the man?'

'Yes,' Kazakov answered, looking at me with what I felt was a sympathetic concern. Then turning to me he continued: 'You'll go with this comrade now. Don't take your things with you. They'll be sent on to you if necessary.'

An automobile was waiting at the gate. The comrade sat with me in the back seat, and we drove off. Again I was enjoying the sight of the city, while wondering where I was being taken, and why. I asked my companion a few questions, but his answers were so evasive I did not repeat the attempt.

From Nevsky Avenue the car turned into Liteyny. 'That's it, the Big House,' I thought to myself. I was not wrong. A few minutes later we stopped before the main entrance, got out of the car and went through the doorway. My companion showed the sentry a pass, and we were let in, then climbed up a carpeted stairway to the top floor where the best-appointed offices of the N.K.V.D. were situated. I had visited them once before, the night I was taken from the Nizhegorodsky prison to Shpalerny prison.

We came to a door marked with some big number. He knocked, and entered letting me in first. It was a large room with big windows. On the right at the wall stood a huge desk lighted by a table lamp with a strong reflector. A man sat behind the desk, in front of it stood an armchair. The rest of the room was drowned in darkness.

The man at the desk raised his head and silently nodded to my escort. The other turned around and walked out. I stepped up to the desk.

'Sit down. Have a cigarette,' said the man in a slightly hoarse voice as he pushed a box of 'Kuzbass' cigarettes toward me. These are the best-made cigarettes in the Soviet Union, sold only to the higher officers of the army and to the agencies of state security. Then, while appearing to look for matches on the desk, he turned the lamp so that a bright beam of light fell straight on my face. Looking at me from behind the desk was the flabby face of a strikingly dark-haired man with a hawk nose that reached down to the upper lip.

I lit a cigarette from the proffered match and remained silent, trying to appear calm. I realized what I was in for.

Some sheets of paper were pushed toward me, in which I recognized my letter to Akulov, Secretary of the Central Executive Committee, about the 'wrecking activities' in the N.K.V.D. At the top, written in a bold hand, were the words: TO BE INVESTIGATED AND REPORTED. G. YAGODA. I felt rather uncomfortable. The dark-haired person asked:

'Did you write this?'

I paused, collecting my thoughts, then said:

'Yes, I did. May I ask to whom I'm talking?'

This time he paused – for great impressiveness.

'I am a special commissioner of the People's Commissar of Internal Affairs. My name is Berdichevsky. Does that satisfy you?'

'Completely. But may I have proof of this? You realize the matter is deeply serious.'

He looked at me as if taken aback, but with no expression of resentment. Then he unbuttoned the pocket of his military blouse and drew forth a little red book – a service identification book – and handed it to me. I opened the book and read that Berdichevsky was really a special commissioner of the People's Commissar, the head of the N.K.V.D. Yagoda. An attached photograph left no doubt as to his identity. I returned the little book. As he replaced it in his pocket he asked:

'Are you satisfied now?'

'Yes, perfectly. Thank you. I'm ready to answer all your questions.'

'My first question,' he said, lifting a pen, 'is this: How is it that your letter to a member of the government doesn't carry the stamp of the prison censor or a stamp from the post office?'

'As I understand you, you have come to Leningrad to investigate my statement?' I asked cautiously.

'That's right.'

'In that case it seems to me the question of how my letter got to the People's Commissar is of secondary importance.'

Berdichevsky's face again showed signs of perplexity. He was on the point of saying something, but checked himself. Then, leaning back in the chair and lighting a new cigarette, he said:

'Very well. In that case you tell your story – everything you have to say,' and he picked up the pen again.

I began, first with a sort of general introduction. I spoke of the great number of perfectly innocent people being kept in jail, of the investigators' beating up prisoners, of people being sentenced to ten years in a concentration camp for trivial offences, of the hostility to the Soviet government that this caused among the population, of men formerly loyal to the Soviet regime being turned into its enemies as the result of undeserved punishment. I spoke calmly, controlling my feelings and trying not to leave out anything.

Occasionally Berdichevsky interrupted me with a question: 'Facts. Instances.'

I named prisoners of whose innocence I was convinced, investigators – some of whom I knew by name, for instance, Golubovich, of the Special Section – who subjected men to torture, but I flatly refused to give the names of the people from whom I had heard these facts.

'Why don't you want to name them?' insisted Berdichevsky.

'I don't know who may happen to read what you're taking down now, and I have positive knowledge of cases where men were turned into cripples for complaining about previous beatings.'

'As you please. But you must remember that your unwillingness to name the source of your information largely depreciates its value.'

'I hope you will believe me – believe in my sincere loyalty to the Soviet government, and will do all that's necessary. You have access to the People's Commissar. It rests with you, to a large extent, to have this evil uprooted,' I argued fervently.

During our entire conversation Berdichevsky took stenographic notes of everything I said. When I had finished he said:

'That will be enough for today. It's late. You'll be taken to a cell and we'll continue tomorrow. You can take the cigarettes with you,' and with a regal gesture of his hand he passed me a box of fine cigarettes. Then he rang the bell.

A uniformed man came in.

'Put him up somewhere for the night. I'll need him again tomorrow.'

The man made a fairly low bow, led me out into the corridor, and we proceeded together. After crossing the very familiar little bridge, we entered the first building of the inner prison of the Big House, and my escort, after a brief talk with the deputy commander of the building, took me to a clean small cell on the first floor, locked the door and walked away.

A quarter of an hour later, as I was about to lie down on the bed covered with clean sheets, the door suddenly opened and a guard brought in my supper: a couple of cold hamburgers with fried potatoes, and a glass of milk. After placing all this on the table he walked out, but returned immediately to hand me that day's copy of *Leningradskaya Pravda* and a book of stories by de Maupassant. I could only marvel. My self-respect grew by leaps and bounds. I began to think that, having been convinced of my sincere loyalty, Berdichevsky might perhaps issue orders to release me from prison. With this hope I went off to sleep.

Nobody awakened me in the morning, and I slept to what seemed like ten o'clock. I had been so dead to the world that I had not even heard the guard come into the cell and put a glass of milk and a roll made of white flour on my table. It all seemed like a fairy tale.

It was already twilight outside when a man came to lead me out. Ten minutes later I was sitting in front of Berdichevsky.

'Well, let's continue,' he said, arming himself with a pen. 'Tell me in detail the whole story of your friend Mikhail B. Try not to leave out anything.'

I was prepared for this question, having come to know Mikhail's case as well as his investigator did. I had spent many a day collecting the material by questioning people who were connected, directly or indirectly, with this suspiciously mysterious story. I was even able to establish links between several circumstances which Mikhail himself had not suspected at first. Clearly emerging to the foreground in all that series of incidents were the investigators Volkov and two other high officials of the N.K.V.D., and behind them loomed the German consulate in Leningrad. The facts smelled strongly of counter-revolution and espionage, not to mention the basest sort of operations by agents-provocateurs.

As on the previous day, Berdichevsky listened very attentively and jotted down my statements in shorthand. When I finished, he said:

'Fine. I thank you on behalf of the People's Commissar for all the information you have given. Now tell me what complaints you have regarding your own case. I'm informed you've appealed against your verdict.'

'I have, because I'm innocent of the crimes for which I was convicted. But I wouldn't like you to lump together the important matters I've talked to you about and my personal case. I wrote to Moscow seeking an investigation of the widespread abuses which are going on, and this is why you've come here. As for my own case, let it take its course. I'm sure I'll be acquitted.' Alas, I was far from being as sure as I pretended.

'As you wish. Now you'll go back, and I'll proceed with the necessary measures,' said Berdichevsky.

'Permit me to ask, what is your own opinion of what I've told you?'

'You see . . .' He paused as if weighing and choosing his words. 'You're mistaken about many things since you don't know the methods we use or the aims we pursue. However, I'll make a thorough study of this matter. But here's my advice to you . . .' He paused again. 'Stop altogether this writing or talking about wrecking activities in the agencies of the N.K.V.D. This can harm you personally. And remember, after the trial is closed, you'll be in our hands again, and it will be in our power to set you free before the expiration of your term if – if your conduct is irreproachable. Goodbye.' He rose, shook hands with me, and telephoned for the man who had brought me to the Big House. Presently we were driving in the evening shadowed streets of Leningrad. This time my escort sat in front with the driver, and I was in the back seat alone.

At the corner of Liteyny and Nevsky avenues where our car stopped for the traffic light signal, a crazy thought flashed through my mind and held me bound for a minute: What if I jumped out of the car? I would get lost in the crowd of passers-by, and they would never catch me. But the minute passed, and we drove on.

I returned to the Transfer prison as if it were my home. The roll had already been called and everybody was in bed. My bed was occupied by a stranger. I asked the deputy commander to put me for the night in some other cell. An unoccupied bed was found on the top floor in one of the cells of the 'socially elect', and there I slept through the night.

In the morning I first informed Mikhail of my experience. We were both naturally extremely interested in the possible results of the investigation. I had given Berdichevsky the names of several persons not in prison, Mikhail's wife among them, who could testify to what I had told him. In this way we were able to learn the next steps of the Special Commissioner.

The next thing I did was to restore my rights to my bed in cell No. 8. The usurper turned out to be an old professor of astronomy who before his arrest observed the stars from the Pulkovo Observatory. His offence was objecting to his daughter's marriage to a man who was an agent of the N.K.V.D. His son-in-law removed the obstacle to his happiness by having the professor jailed for five years on a charge of anti-Soviet propaganda.

On the third day after my return from the Big House, one of my friends who worked in the prison office informed me of a secret order from the N.K.V.D. that I be placed under strict supervision and be sent to a concentration camp with the first departing contingent. This was confirmed the next day when Kazakov called me to his office. I asked for no explanation. He added:

'You've stayed in this prison too long, and should have gone to a camp long ago. My only grounds for keeping you here is the fact that your sentence hasn't yet been confirmed – your appeal hasn't yet been acted upon.'

I thanked him and walked out. I could plainly see the hand of Berdichevsky in this development, and it was a bad omen.

My conclusions proved correct. A week later Mikhail's wife came to visit her husband and told him that she, as well as the other people I had named, had been called for questioning by the N.K.V.D., but the questioning consisted only of threats and advice to keep silent if they wanted to avoid trouble. The most piquant fact about all this was that the investigation was being conducted, on Berdichevsky's instructions, by the very man – the investigator Volkov – to whom all the threads in this unsavoury affair led. Everything was as plain as day.

In the meantime life in our cell went on as usual. Gradually there gathered a fairly numerous group of men who spent six or more months in cell No. 8. Later, two others joined it, Karaman and Zimatzky, both military men convicted for participation in the affair of the Novgorod Insurrectionists, in which I was keenly interested. But they were not very talkative. They hated the Soviet regime with all their hearts and souls, and afraid to incur further punishment for anti-Soviet propaganda among prisoners, which was held even a greater crime than the similar offence among the free population, they spoke very little and spent whole days playing chess.

One February day six new prisoners were installed in our cell. Soon we learned that they were not new prisoners at all. They had done

several years of forced labour in the construction of the White Sea-
Baltic Canal, and were handed ten additional years for agitation,
whereupon they were brought to Leningrad for transfer to other
concentration camps: this was the rule – a man whose term was
extended was transferred to another camp.

In answer to my questions one of them, a solidly built man with red
hair and knocked-out front teeth, who had kept silent up to then,
suddenly announced: 'Everybody who wants to survive must do all he
can to avoid being sent to a camp, since even the best camp is many
times worse than the worst prison.' Having said this, he walked over to
the wall, seated himself on his thin knapsack and took no further part
in the conversation. He aroused my interest.

In the evening, when we lined up for roll call, the red-top remained
seated in spite of the reminder by the elected head of the cell. The
deputy prison commander entered and began calling the roll. Then he
noticed the man seated by the wall.

'Why aren't you in the formation?'

'I'm not in military service,' the man announced, rising.

'Yet you're getting up.'

'Only because I have been taught since my childhood to stand when
talking to a standing man. Although I'm not sure you are a man . . .'

'So, you're a wise guy,' drawled the deputy commander, using the
familiar Russian *ty* (thou) instead of the more formal *vy* (you).

'I'll ask you not to thou me. I never tended pigs with you. Please call
the commander.'

'I'd have called him anyway,' said the deputy signalling to the guard.

We all stood waiting for what would follow.

A couple of minutes later Kazakov entered. The deputy walked up
to him and said something in a low voice.

'This isn't your first day in prison, is it?' Kazakov asked the redhead.
'You ought to know the rule – to line up with the others for roll call.'

'Permit me to make a statement, Citizen Kazakov.'

'Do so, if you wish,' said Kazakov with a shrug of his shoulders.

'My name is Prostoserdov. I'm a Social Democrat, or in your language, a Menshevik. I've spent more than ten years in prisons and
camps and I know the rules. But I don't recognize your God-damned
authority – either your personal authority, Citizen Kazakov, or that of
your supreme chief, the Georgian donkey who sits in the Kremlin. A
month ago I was given an additional ten years, and I don't have to be
afraid of anything.'

We all stood holding our breath at the sound of this thunder. None of
us had ever heard such talk before. Prostoserdov, in a highly nervous
state, spoke in a raised voice.

'I'm not going to enter into any discussion with you,' answered
Kazakov. 'According to rules I should lock you up in solitary confine-

ment, but I hope by tomorrow you'll recover your senses.' Turning around he walked out of the cell followed by his contingent.

A hubbub of voices filled the cell, but nobody went over to speak to Prostoserdov. The latter resumed his seat on his knapsack and started rolling a cigarette of *Makhorka*, the Russian variety of shag. In this position he slept through the night.

Next morning at breakfast I offered him some sugar. He took it, thanked me, and after we finished tea, began to ask me questions about the prison regime.

I told him what it was, remarking at the end:

'You shouldn't have got into such a mess with Kazakov last night. He's quite decent, and we're all convinced under another commander things would be much worse here.'

'I don't care what he thinks of me. I had a talk with him when he was taking over our contingent on arrival here. I've been sentenced to ten years of imprisonment under strict isolation. So let them send me to a political isolation camp. I have no business to be in transfer prisons and concentration camps.'

'Still, there's no point in provoking him for nothing,' I insisted.

'I'll see how you talk after doing time for ten years. How many did they give you?'

'Six.'

'Not much. But don't lose hope. These skunks are very free about adding on years.'

The man definitely attracted me. In the drab colourless crowd which filled the prison, this bold way of talking about the most slippery subject appealed to me a great deal. He inspired instant confidence, although it was a well-established fact among prisoners that men showing so much daring in their talk were, as a general rule, N.K.V.D. stool pigeons. By various rather complicated manipulations I managed to get Prostoserdov a bed next to mine. This led to long conversations between us in which we both tactfully refrained from asking each other questions about our lives before being arrested so as not to arouse mutual suspicion. He told me that he had been a member of the Russian Social Democratic Party since 1924, and practically from the same time, with a few brief intervals, had been a constant inmate of various prisons and camps. A short time before coming to the Transfer prison his term was extended automatically, by a decision in absentia.

As a Socialist he, for some time, received aid from the Society of Aid to Political Prisoners, headed by E. Peshkova, the first wife of Maxim Gorky. The society led a miserable existence, and had a staff of only a few people. With the permission of the N.K.V.D., given separately in each individual case, E. Peshkova was able to send parcels to Russian Socialists held in prisons and concentration camps. But in 1935 the N.K.V.D. struck powerfully at the society and it ceased to exist.

It was about that time that my two former friends, Boris and Vladi-mir, were sent to a concentration camp. They were taken out at night to join the contingent which was being sent to the Svirsky camps lying not very far north-east of Leningrad. Unlike me, they had not appealed against their sentences, considering them fairly lenient. I met them rarely since they were confined to another cell – and I never did hear of their fate.

The conflict between Kazakov and Prostoserdov was finally ironed out. At the next roll call, made by Kazakov himself, Prostoserdov who was lying on his bed was very politely asked by the prison commander not to break the rules of the prison. Prostoserdov got up and joined the back row of the line-up, declaring however that he did so out of per-sonal respect for Kazakov, and not for the sake of observing the hard-labour discipline. This settled the matter.

And then the day came when the most ordinary guard in the corridor handed me a small sheet of paper on which was a typed notice for me from the Supreme Court to the effect that 'having considered his appeal at its session, the court found no grounds for a retrial of the case'. I put my signature under the statement on the back of the paper, indicating I had read the notice, and returned it to the guard, breathing a sigh of relief, since I was beginning to fear that if my case were retried I might get ten years instead of six.

Toward the end of April I was told by one of my friends among the privileged class that preparations were on foot to send a huge party of prisoners with long terms *na etap*, on a journey to a concentration camp. The contingent was to be made up of prisoners from all Lenin-grad prisons and was to proceed to Kolyma, the fathermost region of north-eastern Siberia. Rumours of this transfer had been spreading in the prison for some time causing much apprehension among the in-mates since nobody wanted to get into a concentration camp that was more virtually cut off from the rest of Russia than any other camp. Many stories circulated among the men about the Kolyma camp Some pictured it as a fine place, others as one in which the climate was terrible and work extremely hard, in short, as a death trap from which no one ever escaped. One fact was not disputed by anybody: it was recognized that it was impossible to run away from the camp, and that a prisoner had no chance of returning from there before serving his full term. Most agreed that one must try to avoid being sent to Kolyma at all cost.

The fatal day came. From early in the morning there was a great stirring of activity in the prison. Guards kept informing us of the arrival of large numbers of convoy soldiers, of the movement of automobiles and buses in the prison yard. Office clerks rushed about with folders and lists of prisoners in their hands. Men in the cells, preparing for any eventuality, were writing notes to their relatives to inform them of their destination. Finally, the deputy commander entered our cell, and reading from a list, called out names in a loud voice. Following the prison tradition the man called out answered by quoting the clause under which he was convicted, and the term of sentence. I, too, was called. When all the names were read, the deputy commander shouted:

'Get your belongings ready!'

Then he turned around and walked off.

This was veritable carnage. Those named were all men with sentences of five years and over, men who had been in the prison for many months. Among the victims were all my friends, and many, many others. My preparations were simple, for I had no belongings. All I did was write a postal card to my mother informing her of my likely destination.

Prostoserdov, after beginning to prepare for the journey, suddenly changed his mind, lay down on his bed and announced that he was not going to Kolyma. When, half an hour later, we were led to the *etap* hall, he stayed on his bed.

The hall was already filled with people. The prisoners were lined up on one side. A long table stood in the middle. At one end of the table was the N.K.V.D. doctor, in a white smock. A commission sat at the table: on one side, Kazakov and representatives of the N.K.V.D. handing over the prisoners – on the other side, facing them, the commander of the convoy and representatives of the camp taking over the prisoners. In a word, just like the business transactions in a slave market.

In a loud voice, prisoners' names were called out singly. Each prisoner then took off his shirt and approached the doctor who glanced at his teeth, felt his muscles, and asked the stereotyped question: 'Any complaint?' Then the doctor stamped the prisoner's personal record, and passed it on to the members of the commission. The latter checked the identity of the prisoner, signed the certificate of transfer, and the prisoner was taken to the other side of the hall where the convoy soldiers went efficiently through the contents of his bag, removing money, 'cutting and piercing' articles, and things more valuable. Meantime the prisoner dressed. When a group of about twenty men was collected, they were surrounded by a convoy and led out into the prison yard. The proceedings were handled methodically, in perfect order. The technique was evidently the result of long and intensive practice.

I was standing in one of the back rows waiting for my turn. Suddenly I saw Poggio take off his jacket, lift his shirt, and stretch himself out on the cold cement floor close to the wall. I walked over to him and squatted down:

'What's the matter? Are you sick?'

'Not yet,' he answered, 'but I will be presently. In ten minutes I'll have a high temperature. Stand aside and don't bother me.'

I looked at him in wonder. I had heard before that there were methods of raising one's temperature artificially. A high temperature was the only condition prison doctors regarded as serious, since methods of simulating sickness were so skilled that no attention was paid to complaints of even real illness. But temperature could at least be checked.

Poggio was an experienced prisoner and knew what he was doing. His breathing stopped completely as he lay with his bare back on the cold floor. The terrible inner strain he was undergoing distorted his features. When he was finally called for a medical examination, the doctor, after asking him something, put a thermometer under his arm with an expression of boredom. A few minutes later he took the thermometer out, looked at it, and sent Poggio back to his cell, seriously ill.

My turn came. The doctor's examination was quickly over, and I stood erect before the members of the commission. A few brief questions, and the folder with my personal record was transferred from the pile in front of Kazakov to the growing pile in front of the commander of the convoy. I said goodbye to Kazakov and stepped over to the other side.

There were only a few men left when suddenly there was a loud noise. The door on the opposite side of the hall flew wide open and in came a grim procession, six or seven guards carrying the struggling Prostoserdov and his knapsack. He was brought up to the table and stood on his feet. Then an unforgettable conversation ensued. Banging the table with his fist and upsetting the inkwell, Prostoserdov shouted:

'What are you doing, you bastards? You know I've been sentenced to confinement in prison, not a camp. Can't you respect your own dirty laws? What right have you to send me to a concentration camp?'

This caused a stir among the members of the commission. I heard the commander of the convoy say to Kazakov:

'I'm not going to take this bird, do what you will.'

'You'll take him, dear comrade, whether you like it or not,' Kazakov answered, showing the man some paper. The latter and his associates studied the paper, no longer paying any attention to Prostoserdov who announced he was immediately going on a hunger strike, and demanded to be sent to a camp for political prisoners. At last, the convoy commander ordered that Prostoserdov be taken to the side of prisoners received, and with a sigh put his signature on the transfer document.

Unceremoniously pushed by N.K.V.D. soldiers, Prostoserdov joined our group, continuing to blast the Soviet government – from Stalin downward – for all he was worth.

The man in charge of the departing contingent counted off twenty prisoners and led them out to the hall. Just two were left: Prostoserdov and I. Shaking his hand I said to him:

'Drop it, Nikolay Nikolayevich. What's the good of getting so worked up when you're utterly helpless, and can do nothing? There's a long journey ahead, and you can't break down a stone wall with your head.'

At that moment a guard who had just entered the hall, cried out:

'Prostoserdov! Are you here? Take your parcel: your aunt has called.'

That was Prostoserdov's visitor's day. Although he had formally announced a hunger strike, he accepted the parcel which apparently contained some concealed notes about his personal affairs. Parcels were examined very thoroughly, but people always contrived to hide notes or money inside pickled herrings, the cardboard ends of Russian cigarettes, the seams of linen, and so on.

We waited about half an hour in the almost empty hall. Then the door opened and somebody ordered us to go out.

We came to the back stoop of the prison. A motorbus was waiting there and we were told to get in. We were followed by the members of the commission and some twenty convoy men. The prison gate opened, and I gave a parting glance at my 'home' in which I had spent eight not so very bad months. What was in store for me now?

The bus sped through unfamiliar side streets and soon came to the freight yard of the October (formerly Nikolayevsky) station where it turned in.

On the outside tracks stood a long train containing not less than forty freight cars. It was surrounded by a line of N.K.V.D. soldiers standing at a distance of some five steps from one another and trailing arms. They kept a huge crowd of people from moving closer than twenty yards from the train. The crowd consisted mostly of women shouting and waving their hands to men peeping through the little grilled windows in the freight cars. Nearly everyone in the crowd held packages and bundles apparently intended for the departing prisoners. Many women held babies in their arms. Sobbing and screaming filled the air.

Our bus drove up to the line of soldiers and stopped. Some of our guards came off, and Prostoserdov and I followed them. I overheard the conversation of women who stood near by.

'Look, look. These must be the chief prisoners – twenty soldiers guarding two men!'

We were led to one of the cars, but a supervisor who was bustling around protested:

'No, no, it's impossible. There are more than sixty men in this car as it is. Take them farther down, to the rear.'

After a couple of other futile attempts, the door of one car, on which the number 52 was chalked, opened with a crunching sound. We tossed in our simple baggage and climbed into the cavernous darkness of the car. The door closed again.

We stood in the dark near an iron stove, while a mass of wriggling bodies strove to cling to the tiny windows, shouting, asking questions.

My thoughts skipped from subject to subject.

Goodbye, Leningrad, the city which housed so many of my hopes and disappointments. The city where I felt free for the last time. Was I really free? Here, in that city, I lost this shadowy freedom. Here I left all my former hopes and dreams, my dearest friends.

I don't know how long I was reminiscing like that. A shrill locomotive whistle sounded, and the train pulled off, gaining speed to the accompaniment of an air-rending wailing and moaning from the crowd.

Our course lay eastward, into the unknown.

3. IN THE TRAIN

THE train was moving full speed. Prostoserdov and I had no time to waste. As soon as our eyes were adjusted to the semi-darkness of the car, we took advantage of the fact that the other passengers were still pressed against the windows in a solid mass, so we quickly climbed to the second tier of plank-beds which ran on each side of the car. There we stretched ourselves out.

Several minutes went by, Leningrad disappeared in the distance, and the men began to return to their seats. Immediately many of them claimed the places Prostoserdov and I already occupied. Some vicious-looking bearded faces advanced toward us in a menacing manner, and shouts and curses demanded that we move to some lower plank-beds which had scarcely any light.

Pointblank we refused to comply, although we could see those who threatened us were the roughest kind of criminals, the most unpleasant and troublesome type in the entire category of the 'socially elect'. One had only to hear their highly expressive and pictorial, if limited vocabulary, to recognize them for what they were.

There is only one right recognized in prison: the right of force. The toughs we faced were fearless and resolute, and were accustomed to acting together. A fight was inevitable since we had not the slightest idea of moving down to the lower level which was dirty and submerged in darkness. The shouting grew louder, fists were clenched tight, and bending my knees I was getting ready to kick down the first attacker with a well-aimed blow to his belly.

The first two attackers went down to the floor. But the enemy was plainly stronger than Prostoserdov and I. It would have ended sadly for both of us but for sudden aid from a surprising quarter.

'Hey you! . . .' There followed a string of oaths which would have satisfied the most exacting listener. '. . . Why in hell don't you leave decent people alone? If you want seats on top, kick down the devils on the other side. Well . . . hurry up!' The words were shouted in a deafening voice by a stocky young fellow, my neighbour on the left.

The attack stopped instantly. Grumbling and cursing, our opponents crossed to the other side of the car, and without much argument pulled down three men from the top boards. By their appearance the victims were simple peasants who meekly found room for themselves on the lower plank-beds. Gradually everything calmed down.

I didn't thank my neighbour. In prison all acts of civility are regarded as signs of weakness, or inability to adapt to the life, and anyone who offered thanks was humiliated by establishing his dependence upon his benefactor.

Little by little we learned the make-up of the railway car's population. Nonpolitical criminals comprised about one-half of the total. They were divided into two sharply different groups. The smaller group, which included Vaska, consisted of well-seasoned bandits and murderers, largely with a death sentence commuted to ten years in a concentration camp. On the whole they were quite decent fellows who realized their own worth, feared no person or thing, were able to crack anybody's head without a moment's hesitation, and knew how to make others respect them. To this group also belonged a few prominent robbers whose behaviour reflected a certain sense of personal dignity.

The other nonpolitical group, made up of petty crooks and pickpockets, was a constant source of trouble throughout our long journey. These creatures in the image of man sang prison songs incessantly, bellowing for all they were worth and ending each chorus with shrill squealing. Most of their songs were utterly obscene, and their perpetual swearing was done with variations of the most elaborate kind. One had to be constantly on the alert in order not to have something stolen by them. And these people stole everything, even things they did not need for themselves. The reason for this lay in the fact that stolen articles were used as currency in never-ending card games. After losing everything he had, a man would go on with the play paying his losses with the things he stole from the 'devils', the name applied mostly to peasants sentenced for counter-revolution. These devils, who included all helpless prisoners, mainly of the political category, had a miserable time of it. Downtrodden and frightened to death while still in prison, they did not have the courage to offer resistance to the 'socially elect' dregs of society, no matter how impudent and outrageous the provocation.

Thanks to the intervention on our side, and partly due to our readiness to stand up for ourselves, Prostoserdov and I were at once and for all time recognized as 'special people', and suffered no further attacks, except for one occasion. This happened when one of the petty thieves attempted to steal a pack of cigarettes from us. Prostoserdov thrust out his boot and kicked at the man's face with such force it was covered with blood. By this act he confirmed our moral superiority and earned the approbation of public opinion from the entire carful of men.

There were even more important consequences. That evening, when the train stopped and we received our ration of food, tossed in as usual on the dirty floor, it turned out that by mistake our fifty-four travellers were given fifty-six rations of bread and fifty-six herrings. To distribute those two extra portions rightly, it was decided to elect a headman. The post, as well as the honour which went with it, were offered to Prostoserdov, but he declined because he was still on a hunger strike. I was the next candidate, and accepted the post. From then on I was a headman, and my duties consisted of distributing food and enforcing certain rules of the criminals' own moral code. For example, thieving was permitted and could be applied to anything within the thief's capacity and luck. But there was one exception – bread. Bread was sacred and inviolable, regardless of any distinctions in the population of the car. An incident occurred soon after I had assumed my duties.

One of our petty thieves stole bread from one of the devils on the lower tier of plank-beds. He even had the audacity to brag about it. There was an outburst of general indignation, and I, as headman, was authorized to impose punishment. Since the fellow had already eaten the bread, it was impossible to return it. Getting down from my plank-bed, I pulled the thief to the ground by his feet, and began methodically and for a considerable length of time to beat him with Prostoserdov's high boot, giving the man no chance to rise from the floor. With this part of the punishment over I pushed him, accompanied by encouraging shouts, under the lower plank-bed where, by the decision of all, he was to live for the next three days.

Such was our dreary day-to-day life as the train rolled slowly toward the East.

Whenever our train made a stop, innumerable guards appeared from nowhere and formed a close line all around the train. This was done not so much from fear of prisoners' escaping as to prevent any contact between them and the signalmen, greasers, couplers, and other railway personnel who might happen to be near.

However, measures against possible breaks were not neglected. At every stop, guards with specially designed sticks carefully tapped the walls and floors of every car to discover if any boards were cut. At night this tapping made sleep difficult. In addition, guards made frequent runs over the roofs of the cars, even when the train was in motion, to make certain no holes were cut and that no passengers were preparing without authorization to terminate their journey even if they had to leap from the top of a moving train to accomplish this.

Undoubtedly there were sound reasons for such precautions. In our train, especially, we had quite a number of desperadoes who could have staged a most unpleasant surprise to the commander of our convoy.

Leaving Vologda and Vyatka behind some ten days later, we finally reached the top of the Ural Mountains where we passed the high sign-post set up on a perfectly level stretch of ground and bearing the words: EUROPE-ASIA. But in Asia, too, our progress remained as slow as before.

Prostoserdov was continuing his hunger strike with determination. Despite his long opposition I succeeded in persuading him to drink water, and once a day to eat a little piece of sugar. But even with this relaxation from the rules of strict hunger strikes, on the tenth day he lay motionless, unable to rise. All my arguments about the utter sense-lessness of this self-inflicted torture failed to budge him from his decision, and with complete indifference he watched me consume the modest supplies of food which he had received from his aunt on the day of our departure. I ate only the perishable stuff, hoping he might still change his mind.

We were not fed according to schedule. Deliveries were made once a day, but the actual time, morning, midday, or evening, depended entirely upon how the spirit moved the authorities. However, on the tenth day, at a rather unusual hour, the car door slid open and in climbed a man whose smock pulled over a uniform indicated he was some sort of parody of a doctor. With his fingers he went over Prostoserdov for a few minutes, listened with his stethoscope, then jumped off the car and was overheard reporting to some superior: 'He'll last about three days.'

Prostoserdov was extremely pleased about this visit. We knew part of the convoy was to be kept in Maryinsk, capital of the Siberian Concentration Camps of the N.K.V.D., and, according to rumours, all eight of the women's cars were to be uncoupled, and all sick and aged among the men were to be removed. Prostoserdov hoped he would be included in the latter group, preferring to stay in a concentration camp in central Siberia to the journey to the spot from which no one returned.

At this prospect I was able to make him eat two little pieces of sugar every day instead of one, for I was beginning to fear he might really die.

Our expectations proved correct. On the fourteenth day we arrived safely at Maryinsk. The train was shunted to a special track which was surrounded by several rows of barbed wire, and the sorting out of freight began. We listened intently to the movement beyond the walls of our car. In due time our turn came. The door opened and somebody shouted: 'Prostoserdov! Come out with your belongings!'

I helped him get down from the plank-bed and walk to the door. Men below took him over. I handed him his knapsack, shook him firmly by the hand, and the door closed again. During the few minutes the door was open we saw a fairly large open space filled with prisoners and surrounded by guards. On one side, pressing close to one another, stood two or three hundred women. Various officials, probably from the camps, rushed about with sheets of paper in their hands, shifting prisoners from one place to another.

Back on my plank-bed I lay and listened. By my side, in the place vacated by Prostoserdov, another man was arranging his belongings. He was Vanka, a driver from Leningrad, sentenced for banditry in transport because while driving his truck he had plunged into a platoon of soldiers – his brakes had not held. His death sentence, after his waiting for a month to be executed, had been commuted to ten years in a concentration camp.

A voice outside yelled: 'Prostoserdov!'

'I am he. Article 58, clause 10, term 10 years,' the answer came according to rules. Prostoserdov's voice was noticeably weakened by his hunger strike.

'Are you Prostoserdov? Why did you declare a hunger strike?' asked another man's voice. The man used the Russian familiar *ty* (thou) for the more formal *vy* (you). Since Prostoserdov was particularly sensitive to this form of insult, I knew there was going to be trouble. I was not wrong.

'In the first place I must ask you not to *thou* me,' I heard Prostoserdov say. 'And in the second place, I demand to be sent to a political isolation camp, in accordance with the decision of the Collegium of the N.K.V.D.'

'And who are you?' asked the voice in a deliberately mocking tone, obviously that of a Public Prosecutor. 'An important Trotskyite perhaps? A political prisoner, an eminent figure? Now what do you say? How about being locked in a punitive cell, eh?' the voice continued.

'Don't shout at me. The devil take you all,' Prostoserdov answered in the same tone. 'You're an ass, not a Public Prosecutor. You can't scare me. I stopped being afraid of scoundrels like you ten years ago.'

I whistled at this kind of talk, and wondered what was going to happen.

The Public Prosecutor fell silent, but there was a hum of voices as if the higher officers were discussing the situation. Through the hum Prostoserdov's voice broke in again:

'Do you think if you can put half the population of Russia behind barbed wire, if your Georgian donkey can abuse the people with impunity, you'll secure eternal grace? No, the time is coming for all of you when your heads will be torn off, unless you've cut each other's throats before then . . .'

The consultation must have come to an end, for the door of our car slid open and I saw Prostoserdov sitting on his knapsack, and in front of him a group of men among whom one, apparently the Public Prosecutor, was speaking and waving his hands.

'What! I take this man over? Not for anything in the world! Keep him on your train. I don't care if he dies on the way. Take him back into the car!' he ordered.

A number of guards who had been listening to Prostoserdov's denunciation with evident interest, picked him up under the arms and restored him carefully to his place in the car.

Even after the door closed, Prostoserdov continued for several minutes in the same vein, blasting away at the Soviet regime and its representatives from Yoska – short for Joseph, Mr. Stalin – all the way down. The inhabitants of our car, especially the petty crooks and thieves, heard this diatribe with undisguised joy, and greeted his statements with approval. Strange as it may seem, after this incident

Prostoserdov's prestige took a sharp turn upward among these dregs of society who began treating him with underscored respect.

'Well, how about your hunger strike?' I asked Prostoserdov when he calmed down a little. 'Are you going on with it?'

'To hell with it!' he answered. 'To fight these skunks with means recognized in civilized countries is to humiliate oneself. They only understand machine guns. Let's eat whatever we have left.'

Fortunately I had not yet consumed the entire stock of edibles supplied by Prostoserdov's aunt. I picked out what seemed most suitable for a stomach exhausted by a long hunger strike and gave it to my friend who immediately began his first meal in ten days. The experience of many years made him observe moderation. Moreover, the indignation which still raged within him after the conversation with the Public Prosecutor had a curbing effect on his appetitite since he kept recalling the scene at which I had been an unseen witness.

At length the sorting of prisoners was completed. Some were taken down, some added to our numbers from local offenders, and we set forth again on our long journey.

Time passed slowly, as slowly as our train made its progress eastward. Thanks to the consideration of one of the bandits, we were able to move to a window, a small square opening in the car's wall covered with a metal grille. Through the window we could see the free world outside and breathe fresher air.

At out next stop, which was a small station, we noticed a group of some thirty people standing on the platform apparently waiting for their own train. Acting on the spur of the moment, which surprised me as much as it must have surprised himself, Prostoserdov addressed the crowd with a militant speech, paying no attention to the guard who stood right below our window.

'Look at this trainload of prisoners, comrades,' he said in a loud voice to the people who gazed at him with eyes full of fear. 'The great majority of them are Russian working men, simple folk just like you, who have committed no crime either against our people or our country. The scurvy N.K.V.D. has decided to drive to the Kolyma what's left of the people who haven't yet turned completely into dumb cattle. Our country is ruled by a small gang of scoundrels, headed by that scoundrel of scoundrels, Stalin . . .'

During the speech there was a great to-do among the guards outside. They shouted at Prostoserdov and tried to drown out his speech, but he outshouted them. Their threats to shoot at him were in vain, too, for he knew the convoy commander was held responsible for every prisoner lost during the journey. In the end, to avoid worse trouble, the commander sent a few guards to drive the listeners away, and only when there was no one left on the platform did Prostoserdov stop his speechmaking and contentedly stretch himself on the plank-bed.

This experiment pleased my friend. After that he never missed an occasion for one of these talks with anybody who happened to be within hearing distance of our window. It did not matter whether they were passengers waiting for a train, railway employees, or even the soldiers standing guard near the car. To all of them Prostoserdov spoke on the same inexhaustible subject – the oppression of the Russian people by the Bolsheviks. These speeches were a constant thorn in the flesh of our commanding officers, particularly since the guards of lower rank, as I could see for myself, showed an ever growing interest in and even sympathy for Prostoserdov's torrents of denunciation.

After we passed Novosibirsk, the landscape visible from our window acquired a certain specific character: more and more frequently you could see, some distance from the track, typical concentration camp structures. A small field fenced off with barbed wire, with several barracks set closely together, watchtowers at the corners, and with characteristic wooden arches over the gateway, left no doubt that the place we were passing was almost exclusively peopled with convicts at hard labour. The archways displayed crudely painted slogans such as: WELCOME TO OUR PLACE! LABOUR IN THE SOVIET UNION IS A MATTER OF GLORY, HONOUR, COURAGE AND HEROISM! THE WAY TO FREEDOM IS THROUGH HONEST WORK! LONG LIVE THE SECOND FIVE YEAR PLAN! EVERYWHERE AND ALWAYS WE ARE INSPIRED BY OUR GREAT LEADER, COMRADE STALIN, and many more in the same vein. Reading these slogans I felt uncomfortable and could not understand whether this was imbecility in the extreme or the height of hypocrisy. As for Prostoserdov, these slogans threw him into raptures – they provided fuel for his new speeches. Except for the wretched, downtrodden peasants who feared everything at all times, those in our car always enjoyed listening to Prostoserdov, and the petty thieves and their kind simply hung on his every word. I am sure that, as a result of Prostoserdov's educational work, all these men left the train at the end of the journey in Vladivostok with definite anti-Soviet convictions, although their primitive thinking probably lacked sufficient clarity.

One day Vaska, our first defender at the start of the journey in Leningrad, wedged himself between me and Prostoserdov and began whispering with the latter. Apparently my friend was greatly interested, since whispered conversations between them became the order of the day. For two days I was mystified, but on the third night Prostoserdov woke me up and asked:

'Do you want to make a break?'

At first I could not understand what he was talking about. Then I grasped the meaning.

'Make a getaway? How? Is it possible?'

'It's difficult, but it can be done. When we stopped at Maryinsk I spied out everything while having a talk with that Public Prosecutor. The train is heavily guarded, that's true – there are a couple of guards at the front of each third car. At the end of the train there is a machine gun, a projector, and that special device they call a "cat" for picking up anybody who might cut through the car floor and jump between the rails. But one could take a chance on a dark night. I have already looked it over. One could get on the roof and jump off the moving train. There'll be three of us to try it,' he explained.

I took time to think this over, although from the start the idea of a break held little appeal for me. In the first place, I could be shot down. Next, even if I could get off safely, without breaking my legs, where could I go without papers or money in a territory packed with concentration camps and therefore scattered with control points? Finally, if I hadn't attempted a break in Leningrad where I had real chances of success, there was certainly no sense in doing it here. Having pondered all this, I said:

'No, Prostoserdov, you go ahead without me. I'm not going to advise you. In a matter like this each must make the choice for himself. You've already done ten years, and have at least as many ahead of you. Your case is different. As for me, I'll stay on, come what may.'

'Do as you please. I must make an attempt. To hell with the Kolyma. Let Stalin mine the gold there himself.'

This ended our conversation. But during the following days I noticed conferences between Prostoserdov, Vaska, and another rather decent bandit who lay next to Vaska. Preparations were carried on with the utmost secrecy since there was always the danger that one of the prisoners might throw a note of information about the plot out of the window. Yet, in spite of all precautions, the petty crooks got wind of what was going on, and one of them, climbing up on our plank-bed, began pleading with Prostoserdov to allow him to join in the getaway.

Our plotters were forced to agree that if they succeeded in making a safe break, the others could follow and join them later somewhere along the track.

One night, when my reckoning placed our train near Lake Baikal, I was awakened by Prostoserdov's whispers.

'We're just about ready to go. Goodbye,' he said, shaking hands with me and cautiously getting off the plank-bed. In the complete darkness of the car I could hear only the whispering voices and the rustling footsteps. Then came the sound of creaking iron. I realized they were trying to remove the chimney stack of the iron stove which stood useless in the middle of the car. The lack of coal kept the stove unheated, although April and May in Siberia are customarily cold. The flue cut through an opening in the roof which was covered with sheet iron, and it was wide enough for a man to squeeze through.

The men worked quickly in the dark, but I felt our entire car was awake and listening to what was going on. At length the stack was removed. Someone, lifted up by others, tore the sheet iron cover. For a brief second a bit of starlit sky flickered in the darkness, then it was instantly shut off by the body of a man crawling out. A minute later the scout climbed down. I heard the whisper:

'Two cars away a guard's head is sticking up looking the other way.'

Muffled voices conferred and somebody again crawled to the roof, covering the glittering stars with his body.

Suddenly the train began slowing down as it always did when approaching a station. A figure tumbled down into the car, the opening was hastily covered up, and the chimney was put back into place.

The train came to a stop. Overhead running footsteps of the convoy guard were heard as he checked the car roofs, and came nearer and nearer. Would he step on the thin covering over the hole? He did. In the twinkling of an eye somebody's leg crashed through our ceiling. Yelling at the top of his lungs, the guard extricated his leg. Immediately there were three shots, one after another.

The would-be fugitives crawled hurriedly back to their beds. Prostoserdov wriggled himself by my side. Everyone held his breath.

From outside came the sound of stamping feet, shouts, exclamations. The car door flew open and about a dozen guards, headed by the convoy commander and all carrying small lanterns, burst in.

We lay silent, pretending to be dead to the world. Only Prostoserdov was fidgeting about. But the shouting and swearing of the guards would have awakened the dead, and so we 'woke up', too.

'Who's the headman?' the commander demanded.

I sat up.

'I'm the headman. What's the matter?'

'Why, you, dirty bastards – who's got away from this car?'

'Got away? I don't know. I didn't hear anything. I was asleep.'

'Asleep?' the commander yelled, poking his revolver into my face. 'I'll make you sleep so you'll wake up in the next world!'

'But Citizen Commander, it was dark in the car. How could I see anything?' I said with all possible calm as I tried to cool off the raging commander. I was beginning to get frightened myself since in a fit of fury N.K.V.D. men were capable of anything.

'Well, I'll talk to you later,' the commander said ominously. 'Now, everybody sit up on his bed!' he ordered with fierceness.

Everybody sat up, and the checking began – first by counting the number, then by a roll call. Everyone was present. A certain amount of calm set in.

'Well, who tried to escape? Confess, you . . . and . . . or we'll shoot you all dead on the spot,' the commander threatened. Nearly everyone kept silent. A few mentioned the darkness. A brilliant idea flashed through the commander's head.

'Show the palms of your hands!'

We all stretched out our hands as the commander, holding a lantern, began to examine our palms one after another.

'Ah! Here's one!' the guards shouted triumphantly as they pulled Vaska down from his bed. 'Here's another!' And another man was yanked to the floor. Although dirty, the palms of all the others showed no visible trace of soot from the stack. Prostoserdov outsmarted the commander: he had licked and wiped off his hands before being told to show them.

'That'll be all. We'll look into the rest of this tomorrow. Let's get out!'

The commander jumped off the car followed by the guards who dragged the two unsuccessful fugitives along with them.

Hardly had the door of the car closed when we heard something terrifying – not human cries but beast-like yells from the two luckless offenders. This was accompanied by repeated blows which were audible in spite of the considerable distance from which they appeared to be emanating. Presently the yells turned into a continuous howl which suddenly stopped, almost simultaneously, from both victims. Everything became quiet. A few minutes later our train pulled off. A guard on the roof of our car kept incessant watch.

I was shaking all over. Despite his long prison experience, Prostoserdov, I think, did not feel too well either.

About ten days later, after our arrival at Vladivostok, I met the two fugitives. They were alive, but Vaska had a gouged eye and not a vestige of teeth. He walked stooped like a cripple. The other fellow could not stand up. His internal organs had been crushed, and he was taken to a field hospital where he died in a few days.

Neither of these two men informed on their accomplices, as Prostoserdov had long feared they might. Both he and I agreed that had so-called political prisoners been in the place of the two bandits, neither of us would have fared too well. As for the remaining residents of the car, Prostoserdov and two other men whose word was authority assured them they would tear their heads from their bodies if they made the slightest attempt to give information to the N.K.V.D. officials.

Whether this threat had effect, or whether the N.K.V.D. officials were satisfied with the punishment already inflicted, we never knew. The whole affair had no further reverberations.

Meantime our journey went on. That never ending sensation of a half-empty stomach, customary as it was, became even more unbearable because of the reduction in our water ration to one-third of what it had been. With salted herring an important item of our diet, thirst caused real suffering. It got so bad I was obliged to stop eating herring.

But this, in turn, so weakened my body that I could hardly stand on my feet. I actually fainted twice as I was taking in the food for my carmates, and after the second faint I gave up the duties of headman to Prostoserdov. After that I lay almost continuously on my plank-bed, and the slightest movement of my body produced a sharp pain in my legs, especially under the knees.

On the forty-seventh day after we had left Leningrad we arrived in Vladivostok. Forty-seven days of travelling in a closed freight car, in stifling air, in dirt, without once washing my face. . . . Forty-seven days of lying on a crammed plank-bed extending from one end of the car to the other, of eating food that wouldn't have satisfied dogs.

Having covered 11,000 kilometres, about 6,500 miles, our train finally stopped at the station Vladivostok-Black River. We were ordered to leave our car.

We found ourselves standing on unpaved ground extending for a considerable distance in all directions. It was warm and dusty. Crowds of people were pouring off the train. Apart from us stood a group of women exchanging loud remarks with the nonpolitical male convicts. Judging by the conversation the majority of the women were prostitutes. But not all. The fate of a woman fallen into the hands of the N.K.V.D. is a terrible one, particularly if she is young. A man can sometimes go through all his prison years and not lose his human image. This is difficult to accomplish, especially on a long term, but it *is* possible. A woman can never do it. Once cast into a prison or a concentration camp, she is lost forever, both to her family and to society as a whole. It is a rare investigator who does not take advantage of the helplessness of the woman who falls into his hands. And the situation in prison is beyond description: from the superior prison officials to the last guard, down to the chef in the prison kitchen, everyone has an inviolate right to pick and choose any woman prisoner he likes.

Resistance is impossible. No one will ever come to the woman's aid, and if she resists she is simply raped. There is no one to whom she can complain.

The same conditions prevail in the concentration camps. Women are kept separate from men, but guards in the women's camps are men, and all the powers that be go to the women's camp to amuse themselves. The situation of a woman prisoner is such that 'of her own free will', she soon begins to slide down the path of moral and physical degradation. At the price of 'love' she can sometimes buy herself a certain amount of relief such as being excused from heavy work, getting an extra couple of pounds of bread, and so forth. Moreover, she knows that nothing can be gained by resistance, for resistance is instantly broken down, sometimes in the most ruthless way.

The fate of a woman in a camp is the worst imaginable. All the officials, great and small, have harems. From time to time they exchange their concubines, sometimes take them away from one another by legal or illegal means, or lose them at cards and on bets.

Frequently women prisoners work as servants in the houses of engineers, book-keepers, economists and the rest of the hired technical personnel attached to the camps. It goes without saying, they always perform the duties of concubines as well. As a rule such servants are selected not from prostitutes or thieves, but from formerly respectable and educated women sentenced for counter-revolutionary activities.

The direct result of these conditions is that all women prisoners are victims of venereal diseases. They may contract them a little sooner, or a little later, but they can escape them never. When this happens they are isolated in special, strictly guarded camp quarters where they rot away almost without any medical care.

Before all the prisoners were unloaded, we were ordered to form in a column and, surrounded by a convoy, were marched off uphill to a camp where prisoners intended for the Kolyma region were eventually sorted out, and the healthiest among us chosen to be transferred later to the Vladivostok port and shipped to the north.

With tremendous effort, almost crawling on all fours, I dragged myself up the hill. The acute pain in my legs indicated some disease which must have attacked me on the train journey. We entered the camp, disposed ourselves in a large square in the midst of which a commission, sitting around a table, was holding a session: the act of delivery and acceptance, similar to that in the Leningrad Transfer prison, was taking place, this time in reverse. Another difference was that, unlike Leningrad, the camp could not refuse acceptance of any arriving prisoners. This did away with medical examination, and the whole business was reduced to a roll call and the transfer of each prisoner's records.

Straight from the square we were marched to the bathhouse and disinfection chamber within the camp. In groups of about one hundred we walked into the dressing-room, undressed, and proceeded into the bathroom where, after a quick haircut, we washed ourselves with soap and hot water. While we were bathing, the minor camp officials, mostly from nonpolitical convicts, took our clothes to be disinfected, and went through the contents of our knapsacks and suitcases – some prisoners actually had suitcases. Naturally, when on leaving the bathhouse we were handed our belongings, everything that had any value by camp standards was missing. But I felt absolutely sure that nothing of mine would be lost for at that time my wardrobe presented too sad a sight.

What did worry me was the discovery made in the bathhouse that my legs were covered with bright-red rash, and hemorrhages under the skin showed below the knees. One of the men instantly diagnosed it as scurvy which, as everyone knows, is caused by exhaustion of the body and the deficiency of vitamin C in the diet.

As soon as we put on our clothes we were marched farther into the camp grounds and herded into one of the sheds which was fairly big – 25 by 15 yards – and had two decks of plank-beds, one above the other extending along the two long walls.

During all this shifting around I ran across many of my old friends from the Leningrad Transfer prison: George, Zimatsky, Mikhail, Dabizha, Karoman, and several others. We immediately grouped together on one side of the shed.

The weather was warm and sunny, but I did not leave my plank-bed any more, and my food was brought to me from the camp kitchen by my friends.

The day after my arrival I went to the medical aid station where a male nurse was in charge. He gave me a single look and quickly pronounced my disease as scurvy. He ordered me to take a local medicine – a concoction of conifer needles which he assured me produced miraculous results. I kept drinking this bitter and vile tasting fluid for a long time afterward, but I cannot testify that it helped me.

I kept hoping my scurvy, which was getting worse and worse, would save me, if only for a time, from the imminent journey. But my hopes failed to materialize, for one fine day, when minor camp officials began rushing about the place calling out the names of those who were to go, my name was among them.

The entire camp rose to its feet. Guards were considerably strengthened. Prisoners listed to go were confined to their sheds and forbidden to leave them. Next we were ordered to elect our representatives to receive the foodstuffs for the voyage – a week's supply since, we were told, there would be no kitchen on the ship. The representatives went out and returned a couple of hours later with the food: for the seven-day voyage each prisoner was given 7 pounds of bread, 20 herrings, a big slice of salted *keta*, the fish which yields red caviar, and a can of vegetables one kilogram in weight. Later, aboard the ship, we were surprised to receive the daily ration of a bowl of soup or porridge.

The whole day passed in this confusion. The following morning the shipment of prisoners began. They were put in trucks and driven to the port. Our old Leningrad group stuck together. Under convoy, we walked to the square inside the gate, each of us carrying his own baggage. Mine was light – only the food, but it required all the power I could muster to carry even this, since I could hardly walk.

We got into a truck – twenty prisoners and six guards. One of the higher officials came up and said:

'Soon you'll be taken to the port. Stay seated and don't move. At the slightest attempt to rise the guards will shoot without warning.'

The truck drove out of the camp and sped down a dusty road to Vladivostok. In the most commonplace way we proceeded down the principal streets of this unusual, terraced city, without attracting the slightest attention from the numerous people on the pavements. They were accustomed to the sight of convicts in transport.

We drove into the port. At one of the piers stood a big steamer with its name and port of call written on the stern. I read: *Djurma* – NAGA-YEVÔ. On the smokestack was painted a broad white band with a narrow blue one running through the middle, and the letters DS, which stood for Dalstroy.

Supported by my friends and with great effort I managed to climb to the ship's deck. There we were met by the new guards who belonged the the *Djurma*. The entire group transported in our truck was directed to the stern hatchway. As we descended the steep and narrow staircase we found ourselves in a big hold dimly lighted by three bulbs. The hum of several hundred voices filled the air, and made it obvious that the place was crammed with human beings.

Along the walls of the hold ran four rows of plank-beds in continuous decks, one above another. The space between the decks was so small that sitting was impossible – one could only lie down. My friends, with strong words and organized pressure, wrested a place for me on one of the lowest decks, since I had no strength whatever to climb to a higher deck. I crawled into the dark depth between the decks and stretched out with my bag of food under my head.

In a short time our hold was packed tight. No one was allowed to go to the ship's deck before all the prisoners were put aboard and the ship set off into the open sea. Yet all the toilets were upstairs.

At length, some ten or twelve hours after our arrival, we heard the roar of the engines, felt the ship move. About two hours later we were permitted to go to the deck, but not all of us at the same time. When my turn came I decided to climb up, difficult as this was, since the atmosphere in the hold was unbearably stifling. Somehow I reached the deck and crawled on to a pile of loose ropes.

Fading into the distance, I could still see Vladivostok catching the first rays of the rising sun. On the right was the island of Askold. In port and in the roadstead stood several ships, some of them warships.

I gaped at the retreating shore, and in my thoughts said farewell to Russia. I felt that if I was being taken to the Kolyma in my weakened condition I was destined never to return. Pictures of the past flashed through my mind, but the sharp persistent pain in my legs kept bringing me back to reality.

Soon the shore disappeared, and we sailed into open sea, leaving behind the last island of the Gulf of Peter the Great on the farthest end of which lies Vladivostok.

Late in the evening of the second day after we had sailed, I pulled myself up to the deck for a breath of fresh air. Most of my friends were there, standing at the rail and talking animatedly, but in low voices. As soon as I walked up to them they fell silent, and quickly changed the subject of their conversation. Prison ethics do not permit inquiries about anything deliberately kept secret. But during the next day it was clear that my friends were planning something and Mikhail and I were excluded from their confidence – Mikhail apparently because he was unswervingly loyal to the Soviet regime, and I evidently as his closest friend.

I observed more than the usual comings and goings on the deck and in the hold, and secret conferences held by my Leningrad friends and a few new cohorts whom I knew as men of resolute action. Men kept regular watch on deck, but I could not understand what this was for. Strange faces from other holds began appearing in ours. Plainly, something was brewing.

One day, as I was lying on my plank-bed, Mikhail who had just come down from the deck sidled up to me.

'Do you know what's going on?' he asked.

'I know something is, but what it's all about I don't know.'

'I've found out. Tomorrow we'll be sailing through the Soya Strait.'

'So what?'

'These are Japanese territorial waters. Our fellows want to knock off the guards and steer the ship to one of the nearest Japanese ports. They've already found some allies among the guards.'

'You could be right. Who told you?'

'I overheard it by accident without being noticed. The chief figures are Zimatsky, Karoman, Dabizha and Prostoserdov – the whole project is in their hands. In addition there's a score of desperate cut-throats mixed up in it.'

'What are you going to do?'

'How about you?' Mikhail asked. He wasn't one to get his bearings quickly in a new situation.

'I? I'm going to do absolutely nothing. I can't move – besides, I know nothing. No one has told me anything.'

'What do you mean, no one? Didn't I tell you everything?'

'Maybe. But I didn't hear it. Neither did you – understand?'

'Yes, I do.' He paused. 'But this will be a real crisis, a treason to our country, won't it?'

'And who are you – a Public Prosecutor, an investigator? What business is it of yours? You're not taking part in this affair, are you?' I asked.

'That's true, but still, I can't permit a conspiracy. I must give warning . . .'

'To whom? And what for? For all you know the official you report to may be one of the sympathizers, and you'll be dropped quietly overboard at night and that'll be the end of you.'

'But you know I'm an honest Soviet citizen,' he persisted.

'You were, but no longer,' I snapped. 'Have you forgotten that you were handed ten years for treason to your country?'

'That's true – ten years. All the same . . .'

'Forget it, Mikhail. No good can come from you butting into this business. You're not an N.K.V.D. spy, and nobody will thank you for your information. Sit tight and keep your mouth shut.'

'All right,' he agreed after a long pause. 'We'll wait and see what happens. Anyway, the Japs will hand them back – they have an agreement with Moscow.'

'All the more reason why you shouldn't worry since your dear Comrade Stalin has already taken measures for all eventualities.'

On this we terminated our whispered conversation.

Later, on the deck, after waiting until Zimatsky was left alone, I walked over to him.

'Listen, Zimatsky,' I said. 'I'm not asking you any questions, I don't know anything, and am not interested in anything. But for God's sake look around when you tell anecdotes to your friends. Understand?'

After saying this I turned away. He rushed after me, obviously worried.

'Why, have you heard anything? Who told you?'

'I repeat, I have heard nothing and know nothing. Try to get this straight, and don't forget it when you have to give your answers to the investigator. I'm perfectly certain that you'll have to give such answers, considering your thoughtlessness' . . . and I broke off the conversation with firmness.

Next morning land appeared on the horizon, and by noon we came so close to it that we could see the outlines of mountains with snow-covered peaks. Fishing, motor and sail boats appeared more and more frequently, and sometimes passed very close to our ship.

We were approaching the Soya Strait between Sakhalin and the island of Yezo. Guards began driving the prisoners who crowded the deck into the holds, and I too went down. Only Mikhail was lying on our plank-bed, the rest having somehow managed to stay upstairs.

Mikhail was tormented by doubts.

'I'm sorry I listened to you,' he whispered. 'I should have reported their conspiracy. What are we going to do in Japan?'

'Don't worry. You're not in Japan yet. When you're there I'll tell you what to do.'

'They've even bribed the radio man, I've heard.'

'Heard again? Where? And why do you want to know any more? Remember, the more you know the longer you'll have to talk to the investigator and such talks bring no good to anyone.'

We fell silent. But we both felt tense. Apparently we were sailing through the strait, and if the conspirators decided to act, we could expect events any moment.

There was a shot, then another, then a third. After that everything was quiet again. We listened intently, but nothing more was heard from the deck.

Three hours went by. Then the locked door to the deck opened, and the men rushed upstairs. I, too, got up, and soon saw the group of conspirators, a most cheerless looking crowd. Prostoserdov left his friends to walk over to me.

'You were on the deck, weren't you? What was that shooting?' I asked him.

'Two men jumped overboard when we were less than half a mile from the coast. They were noticed by the guards too late – they were already too far away. The commander gave the cease fire order. They say a radio message has been sent to the Japs to arrest them.'

I asked no further questions, but glanced at him quizzically. For a moment he looked ill at ease, then he said:

'I know you had an idea what was up. It added up to nothing. What can you expect of such people? Zimatsky, at the last moment, got cold feet, and he had all the contacts with the guards. He refused to do anything although everything was ready. To hell with all of them!' Prostoserdov spat vigorously and went down into the hold.

Later in the day I met Mikhail on deck.

'There – and you've been worrying. Can't you see for yourself this was only empty talk?'

'Still I ought to report it to the proper authorities.'

'It would be absolutely stupid to do it now. They would probably be shot, but you wouldn't get along so well either. You'd be asked what you were thinking of before. They'd say you knew what was going on, then you covered up, so you were an accomplice. Say what you will, but I don't recommend it.'

I knew my arguments were sound, and Mikhail soon calmed down. He was phlegmatic and his mind worked rather slowly. As for those who took part in the unsuccessful plot, I firmly avoided discussing all the pros and cons with them. The whole thing had been a failure. Such talk would be useless on the one hand, and dangerous on the other.

For no apparent reason my sickness suddenly took a brief turn for the better and I began to look over the ship. The *Djurma* was still a new steamer of about 8,000 tons. A brass plate on the bridge said that she had been built in Rotterdam, Holland. She was a typical cargo ship, and the whole reconversion undertaken to make it ready for passengers had been confined to the building of the plank-beds in the holds. There was no ventilation, and no provision for the most elementary conveniences. In the four holds, packed to the brim with men, there was not a single table or bench. The toilets were makeshift wooden arrangements built on deck which women, who occupied the fifth hold in the bow, ventured to use only after dusk, and even then only in groups, to protect themselves.

By rough reckoning I figured the ship carried some 2,000 prisoners on our trip. This number was later confirmed in a conversation with the chef who cooked the meals. The women numbered about two hundred.

I was surprised to find how lightly the ship was guarded. There were about one hundred armed guards and no special means for coping with a possible mutiny except locking the holds during the passage through Japanese waters.

Almost without exception the ship's crew consisted of prisoners – former seamen sentenced for nonpolitical crimes. I got into conversation with one of the sailors, formerly a first mate on a ship which had sailed the Pacific, and sentenced to five years' forced labour for smuggling a few pair of ladies' stockings. He told me that outbursts of insubordination were not uncommon, but that the guards were always able to suppress them since they were armed with automatic rifles and had powerful fire pumps at their disposal, and the strong jets of water from a couple of fire hoses were enough to drive the prisoners into the holds which were then locked until the ship arrived at the Nagayevo harbour in the Kolyma territory. As a matter of fact there was such trouble on the *Djurma's* preceding voyage. The Trotskyites among the prisoners went on a hunger strike as a protest against the hideous conditions on shipboard. With the help of the fire hoses all the prisoners were driven into the holds and locked in. But the nonpolitical prisoners did not join the hunger strike, and instigated by the officials, attacked the Trotskyites, inflicting such damage that the hunger strikers had to appeal to the guards for protection. This of course brought their strike to an end.

Today, as I look back, I am of the opinion that the seizure of the ship planned by the conspirators could have been fully carried out by some twenty to thirty resolute and desperate men. The guards were extremely easygoing in the performance of their duties, and it would not have been at all difficult to seize their arms, and with them, the ship. It is another matter whether such seizure could have achieved its object, for it is practically certain the Japanese would have handed us back to the Soviets, with consequences which would have been far from happy for all of us. But the important fact remains that a group of some 2,000 people did not contain even one per cent of resolute men capable of acting together – so downtrodden and demoralized beside being woefully mixed, was the mass of prisoners. And yet three-quarters of these people were sentenced on charges of counter-revolutionary activities. The administration had every reason, indeed, to be easygoing since they knew perfectly well the kind of criminals they were dealing with.

During the voyage we were favoured with good weather. There was hardly any wind, the ship did not pitch very much, and few men on board were seasick. I pictured to myself what it would have been like in a really rough sea when the holds are locked up and hundreds of people lie in the dark in stifling air for many days on end.

The last of the Kurile Islands, seen briefly in the mist of the fourth morning, was left behind and we entered the Sea of Okhotsk, continuing in the same northbound direction. It became noticeably colder and the waves seemed bigger. My illness again took a turn for the worse, and until the end of the trip I stayed almost continuously on my plank-bed, ate nothing, and slept for twenty hours a day. Only later did I learn that when one has scurvy he should sleep as little as possible.

On the morning of the sixth day I was suddenly awakened by shouts coming from the deck: 'Land! Land to the north!' At this, all the men in the hold, pushing one another and as usual cursing with all their hearts, rushed up the narrow gangway to the deck. I followed them.

Far on the horizon a faint coastline could be seen. But gradually the outlines grew more definite, showing the mountainous character of the land. By noon – I stayed on deck all the time – a big peninsula appeared on the starboard side.

The mountains, though rugged, did not rise high, and they were covered with rather sparse woods. We had been moving along the coast for an hour and a half, but no signs of habitation were visible anywhere. Nor did we come across a single ship or even a small boat.

'So this is the Kolyma land on which I'm doomed to spend the next five years,' I reflected. 'What's in store for me here? What conditions of life, what surroundings? Shall I live this out? Don't people say, and they must have reason for saying it, that it's very rare for anyone to return from here?' These were not happy thoughts.

At last the ship made a sharp turn to the east and we entered a wide harbour cutting deep into the mainland. Steep, almost barren cliffs descended into the water, and one could see that the harbour was very deep. On our left the entire shore was covered with a blanket of smoke through which tongues of flame licked out here and there – the woods were on fire. In the distance, where the shore was more level, some buildings could be seen, and farther to the left, under a steep cliff there was a port where a single ship was anchored, and on the stern we were soon able to read her name, the *Dalstroy*.

A long whistle blew on our ship, and presently we stopped a short distance from the pier.

The port comprised a small area, not more than 300 yards wide, literally chiselled from the high shore cliff. It had a few buildings, mostly warehouses, and was covered in a disorderly fashion with piles of cases, barrels of gasoline, bags of flour and various other things.

Our ship slowly moved up and docked at the pier next to the *Dalstroy*. Immediately all guards poured onto our deck, but no efforts on their part could make the prisoners go back into the holds.

A gangway was lowered, but none of the prisoners was allowed to go near it.

It was not until a couple of hours after they had left that we prisoners heard the command:

'Make ready with your things for disembarkation!'

The order came much too late – all of us had been ready for a long time.

Standing at the broadside I saw a small open space on the shore being quickly cleared of boxed-up merchandise and filled with a crowd of guards who had just arrived in automobiles. Some of them held dogs on leashes – big, well-fed sheep dogs.

A gangway was laid directly to the shore and an empty barrel was set at its upper end by the gate. Up on this barrel climbed a camp official who addressed us in words something like this:

'Comrades! You have all committed various crimes against our just worker-peasant laws. Our great government has granted you the right to live, and a great opportunity – to work for the good of our socialist country and the international proletariat. You all know that in the Soviet Union work is a matter of honour, a matter of glory, a matter of valour and heroism, as was said by our great leader and teacher, Comrade Josef Vissarionovich Stalin. Our worker-peasant government and our own Communist party do not inflict punishment. We recognize no penal policy. You have been brought here to enable you to reform yourselves – to realize your crimes, and to prove by honest, self-sacrificing work that you are loyal to socialism and to our beloved Stalin. Hurrah, Comrades!'

The orator's enthusiasm evoked no response in his audience, except that in the back row someone in a loud voice let off a string of obscene oaths. The rest were silent.

The speaker got down from the barrel, and another man, with some papers in his hands, took his place.

'I'll call out the names,' he said, 'and those I've named will announce their presence and walk over to me. After your identity has been checked you'll proceed to the shore.' And he began:

'Smirnov, Nicholas!'

'Here. Article 58—2, 10, 11,' prisoner Smirnov answered, following the ritual as he made his way through the crowd.

'Ivan, Nameless!' The term nameless was frequently used by prisoners who preferred to forget their identity because of repeated convictions.

'Here. Article 162, second part,' a ragged prisoner shouted cheer-fully – a professional thief with a long prison record, who elbowed his way to the gate.

And so it went on. One after another the men walked to the control officials who, besides the identity checked term and date of the sentence, and let them pass on down the gangway. There, guards received the prisoners and stood them in columns at the deeper end of the port.

The sun was about to set. Calling out 2,000 names is not an easy or a speedy job to accomplish. At length I heard my name.

'Petrov, Vladimir!'

'Here. Article 58—10, 11,' I answered as loudly as I could, and sup-pressing sharp pains in my legs and holding on to the handrails, I shoved myself through to the barrel. There I was asked again for my name and the term of my sentence, and this over, was pushed on down the gangway. Failing to keep my balance, I fell, and after rolling over a few times, hit with the full force of descent against the hard Kolyma ground to the accompaniment of loud laughter from the guards.

I was in the Kolyma.

Part II. The Mines of Kolyma

4. MAGADAN–CAPITAL OF THE KOLYMA

I LAY on the ground for a few seconds under the laughter of the guards, and then with difficulty got up on my feet and, mastering my pain, approached the crowd of prisoners, already formed in ranks.

I sat down on an empty crate and became lost in thought, with my head bowed. I don't know how long I remained in this almost unconscious condition, but when I came to myself at the shouts of the guards, the sun was already at the horizon.

Our column had reached an imposing size, and when we left the port area, surrounded by a convoy, and began to ascend a hill, a grey line of new convicts of the Kolyma stretched for three hundred yards along the road. There were no women with us; they were left on the ship until next day, and God knows what they had to go through that night.

Hurried on by the cries of the convoy, the men walked faster. It was very hard for me to walk, and gradually, lagging behind more and more, I found myself in the rear ranks of the column where old men, invalids, and sick men like myself straggled.

Soon lights appeared in front of us and buildings began to come into sight at the side of the road; in another half-hour we entered some kind of settlement and, apparently by-passing the centre, we began to move along dimly lighted streets. The streets were unpaved and very dusty. This dust, illuminated by the light of a lantern here and there, seemed completely to envelop the column, and getting into nose, mouth and ears, made it hard to breathe. The shouts of the guards became louder. Apparently they were in a hurry.

Our procession came up to a high, dark fence, turned to the left, and, at last, crawled through a wide-open gate over which shone an illuminated sign: *Magadan Transit Camp.*

We came into a wide yard and halted. The strong glare of searchlights hurt our eyes. When the tail of the column had pulled into the yard, the gates closed. New faces appeared around us, apparently the local administration. From one side shouts came: 'Quiet! Quiet!' Conversation stopped in the crowd.

An unseen voice shouted:

'. . . and to welcome you to Magadan. Now sit down where you are and you will be taken by sections to the baths. After that, you will be put in tents and you can rest after the road. In the baths you will get new equipment. Life in the Kolyma, Comrades, is a good life; you will soon be convinced of this.'

There was a movement in the crowd and our column finally broke ranks. Some sat down, while others just toppled over on to the dusty ground. My friends and I lay down side by side. Over me was the dark sky, strewn with stars.

Without noticing it, I dozed off. I woke up feeling someone tug at my hand. Mikhail was saying:

'It's our turn to go to the baths now. Get up.'

I looked around. The yard was half empty already; guards came up and, counting off fifty men, led us out of the gates. After walking for a half-hour through dark streets, we came to the baths – a low building made of logs. We entered in a crowd. The baths were of the usual camp construction and arrangement: the undressing-room, where we left all our things; the washing section, where we hastily washed ourselves and were shaved; and finally the dressing-room which we entered comparatively cleaner men. One by one we neared a counter standing by the wall, upon which the equipment was laid.

First cards were filled out, which we signed as receipts for the equipment issued. Then we passed on to a man in a white apron who stood there with a hypodermic in his hand and injected a dose into each man, apparently without changing the needle; it was an inoculation against an unspecified disease. After this we finally went up to the counter and were issued the new things: soldier's underwear, a military shirt, riding breeches, a cap, a towel, and a *bushlat*, a grey coat with a cotton lining, covered with bombazine. Then each of us chose for himself a pair of rude but solid new shoes out of a large pile. Here we quickly compared our new clothing for size, trying to find a good fit, trading pants, shirts, shoes; I managed to find roughly the right size in everything, except for the pants which were much too big for anyone. Tightening my belt – the only item we were allowed to keep of our old things, except for photographs and letters – I went out on the street with the others. In spite of my great fatigue, I enjoyed being clean and dressed in new clothes.

It was beginning to be light already when we returned to the Transit Camp, and we were immediately taken to a large tent arranged in the Vladivostok style – with double shelves on both sides. Climbing up on the top shelf with the help of my friends, I fell asleep immediately.

The day was sunny and bright when I awoke. There was almost no one in the tent. Next to me stood a big piece of bread and a tin cup with luke-warm tea which someone had brought. Having regained some strength, I climbed down and went out into the sunlight.

By the entrance gates there were several buildings of a more attractive type which contained the camp headquarters with the inevitable office for the commander, the dispensary, and the guard room. I came up to the dispensary where there stretched a long queue of sick men, awaiting their turn. Having reserved myself a place at the end of the line, I went off to the side for a short distance and squatted down, leaned against the wall of a small building and warmed myself in the sun.

Suddenly a group of several men got in my light. I looked up and saw that this was the command. They had stopped to look at me. Staggering, and holding on to the wall, I got up.

'Arrived yesterday?' asked a tall, stout man, with special insignia of a medical officer on his military uniform.

'Yes, yesterday,' I said.

'What's your complaint? How are you sick?'

'I have scurvy. I'm not complaining about anything.'

'What were you convicted for? Counter-revolution?'

'Yes, 58 – 10 and 11. Term six years. One and a half already served. In camp for the first time,' I answered, anticipating the next questions.

'What were you before?'

'A student, in Leningrad . . .'

'Ah! So you are a countryman of mine – very good,' said the doctor, patting my shoulder patronizingly. 'But you seem to be pretty sick.'

'Yes, things are bad with me, Citizen Commander. I'm afraid that I'll stretch out my legs for the last time here in your Kolyma . . .'

'Nonsense, we'll have you on your feet in no time. Our medical department is excellently organized here. Have him sent to the hospital,' he ordered, turning to one of his staff. Then, turning to me again:

'Well, goodbye, countryman, and get well. I'll come and check on you at the hospital. Don't get discouraged.' And with these words he walked on. One of the staff remained behind and wrote down my name and tent number. The men standing by the dispensary who had heard my conversation with the Commander with envy surrounded the tall doctor as soon as he had left me, but he went on further without listening to anyone. 'Go into the dispensary,' he said. 'There a doctor will look you over and will see what is necessary.'

The medical director had told the truth. In a couple of hours one of the camp officials came into the tent and told me to get my things together quickly and go to the hospital. I walked out of the tent and in the doorway bumped into two medical orderlies who were bringing in a stretcher. The orderlies caught up with me after I had taken less than ten steps toward the gate, and, having asked my name, which was confirmed by the official, laid me on the stretcher. Outside the gates stood an ambulance.

We started off. Lying on my side, I looked out of the window with interest. I could see the streets of a spacious settlement. All of the streets were unpaved, and narrow boardwalks, built on logs on both sides of the street, served as a path. The houses were all of a monotonous grey-brown colour. They were big and little, built of logs or boards, some having one story, some two. There were not many people in the streets, and very few of them women. I saw no children at all. I caught a glimpse of two or three shops with small show windows, and a big wooden building, evidently some sort of an institution. After this we passed fewer and fewer houses, the road began to go up a hill, and, at last, coming up to a group of large single-storied wooden buildings, we drew up in front of one of the doors.

I was carried into the building, right into the bathroom. I didn't feel at ease lying on the stretcher because I wasn't as helpless as all that, but nevertheless I was permitted no independent movements. They undressed me, put me in a bath, washed me again, and then gave me a warm wrapper and helped me into the ward where there were four beds in addition to mine; three of them were occupied.

With indescribable pleasure I stretched out on the bed which was made up with clean linen, an enjoyment I had been deprived of for a year and a half already. The ward was bright, there were no bars on the windows, the log walls had a smooth finish, and there was nothing to remind me that I was in reality a prisoner. I had not had time to become acquainted with my neighbours yet, when a woman accompanied by an orderly entered the room. She was dressed in white and wore a little cap, and was very young looking.

She sat down beside me, and having asked some short questions as to who I was and the nature of my ailments, she proceeded to examine me carefully, making entries in a notebook and giving instructions to the orderly. Then, with a pleasant word of farewell, she left. Five minutes later the orderly who had accompanied her returned and brought me a huge, soft feather mattress, the like of which I had not slept on even in my student days, remade my bed, brought me another pillow, and informed me that an intensified diet had been prescribed for me and, as medicine, extracts from currants and wild roses. In addition to this, I was to drink lemon juice and eat porridge made from raw potatoes.

My delight reached its furthest possible limits when supper was brought in. The things I found on my plate exceeded all expectations. There was a good soup with rice, well-made bread, a good piece of fried meat with potatoes, and a sweet dried fruit compote – all the things about which I had not even been able to dream for so long.

After supper I began to get acquainted with my neighbours. Next to me lay an old man with an eastern type of face, with intelligent, lively eyes. He told me that he was a Georgian, that his name was Kavtaradze, and that he had once been the secretary of the Georgian Central Executive Committee, but then he had entered the party opposition, joining Trotsky, and after the exile of the latter, the old man had been exiled to Alma Ata. Then, after a few years, he had been arrested again. He was tried in absentia and administratively sentenced to five years in a concentration camp. He suffered from stomach ulcers, contracted in prison. He had come to the Kolyma a month before I had – before that he had been in Maryinsk, one of the Siberian camps of the N.K.V.D.

One of the two others in the ward was a Moscow book-keeper who had received five years for telling anti-Soviet anecdotes; the other was an expert habitual thief who had been caught 'in general' – that is, not for any particular crime, but just because his profession was known. He had been given, also administratively, four years in the camps, not on any particular article of the code, but in absentia on the so-called 'letters', SHE – socially harmful element. Later I discovered that the N.K.V.D. awards 'letters' to all those whom it found hard to convict on a particular article of the Criminal Code, in spite of the prison proverbs in the U.S.S.R. which say: 'If there is a man, an article will be found for him.' I have come across the following 'letters': SDE (socially dangerous element), which is given to those accused of political rather than criminal acts; CR (counter-revolutionary – without verification); SE (suspected of espionage); ST (suspected of terrorist intentions); and for women, SP (suspected of prostitution).

Of our small but quite colourful company I became most friendly with the old man, Kavtaradze. He was one who had been around and seen a great deal in his life – personally and closely acquainted with Stalin as well as with the other Caucasians then at the helm: Ozhzhoni-kidze, Yenukidze, Mikoyan, and the rest.

He spoke carefully and with restraint in telling me the story of the party oppositions, not as we knew it from the papers but as it had actually occurred. Never accusing anyone directly, he characterized the party leaders so vividly that the picture of eternal quarrelling and intrigue within the party stretched out in front of me in all its colour. It was Kavtaradze who warned me that in the camp I would meet two categories of political prisoners, former members of the All Union Communist party. One of these, the minority, had gone into opposition on idealistic grounds and had remained irreconcilable to Stalin's rule; the other, the majority, had been in opposition earlier, counting on its victory, but had confessed its sins after the defeat of the Trotskyites. These last, even after finding themselves behind the barbed wire of a concentration camp, continued to praise Stalin and the general party line as much as they could, and made every effort to prove their loyalty to the regime by writing reports on their fellow prisoners. The 'confessed ones' were proud of the name 'General Liners'* which they had received, but for some reason the high administration of the Kolyma didn't think much of them.

* From 'General Line of the Communist Party', headed always by Stalin.

And so my days passed – in conversation with the old Georgian, in reading a few books, which found their way into the ward, and in the local daily newspaper, on whose masthead was printed the warning: *Not to be circulated outside the camp*. Incidentally, it was as hard to imagine the picture of life in the Kolyma from this paper as it was from any other Soviet papers in general.

Every day Elena Vasilievna, our doctor, visited us, always treating everyone with great consideration. About ten days after my entry into the hospital, she sent me to be X-rayed, and the next day sympathetically told me that I had tuberculosis. A blood analysis confirmed the unpleasant discovery in the form of Dr. Koch's microbes. This then had been acquired in prison.

In addition to vitamin extracts, other medicines were added to my daily ration, and my diet was further strengthened. I began to feel better; apparently the scurvy was leaving me.

Once my saviour, the military doctor who had sent me to the hospital, visited me. He turned out to be the head of the medical administration of the entire Kolyma, the medical aide to Berzin himself – Berzin, the boss of Dalstroy, who had unlimited powers in the whole region.

Entering the ward, the medical director recognized me immediately, questioned Elena Vasilievna about me, and again asserted that there were no diseases which could not be cured in the Kolyma, cited the especially healthy dry mountain climate of the region. He assured me that my tuberculosis would leave me as if by magic as soon as I arrived at the north – the region of the gold fields. This assurance proved correct after the lapse of a year and a half.

Kavtaradze also told me about Berzin, the director of the N.K.V.D. trust, Dalstroy. Edward Petrovich Berzin, a Latvian by descent, commanded one of the regiments which upheld the revolution in the civil war. He had at one time been the commandant of the Kremlin, and later together with Stalin, a member of the Revolutionary War Council of the Southern Front. Afterward he occupied various positions in the Cheka, G.P.U., and N.K.V.D., and before his appointment to the Kolyma, had been the director of another camp, Red Vishera, in western Siberia. In this, one of the northernmost camps of the Soviet Union, he had done so well in the eyes of Moscow, that when Stalin ordered a concentration camp for the mining of gold on the Kolyma to be organized, Berzin turned out to be the leading candidate, and he arrived there accompanied by a group of his former assistants, as the all-powerful boss. Berzin's arrival in the Kolyma in December, 1931 is considered the date of the founding of Dalstroy.

Among the thoughts which occupied my mind at that time was the one of my last Leningrad affairs, about my revelations, about Berdichevsky's visit and the consequences of that visit. Having thought it over very carefully, I decided to raise the whole matter again and wrote a detailed report, addressed to Berzin, which contained the story of Mikhail, and in addition an account of my adventures in Leningrad after Berdichevsky's arrival. A few days after I sent off this report, I was summoned to the office of the chief surgeon of the hospital. When I walked in I saw a youngish looking stranger with an extremely pleasant appearance. I managed to spot the insignia of the N.K.V.D. underneath his white garment.

This man informed me that his name was Andrey Andreyevich Mosevich, that he was the chief of the Secret-Political Branch of the N.K.V.D. in Dalstroy, and that Berzin had instructed him to investigate my report. I felt well-disposed toward him at once, and without misgivings I told him the whole story quite frankly. He interrupted me occasionally, asking questions and taking notes of some sort. However, his familiarity with Leningrad affairs struck me as somewhat strange.

When the conversation had ended, he shook hands with me warmly and told me that he would take all necessary measures and that I was not to think about this affair any more.

Returning to the ward I asked Kavtaradze if he knew Mosevich. It turned out that Mosevich was well known to all the local Trotskyites and that it was because of him that the majority of the General Liners' reports had no consequences for the irreconcilables. Kavtaradze also informed me that before coming to the Kolyma, Mosevich had worked in the Leningrad N.K.V.D. I sat up straight in my bed when I heard this.

'What? In the Leningrad N.K.V.D.? Why didn't you tell me before?'

'Because you didn't ask me. He worked there before the assassination of Kirov, when the entire head group of the Leningrad N.K.V.D. was arrested, sentenced to various terms of imprisonment, and sent to the Kolyma, thanks to the intercession of Berzin. All of them, Medved, Zaporozhets, Fomin, Yanishevsky, Mosevich, and the others occupy important positions in the Kolyma, although technically they are prisoners. Well, what do you expect? Crows don't peck out each other's eyes!'

My morale dropped immediately. I had scarcely arrived here when I had already made my position worse by complaining to Mosevich – a very influential figure in Dalstroy – about his Leningrad colleagues. This could cause the most unpleasant consequences for me. The irony of the whole situation was amusing though. Men are arrested for such a famous crime as the assassination of Kirov, sentenced to five or ten years of penal servitude, then suddenly they turn out to be the big bosses in one of the biggest camps of the U.S.S.R.

That conversation with Mosevich was my last conversation on that subject. After that I never said a word to anyone about my investigations in the field of internal plots within the organs of the N.K.V.D., and tried to forget about it completely. A healthy instinct of self-preservation took the upper hand over what remained of my idealistic loyalty to the Soviet regime.

Later I met Mosevich once again in Magadan. After talking a bit on various unrelated subjects, and just before taking leave of me, Mosevich looked at me searchingly, apparently expecting me to question him about the measures he had taken in regard to that affair. I looked back at him with a simple, innocent look. At last he could no longer contain himself.

'Do you remember our conversation in the hospital?'

'Conversation in the hospital?' I knitted my brows with surprise. 'I remember that you and I talked about something, but for the life of me I can't remember what it was.'

'Have you really forgotten?' asked Mosevich with a slight smile.

'Cross my heart and hope to die. What *did* we talk about?' I answered, with a look of amazement.

'Well, isn't it a pity, I've forgotten also,' answered Mosevich. 'Well, it's not important. Goodbye. I predict that you will go far if you are careful and make no slips. If you need anything, you know where to find me.'

I thanked him and said goodbye. It had been a good lesson. But how many other mistakes would I still make in the future. . . .

Time went by. The symptoms of scurvy no longer bothered me. I got stronger and I walked briskly around the corridors of the hospital. I even began to feel oppressed by the monotony of the surroundings. At one of Elena Vasilievna's visits, I asked her to discharge me.

'Are you bored already?' She was genuinely astonished. 'Everyone here tries to stay with us as long as possible, but you want to leave us. Well, if that's the way you feel, I'll discharge you in a couple of days.'

She kept her promise, and soon I was walking through the entire settlement, accompanied by an official sent from the camp, having traded my hospital wrapper for my prison uniform, with a supply of anti-scurvy extracts in my pocket.

Instead of taking me to the Transit Camp, my guide led me to another camp, situated almost in the centre of Magadan. The open gates and the lack of a sentry there made me like the place immediately. We entered a small building right by the gate on which there was a sign that read: PERSONNEL ALLOCATION OFFICE. I gave my sealed envelope of documents to an official seated at a desk.

Looking over my papers hurriedly, the official asked me what I knew how to do. I began telling him, but he cut me short:

'Do you know how to make designs?'

'Of course, I studied at the School of Building Techniques.'

'That's fine. Tomorrow you will go to work at the Building Office.

We have a request from them for a draftsman. And now they'll show you where you are going to live,' he said, and he began to give directions to a middle-aged man sitting at the door.

We left the Allocation Office, went into the interior of the camp up to a long barracks where we entered. It was empty, except for an old man who was cleaning up the spacious room which was divided into sections by light partitions. Along the walls stood wooden beds with mattresses, covered with uniformly grey blankets. Night tables stood between each bed. It was comparatively clean.

The old man, who turned out to be in charge of quarters, showed me to an unoccupied bed. Then he took me to the camp supply room where I was issued bed linen and a blanket, and also the food cards. On the way back he showed me the camp mess hall.

Between five and six o'clock in the evening the barracks began to fill up with the men coming back from work. Most of them, noticing my presence, asked me no questions and went about their own affairs. This was somewhat strange.

Suddenly the familiar figure of Prostoserdov appeared. At first he didn't recognize me, but when he did, he couldn't believe his eyes – I had changed so much in the hospital.

We sat down on a bed beside each other and in a low tone began to exchange our impressions of the period of time which had passed.

I asked him about the people living in the barracks. The answer was not encouraging:

'Without exception they are all Trotskyites. The trouble is that out of forty men there are only about five decent ones. The rest are all General Liners and terrible stool pigeons. On the second day after I arrived in the barracks I was summoned to the N.K.V.D. and shown three reports stating that I had cursed Stalin.'

'With whom did you speak?'

'Mosevich. Do you know him?'

'I do. And what did he tell you when he showed you the reports?'

'That I should stop reviling the Soviet regime, or things would go badly with me.'

'And what did you say?' I was very interested.

'I said that the possibility of cursing at Stalin is the only joy that I have in prison and on forced labour, and that it is impossible for me to renounce this pleasure.'

'And . . .'

'He answered that I am not on forced labour but that I am working as an accountant, but that he could send me to the gold fields where I would have every reason to curse. Then I promised him that I would hold my tongue as much as possible, and we parted friends.'

The picture was clear. It was necessary to watch oneself very carefully to avoid getting into trouble. However, the General Liners, seeing that I was acquainted with Prostoserdov and that he had warned me about them, did not try to involve me in provocative political discussions and our further relations were limited to purely everyday matters.

But it was very interesting to watch this crowd. These former Communists couldn't live without politics. They discussed even the most minor questions from the point of view of dialectic materialism and the general party line, reading newspapers through and explaining to each other the political meaning of each event. They were all literate, and among them there were some so-called 'Red professors', graduates of the Academy of Marx-Engels-Lenin-Stalin.

More than anyone in the world they cursed Trotsky and other opposition leaders and lauded Stalin to the skies, finding such wonderful qualities in the man that sometimes I began to think that they were just ridiculing the poor Georgian. But the most interesting part came when, after quarrelling among themselves about a cup taken without permission or about a towel knocked on the floor by mistake, they would begin to remember the opposition activities of the offender.

'Don't you remember, Nikolai Abramovich, how you went to Moscow in 1926 to pay your respects to Trotsky?' one would jeer.

'Why I went there, you don't know, but I have definite information that you circulated Radek's proclamation illegally!' Nikolai Abramovich would answer.

'Naturally, you know about that, most respected one. After all I got them from you. You took advantage of my political inexperience!' the first would say.

'So! You were innocent then, were you? And I thought that you already had a wife and two children, and that you had been to the doctor several times to be cured for nasty diseases . . .' Nikolai Abramovich would announce in an annihilating tone of voice.

And so it would go. Two of them would get into an argument, each trying to better the other. Then, a third one would mix into it. The original ones would attack him and list his entire genealogy. These Trotskyites knew each other perfectly. I think that Mosevich had several extremely detailed biographies on each of them, written by one of the others.

As soon as Elvov (formerly Gubelman – Yaroslavsky's secretary) returned from work – he also worked as an accountant, but in a better place, the N.K.V.D. mess – he would lie down in his bed. Always he had with him Stalin's book, *Questions of Leninism*. He would sink his face into the book and just lie there, speaking to no one.

Once I came up to him and saw that he was holding the book upside down. I sat down on his bed and asked him in a low voice:

'What sort of reading are you doing? The book is upside down!'

'Sh-h-h' – His eyes opened wide. 'No one should know this. I have read this book 666 times in its proper order, and I have learned it by heart like a poem. Now I'm reading it upside down, and I'm going to learn it by heart backwards from end to beginning. But the main thing is,' and here he looked toward his colleagues, 'this book is something like the Bible – it drives devils away. If a man is reading Stalin, he must not be disturbed because he is attaining the highest wisdom.'

I just shook my head.

In spite of his cheerful character, Elvov was a deeply unhappy man. He was terribly tortured by the separation from his family – a wife and three little girls, from three to eight years of age. He sent them all his earnings, wrote letters home every day, and once when I awoke at night I saw him half covering himself with a blanket and looking at the photograph of his little girls and crying like a child. The poor man had been recently given eight years in prison for attending underground Trotskyite meetings in 1928.

I reported the next morning to the Magadan Building Office, accompanied by a camp chaser – a man who accompanies prisoners to work. I was taken to the Construction Section, introduced to the head engineer, a pleasant little Georgian, Kotetashvily by name, and was seated at a drawing board and shown some sample work to do. Naturally I made every effort over it, and the result was satisfactory.

During the lunch hour, my neighbour, also a draftsman, told me that of the eight men working in the Construction Office, four were prisoners, and four had come to the Kolyma on voluntary applications. Although the free workers were also engineers and draftsmen, they preferred the prisoners, among whom there were two very good engineers, to do the hardest jobs.

In a few days I got to know the voluntary workers in the camp who worked as technical-administrative personnel.

The story behind these people turned out to be an extremely interesting one.

At the end of 1931, when the creation of Dalstroy was decreed by Moscow, Berzin realized what difficulties he would encounter in the Kolyma in the organization of mass gold mining, and he persuaded Stalin to grant privileges and incentives both for the future forced labourers and for the voluntary technical-administrative personnel.

In several of Russia's big cities like Moscow, Leningrad and Odessa, agencies of Dalstroy were established. It was their mission, in addition to the purchasing of food and technical supplies for the Kolyma, to recruit voluntary personnel. The conditions of work at Dalstroy were marvellous. As a minimum, employees received sixty per cent more than the salary established by the government for Moscow. At the end of every six months, the pay was increased by ten per cent until it doubled. The contract was for three years, including eight months vacation with pay. An employee who voluntarily gave up his leave was reimbursed for it.

The contract could be extended automatically for two years, including a five months' leave. Transportation was paid for in both directions. Expense accounts were paid on the spot – two months' pay. Upon final separation, another month's pay was given as separation wages.

To all this special incentives were added – men serving in the Kolyma were exempt from military service. In addition, and this was probably the biggest attraction for the public, the N.K.V.D. had no right to arrest a voluntary Kolyma worker without personal permission from Berzin in every individual case. And he very seldom granted such permission.

These conditions attracted a large number of volunteers. But they were hired with care. A preliminary investigation by the N.K.V.D. was mandatory. It became a tremendously desirable thing to get into Dalstroy, in spite of the far-away location and the severe climate of the region. People used all their friendships and connections to get to these, by Soviet standards, heavenly places.

But thanks to the established obstacles, the Kolyma often received people who were perhaps politically reliable but technically only half qualified. To overcome this circumstance, Berzin had Stalin's permission to use Kolyma prisoners at his discretion even in the most responsible posts. I won't take Medved, Mosevich, and other Leningrad men sentenced in connection with Kirov's assassination as an example. These people were special cases because of their long membership in the N.K.V.D. But apart from them, in Magadan, and especially in the gold fields in the taiga, many prisoners worked as field-bosses, chief engineers, foremen, and so on. In those years one could very easily find among the prisoners very great and highly qualified specialists, some of whom were placed in concentration camps just for that very reason – so that their services could be more easily and cheaply exploited.

Under Berzin, the prisoners were also very well paid in the Kolyma. They received the pay of voluntary workers, without the rises, and only 500 rubles were retained for the benefit of the camp in the case of the white collar workers, 280 in the case of labourers. Voluntary labourers, however, belonged exclusively to that category of prisoner who had finished his turn and preferred remaining at Dalstroy to going home.

In those days in the Kolyma there was also a very high credit for working days – a shortening of the sentence for those who worked. Men sentenced for criminal acts received credit for 100–150 days per year, and sometimes for two hundred. Those sentenced for counter-revolution only on 58–10 (agitation) received fifty days credit per year. Only the remaining others who had been sentenced on the more serious articles of the code received no credit at all.

The sum total of all this is what created the exceptional conditions in the Kolyma which enabled Berzin, in such a comparatively short period, to achieve such significant results – to organize and launch the greatest gold-production trust in the Soviet Union and in an almost deserted, wild and severe region. People worked there, as distinct from the rest of the Soviet Union, willingly, and not from fear.

As I have already said, I was accepted as a draftsman in the Construction Office. At first my duties in the office were limited to copying various drawings. But at the same time I kept my eye on designing. My knowledge which had survived from the time I lived in Moscow and studied in the Building Technical School helped me in the task of familiarizing myself with this new branch of construction. It turned out to be not complicated, and rather interesting. There was a lot of work in the office and at the end of my first month there, I was able to undertake independent designs and simple technical calculations.

A direct result of this success was a rise in my pay. In our office we were paid according to the amount of work done. The first month, in my capacity as a draftsman, I made 800 rubles – minus 500 for the camp, leaving 300 for myself; the second month, when I had completed more serious work, I received 1,000 – 500 for myself; the third month 1,200 – 700; the fourth 1,300, and so on.

All in all I became the possessor of a somewhat substantial sum of money, more than I had ever had before my arrest. I was able to send money to my mother, who needed it all her life, and in addition to this I was able to dress decently. Expenses for life in camp were insignificant, and although, officially, clothes were not sold to prisoners, it just naturally happened that everyone was able to get everything. There were voluntary employees working in our office, not too good at their specialities, but nice fellows. For small services, such as making an extra drawing, they bought us anything we wanted in their own stores. By the end of my stay there, I became such friends with my fellow workers that they used to ask me themselves, all the time, whether or not I needed anything. In this way I acquired two suits, a watch, shoes, underwear, and other things which I could not have obtained in freedom, and I received permission to eat outside of camp in a very good mess for the more privileged prisoners. I always had all sorts of good things to which I continually treated my less fortunate friends.

Finally, and this I considered a great success, my various voluntary acquaintances began to invite me to their places where we whiled away the long evenings playing cards. I received a special pass which gave me the right to leave the camp at any time and I completely ceased to experience the discomforts of camp life.

In those years, in comparison with the rest of the U.S.S.R., the Kolyma was in an especially privileged position in regard to the presence of various goods and produce. In the Kremlin the efforts of

Dalstroy in increasing gold production were much appreciated and a full measure of everything was shipped out there.

Magadan, as I saw it in 1936, was a rather sad sight. The only brick buildings were the post office, the automobile repair plant, and the power station. Everything else was made of wood, mostly of logs. With the exception of the Kolyma Highway, all the streets were unpaved. After the rains the mud was impassable, and even on the platforms built next to the houses, one had to walk with great care. The illumination was very dull, and few corners had street lights. Three-quarters of the population were prisoners.

Attacks and robberies were rare, because the careful administration retained only the quiet elements in town – those convicted under the less serious counter-revolution charges, and the best part of the privileged class, embezzlers, speculators, chiselers, bigamists, the most flagrant violators of the alimony laws, and others composing the cream of Kolyma society.

Two-thirds of the military guard were composed of prisoners, but only those 'socially elect' who had completed more than half of their terms were accepted for duty in it. The military authorities did not interfere with the life of the camp's permanent inhabitants very much. Anyone who got into trouble – for theft or for being caught making love – was immediately shipped to the gold fields, which was considered a very heavy punishment.

The voluntary part of Magadan's population lived in no less discomfort than the prisoners. There was nowhere to spend the large sums of money they earned. Cards were popular here, too. The shabby little theatre which usually showed movies, but which sometimes gave stage performances put on by dramatic talent from among the prisoners, could not hold all those who wanted to attend. Men wore themselves out in the search of alcohol – the sale of which was rationed in the Kolyma – and if they found any they would drink themselves into unconsciousness. There were cases of men whose time was finished and who could have gone home on leave, but they had drunk and gambled away all their money. Then these men would draw their compensation pay, gamble away the rest out of regret, and remain for another term.

The female question was the crucial one. There were few women in Magadan, and most of them came in search of easy earnings. A beauty would arrive for three, perhaps five years. She would work somewhere for appearance's sake, attach herself to some director with a large salary, save her own money, live on his, and in addition, grab all she could out of him. After bleeding him dry, she would attach herself to the next man.

Occasionally husbands and wives would arrive together. But all these marriages easily dissolved in the Kolyma. Sometimes even on the ship on the way from Vladivostok wives changed husbands a couple of times before finding a 'suitable' one. After they arrived in Magadan, such things would happen as a rule. I knew one couple – our book-keeper and his young wife. After coming to Magadan, by mutual agreement they pretended that they were strangers to each other. He got a good job and she did, too. But the girl immediately started going 'from hand to hand', but cleverly. Finally, at the end of the agreed period, she had managed to fleece ten men and had earned several times more than her husband. And when the period ended, the enter-prising couple went home, the best of friends. This satisfied pair almost ruined themselves giving a farewell party. I think they took 150,000 home with them.

Scandals often happened because of women, even up to the point of shooting. But these affairs were usually covered up and every attempt was made to prevent any consequences.

However, the problem was often solved thanks to the women prisoners, because the bachelors in more or less high position chose maids for themselves according to taste from the women's camp.

The correspondence which had been established between my mother and myself was a source of great joy. I didn't write anyone else, but I wrote to her very often. My large amounts of money made it possible to send telegrams of fifty words or more. Officially, all correspondence was subject to camp censorship, but this regulation remained on paper only, since no one could prevent me from going to the post office and sending a letter or a telegram. Letters took about a month, but only during the period of navigation. From December to April, when the sea was frozen, the telegraph was our only means of communication with the 'mainland' as we called all of Russia west of Vladivostok.

Month after month passed in this way. The mild and damp autumn came, and with November the first snow fell. In general the entire coastline of the Sea of Okhotsk has a climate which is very different from the inland part of the Kolyma. There are no severe frosts; the winter lasts only four months, and it is never too cold. The minimum temperature recorded in Magadan is 45 below zero, Fahrenheit.

I had become so accustomed to my life in the Kolyma capital, so used to the surroundings, and so engrossed in my work that I was almost satisfied with my position. I developed a group of friends and acquaint-ances in the camp and outside of it, and even had connections in the Main Administration of Dalstroy.

My technique of designing improved steadily and after a few months I was able to complete jobs independently which were supposed to be done only by engineers. Once I even received an extraordinary reward – a good coat for the fast completion of a heating plan for a large brick house which was being built on the Kolyma highway.

However, I suspect that this reward was a false one, and that the coat had been bought with the secret contributions of my voluntary colleagues.

But the greatest pleasure for me was an event which rarely happened in camp.

Once, while I was working, I was summoned by the office manager.

'How do you like it with us?' he asked.

'Very well. So well that I am ready to sign a contract before the end of my term,' I answered.

'What would you like more than anything else?' probed the manager, smiling.

I stood in bewilderment. What else did I need? As a counter-revolutionary, I couldn't be freed before the end of my term. Money? I had enough for my needs . . .

'I don't know, Mikhail Andreyevich. I don't seem to have any special wishes. I'm satisfied with everything.'

'Well, how about this?' He stretched a paper toward me. I took it and saw that it was a special N.K.V.D. document which gave me permission to live outside the camp, within the territory of Magadan. Signatures, seals, and even my photograph were all in order. I thanked him warmly and rushed back to my office to show everyone this amazing document. It was immediately decided that I would move into the voluntary workers' barracks, not far from the office, where two of our office workers lived.

That same evening I shifted all my things from the camp to their house, where I occupied a bed in one of my friends' rooms. The room was not big but it was sufficient for two. I felt at the height of my bliss.

However, the new situation brought new temptations with it. In the camp I had led a Spartan life, only occasionally had I visited friends to play cards or go to see a family of imprisoned Trotskyites – a man, his wife, and a child, who had a permission similar to mine and lived modestly in one of the city dormitories. Except for these two places, I limited myself to short walks.

Now the situation had radically changed. As soon as it was evening, my friend would take me to one of the rooms in our house where a card game was in progress, if, indeed the company had not assembled in our room. And I was forced to play. In spite of the fact that most of the people living in our house treated me pleasantly, I had to be on my guard always, never forgetting my position. In the card games I was more afraid of winning than of losing, and I won most of the time. If I tried to play in a small way they were insulted. Once I tried to return my winnings to the heavy loser – another *faux pas*. Not to go at all was also impossible. I liked my sleep, but they would sit until three or four in the morning, sometimes until dawn.

In other words, my new life was a constant source of worry. It was worse when there was a liquor ration. Everyone would get completely drunk, and start to argue and fight. They would break into the two or three rooms where married couples resided. It was not good to drink, but you couldn't refuse. Sometimes I seriously contemplated giving up the free life and returning to camp. But I didn't have the courage.

And that is how the time passed – cards, drinking bouts, and fights. But my free life ended suddenly, and in the most unexpected manner.

A family had arrived on the last boat from Vladivostok and settled in our house – a middle-aged couple with a fifteen-year-old daughter. The parents worked in the main office, while the daughter usually remained at home.

Once, returning from work a little earlier than usual, I lay down on my bed with a newspaper, but before I had read ten lines, I heard a penetrating childish scream. There was no one else in the house – they had not returned from work yet.

'Help! Save me!'

I understood immediately that it was the newly arrived girl who was screaming, and without thinking I forced my way into the room, tearing the hook off the door with the strength of my push.

I got there just in time. The girl was rushing around the room in a torn dress, pursued by my neighbour, a mechanic from the auto repair shop, a healthy fellow, a member of the Komsomol. I grabbed him by the arm, but he lunged at me, demanded that I get out, swearing and saying that that counter-revolutionary swine had no business there. I hit him in the face with the full strength of my fist, and a fight started, a fight which I had no chance of winning since my opponent was stronger than I. The parents and the other neighbours returning from work saved the situation. We were separated, and my opponent, cursing wildly, announced that things would go badly with me.

I returned to my room feeling very badly about what had happened, because in spite of the approval of all the people in the house for my action, I knew that he would always be right, that the law was on his side, and that I was really in trouble. My smashed and bleeding nose did nothing to cheer me up.

In less than two hours, during which I took the only action that was possible – I informed my boss about what had happened – two officials from the N.K.V.D. arrived at our house together with the insulted Komsomol man, and ordered me to collect my things. The weak protests from the parents of the girl were ignored.

I packed quickly and they took me to the camp, confiscating in advance my permission for residence in town. They took me to the very centre of the camp where the guard house was, and there my escort turned me over to the soldiers on guard.

The soldiers took my suitcase away, and, with a hard blow on the head, pushed me into a dirty, half-dark cell, with bars on the windows. Still dressed, I stretched out on the rough bed whose mattress had been removed, and began to curse myself in every possible way, taking an oath never as long as I lived to interfere with any affair which did not directly concern me. Let them kill a child on the spot – and I wouldn't move a hand to save it.

I promised myself that I would always be humble and submissive to everyone more powerful than I, always to know my dog's place, and to refuse all privileges which did not correspond to my position. . . .

Belated repentance! I understood the hopelessness of my position only too well. To interfere with the affairs of a volunatry employee, and in addition to beat him on the face and other parts of the body, was an unforgivable act for a prisoner. I knew that punishment was always meted out for this, and very severely.

The minimum punishment would be – exile to the gold fields. And they could decide to add on five more years to my sentence for hooliganism if they wanted to. However, I was not too much afraid of the latter, because in such a case my Komsomol friend would have to appear at the hearing, and his role also would not be an enviable one.

Through the walls I could hear the guardhouse slowly filling up with people. Apparently my incident had served as an impulse for a purge of the camp of all manner of disturbing elements, which was initiated from time to time. Finally, two men were pushed into my cell whom I recognized as two of the Trotskyites. One of them informed me that Prostoserdov had been arrested too and was sitting in the next cell.

'Nicolai Nicolayevich, are you there?' I shouted.

'You here too? By what fates? What did I tell you?' his vigorous voice sounded. 'They're all bastards! Our paradise here didn't last long. Wait, they'll show us soon where crayfish spend the winter. And our Berzin is just as much of a swine as his boss in Moscow.'

It was clear to me now that we would start for the north that day.

They brought us each a piece of bread. I had lost the habit of eating such food, but there was nothing to be done about it. I was hungry and ate every crumb. We demanded water. Instead we were brought snow in a cup. This was a sheer mockery because the camp had a water main, but we were hardly in a position to argue. We began to wash the bread down with snow.

I regretted my lost things and my work, but experience had taught me already never to surrender to unnecessary regrets, and I was almost calm.

At last the guards came into the house and herded us all out into the yard. Directly in front of the door, black against the snow, stood an open truck with its motor running. The camp commander stood there, and one by one we approached him. He was making up the roster on the spot. I didn't even try to explain anything to him, seeing his angrily smirking face.

'Ah, and the volunteer is here too? That's nice!' he said.

I climbed silently into the truck after the others. The guards climbed aboard.

We were on our way.

5. MY FIRST ACQUAINTANCE WITH THE MINES

ALTHOUGH November in Magadan is not cold, as I sat in the moving open car I felt sharply that it was no longer summer. I buttoned my topcoat and turned up the collar, but it did not help.

We came out upon the Kolyma Highway, turned right, and drove along the straight ribbon of road leading directly to the high mountain pass in the distance. I looked back at the sleeping city, lit here and there by street lamps, and now receding rapidly.

For the last time the lights of Magadan flashed in the distance and vanished. Against the dark sky we could see only the standing figures of our four guards, posted at the corners of the truck with rifles in their hands. They were warmly dressed and not afraid of freezing, but I began to shiver violently and could no longer feel my feet, clad in light shoes.

Once across the pass, the driver added speed, although the highway lay under a thick layer of snow which had not been cleared away.

The Magadan Sovhoz, where vegetables were grown in hothouses for the higher local officials, flashed past, and the last building disappeared from sight. Beyond them the road was totally deserted, except for a rare car going toward the city. According to Kolyma rules, cars and trucks coming from the taiga shut off their headlights and stop, making way for those from Magadan. The road was narrow even in summer; in winter, when its outlines were marked only by lines of twigs stuck into the snow, there were frequent accidents.

The moon rose. Snow began to fall, and gradually the prisoners huddled in the truck were covered by a thin but fairly solid white blanket. The snow melted a little with our breath, and soon trickles of cold water began to crawl down our collars, sending our spirits even lower. My teeth chattered, and I tried to prevent severe frostbite by moving my feet constantly despite the protests of my neighbours. For my hands I feared less, but I did not want to lose any toes.

It was daylight when we drove into a small settlement. We had reached Atka, which housed the 2nd Auto Base of Dalstroy. It consisted of garages, depots, repair shops and living quarters for the workers and prisoner employees. In the entire village there were less than twenty free employees.

Our truck stopped at the camp club. The guards ordered us to climb out and go into the building.

The club was a large empty room with several benches and a large stove in the middle – a homemade affair made of an empty petrol barrel. A bright wood fire was burning in the stove, and everyone rushed toward it. My first thought was to remove my shoes and rub my numbed feet to restore circulation. It took fully thirty minutes of effort before the dead numbness gave way to sharp, cutting pain. I was happy that I had saved my feet.

Meantime, dinner had been brought: bread and gruel, still hot, and we greedily swallowed it. There were twenty-five of us. Many were known to me. The group included five or six criminals who were being deported to the taiga for various offences committed in the Magadan camps.

The political prisoners were being deported as a result of denunciations or for impertinence to authorities. Prostoserdov was one of these. He told me how it had happened. All the prisoners of his barrack had been taken to the baths and there given some of the usual injections. I do not know what bee had bitten Prostoserdov, but he refused point-blank to be stuck and was rude to the doctor. When the group returned to the barracks, Prostoserdov was summoned to the camp commander, who proceeded to lecture him on proper behaviour in camp, lamenting the slackening of discipline which led to such deplorable incidents as my attack upon a member of the Young Communist League. Prostoserdov flared up again, saying that if I beat up a Komsomol member, there must have been sufficient provocation for it, and that there were too many scoundrels about who deserved a beating, not only in Magadan but also in Moscow. . . . As a result of this outburst, Prostoserdov was led off from the director's office straight to the punitive cell.

This stocky, red-haired man smoked a cigarette and with great gusto reviled the entire Soviet government, explaining to me that he now considered himself free from the promise given to Mosevich.

The chauffeur of the Atka auto-base entered the room to see whether he could do some trade with the men. I offered my new coat, demanding some warmer clothing in exchange. The customer took a liking to the coat. He left and soon returned with a sheepskin-lined coat in fairly decent condition. Later, when we had arranged ourselves again in the truck and it began to move, a young fellow came running from around a corner, shouting that I was wearing a stolen coat and demanding its return. Of course, he did not get it back – it warmed me not a whit less for being stolen.

The rest of the trip was somewhat easier. The sheepskin coat was big for me and I managed to sit in such a way that it covered my feet. The high collar saved my ears, and I kept my hands warm by tucking them deep inside the sleeves.

We climbed down from the truck and were taken to a special tent assigned to transient prisoners going north. We were soon given supper, but sat up for a long time before going to sleep, trying to get warm after the freezing journey. There was plenty of wood and the fire in the stove burned brightly. At length we lay down on the bare benches along the walls and slept.

We were awakened and started out again when it was still dark. Two hours later, when it began to dawn, I saw ahead of us a small settlement, and beyond it a wide river with steep banks which could only have been the Kolyma River. We stopped at the turnpike, while the leader of our guards went to find out whether we could continue. We took advantage of the opportunity and clambered out of the truck, stamping about and running back and forth to warm up. The guards were unconcerned, since there was no danger of our escaping – indeed, there was nowhere to go.

The leader returned and told us that although the Kolyma was already frozen, the ice in the middle of the river was still thin and we would therefore have to walk part of the way. I immediately protested, categorically refusing to go any further unless I was given felt boots. Two other men, who had also been seized in Magadan without adequate clothing, joined me, and the rest supported us. The demand, incidentally, was a legitimate one and in accordance with local rules. Soon one of the guards who had left the group returned with three pairs of old felt boots and we immediately put them on. I stuffed my shoes into the pockets of my sheepskin coat, for any future eventuality.

The guards ordered us to get into the truck again and with screeching brakes it crawled down the narrow road and on to the ice-bound Kolyma. A road leading to the left bank was cleared in the thick snow which covered the frozen river, and on either side of it, at intervals, there were holes cut in the ice to gauge its thickness. Dense fog rose from these openings.

Somewhat to the right groups of people were pottering about on the ice. I guessed from certain signs that they were building a bridge over the Kolyma, which was half a mile wide at that spot. There was no mechanical equipment whatever in this work, and it was difficult to understand how these people could work in the water in a frost of 40–45° below zero, Fahrenheit.

Slowly our truck moved down from the bank along the crackling ice. As we approached the middle of the river, this unpleasant crackling became ever louder. Finally, even our imperturbable guards could endure it no longer. They jumped off the truck and ordered the driver to stop while we got out.

We had barely time to stop when there was a deafening crash – the ice broke under the front wheels and the truck, resting on its frame, began to keel forward. The driver immediately reversed the engine, the wheels whirled backward and the truck slowly began to climb back, its sunken front wheels cutting a swath in the thin ice.

Urged on by the excited guards with levelled rifles, we all clutched at the truck, dragging it back, throwing our own bags and coats under the slipping wheels. Glancing back, I saw another truck which stopped behind us, nearer the shore. I ran to it, spoke briefly to the driver, took a steel-wire rope from him, tied one end of it to the bumper of his car and ran with the other end to ours. The driver's assistant followed me and helped me to tie it to the back of our truck. Then we called to the driver to back up. Picking up our bags, we stepped aside. The steel rope stretched taut, the cracking became louder.

Suddenly, glancing back, I noticed a crevasse forming over a rather large area in the snow and spreading rapidly. 'Get back!' I shouted wildly, rushing toward shore. The guards and the prisoners followed me, falling and foundering in the deep snow.

I had barely jumped across the fatal crevasse when the entire floe broke off and began to sink under the water, which rapidly flooded over the snow.

About five of the men, stranded on the huge floe, struggled toward the ice bank, the water already reaching to their waists. The driver's seat of our truck was already submerged, together with the driver who had not managed to jump out in time. Some of the men who had saved themselves ran toward shore, with the guards in the van. Several of us waited on the edge of the intact ice for the rest, who half-walked, half-swam across the breach.

Four of the men succeeded in reaching the shore and we pulled them up to safety. But one unfortunate soon sank and disappeared under the water. The truck was also gone.

Returning to the bank, we walked to the bridge-building site, where several large bonfires were blazing. Still excited over our recent escape, we heatedly discussed the incident. The building workers who were sitting around the fire cleared a space for us, and our four soaked comrades were advised to undress at once. Wrapped in borrowed coats and sheepskins they warmed themselves by the fire while their own clothes were drying. The guards sat down with us and tried to discover the names of the accident victims. The name of the drowned prisoner – a Trotskyite – was recalled, but no one knew the driver even the number of the truck escaped anyone's notice. The guards made out a report about the loss of the truck and two men, and began to hurry us on, anxious to get going again. The protests of the soaked men were of no avail. Some of the others tried to support them, but the guards walked away a few steps and levelled their rifles, declaring that we had five minutes to get ready, after which they would open fire.

This argument was irrefutable, and we were obliged to comply.

Stretching out single file and accompanied by the guards, we crossed to the left bank without further mishap, walking along the boards which had been laid over the ice by the bridge builders. We climbed the steep bank, and ten minutes later we were in the small settlement which housed the workers.

We were brought into one of the tents, where we hastened to build a brighter fire, recklessly destroying the supply of firewood piled on the floor. The guards departed somewhere to clear up the question of our further transportation, and our wet and violently shivering comrades had an opportunity to dry out and get warm.

Soon one of the guards returned with four large loaves of bread, which he managed to obtain for us from the camp commander, and told us that an hour and a half later a truck going in our direction would pick us up and take us as far as Yagodnoye, which was farther north.

The sole advantage of a prisoner's life consists in his never having to plan or worry about anything; that is what the authorities are for – it is their job to foresee every eventuality in life. When a Kolyma convict is asked what his own opinion is on any matter, he invariably replies: 'Why should I worry about it? Let the authorities do the thinking – they read the newspapers, they go to the baths, they talk over the telephone. Let them rack their own brains.'

Some two hours later, when it was already quite dark and the frost became sharper, the truck finally came, and soon the village disappeared behind us in the snowy distance. The only difference between the roads on the right and the left banks of the Kolyma was that the new road was even narrower, worse and more desolate, and that there were no mountains near by. We were driving along the valley of the river Debin, a tributary of the Kolyma which joined it near the place of our crossing.

It took us six hours to reach Yagodnoye, which is no more than some seventy miles from the left bank. Several times our truck foundered in snowdrifts and we had to climb out and pull it back, spurred on by the shouts of the guards. Once, when we were again moving along the narrow gorge of the left bank of the Debin, we skidded on a sharp turn of the slippery road and nearly plunged over the edge. As we pulled the truck back on to the road, labouring up to our waists in snow, I glanced down and momentarily imagined how it would have felt to be plunging into the ravine. The vision left me queasy and depressed.

A heavy snow began to fall once more, but soon we saw the lights of Yagodnoye. We drove along its single street, which was, however, wide and well-lit, and turned into the courtyard of the local camp, where we were quickly assigned to one of the tents. Everyone received a bowl of gruel and a mug of hot water with bread; after supper we were ordered to go to sleep. This time we slept like kings, for though there was no linen, our mattresses were clean and stuffed with fresh straw.

I woke early, dressed and went out into the yard. Overnight, the snow had piled up to a depth of at least seven or eight feet, and there were no traces of the road by which we came.

The sun rose and the snow glittered so dazzlingly that it hurt the eyes. Prostoserdov came out of his tent, and we walked down the trodden pathway into the street.

Yagodnoye is one of the best managed settlements in the taiga. It is the seat of the Road-Building Administration, which was headed at the time by Fomin and Zaporozhetz, members of that company of N.K.V.D.-men who had been expelled from Leningrad to Kolyma after Kirov's assassination. Yagodnoye owes its gay and pleasant appearance to the energy of these two men. Moreover, the forests surrounding the village have been preserved intact, although as a rule timber is destroyed mercilessly and recklessly in the vicinity of settlements.

We returned to the tent just in time. We were already being summoned by the hoarse shouts of our old friends, the guards, who ordered us to finish our breakfast and get ready to move on. A half-hour later we fell into formation outside the tent and everyone was given a pair of mittens and a wooden shovel. We were told to leave everything behind, except the bag of bread which had been brought from the bakery.

Leaving the camp, we walked to the northern boundary of the village. Where the path ended, we had to clear our own way north. We proceeded at a snail's pace, since only the first two men could work, while the rest stamped about aimlessly behind them with the useless shovels in their hands. I suggested that several men climb ahead over the unbroken snow and begin work farther on. The guards pounced on my idea and soon our contingent was spread over a good two miles; as the cleared sections were joined, those in the rear moved ahead.

The short northern day was already drawing to a close when we heard behind us the whirr of a motor and saw a snowplough which was rapidly catching up with us. It was a welcome relief, for we were thoroughly tired by that time. Stepping aside to make way for the machine, we dined on bread and salted fish, washing both down with snow.

It was somewhat galling, however, that all our work in clearing the seven or eight miles of unnecessary road, which left us barely able to drag our feet, had been for nothing. Our path was quite destroyed by the snowplough, which left instead a wide and rather firmly packed road.

After dinner, we resumed our trek. By sunset, according to my calculations, we had walked close to 12 miles since leaving Yagodnoye. We hoped to reach our destination that night along the cleared road, when we suddenly caught sight of the returning snowplough, which was widening the already cleared road. The driver told us that the road was cleared only for another mile and a half, and that, if the machine did not break down, he would resume work the next day.

Soon we came to the end of the road, and, under strict orders of the guards, again took up the shovels. As darkness gathered, our convoy became even more gloomy and their shouts even more vicious, but the work no longer went on as energetically as it had in the morning.

It became altogether dark. Stars shone in the clear sky and luminous, quivering threads stretched from horizon to zenith – reflections of the northern lights.

In this vague and strangely irritating light, we continued to poke the snow with utterly exhausted hands. My system had long been abandoned, for now blows of fist or even rifle butt could not force the men to climb into the deep snow.

Finally, a couple of my fellow travellers and I volunteered to climb ahead, for which we received immediate permission. Straining the remnant of our strength, we struggled forward to overtake the rest, helping each other, trying to walk in one another's footsteps and ignoring the fact that our felt boots were filled to the top with snow. When we were about two miles ahead of the column, we stopped, panting for breath. Then, according to our plan, one man began to clear a path forward and the rest climbed uphill to gather the sticks of brushwood which protruded above the snow – leftovers from recent woodcutting operations in the area. Fortunately, we soon discovered under the snow a whole stack of cut wood, and by the time the rest of the contingent reached us, in a cleared area at the side of the road, a huge bonfire was blazing.

Our psychological stratagem proved successful. Long realizing the senselessness of our work and forcing us to move forward for no reason but sheer obstinacy, the guards would never have permitted us to build a fire had we asked them. Now, however, faced by the accomplished fact, they relented and declared the end of the work-day.

It was almost midnight . . .

The men literally dropped upon the snow with fatigue. We shared the remnants of the bread we had received in Yagodnoye. Someone had a tin can in which we immediately set to boil the simple Kolyma tea – a brew of nothing but snow. The guards also ate – white bread, sausage, and cheese, washing it all down with vodka from hip-flasks.

We sat around the huge fire. The side of the body facing the fire was roasted, while the rest froze. But the men fell asleep sitting and lying around the fire, insensible to the discomfort.

By morning it was snowing again and became somewhat warmer. Several volunteers – and such are always found, odd people! – had kept the fire going all night. The guards also slept. Had we wished to, we could easily have disarmed and killed them and regarded ourselves free. But such a wild thought never occurred to anyone: the geographic situation of the Kolyma camp, the snows and the forests, and, in summer, the impassable swamps, were the best of guards. There were remarkably few cases in the history of Kolyma when some incorrigible adventurer decided to escape, hoping to cross, without any means of transportation, the desolate and trackless region which stretched for nearly two thousand miles between Kolyma and the rest of Russia.

When dawn began to break, the guards awoke and roused us. Furious at the unforeseen delay, they scattered the fire and forced us to resume our laborious trek.

Although our rest had been insufficient, we were feeling better in the morning, and the work was soon going full blast. By sunrise, two hours or so later, we had moved forward about two miles, despite the protests of our hungry stomachs. I do not know how far we would have got at that pace, but soon the situation was saved by the snowplough which had again caught up with us. Allowing it to overtake us, we followed it with quickened steps along the cleared road.

It was pitch dark when we finally saw the lights of some settlement in the distance. I do not know where we drew energy after the hungry and almost uninterrupted trek of two days, but this last mile we walked with quickened steps.

We entered the street of a small village, turned right somewhere, and, crossing between dark buildings to the next street, approached a long one-story house lit by an electric bulb over the entrance.

The guard knocked, but there was no answer. Then with a violent tug at the door he broke the latch and we entered. It was the building of the Allocation Office of the Northern Mining Administration. In the middle of the room, between the tables, a stove was burning brightly, and in the corner on a bench a watchman was fast asleep, his coat serving as pillow and mattress. The chief guard woke him rudely and ordered him to guard us until morning, after which the convoy departed.

Piling up our quite useless shovels in a corner, we quickly undressed, for the first time since the beginning of the trip. Every bone in my body ached, my stomach seemed contracted from hunger, and I felt near collapse from the fatigue of the preceding days. Even Prostoserdov was subdued. We arranged ourselves around the stove.

After brief negotiations with the watchman, I exchanged the shoes which I had carried with me since our departure from the left bank for a large chunk of bread and a package of makhorka. I roused Prostoserdov and we replenished our strength. Afterward, warmed and happy, we fell asleep till morning.

The watchman woke us a half-hour before the beginning of office hours. We rose, still aching all over after our journey, washed ourselves somehow, and set out to wait for further developments.

When the employees assembled and the chief arrived, our head guard handed him the list of our names and the bundles of our documents, awaiting further orders. The decision was soon made, but we were not told about it.

Four new guards conducted us across the village in a north-easterly direction.

The settlement, called Camp Khattynakh, was the centre of the largest mining district, the so-called Northern Mining Industry Administration. The nearest mine – the Vodopyanov – was only half a mile away, on the other side of the defile. Our way, however, was more distant. Crossing to the side of the mines, laboriously climbing the narrow footpaths across the torn-up earth, we passed the mine and followed the road cleared in the snow.

After more than an hour's walk, we came to another mine and soon learned its name as well, since its entrance was graced, according to camp custom, with a wooden arch bearing the legend: WELCOME TO LOWER KHATTYNAKH.

When we reached the top of the hill, we saw the camp itself – a small settlement of the usual tent type, with a mess hall and bakery in the centre. A small distance away was a group of log cabins, apparently the dwellings of free employees.

In the 'U.R.B.' (the camp's allocation office) tent we were delivered to the camp commander, who signed a receipt for us.

For about an hour we stood at the barrier while the commander studied our documents. He was apparently a man of doubtful literacy: he asked an elderly assistant in a sweater who sat next to him to read for him both the written papers and the typewritten ones.

Finally, calling out by name all the political prisoners, he led us to a small empty tent near by.

Soon there was a whistle, and the camp 'elder' (*Starosta*) conveyed us to the kitchen-mess hall, a large, filthy, steam-filled room where we received bread and a bad, typically camp-style dinner. We were ending our meal when the dining-room began to fill up with workers from the mines. Postponing acquaintance, I returned to our tent, accompanied by Prostoserdov and several Trotskyites.

We lay down on the beds and smoked makhorka cigarettes, discussing the situation. The general impression produced by local conditions was very depressing, even if it were not for its striking contrast with life in Magadan. The mine was small, the authorities stupid; there was dirt everywhere, the tents, ice-crusted even inside, were cold, and the food in the dining-room was vile. All this promised no good. This was real *katorga* – penal exile to hard labour.

We knew that in winter the working day in the mines was nine hours. This meant getting up and going to sleep in the dark, since the northern day was not much longer than four hours. As for work in the mines, we knew what it meant – digging in the pits with pick and shovel.

True, there was better work, too – preparing lumber and firewood,

cleaning the camp, clearing roads, and so forth. After careful consideration, we decided to demand assignment to such work and to refuse to
go into the pit. Soon we fell asleep and slept until our tent-mates, old-
time camp inmates, returned from work. They were all known as
Trotskyites, although they included one anarchist – the first I ever
saw – a couple of traitors to the homeland, and one Socialist-Revolu-
tionary.

What they told us about conditions of work in the pits merely confirmed our decisions – the mine was considered the worst in the
Northern Administration and was maintained on a punitive status.
The workers were always accompanied by several guards, who were
free to beat up at will those who in their opinion were lagging at work.

The mine director, Sedykh, was a habitual drunkard, never seen
sober. The camp commander was a fool, and fond of pushing in the
prisoners' teeth. In the kitchen there was endless thieving and the
prisoners' rations were plundered mercilessly. The prisoners were
cheated and tricked out of their wages by various means, so that they
seldom received more than 200–250 rubles, the rest being appropriated
by the administration which submitted falsified reports. In short, the
picture was clear and very unpromising.

On the following morning, when the whistle blew, we remained in
bed instead of going to roll call. Through a small window we saw the
entire camp population form into ranks and the commander delivering
a speech.

Suddenly our door flew open and the camp elder entered with his
assistant:

'Why are you not at roll call?' he asked in a raised voice.

'We want to know first where we are going to be sent to work,'
replied Bocharov, one of our men.

'Where? Where do you think you are? Are you playing the fool?
Isn't it clear what work you have to do here?'

'All right, my friend,' answered Bocharov, 'we won't waste time in
speaking to you. Let the commander come . . .'

'The commander will come, but look out, it will be worse for you.
Those who do not come out at once will have to answer for it.' He
threw out the threat as he left.

One group began to stir. One after another the 'genliners' got up,
dressed silently and went out. Only six or seven men remained.

Half-hour later our door opened again to admit the camp commander, attended by a numerous suite of camp 'foolers'. 'Foolers' is the
collective nickname of the entire camp staff, usually drawn from among
privileged prisoners. The nickname derives from the word 'fooling
around', as opposed to 'toiling'. A 'fooler' is the opposite of a 'toiler'.

And so our tent was filled with various officials, beginning with the camp commander and the elder, and ending with all the other idlers, seekers for a little excitement. It was obvious that concerted group refusal to work in the mine was a novelty in the camp.

When the commander entered we rose and stood before him. From his very small height, his arms akimbo, the commander gave us a devastating look which, however, did not frighten us.

'So these are the refusers?' he asked, without addressing anyone in particular. The elder jumped to his side:

'Yes sir, Citizen Commander, these Trotskyites refused to . . .'

'Why?' The commander turned with a menacing frown, to Prostoserdov, who stood at the end of the group.

'With your permission, Citizen Commander, we are all educated men, unaccustomed to hard physical labour, and we therefore request to be sent to some easier work.' The irony of Prostoserdov's reply escaped the commander, who said:

'We have no other work at present . . .'

'We can wait . . .' Prostoserdov gladly interrupted him. The latter again failed to perceive the irony.

'Here everybody must work. And every day. Education is no hindrance to work in the mine. Our mine is small, but we have eighteen professors here, not counting the engineers and doctors – all working in the pits. Only invalids are sent to the woods. Are you an invalid?' he asked Prostoserdov in a business-like manner.

'No, but if I go into the mine I'll surely become one. That is why I am asking for something else . . .'

'I see you are simply a loafer!' the commander exclaimed and turned to the next man.

'Why are you not at work?'

'I do not feel well . . .'

'Did you go to the infirmary? Where is your certificate?'

'They gave me no certificate . . .'

'Another loafer! And you?' he turned to me.

'Citizen Commander, I request to be assigned according to my speciality,' I replied, not a bit daunted by his angry tone.

'We have no other specialities here except that of miner. You are all loafers here. This is my final word to you: I give you five minutes to dress and go to work. Those who do not comply will go to the punitive cell on a hungry ration. I'll show you . . .' He concluded with an oath, striding out of the tent. The 'foolers' filed out after him.

Three of us – Bocharov, Prostoserdov and I – were the only ones really determined to persist in refusing to work in the mine. The rest dressed hastily and left. Bocharov, a tall man, middle-aged but still strong, a miner from the Don Basin and a party member since 1916, declared: 'They can crush me, they can do whatever they please, but I

will not work on this "katorga". I fought throughout the whole civil
war, I was captured by the Whites and put to every possible torture,
but I've never yet suffered such indignity. And I never was a Trotskyite. They foisted this on me only because I spoke a few heated words to
the Secretary of our Party Committee. They tortured me at the
investigation, though I have never committed any crime, and sent me
to concentration camp for five years. And now I am expected to work
for that scum! Never in my life!'

The door opened, letting in a tall guard wearing a sheepskin coat
and carrying a rifle.

'Well, how many of you are left here? Three? Come on, then, get
ready with your belongings. We'll go to the punishment cell!' he
ordered cheerfully.

'Don't you come on us, you bastard! We are not going anywhere!'
Bosharov shouted angrily.

'We like it here well enough,' I added.

The guard was obviously taken aback, but he did not lose his equa-
nimity and levelled his rifle at Prostoserdov.

'Get ready, quick, or I'll shoot!'

'Go on and shoot, —— —— —— !' Prostoserdov swore at him. 'They
won't pat you on the head for that either . . .'

Apparently the guard knew this as well as we did.

'So you will not come of your own will?'

'No!' we replied in chorus.

'All right!' he said threateningly, and fired two shots into the
ceiling. The tent filled with thin smoke.

Almost immediately the shots attracted eight other guards, led by a
squad commander, a little pockmarked man. Our guard jumped to
attention before his superior.

'Permit me to report, Comrade Commander, these Trotskyites
refuse to go to the punishment cell, and they are swearing, too . . .'

'Go on, take them all! Put down your rifles!' the squad commander
ordered.

The guards leaned their rifles against the wall and energetically
threw themselves upon us.

A few minutes later we were lying on the floor, tied hand and foot by
the soldiers' belts. Then each of us was carried out of the tent by two or
three guards, assisted by some 'foolers' attracted by the noise. We were
dragged somewhere to the side, toward the hill. This was the first time
in my adult life that I was carried, and, though it was done quite
carelessly, I must confess that it was not altogether unpleasant.

Soon we were brought before a small cabin. There we were
dropped on the snow and untied. Meantime, a guard unlocked the
door and the others dragged us inside one by one. As we were pushed
into a small side cell, each of us received a stiff blow on the back of the

neck in parting. However, Bocharov managed to give a solid punch in the jaw to the camp elder who happened to be within arm's reach.

The cell was extremely uninviting: a tiny barred window high in the wall, a continuous bench of unhewn planks along the wall, an iron stove. An electric bulb in the corridor outside shed some light into our cell through a hole cut in one of the walls. It was dirty and cold.

My comrades swore incessantly. Prostoserdov built a fire in the stove with some of the wood that was piled on the floor, but the temperature in the cell was scarcely affected. The punishment hut was poorly built and the walls failed to retain warmth. And outside there was a frost of at least 40 below, to judge by the thick cold mist which limited visibility to about twenty yards.

When we calmed down a little, we decided that the best thing in our situation was to declare a hunger strike. We knew that, under prevailing regulations, hunger strikers were removed from the jurisdiction of the camp and placed directly under that of the local N.K.V.D., and we felt that we had nothing to lose from such a change. Accordingly, when the punitive ration was brought in, a couple of hours later – prisoners in the punishment cell are allowed a half-pound of bread and a bowl of wretched soup daily – we refused to accept it and, obtaining a sheet of paper from the guard, wrote a declaration of hunger strike. The guard shrugged his shoulders, brought more wood, and left.

Hours went by, but we were not bored. My companions were interesting men, especially Bocharov who had seen much and was full of stories about party affairs, so that time passed quickly in conversation. Bocharov had been under disfavour for some time before his arrest and worked as an ordinary miner despite his long party experience. But until 1934, he was always engaged in leading party work in Donbas and in Moscow.

One day passed, then another. On the third morning visitors came to our tiny cell – seven or eight of them, headed by a short blond man in a fur coat whose walk was unsteady. Obviously, he was drunk. As we learned later, it was Sedykh himself, the director of the mine. He was followed by the camp commander and his assistant, our old acquaintance Brukhnov. A fat elderly woman about whom we had also heard before, Nina Petrovna, the local representative of the N.K.V.D., was also on hand. Then the little pockmarked commander of the guards showed up, along with some others.

Rocking slightly, Sedykh addressed us:

'So you are the men who refuse to work?'

'We don't refuse to work, we merely request to be assigned to other jobs, and not to the mine,' Bocharov answered for the group.

'Are you Trotskyites?'

'No, we are not Trotskyites . . .'

'Crooks? Why did you not say so before?' Sedykh turned to the camp commander, who hastened to explain:

'They are not Trotskyites, just general *contras* (counter-revolutionaries), equivalent to Trotskyites.'

'Oh, so that's it . . .' Sedykh drawled. 'Now I see. Well, my friends, for Trotskyites and others of their ilk the law prescribes only one kind of work – in the pits. So you had better cease your hunger strike and go to work. Remember what the great Stalin teaches us: In the U.S.S.R. work is a matter of honour and heroism.' He concluded with a resounding hiccup. Then the fat carcass of Nina Petrovna came forward, wafting a strong odour of vodka. Her beady little eyes rolled about in her pasty face as she declared:

'You will also remember that a hunger strike is in itself a counter-revolutionary act and that you may suffer grave consequences, including a lengthened term.'

At this Prostoserdov spoke up:

'Don't try to scare us, citizeness. We've been threatened before. I've seen more officials in my day than you have seen prisoners. You were told that we refuse to go into the mine, and if we croak of the hunger strike, you'll be answerable. See?'

Nina Petrovna's eyelids flapped somewhat helplessly. It was said that this woman had been a partisan and after the civil war had made quite a name for herself by her work for the G.P.U.-N.K.V.D. But she was ruined by her passion for the bottle. Only in the camp was she able to freely satisfy her cravings. Unaccustomed to being addressed in such a tone, she was taken slightly aback. She answered:

'Oh, so that's the kind you are? In that case there's no sense in talking to you. I'll send a report to Khattynakh, and let them decide what is to be done about you.'

The drunken Sedykh again attempted to persuade us to go to work, but without success, and they soon left.

Another day passed, and we entered the fourth day of our hunger strike. We were beginning to feel quite weak. The camp's male nurse came to examine us, and an hour later Brukhnov came and declared that, under orders from Sedykh, we would be assigned to cleaning the camp instead of the mine, and that we might therefore end our hunger strike. He added that we were granted three days for recuperation.

With lighter hearts we left the punishment cell, for we were not at all happy about the prospect of ending our days in that accursed hole.

In the camp we received special rations to restore our strength: a little butter, several cans of evaporated milk and a loaf of white bread. We returned to the Trotskyite tent. When our tentmates returned in the evening from their work, they showered us with questions; after they learned the results of our sojourn in the punishment cell, the hypocritical sympathy of the 'genliners' gave way to unconcealed envy.

On the following morning I went to the infirmary to see my old acquaintance, the male nurse, and to complain about the constantly increasing pains in my chest – the result of the tuberculosis. He turned out to be a once prominent professor of a Moscow clinic exiled to camp for telling anti-Soviet anecdotes. He decided that I needed an X-ray examination, for which I had to go to a larger mining settlement, the Vodopyanov, which we had passed on our way from Khattynakh to Lower Khattynakh. He gave me a pass, and the next morning I was walking along the snowy road on my way to Vodopyanov, accompanied by a guard.

When we arrived, the guard left me at the door of the hospital and vanished, apparently to look up some friends, instructing me to meet him at the same place at 5 p.m. It turned out that the X-ray laboratory had been closed for several days, as the radiologist was himself in the hospital, recovering from one of his periodic drinking bouts.

Having several hours at my disposal, I decided to take a walk across the valley to Khattynakh, the seat of the administration of the northern group of mines, and try my luck in obtaining a transfer from our mine to some other place.

Following the familiar path, nearly breaking my legs among the heaps of turned-up frozen earth, I made my way across the mining area and entered the settlement. My first thought was to find the local building organization.

Inquiring of passers-by, I soon came to a small tent, the entrance to which was graced by a double sign: DEPARTMENT OF CAPITAL CONSTRUC-TION – COMMANDATURA OF CAMP KHATTYNAKH. Inside, the tent was divided into two sections by a thin plywood partition. I entered the left half where, at four tables, I saw four men who were bending over some plans and other papers. Over one of the tables was a sign: CHIEF OF THE CAPITAL CONSTRUCTION DEPARTMENT. It was to him that I addressed myself, with due humility.

In a few words I told him my story. It immediately transpired that we had mutual acquaintances in Magadan. The chief, Sukhanov, was still a very young man. He listened to me with great sympathy, asked what I could do, and finally said goodbye, promising to effect my transfer from Lower Khattynakh.

At the appointed time I was back at the Vodopyanov Hospital, but I had to wait for a long time before my escort finally appeared. On the return trip I was obliged to support him and carry his rifle, for he had so thoroughly filled himself with liquor that he was barely able to walk.

The other two days of our recuperation period passed without further incident, and on the third day, when the whistle called the camp's population to work, we all dressed and went out to morning roll call.

We stood somewhat apart from the others, waiting to be assigned to one of the brigades. Catching sight of us, the camp commandant, Brukhnov, who was in charge of roll call, said something to one of his retinue who approached us with orders to join the brigade standing in the formation nearest to us.

We immediately made inquiries of some members of the brigade and, finding they were miners, again stepped aside. Brukhnov flew at us, shouting:

'Why did you leave the brigade you were assigned to?'

'Because you yourself told us that Sedykh ordered our assignment to camp chores,' Bocharov answered reasonably.

'I am master here!' little Brukhnov roared and blustered. 'I make assignments wherever I please. If I wanted to lend you to the kitchen duty yesterday, I would have done so, and if I want to send you into the pits today, you'll go into the pits!'

'Don't try such jokes with us, now,' Prostoserdov suddenly raised his voice. 'You can fool around with the others, but we've said once that we are not going to work in the pits, and that's how it stands. It will be our way, not yours. Understand?'

'Oh, so that's how you talk!' Brukhnov hissed through his teeth. 'Then I'll show you a thing or two. Hey, guards, come here!' he shouted. Several guards came running.

'Take these counter-revolutionaries to the *kartser* (punishment cell), on hunger rations,' he ordered. 'They are to be kept under the strictest regime! I'll rot them in the punishment cell, I'll teach them how the Soviet government fights saboteurs.'

Again we were dragged off to the punishment cell. Although this incident might have jeopardized my future transfer to Khattynakh and it would have been more prudent to go into the wretched pits until the order came through, I nevertheless joined Bocharov and Prostoserdov, both because of a feeling of solidarity and because my pride, not yet completely destroyed by the two years in prison and camp, rebelled against the arbitrary tactics of that hooligan Brukhnov.

Ten minutes later we were in our old cell. My companions energetically swore at Brukhnov, at the camp system, and at the 'Iron People's Commissar', as the current chief of the N.K.V.D., Yagoda, was officially called. Neither did they spare Stalin himself – the inspirer and founder of the penal method of governing Russia.

Needless to say we resumed the hunger strike interrupted three days earlier, telling the guard who brought our dinner to go to hell.

This time, infuriated at our disobedience, Brukhnov apparently decided not to confine himself to keeping us in the cold and dirty punishment cell, but devised a new method of annoying us.

On the following day the door of our cell was flung open and the pockmarked chief of the guards entered quite drunk and carrying a revolver, and followed by three other guards.

'Hey there, get up! We are going to search you now,' he declared.

Properly speaking, there was nothing for which to search or find, but as a matter of principle we decided not to allow those scoundrels to rifle our pockets.

'Go to the devil, all of you!' cried Prostoserdov. 'We are hunger striking, and you have no right to enter at all!'

'We'll soon show you our rights!' squealed one of the soldiers. 'Grab them, men, and search them!'

The guards advanced with outstretched arms. I seized a log of wood lying near the stove. With one blow I turned over the burning stove, with another I shattered the window. The glass splintered and the cell became filled with suffocating smoke. Apparently somewhat cowed, the pockmarked chief opened fire – true, not at us, but at the broken window. The other guards stopped hesitantly, and we jumped up on the sleeping bench, preparing to resist all onslaughts.

Emptying seven cartridges, the chief of the guards seemed to have found new inspiration, and, with the cry, 'Forward, boys, get them!' he threw himself into attack.

I dropped almost at once, felled by a blow on the head. When I came to I saw that we were once more alone; Bocharov and Prostoserdov were groaning and rubbing their welts and bruises, and the fierce Kolyma frost filled our cell through the broken window.

It had been simple to knock out the window in the heat of battle. But now, when the excitement had subsided, the frost was no joking matter. It is true that the stove was back in its place, set up by the guards, and there was even enough firewood, but we came to the conclusion that in addition to the voluntarily assumed pangs of hunger, we must also endure torture by frost. Therefore, wrapping ourselves closely into our quilted coats and gathering up our feet, we sat down on the bench and began to wait for further developments.

Soon the guard on duty looked in through the peephole in the door and saw that the fire was out. He came in and lit it again. As soon as he left, I picked up a jug with half-frozen water, broke the crust of ice and poured the water into the stove. The guard who watched the proceeding, entered again and relit the stove once more. Since there was no more water, I pulled out the burning logs with my hands and threw them out of the broken window, where they sank into the snow.

This somewhat baffled the guard. Some time later we saw that the broken window was being boarded up from the outside with a piece of plywood that was nailed securely to the frame. After this, the patient guard, still silent, again lit the stove and began to watch us. I talked it over with my companions, then pulled up the iron chimney, stuffed my mitten into it, and replaced it on the stove. The cell immediately filled with smoke and the fire went out for lack of a draught.

The nonplussed guard ran out and fired three shots to call the patrol leader. A few minutes later we heard the following conversation:

'Comrade Commander, these Trotskyites want to freeze to death . . .' And he told the whole story.

'To the devil with them, pay no attention!' his superior answered.

'I am afraid we'll be called to account for it, Comrade Commander. They must be people with connections, or they would not have so much nerve. A Trotskyite – he is always quiet, but these are like madmen. You know, today a man is a Trotskyite, tomorrow he may be a director of a trust . . .'

The rest was inaudible.

The stove did not burn any more, the cooled smoke made our eyes smart, we felt depressed, hungry and miserable. Towards night it became colder. We could not fall asleep. Sitting in the corner, I heard Prostoserdov's teeth chatter.

Throughout the following morning the guard did not move away from the peephole in the door, watching us constantly. Then he entered the cell. It was yesterday's guard – he had again returned to sentry duty. Sitting down on the edge of the bench, he began to speak to us in a conciliatory, persuasive tone:

'Say, fellows, why raise all this fuss? You are knocking yourself out for nothing – they have the power and you won't get anywhere. There is nothing but scum all around nowadays, all these N.K.V.D. men, one scoundrel worse than the next. Give up your hunger strike and go into the pits. Do you know how to stall? Just pretend you are working, but take it easy, save your strength. And so, easily, quietly, your term will be up before you know it. Why torture yourself . . .'

Prostoserdov answered him:

'You don't understand, my friend. They are all scoundrels, and if they want to, they'll drive anyone to the grave. But that is not the point. The trouble is not with the camp authorities, but with the whole Soviet system which destroys innocent people . . .' And Prostoserdov proceeded to make his usual speech. The guard began to glance over his shoulder at the door more and more often, and finally rose and left without a word, closing the door behind him.

In the evening my old friend, the male nurse, came to our cell, accompanied by Nina Petrovna. We sat motionless, numb and stiff with the cold. Nina Petrovna asked something, but Bocharov only swore. After a short discussion, carried on in whispers, they left.

Fifteen minutes later, our friendly guard re-entered the cell, and, with a happy face, announced that we were free to return to our tent and that our punishment was unconditionally revoked. He inquired whether we were able to walk by ourselves, and, reassured, he let us out.

We returned to our tent in such a condition that the others stared at us as if we were ghosts – bearded, incredibly filthy, black with soot, emaciated, we could easily have frightened any nervous man.

Without answering their questions, we stretched out on the beds and finally after warming up a bit, fell asleep.

In the morning we were brought reinforced rations – the same dairy diet – and were told by the camp *starosta*, who spoke with eyes carefully averted to avoid looking at us, that we could go to the baths if we wished to. This was most attractive to us. In the bath-house we learned that it had been heated almost especially for us. Shaven, clean, and feeling much better we returned, wondering at the miraculous happenings.

Finally, the riddle was solved. I was called to the U.R.B. and told that an order had come from the administration with strict instructions to lend me immediately to the 'centre', and that Brukhnov had already written in reply that I was slightly ill and would be brought there in two days.

Apparently past experience had led the local authorities to fear that, once in the administration, I might cause them unpleasantness, which was quite possible, since at that time there were many prisoners in responsible posts. Besides, unaware of my illegal visit to Khattynakh and knowing that I had come directly from the capital, Magadan, they could easily have supposed that I had powerful protectors.

As a result, during my last days at the mine, the administration treated us with the utmost consideration and attention possible under camp conditions. My friends received personal assurances from Sedykh himself that he would find them 'warm spots'. Nina Petrovna urged me in the friendliest manner to forget bygones, and assured me that the guard commander who had searched us in the punishment cell had already been severely reprimanded for this indiscretion.

Sincerely, though with a gratifying sense of my own superiority, I promised her to do nothing against the local officials. And indeed, even had I found the opportunity to revenge myself on my oppressors, I would not have done so, knowing that this would merely create for me new enemies, which is always a dangerous situation for a prisoner.

In conclusion, we were given complete new outfits, and a couple of days later, warmly dressed and wearing new felt boots, I entered Khattynakh, where I was to spend the next period of my imprisonment.

6. IN CAMP KHATTYNAKH

ON arrival, I was sent to the local 'lager' (camp), the usual group of heated tents situated somewhat apart from the free settlement.

I was pleased that the lager seemed to be almost a part of the settlement, without a sign of fences or guards. It housed prisoners, employees of the administration and the commandatura of the village, and workers who supplied Khattynakh with wood and water. In accordance with Kolyma custom, the latter was brought in its dry form in bags. Several dozen men with long picks were always working on the ice of the small river which divided Khattynakh from Vodopyanov. These were the local version of an artesian well.

On the morning following my arrival, I reported at the Building Section, where I was greeted warmly by the prisoner employees, benevolently by the free employees, and somewhat officially by the department head, Sukhanov. I received an immediate appointment to the brigade of carpenters engaged in the construction of a wooden building for the printing shop of the local newspaper.

I was a brigadier. The work was simple, and the workers amiable. The foreman, Kruglikov, was a very decent man despite his past as a bandit, or perhaps because of it.

We worked only eight hours a day, without overstraining ourselves; no one drove us, and we smoked and rested to our hearts' content. Nevertheless, the work proceeded efficiently, and our earnings for the first month exceeded five hundred rubles.

The tent which housed only the workers and employees of the Building Section was warm, even clean according to camp standards. The traditional card games were not too much in evidence. Moreover, there was almost no thieving, which was also a sign of the respectability of the population.

On especially cold days in January and February, workers were issued allotments of alcohol at lunchtime. These were given out in the department warehouse and consisted of 2–4 ounces per man, depending on conduct and efficiency at work. Generally, alcohol was highly prized and was referred to by everyone, including the free employees, as liquid gold. It is true that the latter received a monthly allowance of half a quart of the precious liquid, but what was half a quart to thirsty Kolymans? The alcohol for the prisoners was issued separately, by the administration warehouses, and in fairly large quantities. This was why the warehouse-keepers of departments employing workers, such as the Building Section, the Commandatura, and the Geological Prospecting Section, were always surrounded by the most obsequious attentions of the free staffs of the administration, and our warehouse-keeper, the prisoner Vasya Khudiakov, was justly regarded as the most influential person in Camp Khattynakh. Even the commander of the local camp fawned upon him, especially when he was drunk, cadging a sip of the fiery liquid. In order to make ends meet in his reports, Vasya was obliged to dilute the alcohol issued to the prisoners with clear cold water, which provoked just complaints on the part of the labouring masses.

This Vasya Khudiakov was quite a character. Condemned to five years of penal labour for some complicated machinations and combinations in the warehouse of a Moscow factory, in camp Vasya developed his natural talents to their full scope. As a warehouse-keeper he was irreplaceable. Should the truck tyres be worn to shreds and no replacements available in the warehouse, Sukhanov need only call Vasya and tell him: 'Vasya! Get some!' And before there was time to look, the truck had new tyres. Or there might be a shortage of lumber for building. Sukhanov would call Vasya: 'We need three truck-loads of lumber, and quick!' And in the evening Vasya would get ready, take along a couple of quarts of alcohol, and drive out in the light sleigh to the highway along which lumber was transported for the mines. He would stop one truck, then another, whisper a bit with the driver, slip him the coveted bottle, and lo! – in the morning there was enough lumber for construction.

Vasya did not live in the camp, but like a free employee, in a little room attached to our carpentry shop, together with the manager of this shop, Stepanov, also a prisoner, sentenced to five years of penal labour for counter-revolution, which in his case meant belonging to the Dukhobor religious sect. Vasya lived there unofficially, thanks to his influence over the camp authorities who depended on his good will in the alcohol situation. But Stepanov, who was an expert worker, was allowed to live as a free employee because our shop made special cases for gold. The boards for these cases, made of dried ash, were brought especially for this purpose from 'the continent'. The cases were of a strictly specified size and had to be of perfect construction. The smallest cracks or knots were ruled out. These cases were built throughout the year for all the Kolyma mines. In the summer when washing began, they were collected from us by representatives of the N.K.V.D. field service and taken to the central gold-receiving office. There each box was filled with a double leather bag containing 20 kilograms of gold dust, the lid screwed down, and the precious load was sent to the airport whence the gold was flown directly to Moscow, to the special N.K.V.D. plant named after Yagoda.

The quantity of the gold mined was considered a top secret, but Vasya Khudiakov once admitted to me, in a tipsy state, that approximately 4,000 cases had been delivered to the N.K.V.D. in 1936. Later this figure was confirmed by other sources.

Camp Khattynakh was at that time a small settlement. It had not more than eight hundred inhabitants, about two hundred of these being free workers. In the summer its population shrank, since half of its workers were sent to the mines for the entire washing season.

When I came to Khattynakh, the chief of the administration was Berkovitch, a prisoner. But soon he was replaced by a free employee, the Communist, Kaulin, a Lett and a comrade of Berzin's in the civil war. For a long time the chief engineer of the administration was Mark Eidlin, a clever man and an expert in his field, who had been sent to the camp for wrecking. The chief geologist, Voznesensky, had just completed his term, as had the head of the supply department, Lubinov. The head book-keeper was also a prisoner, and even the chief of the Planning Section, who handled all the secret and top secret figures concerning gold and the number of prisoners, was also a recently freed specialist who had served a term for counter-revolution.

Needless to say, all these officials, regardless of their past and present position, lived outside the camp, in private apartments assigned to them by Dalstroy.

We also had a Communist cell, headed by a most charming man, Vasily Katz, but neither at that time nor afterward did I understand what the role of the party was in Kolyma.

A similar situation existed at the administration mines as well: everywhere there was a preponderance of prisoners in official posts. At the Vodopyanov mine the chief engineer was Lapin, who had once owned mines himself on the Lena River. The directors of the Berzin and Shturmovoy mines were former heads of the Leningrad N.K.V.D., condemned in connection with the Kirov assassination, Yanishevsky and Gubin; my friend Sedykh, the chief of Lower Khattynakh, and even Brukhnov, the camp commandant at Lower Khattynakh, were all, as I discovered, former prisoners who had recently completed their terms and who had voluntarily chosen to remain in Kolyma.

If this was true of the top administrative levels, it may readily be imagined that approximately three-quarters of the middle and lower levels were also made up of prisoners. Despite this, however, the work was no less efficient than it would have been under a free administration. The whole piquancy of the situation in the Soviet camps resides precisely in the fact that the prisoners in them are not criminals but people in every way as good, and often far better, than the free employees.

It is a well-known fact that the population of the U.S.S.R. is divided into three categories, which are today almost equal in numbers: prisoners, ex-prisoners, and future prisoners.

It is difficult to find in the Soviet Union a company of three adult men, at least one of whom has not at some time been subject to represssions, either through investigation or trial, or imprisonment in a camp.

Although my life in Camp Khattynakh was not as pleasant as it had been in Magadan, it was nevertheless rather fair, and I soon became accustomed to it. I worked conscientiously, and the results soon became apparent. At first I was appointed foreman, and later Sukhanov transferred me to a job in the Building Section office.

Summer came, and our building activities declined somewhat, though not as sharply as in former years. Nevertheless, several brigades of workers were sent off to the mines to work at mining, washing, and building gold-washing apparatus.

But in the office there was as much work as ever: we were preparing projects for winter construction work.

Since our section was also in charge of the building units of the mines, its employees occasionally had to visit the various mines to observe building work, give instructions, determine local requirements for materials, and so forth. Such trips were extremely pleasant affairs, as we were always welcomed as visiting authorities from the centre, especially since we were empowered to halt the financing of all illegal, or unplanned works. And since there was more infraction of the law in Kolyma than there was compliance with it, we always had an effective means of influencing the local mine officials up to and including the threat of prosecution and trial. However, such extreme measures were seldom resorted to.

Under Soviet procedure even such petty construction activities as ours had to be approved in Moscow, by the Ministry, and the latter, lacking any knowledge of the actual local needs, often included in the plan completely unnecessary units and omitted the essential ones. As a result, a mine might be in need of a bakery, but would be required by plan to build a bath-house. Or it might need a bath-house, but the plan would provide money for building breeding kennels for blood-hounds; or else money would be allotted for the construction of a communal dwelling, while the mine director wanted to build a new house for himself, with but a single apartment. Then a series of complicated combinations would begin. In its reports, the mine would show the building of a dining-hall for prisoners, when in fact a dormitory for the guards had been erected. Naturally, the bank knew nothing and issued the money for a dining-hall. The bank was not concerned with whether the kennels were needed by the mine: if kennels were ordered, they had to be built! But under Kolyma conditions, when all local power was in the hands of Dalstroy, and the bank's sole representative was the ever-hungry inspectress Sveshnikova, the bank's actual powers of control were reduced to zero.

However, within the mining administration, the construction activi-

ties were also controlled by the Building Section, which in effect said
to the mine: 'You may break the law, but only with our permission.'
And the mine director knew that if our section should report his
illegal building work to the bank, the money would be stopped at once,
and, if things took a bad turn, he might even end up on the defendant's
bench. If, luckily, his mine fulfilled the gold production norm, he could
reasonably expect leniency and, in the worst case, even appeal to Berzin
who always regularly visited the mines and personally appointed their
directors. But if, in addition to everything else, the mine produced less
gold than was required of it, then no power on earth could save the
mine administration from serious difficulties.

Once, ordered by Sukhanov to inspect the construction work in
Lower Khattynakh, I mounted a horse and followed the familiar road
to the mine. A half-hour later I was already at the house of the mine
director, my old acquaintance, Sedykh. When I came in sight I set the
horse off at a gallop, and, dashingly reining in at the entrance, I
carelessly threw the reins to the orderly who ran out to meet me,
jumped off the horse, and entered.

I was expected. The mine director was in his office with the camp
commandant Brukhnov, who rose as I came in and hesitantly offered
me his hand. I pressed it warmly, wishing to show that I harboured no
ill-will toward him for our past encounters. And indeed, could I have
done anything else? Being outside the power of Sedykh and Brukhnov
at the moment, could I be certain that capricious fate would not again
bring me to this mine? Besides, my friends were still there, and I knew
very well that any unpleasantness between me and the mine officials
would automatically be avenged on them.

All these considerations did not prevent me from experiencing a
certain moral satisfaction at all the attentions with which Sedykh
welcomed me. Giving me no time to mention the reasons for my visit,
he hurried me off to the next room where the table had already been
set for dinner, and the dinner was an excellent one, with all the required
trimmings, including the sparkling decanter of vodka.

There gathered around the table the familiar company of local
officials, with the exception of the commander of the guards, that little
pockmarked lieutenant who fired his gun in the punishment cell during
the search. I duly appreciated this display of tact on the part of Sedykh.

Generally, on closer acquaintance, they proved pretty decent men
or, at any rate, not vicious ones. But one thing was characteristic of
them all: they did not regard the prisoners who were in their charge
and dependent on them as quite human, although some of them had
been in the very same shoes in the past. Their attitude toward persons
who had lost their freedom was very similar to that of the whites
toward the Negroes in the United States during the period described
in *Uncle Tom's Cabin*.

This attitude had entered into the very blood of these men, for almost unlimited power over living beings, deprived of nearly every right, inevitably awakens the specific instincts of arbitrary tyranny, absolute intolerance of any opposition from these 'lower creatures', and complete irresponsibility in dealing with them. True, the illiterate fool Brukhnov was proud of having at his command and working as common miners eighteen professors. But his pride grew out of his awareness that all these people, better and more intelligent and more honest than he – the flower of the nation – were in his hands, while he, a fool who could not write his own name, could exercise his power over them at will, in any form and with total impunity.

After dinner, which ended in the traditional drinking spree, Sedykh, barely able to manage his tongue, suggested that I rest in one of the rooms set aside for guests. Seeing that it would be quite futile to speak about business, and though I had drunk very little, I accepted his suggestion, for the revel had become altogether too wild.

In the morning I waited almost until noon for Sedykh to get up – he rose at dawn for roll call, then went to sleep again. Finally, he received me and introduced me to the local book-keeper whom he had summoned and with whom in fact I had to deal. In the course of a couple of hours I obtained all the necessary information, then inspected the buildings under construction, took down the required notes, and bade goodbye to Sedykh who made no effort to detain me. In the evening I was back at Camp Khattynakh. I had not drawn up any reports while I was at the mine, although I had found several clear violations of the laws.

Sedykh was lucky. Several 'nests' – rich gold-bearing veins – had been found in his field, and Lower Khattynakh was ahead of the other mines in fulfilling the plan for gold production. Thanks to this, all transgressions against the law for which any administrator in the U.S.S.R. would inevitably have been sentenced to a five-year term in concentration camp were in this case overlooked.

My next expedition was to the Berzin mine, in the valley of the river At-Uryach. This mine was administered by a most charming and clever man – also a prisoner – Yanishevsky, who had been the head of the Foreign Section of the Leningrad N.K.V.D. He met me very cordially, like a decent human being. He lived with his wife, who had been permitted to join him six months after his arrival at Dalstroy. Although I had completed my inspection on the first day, I accepted Yanishevsky's invitation to spend two more days with him. Since there was nothing especially important to call me back to Khattynakh, I was delighted to remain.

Yanishevsky was an extremely interesting man. In Leningrad he had been in charge of problems of espionage, counter-intelligence, and the

Russian white *émigrés* in Finland and the Baltic countries. He spoke
several languages fluently and represented the best type of Soviet
administrator in such a dubious institution as the N.K.V.D.

He appreciated the fact that I refrained from asking him any
questions or making embarrassing inquiries into his past activities, but
one evening after supper he lifted for me somewhat the curtain shroud-
ing N.K.V.D. activities and told me a few things which I had never
remotely suspected.

He told me about the tremendous role of provocation as a method
in N.K.V.D. practice. It was the duty of secret agents to constantly
engage people in provocative conversations, criticizing Soviet policies to
win their confidence and to draw them into expressions of discontent
with Soviet life and the Communist party. Those who were unable
to hold their tongues found themselves in prison on the very next day.

He also told me that the prison regime in camps and especially in
prisons where people were kept during the investigation period had
been made in recent years the object of scientific study by a group
of eminent psychiatrists who observed the effects of the various regimes
on the mental condition of the prisoners. Their reports were studied
by a collegium of the N.K.V.D. which subsequently issued instructions
to prison wardens and camp directors concerning changes in the treatment of prisoners calculated to dull their minds as rapidly as possible.

I learned from him that the local N.K.V.D. offices had general
instructions from 'the very top' to pay especial attention to 'weeding
out' the old intelligentsia – scientists, engineers, doctors, teachers –
using every available pretext to this end whenever preliminary inquiries
revealed that a given individual in this category was not vitally essential
to the enterprise where he was employed. As a rule, these people were
doomed to hard physical labour in the camps, aimed, in the final
analysis, at 'gelding' them. Mortality in the camps was highest among
the intellectuals. It often happened, too, that a local N.K.V.D. office
received orders from the centre to arrest certain designated persons
who were required for work on one of the construction projects of
'Stalin's Five-Year Plan'. These fortunate people had no need to fear
physical labour – they would be employed in their speciality wherever
they were sent, but they had to submit without a murmur to living
without the barest comforts and working either entirely or almost
without remuneration. The nature of their crimes was in such cases of no
consequence: they were tried in absentia in Moscow and all they were
told was the article of the Criminal Code under which they were
sentenced and the term of their imprisonment.

Another thing he told me – this, incidentally, I had known before –
was that Dalstroy's Kolyma camp was unquestionably the best in the
U.S.S.R., both in its regime, with the lowest mortality rates, and in the
cultural level of its adminstration. That was due to the fact that Stalin

attributed great importance to Dalstroy's efforts to increase the gold output.

During this visit to the Berzin mine I also met, quite by accident, my old friend, Mikhail B., whose acquaintance I had first made on the night after my trial in the cellar of the Leningrad Transfer prison, and whose affair I had so laboriously and so vainly tried to disentangle.

Although he was very thin and dressed in a greasy, dirty chauffeur's uniform, I recognized him at the first glance. He still retained his usual phlegmatic manner. We greeted one another warmly, but, as was his custom, with restraint.

Mikhail immediately told me a happy bit of news: the petition which I had written for him in Leningrad was crowned with unexpected success – the Military Collegium of the Supreme Court of the U.S.S.R. reviewed the case and changed his sentence. Without a new investigation the paragraph of the Criminal Code under which he was sentenced was changed and his term reduced: instead of the dreaded 58–1A (treason to the fatherland) and a ten-year sentence, he had now a mere five-year term for revealing military information. The unpleasant aspect of the situation was that Mikhail's wife and daughter had been exiled from Leningrad to somewhere in the province soon after his departure to the Kolyma, and that almost all his property was lost.

'Well, are you still for the Soviet regime?' I asked him.

'More than ever,' he answered firmly.

'And you are pleased with your fate?'

'No, but I believe that soon I shall be freed altogether,' he said significantly.

A day later I left the mine. But I recalled this conversation much later, at the end of the year when I was suddenly called to see Bazhenov, the N.K.V.D. representative for the Northern Administration. As I sat in his anteroom waiting to be called, the door of his office was suddenly flung open and I saw emerging from it, emaciated and bearded, my Leningrad friend, Kirill Dabizha, who had arrived in Kolyma with me. Two guards came out of the other door, and, allowing him to step forward, followed him out into the street.

From the office Bazhenov's voice called out my name, I rose from the chair and entered. I knew already what I was wanted for.

'Sit down.'

Bazhenov immediately launched into the matter at hand:

'What do you know about the preparations for a mutiny on the ship *Djurma* in the summer of 1936?'

'Are you referring to the trip on which I came to the Kolyma?' I asked, trying to gain time and think over the situation.

'Exactly. What do you know about the affair?'

'Apparently you know all about it?' I asked again.

'Yes, I do, but perhaps not all. Go on, tell me about it!'

'I can tell you very little. You probably know that I was sick with scurvy during the trip and could barely move . . .'

'Yes, I know. Go on!'

'When we were approaching the shores of Japan, there was a rumour in the hold that a group of prisoners was planning to seize the ship. I recall that I paid no attention to this talk, considering such an idea senseless and, perhaps, merely the figment of somebody's imagination. I turned out to be right. There were no incidents whatever on the ship during the trip.'

'And who spoke to you about the preparations for the seizure?'

'I don't remember any more. You know, it was a year and a half ago. But I think I can name one man . . . It was Mikhail B.'

'From the Berzin mine?'

'Yes.'

'That I know. Who else?'

'I cannot recall anyone else.'

'Who was planning the mutiny?'

'I do not know. I spoke to no one, and the people around me distrusted me, knowing my firm sympathies for the Soviet government.'

'I will help you. Do you know the names of Zimatsky, Karoman, Dabizha, Prostoserdov?'

'I remember the names, but I cannot tell you anything concerning their connection with this fantastic story.'

'Very well. We shall leave it at this for the time being. I really ought to arrest you and investigate your record thoroughly. But I shall leave you temporarily in the camp and shall call you again when necessary.'

We said goodbye.

I left Bazhenov with a feeling of thorough disgust, reviling Mikhail for his accursed devotion to the Soviet government which prompted him, after a year and a half, to revive this absurd story and destroy people. At the same time I did not understand why I was allowed to go free. This puzzle was answered when I returned to the office. Sukhanov immediately called me inside and asked in a lowered voice:

'You saw Bazhenov?'

'Yes. You know?'

'I do. He called me in this morning and asked whether I could spare you in the event you were arrested. I said "no" . . .'

'Thanks.' I pressed his hand warmly.

However, the affair was never brought to any conclusion. Some time later I learned that Prostoserdov had been arrested. He again declared a hunger strike, and after a month in the solitary cell for prisoners under investigation – toward the end he was administered artificial feeding – he was sent to the punitive section of the Shturmovoy mine. About the others I know nothing. Only once, I met the girl who worked for Bazhenov at the club, and, though I asked her nothing, she approached me and told me that all the documents relating to the affair of the *Djurma* mutiny had been sent for final decision to Magadan, to the central N.K.V.D., and that as yet there was no answer.

The events described above took place at the end of 1937. By that time my position in the department was already sufficiently secure. Sukhanov had become accustomed to me, I managed my work quite easily, and my relations with everyone I came into contact with in the course of my work could not have been better. I was already well known to the entire small population of Camp Khattynakh and the administration of the northern mines. I was a frequent guest at the homes of free employees, and, with Bazhenov's permission, I lived in the small room off the carpentry shop together with Stepanov and Vasya Khudiakov.

I was on especially friendly terms with the local geologists and topographers. In contrast to the rest of the free employees who came for various accidental reasons, the geologists and topographers came to Dalstroy because the very nature of their work involved residence in distant regions.

I respected and liked these people all the more because as a rule they were free of prejudice against prisoners, fully realizing that there were few real criminals in the camp, most inmates being merely unfortunate victims of bad luck, and that the path upon which they had found themselves was open to every citizen of the U.S.S.R.

I began to frequent a certain small circle of young geologists, and though several of them were members of the Young Communist League, this did not interfere with our friendly relations. With one of the young women, Irina K., who had only graduated from the Leningrad Mining Institute that spring, my relations soon passed the boundaries of mere friendship. Remembering the incident which led to my expulsion from Magadan, I was very careful. I knew very well that friendly relations between prisoners and free employees were generally frowned upon, and that any degree of intimacy was severely punished under the strict camp regulations. That being the case, my danger was as great as Irina's, but I had to think of her above all, since for me a scandal might mean only a lengthened term or possibly assignment to work in the pits, while for her it would lead to a minimum punishment of three years in prison. Therefore, we almost never met outside the general group, and the few meetings alone were surrounded by endless precautions and usually took place either somewhere at the mine, as if by accident, or at some distant geological prospecting sector where she came ostensibly in connection with her work.

This complicated affair was very short-lived. Once Irina telephoned me to say that she had to see me at once. We agreed to meet on the same evening at the house of a friend across the river. I came as soon as it was dark, and found Irina already there, waiting for me. My friend absented himself, and she immediately said to me:

'Today I was told at the office that I am being transferred to the newly organized Western Administration. What shall I do? It is almost impossible to refuse the transfer.'

'If it is impossible to refuse, you will have to go . . .'

'But I do not want to leave you! Help me to think of some plan. You know everyone here. It is easier for you.'

'Would they consider any personal circumstances? What arguments can you give?'

'No, they will not. The order for my transfer is signed by Berzin himself, with the consent of my local superiors, and I cannot think of any convincing arguments. I see only one way . . .'

'And what is that?' I asked, guessing what she had in mind.

'To declare outright that I do not wish to go because you are here.'

I took her hands in mine and thought about it, trying to foresee every possible result of such a declaration. First – Irina's expulsion from the Komsomol. Second – difficulties because of the violation of her contract, in which she pledged herself to absolute obedience to all orders of Dalstroy. Third – the only path that could be pursued after an open declaration of our relationship was to endeavour to gain recognition of it by the authorities in the form of a permission to marry. Supposing that we were to succeed in this, since I had enough influential contacts to be reasonably hopeful of obtaining such a permission – what then? At the moment I occupied a certain position in the administrative office, commanded a degree of respect. But I had no assurance that my situation would not change over night, that I would not be sent into the mines, to heavy labour, where Irina would not be able to follow me. What would be her position in such a case? And what could it lead to?

At this point in my reflections, I mentally drew a line. Looking into her expectant eyes, raised to mine in the hope of advice and help in a question that was to decide our common future, I said:

'No, Irina, nothing can be done. It is even impossible to foresee all the results of the step you are proposing. Tomorrow I shall try to see whether anything can be done without declaring our relationship. If my effort to detain you here proves fruitless, you will have to go . . .'

The young woman who had tried to control herself now broke down into bitter tears. Sobbing, she spoke:

'I knew that you would say this . . . I thought so myself . . . But what are we to do? I do not want to, I cannot go . . .'

'Fate must be against it, Irina. We met by accident, at the world's end. Our relations were never serene and cloudless, and now we must part. Try, if you can, to forget our friendship. Our future is too dark and uncertain to bind ourselves with promises, especially you . . .'

'No, I will wait until you are freed . . . I do not know, I never told you . . . Perhaps you would already be free if . . .'

'If what? What is it?' I raised my head and looked into her eyes.

'Already a month ago Bazhenov suspected our relations, although he had no proof. You know that he persistently courted me . . . And once he told me that he could do very much for me, up to . . . freeing from camp any prisoner I chose, if I . . . married him! I could not buy your freedom at this price . . . And now I regret it . . .' And Irina again broke into weeping.

'Don't regret it, Irina. Even if you had paid this price, nothing would have come of it. He would have got what he wanted, and I would have remained in camp anyway. And in any case, even if you had done it, it would not have helped in our relationship. You did well, it could not have been otherwise. And now – let us say goodbye . . .'

In total darkness we walked across the rutted gold field and separated at the entrance to the village, each going in a different direction.

The following day I met our chief geologist with whom I was friendly, and tried to determine the seriousness of the order which sent Irina west. I knew that it was often possible to circumvent orders from the centre if the local authorities chose to disobey them. He showed me the order and I saw at once the hopelessness of the situation: a new mining administration was being organized on direct instructions from Yagoda, with plans for a high gold output. The order was very strict. Guessing what I wanted to ask him, the chief geologist said:

'It is absolutely hopeless. The order is too strict, and I may get into serious trouble if I do not comply. I am very sorry . . .'

There was nothing left but to telephone Irina and tell her about the failure of my attempt . . .

I never saw her again, and two years later I learned that she was married, and apparently quite happily.

At that time preparations were in full swing for the first elections to the Supreme Soviet of the U.S.S.R. to be held in the Kolyma. The free employees held meetings, organized election districts, painted placards and slogans. Incidentally, the entire technical work of these preparations was done by prisoners – carpenters, joiners, painters, artists, etc. The candidate put up by the party organization of Dalstroy was, naturally, Berzin, the popular boss of the Kolyma.

Berzin's name was already on all the placards and proclamations in every club and every public square in Kolyma. Already the local newspapers published resolutions to nominate him as candidate for the Supreme Soviet of the U.S.S.R. from the Kolyma electoral region.

Then suddenly something broke down in the election machinery.

One week before the voting all portraits of Berzin and all the slogans with his name vanished as by the waving of a magician's wand. The newspapers printed Berzin's statement withdrawing his candidature, and on the following day the voters were urged to cast their ballots for a new candidate, proposed by a bloc of nonpartisans and Communists, a man nobody knew – the new chief of the N.K.V.D. for the Far East. People who at first took the new constitution seriously, shrugged their shoulders with amazement and incomprehension. Later it was explained at the closed party meetings – and party secrets, it must be said, were as closely kept as the *secrets de Polichinelle* – that Berzin withdrew his candidature in compliance with the categoric demand of the Central Committee of the All-Russian Communist Party (Bolshevik), sent in from Moscow without any explanations. The new candidate represented an absolute question mark to all the residents of the region in which he ran. Despite this, all members of the party, Young Communist League and trade unions were instructed to give an all-out support to his candidature.

Election day came. On special instructions directly from the new N.K.V.D. head, Yezhov, a reinforced military guard was thrown around all the camps, ostensibly in order to prevent anti-Soviet demonstrations. I remained free along with several workers, since it was necessary to set up a festive illumination on the roof of every village house. With the permission of my friend, a member of the election committee, I entered the club hall where the urns were already prepared for the balloting and took a closer look at the mechanics of the election.

The entire local officialdom sat at a large table, presided over by Katz, secretary of the party organization. The voters approached the table one by one and picked up two forms – there were two candidates, one to the Soviet of the Union, the other to the Soviet of Nationalities who had not been publicized at all, so that no one remembered his name afterward. Putting the forms in envelopes and sealing them at once, they entered the booth where the urn stood and, after dropping the envelopes in it, immediately left the hall.

When I came with the workers the following day to dismantle the booth, I found that it contained both an inkwell and a penholder, but the inkwell was empty, and the penholder had no pen. Theoretically, the voter who wished to cross out the candidate's name on the form – the only method of voting *against* – would have found himself in a quandary, for no one in Kolyma owned any fountain pens. However, everything turned out well, even too well: the committee which counted the votes made some miscalculations, and the official government candidate received twelve more votes than there were voters in Kolyma.

Several days after the elections Sukhanov informed me that I was being sent to Magadan on official business, to submit to Dalstroy our construction plan for the following year. I received a new furlined jacket at our depot and made inquiries as to when the next administration truck was going to Magadan for supplies. On the appointed day I sat with the chauffeur in the heated truck, travelling south, to the sea, to Magadan whence I had come a year before.

This trip along the winter road passed without adventure. Sitting in warmth and comfort, chatting with the driver, I marked with pleasure the contrast between my present method of travel and the one by which I had come north.

We covered the four hundred miles to Magadan in little more than twenty-four hours, during which we drove almost continuously. The endurance of Kolyma chauffeurs is something to be wondered at. Driving along such poor roads always demands special attention: sharp turns, uphill and downhill, cars and trucks going the other way and always difficult to pass on the narrow road, the slippery surface of the road – all this should be extremely fatiguing. And yet we drove as though these difficulties did not exist. Only once, toward morning, the driver dozed off for fifteen minutes, parking the truck on a wider section of the road without shutting off the motor. Indeed, it was impossible to shut off the motor because the temperature was 50° below zero, Fahrenheit, and the water would have frozen at once, splitting the radiator.

On our arrival in Magadan, I made an arrangement with the driver concerning our day of departure and proceeded to the familiar camp of the Building Office where I intended to sleep during my stay.

But in the Building Office and at my former place of work I found many old friends and acquaintances who immediately extended to me a series of invitations. They welcomed me very warmly, expressing regret that I had to leave for the taiga so suddenly, and so on. I also learned a piquant bit of news: the member of the Young Communist League with whom I had fought the ill-fated fight that had sent me to the mines, had married a month before my arrival, the girl whom I tried to protect at the time.

Having spoken to all my old and new friends, I proceeded to the head office of Dalstroy, to the Department of Capital Construction, where I was sent from Khattynakh with our plan for 1938.

There I was also met by old acquaintances. After a short talk with them, I was received by the chief of the Planning Section, Mikhail Nikolayevich Surovtzev, whom I had known before and to whom I now submitted all my papers. To supplement the written reports, I told him in my own words about the state of affairs in the north, relayed all the necessary greetings sent by people he knew, and also gave him the bottle of alcohol I had brought as a present. Our plan, as well as the bottle of liquid gold, were accepted graciously by the esteemed chief, who ordered me to remain in Magadan for a few days longer in order to be available should any explanations prove necessary. Every morning at nine I was to report at the head office for an hour or so, and the rest of the time was my own.

I also utilized my stay in Magadan to secure, for any eventuality, a certain number of well-wishers who had influence in camp affairs, people employed in the Allocation Administration of the camps. These acquaintances were made either at cards or over drinks. I became especially friendly with a certain member of the Young Communist League, a recent arrival, who was astonished to learn, toward the end of our conversation, that I was a prisoner. To his honour it must be said that this discovery did not affect his attitude toward me, although, working for the Central Allocation Office in Magadan, he was already beginning to develop the usual sense of enormous superiorty over prisoners generally.

I successfully wound up my affairs at the head office, my driver was ready to leave in time, and after a four-day stay in the Kolyma capital, I departed north, where I arrived without further adventure.

While I was still in Magadan, I heard from a number of usually well-informed people that great changes were looming in the position of Kolyma prisoners. It was said that the former N.K.V.D. chief Yagoda, recently shot in Moscow, maintained close ties with Berzin, and that Berzin was living out his last days as head of Dalstroy. It was also said that the latest transport arriving in the Nagayevo port brought an entirely different type of prisoner from the earlier ones – terribly emaciated, worn out by their imprisonment, these people had been caught up by a new wave of repressions which had rolled across Russia. This wave was already nicknamed 'Yezhovshchina', after the name of Yagoda's heir – Nikolay Yezhov. On orders from the latter, the last remnants of liberalism in the camp system were being hastily liquidated, and the general regime of prison life, methods of investigation, and work in the camps, were everywhere taking a sharp turn for the worse.

These rumours had already preceded me, and when I arrived in Khattynakh, Sukhanov confirmed to me much of what I had heard in Magadan. Two newcomers appeared in the settlement – party members recently arrived from Moscow. They called a series of secret party meetings which were attended by people from all the administration's mines. In the administration itself the authorities were visibly nervous. Even Sukhanov went about darker than a cloud.

In the middle of December a friend of mine from the Supply Section who had gone to Magadan on business returned with what was no longer rumour but real news. When everyone was already expecting the end of the navigation season because of the early freezing of the Sea of Okhotsk, a whole fleet came to Nagayevo, accompanied by an ice-cutter. The fleet included three or four ships, one of them the large new steamship purchased in England, *Nickolay Yezhov*. In addition to five thousand prisoners, the ships brought a whole army of soldiers and a large group of Chekists from Moscow.

New developments followed in rapid succession. The administration received an order from Dalstroy stating that Berzin was no longer the chief and had surrendered all affairs to Yezhov's appointee, Commissar of State Security, 3rd Grade, Carp Alexandrovich Pavlov. This information was followed by a long list of new appointments and transfers: the former directors of Dalstroy administrations, departments and mines were replaced by new personnel, 'reserve Chekists' who had come with Pavlov. Our administration was relatively less affected by these changes: we were assigned a new assistant director; a new post was established, that of head of the Political Section, to be occupied by another unknown; and several officials were replaced, including the chief of the administration camps and several people at the mines.

Furthermore, people arriving from Magadan said that Berzin and several of his closest assistants were placed, under strong guard, on the ship which sailed to Vladivostok, accompanied by the ice-cutter. In addition, it was said that during this winter there would be no interruption of navigation and that the ice-cutter would remain in Nagayevo in order to cut a path for the ships in the 50–80 miles belt of ice along the shore. This measure was prompted by the fact that all existing camps in Siberia were so crowded with prisoners that it became necessary to relieve the overflow by sending at least several thousand prisoners to Kolyma.

The next bit of news I received from a friend who worked in the Planning Section. He told me that Moscow revoked the earlier plan for gold production for 1938 and sent in a new and much higher one. Our administration was to receive an additional 30,000 prisoners which would double its current number.

New rumours spoke of arrests among the free employees of Dalstroy throughout Kolyma. In our region, in the north, the chief engineer of the administration Eidlin was arrested, as well as the chief engineers of three mines, including Lapin from Vodopyanov. There were also rumours of the arrests of Medved, Mosevich and Fomin – from among the heroes of the Leningrad trials after the assassination of Kirov. At the Shturmovoy they arrested Gubin, at the Berzin mine, Yanishevsky. The mine itself was renamed 'At-Uryakh'.

There were endless secret conferences of party members with the head of the Political Section who had come from Magadan. Barbed wire was rapidly being thrown around the camp, with high watchtowers in the corners on which searchlights and machine guns were set up . . .

Once, late at night, while Khudiakov, Stepanov and I were asleep in our room near the carpentry shop, someone knocked violently on the door. I opened it. Sukhanov entered, looking very upset.

'What has happened?' I asked.

'Be prepared for very unpleasant things. There has just been a meeting of the leading personnel of the administration. We were informed of new instructions from Pavlov, the new chief of Dalstroy. We are ordered to remove immediately from administrative posts all prisoners sentenced for counter-revolution and send them to general work at the mines. All the other prisoners can remain temporarily only at the most common, nonresponsible work.'

'Oh well, let us say goodbye then. We have worked together for a while – that's enough,' I said bitterly.

'Let us hope this wave will pass and I shall be able to pull you out again. In case of extreme need, I shall do all I can to help you. Do not lose touch with me, and I will follow your movements. I shall make an attempt to persuade Kaulin to detain you, but I am afraid it is hopeless,' Sukhanov said.

'Thank you. And what else did they say at the meeting?'

'There will be a great change in the position of the prisoners. Everyone will live in camp, behind barbed wire, and under strong guard. They will be taken to work under convoy. Wages will be reduced to a minimum. The diet will be worse. People sentenced for terror, espionage and treason will be isolated and kept apart. These are the chief points. And now I must go.'

We began to discuss the situation and were still talking when there was another knock at the door. We opened it, and two guards entered.

'Hurry up, get dressed and collect your belongings!' one of them ordered.

In ten minutes we were ready. We feared the worst, but for the time being we were merely taken to the camp, to the same tent where I first lived on arriving in Khattynakh. My friend Badyin welcomed us like a host and soon found us places, where we slept for the remainder of the night. In the morning I came to the office.

Sukhanov had gone directly from home to the chief of the administration and came to the office about 11 a.m. Summoning me, he said:

'Nothing can be done. Kaulin is trembling himself: he may be arrested any moment, he is the only administration chief in Dalstroy appointed by Berzin to be still untouched. Yesterday they arrested Epstein, Berzin's right hand in Magadan. I asked that you be left at least as a building worker – it would still be easier than work in the mine – but Kaulin refused pointblank. Generally, more than half of the employees will be sent to general work. For the time being, I am sending Khudiakov and Stepanov to lumbering jobs. But with you it is more difficult, you were more prominent here, and then you have been here only a relatively short time. Meantime, you may remain at work. They will pick you up when your turn comes . . .'

He was right. That night a virtual pogrom was carried out in our tent. About half of its population was roused soon after midnight, and an hour or so later I was already leaving the camp under strong guard for an unknown destination. The truck was packed with people. Behind us followed three more trucks.

The moonlit settlement, blanketed in snow, was again left behind in the distance.

Part III. Black Times in the Gold Fields

7. BLACK TIMES

THE settlement faded away in the distance. Dressed in a warm short winter coat, new felt boots, and a fur cap, I sat in the back of the car contemplating the ups and downs of fortune and the surprises which might be in store for me. The car moved slowly since the roads, after the recent heavy snowfall, had not yet been cleared for traffic. Criss-crossed with ditches and looking strange in the moonlight, the outlines of the Vodopyanov gold mines floated by and disappeared. The road turning off to the distant Shturmovoy gold mines was also left behind, and we began to climb a steep and winding road to the top of the ridge beyond which lay Yagodny.

On the way up, a little off from the road, we passed a few long and unpleasant-looking barracks. At one time those barracks had housed a road-building unit, and were called *Serpantinnaya*, but since the completion of the road to Khattynakh they had been empty for over a year. I recalled that a few days before, by orders from Magadan, Serpantinnaya had been transferred to the district section of the N.K.V.D. which sent two brigades of men there to carry out some secret work.

I knew the nature of those 'secrets'. The little camp was to be fenced with three rows of barbed wire, watchtowers for sentries were to be erected every twenty-five yards, and commodious house for officials and guards would be built as well as a garage. What puzzled me was the garage. It was not usual to build a garage in a small camp like this, especially since only three miles away were the big garages in the Khattynakh camp and in the Vodopyanov gold mines.

We soon reached the camp At-Uryakh. We were ordered to stand on one side by the fence, and were not allowed to warm ourselves in the tents although the long trip had nearly frozen us. In our group, numbering from fifty to sixty, I soon found men I knew, and we began talking among ourselves in low voices, conjecturing as to what we could expect. On the whole, we agreed nothing good could happen. To me it was also clear that the trick Prostoserdov, Bocharov, and I had used a year earlier at Lower Khattynakh could not be repeated. The whole situation had utterly changed, and I was certain no hunger strike could help matters, whereas any disturbance of this kind was bound to lead to many serious complications. The others agreed.

Almost an hour later, when we were all quite stiff with cold, guards appeared again, we were lined up in a column four deep, and were escorted out of the camp.

When At-Uryakh was far behind and we had climbed a fairly steep hill up a barely distinguishable snow-covered road, I realized we were going to the Tumanny gold field which only a short time before had been opened in the Tumanny Valley which lay between the Khatty-nakh and At-Uryakh valleys. We could not imagine a worse destination.

The road, running continuously through the woods, got steeper and steeper. The guards gave up any intention of keeping us encircled since that would have made them walk over deep unpacked snow. Accordingly they split up into two groups, a smaller one which walked in front, and a larger one, bringing up the rear.

The changes which had taken place since Pavlov's arrival in the Kolyma applied to guards as well. With the exception of a few privileged prisoners who had not more than six months left to complete their terms in the camps, all other prisoners in this category were dismissed from service as guards. The number of guards was greatly increased by reinforcements which came from Vladivostok. Everywhere new barracks were being hastily built for them. A week before the last raid I had had a talk with a friendly guard about the methods the N.K.V.D. used for recruiting troops which included camp guards. This is how it was usually done.

During their service in the Red Army all soldiers were constantly under observation of the army commissars and political instructors who made a careful study of each man's psychological aptitudes and political sympathies. Toward the end of their army tenure the most reliable of the men were transferred to the N.K.V.D. troops of internal defence. Here they were offered higher pay and numerous privileges to make them sign up with the N.K.V.D. on a voluntary basis for a period of from three to five years, or for permanent duty. Many soldiers were tempted by these offers since the Red Army pay for an enlisted man was 30 rubles a month, whereas guards in the Kolyma region received 500 to 800 rubles a month. Those who volunteered for this service were usually men not well adapted to normal working life because they were not too bright, lacked professional skills, or preferred an easy life. As guards in our camps they really did have a pretty easy time of it. They were not bothered with drill, their duty hours were usually short – on the average not more than four or five per day – and they were excellently fed. They had little to complain about. A considerable percentage of these guards were members of the Young Communist League, wholly convinced that their happy life was possible only because of the Soviet government. They were therefore most ready to defend that government from the disarmed and helpless 'enemies of the people' who were held in concentration camps. In fact they were systematically indoctrinated with the idea that camp inhabitants were all dangerous criminals whom one could treat like the scum of the earth with complete impunity. Particularly well trained ideologically was the contingent of guards which arrived at the Kolyma with Pavlov. They did not even talk to the prisoners, and without ceremony cut short all attempts to draw them into conversation. Instances of guards using their fists on the slightest provocation were becoming more and more frequent.

Some four hours after we had set out from At-Uryakh, when it was already quite light, we saw the Tumanny gold field below us in the valley, and in another half hour, completely famished and worn out by the journey, we reached the camp. Some prisoners, unable to carry their suitcases, dropped them by the wayside after taking the most valuable things for themselves and giving the rest to other prisoners. Since the guards allowed no one to halt, the emptying of suitcases was done hurriedly while the men marched forward.

At the gold field, after the roll call and registration, we were escorted to various tents. The camp was small, containing only about ten tents in all. Six or seven of the big ones were used for housing the counter-revolutionists, and three or four of the small ones were occupied by the criminals. As I had expected, the tents had been put up very recently and were of flimsy construction. A shaky wooden framework was covered with tarpaulin, while the walls inside were lined with ply-wood sheets which were loosely put together and let in the cold air.

In every big tent two stoves made of petrol barrels stood in the central passageway. But even when the stoves were red hot and one could scarcely stand close to them, just three steps away by the walls the temperature was freezing. In the old gold fields it had been the custom to cover the walls of such tents with moss going up four to five feet on the outside, but this had not been done here. Only the thick layer of ice which covered the ply-wood walls at the bottom helped to a certain extent to keep some warmth inside the tent.

We laid our things on our bunks and, leaving one of our men to guard them, went out to look over the camp.

The general impression we got did nothing to cheer us up. The camp grounds were not cleared after the last snowfall, and only the open area near the gate where prisoners were mustered showed any trace of clearance. Although the camp was a new one, the tents were made of used material. However, one thing in our camp was unquestionably new. That was the barbed wire which thickly encircled the camp territory. It had not even had enough time to get rusty.

A new building was also next to the gate – a control booth and house in which about a dozen guards were always on hand. On each of the six turrets, which were part of the camp security system, a sentry in a sheepskin coat was standing in the cold wind stamping his felt-shod feet.

The dining-room was disgusting, and clearly had been built so as not to encourage the men to stay in it any longer than necessary for gulping their breakfast, dinner, or supper. The shabbiest of all tents, this one did not even have a ply-wood lining on the walls, and gave no protection against ordinary wind, let alone the frosts of 50° below zero. From an adjoining kitchen steam poured into the dining-room and, cooling instantly into snow, formed a slippery skating rink surface on the floor. Men slid and fell flat with the dishes they carried.

It was said by some that soup still warm when received in the kitchen would become covered with ice during the period of time one man would wait for a spoon from another who had finished with one. This probably explained why the majority of men preferred to eat without spoons – forks and knives were forbidden at all times – and drank their soup as if it were tea, helping when necessary with their fingers.

The men, too, were quite different, as I found out later that first evening when our tent became filled with prisoners returned from work at the mines. Their faces all showed signs of frostbite, although the winter was only three months old and the most severe frosts were yet to come. The majority of them were so dirty looking I was willing to wager that some of them had not washed their faces for weeks. Their clothes were like nothing I had ever seen at the Kolyma – everything from the torn felt boots to the incredibly dirty rags wrapped around their necks instead of scarves, their burned and tattered winter coats.

The men had starved, worn-out faces, quiet voices, were completely absorbed in themselves and uncommunicative. Their range of interest was limited to work and food, and more food, and food again. Besides work and food the other questions discussed among them were tobacco – the eternal Kolyma shag – and the cold.

They came to the tent after having supper in the dining-room. They had rushed there as soon as they had returned to the camp from work – and immediately crowded around the stoves, coming so close that one feared they would catch fire. Indeed, now and again one heard voices: 'Look out! Your coat's burning!' The repulsive smell of burning rags would come up and bite into your nostrils.

The sight of these creatures who had almost lost the image of man made me feel distinctly uncomfortable. The possibility of becoming one of them seemed anything but attractive. I felt the necessity to do something about it at once, and even before the men started for their plank-beds I set out on an inspection tour of other tents.

I soon found what I was looking for. One of the neighbouring tents seemed markedly different from the others. It, too, was occupied by prisoners, but from the appearances of both the tent and the men inside, I realized that here were the 'old guard' of the Kolyma, and not the caricatures of human beings I had seen in the first tent, men who had bee.· at the Kolyma only two or three months. These were men that had already spent one or more winters there. They were incomparably cleaner. Even in the extremely harsh conditions of their life in camp they had managed to wash their faces every day, and when they could not get water, they had used snow. They were better dressed, too, thanks to the better clothes they had been able to preserve somehow from the old pre-Pavlov days. These old-timers were more self-possessed. They did not crowd about the stoves, but sat on their bunks either doing something or talking about their affairs. Even from the outside their tent looked different. You realized that the men who lived there tried by themselves, as far as they could, to make the tent warmer by covering it with moss and snow.

As I entered I asked an old man who sat at the door on guard duty against possible thieves, what brigades lived there and who were the brigadiers. He pointed to a tall grey-haired man who, despite his age, looked exceptionally strong. The man's name, I was told, was Kachanov. I walked over to him.

'What do you want?' he asked none too affably.

'I came here today. Take me into your brigade.'

'How long have you been at Kolyma?'

'A year and a half.'

'Did you work in the mines before?' Kachanov continued.

'No. I worked in Magadan at first. And during the past year I served in the administration in Khattynakh.'

'You won't do for our work,' said Kachanov, giving me a critical once over. 'We manage to get along because we work more and better than the others. You won't be able to stand our work. We have picked men in our brigade.'

'Give me a try, Kachanov,' I persisted. 'I'm not as weak as you may think.'

He paused for a second, then rose to his feet and donned his cap and mittens.

'Let's go. I'll speak to the man who assigns the jobs.'

We walked out of the tent and soon found ourselves in another, smaller tent which served as the camp office. It was brighter, warmer and much cleaner than the tents we lived in. Kachanov called one of the functionaries who were sitting at several tables – they were obviously of the 'socially elect' category – and said, pointing at me:

'I'm taking this one into my brigade. Make out the papers.'

Then he turned to me and added:

'When you're through with this, pick up your things and move over to our tent.' With this he left.

Everything suggested that I had chosen the right course. The authorities knew Kachanov and reckoned with him since his brigade was the best in the gold field and in output surpassed any other by three or four times. The man who handled assignments entered my name on his list, issued dinner coupons, and let me go. I left the office, walked quickly over to my tent, told my friends of my new arrangements and advised them to do the same. Then I carried my simple baggage to Kachanov's tent and got myself a berth on an upper deck in the corner of the tent. Everyone was already asleep, and without wasting time I followed their example.

I was awakened by a light push. Opening my eyes I saw the elderly man I had first met guarding the door.

'Time to get up,' he said and went off to wake up the others. Quickly I put on my clothes, and from a can which stood on top of the stove, scooped up a mug full of water. The orderly had melted some snow during the night. I washed my face over a bucket outside the door, and in five minutes was ready. Nearly all the others were on their feet, completing their simple toilet. Bread and two big iron containers of soup were brought in from the dining-room. As a special privilege, the Kachanov brigade was allowed to take food for all its members at once and eat it not in the dining-room but in its own tent where there were two long tables and four benches. This was much more pleasant and comfortable. I did not take the soup – it smelled much too objectionable – but I took the bread, and with sugar I had brought from Khattynakh made some 'snow tea', which completed my breakfast.

The piece of bread was quite big, weighing over two pounds. Walking past me Kachanov said:

'You will be getting the same amount of bread as the rest of the brigade if you qualify to stay with us. There are four rations of bread here – 1,300, 1,000, 800 and 400 grams. Also there is a 200 gram punishment. We get one kilogram each. In the tent where you were first, the men get 400 grams. You don't have to worry about things left in the tent. Ours is a good orderly. Nothing will be stolen.'

A steam whistle was heard and we all began to file out of the tent.

It was completely dark, and only a few scattered lamps could be seen. After walking past several tents, we came to the open ground fronting the gate which was lit by powerful searchlights. There we lined up in three rows. Only one other brigade, also made up of old-timers, stood beside us. It was intensely cold, but I was warmly dressed. Gradually men lined up around the open space. Shouts drifted out from the tents, as did loud swearing and cries from the dining-room.

'That is the headman and the assigner, gathering the *dokhodyágas* for the muster. These fellows are always slow in mustering up,' a man next to me explained.

The word *dokhodyága* I heard for the first time. It is applied in the camps to the men who have been reduced to such a low level mentally and physically that even as workers they are of very limited value. The name *dokhodyùga* is derived from the verb *dokhodit* which means to arrive or to reach. At first I could not understand the connection, but it was explained to me: the *dokhodyágas* were 'arrivists', those who had arrived at Socialism, were the finished type of citizen in the Socialist society.

Little consideration was shown in the treatment of these *dokhodyágas*. They were being reprimanded constantly, and received frequent cuffs on the head from the camp officials and guards. Having finished eating their bread – the *dokhodyágas* always gobbled up the entire day's bread ration at breakfast time – they formed in brigades. The open space was now filled with people.

After leaving camp we at once turned to the left down a winding well-beaten path in the snow and without keeping formation began descending to the mines. Our brigade being Stakhanovite – workers who surpass the established normal output – it was accompanied only by a single guard. It is difficult to say why he was there, but the new Kolyma regime demanded his presence, and he trudged along at the tail end of a long file of men, his feet getting tangled in the folds of his long winter coat.

It was entirely dark. Only the stars shed some light on the landscape, and the searchlights at the mines glittered in the distance. Then the searchlights went out abruptly and we were told to halt.

The air was shaken by blasts. There were seven or eight concussions in close succession. We set off again. When we reached the working site, the searchlights were blazing again. They had been moved away during the blasting operation to keep the lamps from being smashed.

Close by there was a toolshop in which we got our crowbars, spades, and pickaxes. Our brigade's tools were in perfect condition.

The excavation, where a considerable quanity of hard-frozen soil had been blown up just before we arrived, presented a sight of large and small rocks and hardened lumps of clay piled helter-skelter on top of one another. Separating into pairs, we went to our assigned spots and began breaking up the rocks.

Meantime, horses were brought up to cart away the broken soil. The procedure of work was as follows. A two-wheeled cart made up of a big box-like receptacle was placed horseless near every pair of work-men. As fast as we could, we filled the box with broken soil, after which a horse was harnessed to the cart to pull it off to the dumping ground. During the horse's trip to the dump and back we had to fill another cart. This went on for the entire day.

The dumping spot was just outside the gold-bearing area, and only 'empty' soil which covered the gold-bearing sands was cast off there. This work of removing the upper empty layer of soil constituted the winter cycle of the mining operation. In summer, as soon as the warm rays of the sun began sending water to the Kolyma streams, work started on mining and panning the sands released during the winter.

Filling the carts one after another with heavy soil, I did not notice the coming of dawn, extinction of the searchlights and the rising of the cold winter sun over the surrounding mounds.

The steam whistle shrieked to signify a break for dinner. Without wasting a minute we all rushed to the camp. Our excavation was only a quarter of an hour's walk from the dining-room, so during the one hour break, especially when one managed to be among the first to get to the dining-room, you had a chance to get a little rest. Those who worked farther away were worse off. Panting, they would reach the dining-room about the time we were finishing our simple and fairly unappetizing meal. They barely had time to gulp down their soup and porridge before being egged on by the guards to hurry back to work.

The short winter day came to an end – the searchlights went on again, but we were still hard at work. The horses showed signs of fatigue, so did the men. The air felt noticeably colder, and we had to don our discarded coats. A foreman came to our excavation and ordered us to wind up our work: it was ten hours since we had begun loading those cursed carts. The horses were led away. I thought we would now return to the camp to rest and warm ourselves. But no such luck. We had to pick up our tools and walk over to another nearby excavation where the same kind of work was done, except that instead of horses, dump cars on rails were used for removing broken-up soil.

Rails crossed the excavation in different directions leading to the spots where little black figures of men were seen working. Cars were rolled up to the men, loaded by them and rolled away to the main line, over which an endless cable was perpetually moving. The cars were hooked to the cable and pulled away into the darkness. Empty cars came back the same way.

We stayed working in the new place for an hour, until Kachanov ordered us to lay off. We gathered our tools and carried them to the toolshop. After that about half the men went to the camp, while the other half, picked out by Kachanov, went off carrying hatchets to the wood up the hill, some two or three miles from the excavation, to cut firewood for our tent. I was included in that second group. So tired that we could scarcely feel our legs, we trudged on up the hill. From behind came shouts of foremen on the rail-equipped excavation where men were still at work. Stumbling in the deep snow we finally reached a spot where a number of trees had survived the previous tree-cutting expeditions. Our hatchets went into action, and half an hour later we were trekking to the camp, each man carrying a heavy log on his shoulder. Dumping the logs outside our tent, where other men of our brigade immediately began sawing and chopping them, we dashed to the dining tent to gulp down the can of porridge and the can of soup which constituted the camp supper.

After a quick meal I returned to our tent, washed my gullet with a quantity of boiling water with sugar, and went to sleep.

The following day was a Sunday, supposedly a day of rest. Nevertheless, we had to get up at eight o'clock, were given wooden shovels, and were ordered to clear the snow within the camp. Several groups of prisoners were sent under escort to the woods to cut firewood for the kitchen and administration buildings. The Kachanov men were freed of this task, but others were compelled to go regardless of all considerations. All we were obliged to do that Sunday was to clear a section of the camp of snow, and about a dozen men were sent out to get 'dry water', ice from the stream. The ice was brought in sledges or in bags carried over the shoulders, and was used in the kitchen and bathhouse. Men were taken to the bath-house one Sunday a month, and since our turn did not come up that day, we were left undisturbed after midday.

Two dust-covered electric bulbs lit our tent. Some men were sleeping, some just lying on their plank-beds. Others warmed themselves near the red-hot stove or played dominoes which they had made themselves. Playing dominoes was the only amusement the prisoners had.

Days went by one after another in an unchanging row. My work took all my strength. I was not too strong, and it was difficult for me to keep up to the average working level of the brigade. I caught several sidelong glances from Kachanov and understood his uneasiness, since he could not possibly have dependents in his brigade: they themselves were able to live only by working like dogs, which brought them somewhat better rations, and occasional small favours from the administration. To keep physically weak men in the brigade would have meant lowering the average output. Nor would anyone have wanted to work for others. I was therefore obliged to strain my powers to the limit to avoid the alternative – being put out of the brigade and having to join the ranks of the *dokhodyágas* with all to which that inevitably led.

By the time spring set in, I secured the job of horse driving as a permanent assignment. I came to terms with Kachanov, renouncing all privileges such as extra handouts of food and tobacco, as well as waiving the monthly wages of 40 to 50 rubles which we were paid, provided he kept me in his brigade.

Days were growing longer and longer. On the high grounds dumped during the winter, gold-panning equipment was being hastily set up. On the side of the hill, work was being completed on a drainage channel running the length of the gold field. On the site where we worked in winter a stream called Tumanny flowed across in the summertime. During the winter months the ice was removed and the hard earth which covered the gold-bearing sands was also carted away. To prevent the mines from being flooded by the spring flow of water, a dam was constructed far above the gold field to carry the water into an artificial channel made of wood and raised in some places as high as sixty to seventy-five feet above the excavations. From this channel water was to be diverted into the gold-panning construction, there to wash the gold-bearing sands which had thawed off under the warm sun, and to separate the precious metal from stones, clay and sand.

Below, in the middle of the mines, a drainage ditch was being dug to carry away the water from the panning constructions and the section of gold-bearing area which was being mined. It is impossible to mine sands in water, since gold is washed off and sinks. As the sands are being mined, the drainage ditch is dug deeper and deeper.

With springtime I had to leave Kachanov's brigade. I was no longer of equal value to his other men, and without waiting until he would tell me to go, I spoke to him myself. He nodded approvingly.

'I'm glad you've realized it yourself,' he said. 'Your two friends are stronger, and they may stay. You look for something else, more suitable to your strength. Take your time – I'm not rushing you. When you do find something, tell me and I'll report to the man who makes assignments.'

An accident helped me. One day at the excavation I saw a geologist from the Khattynakh with whom, at a time when I was in a better state, I had spent many pleasant hours. I hesitated to walk over to him and let him see the changes the last four months had brought about. But I overcame my reluctance.

'How are you, Dimitry Alexeyevich?' I said as I approached him, having chosen a moment when there was no one else near him.

He looked at me with a puzzled expression.

'Who are you? And what do you want?' he began, but suddenly recognizing me exclaimed: 'Is it you? What are you doing here?'

I pointed to the shovel I was holding. He understood.

'Yes, I heard you were sent to a gold field, but I didn't expect you would have to work as a miner. Bad luck. Can I do anything for you?'

'Are you going to be here long?' I asked.

'About two weeks. I've been sent here to check on the exact boundaries of the gold deposits.'

'If you can do it, get me transferred to the brigade working on the central drainage ditch. The work there is somewhat easier. All you have to do is to say a few words to our checker who will be here toward the end of the day to see if all the men are at their jobs.'

'I know. I'll speak to him. What else can I do for you?'

'Thank you. I'll manage the rest somehow by myself. It wouldn't be safe for you to make requests for me. So I won't ask for anything else. When you return to Khattynakh give my regards to our friends.' With this I walked away, for he was beginning to look around with a certain uneasiness to see if anybody was watching his private conversation with a criminal counter-revolutionary prisoner.

He did more for me than I had hoped. Two days later I was called to the office of the head of the section – he was the man who had killed my horse – and was told that I was appointed as head of the brigade which worked on the ditch. This was excellent. It is true a brigadier was not a foreman, and had to work with his men, but he worked less.

The brigade I got was a choice one – all picked men, *dokhodyágas*. There were about thirty of them, all of 'the 1938 import', which meant as workers they were less than third-rate. At morning musters I had to do quite a bit of running around to get them together. They crawled away like roaches. Some would not leave the dining-room until they got an extra dish of soup; some would be rooting in the pile of refuse outside the kitchen; some would be standing in the crowd always waiting outside the camp dispensary in the hope of getting released from work for a day or two.

This dispensary was a remarkable institution. A male-nurse, sentenced to five years for doing abortions, was in charge. He was a therapist, a surgeon, and a specialist in every kind of disease. The principal purpose of the dispensary was to release sick prisoners from work, and only the doctor's notes were recognized for such purpose. If a man was too sick even to wait his turn at the dispensary, his condition was disregarded, and at the morning muster he was forced to go to work. The only ground for release was having a temperature of one hundred degrees or more. Exceptions were the cases of obvious physical injury, or when the male-nurse acted as surgeon: he loved amputating frost-bitten toes, and in such cases granted the patient a couple of days' rest. He even attempted to remove the blind gut in cases of appendicitis, but after three or four deaths he was forbidden to try again.

Even in cases of patent sickness, it was not always possible to get release from work. Patients were admitted to the dispensary only after 8 p.m. when men were beginning to return to the camp, and examinations took place for only two hours although sometimes there were over a hundred waiting. In addition, the camp commander limited release notes to from twenty to twenty-five a day, and if this number had been reached, a man was driven to work even if he had pneumonia and a temperature of 105°. The only drugs the dispensary possessed were soda and iodine.

My brigade was made up of regular dispensary visitors, and presented an appearance which made the more cheerful camp officials burst out laughing when they saw it. Gathered together the members of my brigade resembled a flock of plucked and famished crows. In their tattered black coats, in caps that looked like monks' cowls, with sores covering their faces (the result of frost-bite) they were a weird and fantastic spectacle.

Fortunately for me, their physical helplessness was obvious to everyone, as I would have got into a great deal of trouble, including solitary confinement, for the poor work of the brigade.

I was allowed to continue living in Kachanov's tent and to receive the Kachanov bread ration of two pounds. Members of my brigade received only one pound.

One day, in a fit of hilarity, the camp commander christened my brigade 'the brigade of wet hens'. After that, at every muster the headman of the camp, a notorious Moscow bandit, would shout, bursting with laughter:

'Brigade of wet hens! Step forward!'

To this I had to answer:

'Here! Twenty men in formation, eight released on account of illness, three hiding somewhere and cannot be found.'

The headman yelled:

'Checker! Find the missing men at once. They are rooting in the refuse pile at the kitchen. Lock them up in the detention house!'

Then we marched off to work, to dig our ditch.

My brigade was made up exclusively of former members of the intelligentsia. One of them was Isaac Brevda, a former professor at the Military Medical Academy and an expert in plastic surgery. He was a little, weak, and hounded man who had been accused of terrorism, although he started with fright at the very mention of the word. Another man, Vladimir Steklov, was the son of the well-known Bolshevik Yury Steklov-Nakhamkes, one of the veterans of the revolution and former editor of *Izvestia*, who too was jailed in an isolator, either in Syzran or Yaroshavl, for joining the forces of the anti-Stalin opposition. Still another, Nekrasov, a professor of meteorology and an old man, had been sentenced for espionage, although he could not understand what it was he had done to make him a spy. Then there was a former member of the Communist party and a director of some trust, by the name of Ginzburg. There were also engineers, teachers, doctors, and artists. All of them had been seized during the wave of political reprisals launched by the head of the N.K.V.D., Yezhov, and all reached the Kolyma in a condition unfit not only for work, but for living. Brevda, usually uncommunicative, once told me of the tortures he had undergone during his investigation. This tiny man who had given his whole life to science, was forced to stand by the wall without budging from his spot for two days on end. The investigators repeated this treatment several times, until the veins in Brevda's feet began to burst. He was also tortured by light, forced to gaze at a 2,000 watt lamp for several hours, and beaten up every time he tried to close his eyes. He was 'played ball with', when the investigators, taking advantage of his small size and light weight, had tossed him from one end of the room to the other and occasionally dropped him on the way. At the interrogations his glasses were taken away from him, and being extremely nearsighted he could not read the records of interrogation which he had to sign. His wife was also held in some camp, but in which he did not know. The same was true of his daughter who before she was sent to a camp had been brutally raped by an investigator. I believe the reason for his jailing was some contact he maintained with foreign scientists. He had been tried in absentia and sentenced to ten years in a concentration camp.

A different type of man was Vladimir Steklov. Still in his early twenties, he had belonged to the Soviet aristocracy. Despite what had happened to his father and himself, his mother continued to be a member of the Executive Committee of the Communist International, lived in the fine Hotel Metropole in Moscow, and led an easy life, from time to time sending her son magnificent parcels. Steklov told many stories of his life in Moscow, and of all the adventures of the upper set of the Soviet's gilded youth – he had mixed with the company which included Stalin's own son. If only a quarter of what he told was true, one could only wonder why it was necessary to have the revolution at all. During the time his case was being investigated, he, too, tasted the pleasures of N.K.V.D. procedure and had a couple of his ribs broken. But he was still a wonderfully strong and healthy fellow, and was put in my brigade simply because he refused to work any more than he could help, believing that in camp life one had to save his strength. Steklov was sentenced to only five years because, as he explained, he was guilty of no crime except being the son of a man who opposed Stalin.

Nearly every member of my brigade must have had a personality of some interest at one time. But oh Lord, how incredibly alike they were when I met them! They were all equally dirty, famished, tattered, broken down and reduced to the lowest level of humanity. It was hard for me to perform my hideous duties of brigadier, but I think it was better for them that I was their brigadier than somebody else.

With the first rays of spring sunshine the population of the gold field began to increase at a rapid rate. Three big contingents totalling about a thousand men came one after another from Magadan, and in smaller parties arrived the usual reinforcements from among the Kolyma old-timers, transferred to the gold field from other departments of Dalstroy. By the middle of May there were over two thousand men working as miners in our gold field, and this was one of the smallest in the Kolyma region.

Activities at the excavations were now carried on in two full shifts that worked day and night. The only breaks, half an hour long, were between shifts when the necessary blasting was done. Another electric station, with power derived from a mobile engine, was set up on a separate section, a score of boilers were brought over, and finally, 'Marion', a brand-new American excavator, arrived.

During this period of my stay at the Tumanny gold field, the practice of 'conserving one's strength' became a mass characteristic of the prisoners. When there was no official near by the man at work moved slowly with minimum exertion, halted as frequently as he could to have a smoke, took time to roll his thin cigarette, walked around to look for a match, and so forth. But with an increased number of supervisors, the method of 'conserving strength' underwent a change. Men pretended they were working with great energy, whereas in crushing rocks they put no force in their pickaxes, and in loading wheelbarrows lifted with their spades only half or less of what they were supposed to lift. They moved the wheelbarrows slowly, and often upset them. As you looked from the side, you saw a man pushing a wheelbarrow and apparently straining every effort so that even the veins on his forehead looked swollen. But one glance at the barrow and you saw it less than half filled, light enough for a boy to push. During the time it took the man to wheel his barrow to the panning structure, with a couple of upsets on the way, his two team-mates, who were filling the next barrow, were able to snatch a good rest. This practice had a special name: dimming. You asked a worker, 'Well, how goes it?' He would wink at you and answer, 'All right. Just dimming a little.'

However, the authorities soon began to see through all this, and woe to him who was caught with a half-empty barrow. A resounding cuff on the head sent him, along with his wheelbarrow, flying for several yards off the runway. But this didn't improve matters much. The men realized too clearly that any overexertion at their exhausting work would soon land them in the brigade for the unfit, with its reduced ration of bread from which it was a straight road to the common grave.

Even in the early weeks of the brief Kolyma summer, the men revealed a tendency to die at a rate never before known in the region. Frequently this happened all of a sudden, sometimes even while the man was at work. A man pushing a wheelbarrow up the high runway to the panning apparatus would suddenly halt, sway for a moment, and fall down from a height of twenty-four to thirty feet. And that was the end. Or a man loading a barrow, prodded by the shouts of a foreman or a guard, unexpectedly would sink to the ground, blood would gush from his mouth – and everything was over.

The death rate was particularly high among men brought to the Kolyma during the last six months. Their body resistance had been undermined in jail before they were shipped to the gold fields, and they simply succumbed under the violent pace of work.

The section head ranted more and more desperately, the foreman and brigadiers grew more and more vicious, but the gold field stubbornly refused to fulfil the plan, and it was reported the head of the gold field, Svirin, who under Berzin had been awarded the Order of the Labour Red Banner, had many unpleasant moments when talking over the telephone or face to face with the head of the Dalstroy.

Reinforcements were sent over – some fifteen men of the Young Communist League picked for the jobs of section heads and foremen, trained to hate all prisoners as enemies of the people and saboteurs. More guards, too, appeared at the excavations. Swearing at the men grew louder and more obscene, blows and cuffs on the head became more commonplace, and the men spat out their knocked-out teeth more frequently.

I ran up and down the ditch all day trying to stir up my men who stood on small planks thrown across the ditch poking their long crow-bars in the muddy water. I knew that if I failed to keep strict watch over them, the consequences would be bad for them as well as for me. Nevertheless, the little professor Brevda was sent toppling into the ditch several times. Steklov got his face battered, and many others received punishment which sometimes was, and sometimes was not, deserved.

I repeatedly asked section head Kuznetzov to make me an ordinary worker in the brigade, but he only berated me, threatening me with solitary confinement, and ordered me to stay where I was.

The last snow had long since melted away, the panning units numbered five instead of the original two, and there were three thousand men working in the mines in two shifts, but the prescribed quotas of gold output were never reached. Rumour had it that at other gold fields things were even worse.

There was a standing order by the administration promising a premium for nuggets of 100 grams and over at the rate of one gram of alcohol for every gram of gold. An earlier rule, under Berzin, had been different: the administration paid 1 ruble 20 kopecks per gram for nuggets of 50 grams and over, and gave the finder the right to use the money for purchasing any products in the camp store at established prices. When Berzin was replaced by Pavlov, the old offer was withdrawn. The result was that several cases were uncovered where prisoners who found big nuggets threw them away into the bushes rather than hand them over to the authorities. They were put to death, but it did not make the prisoners any more keen on looking for nuggets. It was then that Pavlov's new order offering alcohol was issued.

One day, helping Brevda rake the broken-up earth out of the water-filled ditch, I raked up a nugget as big as a hand. I rushed with the nugget to the section office where I triumphantly laid it on the table in front of Kuznetzov. We took it to the cashier's office where it was found to weigh over four pounds – the biggest nugget ever found at Tumanny. I became the hero of the day. The same evening, with all the solemnity possible, I was handed my premium for finding the nugget – two quarts of alcohol. Later I learned that Kuznetzov, too, was given a reward – 1,500 rubles.

In places the deposits were incredibly rich, and there were days when each of the five panning units took off up to 40 to 50 pounds of gold at each shift. As regards the quantity of gold mined, the gold field was now getting its assigned quotas. But the 'volume indices', the number of cubic metres of panned sand, were far from met. The daily measurements of the work done at each shift were woefully small even for the best brigades. Despite the heavy death rate there were more than enough workers, but the amount of gold-bearing sand produced per man was three times less than in the preceding years.

The same situation prevailed at all the Kolyma gold fields: the productivity of labour kept constantly falling off. Taken as a whole, the operational plan of Dalstroy was not being fulfilled, not only in volume of sand mined, but in the weight of gold as well.

Those in authority were raging and getting more savage. Yet a limit was reached when new contingents of men which kept arriving failed to increase the output, for these men were utterly unfit for the work they were forced to perform. To increase manpower for the panning operation, all other work, including that in the administration offices, was either stopped or drastically cut down. The privileged ranks of prisoners who held various official jobs in the camp were reduced to a minimum, and the men were sent to the excavations. Even the hired volunteer office personnel, accountants, book-keepers, economists, secretaries and so forth were formed into a brigade and made to join in the work – a sight never before seen in the gold fields. To be sure, they worked only eight hours a day, and in the matter of efficiency were worse than the weakest brigades of prisoners, from whom they were kept some distance away, but we were delighted to see them work as they did. For their part, they were very nettled at the change in their position. But those were the orders of Pavlov, and he was the terror of the Kolyma, a dictator with absolute powers over life and death for everybody.

However, the 'plan' figures were still not met. A new order came from Pavlov – it was secret, but we learned about it in no time. By this order new brigadiers were to be appointed in the mining brigades of counter-revolutionists from the carefully sifted ranks of the socially privileged bandits and gunmen. The new brigadiers were given official permission to apply strongarm methods with saboteurs. I believe only Kachanov was left at his job. In all the other brigades there appeared the well-fed faces of the former bread-cutters, bath-house attendants, barbers and other functionaries of the camp administration. Bitterly resenting the change from a quiet life to that of working twelve to fourteen hours a day in the mines, these fellows found pleasant relief in working off their resentment on the men under them. Blood and knocked-out teeth became still more common, and the air was filled with the most obscene language. Even the well-practised foremen from among the members of the Young Communist League at first shied away from these bandits. But they got used to them soon and themselves adopted the new style of work.

However, the plan figures still were not met.

In the early part of July a new order by Pavlov was read to us at the morning muster. It announced the introduction of a 14-hour working day and authorized section heads to hold the brigades at work overtime until they fulfilled their daily quotas.

Although the summer days at the Kolyma are very long, lasting from eighteen to twenty hours, and although the muster was held at dawn, one could often see the figures of miners dragging themselves through the entrance gate of the camp in complete darkness.

Mortality reached unprecedented figures. In my own brigade, despite the comparative lightness of our work, there remained less than half the men I had received at the beginning of spring. The others were all written off and buried in the nameless common grave. Nevertheless, the number of my men now exceeded one hundred since more and more were found utterly unfit for work in the mines and were therefore transferred to my brigade. There was no special surveillance over my men since it would have been quite useless, but they were bawled out and beaten up in passing, so to speak, by everybody who felt like doing it. It was increasingly difficult, with the men I had, to keep incessantly deepening the ditch which was our task. Only when the head of the gold field, Svirin, agreed to let me have four extra good workers was I able to save the mines from imminent flooding. Now I constantly had to get into the water with a pickaxe and shovel myself. The five of us did more work than the whole hundred *dokhodyágas* put together.

My brigade had one immense advantage over the others. It worked only one shift and did not have to meet volume figures. We were therefore able, after fourteen hours of work, to return to the camp. Miners were in a much worse position. There were cases when men worked for two days on end without a rest.

Still the 'plan' was not being fulfilled.

In August one more order came from Pavlov. As read at the muster, it charged the prisoners with 'adopting the tactics of counter-revolutionary sabotage' and decreed that this be fought with all available means, including trying the offenders by an N.K.V.D. *troyka* (a three-man court) which was given the right to pass the death sentence on malicious saboteurs.

Late that night I had a conversation with my friends Badyin and Lebedev who were still working in Kachanov's brigade. They had changed so much one could hardly recognize them: they had grown terribly thin, stooped, and looked dried up. At the age of twenty-two and twenty-five respectively these two boys looked like old men.

Mikhail Badyin said:

'We are in a bad way, boys. The end is near. Our bosses will get us one way or another. What are we to do?'

'What can we do? Only what we're told. We have to work until we drop, and are thrown into a common grave with lime poured over the top,' answered Sasha Lebedev with complete indifference. It sounded odd from this quiet and modest boy, a former student and poet of some talent who even that winter had been composing verses at night.

'Look, boys. We have to make a break,' Mikhail whispered.

'Nonsense! Where can one go? Have you ever heard of anyone escaping from the Kolyma?' I asked.

'I'm not proposing an escape from the Kolyma. All we have to do is make our way to the state farm Elgen which is only fifty miles away. There is a camp there, too, but work is easier. We'll be able to rest up.'

'No, Misha, I'm not going. If they catch us, they'll beat us up and clap on another five years.'

'Do you still hope to live out your term?' Mikhail asked me caustically. 'Better pray to God to survive this year.'

'I'm not going to try any breaks,' Sasha declared.

'Neither am I,' I said.

'Well, you can stay. I'm going away tomorrow. I'll go right over the hills. But mark my words, Vladimir. They'll soon be going after the brigadiers, and your number will be up, too.'

This ended our conversation. The following day Mikhail did not come back to the tent after work, and Kachanov handed in a report of the break.

Two days later Kachanov came over to me at the excavation and said that he had seen Mikhail, covered with blood, being dragged by two guards to the solitary confinement cells. He had been caught on one of the mountain passes near Elgen by a guard at a secret post.

And next day, at morning muster, the camp commander read a statement announcing execution, by a firing squad, of forty men from our gold field charged with counter-revolutionary sabotage and breaking of camp discipline. Among those named was Mikhail Badyin.

I could not even write to Mikhail's mother about his death. We were not allowed to send letters, and I would not run the risk of sending one through some hired volunteer office worker from among those with whom I was friendly. I knew though where Mikhail was shot. It was in the small camp near Khattynakh, called Serpantinnaya, which was made the execution centre for all prisoners of the Northern Administration. I had been puzzled by the garage which was being built there. Later I learned it was used to house two tractors, the engines of which produced enough noise to deaden the sounds of shooting and cries of the men. However, after a short stay, the tractors were moved to some gold field, and the automobile drivers who passed the camp at night sometimes heard the proceedings there with the utmost clarity.

Wholesale arrests began in the camp. As a rule the charge was systematic underfulfillment of quotas. Since no man in the gold field could possibly fulfill them, the failure was ascribed as criminal when the worker completed less than fifty per cent of the quota.

It was absolutely impossible to measure accurately the exact performance of a worker, and the estimate made depended entirely upon the attitude of the foremen. The foremen made daily measurements in a rough and ready fashion with the help of a tapeline, and made their reports to the office where the volume of excavated sand was translated into percentages of the daily quota fulfilled by each brigade. In doing this a practice was systematically resorted to whereby a certain amount of work performed by the less efficient brigades was stolen from them and credited to the better brigades as a means of encouraging them. But the foremen were not altogether free in recording their measurements. Once a month a measurement of the mine's entire output was made by surveyors with instruments of great accuracy. The engineers measured the depth the mine increased during the month, and compared this with the added up measurements of the foremen. When the figures disagreed – and they always did, and to a great extent – the foremen were merely reprimanded. Now, by Pavlov's new order, foremen guilty of excessive measurements were to be put on trial. The same order stated the fact that six foremen had been executed for deceiving the state. It was natural that the foremen often went to the other extreme – charity begins at home – and deliberately gave lower figures.

The official figures for labour productivity immediately dropped heavily.

Then the firing squad set to work.

A representative of the N.K.V.D. three-man court – the *troyka* – appeared at the gold field. He held conferences with the section heads and demanded lists from them of malicious saboteurs who systematically failed to make their quotas. The section heads had no alternative but to prepare such lists and to include in them the least able workers who lowered the average labour productivity for that section.

At night guards entered the tents and with the assistance of the camp's headman and the tent orderly picked out the sleeping men from their lists and dragged them away.

A day or two later, at the morning muster, we learned from the camp commander that various people had been sentenced to death for sabotage by the *troyka* and that the sentences had been carried out.

Failure to fulfil the quota was not the only crime punishable by death. A sick man who did not go to work and who stayed in the camp without obtaining permission to do so from the dispensary was sent to Serpantinnaya to be shot.

It was sufficient to show lack of due respect in one's answer to a section head to be reported by the latter as a saboteur and disappear next day from the camp.

Early in September my friend Sasha Lebedev met his fate, too.

I was working in the ditch directly opposite the excavation where Kachanov's brigade was working. A few days before this brigade had acquired a new foreman, a Young Communist League member who was anxious to win distinction and earn advancement by a show of energy. That day he appeared at the excavation, looked it over, and noticed that one of the workmen, taking advantage of a free moment after loading a barrow, lit a home-made cigarette. The foreman rushed across the excavation, and with a blow of his hand shoved the burning cigarette into the man's mouth. The man crouched, covering his face with his hands, while blood showed through his fingers. With a stream of oaths the foreman continued beating the worker on the head, then hit him in the chest. The man fell to the ground. Then the foreman began kicking the man with his heavy iron-studded boots. At that moment Sasha Lebedev rushed up. Seizing the madly cursing young fellow by the throat with one hand, Sasha pommelled his face with the other. Taken by surprise the young foreman put up no defence, but broke away and took to his heels.

Everybody was silent for a moment; then work resumed. I walked to Sasha.

'Whatever did you do? You know what you'll get for this?'

'I don't care. Let them shoot me. What difference does it make whether I die a little sooner or a little later?' he answered.

At that moment the foreman appeared at the entrance to the excavation. He was accompanied by three guards trailing arms.

'Which one?' one of the guards asked the foreman as he pointed at us.

'That one, in a black shirt,' the foreman replied, his finger pointing at Sasha.

The guards came over. One grabbed Sasha's arm and began to twist it. The other two stood by, their rifles covering the workmen who held their heads down, afraid to lift them and look at what was going on. Sasha offered no resistance, uttered not a sound, although his twisted arm must have been very painful. The foreman, secure under the guard's protection, now plucked up courage, and dashing over to Sasha hit him twice in the face. Then turning to me, he hit me, too, in the chest, toppling me over as I stumbled over a shovel that lay behind me. Blood rushed to my head. No one had done that to me since my first days in the Kolyma. But I checked my impulse, and stayed on the ground.

The guards led Sasha away, pushing him on with their rifle butts. The foreman followed them. A couple of hours later he came back, and started to bawl out Kachanov. The latter stood in silence, although this always reserved and calm man, I felt, was ready to crush this whipper-snapper to pieces. The foreman then walked over to the worker he had beaten up, and hit him twice in the face.

In the evening, when after work I called at the section office, I was told by the assigner that the foreman had turned in a report charging Sasha and me with an attempt to murder him. The section head, Kuznetzov, immediately forwarded the report to the N.K.V.D.

That same night I was awakened by Kachanov. I saw a guard standing by his side.

'I've just come from the N.K.V.D. where I was taken for questioning,' said Kachanov. 'Put on your clothes quick, and he – ' he pointed to the guard ' – will take you there, too.'

I was ready in a minute. That evening, preparing for any eventuality, I had already given my mother's address to some of my friends, asking them to try to let her know if anything happened to me. Escorted by the guard I walked out of the camp, and five minutes later I was in the little house in which the gold field N.K.V.D. had its office. I was taken into a room where sitting at the table I saw my old acquaintance from Khattynakh, Bazhenov, and our local representative of the N.K.V.D.

When he saw me, Bazhenov said to the other man:

'Well, you can go now. I'll finish the case.'

The man left, and Bazhenov and I were left alone.

'So we meet again,' Bazhenov said. 'You're in a bad way, Petrov. We'll have to shoot you.'

'If that's what you've decided to do, there's nothing I can say.'

'How did you come to attack the foreman? Tell me all about it.'

I told him what had actually happened.

'Kachanov gave the same story. But the foreman tells the opposite. Who am I to believe?' asked Bazhenov.

'You will believe those you want to.'

'Yes, those I want to. I really don't know what to do with you. The simplest thing would be to have you shot. There are more than enough grounds for that. How old are you?' he asked suddenly.

'Twenty-two,' I answered.

'H'mm. It's not very interesting to die at twenty-two with a bullet in one's neck. Well, all right. You can go now. You'll be told later what to do.'

'And what's going to happen to Sasha?' I asked, turning to him as I reached the door.

'He'll be shot, of course. What do you think he was going to get – a decoration?'

I turned around in silence and walked out. The guard who had brought me there was standing in the hall. He stopped me, and opening the door into Bazhenov's room asked:

'Is he to be taken to Serpantinnaya, Comrade Commander? The car is still waiting.'

Bazhenov paused. My heart began to beat violently.

'Take him to the camp for the present. We'll see later,' Bazhenov said at last. I caught my breath.

A few minutes later I was back in my tent, and lay on my berth. Everybody, except Kachanov, was asleep. He walked over to me.

'Did they let you off?'

'Yes.'

'And Lebedev?'

'He's to be shot. He must be on his way there now with the others.'

Kachanov was silent for a minute. Then he got up and said in a whisper which could hardly be heard:

'When will we begin shooting them?'

With this he went to his place.

I did not sleep the whole night, thinking all the time. In the morning, at the muster, the announced list of men who had faced the firing squad contained the name: Lebedev, Sasha.

The foreman for the Kachanov brigade, a vicious member of the Young Communist League, was always walking about, constantly finding fault with the men, bawling out one, hitting another. He had a big black eye – Sasha's souvenir – and this infuriated him since it made him the object of his pals' jokes. Even the Young Communists, though, disliked him. He took out his resentment on every prisoner he met. Nobody ever dared offer resistance. This was unthinkable anyway since the mines were overrun with armed guards. In a section some distance away two workmen were killed on the spot for disrespect toward their superior officers.

Late one evening, after turning in my daily report on the brigade, I proceeded from the section office to the smithy to leave a pickaxe which had been left for fixing at the place of work by some worker. The smithy was beyond the dumping grounds, in a fairly isolated location. As I walked along I suddenly saw the hated foreman in front of me.

Instinctively I felt something was going to happen. The place around was wild and deserted. I mended my pace to catch up with him. He looked back, but did not recognize me in the dark, and strode on. When I caught up with him, before I fully realized what I was doing, I raised the pickaxe and with one swing hit him on the head. He dropped without making a sound. All I heard was the cracking of his skull.

I looked around, then turned and ran back to the mine. As I reached the ditch I threw the pickaxe into it. That done I went straight to the camp, stopped in the dining-room, had my supper, talked to a brigadier who happened to sit next to me, walked to my tent, and, as usual, went to bed at once. Strange as it my seem, I fell asleep instantly.

The foreman was picked up next morning. He was alive, but unconscious. There was a great commotion at the gold field. The foreman was sent to a hospital in Khattynakh. Some time later a report came from there that the man's life had been saved, but that the injury had turned him into a complete idiot. The fear that he might recover consciousness and, if he had recognized me, mention my name, was now gone.

Both the gold field authorities and the N.K.V.D. were greatly disturbed by the incident. Their investigation brought no results – there were no clues of any kind. The direct consequence of the case was a certain restraint among the officials. They lashed with their tongues as before, but no longer let loose their hands.

Although the uniforms and characteristic blue-topped peaked caps of the N.K.V.D. agents were conspicuous everywhere in the mines, the number of men sent out for execution not only did not increase after the incident with the foreman, but, if anything, decreased.

One afternoon I was checking the work of my brigade and walked to the farthest lower end of the gold field where the main ditch ran through. I sat down on a stone to roll a cigarette.

I heard footsteps. I glanced around and instantly jumped to my feet. Before me stood Bazhenov.

I noticed right away that he was quite drunk although fairly steady on his legs. His collar was open, and he had his belt with the dangling revolver slung over his shoulder.

'Well, how goes it, Petrov?' he asked, gazing straight in my eyes.

'Pretty fair, Citizen Chief,' I answered. 'My ditch is in order, my men are working, and we are not delaying the main work.'

'How many men left your brigade during the past month?'

'Eighteen.'

'What percentage does that make?'

'About twenty.'

'Where did they go?'

'Three were sent out on penalty duties, five were charged to the dispensary, one died at the excavation, two were transferred to a mining brigade . . .'

'That adds up to eleven. Where are the rest?'

'The rest have been sent to Serpantinnaya,' I said with difficulty.

'Are those charged to the dispensary still alive?'

'No.'

'Did you try to kill the foreman?' Bazenov asked all of a sudden.

I had a feeling of calmness, and fully realized the importance of my words as I answered:

'I did.'

Bazhenov nodded, as if he expected this answer.

'Just as I thought when I was told of the incident. Tell me, are you sorry?'

I shrugged my shoulders. 'I don't know. At all events, I'm not bothered with pricks of conscience, and I sleep well.'

'And how would you behave if you found yourself in the same situation today, two weeks after that event?'

I answered after a pause. 'It's difficult to say. In all probability I'd do the same thing. On the other hand, I might not.'

Bazhenov paused and looked away from me. I waited.

'Tell me, Petrov, do you hate us very much?'

'I can speak only for myself. I have no feeling of hatred for you personally, if only because after the incident with Lebedev you had every opportunity to send me to Serpantinnaya, but didn't. As for the general question,' – here I paused to think – 'I can make no generalizations. As far as the prisoners are concerned, there is a complete reciprocity of sentiments. We return what we get, with the difference that you are able to express your attitude freely, and we are not.'

Without saying a word Bazhenov turned around and walked up along the ditch. Having taken a dozen steps he shouted:

'Petrov!'

I walked up.

'You can sleep peacefully. I'm not going to send you to be shot. At least not now. But watch your step – it's very easy to stumble.' And Bazhenov disappeared behind the bend of the ditch.

Only after he was out of sight did I feel a slight shiver throughout my body. I lit a cigarette and turned my steps toward the place where my men were working.

In September a rainy season began. An unpleasant drizzle kept falling from the dull sky, ceaselessly, for hours and days. The Kolyma soil, frozen almost to the surface, absorbed no rain water at all. The water level at the upper drainage ditch reached a menacing height. Our lower ditch was also near overflowing, and we had to do more and more work.

Approximately at that time a wave of suicide swept the gold field.

The first to end his life was Professor Nekrasov, a member of my brigade and a former meteorologist, who hanged himself on the high struts of the main ditch. I was the first to learn of this from my men, and I sent one of them to inform the section head while I went to the place of the accident. There, the old professor, always close-mouthed and now forever silent, was swinging slowly on a rope. He gazed at me with bulging, unseeing eyes, and his mouth with knocked-out teeth was hanging wide open. A slip of paper stuck out from his blouse pocket. I took it and read:

'I die because my death is inevitable. A little sooner, or a little later, I'm sure to lose my life. I have no strength to go on suffering the present torture. I ask comrades who know the address of my children to inform them of my death.'

I shoved the note back into the pocket. The section head and a few other men came up. I waited until the guards took down the body, then returned to my work.

A few days later one of Kachanov's men hanged himself at night in the latrine behind our tent.

Then in another couple of days one of the Trotskyites opened up the veins in his arm.

One of my men drowned himself in our ditch in broad daylight, and nobody made any effort to rescue him, although several men saw him drown. When I came over to the dead body as it was dragged out, and asked one of the workers who witnessed the suicide why he had not tried to rescue the man, he answered:

'That is none of my business. When a man drowns himself, it means he doesn't want to live. What right have I to interfere with him if he thinks death is better for him than life?'

It was difficult to contradict this, and silently I began to write a report on the incident.

Except for this period, suicides were extremely rare. Men desperately clung to life. Almost all of them lost any ability to react to their surroundings. Nothing aroused a feeling of indignation, a desire to avenge oneself. Men were seized with complete apathy hand in hand with the purely animal instinct of self-preservation. I saw men beat up a man who stole a chunk of bread from another prisoner. The beating was unbelievably savage, but the victim did not seem to care – he only said something and, covering his head with his hands, with his mouth bleeding, tried to swallow the last bit of the stolen bread.

A man lying next to you dies, a friend. What of it? He dies today, I will tomorrow. Why feel sorry about him? And the one who stays alive – the first to discover the death of his friend – without saying a word about his death to anybody hurriedly searches through the wretched belongings of the dead man in the hope of finding a piece of bread or something which can be exchanged for bread in the kitchen.

Those who were more impressionable and sensitive were the first to die, for their strength was undermined not only by the conditions of their life, but also by their inner suffering. It was dangerous and almost impossible to think of one's family and friends, one's past and future. You had to think only of how to survive in this life – how to get an extra amount of calories, to avoid the slightest conflict with the powers that be, which led to an instant dispatch to Serpantinnaya.

Human nature there was laid bare with particular clarity. It is easy to be honest and decent under normal conditions – with a home, a family, and friends, doing normal work, respected by others, and with respect for oneself.

But in conditions where the struggle for life is carried on in the most primitive form, where the question 'to be or not to be' has to be decided at every moment, where there is no future and no hope of any improvement – in these conditions a man reveals his true nature in a surprisingly short time. The first sign of the man's regression is external – he stops washing himself and taking care of his appearance. If a man is utterly dirty, overgrown with hair, wearing tattered clothes, showing frost-sores on his skin, one can be sure he is capable of any abominable act. He will steal anything available, be it bread, a handkerchief, or some valuable tool. If he has done anything wrong he will try to shift the blame on someone else. He will tell lies at all times, whether or not it is necessary. He has sunk to the bottom. He does not feel blows and has lost sensitivity to everything. I saw one such fellow, formerly a book-keeper, eat his own excrement when promised three pounds of bread by a drunken company of higher officials if he would do so. What would this man have done three years earlier, if at that time he could have seen himself? Probably he would have hanged himself. But once in a concentration camp, where life is the only thing a man still has, he begins to cling to it with every ounce of energy. He turns into an animal in the lowest sense of the word.

Very few men, not much more than one or two per cent, manage to preserve themselves. These are the strongest, the 'real' men. A more numerous group are those in whom the fierce struggle for existence has developed an ability, in a varying degree, to compromise with their consciences – with what is called decency, moral principles.

The greatest number, of course, are those who have lost the human image, who had forfeited the right to call themselves men. These always existed in concentration camps, but became particularly numerous in the Kolyma from the summer of 1938.

The Kolyma summer was fast drawing to an end. Night frosts grew stronger, and in the morning, when my men came out for work, they began the day by breaking up the ice which had covered the ditch during the night. It became increasingly more difficult to make men go into the icy water in leaky rubber boots.

The time was near when in previous years gold panning ended and things grew more quiet in the gold fields. But not that year: Dalstroy was still far from fulfilling the plan of gold output for 1938 approved by Stalin. Although certain gold fields such as ours, which delivered over five tons of gold during the panning season, achieved their quotas, the majority of Dalstroy gold fields delivered hardly one-half of what was required.

The first snow came about the middle of September, but panning continued, although shortage of water made it necessary to stop work on three panning constructions. There were too many men for these operations, and half of the miners were therefore transferred to winter work – to removing the upper layer of empty soil and so prepare the gold-bearing layers for the next year. A new section was marked off about a mile below the mine area of 1938, and it was there that the mining in the next season would have its centre.

An order by Pavlov informed us that after the fifteenth of September the workers not engaged in panning would be allowed to rest every second Sunday. My brigade was permitted to take rests one Sunday for one-half of its members, and the next Sunday for the other half. In this way every man got one free day a month, and I took advantage of my first holiday to sleep the whole day – the first time in four months that I really got a decent sleep.

8. A HARD WINTER

THE washing season was over, but . . . washing continued. It was still summer when the digging of a drift – a horizontal mine – was begun in one of the sectors of the field, in the high flank of the mine, where the gold-bearing stratum went deep under the surface of the earth. This was done in order to avoid too much excavation work in uncovering the auriferous sand.

At the beginning of September, hurried construction was started on a 'heater', a large wooden barrack, at the entrance to the mine. In the barrack a primitive washing apparatus was set up. While there was still enough water in the upper ditch and the large washing apparatuses were operating in the field, the sands mined in the pit, very rich in gold content, were wheeled outside, heaped up, and sent to be washed as they thawed out, although the washing site was almost half a mile away.

A short time before the water froze completely solid, I received instructions from the section boss to flood the drifts somewhat above the mine. We rapidly constructed a series of successive dams which made it impossible for the water to escape, and destroyed the flank of the upper ditch in order that the water which was not yet frozen should drain off into the dam. Thus, during the last week, we succeeded in creating something like a skating rink of completely frozen brownish-yellow water, more than five feet deep and extending over approximately five acres. This was our water reservoir for winter washing, a thing hitherto unheard of in the Kolyma.

Technically, the work proceeded as follows: in the mine drifts the workers bored and blasted the sands, which were then raked away and heaped into a single pile. The ends of steamhoses connected to boilers standing outside the barrack were then driven into the pile. The steam was released and the sands were thawed out somewhat. Then they were carried in wheelbarrows to the panning unit. Carloads of ice were also thawed out by steamhoses, and the sands were washed with the water thus obtained. After the washing, the water flowed off into a deep pool where it was allowed to settle and later used again.

From the technical point of view, winter panning under such conditions bordered on insanity, since, in the first place, the sands were never thawed out properly, and, second, the apparatus was extremely inadequate. Geological analysis established that close to three-fourths of the gold was carried off instead of being retained in the apparatus. However, the plan for gold production fixed for Dalstroy remained unfulfilled, and Moscow demanded gold. According to computations by economists, each gram of gold obtained during winter washing cost approximately four times the number of working hours it required in summer. Despite these facts, panning continued.

When we finished the outside work, my brigade was dissolved. Together with a small group of workers, I was transferred to work in the mine, digging small ditches down which the water would drain off from the piles of thawing sand. The rest were sent to the woods to cut lumber. My men were useless in the pits – the least wind threw them over. The other miners took up the usual winter tasks in the gold field.

Things became somewhat calmer. There were scarcely any shootings now, but the mortality rate did not diminish since the physical resistance of the prisoners, undermined by the difficult spring and summer, now disappeared entirely under the hard winter conditions. It must also be added that the diet of the workers deteriorated dreadfully with the end of the large-scale washing. 'There is no gold, so they give us no food,' I was told by an acquaintance, an employee of the local Supply Section.

Work in the mine held one vast advantage – it was relatively warm. There was no snow, no icy piercing wind, and it was possible to work only in the quilted jackets, without coats or sheepskins. The steam which thawed out the sand also lent some warmth to the air. The water in the draining ditches froze only at the very exit of the mine.

But there were also disadvantages. The felt boots that we were given in place of the summer army shoes were always wet, never quite drying out – rheumatism was guaranteed. Then, the air in the pit, where there was no ventilation whatsoever, was filled twice daily with the poisonous fumes of blasted ammonal. Only thirty minutes were allowed for the clearing of the fumes through the entrance of the mine, after which the workers were driven back into the pits to continue their work. Many of them succumbed to the poisoned atmosphere and coughed violently, spitting blood and often particles of lung. After a short time, these were usually sent either to the weak squads for lumbering, or to their graves. Mortality was especially high among the men who carted the wet sand from the barrack after the washing. From the steamy, damp atmosphere of the heater the perspiring wheelbarrow-pushers slipped through the opening, which was covered by an old blanket, rolling out their wheelbarrows into the piercing 50° below zero frost. The time limit in this work was, at the most, one month, after which either pneumonia or meningitis dispatched the worker into the next world.

Apart from the foundation of the rolling-out drifts, there were almost no reinforcements in the mine. The permanently frozen ceilings held quite solidly, and only now and then, thawed out by the steam, a lump of frozen rock split off and crashed down. If, luckily, the crumbling part of the ceiling was noticeable beforehand, the men had time to run quickly across the dangerous spot, after looking to gauge the imminence of the fall. But there were also unexpected falls, breaking bones and smashing skulls.

The mine was lit by portable electric lights which were carried outside before every blast. On the whole, it was fairly satisfactory.

I appreciated my relatively easy job in a warm place, and my water works were soon in ideal order: the water ran off without a hitch from all the drifts of the mine to the exit. One day the section boss, Kuznetzov, entered our mine and praised my work:

'Good fellow, Petrov! So you say the water is running, eh?'

'It is running, Citizen Chief!' I replied as cheerfully as possible.

'And how many men do you have working at the ditches?'

'With me? Eight.'

'Oh-h,' the boss wondered. 'There are too many of you here. I'll tell you what: leave four men on the job, and yourself, with the rest, get down to some other work. You will drill.'

It was impossible to protest. On the following day, with a last look of regret at the ditches which saved me from certain death, I went away to one of the drifts, with an assortment of steel drills and a six-pound hammer. As a workmate, I was assigned a Polish priest, Studzinsky, who fortunately was conscientious and did not try to ride me.

The drift turned out to be a bad one – very low. One had to lie on his back, holding the drill horizontally and turning it after each blow by his partner, who worked on his knees in an extremely uncomfortable position. Every now and then we changed places. When the opening was deep enough, a longer drill was substituted, until the opening was three feet deep. At the end of the shift, before charging, the foreman came and measured all openings, and woe to those who bored less than ten yards per pair of workers – the following day they would receive one pound of bread instead of two. And ten yards of drilling is not a joking matter, especially when the drift passes through solid, frozen rock, and when the layer of gold-bearing sand is thin.

My new job did not please me at all, since I saw clearly that one could not last long at a work which demanded such excessive physical effort. Although we now rested every Sunday and those who worked in the mines were not sent to any other job on rest days, the eleven hours per day in the poisoned atmosphere was a sufficiently exhausting affair.

A week after I had begun, I was given another partner: the first was killed by a large piece of rock that fell from the ceiling. The new one was much worse and I had to work most of the day with the hammer since he would gasp for breath after the first ten or twenty blows. Moreover, he often missed his mark and, instead of hitting the drill, hit my hands which turned it. The ten-yard norm cost enormous effort . . .

During the rare, lucky days when we struck relatively soft ground and finished our drilling an hour or two before the end of the shift, we crawled away into some out of the way corner of the mine, spread our coats on the frozen earth and were immediately asleep, until the departing shift woke us before the arrival of the blasting squads.

This perpetual sleepiness nearly cost me my life. One day, having completed the required ten yards, I climbed into a dark corner and at once fell asleep. I was awakened by a deafening crash. In the absolute darkness I was surrounded by flashing bursts of blue flame and thunderous, shattering explosions. The stifling ammonal gas filled the air.

I instantly realized that the other workers had forgotten to wake me before leaving and that the detonation squads had lighted the fuses throughout the mine and also run out. Jumping up and quickly orienting myself in the flickering light of the exploding drifts, I rushed to the mine entrance. In one place I ran under an explosion and was showered with a hail of fragments. I could not breathe, my legs seemed to fail and finally I stumbled against a ladder and fell. Fortunately, I carried my coat on which I had slept and which I remembered to pick up despite my hurried escape. As I fell, I tried to wrap it around my head, and almost immediately lost consciousness.

I came to an hour later, lying on the snow near the mine. The workers of the new shift found me near the entrance and pulled me out into the fresh frosty air, hoping that I was not yet altogether dead. Luckily for me, when I stumbled in the darkness of the mine, I fell into a narrow ditch which ran along the wall of the passage and was thus lying near water. And the ammonal gas, being lighter than air, was more concentrated under the ceiling than at the ground; furthermore, the gas is water-soluble. It was only through this combination of circumstances and thanks to the coat which I had wrapped around my head that I remained alive.

Regaining consciousness in the cold air, I rose from the snowdrift and staggered back to the camp. When my comrades saw me, they gasped. Kachanov came over.

'Where did you get so battered?' he asked.

'In the mine. Why, is it very noticeable?' I replied.

'Take a look at yourself in the mirror! Let's have a mirror, whoever has one!' he cried. A mirror was brought. I glanced into it and was horrified – my whole face was bloody.

I washed myself with water from a tin can and, taking another look in the mirror, found several small wounds on the right side of my neck, which were still bleeding a little. I had to go to the dispensary.

After a long wait I was received by the male-nurse. He was irritable. 'What nonsense will you trouble me with now? The devil, taking up my time,' he grumbled as he examined the cuts. 'A few fragments stuck in the neck, a great matter!'

'I'm afraid of infection,' I explained humbly.

'And what if there is an infection? A terrible calamity! All right, I'll operate. Sit still!' Taking a dirty and dull lancet he poked at the small splinters of rock embedded in my neck. When he was finished, he painted the wounded area generously with iodine and, tearing off a sleeve from a night shirt lying in the corner, he ordered me to bandage my own wound.

Returning to the tent, with the help of some friends I managed to bandage my neck. My only regret was that I was not hurt more seriously and had no grounds for asking the medical assistant to free me from work for a couple of days. But it was better not to enlarge too much about my accident, for that might make it necessary to explain how I remained in the pit after the end of the shift: sleep during working hours was illegal and could have landed me in the punishment cell.

My wound ached dully and a few days later I discovered that an infection had set in. After a week my neck and cheek swelled enormously and I could no longer sleep. I was again obliged to go to the dispensary.

'You again!' the male-nurse greeted me, swearing furiously. 'What now?'

I unwrapped the rags and showed him what had become of the initial wounds. He rapidly glanced at the swollen cheek, felt it in a few places, making me cringe with pain, then took his lancet again and without a word made several incisions in the swelling. Pus flowed out. I felt a little relieved, and wrapping the wound again with the rags I left the dispensary, vowing that I would never return there.

I nursed my swollen cheek for over six months. The pus broke through several times, after which the wound festered again. I became the laughing-stock of the camp officials, with my bandages over the swollen cheek. The whole affair so disturbed me that my capacity for work soon ceased to satisfy the mine director and he chased me out to surface work.

The winter was still in full force when I left the warm pit. I was assigned to a brigade of miners composed of novices, and one of the weakest at the gold field. Kachanov refused pointblank to take me into his brigade, and I did not insist, realizing the groundlessness of any attempt on my part to join a strong brigade in my physical condition.

My new brigade worked on the mechanical dumper: in the pit the workers loaded the blasted rock in large wooden cases on sleighs; these sleighs were then raised to the cable which ran the length of the drift attached to it by special hooks, and dragged out to the dumping ground.

At the time I was pretty depressed, since I saw I was inevitably slipping into the ranks of *dokhodyágas*, into the weak brigades from which there was no return. My strength ebbed catastrophically. My new brigadier, an ex-Trotskyite – with the end of the washing, the bandit brigadiers returned to their easier tasks in camp such as the kitchen, the bread-cutting room, etc. – seeing my patent uselessness for work in the mine, sent me to the dumping ground only a week after my transfer. Four or five of us were on this job. It was our task to receive the cases of rock carried up from the mine, detach them from the cable, roll them to the edge of the dumping ground, turn them over and send them back empty, attaching them to the returning cable. We were also required to take care of the snow path along which moved the sleighs with the cases, keeping it always slippery and covered with snow.

A high derrick was driven into the highest ledge over the dumping ground. It had two pulleys over which passed the cable connected below to the electromotored windlass. This derrick was moved from place to place as the dumping heap grew.

The new work was easier, especially toward the end of the working day, when the foremen's shouts urging us on to greater effort no longer sounded as frequently in the pit and fewer cases rose to the surface. We also had a fire going constantly near the dump and were able to warm our hands from time to time.

But the work had a serious drawback as well: above ground it was much colder than below in the closed pit. The wind, not very strong but piercingly cold, numbed the whole body, and no clothes afforded enough protection.

In the usual confusion of the bathing procedure I lost my own good clothes and received the oldest and worst ones instead. Now I wore old torn felt boots and a dirty quilted coat from which the cotton hung out on every side, and whose hem was so torn that I looked as if I had just been attacked by a pack of dogs. In this outfit every day in the total darkness of the Kolyma mornings I climbed to the hill over the dumping ground, lit by a small searchlight. We quickly started a fire with pieces of wood especially brought for the purpose, parts of broken cases and sleighs, spread fresh snow over the path along which the cases loaded with rock moved up, and prepared to meet them as soon as the cable began to move. A prickling, burning wind pierced us to the marrow. It was almost continually necessary to rub the face to prevent frostbite, and from time to time we had to pull off our felt boots and warm our feet, wrapped in rags, at the fire.

During the busiest hours we were somewhat warmed by movement, but the rest of the time the fire was the only lifesaver.

At the beginning of the winter a new order from Pavlov was read to us. Before this order, according to the rule established by Berzin, all work ceased in the mines in winter whenever the temperature dropped to 50° below zero. The new order changed the figure to 60°. But even this could not be verified, since the only person at the gold field who had a thermometer was the director, and the instructions to stop work came by telephone from the administration in Khattynakh. As a result, only three days during the winter of 1938–9 were declared non-working days because of low temperatures, as against fifteen days during the winter of 1937–8. But even on these days all the workers were sent to the mountains to cut lumber.

My work at the mine ended most unexpectedly. One especially cold day, when the simplest sudden motion of a hand in the air caused a noticeable swishing sound, we had to work particularly hard. One after the other the cases of rock rose from the mine which was shrouded in milky-white fog. On that day our mine was being visited by the administration chief Mendzyrzhetsky, with a whole retinue, and the foremen were bursting out of their skins to stir up the workers.

The four of us above were obviously not enough to cope with the job. More and more full cases piled up at the ridge of the hill and we could not work fast enough to unload them, barely managing to detach the arriving ones and roll them aside.

It was my task to meet each case, allow it to come as closely as possible to the derrick over which the cable passed – in order to reduce the distance that would be necessary to drag the cases by hand – and detach the heavy, clumsy hook made in the district forge. Detaching one case, I ran to receive the next. This required great agility and quick thinking, because the undetached hook inevitably crawled to the derrick and broke it, halting the activity of the entire mine for at least a half hour.

Having just detached several cases, I stood clapping my mittens at the entrance to the dumping ground. Suddenly I saw – visibility was limited to fifty yards or so – six or seven cases emerging from the white fog, attached to the cable at intervals of not more than two yards. Calling to the others to clear a space for them, I jumped up on the first case, preparing to undo the hook. When it was about three yards from the derrick, I hit the latch of the hook with my hand, but it did not open: the hook was poorly made and the latch caught. With all my strength I desperately hit the hook again and again, unable to detach it. Before I noticed it, the hook came up hard against the pulley. My left hand was caught between the cable and the pulley, then the hook struck the derrick, which was nearly nine feet high, and I saw that the derrick was bending. At the same moment I heard the sound of snapping wood.

My workmates on the ridge raised a cry and waved their hands to tell the mechanic at the windlass below to stop the machine. But it was too late. The derrick broke. Holding with both hands to the cable and still feeling no pain in my left hand, I was already hanging sixty feet up in the air. The case on which I stood slid off the sleigh and tumbled down, followed by the next one . . . The cable still moved.

I looked down and saw a group of men coming to the hill from the windlass. They were shouting something.

Finally my hands unlocked and I dropped. . . . Only one thought flashed through my mind: 'Am I alive or not?' Almost at once I felt my whole body strike with a dull thud the stones, lightly covered with snow, at the base of the dumping ground and heard the crashing of heavy rocks and cases flying down the slope one after the other.

Then I lost consciousness. I came to from a hard blow on the side and violent cursing. l did not stir, recognizing the voice of our camp commander. He continued to kick me with his felt boot, but my body seemed to have lost some of its capacity to feel. Besides, my right arm and shoulder were pressed down by a heavy rock that had fallen from above, and I could not move my feet.

The blows ceased. I heard approaching voices, and a group of people stopped near me. I stubbornly kept my eyes shut: it was to my advantage to be considered dead, or at least seriously injured, if only for the first few minutes after the accident, for accidents usually ended unpleasantly for the culprits who allowed the derrick to break.

Suddenly among the voices of the people who stood above me discussing the question of stopping the windlass, I distinguished that of Sukhanov. He came nearer to look at me and apparently recognized me at once:

'Why, it's Petrov!' he said with astonishment.

'Who is Petrov?' another voice asked.

'He worked in my section last year,' Sukhanov answered.

'Hey there, why don't you take the man away?' the other voice asked, in a tone of authority.

'At once, Comrade Chief!' the camp commander hastened to reply obsequiously. 'Hey there! You, at the dump! Come here!' he shouted.

A minute later I heard more orders:

'Take him to the windlass shack, then we'll see!' the commander told the men. And I felt myself being freed from under the rocks and lifted up. Five minutes later I was carried somewhere. Half-opening my eyes, I saw that I was in the room where the windlass was set up.

Putting me down on the floor, the carriers left. The windlass clattered again.

After a while, when I was certain that no one was there except the machinist, I opened my eyes and sat up. Then I crawled to the brightly burning stove.

'Oh? So the corpse has come alive! Hurrah!' cried the machinist, my old friend Vanka, a jolly, cunning ex-bandit. I nodded to him. Coming over to me, he helped me to get up and sit down on a wide stool covered with a sheepskin coat. Only then did I feel how badly I had been mauled in the fall. With an effort I pulled off the mitten from my left hand; the mitten was filled with caked blood, and the skin on my hand was badly grazed, but the bones apparently were uninjured.

'Say, but you've had a drubbing!' Vanka said admiringly. 'Did the chief send you here? There is a whole crew of them here, bosses from Khattynakh. They came in to warm up . . .'

'Yes, the chief . . .' I answered shortly.

'All right, sit there, get warm. I guess you are not up to talking much now,' said the machinist, returning to the windlass.

Although my arm and whole body ached sharply, I enjoyed the warmth and rest. Before my closed eyes I still saw the approaching cases, one after the other . . .

Suddenly Vanka jumped over to me, having seen something in the window through which he looked out at the dumping ground.

'Lie down, quick! Put on your mitten and close your eyes. The camp elder is coming!' he whispered, helping me to the floor. I understood and stretched out. The door banged.

'Well, how is that scoundrel? Alive or dead?' asked the elder.

'Alive, it seems, but pretty bad. I am afraid he'll give up the ghost any minute,' Vanka answered.

'The devil take him altogether! He would drop down out of the sky just when the bosses were coming over,' and the elder let out a string of unprintable oaths. 'It turns out he worked in the administration once, one of the fellows with Mendzyrzhetsky recognized him and now I am told to take him to the infirmary and free him from the mine if he stays alive.'

'But how can he get to the infirmary?' Vanka asked with well-feigned doubt. 'It is an hour's walk.'

'The camp commander sent for a sleigh,' the elder answered.

My spirits rose. To make sure of things, I groaned to confirm my condition.

'Lucky fellow,' Vanka said. 'Now he'll have a rest . . .'

'The devil take him, instead of rest!' the elder swore again. 'As soon as he comes to, I'll chase him back into the pit!'

'You'd better think twice before you do it. If he really has a "hand" in the administration, you may wind up in the pit yourself,' Vanka observed quite reasonably.

'Oh, well, they don't coddle contras so much nowadays . . .' the elder grumbled.

'That's just why I'm saying it,' my counsel went on. 'If they don't coddle contras nowadays, and yet they stood up for this one, his "hand" must be a pretty strong one. See that you don't break your own neck.'

'We'll see about that when the time comes,' the elder remarked vaguely and left. When his steps died out, I sat up.

'Congratulations!' said Vanka, coming over and putting an already rolled cigarette into my mouth. 'It seems you'll get out of the pit. Those bastards,' he nodded in the direction of the door, 'put on a show of nerve, but they are shaking for their own skins, along with the camp commander. Don't be afraid.'

'I am not afraid. I lost all the fear I had last summer,' I replied.

'The main thing, fake sickness as long as you can. There is no sense in playing fair with them. Look them in the eye without blinking and lie that you cannot walk.'

'Oh, I can look them in the eye, all right – this is my third winter in Kolyma and my own eyes were frozen out long ago . . .' I repeated the current local saying, inhaling the makhorka with pleasure.

'They're here!' Vanka cried a few moments later from the window where he kept close watch. 'Throw away the cigarette!'

When the door opened, I was lying motionless, with closed eyes, on the floor. I was picked up, and this time I cried out with real pain. Carrying me out of the windlass shack, the men threw me into the sleigh without ceremony or care, and we drove off.

When we arrived at the camp I was dragged directly from the sleigh to the dispensary. The elder followed me. The men woke the drunken male-nurse who was generally never seen sober. Pulling on a dirty, once white smock and swearing, he began to examine me. The elder whispered something into his ear. The medic glanced at him with astonishment, shrugged his shoulders and said:

'It is all the same to me. For my part, you can leave all the malingerers in the camp.' Sitting down at the table, he wrote a note freeing me from work for three days and certifying that, in view of my physical condition, I was unfit for work in the mine. Handing me the note, he asked:

'Well, are you satisfied? Must I look after you, or will you get well on your own?'

Restraining my joy for form's sake, and at the same time wincing with unfeigned pain, I replied:

'I think I'll manage myself. I won't trouble you any more . . .'

'All right, get out! There's enough work here without you. I amputated more than ten frozen fingers today already . . .'

I reached the tent in a state verging on complete ecstasy: three days of rest, and goodbye to the mine! My hopes of surviving the winter too, to remain alive and not follow my many friends, were revived once more.

For three days I was blissfully happy.

On the evening of the third day I went to the camp office to find out where I was to report for work on the following day. The elder conferred with the foreman and told me I would work in the woods, at lumbering. I expected that and asked what the output norm was. When

I heard that it was 2 cubic metres per man, I requested not to be assigned to any brigade, but to be given one team-mate with whom I might work as a separate team. I did this because I knew that lumbering was done by the weakest brigades whose output was very low and whose members therefore received only one pound of bread a day and the vilest of food at the mess hall. Joining such a brigade, I would have been reduced to its general ration category no matter how hard I worked, since the output was determined by the whole brigade.

Telling me to wait, the elder went in to see the camp commander. Five minutes later he returned:

'The devil with you! The commander says that it's all right. You can take Alexeev, from the fifth tent, as your team-mate. I'll tell the foreman, and you'll get the tools at the warehouse tonight,' he said, writing a note to the warehouse.

I emerged from the office triumphant. Working outside of the brigades was the ideal of all who had not yet lost the desire to fight for existence. Working alone, I was responsible for myself only and earned as much as I produced. I knew that the norm of 2 cubic metres was not too difficult for a normal person, although the *dokhodyàgas* in our camp produced on the average not more than half a cubic metre per person and were never taken off the punitive ration.

After I received the tools – a saw and two axes – I found Alexeev, who turned out to be a morose young fellow of about twenty-five. He took the news that we would work together quite indifferently. In preparation for the next day we thoroughly sharpened our saw and axes, knowing that sharp tools made the work much easier.

In the morning, when the roll call was almost over, the camp elder called out:

'Petrov's team! On your way!'

'Here! Two men! Both present!' and we briskly walked out of the gate, catching up with the brigade of lumberjacks.

We caught up with them very quickly as these *dokhodyàgas* moved with the speed of tortoises, although three well-fed, warmly clad guards in the rear did their best to prod them on. As they walked they talked about the same inevitable subjects: food, makhorka, and work, finishing up each other's thin cigarette stubs as they went along – as soon as one man lighted up, tens of voices were already asking him not to forget to give them the stub for a drag or two. They walked calmly, without hurrying, philosophically ignoring the prodding of the guards.

The sleigh road along the snow led uphill. After an hour's walk, we were overtaken by the lumbering foreman, a stocky fellow from among the criminals, and we speeded up a little, since he swore energetically and generously administered blows on the back of the neck to laggards.

At the end of the second hour we reached the lumbering site. During the year of the mine's existence, all forest directly adjoining it was cut down and the work sites moved farther and farther away.

The foreman knew that Alexeev and I were to work separately and, vaguely pointing out the place where we were to operate, he left us alone. While *dokhodyágas* stamped about stubbornly reluctant to begin before a fire was started and they could warm up after the walk, Alexeev and I went deeper into the woods and chose our starting place.

The snow was very deep, piled more than three feet high, and we had to stamp about for a long time to pack it down around each tree so that we might cut as low as possible. After toppling about ten trees, we made a small fire to warm our chilled hands.

After a half-day we sat down by the fire and replenished our strength somewhat with the bread and herring we had saved from the previous night's supper – washing down our simple breakfast with hot water from a tin can which Alexeev had providently brought.

From all sides we heard the sounds of work, clear and sharp in the still frosty air. At times they were reinforced by the familiar swearing of the foreman and guards. We did not join the rest and were not curious to know how their work was proceeding. Camp life generally breeds in people an almost morbid desire for solitude, a wish to avoid as much as possible any association with others. The longer a man lives in a camp tent, in unavoidable contact with hundreds of people, deprived of the opportunity to choose his own society, the more he tries, at least for a time, to withdraw from the rest. As a rule this is impossible, and therefore Alexeev and I were only too happy to remain alone. He was a taciturn man. We were silent for the most part, only exchanging occasional brief remarks.

It was not yet dark when we completed a pile – exactly 4 cubic metres. We added some wood to the fire, which formed a deepening well as the snow around it melted, made ourselves snow armchairs, and sank into them as comfortably as we could, thinking our own thoughts . . .

We were roused by the foreman's voice:

'Taking your rest early, you devils! Where is your stack?'

I took him to it. Grumbling to himself, he measured it from every side, but it was difficult to find any pretext for scolding, and, brightening up somewhat, he returned to the fire, to roll himself a cigarette.

'If everybody worked like that, there would be less trouble. But all the bastards think of is to stick to the fire – you cannot tear them away. The damned wick [wick was a synonym for *dokhodyága*] may be on fire already, but still he is pushing right into the flames. And how does he chop trees? The son of a bitch couldn't chop off a chicken's head with blows like that.' He concluded his tirade with a string of oaths.

Finishing his cigarette, he rose.

'Time to go. It's dark already.'

I got up, and so did Alexeev, who had not spoken a word. We walked toward the bright fires burning in the distance. Approaching the others, I stopped for a moment, struck by the picture: tongues of flame rose from the huge bonfire around which were huddled several score of black figures, sharply outlined against the bluish-white snow; under the black monk-like cowls, the faces lit by the bright flames were incredibly dirty, with dark stains – traces of frostbite on cheeks and noses. All this combined to give the impression of a strangely wild, not quite human assembly. The sitting men muttered quietly among themselves, and their talk was drowned out by the loud, resonant voice of the guard swinging his rifle as he walked among them in a warm coat, mittens reaching to his elbows, felt boots and a large fur hat with earpieces.

'Scum and bastards, every one of you. For your crime the Soviet government brought you here, leaving you your heads and hands to give you a chance to earn a right to life by honest labour,' he bellowed. 'And all you think of, you scoundrels and saboteurs, is to continue your counter-revolutionary sabotage in the camp, sitting on your punitive rations and dying out like flies. Serves you right. The fewer parasites like you, the sooner the socialist revolution will triumph throughout the world. How many cubic metres did you do today? Hey, you, brigadier, I'm addressing you!'

'Eighteen,' someone answered reluctantly from the sitting circle.

'How much is that per man?' the guard continued his interrogation.

'.45 cubic metres,' was the reply.

'There you see! Aren't you scoundrels, aren't you saboteurs? You ought to be sent into the pits, all of you!'

'We have all been there already. That's why we are here now . . .' someone said. 'You ought to get a taste of the pits yourself,' muttered someone else. The guard heard him and flew into a rage.

'Get up, you sons of bitches! Hurry up now!' He rushed at the crowd, swinging the butt of his rifle. The 'sons of bitches' dropped on the snow, trying to cover their heads and faces against the blows of the rifle and the new, hard boots. The guard quenched the fire, wildly kicking the snow into it. The foreman joined him.

Firing a shot into the air, the guard signalled to the two others who watched another group some distance away, and soon we were walking in the direction of the camp. It was totally dark, and only the stars and the northern lights illuminated our way. An hour later we were in camp. The return trip was shorter, both because we walked *from* instead of *to* work, and because the road campward was downhill.

Several days passed. On the whole, I was pleased with my new occupation and felt fairly well – the pain of the fall had disappeared, and even the famous swelling on my cheek and neck had begun to go down a little. The only trouble was that those wretched wicks were kept at work too long – twelve hours per day, not counting the trips to and from the work site. Very little time was left for rest and sleep.

However, matters soon improved. After waiting a week and making sure that the foreman was honestly showing in his daily reports that Alexeev and I fulfilled our norm, I went to the camp office one evening after work, and, taking advantage of the elder's absence, stepped directly into the office of the camp commander.

'What the devil do you want?' he asked me.

'Citizen Commander, I should like to request that Alexeev and I be permitted to work independently, without being tied up with the nearest brigade.'

'What else?'

'Allow us to go and to return by ourselves, without waiting for the rest. The norm will always be fulfilled. Otherwise we must waste too much time with those *dokhodyágas*. If we rested better . . .'

'And what do you think you were sent to Kolyma for – to rest?'

'I know that we were sent to work. And you know, Citizen Commander, that we work conscientiously,' I tried to persuade him. He considered it for a while.

'Very well. Only instead of 4 cubic metres, you'll have to produce five. And you'll each get two pounds of bread. Tell the supervisor I allowed it.'

In a happier mood I left the office and told the supervisor about my conversation with the commander. He refused to believe me and went in to verify it, but returned at once and nodded.

'All right, you can go now. The guards and the foreman will be notified.'

From the following day on, Alexeev and I, leaving later after roll call than the others, quickly overtook the crowd of *dokhodyágas* and, by the time they came and began work, we already had almost one whole cubic metre in our stack. Completing our norm by six o'clock, we called the foreman who measured the pile and dismissed us with a note that we were permitted to return to the camp. Without such a note the guards at the gate allowed no one to enter before eight, while normally the lumber workers did not return from work before ten. Roll call began at 6 a.m.

My calculations proved correct. The work in the forest was not as exhausting as mining and it could be fulfilled without too much difficulty by a man who had not yet altogether lost his strength. And the additional pound of bread, even of such half-baked and vile tasting bread as we were receiving at the time, mixed with bran, was of considerable help. Moreover, we were paid, for the first month, 40 rubles each, and could now buy makhorka and sweets at the camp commissary, even if in microscopic quantities. Alexeev somewhere procured several kilograms of herring and we had supplementary breakfasts for a whole month, making it unnecessary to save some gruel or salt fish at dinnertime for the next day. At 7 p.m. we were already in the camp, had time to dine before the others, and were able to sleep from 10 p.m. to five in the morning.

About that time we began to cart wood from the forest to the mine. The horses were all being used in the pits, and the inventive administration decided to use men as draft horses, preferably selecting the weaker men. From four to six men were harnessed to a sleigh loaded with lumber. The load itself was not too great, especially since the road was almost entirely downhill, but the human horses had to exert tremendous effort to move the sleighs. They would constantly fall on the downgrades, or be knocked off their feet by a sleigh that would slide down the slippery places.

Shortly before Christmas heavy snowfalls began, cutting off our mine completely from the rest of the Kolyma. There was so much snow that some mine workers were transferred to the work of clearing a road. In the meantime, the last food reserves for the prisoners were exhausted.

First of all, as usual, the salt disappeared, and in all the dishes we were served in the dining-hall it was replaced by herring. Soup with herring, gruel with herring. Then the cereal gave out, and there was no more gruel. There remained only soup with bread, the soup consisting of nothing but water with a small mixture of flour. Then, for three days, all workers received only a half-pound of bread per person, and on the morning of the fourth day everyone received a double portion of the same soup instead of bread. On the following day again there was no bread.

Real famine set in at the mine. Five thousand men did not have a piece of bread. But everyone worked as usual – twelve hours a day. The prudent administration put all guards on duty, fearing a hunger rebellion. These fears were groundless – the browbeaten and worn-out men were incapable of any energetic action.

Exhausted by long years of half-starved existence and inhuman labour, people spent their last remnants of strength in working. And died. During those days the nameless graves under the hill swallowed fifteen or twenty men every day.

In the evening of the fifth day, barely dragging our feet, my teammate and I went directly to the dining-hall on returning from work. Alexeev's eyes were burning feverishly. We had just come into the mess hall when our nostrils were struck by the smell of meat. From the kitchen window we were given a plate of soup each, and what soup! Large chunks of meat floated in it. Alexeev began to gulp it down at once, but I was seized by a sudden suspicion, knowing that the roads had not yet been cleared. Since there were few people in the dining-hall, I went to the window and called the cook, whom I knew, to ask what kind of meat it was. The cook laughed, immediately guessing my thought. His fat face shone. 'So, you are afraid it is human meat? No, not yet. Calm down and eat it. Today they slaughtered three horses at the stable. They say that one died himself, but what's the difference?'

I agreed that it made no difference and returned to the table to eat my portion with great relish. After supper we went to our tent to sleep.

On the following morning we had the same thing for breakfast: half-soup, half-stew of horse meat. And as usual, at six in the morning, in total darkness, we were sent off. After we had walked a few hundred steps, my team-mate suddenly said:

'Do you know that today is Christmas?'

I did not know, for I had long ceased to keep count of the days – it was easier that way.

'Listen, let's not hurry, work is not a bear – it will not run off to the woods. Let us go and sit down awhile, warm up . . .'

'Where?' I asked Alexeev.

'Along the road. I have a friend, a machinist at the windlass, on the mechanical path. He has a warm shack and we can sit there till sunrise.'

Forty minutes later we turned off the trodden snow path leading to the forest, and soon were approaching the windlass shack. I immediately recognized the place. And my old friend, the machinist, welcomed us warmly.

'Come in, dear guests, sit down by the stove!'

I sat down at once near the brightly burning stove, and my companion walked away to the side, turned from us and stood motionless.

I glanced at him questioningly. The machinist caught my glance and also looked at Alexeev. I suddenly caught a new expression in the eyes of this confident and cheerful bandit – a curious mixture of respect and – fear.

'Have you known him long?' I asked the machinist quietly.

He nodded:

'Yes. About two years.'

At that moment a shout was heard from the distance – 'Start the windlass!' – and the machinist began work. The windlass clattered.

Looking at Alexeev, I saw him kneeling, with his head on the dirty floor. His pose left no doubt – he was praying. Something long forgotten stirred in my breast. The machinist also glanced at my comrade, silently, although jeers at the least expression of religious feeling, often verging on vicious insults, were common not only on the part of the administration, but generally among the criminal elements.

I do not know how much time passed. Alexeev rose, and with a brief 'Come on' walked out of the shack without looking at us. I followed.

It was beginning to dawn. We walked silently. With an enormous effort I tried to drive from myself the pictures of the distant past, pictures of early childhood that had been awakened by my comrade's action. Christmas! The happy winter holiday, happy especially for children. Decorating the tree, all the festive preparations, friends, guests, merriment, laughter . . . For a second the thought flashed upon me: 'When did I laugh last?' And I answered myself: 'More than a year ago.' Yes, Christmas! My fourth Christmas in a prison or a concentration camp. Before me there were two more. Would I live to see them?

In camp that evening we learned that the first tractors with food had come along the cleared road that evening. But we still had the same supper – horse meat stew. The next morning we had it again for breakfast. The menu was not improved because the administration did not want to create a holiday impression, no one was to feel that the food had been brought for Christmas.

In the morning we came to the forest even hungrier than before. We had barely felled several trees when the foreman appeared, calling out to me:

'Stop making a fool of yourself! Nobody is working at the field, and you are still at it. Make a fire and sit around till dark. And then – back to camp. Here is your note to the guards,' he said, tearing out the prepared slip from his notebook. We obeyed. That day we cut only enough wood to keep the fire going. But our empty stomachs made themselves felt. It was not yet dark when I rose from my place.

'I'll take a walk to the free settlement to see if I can find something to eat,' I said. Alexeev nodded silently and I went.

I had a slight opportunity at times to procure some food for myself; several free employees at the mine knew me from better days, and occasionally they fortified me with bread or some other edible. I now went to their houses, impelled by the pangs of hunger.

But luck was against me. The territory of the free settlement swarmed with guards – the state of alarm was still maintained at the mine. Knowing that prisoners caught on settlement grounds were immediately sent to the punishment cell, I was very careful. Finally, stealing along the shadows of houses and barracks, I reached the house where lived my acquaintance, the mine economist. I looked through the lighted window – the room was full of people, a party with singing and laughter was in progress. It was impossible to call out the man I needed. And my other acquaintance, the book-keeper who had given me a large loaf of bread two weeks earlier, was not at home.

Returning to the camp, I was consoled by the fact that we were each given half a pound of bread with the now thinning horse soup. After supper I went to sleep.

On the following day the usual food norms were restored: again we received gruel and salt fish, and, most important of all, I was again given two pounds of bread daily. Life resumed its course.

By the end of winter, despite the chronic lack of sufficient food, I grew stronger working in the forest in the fresh mountain air, and was able to sleep seven hours every night. My team-mate was still Alexeev, although he had become completely silent. There were days when we did not exchange words, working silently, and silently sitting by the fire after work.

The snow still lay thick everywhere and the frosts reached 20–25° below zero, especially toward morning. Then an unpleasant incident occurred to me – I was sent to the punishment cell.

One morning, when roll call had already begun, I was in the dining-hall, finishing a muddy liquid that was called tea. Suddenly I received such a hard blow on the back of the neck that I bit my tongue. Since childhood, any physical violence always provoked me to an automatic, purely reflex reaction. I immediately jumped up and, without glancing back to see who the assailant was, I swung the cup and hit backwards, over my shoulder, with all my might. The blow hit the target: someone howled with pain. I finally looked back and stood petrified: before me was the guard who had come to the mess hall to drive out all laggards. Jumping back, he aimed his rifle at me and ordered me with an oath to go to roll call. I understood his indignation, for the cup had hit him in the nose and it was bleeding. My fighting spirit departed instantly. I knew that I would not fare well – I had committed one of the gravest crimes according to camp standards.

The injured guard brought me to the square before the gate and forced me to lie down on the snow near the fence. I obeyed without protest, knowing that a man of his type would not hesitate to fire at me, and I did not think it would be the height of wisdom to let myself perish so stupidly after four years of imprisonment. I was still lying on the snow, watching the end of roll call, seeing Alexeev looking in all directions in search of me then finally leave. It was cold and unpleasant, as it always is when one is conscious of having committed an irreparable blunder.

My guard called one of his colleagues and told him in a lowered voice about the incident in the dining-hall. The latter went to speak to the camp commandant, then returned and ordered me to get up and walk. I did not ask where, unerringly guessing my destination. Along the narrow, well-trodden snow path we passed the camp, walked up-hill about a mile in the direction of the mound, and came to a small building. Even before we reached it, we were stopped by a shout:

'Halt. Who is it?' My guard replied, 'It's all right,' and another soldier, trailing his rifle, emerged from a booth near the building. Exchanging a few words with the sentry, my guard turned back toward the camp, and the remaining one ordered me to the punishment shack. Unlocking the door, he let me in and closed it again.

At first I could not see anything: after the dazzling white snow this windowless room seemed absolutely dark. Standing at the door, I only heard the voices of several men and the usual swearing. Only after several minutes, when my eyes became accustomed to the darkness, I realized that I was in the small and only room of the punishment shack, weakly lit by the daylight seeping through the cracks in the log walls and the feeble flame from the open doors of the stove. Someone from the upper bunk called to me:

'Hey there, pal, climb up here and tell us what brought you here!'

I climbed up and found four men, all unknown to me and dressed only in their underwear – obviously criminals. Briefly telling my sympathetic listeners about the unlucky incident, I asked why there were so few men in the punishment cell.

'Here we have only clever men. All the idiots went to work.'

'Is not everyone required to go to work from the punishment cell?' I asked.

'No, we have full freedom, as under the Czar. The only difference is in the bread ration: those who work receive one pound, those who don't, a half-pound a day. We decided it wasn't worth knocking ourselves out for twelve hours for an extra half-pound of bread. It's true, the bastards took away all our clothes, but that's not so bad – while the shack stands we won't freeze. Kolka! Get some firewood!' ordered the terribly emaciated, bearded man who spoke to me, and who apparently commanded a position of authority.

The young fellow jumped off the bunk and began to rock the rods of which the lower bunk, already half-dismantled, was made. Pulling out a few sticks, he pushed them into the stove and clambered up again.

'Good boy, Kolka!' the bearded man praised him. 'This is my wife!' He introduced the boy. I nodded. Homosexuality among criminals was no secret to me. I had even heard about cases where male prisoners, including politicals, had been raped by thieves and bandits.

The criminals continued their card game, and I stretched out on the bunk and soon dozed off. I woke up feeling that someone was rifling my pockets. One of the company of players sat bending over me. Apparently while I slept they decided to see whether I had anything of value with me.

'What do you want?' I asked.

'Let us see what you have,' he ordered.

'Why didn't you say so in the first place, instead of shoving your hands into my pockets?' I said, trying to keep up my courage, and, sitting up, I began to turn out my pockets. But I had nothing of interest to the thieves besides half a package of makhora and the scarf around my neck – the last relic from Kattynakh. They took both things and left me alone.

'Will you go to work tomorrow?' asked one of the players.

'I'll go. I cannot refuse, or they'll make me a saboteur before I know it.'

'Just think of that, a great matter!' commented the bearded man. 'We've all become saboteurs here, except Kolka. Last summer they told us our terms would be lengthened by three years and that our article of the law was now 58–14. But we . . .' and he swore again.

'So you have been here since summer?' I asked.

'Yes, almost without a break. We'll go out to work for a few days now and then, get some provisions from our friends in camp – and back to bed. That's how we live.'

I was surprised, but not too much. I knew the astonishing endurance of criminals generally. Neither hunger nor cold nor beatings could break them down. They were a hardened element. From childhood they had been accustomed to living in the street, to spending winter nights in cold railway stations, in parks or in doorways, to stay hungry for weeks, almost without a piece of bread, and always dirty, ragged, and very often suffering from venereal disease. These people could adapt themselves to any condition, and it was very difficult to break them down. They were really capable of enduring half a year in the punishment shack, in those inhuman conditions. A tough element . . .

It was late at night when the others returned from work. Some dark figures stirred below, near the stove. Two guards entered with lanterns.

'Off with your hats, mittens and boots, make it quick!' one of them ordered. Everyone began to undress hurriedly. I also had to follow the general example. Then, one the guard's instruction, two men collected all the felt boots and the rest of the rags and carried them outside. The door remained open and it became very cold. When the men returned, the command was given: 'Four men are to go for firewood!'

Rapidly deciding who was to go, four men left the shack and went barefoot across the snow, disappearing somewhere into the darkness in the company of the guards. Ten minutes later they returned with armfuls of wood. The door closed. Soon the stove was burning brightly and the reflection of the flames on the walls lent some light to the room. A little old man whom everyone addressed as 'daddy' settled down near me. For a long time he fussed about, trying to wrap his feet in a rag which he pulled off from his neck. Finally, he quieted down and lay back, sighing.

'What kind of order do you have here, daddy?' I asked him.

'As you see, they torment good people, the infidels,' the old man replied. 'Every evening they take away our hats and boots. And what for? They don't know themselves. "So that no one runs away," they say. And who will run? And where? First, they take your boots, then they make you walk a hundred steps in the snow for firewood. And who brings the firewood if not we ourselves, from the woods? You'd think they'd let us carry it right in. But no! First, they make us throw it down in the yard, and then run for it barefoot. It's lucky, too, if they send out four men, as tonight, so we'll have almost enough wood to last till morning. But if somehow we anger the guards, they'll send out one man only – and what can one man bring? Oh, what a life!'

The old man fell silent. And indeed, after such a life even the camp seemed like a paradise. Everything in the world is relative. Only now was I able to appreciate the advantages of obedience in camp . . .

'Have you been in the punishment shack long, daddy?' I asked.

'Since Christmas, sonny,' the old man replied. 'They put me in because I prayed aloud to the Lord in the woods – seeing it was a holiday – both for myself and for others . . .'

'Are you of the clergy, daddy?'

'Yes, son. I was vouchsafed the honour of holy orders. But now it is nearly ten years since they wrecked our little church and sent me to camp. At first I was in Solovki, then on the 'B.B.K.' – Baltic-White Sea Canal – and now I've come to Kolyma. Everywhere it is God's land, but in this spot of His earth they torture people too much. And there is not enough bread for such work . . .' The old man sighed,

In the morning, having received our hats and boots, we walked up-hill with old and dull axes in our hands. There were not many of us, about fifteen men and four guards. The punishment shack inmates worked at lumbering, but this work was a pure formality, since even I could be regarded as a Hercules in comparison to the others.

For the whole day we cut about two cubic metres of lumber, not counting what was used to keep up the fires – ours and the separate one for the guards. Against expectation, the treatment of the prisoners by the guards was not worse than that prevalent throughout the camp. They swore as usual, but more from a sense of duty than for pleasure. They did not beat the prisoners, and did not drive them.

About midday another soldier came and brought a sack of bread, cut into one-pound portions. Then two prisoners from the camp, accompanied by a guard, brought a pail of cold, freezing gruel and five or six bowls for all of us. This was our combined breakfast and lunch. We dipped the bowls directly into the pail for the gruel, and ate it with the aid of the bread and our fingers, since spoons were not given to punishment-cell prisoners. Several lucky men received their portion of gruel last and were therefore able to warm it over the fire before eating. Those who did not work, remaining in the shack all day, received only bread in the evening, a half-pound each, which, together with melted snow, constituted their entire daily ration. I cannot say that this method of dining and the quantity of food received pleased either my appetite or my esthetic sensibility.

Work ended approximately two hours after lunch, when everyone settled around the fire for the rest of the day. All these men, each a political, had already reached the degree of exhaustion which leaves only one way open – to the grave . . .

My neighbour of the previous night turned out to be a little old man of about sixty, dressed even worse than the rest, although it would be difficult to imagine that any clothes could be worse than those worn by the group. He was in camp, but he knew neither the article of the Criminal Code under which he had been sentenced, nor the term of his imprisonment. When I wondered at it, he replied:

'No one told me, and I did not ask. And why should I know, sonny? How much longer can I live here anyway? Perhaps two or three months. It is time to die. And I am not frightened of dying. I've lived out my lifetime in the world, now it is time to take my rest. But for those like you, it is much harder. You're young, you have not seen enough of life and trouble. But don't you fear, sonny, you'll live,' he concluded with unexpected certainty. 'And you'll be happy yet.'

The old man enjoyed everyone's affection, and even the guards were indulgent to him. Once, when a soldier uttered an especially long and obscene oath, the old man came over to him and said:

'There, now, why do you swear like that, son? What's the good of it? You'll get used to swearing, and what will it bring you to? You're still young, soon you will marry, have children, and you will have the habit and continue swearing so that all good folks will shun you!'

'Go along, daddy,' the guard replied. 'Don't forget to whom you're talking! Where do you think you are?'

'In Kolyma, they say, sonny. Why?'

'Not in Kolyma, but in a concentration camp, and you are a counter-revolutionary and an enemy of the Soviet government.'

'God be with you, darling, I am nobody's enemy. As for the camp, what difference does it make, the camp or any other place? The sun shines everywhere, and everywhere there are people.'

'All right, there's no sense wasting my time in talking to you. Get to the fire, daddy.' The guard ended the conversation, and turned to the others with embarrassment.

In the evening, gathering firewood, we descended to the shack, threw the wood down in the yard, and repeated the same procedure of undressing and going barefoot across the snow to bring it in. I was one of those elected for the run.

Thus one day followed another. This was now almost the lowest ebb of camp life. I felt that I was beginning to sink into apathy, into indifference to everything – the surest symptom of giving way. Even the purely animal sense of hunger somehow lost its potency. I ceased washing myself – although in fact all I could do was to rub myself down with a bit with snow on arriving in the forest. I no longer noticed the revolting atmosphere of the punishment shack, its filth, smell, or cold. The strongest human instinct – that of self-preservation – became somehow atrophied for the time being. And yet I would not admit the logic of the four criminals who remained in the shack to preserve their strength, since being out in the fresh and clean air of the woods seemed to me the only possible condition of aliveness. I became noticeably weaker, but it did not worry me too much. Several days after my coming to the punishment shack one man died, then two others. On the days following their deaths – they usually died at night – the old priest always remained in the shack to pray over the corpses until the arrival of the sanitary workers who took them away. He was regarded as a somewhat abnormal eccentric, and on those days the guards gave him the usual portion of those who worked – one whole pound of bread.

Then he also died – though not in the shack but in the woods. He sat silently at the fire, his head bowed over his hands. When we all rose to return to our cell, he remained seated. Someone touched him, and he fell over. The guard came and looked at him.

'Daddy is done for. Leave him here. Tomorrow they'll take him away.' And we went down, not knowing just when the old man had died. We were even more depressed and heavy of heart than usual – everyone was used to the old man and fond of him.

In the morning, when we returned to the forest, the corpse was lying as we left it, covered with the thin layer of snow that had fallen overnight. It was only at dinnertime that men from the camp came to carry the body away.

One day we were not taken out to work. Instead, we were given hats and felt boots and lined up in the square before the punishment shack. The camp commandant and two other officials came from the camp and critically examined everyone. I and two others were ordered to step aside. The rest were driven off into the woods, but we were told:

'Soon the washing season starts – there's no sense in your loafing here. Go to the camp. Tomorrow is rest day, and the day after to-morrow you'll go to work at ditch-digging.'

This news neither grieved nor gladdened me. I was indifferent to everything. Descending to the camp, we met a group of three men who were being shoved and angrily cursed at by a guard as he led them to the punishment shack.

9. AT THE BOTTOM

I HAD come to the most critical period of my life in camp. At times I felt that I was losing the last remnants of resistance to camp conditions and was surely becoming a typical *dokhodyága*, a candidate for death – a member of the corporation of wicks who had become so numerous in Kolyma in 1938–9.

On my return from the punishment cell I went to the camp barber shop. But when I looked in the mirror, the figure that looked back at me filled me with terror. I saw an old man of indeterminate age, pale, emaciated and bearded, in broken glasses tied over the nose with a string, with a still swollen right cheek, wearing an old hat that once was made of fur and a filthy quilted coat. It was most disconcerting to realize that this suspicious looking person was none other than myself.

This realization awakened in me a burst of energy. From the barber shop I proceeded to the baths, although it was not yet the turn of my tent to bathe and I was obliged to raise a scandal to be allowed in. In the baths I was lucky. By some odd accident, my upper clothing disappeared: either someone had put it on by mistake, or else it was lost. Everyone had already left the building, but I still sat by the stove in my underwear, waiting for some clothes. Suddenly a young fellow came in, nattily dressed in a new outfit, with a yellow leather officer's belt tightly drawn across his cotton quilted jacket, in new felt boots and fur mittens reaching to his elbows. At first he passed me by with a mere glance, then he returned, looked again. I recognized an old acquaintance, a brigadier over a group of carpenters who had worked for me in Khattynakh when I was foreman.

He greeted me very warmly. He had been assigned to our camp a week earlier and, as one of the privileged prisoners – he was a former book-keeper imprisoned for a large embezzlement – was immediately appointed a warehouse-keeper in charge of clothing and food supplies.

He ordered a new set of clothing for me and invited me to come to see him later in the evening, promising to arrange something for me.

For a long time I had not felt as well as I did that evening when I returned from the depot with several cans of preserves, a loaf of white bread and a bottle of liquor, and had a party on my bed, to which I invited Kachanov and two or three other friends.

This apparently insignificant incident roused me from the dull lethargy into which I had sunk. To feel myself washed, shaved, in new clothes, even if of standard camp style – and also well-fed and slightly drunk – what could have been better?

And on the following morning I was already going out to work with a brigade of *dokhodyágas*. This brigade worked on the construction of a new ditch, passing high over the pits. There were many men, but little order. The workers were all selected; merely to move from place to place was a problem to them, let alone to work.

I liked the work. It was not difficult. We were not shouted at much since the foremen knew it was a futile effort -- everyone was too weak. Although snow still lay everywhere, the sun was becoming warmer. The air was pure and fresh.

In those days one often saw people in camp who stood on all fours, growling and rooting about in the filthy garbage near the tents and, especially near the kitchen, looking for anything even remotely edible and devouring it on the spot. They had become semi-idiots whom no amount of beating could drive from the refuse heaps.

Although it was already quite warm – only at night did the temperature fall below zero – these wicks did not work but dozed all day by the fires. At all times there were ten or twelve of them sitting there without speaking, their spades placed under them for greater comfort, their dirty gnarled fingers stretched to the fire, their eyes closed with pleasure. Only from time to time would there be a hoarse exclamation: 'I'll trade a herring for a slice of bread!' or 'I'll trade a match box of makhorka for a herring!' Occasionally one of them would respond to an advantageous offer and the deal would be made at once. If anyone lit a cigarette, ten voices would rise at once, begging for the butt. And then it would be smoked until it burned the lips. For the first time I saw these people use a new method of smoking: one would pull on the cigarette, and then exhale the smoke into the open mouth of his neighbour, who would try, choking and gulping, to breathe in all of the processed smoke. The tobacco situation at the mine was quite difficult.

I had been working on the ditch for nearly a month when I was called to the office one evening and told that I would be sent elsewhere on the following day. I was not informed where I was to go.

On the following morning, when roll call was over, the elder told me to join a group of about ten workers standing at the side. I knew some of them and understood what my new occupation would be: I was assigned to the grave-digging brigade.

We started out, past the mine, past the punishment shack, uphill to the mound. Our tools were stored in a small booth. A wide square was cleared of snow, and in it two pits were dug, about ten by thirty feet. One of them was shallow, apparently it had been just begun, but the other was finished and already – nearly full. Standing at the edge, I saw clearly the outlines of the corpses under the layer of lime. A barrel with lime stood near by, ready for use.

We began to work, drilling vertical holes arranged in chessboard order, in the unfinished pit. When the holes were about three feet deep, they were charged with ammonal and blasted, after which we had to clear away the earth and rock, and drill again. The work proceeded quietly, and slowly. There were no guards about, and the workers were all fine fellows. The blasting was done once every two days. A huge bonfire was always burning near by, and we spent a good half of the working day sitting by it. I fell to talking with the senior grave-digger, a cheerful young man.

'I am a veteran grave-digger,' he told me. 'Even before I came to Tumanny, I buried men at the Berzin mine. The mine was a large one – at that time it employed six or seven thousand prisoners. The camp had to have one grave-digger, and I used my connections to get the job. What a life that was! No worries, no troubles, no control of any kind. The work was easy enough. In 1936 I buried only three men, in 1937, four. What a job! In the summer I picked berries and toasted myself in the sun. The output was always one hundred per cent, the food was fine . . . And though I was not socially preferred, I was considered something of a camp official. The criminals hate to dig graves.'

'And how was it last year? And now?' I asked.

The veteran grave-digger only shrugged his shoulders.

'Now there is almost no difference between working here at grave-digging, and slaving in the mine, except that you are not being pushed around. The work is the same as everywhere else – they drive you to death. Last year there were four of us, then six, and by winter we had fifteen men. Last year we dug more than ten pits.'

'And how many corpses go into one pit?' I asked.

'That depends. As many as it will take. Sometimes thirty, sometimes more. In summer, though, they swell up too much, you can't keep the graves open too long. And the smell, of course . . .'

The man exuded an atmosphere of philosophic serenity.

On my third day with the grave-diggers two corpses were brought in a sleigh from the camp morgue. We left our work and went to the other pit. Wrapped in dirty blankets, the corpses were dragged from the sleigh to the edge of the pit. The blankets were pulled off and we saw that the bodies were naked. Small woollen plaques with their names and camp numbers written on them in indelible pencil were dangling from their necks. Someone brought a rope with a noose which was thrown over the legs of the first corpse. The other end of the rope was thrown across the ditch. Another rope was slipped over the corpse's neck and two men on the other side began to pull the cord holding the legs. We kept the head on our side. When the workers across the ditch caught the legs, they loosened the noose and the two teams began to lower the body into the pit. It settled neatly over the others, the ropes were pulled away, and the same procedure was repeated with the second corpse. After that the sleigh left – with its blankets – and two of us poured freshly slaked lime over the bodies until the outlines lost their sharpness.

Then we rested, smoked, and returned to drilling holes in the new pit.

'It is lucky we have enough lime nowadays,' said the veteran grave-digger. 'Last summer we had no lime for six weeks – it was hard to catch your breath.'

'Do they notify the relatives when someone dies?' I asked. 'What do you think?'

'I know that they don't. In the camp they make a record that prisoner so-and-so died of such-and-such an illness and send the information to Magadan where his name is struck from the lists. If it was a political prisoner, his death is reported to the N.K.V.D. in Moscow. And that is the end of it. But the prisoner's name is not always known in camp. Think of yourself, for instance – you worked on the ditch, did you know many of the men by second name?'

'No, hardly anyone,' I admitted.

'There, you see. You worked with people for a whole month and did not know them. How then can the camp supervisor know everyone by sight, when there are five thousand men? Especially when all the wicks and *dokhodyágas* look exactly alike?'

This was difficult to dispute. However, I still asked:

'But what do they do when it is necessary to send the name to Magadan so that it might be crossed off the lists?'

'Oh, there is a special category of unascertainables. Imagine that it is war time: a bomb falls and blows up ten men into bits. Who can find out their names? Nobody. And so it is here, too.'

And indeed, the man's logic was incontrovertible. I had no reply to it. At war it is the external enemy that is destroyed, in the camp – the internal enemy. The essential facts are the same. A corpse would be brought to us, under the mound, thrown into the pit, covered with lime – and that was the end of it. To seek out the name of the particular scoundrel who died, and then go to the trouble of informing his family – well, that would contradict all the fundamental traditions of the Soviet government and its punitive policies.

The work was easier than ditch-digging, but naturally, I did not like it. It went against the grain to handle the corpses, though not too many of them were brought while I was there – in the course of two weeks we buried seven men.

It was becoming warmer. Despite the lime, the pit with the corpses gave off the sickening, sweetly sour smell of putrefaction, not very strong but persistent. The last corpses were lowered directly into the water which had filled the pit as the snow melted under the rays of the spring sun. By the time we finished the new grave, about nine feet deep, the old one was full and we covered it with earth. At the same time as the snow melted, we added earth to the previous year's graves which were marked by hollows filled with water.

Finally, I could not endure this type of work any longer. One

evening I went to see the camp commandant and asked to be transferred.

'Why? Is the work difficult?' He was genuinely astonished.

'No, it is not difficult, but I don't like it. Send me to lumbering.'

'No, that I cannot do. Spring is here, and any day now the washing
season will start and all work will fold up except mining . . .'

'And grave-digging under the mound,' I slipped out imprudently.

The commandant looked at me, wanted to say something, but
restrained himself. Then he gave me an odd glance and said:

'Yes, mining and grave-digging. Exactly. From these two jobs we
shall not remove any workers. You can choose whichever you prefer.'

'Very well, send me to the mine,' I said.

Apparently the commandant did not expect this answer, since grave-
digging is far easier despite its unpleasantness. He looked through some
lists and said:

'As you wish. But look out, hold your tongue among the prisoners
concerning the cemetery business! You'll go into a mine brigade . . .
No, wait. You worked on the ditch last year, didn't you?'

'Yes, I did.'

'Good. I'll suggest to the section head that he give you another ditch-
diggers' brigade.'

'No, Citizen Commandant, not for anything in the world. I want to
be only a common worker. I am not yet tired of living. And I'll be able
to work.'

'Afraid of being shot?' he asked with a wry grin.

'Maybe. . . . I'll accept no responsibility,' I said firmly.

'The devil with you. There will be six of you. The Kuznetsov
section needs a ditch-digging team. Look up Sokolov in the third tent
and tell him I sent you. Tomorrow you'll join the team at roll call.'

I found Sokolov, and the following day we went to work in a
distant sector headed by Kuznetsov, my boss of the previous year.
We received two pairs of high rubber boots, still quite new, shovels and
special picks up to three feet long, for the ditch work. Soon we were
going full blast, standing knee-deep, and deeper, in the icy water of
the central ditch. I had become accustomed to this work the previous
year, and it did not tire me too much. Its great advantage was that it
was not measurable and we were not expected to produce any norm of
cubic metres. Therefore, we were not driven on like the rest of the
miners. It is true that sitting on the job was also impossible if one
wanted to avoid unpleasantness, but if one remained in the ditch, one
could take a rest leaning against its wall and smoking all one wished.

I was certain that if I was not removed from the ditch, I would be
quite capable of surviving the summer, even on the usual half-hungry
ration. The only risk I faced, and that quite consciously, was contract-

ing acute rheumatism. But there was nothing to be done about it.

The situation in the mine was a close repetition of what had taken place the preceding year. The mine had expanded and now employed more than six thousand men. The only difference was that now the overwhelming majority of them were *dokhodyágas*, to a greater or lesser degree; the percentage of real workers of the old-style Kolymans was three or four times lower than the previous year.

One day I had a talk with the norm-setter of the mine's Planning Section – a free employee. He told me that the productivity of labour in the pits was approximately three-fourths of that of the preceding year, and only one-fourth of that of 1937. The situation was partly corrected by the presence of three excavators which managed to do some of the work despite the difficulties of operating in perpetually frozen soil. I asked how the large 'Marion' excavator of American origin, imported a year earlier, was functioning. He thought for a while.

'Marion, Marion . . . I remember we had one by that name. But where is it? Last year I heard that it was working poorly and very little: some mistakes had been made in assembling it, then there was some breakage, and it stopped working altogether. I have no idea where it is now, though I know all our sections . . .'

'I remember it was said last year that it was paid for in gold, something like $20,000, apart from transport costs,' I remarked.

'I know. I was a member of the procurement commission. But you may kill me – I cannot recall where it is.' And getting up from the over-turned wheelbarrow by the ditch on which he had been sitting, the excited norm-setter went off somewhere. I followed him with my eyes and then returned to poking about in the muddy water.

Two days later I saw him again. He came to where I worked and sat down on the embankment.

'You've started something now. There is quite a mess. I ran through every mine looking for the excavator, and then reported to the director that it had disappeared. He raised everyone to their feet and now we are all running about searching for it . . .'

I burst out laughing. The supposition that a huge excavator could disappear without a trace from a relatively small gold field seemed extremely amusing. The fact that picks and shovels, wheelbarrows and wagons were lost by the hundreds in the blasting operations, to the complete indifference of everyone, that the rails of the mechanical tracks rusted through and vanished under piles of rock and ore, that building timber was burned in the ovens and boilers – all this was perfectly normal and taken for granted in every Soviet enterprise. But an excavator! A huge, expensive imported machine! This was too much even for the camp administration. No one could have stolen it, especially since, when it was last seen, it was inactive, broken by unskilled mechanics. Besides, who would steal an excavator at the gold fields!

Looking at me with chagrin, the norm-setter said:

'Well, what are you laughing at? Do you know what trouble this might mean for me? I was one of three persons who signed the inventory of October the first, certifying the presence of a "Marion" excavator at the mine. And now it is not here. It is true that formally the warehouse-keeper of the 3rd Section is responsible for it, but the trouble is that he was transferred six months ago to the new Western Mining Administration, and the transfer was so hurried that he had no time to explain all his affairs to the new man. And now no one can say who will be answerable.'

I understood all that, knowing the system of complicated book-keeping controls in Soviet institutions, a system which, however, was quite powerless to eliminate the crying inefficiency everywhere. And yet the very fact of the disappearance of an excavator was too ludicrous!

This affair occupied the entire camp administration for quite some time. The search for the vanished machine remained without success. To divest itself of responsibility, the authorities officially demanded, in a special letter to Dalstroy, that criminal charges be brought against the former warehouse-keeper who was now in the West, and who was less guilty than anyone else for the loss, since his responsibility was purely nominal. Some time later we learned that the warehouse-keeper was sentenced to three years in camp – he was a free employee.

The puzzle of the excavator's disappearance was cleared up in the fall, and then quite by accident. The geologists found that one of the previous year's dumps was lying on ground with a high gold content, and it was necessary to carry it to a new place, which had already been mined. One of the new excavators was assigned to this work since the earth to be moved was not frozen hard and therefore the excavator could be of use. One day the scoop of the excavator caught against something in the dump and broke; the men began to dig, and found, under a solid layer of earth, the vanished 'Marion', thoroughly rusty and battered. How this huge machine could have been buried under the refuse without anyone seeing it or taking note remained a mystery. In the field records the excavator was written off as iron scrap. And I have never learned what became of the hapless warehouse-keeper.

Occasionally I received letters from my mother. They took a long time to reach me, sometimes two months, and many were lost on the way. Mother sent me food packages, very small ones, with some toast, makhorka, a tiny bit of lard. Knowing her own difficulties, I soon wrote to her to stop sending them. Her sacrifice was especially senseless since most of the food was stolen without shame or pity. All packages went through the hands of an official in the Khattynakh post office, one of the 'socially elect', who checked them. As a result, the addressee received only a part of the package, at best, and very often nothing at all. All the loot was divided among the foolers by the camp administration and constituted a considerable part of their income. Out of two packages from my mother, I received only toast. Two were lost altogether, and only one, very small and meagre in content, actually came intact.

About that time I had a minor adventure which broke to some extent the monotony of my existence.

One day, after lunch, when I was already digging in the muddy ditch, a certain N.K.V.D. official appeared in the next field. He walked unsteadily and seemed to be bestially drunk. His cap was gone, his blouse was unbuttoned, and his eyes wandered over the field. Glancing sidelong at him from time to time, I continued to work.

Suddenly his eye was caught by three bowls lying on the ground. These bowls were often used by the workers to bring back the gruel received at lunch so that they might eat it in the relative quiet of the field instead of the crowded and noisy open-air summer dining-room. Walking up to these bowls, the official kicked them so violently with his boot that they rolled away in all directions and he apparently hurt his foot.

'Who brought these bowls to the field, you damned contras?' he bellowed.

Everyone remained silent, concentrating on the work.

'Who brought them, I am asking again, you scum, bandits, scoundrels . . .' he continued to yell drunkenly, peppering his shouts with choice expletives. The men kept quiet. Then he pulled out his revolver from its holster.

'Oh, so you're silent, you bastards. Who is the brigadier? Tell me, or I'll shoot you all like dogs! You were brought here for counter-revolution, and you start out here by stealing Socialist property!' he shouted, pointing at the tin bowls. The brigadier approached him.

'I am listening, Citizen Chief . . .' he spoke falteringly.

'So you are the brigadier, you blasted bandit!' the hero yelled, unsteadily pushing his left fist into the brigadier's face. 'Tell me at once who stole these bowls from the mess hall?'

'No one stole them, Citizen Chief. They'll be taken back at once.'

'Shut up, you scoundrel!' squealed the official. 'If you don't point out the thieves at once, I'll kill you on the spot!' And he shoved the muzzle of the revolver into the brigadier's face for greater emphasis. The brigadier grew noticeably pale.

'Here is one,' he said, pointing to a worker, 'and the others I have not noticed . . .'

'So it is you, bastard!' The official walked unsteadily up to the worker at whom the brigadier pointed and grabbed him by the throat.

Then he pushed him, but lost his own balance, swayed and fell. This
filled him with altogether uncontrollable rage. Yelling something, he
raised himself up and suddenly began to shoot. Once, twice, three
times. Suddenly I felt that something singed my right leg. I looked
down – there was a hole in the rubber boot. When I turned down the
boot, there was blood, though not too much of it. The bullet only
grazed the skin. Guards and other officials came running. A group
gathered around the N.K.V.D. man, who was helped up. Two workers
lay on the ground. The drunk was led off, then the two were carried
away. One worker was killed outright, the other was wounded. Climbing out of the ditch, I walked up to the section boss, Kuznetsov,
limping slightly.

'What do you want?' He turned to me.

'I have also been injured a little, Citizen Chief,' I said, turning down
the boot and showing my wound.

'The scum . . .' he muttered. 'All right, go back to camp and take a
rest today and tomorrow. Here is a note to the guards to let you in.'
He wrote a few words on the slip of paper he tore from his notebook.

Happy at the respite, I returned to camp, almost forgetting my
wound. I did not even trouble to go to the infirmary, but made my
own bandage. This was indeed a happy incident. I gave Kuznetsov's
note to the overseer so that I would not be awakened in the morning
to report at roll call.

Nevertheless, I was awakened, though a little later. The overseer
stood before me:

'Get up!' he ordered.

'But I am excused from work today. You know it!' I argued.

'You are not going to the mine. A car is leaving now for Khattynakh, to pick up some iron and we need three loaders. It is an urgent
business and we have no free men. You'll rest tomorrow . . .'

I was not even listening to him as I hastily pulled on my boots. A
trip to Khattynakh! What could be better!

Fifteen minutes later I was on the way, in the truck, and after an
hour and a half we were in the depot territory in Khattynakh. Pulling
up to the pile of iron prepared for our field, we began to load the truck.
The driver fussed around the motor, which was somewhat out of order
– or perhaps this was only an excuse – and then declared that we would
not go back until evening. No one argued with that, and when we
finished loading, I walked out to Khattynakh where I had not been
for a year and a half.

The settlement had changed noticeably during that period. There
was a row of buildings which had not been there in my time; buildings
which had been begun when I was there were now finished and there
were many other new ones in various stages of construction.

I found the Building Section which was now in another, larger tent.

Opening the door, not without a certain agitation, I saw a large room filled with people. Men sat, as of old, behind tables and drawing boards, but, apart from Sukhanov and one other man, everyone was new and unknown to me. Waiting until Sukhanov was free, I approached him. I am afraid he took me for a ghost from another world, for his face expressed utter amazement.

'Do you recognize me?' I asked.

'Of course. But how did you get here?'

I explained.

'Well, tell me how your affairs are going.'

I told him briefly about myself, about what had happened since our last meeting when I was lying under the heap of rocks on the dump in Tumanny, and I thanked him for his help.

'Oh, nonsense,' he waved me away. 'What is there to be thankful for?'

I asked him not to forget about my existence and to pull me out of the mine if there should be an opportunity.

'I tried,' he answered. 'I've tried several times, but thus far without success. Perhaps in the fall, after the panning season, it will be possible to do something. I always have you in mind. Do you need anything now? . . .' he hinted. I thanked him again and refused, saying that I would take care of all my other problems by myself. Bidding him good-bye, I left.

In the small room off the carpentry shop where once I had lived, I found Stepanov, the shop manager, whose term was soon to end and who therefore enjoyed certain small privileges. Vasya Khudiakov was not there. Long before my visit, he had been arrested and sent to Serpantinnaya, a place from which no one returned. Stepanov invited me to stop by later, in the evening, when he would have some food products prepared for me.

From there I went to the Vodopyanov mine, to my friend who was connected with the mine Supply Section and therefore commanded practically unlimited quantities of the provisions I needed. He received me well. We dined together, discussed various topics. Suddenly he said:

'We have a friend of yours here, from Lower Khattynakh. His name is Prostoserdov. He tells me he knows you.'

'Where? How is he? I never thought he would survive the last year.'

'He survived, but what's the good of that? He has not long to live. He has been on a hunger strike, on artificial feeding, for more than six months. He is in the hospital. If you want to see him, I can arrange it. . . .'

Half an hour later I was admitted to the local hospital which held about ten beds, and on one of these I recognized, or rather guessed, my once energetic, life-loving Menshevik. I came over and sat down on the edge of his bed. He recognized me and nodded. He was a frightening sight. He no longer had any teeth, half of his hair had fallen out, and his state of emaciation was difficult to imagine.

'Well, how do you like me?' Prostoserdov tried to smile. 'There's nothing for it, my friend. They've done me in, finished me off, the bastards . . .'

'Is it worth while to keep on these hunger strikes, Nikolay Nikolaye-vich?' I asked.

'Now it is all the same. Last summer I survived by chance, only because I was hunger striking. And now it will make no difference. If I stop the strike, they will immediately take me to Serpantinnaya. The deputy told me so some time ago. Better to die here, on the bed, than be shot in a hole like a dog . . . And you are still holding up?'

'For the time being,' I answered vaguely. 'Who knows how long it will last.'

'Keep going. Try to get out of this damned camp. Perhaps some day you'll meet my comrades. Tell them there was one Prostoserdov, but he died ingloriously. If only I could kill one of these scoundrels in parting, but I haven't any strength left,' he said, raising his hand with an effort.

'Oh, Nikolay Nikolayevich, it is difficult to survive here. I still have more than two years to go . . .'

'Try! Did you see in the papers about that Georgian scum playing a love and friendship game with Hitler? That means war any day now. It is hard to say who'll outwit whom, but my whole hope is that the dogs will quarrel. Hitler is also a scoundrel of the first order, but he doesn't come up to our Georgian donkey's ankle. He's cunning, the swine . . . Still, perhaps the Germans will string up our Joe. No matter what, our people will be able to breathe easier. I shall not see what is to come, but you try to hold out . . .'

'Would you like me to send any message for you to your friends in Russia?' I asked.

'I am afraid there is no one left. I learned that in 1937–8 everyone was shot mercilessly. And even if anyone survived . . . No, it is better not to. Perhaps you will now come out of the tent and they'll pull you in by the collar and demand to know what I said. Thanks. I trust you, but my mind is easier this way. Unless you meet a Socialist some day by accident – then you can tell him about me. And now you had better go. . . .'

We said goodbye. Outside the tent the medical assistant was sitting in the sun and I approached him.

'What is Prostoserdov's condition?' I asked.

'He may last three or four days. Why?'

'Nothing. I merely wanted to know,' I answered, and quickly walked away.

Late in the evening, well loaded with the provisions collected from various old friends, I returned to Tumanny and arranged a real feast for my friends. The supervisor kept his word and did not send me to work on the following day.

Time was passing. I continued to work on the ditch. It was not easy, but it was less exhausting than the mine. The rains came. Men pushed wheelbarrows along wet and slippery gangways, fell and injured themselves. They returned to the tents late, wet to the bone, and went out to work again on the following day in the rain and in clothes that had not dried overnight. I still managed to hold my own, although the rheumatism which I contracted in the ditch became ever more severe.

Finally, the rains became continuous. The water in the ditches, especially in the upper drainage ditch, rose with menacing speed; the previous year's experience, when the ditch was built, had been disregarded since it has been thought that the rise in the water level had been unusually high that year. The mine was again in danger of being flooded.

One day, running past us, the section chief Kuznetsov ordered our entire team to follow him at once. As we walked, he continued to remove men from their work until he had more than a hundred workers. Finally we came to the upper ditch, where the water had already reached the banks and was obviously still rising.

'Take all these men under your command,' Kuznetsov ordered me, 'and warn everyone that if the water overflows into the pits, every second man will be sent to Serpantinnaya.'

With these words he left. The situation was clear and there was no need for discussion.

Briefly explaining to the workers what was to be done, I told them about Kuznetsov's threat. A part of the squad began to cut out slabs of turf from the surrounding land, several men were sent to prepare wooden poles, and the rest carried the turf and laid it in rows along the threatened bank, raising and reinforcing it.

The rain poured down without let-up and the length of the endangered bank grew as the water rose. Kuznetsov came running again and I asked him to send more men, since the number at my disposal was insufficient to stem the tide.

'How many do you need?' he asked.

'For the time being, fifty. And another fifty by evening if the rain does not stop.'

'Very well. You'll have the men at once. But hold it back, Petrov, I beg you. We are stopping work in the lower sectors. In one place a ditch was broken through, in another a pit was flooded and the dykes were carried away.'

He ran back. Soon more workers arrived and we continued our

efforts, paying no attention to the rain. In the meantime the men who were sent to the woods began to bring in the poles. These were thrown across the ditch and driven into the semi-liquid earth, reinforcing the threatened bank.

It was already growing dark when a whole group of people headed by the mine director, Svirin, came to our work site. They stood and watched us. I approached them.

'Will you hold back the water?' Svirin asked.

'For the time being it is held. What will happen later is hard to tell . . .'

'In an hour you'll get a relief shift – the men from the flooded pits are resting now. Keep on the job those who work best, who are needed most, and dismiss the others. You will remain here – the ditch is your responsibility. Supper will be brought. How many men will you need?'

'Two hundred for the night. If I need more, I'll let you know. Tell them in the camp to send out an additional hundred in case of emergency,' I said, feeling myself the master of the situation.

The officials left, and I sent half of the men to the forest for firewood. When the new shift came, a series of fires were blazing along the bank, illuminating the area and permitting the men to warm themselves from time to time. Several pails of gruel and supplementary bread were brought, and everyone dined well on the generous portions.

All night, almost without sitting down, I had to supervise the work of the men who evinced a quite natural tendency to stay by the fires and doze, despite the rain. Before dawn Kuznetsov came running, greatly concerned about the ditch. I was able to reassure him to some extent.

'I am afraid the whole field will have to stop work tomorrow,' he said. 'In the 5th Sector a huge waterfall poured into the pit. Look here, Petrov, all our hopes rest on you. I'll be back in an hour. Do you need more men? Now we have as many as you want, and tomorrow I'll have two thousand on my sector, if necessary.'

'We'll manage till morning, and then send us a new shift, as early as you can. About three hundred men.'

'Even a thousand. Well, hold out!' He disappeared into the darkness.

By morning the water level in the accursed ditch again began to rise and I had to detain the night workers for a couple of hours even after the arrival of the new shift. Everyone was wet and angry.

Below, on the sector, the work went on at full speed. It was obvious that nearly half of the field's workers were now there. Several of us were brought breakfast, far better than the usual one, and before noon Kuznetsov came again, accompanied by the warehouse-keeper.

'We are issuing alcohol,' he announced. 'The men will come one by one!'

That was a clever idea. Every man received three ounces of alcohol –

a solid portion that soon raised the spirits of the rain-soaked, exhausted workers. After the distribution, Kuznetsov called me over and said, giving me the bottle:

'This is for you. If more is needed, I'll send it again in the evening. Only try to hold it back . . .'

'Order a good dinner to be brought,' I said. 'What are they doing at the field?'

'My sector is the only one working. I have 1,500 men today. Oh yes, there is news: yesterday Soviet troops entered Poland . . .'

'Is it war?' I asked, recalling Prostoserdov's words.

'Not exactly, but something like it . . .'

However, there was no opportunity to think about the war. The accursed ditch was barely holding.

'Citizen Chief, send us some empty sacks, the more the better. The turf cannot hold the water.'

'Good. I'll send some men to the warehouse at once.'

At that moment a worker came running from the mine, shouting:

'Citizen Chief, go down. Pavlov himself is here. He is inspecting the pits . . .' Kuznetsov hurriedly ran down.

But he did not forget the sacks. Soon they brought us two large piles of them. I assigned some of the men to filling them with clay which others were digging right there, and the rest were bringing turf and poles. I was quite hoarse with shouting, and I hardly noticed the rain.

Someone said that a leak had broken through the side of the ditch in one place. I went to inspect it and found that the break was considerable: the most unpleasant aspect of the situation was that the leak could not be repaired from the outside. I ordered poles to be driven in, lowering them into the water of the ditch, on the inner side, and filling in the space thus formed with sacks of clay. However, the leak did not stop, although it grew no larger.

Suddenly I saw a whole company coming up from the mine, led by Pavlov, who was known throughout Kolyma by his extraordinary height and size. He came to the place where we worked and stopped.

'Oh, there is a leak here. The water may flood the mine any moment now. Who is in charge here?'

Kuznetsov pointed at me.

'Hey you, look sharp – if the ditch breaks through, things won't look so well for you. Drive in new poles! Get busy! The devil take you all!'

I did not need his threat to know that things might turn out badly for us. In the presence of the authorities the men moved about with unprecedented energy. Pavlov watched our work, then gave a shout:

'At this rate it will take you three years, you stupid devils. Get into the ditch yourselves and pack down the sacks!'

'It is cold, Citizen Chief,' someone ventured to say.

'Cold? Oh, you . . .' He swore, went to the edge of the ditch and jumped into the water fully clothed.

'Hand me the sacks, quick, you miserable wicks!' he roared.

The sacks were passed on one after the other. I felt the awkwardness of my position and climbed down into the water after Pavlov. There we stood, the icy water reaching to our chests. We lowered the sacks and packed them down with our feet and with long poles.

'The leak has stopped,' someone in Pavolov's retinue shouted to us, and we climbed out of the ditch. Pavlov looked about him with triumphant self-satisfaction.

'That's how work should be done!' he said, leaving the site in the company of the other officials.

'It is easy for you to talk,' I thought, emptying the water from my boots and trying to wring my shirt and trousers as I sat on a log near a large bonfire. 'You will go back to a house now, change to dry clothes, fill yourself with liquor, and the devil may take the rest of the world . . .'

The infernal rain was still coming down – it was the third day of continuous downpour.

An hour later Kuznetsov came again with some alcohol. He was quite tipsy himself. He told me that work was halted in nearly all the northern mines, and that Pavlov had commended him.

The second sleepless night came. Despite the liquor, I could barely move my feet. One of the workers said to me:

'What are you knocking yourself out for? Open the side of the ditch and let the water flood down – let them choke on it there. What need do you have for this damned gold?'

Strictly speaking, he was right. I had no reason to exert myself. However, nature had its way, and in my twenty-three years I had not yet reached that age of wisdom.

Toward morning the rain stopped, and Kuznetsov, beaming as if it were his birthday, allowed me to return to camp, together with the bottle which still held about a pint of alcohol. Coming to the tent, and barely managing to undress, I dropped into my bed and fell asleep.

I did not go to work for three days – which was the highest possible reward under camp conditions. In addition, I received a new blouse and trousers, and all the participants in the expedition received, collectively, one bottle of liquor.

At the end of September there was another special rest day – the day of the all-Union census, although it had reached us rather late. All movement of men was stopped, and everywhere there were reinforced patrols. We were lined up into a long queue before the camp office where a few men were admitted at a time. In the office there sat five or six men from Khattynakh, filling up the census cards. The cards were uniform and nothing in them indicated that the registered man was a camp inmate, except, perhaps, for the tiny cross which was made in the right-hand corner by the interviewer when the man questioned replied that he was a prisoner.

It was becoming colder and colder. Snow fell. Although Dalstroy had fallen far behind the gold-output plan – it was said that the 1939 plan called for 250 tons of gold – no preparations were made for winter washing that year.

It is true that the panning continued to the very last day, until the water in the upper ditch was completely frozen. Then everything was stopped and all workers were sent to the usual winter works: preparation of the auriferous sands for the following season, lumbering, building. No more was heard about shootings. Apparently they had ceased. No new reinforcements came from the mainland and men were dying off quietly – not too intensively, but at a steady rate.

When the summer work in the mine was over, I was sent far from the camp to the forest, where a brigade of carpenters was preparing materials for the construction of a new house. Our work site was more than twenty miles from the camp, and we therefore lived where we worked, in a low, soot-blackened barrack, without windows, and lit by a kerosene lamp. It was almost completely hidden under the piled-up snow.

Life here was quieter and easier than life in the camp – there were no guards, no overseers. We worked moderately, from dawn till dark. Firewood was abundant. We kept warm, and the men were not bad fellows. Yet my mood was growing darker every day.

My closest friends among the workers were two still young men who had until recently been in the armed forces – one as a senior lieutenant in the Far-Eastern Army, the other as an important official of the Moscow Voyentorg, the central procurement organization serving the Soviet officers. Both were sent to camp during the purge which swept the Red Army after the famous conspiracy of the Soviet Marshals – Tukhachevsky, Yegorov, Yakir, Uborevich and the others who were shot in 1937. The purge liquidated – by shooting and imprisonment – not less than 80 per cent of the entire commanding personnel of the Red Army, from majors up. Perhaps this was part of the reason for the disgraceful failures of the Red Army during its attack on Finland, the muted echoes of which reached even us. Few of the arrested officers were sent to Kolyma; most of them were imprisoned in specially organized camps with a particularly severe regime.

I gradually grew closer to my comrades, the former army men, Andrey K. and Nikolay B., while we worked in the forest. Later, when we knew each other better, Nikolay asked me whether I would like to escape from the camp and from Kolyma. While he served in the Far-Eastern Army, he had at one time taken part in punitive expeditions against gangs of escaped prisoners and peasants who had fled from the collectivization. Knowing the Siberian taiga very well, he was certain that he could reach the places inhabited by free men, somewhere in the Yakutsk region. He told me that Andrey also wanted to join him and that they had already prepared one pair of skis and would soon have another pair. They also had a compass and a small reserve of food.

Although I was fully aware of the enormous difficulty of escape across the vast distances and the possibility of pursuit, in my state of desperation I was ready to take the risk. I had much more at stake than Nikolay and Andrey: they still faced about eight years of concentration camp each, while I had only one year to go. In case of capture, if we were not beaten to death by the guards or torn by the savage blood-hounds which constantly accompanied them, our term would be lengthened by three years. To them the difference was not great, since it was obvious that it would be impossible to last even half of their terms under current camp conditions, but to me three additional years meant very much. Moreover, they were far stronger than I was physically, not having spent all their strength as yet in gold mining. I was somewhat concerned about the season of the year, but Nikolay assured me that in the summer flight was not possible, both because of the swamps and impassable bogs which abound in Siberia, and because of the mosquitoes and gnats which were a constant torment even in camp.

I argued that at the first encounter with natives, they would seize us and deliver us back to the camp, since it was known that the admini-stration paid large rewards for every returned fugitive, not in money, but in even more tempting alcohol. This alcohol caused whole tribes to die out, but this did not diminish their uncontrollable greed for it.

Finally they convinced me, or rather I convinced myself. We began preparations for the escape. Andrey made skis for everyone, secreting himself away in the woods to do the work. We laid in a store of food, matches and liquor, exchanging our last valuable things for these com-modities. When I made one of my regular trips to camp for food supplies for the entire brigade, I made every effort to collect from my friends among the free employees some sugar, egg and milk powder, lard, and so on. A warehouse-keeper I knew gave me a pint of alcohol. Preparing for the trek, we almost ceased talking to one another to avoid any possible suspicions among the other workers. Only at night and then in whispers did we talk about our plans. Naturally, we kept all our supplies not in the barrack, but in the forest, under the roots of a large tree felled by a storm.

Finally, everything was ready and we only had to wait for the appropriate moment. It was very important that we should not be missed at once by the others who would report our disappearance in the camp whence a pursuit would be sent immediately.

We were helped by chance. A foreman came from the camp and said that, beginning with the new year, it would be necessary to start new operations in the forest to fell timber for the construction of a camp club, and that it would be necessary to find a suitable site for this work with trees of the proper size. He himself selected my two comrades for the job, instructing them to take along enough food for several days as it was impossible to tell how long the search would take. I volunteered to accompany them, but permission was refused. Then I obtained authorization to return to camp, saying that I was feeling ill and had a high fever. The brigadier granted me the necessary permission. In the camp I found my friend, the warehouse-keeper in charge of supplies, and begged him to secure for me a pass to Khattynakh, where various delicacies were then being distributed to the free employees for the holidays, promising to share with him everything I obtained. For a long time he refused to make use of his influence in the camp office, on the pretext that the commandant was sure to refuse his request since there was no good reason for it. I told him that it was possible to obtain a note from the infirmary that I was going to the Khattynakh hospital for treatment for several days. The warehouse-keeper, who was connected with the medical assistant through various liquor deals, easily obtained the certificate, and I received a week's pass to Khattynakh and back.

With the pass in my hands, I returned to the forest and showed it to my friends. Circumstances were arranging themselves most favourably. We drew up a plan and an itinerary for our escape. In order to go west from Tumanny, it was necessary to cross the highway which connected Khattynakh with Yagodnoye – all familiar places. We agreed that they would start out early in the morning, taking along my skis, and I was to leave later, cross to the gold field, and thence go, by a car travelling in the same direction, to the ridge where we would meet near the pole of the high-voltage line.

I could not fall asleep on the last night before the escape, constantly thinking about the step I had decided upon. However, in the extremely nervous state I was in, I gave no thought to what awaited me on the way, and certainly none to what was to be in the unlikely event that the escape succeeded and we reached the Yakutsk region.

Early in the morning of the following day my friends left. I listened to the conversations of the other workers: no one entertained the slightest shadow of suspicion of flight, or even of its possibility. Somewhat later I left, too. Reaching the field with the sack behind my shoulders, I almost immediately found a truck which was going to the warehouses

of the administration Supply Section, near the Partisan mine, not far
from the spot where we agreed to meet. Several hours later I was
already at the warehouses. Having approximately calculated the time,
I was not in a hurry to go on – I had only two miles to walk to the
ridge. I was allowed to go into the watchman's quarters to warm up.
The people were all strangers, but they gave me a good meal and a
drink of liquor. All watchmen were from the privileged class.

It was already dark when I was preparing to set out again. The
watchmen came and went. Suddenly one of them ran in with the
joyous announcement that a motion picture was to be shown in the
large office tent and everyone rushed out, forgetting about me. Glancing
about me, I took some watchman's rifle which hung over a bed and
which I had noticed before, and also walked out into the darkness of
the night. The frost was sharp, but I walked rapidly. The road was uphill; and I soon felt warm. An hour later I reached my destination: my
friends, who had come a half-hour earlier, were already waiting for me
at the pole. My new acquisition filled them with enthusiasm. Taking
the rifle from me, Andrey immediately found that it had five cartridges.
That was not much, but better than none.

I put on my skis and we started out, deciding to walk as far as possible during the first night. Fortunately for us, snow began to fall and it
became slightly warmer. Nikolay led the way on skis. I followed, and
Andrey, with the rifle slung over his shoulders, brought up the rear.
Each of us carried on his back a well-filled sack with provisions. We
also had two woollen blankets. My spirits rose. I felt as if we were boys
engaged in some wild prank.

I had not run on skis for a long time and it was somewhat difficult
for me to keep up with Nikolay. However, it was not too dark, despite
the snow clouds, and I clearly saw the tracks of my comrade's skis.

We came to the descent and it became completely easy. From somewhere below I heard Nikolay's voice: 'Come on down! It's safe. There
are no trees!' With a strong push, I slid downhill. Nikolay waited
below. Andrey joined us, we rested for five minutes, and went on . . .

Dawn found us already over the second pass, totally exhausted by
the night's run. Since the snowfall had not stopped, we went into the
depths of a small wood on the slope of a hill and made a fire on which
we boiled tea, heated a large tin of preserves – peas with meat – and
breakfasted with fine appetite. After our meal, banking our fire, we
went to sleep on our blankets.

When dusk fell, Nikolay awakened us. We decided to walk at first
only at night, since it had been said that fugitives were sometimes
pursued by airplanes from which people could easily be spotted in this
totally unpopulated region. The snow covered our tracks, and made
the usual search more difficult.

Quickly making ready to proceed and destroying the traces of our camp, we began to ascend. Despite my high spirits, my body was aching painfully after the previous night's trek, and I was barely able to keep up with my companions, who urged me on and with whom I caught up only on the downhill stretches. While I was catching up with them, they managed to get some rest, and too little time was left for me to recover my breath. I felt that my strength was ebbing rapidly.

We ate twice a day: solidly in the morning, before going to sleep, and lightly in the evening, before setting out.

Gradually I regained my sober senses and began to think more seriously about the step I was undertaking. At the second camp, when, according to Nikolay's calculations, we had already covered not less than 50 miles, I suggested that we check our food reserves. Spreading out the contents of our bags on a blanket and dividing them into rations, we found that the provisions would at most last us for 20 days of travelling. We had to cross about 1,300 miles, roughly computed on the basis of a straight line. However, in the mountainous region this distance was turning out to be greater. And we had enough food to last us for only about 500 miles, if we should continue at the rate of 25 miles a day.

My friends argued with me. They insisted that we could easily cover 30 or even 35 miles a day, that our rifle held five cartridges with which we could shoot some animal, and that, finally, there was 'His Majesty, Chance' which should help. But all this failed to convince me.

'I'll tell you what, my friends, let us speak frankly. In these two days I've found that I am not a fit companion for you. You can cover more ground than I, because you are stronger and healthier, and I will merely delay you. Since you have firmly resolved to escape at any cost, go on and God be with you. But I shall return. If I survive, I'll live. If not – then that's my fate. You know, I have only one year left in camp . . .'

'You are right, Vladimir,' said Nikolay. 'I would not have begun this conversation myself, and we would have gone on together wherever the road might lead us. But since you have brought up the subject, I must agree with you. It will be too difficult for you to make the trip, and you still have some chance to last your term. We do not have this chance . . .'

'All this is true,' remarked Andrey, 'but you are forgetting that Vladimir cannot return to camp, that he will have been missed and will inevitably get three more years . . .'

'No, I don't think so. I'll try to deal with this somehow. I was given a week's pass, and only two days have gone by. I'll have enough time to return.'

And so it was decided. We checked our food supply once more, and I took a three-day ration. The rest would last my friends for about a month – half of the way if they should really cover 30 miles a day.

And what then? . . . None of us wished to think about it since all speculation was futile. Then we went to sleep.

In the evening, before we parted, Nikolay explained to me how to guide myself by the stars. Besides, I depended on my good visual memory which had never betrayed me. Although we had walked mostly at night, the outline of the region was sufficiently visible.

We embraced warmly, wished each other luck on the journey, and went our separate ways: they vanished in a westerly direction, and I turned back, eastward.

I walked rapidly, and it seemed to me that I was moving faster than I had on the previous nights. Uncertain of my strength, I tried to cover as much distance as I could from the start. Ascents and descents alternated as before, and I found my way mostly by intuition, only looking from time to time at the glimmering polar star and the Big Dipper that shone brightly in the dark sky.

I did not feel the cold at all. Indeed, very soon I had to take off my fur mittens and lift the earflaps of my cap, tying them over the crown, for the movement made me feel quite warm. I had no bag over my shoulders – all the provisions were stuffed in my pockets – and it was easy to run without a load. Moreover, I was spurred on by the realization that I had just escaped committing an act of unforgivable folly.

I thought that for the first time in my five years of imprisonment I was totally free, without a living soul for dozens of miles around. The scene was utterly silent. The snow-covered mountains, my own motion, the starry sky – all this was soothing to the nerves. I did not think of what awaited me on my return.

I followed the route so exactly that by dawn I had reached the site of our camp of two nights previously. I built a fire, ate, and fell asleep right there, on the snow. Twice I was awakened by the cold and I added some twigs to the fire.

Thoroughly chilled, I got up after not more than three or four hours of rest, dined, and set out again without waiting for darkness: I distrusted my strength.

About midnight, perhaps later, I turned left and made a detour instead of climbing the next hill – I wanted to reach the valley of the river Khattynakh on the other side of the mountain ridge, since this would shorten my way. I decided that it would be best not to return directly to Tumanny, as according to the pass I still had three days of my leave.

I now walked with difficulty. The previous day's energy had disappeared without a trace. Twice I lost a ski on the downgrades, and it took a long time crawling about on the snow to search for it. I felt that I would not last long.

Another hill. An ascent, then level ground for a while, then another descent. Suddenly I felt that the descent was becoming too steep and stopped short, catching sight, almost at the same moment, of the light of electric bulbs far below . . .

I had stopped just in time: only then could I see that the hill broke off almost perpendicularly before me, and in another moment my journey would have ended most ingloriously.

I tried to make out where I was. Very few lights were visible – not more than ten, and they explained little. I could see a couple of dark barracks . . . It was only when I saw the bright lights of automobile headlamps on the other side of the canyon, almost on the same level with me, descending the hill in zigzag movements, that I realized that I had almost reached my destination: the river Khattynakh lay in the valley, and I actually stood directly before the dreaded Serpantinnaya, the former road station, where several thousand people had been shot during the past two years. The gorge below was the notorious graveyard where the executed men were buried.

Changing my direction, I went left and down, and a half-hour later I was already in the valley. About 200 feet from the road I removed my skis and walked the rest of the distance. An hour later I was already entering the sleeping Khattynakh, still not knowing what I was going to do there. Luckily, I met no one.

Finally, arriving at a definite decision, I cut across the settlement area and knocked at random at one of the tents. After some time the door was opened and I entered. The trip must have left its marks on me, for the old attendant only gasped.

'Where did the devil bring you from?' he asked.

'From Tumanny. I walked two days, daddy . . .'

'Why didn't you catch some car or truck going this way?' he wondered.

'I had no luck. Nobody wanted to take me . . .' I replied.

'Do you have a note to the hospital?'

With numbed fingers I found the note and the pass I was given at the mine, and handed them to the attendant. I was barely able to stand. The old man examined the documents and said:

'It's night, and no one is here, neither the doctor nor the male-nurse. I am the only one here. In the hospital office everybody is also asleep, and I don't know what to do with you,' he said, looking at me with concern. Then, apparently coming to some decision, he told me:

'All right, get undressed. I'll shave you, then you'll wash yourself and go to sleep. Warm yourself at the stove in the meantime while I prepare a bath. I may get into trouble for letting you in, but the devil with it.'

He left, and I literally dropped near the gaily burning stove and fell into a deep sleep. Later I felt vaguely the old man performing his various manipulations over me. How he did not cut my throat or drown me in the bath is still a mystery to me.

In short, when I woke, I was lying on a bed in a tent dimply lit by tiny windows. Before me stood a doctor, whom I knew slightly from the past. He held a thermometer in his hand, and spoke to the nurse who stood near by with a notebook:

'Petrov, Vladimir. Temperature 103° . . .'

Seeing that I had opened my eyes, he sat down near me on the bed and silently began to tap me and listen to my breathing. Then he said:

'It may only be the 'flu, but it may also be pneumonia. We shall soon see. When did you arrive at the hospital?' he asked when the nurse stepped aside.

'Three days ago, doctor,' I said, looking him straight in the eye.

'Three days? But the night duty attendant wrote that you came . . .'

'. . . three days ago,' I repeated.

'Of course, judging by your pass, you left Tumanny four days ago,' he said wonderingly. 'But the attendant . . .'

'The attendant made a mistake, doctor, and if you really want to save my life, you'll enter in the registration book that this is my fourth day at the hospital,' I said insistently.

The doctor rose.

'It is strange . . . I don't understand it at all . . .' he muttered, leaving.

Soon they brought me dinner and some medicine. The dinner was not too bad, but I had no appetite at all. I kept thinking of the possible turn of affairs.

In the evening the doctor again approached me and sat down on my bed.

'They telephoned from the mine, asking whether you were here and when you came . . .'

'And?'

'And I said that you were here and that you arrived three days ago,' the doctor said significantly. I silently pressed his hand.

'I am not asking you about anything, Petrov,' he said. 'But I hope that you will not let me down.'

'No, of that you may rest assured. Thank you . . .' I replied.

The doctor left, and I fell fast asleep.

Fortunately, it was only the 'flu. Several days later I was already feeling much better, and my temperature dropped to normal. My appetite returned, and with it my energy. My expedition was remembered as in a fog, as if it had all been a dream.

When I was discharged from the hospital, I was given my pass, with a note certifying that I had been under treatment for ten days. I thanked the doctor and went directly to the Building Section. However, luck was against me. Sukhanov had gone on business to Magadan but Ivanov told me that the chief was bending every effort to obtain my transfer and might achieve some results in Magadan. He also told me another bit of news – Pavlov was no longer in Kolyma.

The facts were interesting: during one of his telephone conversations with Moscow, Pavlov had quarrelled violently with Beria, the N.K.V.D. chief, when the latter sternly reprimanded him for falling behind in the gold output plan, and tendered his immediate resignation. Beria refused to accept it and ordered Pavlov to remain at his post.

Then Pavlov talked by radio-telegraph to the military-naval base in Nikolayevsk-on-the-Amur and demanded that a mine-carrier be sent at once to Nagayevo since the navigation season was over and no more ships were expected. The mine-carrier was sent – no one would have dared to deny the request of such a high official as the chief of Dalstroy – and Pavlov left for Vladivostok on his own initiative, without permission from his superiors. There he boarded a special train for Moscow where, according to rumour, he was either arrested or placed in a Kremlin hospital. At the moment Dalstroy was directed by Pavlov's assistant, Senior Major of State Security, Yegorov – a Senior Major in the N.K.V.D. is equal in rank to a division commander in the regular army. A new chief from Moscow was awaited.

On the following day I was back at Tumanny, and the first thing I did was to go to the warehouse-keeper who had obtained my ill-starred pass. Explaining that I had really become ill on the way to Khattynakh instead of merely feigning illness, and spent ten days at the hospital, I proceeded to the camp office where I repeated the same story to the camp elder. He glanced at me very suspiciously, went to the commandant's office, where I was called five minutes later. I entered.

'Where are your friends?' the commandant asked without warning.

'What friends?' I wondered, as naturally as I could.

'Stop playing the fool!' the commandant bellowed, banging his fist on the table. 'I'll kill you on the spot! Where are K. and B. with whom you ran away?'

'I did not run away anywhere . . .' I muttered, feeling that my heart was in my heels. 'You know that I was at the hospital.'

'And for whom did you collect food at the camp and the mine before you left?'

'For them. That is true. They asked me to, and they gave me money for it. But you know that this is often done in camp!' I exclaimed. 'And then they were sent to look for timber for the club . . .'

'All right, the N.K.V.D. will find out the truth. A search party has been sent out for them, and their tracks were found. They'll be caught, and then all your tongues will be untied. Get out!' he shouted.

The following morning I was not permitted to leave the camp, and about noon I was travelling in the company of two guards in the direction of Khattynakh. Descending from the ridge past Serpantinnaya, the truck stopped, and I was thrown out without ceremony. The guards also climbed out. The truck went on, and we remained standing on the road, stopping the passing cars and inquiring their destination.

I began to guess the goal of my journey, and my spirits fell altogether.

Finally, a truck going to Shturmovoy stopped to pick us up, and we climbed in. It was useless to attempt conversation with the guards, who chanced to be surly and vicious. But I already knew that I was being taken to the notorious Eighth Unit.

Since the summer of 1938, that summer of unhallowed memory, there were three degrees of punishment in the camps of the Northern Administration. The highest was shooting in Serpantinnaya; the second – almost equivalent – was exile to the Shturmovoy mine, to the separate camp at panning Unit No. 8; the third and mildest, imprisonment in the local punishment cell at the camp where the culprit lived.

It was rumoured about the Eighth Unit at Shturmovoy that no one could survive the regime there for more than a month, and that even more people passed through this camp than through the butchershop at Serpantinnaya.

I once visited the Shturmovoy and was soon convinced that I was not mistaken as to our destination. The guards ordered the truck to turn off the road leading to the mine settlement and the main camp, and to drive up to a group of three tents surrounded by several rows of barbed wire, with watchtowers at the corners of the fence and with a double gate.

At the gate I was left in the charge of the local guards who let me in and suggested that I find any place I wished for myself. I inspected the three tents which did not have a living soul in them. I was numb with fear. The tents were full of gaping holes through which blew the cold winter air. The broken iron stoves were not lit. The filth was unbelievable. The beds had neither mattresses, blankets, nor pillows. Only here and there dirty rags lay strewn about.

Seeing that there was nothing to choose from, since all tents were the same, I went into one of them and began to pace from corner to corner, to warm myself a little. I paced for a long time . . .

It had been long dark when the men returned from work. They brought some firewood and the stoves belched forth smoke from all their holes, creating an illusion of warmth. The tents were lighted only by the fire in the stove – there were no lamps. Only the yard was lit by the dazzling searchlights set up in the watchtowers.

I had seen a great variety of men during my stay at Tumanny, among them many like those who sat around the stove in the smoke-filled tent, but I had never seen such a complete collection of typical *dokhodyágas* and wicks.

Some semblance of dinner was brought in, apparently delivered from the mine – a mixture of soup and gruel. The tent which held God knows how many people was given only one pail and several bowls. How many groans and shouts sounded around this miserable pail! The men fought and swore, although both were done without any energy or expressiveness. In order that no one might accidentally receive two helpings of dinner, every man had to come up to the stove where an elder of some sort checked him, marked something down on a sheet of paper, and the prisoner then received his portion. Because there were so few bowls, the dinner lasted a good two hours. The men devoured the food on the spot, without spoons, greedily clacking and gulping down the vile brew and scraping the bowls dry with their fingers.

I did not eat . . .

We were driven out to work in the total darkness of the Kolyma winter morning. The work was of the usual kind, in the mine. The inmates of the camp of the Eighth Unit worked on the mechanical path, isolated from the rest of the mine by a heavy guard posted on all sides. The guards also served as foremen, driving the workers on with blows and oaths.

In the light of the day the prisoners were even more terrifying than by night. It was obvious that all, without exception, were *dokhodyágas* who had attained socialism, yet had become complete wicks. Their collective and individual lives were clearly in the last stages. There were no criminal elements here; for them the punishment would have been too severe – they may have robbed or stolen in camp, but they were, after all, privileged prisoners.

On the distant dump, where the mechanical path led and where infrequent cars with rock rose from time to time, there laboured other mine workers. At the ascent to the dump a guard was pacing back and forth, closing the chain of patrols on our side.

The tools were almost useless and we had to work practically with our bare hands: the shovels were bent and broken, the picks dull.

I worked silently, mentally congratulating myself on making the acquaintance of the Eighth Unit. My stomach was desperately empty – in the past two days I had eaten only the half-pound of bread which I had received before work. When the lunch siren sounded, they brought to us, right in the mine, some pails of food, apparently the same as last night's, and the scene I watched in the tent was repeated here, the only difference being that now the guards did not allow anyone to relish the lunch, but drove the men on so that they choked in order to swallow the revolting liquid as quickly as possible and return to work.

The situation became quite clear to me: no one could leave the Eighth Unit alive. It was imperative to escape, but how? The only way was over the dumping ground.

It became dark, and the mine was lighted only by the three search-lights. The work, or rather the semblance of work, continued. Four other men and I had just filled a car and rolled it to the central path where we attached it to the cable that carried it to the dump. The others returned, and I went for the next empty car which was coming down from the dump.

Instead of that, I took one of the several which stood on the reserve path and slowly rolled it toward the mine. As I crossed the shadow of the high ledge, I stopped the car for a moment and climbed in as quickly as I could, doubling up at the bottom so as to occupy the least possible space.

Did anyone see my manoeuvre? Would my car be taken into the mine for loading? These questions tormented me as I lay huddled in the darkness. I do not know how long I lay there. Suddenly I heard shouts:

'Hey there, you stinking devils! Why don't you work? Take the car!'

Some people came up and I felt the car moving. They pushed it from behind, walking with bowed heads, and did not see me. It is true that the cars were quite high, and one had to look down carefully to see their bottom. Fortunately, I was taken to a dark mine. A few minutes later I felt the rocks and clods of frozen earth strike my body. Covering my face with my hands, I tried not to breathe.

Those damned wicks worked at a tormentingly slow pace! I was thoroughly chilled in the iron box of the car. Finally they more or less covered me with earth. I was not afraid of suffocating – that would require much more earth than those men threw in. Someone said:

'All right, it will do. The case is full. Roll it away!' And I rode off.

The car was rolled to the cable and attached. My carriage moved on, clattering evenly. I freed my face a little to make it easier to get my bearings. The angle of the car told me that the ascent had begun. How long was the path to the dump? I gradually freed myself of the thin layer of earth that covered me. When I raised my head and looked out, the light burning at the dump was already much nearer than the mine below. I quickly rolled over the edge of the car, jumped aside two steps, and rolled downhill. For a second I heard voices from the dump:

'The sons of bitches are sending up empty cars . . .' They must have spoken about my box. Or perhaps they did not.

Tripping over the rocks and the snow, I rapidly put distance between me and the accursed pit. Having taken my bearings during the day, I knew that I was walking toward the field.

Coming to the next pit and making certain no one worked there any longer, I descended and continued my way in the snow by a more convenient road than that above. In half an hour I came to the field.

With great difficulty, after much wandering, I finally located the carpentry shop. To avoid drawing suspicion to myself, I did not ask anyone where it was, for the Shturmovoy mine was a strict one.

As I expected, no one was in the carpentry shop which stood somewhat apart from the other buildings. Entering, I buried myself in a large pile of wood shavings, and fell asleep as soon as I felt warmer. But I slept lightly, waking up at the least sound.

Toward morning, when I heard the first steps and voices outside the window of men going to work, I shook off the shavings, came out of the workshop and sat down under the roof of the open shed near by. Workers came to the workshop, but no one paid any attention to me. Suddenly I saw a familiar face – the head of the mine's Building Section, whom I had met two years earlier while inspecting the local building works. I approached him at once, but it required much persuasion to convince him that it was really me. Finally he believed me and became a little friendlier. I asked him to telephone Sukhanov at Khattynakh to tell him that I was at Shturmovoy, assigned to the Eighth Unit, and that I begged him to do what he could to save me. The head of the Building Section was astonished and looked at me suspiciously, but he agreed to do as I requested, and went to his office. I remained in the yard, waiting.

A little later the door of the office opened, and I was called in. The telephone receiver lay on the table.

'Sukhanov wishes to speak to you,' said the official.

I took the receiver:

'Hello.'

'Is that you, Petrov?' Sukhanov's voice asked me.

'Yes, Constantin Grigorievich!'

'What devil carried you to the Eighth Unit?'

'There has been a misunderstanding. Two men escaped from Tumanny, and I am accused of complicity. It happened while I was lying at the hospital.'

'What nonsense! And I have good news for you. I arrived from Magadan yesterday and brought an order for your transfer to the administration. The order was signed by Yegorov himself, chief of Dalstroy.'

'Thank you, Constantin Grigorievich! But what shall I do now? I'll be dragged off to the Eighth in a few minutes . . .'

'I'll tell you what. Go to the camp office in an hour. The order will be transmitted by telephone, and your punishment will be revoked. I am going to the administration chief now. Give the receiver to the engineer . . .'

I handed over the receiver, beside myself with joy and still unable to believe anything. When the engineer concluded the conversation, he turned to me. Now he spoke most cordially:

'Stay here. In about an hour and a half you'll go to the camp office. Everything will be all right. Are you hungry?'

'Very.'

'Excellent. Have your breakfast,' he said, taking bread and some cans from the closet. Then he said something to the watchman who left the office, and occupied himself with his own affairs. In an hour I asked whether it was not yet time to go. He said:

'Wait. I sent the watchman to the office. He is a clever rascal, and he'll hang about until he learns that the message is here. Then you will go.'

Soon the watchman ran in.

'Hurry up. They just received the communication and took it to the camp commandant.'

I walked rapidly, accompanied by the engineer. Entering the camp office, he came with me directly into the commandant's room.

'Did you receive an order summoning Petrov to Khattynakh?' he asked the commandant who sat behind a desk.

'Yes. He is at the Eighth Unit. I have already sent an order to bring him here.'

'Very well. Here he is,' said the engineer, pushing me forward.

'How did you get here?' The commandant looked at me with astonishment. He addressed me in the formal 'you', which did not escape my attention – that meant the message was an important one.

'With your permission, I ran away from the Eighth Unit, Citizen Commandant. I ran away last night.'

He merely stared at me.

'Ye-es . . .' he drawled. 'But those scoundrels can't be watching their men carefully. There are about twenty guards at the spot!'

'Well, I did, Citizen Commandant.'

'You're lucky. If Yegorov himself had not sent for you, you would be in a bad spot . . .'

And he issued the necessary instructions.

By evening I was already in Khattynakh, in the same tent from which I had been taken to the mines more than two years earlier.

Part IV. The Way to Freedom

10. ON THE WAY TO FREEDOM

IT took me a relatively short time to regain the appearance of a human being. I was met warmly at the Building Section. By common effort my colleagues dressed me in a variety of assorted clothes, and I was able to discard the rags I had been wearing during the preceding period. I began to recover rapidly. My position could be considered fairly secure as my job in the department of the mining administration had the most exalted confirmation of the head of Dalstroy, and the small fry among the local camp officials could not seriously harm me.

I returned to my old occupation – preparation of building estimates. At first I was very busy, staying at the office 12–15 hours a day, and only gradually realizing how far I had fallen behind, living at the gold fields, in almost total ignorance of the events taking place in the world.

I learned that during the past half year there was war in the West between Germany on the one hand, and England and France on the other. I was especially astonished at the fact that all the sympathies of the Soviet government were on the side of Germany with which the U.S.S.R. had concluded a friendship pact after many years of bitter anti-Hitler propaganda. Under camp conditions, this friendship with Hitler reflected itself in a series of privileges to prisoners of German origin. Those who had retained their German citizenship were freed and sent back to Germany, and the Russo-Germans were immediately placed in a favoured position: an example of this was provided by the case of the mechanical engineer Fritz, who was given a job in our department, while serving a ten-year sentence for espionage – an extremely rare case in the history of the administration. In the department he was nicknamed 'friendly power' and enjoyed a number of freedoms inaccessible to contras of Russian origin: freedom of movement in the settlement, the right to obtain supplementary products, to send home telegrams and money, and so forth. In contrast to the rest of us, Fritz always went about in a brand-new outfit.

The partition of Poland brought to Kolyma a certain number of Poles from the liberated regions of the Ukraine and White Russia, Galicians and Polish Jews. These, however, were never sent to our administration, but were kept carefully apart from the 'old' Soviet citizens somewhwere in the Western Mining Administration, away from possible contact with the other camp inmates. According to rumour, their number was not great, and the conditions of their existence were far below the average Kolyma level.

People greedily read all available newspapers: the events shook everyone. As a result of the pact with Germany, the U.S.S.R. expanded its western frontiers. The Leningrad Military District fought Finland, but there were muffled rumours that the little country was fought not only by one military district, but that a partial mobilization had been carried out throughout the U.S.S.R., with the exception of Siberia and the Far East, and that the westward movement of troop units was in full swing.

In our group political questions were never discussed; newspapers were read avidly from cover to cover, the free employees relayed to us the news they had heard over the radio – there were, of course, no radios in the prisoners' barracks – but everything was spoken and heard without comment. Indeed, no comment was needed: it was clear enough that the Soviet Union had entered into active international politics, taking advantage of the dependence of a Germany that was waging war in the west on its eastern neighbour. What this could lead to we did not question nor ponder.

Against this background of large events, there were some local developments as well. A new chief of Dalstroy appeared in Kolyma. He was Ivan Fedorovich Nikishov, member of the Supreme Soviet of the U.S.S.R. and Commissar of State Security, 3rd Grade – a rank equivalent to that of lieutenant-general in the army. Soon the 'line' of the new chief became evident, a 'line' that was, of course, in consonance with both Beria's and Stalin's policies. New works were developed in Kolyma, the geological activities were stepped up, the new Western Administration was expanded, and a South-Western Administration was set up – located geographically in the east. The new projects also included a tin mining administration on the Chaun Gulf, on the shore of the Arctic Ocean, the Anadyr Geological Base, an expedition to the mouth of the Neva River on the Indigirka, and a plan for the opening of a mining administration on the river Yana.

The road-building administration was being transferred from Yagodny to the far west, in connection with the shift in the relative importance of road works, and our own Northern Administration was to be transferred to its new location in Yagodny, which we thoroughly welcomed, since the road settlement was much more comfortable and well equipped. The road administration officials, headed by Zaporozhetz, furiously resisted transfer to the wild and undeveloped west, but without success. Incidentally, Zaporozhetz was the last remaining member of the group of leading Leningrad N.K.V.D. officials exiled to Kolyma after the assassination of Kirov. The rest, headed by Medved, had been taken back to Moscow a year earlier, where, according to rumour, they had been shot by Yezhov shortly before the latter's own fall.

Our department's building activities expanded considerably during the period that followed my return from the mines. The main task was the construction of a 3,000-kilowatt electric power station on the river Taskan, which was to supply electric power to the entire northern group of mines. The work was done by a contracting office under our control. But the ill-starred powerhouse was beset by endless mishaps from the outset.

In Pavlov's time an engineering-geological expedition had been sent to the mouth of the Taskan to select a building site. Despite the constant pushing by Pavlov himself, the survey of that area prolonged itself. Pavlov lost patience and made a personal appearance on the spot in the middle of winter, mercilessly berated all the geologists, cast his ruler's eye over the region, pointed out a site for the erection of the powerhouse, and ordered immediate excavations. Within a week about a thousand workers were herded to the spot, and all winter they dug the ground for the foundations of the powerhouse. However, when the snow melted, it turned out that the spot chosen was in the middle of a swamp and there could be no question of building anything there. Everything had to be started anew. Fortunately for the geologists, the head of the prospecting party had succeeded in obtaining from Pavlov a written order for the starting of operations on the spot determined by the eccentric's whim, and therefore no reprisals followed the initial fiasco.

By the time I arrived at Khattynakh, the work at Taskan was already going full blast, as was the construction of a high-voltage line connecting the powerhouse with the mines. But the financial state of the project presented a sad picture as a result of the enormous over-expenditures on the unnecessary work of the first winter.

Another big construction job carried on by our department was the laying of a single-track suspension railway. By that time the problem of supplying the mines with construction lumber and firewood had become extremely complicated, since all more or less suitable timber had been ruthlessly destroyed within a radius of 30–40 miles. The nearest forests of suitable size were located along the upper reaches of the Taskan River, separated from the gold fields by a wide stretch of impassable swamps. The lack of transportation facilities and the general acuteness of the problem made it necessary to find some way out of the difficulty; as a result, it was decided to build a suspension railway on piles dug deeply into the earth. Along this railway, suspended cars were to ply back and forth, carrying lumber to the fields. The road was to be laid directly across the swamp, and its total mileage, to begin with, was to be 25 miles.

Two talented constructors were found among the prisoners working in our department – the railway engineer Kasyanov, and the constructor Wallerstein, who developed the detailed plans for the entire project. The authorities seized on the idea and pushed the work in every possible way. Direction of the project was entrusted to Kasyanov who left for the area soon afterward with a large group of workers. Despite the warnings of Kasyanov himself and the cautious Sukhanov, the head of the administration, Mendzyrzhetsky, obtained Pavlov's approval of the plans, and several hundred people were assigned to the railway construction work during the very first winter.

Since the Industrial Bank refused to grant any funds for so risky a venture, some simple book-keeping manipulations were indulged in, and the financing was started at the expense of basic production – the expense of costs per gram of gold.

The whole story ended ingloriously. Work went on for about eight months, but when spring arrived it became clear that the implacable swamp would brook no intrusion: all the piles that had been driven into the earth in winter began to settle down and sag in various directions as the ground thawed out. The road laid over them, with here and there the rails already in place, turned into such a bent and twisted line that there could be no question of moving cars with lumber along it. Work was stopped. A part of the construction timber that went into the road was salvaged for fuel, and the rest was abandoned without use. The administration wrote off a loss of about a million and a half rubles.

While the work on the suspension railway was still in progress, I had to make several trips to the location, not far from the Taskan village where a deer-breeding Sovhoz was run by a tribe of Orochels.

It must be said that the local natives were everywhere pampered and coddled as no ordinary mortals. The smaller the tribe and the more backward culturally, the more attention it received from the Communists and the government. This was called the Stalinist policy concerning nationalities. The question of nationalities in Kolyma graphically illustrated the general policy.

Before Dalstroy was organized, Kolyma was inabited by several scattered nomadic tribes of deer-breeders and hunters: the Tungus, Orochels, Yukagirs and others. They were supplied with necessities by the trading stations of the Fur Trust in exchange for valuable furs; in the process they were cheated mercilessly since they had no realistic conception of the value of the furs they surrendered. When Dalstroy was organized, the life of these primitive children of nature became immeasurably more complicated. While Berzin was still in charge, the government began to settle the natives in villages built by the camp inmates. The nomads found it extremely difficult to adapt themselves to a settled existence, but this was dictated by Stalin's policy for nationalities. Later, in the early thirties, under directives from Moscow, these savages were collectivized and subjected to the general anti-Koulak drive. As a result, the newly created villages became completely disorganized: the natives ran away to the taiga and the distant tundras, whole tribes escaped to Alaska across the ice of the Bering Strait, driving before them the herds of deer that survived the collectivization. With enormous difficulty, at the cost of promises not to touch the natives' property and various other bribes, the government succeeded in bringing back some of the savages to the villages built for them. The villages were called *Sovhozes*, although they bore little resemblance to the Sovhozes established in Russia proper: the natives did not recognize the Socialist character of their property, and their mood had to be respected.

The government set up district Soviets of deputies of the natives; Magadan was the seat of the Regional Soviet, These Soviets were independent of Dalstroy and only natives enjoyed the rights of voting and election.

However, the game of parliamentarianism did not amuse them: they constantly demanded various bribes in return for their acceptance of the Soviet system. These bribes included cloth, alcohol, hunting equipment, and food. Occasionally the natives did some work for Dalstroy, naturally on an entirely voluntary basis and for good compensation. Under pressure from the party organization, our department also had to sign a contract with the natives in connection with the building of the suspension railway: we contracted the Taskan Sovhoz to transport lumber for us by deer. During one of my trips I came to realize the justice of Kasyanov's complaints against 'those damned Asiatics'.

One of these heroes would harness a pair of deer in a sleigh and take off to the woods where he would appear three or four hours after the beginning of work; no one would presume to comment on his lateness. Then he would load one log on his sleigh, choosing the thinnest and lightest, and set out on his trip to the building location. After a half-hour or so, his deer (small and weak) would tire and stop to rest. The native would then climb out of the sleigh, take out his saw – stolen from the building site – and cut off a part of the log to make it easier for the deer. Whether because of the lighter load or because they had rested, the deer would resume the journey. After a while the scene would repeat itself: the deer stop, the log be shortened by another metre, the driver get back into his place and again travel a short distance. As a result, instead of the needed long pole, the builders were supplied with a short stump useful only as firewood. In the course of a day's work, the native would bring two or three such stumps, but his wages were 20 rubles a day, and he also had to be treated to regular drinks of liquor. With great difficulty we rid ourselves of the onerous contract with this Sovhoz, which brought us nothing but losses . . .

These natives knew almost no Russian – at any rate when they did not wish to understand what they were told. They were unbelievably dirty: according to their customs, a man was not meant to wash from birth until death. Once, arriving at the Sovhoz, I witnessed an amusing scene. A new bathhouse had just been erected for the villagers. It was built, of course, by camp inmates on orders from Magadan. But when the baths were ready, no one wanted to use them. Several members of the Young Communist League vainly tried to persuade the natives to go and wash themselves and thus to partake of Socialist culture. Finally they found one old Orochel, a chronic drunkard, tempted him with a bottle of alcohol and a new shirt into agreeing to wash, and led him off to the baths. Behind them walked the old man's numerous relatives, howling aloud as at a funeral. At last the pioneer of civilization was brought into the bathhouse. I went in, too, interested in the sequel. Once in the dressing-room, the old man became refractory and categorically refused to undress. Persuasion was of no avail. Even an advance payment of several swigs of alcohol failed to inspire the savage with the courage to go through with the ordeal to the end. Then the Komsomols – there were about five of them – lost patience and undressed him forcibly, ignoring the screams and the desperate resistance of their victim, after which they dragged him to the soaping room and there washed off the accumulated dirt of his sixty years of existence.

When he was led out of the baths afterwards, dressed up in his new shirt and scrubbed to a shine, the unfortunate one sobbed like a child and covered his face with his hands in shame. As soon as his family, who waited for him at the entrance, with other curious kinsmen, caught sight of the unnaturally clean colour of his face and hands, they wailed desperately in their dialect and scattered from him in all directions. The sufferer, clutching his honestly earned bottle of alcohol, ran after them, crying . . .

And so the baths remained without further users.

The village also boasted a library, which stood empty for want of literate readers, as well as a male-nurse who was never consulted.

I looked at all this coddling of the natives and thought bitterly about the true carriers of human culture who were being mercilessly exterminated in the nearby camps. How many centuries of progress would have to pass before these savages could produce scientists, writers, engineers and doctors like those who were perishing by the thousand at Soviet penal labour!

March was especially snowy. For a couple of weeks the northern mining area was cut off from the shore, from Magadan which fed all Kolyma. Days of hunger set in once again. Feeling the unpleasant emptiness in my stomach, I thought of those who were at the mines and who surely fared much worse than men like me who had managed to get jobs with the administration. The snow was so high that in many places it was easier to pack down a new road on the snow at the height of six or nine feet above the highway instead of clearing it. And when the snow began to settle down under the sun's rays, we found that our road ran over a number of cars stranded on their way during the blizzard and snowed under.

When the first trucks arrived from Magadan, I received three letters from my mother – the first in a whole year. They were in answer to the telegram I sent after my return to the administration. In the restrained words and expressions of my mother's letters I read about the difficult life – scarcely better than my own – which she had led at home. In one of the letters I read: 'I learned recently that your father is in a place similar to yours. He has been there for the past year and a half and will return seven years after you . . .' This meant that my father had been sent to a concentration camp in 1938, and was sentenced to ten years.

In another letter my mother wrote that I was the unwitting cause of great difficulties encountered by my younger brother in his efforts to secure an education. Apparently someone had learned that he had a brother in a concentration camp, and he was thrown out of the institute . . . Mother also wrote that she had worked during the preceding summer, together with the pupils of her school, in a *kolhoz* at some farm labour, and that she received as compensation two pounds of sugar and a pound of candy, which she was saving for my return . . . It was far more painful for me to read her letters than to endure my own life in camp.

The newspapers and radio brought news that great events were about to break in the West, events that would change all life in the U.S.S.R. But in what direction? This no one knew. We occupied the Baltic countries – Estonia, Latvia and Lithuania – after the annexation of eastern Poland, but, by all indications, it was only a beginning. The public speeches of the chief of the Political Section, and the private statements of the top officials contained ever more frequent mysterious hints about the coming greatness of the Soviet Union and the tremendous role it was to play in the future. But no one spoke clearly and openly, either in Moscow or in Kolyma, and therefore the ordinary man preferred to keep silent and think his own thoughts. A few of the free employees voiced a desire to return to Russia before the expiration of their contracts, but the administration rebuffed all such attempts.

During one of my trips to Taskan, while I waited on the left bank for a car travelling in my direction, I entered the roadside dining-room for chauffeurs and asked for a glass of tea. The face of the man at the

counter seemed strangely familiar. I sat down with my tea directly
opposite him and looked at that face, graced with its long moustache,
trying to recall who it might be. Noticing my stare, the man obviously
felt uneasy and tried to move away so that I would not see him too
clearly. Suddenly I remembered. Getting up from my table, I approached him and said, looking straight into his eyes:

'Why, hello, Comrade Zakharov!'

With a startled look, he recoiled from me, muttering:

'You are mistaken, comrade, my name is not Zakharov.'

'Don't try to pull any wool over my eyes! You probably don't
recognize me. You have known many like me, but to me you were the
only one. Now I am sure I am not mistaken.'

He began to whisper.

'For God's sake, don't tell anyone you know me. You see, I am in
the same boots now as you are. I beg you . . . You know our chauffeurs:
if they learn that I used to work for the N.K.V.D., they'll kill me.
I wouldn't have a week to live . . . I beg you . . .'

'But please, don't worry, I haven't the least intention to expose you!
You can live out your life as far as I am concerned. I don't even blame
you for my sentence to Kolyma. If it hadn't been you, it would have
been someone else . . .'

The face of my old investigator brightened.

'Thank you. Thank you. You know that I tried to be a human being
even in that filthy job. You know that I never raised my hand against
anyone. But you understand . . . Our position . . .'

'But how did you manage to make the jump from investigator to
prisoner? A rather sad conclusion to such a career . . .' I also whispered,
to spare poor Zakharov unnecessary anguish. Fortunately, the dining-
room was nearly empty and no one listened to us.

'In 1938, under Yezhov, during the purge of the N.K.V.D., I was
arrested on charges of excessive liberalism toward prisoners. They gave
me three years and sent me to Kolyma. The only thing they did – as a
mark of leniency – was to keep out of the records that I was an investigator and to change my name: you know how we and former prosecution officials are dealt with in the camps . . .'

I knew. It was true that the criminals – the most active camp
element – harboured an organic hatred of all who were or had ever
been connected with the militia, N.K.V.D. or the prosecution department. They almost always found some way of liquidating their
enemies, or, at best, of poisoning their whole existence. I asked:

'And what is your present name?'

'My name is now Fedorov. But, please, promise me . . .'

'I tell you again, don't worry about it.'

'Where are you going – to Taskan? We'll take care of it at once. Hey
there, brother!' he called out to a chauffeur sitting in the corner. 'Are

you going to Taskan? Take along this man, will you?' The driver looked up.

'This one? All right. It's time to go. Come on.' With a nod to Zakharov, I left the dining-room, and followed the chauffeur.

On the way back, I had to stop again for a lift on the left bank, and went into the same dining-room. But the man behind the counter was a stranger. When I asked where Fedorov was, he glanced at me and said:

'There is no Fedorov here any more. Two days ago he was transferred, I don't know where. He asked for the transfer himself . . .'

I understood. Zakharov never quite believed me and felt that it was safer to leave the place where he had been recognized.

By midsummer our mining administration was finally transferred to Yagodny, replacing the road administration which was sent West. Yagodny was far more pleasant to live in. It did not have that specific camp atmosphere. Instead, it was surrounded by green things, woods and grass; the river was not muddy and dirty like those that passed through the gold fields, but clear and even suitable for bathing. The houses were clean and neatly built, and the road cutting across the village was smooth and level. We were all very pleased.

Sukhanov went to the Crimea on several months' leave, and his functions were taken over by our chief engineer, a very young and pleasant fellow, one of the Komsomols. It was easy to work with him – he never interfered in my tasks and never opposed my suggestions.

Time passed, and day followed day almost unnoticeably. There was much work, work that had become interesting, that occupied all my thoughts and all the hours of the day. I became accustomed to paying no attention to the conditions of life in camp, returning to my barrack only late at night to sleep and leaving for work among the first in the morning. I enjoyed relative freedom, having a 24-hour pass and obtaining, wherever necessary, special passes for trips to work locations.

Once I went to the building site of the high-voltage line, to the At-Uryach field, where a sub-station was being built. The local chief was ill, after drinking by mistake some kerosene instead of alcohol. I found him in bed, with a greenish-yellow face, but still full of his usual vitality. He ordered his servant to prepare dinner and remarked, in the course of our conversation, that the servant was a professor of psychiatry who had been sent to camp for unknown reasons after many years of work in one of the larger clinics in Moscow. He treated his professor benevolently, addressing him by name and patronymic, but with a certain contemptuousness which even the best of the free employees seemed unable to escape in their relations with prisoners.

Winter returned with its strong winds and frosts. There were no changes in my mode of life. At moments I began to realize that in some six months my term would be completed and I would again acquire some semblance of a free man. I knew that I would never regain the old rights which were theoretically at my disposal before my arrest: a term in prison, especially for political reasons, always remains as a blot on a man's biography in the eyes of the authorities. Wherever I went, wherever I tried to obtain work, I would always be followed by a 'tail' – my prison record, which would be sent from one N.K.V.D. office to another as I moved from place to place.

The doors of educational institutions would also be closed to me forever, as would many enterprises and offices. My passport would carry a notation which would prohibit my living in the capital city of any Republic, in important industrial regions, near the seashore, or within 60 miles of any Soviet border.

I also knew that under the least suspicion, in every purge, I would again, without question or hesitation, be sent to a camp, behind barbed wire, without trial or investigation; that my company would always cast a shadow on people with whom I associated; that I was deprived of the right to serve in the Red Army and that, in case of need, I could be mobilized only into a construction battalion or some other auxiliary service, with a punitive regime . . .

I knew all this to the last detail from friends working in the camp administration and therefore liberation from camp did not seem so great and desirable an event as it might have under different conditions. Inwardly I had already decided to remain as a voluntary worker for Dalstroy, that penal kingdom where at least a former prisoner did not represent some special phenomenon, where I was known to many officials and where, even under prevailing circumstances, I had a definite reputation and standing.

True, even in Dalstroy there was a dividing line between free employees and ex-prisoners – but here it was at least overt, and my future legal position was quite clear, so that I did not risk striking unforeseen obstacles at every step and receiving heavy moral blows to my self-esteem. I knew the precise extent of my few rights and adhered to them.

It was during the Soviet holidays – the anniversary of the October Revolution. I received an invitation to a party on that evening given by a group of free employees. Several days before the holidays Sukhanov came back, but he knew nothing about it. For considerations of prudency, I did not inform anyone of my impending infraction of camp discipline. Hobnobbing with free employees was officially prohibited, but usually it was overlooked, and I decided to risk it this time. But the affair suddenly became complicated by telegraph instructions from Magadan which ordered all prisoners to be locked in the camp and kept under reinforced guard during the first day of the holiday.

I rushed about the camp, trying to think of some way to get out and arrive at the party in time. To ask the commandant's permission was useless – he would merely gloat over denying it.

Evening came, cold and quiet. I put on my good suit, bought a short time before, and left my tent. Circling around the barbed wire fence, I found a place that was relatively less brightly lit by the searchlights in the watchtowers, and, making sure no one was near by, I lay down on the snow and began to wriggle out under the inner row of wire. I succeeded perfectly, without my clothes once catching on the barbs. There was yet another fence. I had just begun to spread the wire, when I heard a shot and a cry: 'Lie still, or I'll shoot!'

Still not entirely certain it referred to me, I nevertheless stopped on the spot, knowing that, under camp rules, the soldier could kill with impunity anyone he saw in the space between the two wire fences. Alas – very soon I found that the cry was addressed precisely to me! Two other guards came running in response to the shot, and talking something over with the sentry on the watchtower, they approached me and turned their flashlights on my face. They could not but recognize me – by that time the whole settlement knew me. Despite this I was ordered again to lie still without moving. One of the soldiers left, and the other stood over me with the muzzle of his rifle staring right at me.

I was extremely uncomfortable and very cold. The snow melted a little under me and my light coat, put on especially for the short trip to the house of my friends, quickly absorbed the moisture and froze. At my least movement, the guard emitted a threatening growl and shouted: 'Don't move! I'll shoot!'

Then his companion returned and whispered something quietly in my guard's ear. The latter only said, 'All right!' and nodded.

Hours passed. I was frozen to the bone and no longer could feel any hands and feet. I thanked fate for my not having perpetrated a desperately foolish thing – putting on my shoes instead of the felt boots. I lay there and thought with anguish about my friends making merry in their warm, cosy room, waiting for me, then giving up waiting and pouring out cups of life-giving liquor for everyone; what would I not have given at the moment for one sip of that nectar!

After a time the guard was relieved by another. I tried to enter into negotiations with him, but in reply received only a few nasty warnings which made me decide to submit and wait for what would come next. I still cannot understand how I escaped freezing to death that night. From time to time the guard called out to me, and I replied with some word or phrase. Then I decided to outwit him and pretend that I was freezing, and stopped answering either his shouts or the kicks of his felt boot, or even the prodding of his bayonet across the wire. My calculation proved correct – apparently the authorities did not include my freezing to death in their plans. After several unsuccessful attempts to get an answer from me, the guard fired a shot into the air. Immediately a second guard appeared, then a third. The first one said:

'It seems he froze, the son of a bitch.'

'You think so?' the other replied. 'Let's try. Hey you, answer!' he shouted to me and poked his bayonet painfully into my back. I kept still. After some more yelling, one of them said:

'We'll have to drag him to the punishment cell. Perhaps he'll come to,' and spreading the wire, they dragged me out by the feet to the territory of the camp and from there to its far corner where the punishment cell was located. The soldiers who guarded that institution opened the door and I was pushed in. I lay on the floor in the lifesaving warmth of the cell, feeling the numbness of my hands and feet giving way to a sharp, cutting pain, a sign that I was thawing out. Two or three other unfortunates who remained in the punishment shack after the usual holiday amnesty came over and pulled me to the centre of the cell, nearer the brightly burning stove. Recognizing me, these fellows, who turned out to be acquaintances from among the criminals, gave me first aid, and rubbed my hands and feet to restore normal circulation. Soon I was able to move about freely. My story about the attempted escape provoked a string of colourful commentaries about the authorities and the guards. They unanimously expressed their conviction that I had nothing to fear and that the camp authorities would not dare to keep me in the punishment cell at the risk of a scandal with Sukhanov. However, I did not share their optimism, and I was not mistaken.

As soon as dawn began to break, the doors of the punishment shack opened, and two guards came in and ordered us to make ready to go. No one paid any more attention to me. When we left the shack, we were taken to the gates of the camp, where a truck was already waiting with its motor running. We climbed in – altogether six of us. The guards followed and we started.

I tried to guess where we might be going. The mine was ruled out: in order to send us to the mine, it would have been necessary first to make the transfers formal through the Allocation Office which the camp commandant could not have done since it was a holiday. Consequently, there remained only the places directly connected with the Yagodny camp. Of these, the only possibility was lumbering work in one of the forests as it would have been absurd to send me to building work where I was among the 'bosses'.

Only several hours later did I realize that I was being taken to the most distant lumbering site, a spot along the At-Uryach River. The truck stopped and the soldiers drove us deep into the woods along a footpath; some time later we emerged in a clearing where a low hut stood, three-quarters submerged in the deep snow. It was the barrack of the charcoal burners who burned charcoal for the needs of the settlement commandatura. Leaving us with the brigadier, the guards departed.

I felt miserable, if only because I was dressed far too lightly. Besides, I was angry at the absurdity of the entire incident which, on the whole, had been caused by my own foolishness.

The charcoal burners' hut was dark and sooty – even more depressing than the one in which I had lived for a time a year earlier and from which I undertook my attempted escape to Russia. It was lighted by a burning splinter, and the charcoal burners were all old and unshaven men, so that I had a feeling that I had been plunged somewhere into the Middle Ages. However, I could not allow myself to lose time. I knew that no one would ever find me in that hole, and that Sukhanov was already raging in Yagodny, not knowing where I disappeared, while the camp officials were spinning out unlikely fables to account for my absence and refusing to tell him where I was. The brigadier of the charcoal burners, who dozed by the stove – charcoal burning does not require the constant presence of the workers on the spot – told me amiably that if I wished, I could go out to work the next day, but if I didn't, I might rest another day or two. The prospect of rest did not tempt me in the least, and I left the hut. Taking advantage of the fact that the woods were not yet totally dark, I found the footpath by which we had come an hour or two earlier, and followed it until I came to a road in the snow which, judging by the tyre-tracks, was used by cars. I turned left and walked as quickly as I could, to warm up somewhat with the motion.

There was a noise behind me and a slowly moving truck appeared, loaded with timber. I stopped and signalled to it. When it drew up alongside of me, the truck stopped and the chauffeur's face appeared in the window:

'Where are you going?' I asked, in the authoritative tone of an official. He looked at me and was apparently convinced by my clothes.

'To Upper At-Uryach, I am carrying poles for the high-voltage line.'

'Fine,' I said, opening the door and climbing in beside him. 'Do you know where the sub-station construction site is?'

'Of course, I do.'

'You'll let me off there,' I ordered, in a tone that brooked no contradiction.

The truck started. Warming up, I dozed off, tired by the events of the past twenty-four hours. I awoke when the truck stopped. Behind the frost-covered glass I saw the figure of a sentry. We were at a control post. The sentry opened the door and demanded the driver's documents. He examined them and asked:

'Who is that with you?'

'An official from the Building Section. He's asleep.'

'What official? From Yagodny? A prisoner?' the soldier asked, apparently forewarned by the guards who brought me to the woods.

'No, ours, from Upper At-Uryach. A free employee.'

There was a second of agonizing silence. The bright ray of a pocket flashlight slid up and down my body. The guard hesitated whether he ought to wake me or not. 'All right, go on!' he said at last. The truck started, and I breathed more freely.

Late in the evening I climbed out at the sub-station and went into my friend's room.

'Petrov! Where do you come from?' he exclaimed.

I told him briefly about the state of affairs, and he roared with laughter. 'And Sukhanov, I hear, has already raised a row at the camp. The commandant got a thorough dressing-down. I'll telephone at once,' he said, picking up the receiver. 'Hello, hello, operator, give me Yagodny.'

'Yagodny? Sukhanov's apartment, please. Sukhanov? Hello. Do you recognize me? I have news: my detectives have tracked down your fugitive. Petrov has been caught and bound, and now he is lying right here on the floor, by the stove. What? . . .'

I tore the receiver from his hands:

'Hello, Constantin Grigorievich . . .'

And Sukhanov's voice replied:

'What the devil, Petrov? You always manage to land in some mess. Come here at once. I have a man here from the electric station. He has been waiting for you all day . . .'

'I would be glad to come, Constantin Grigorievich, but I am afraid they'll seize me again in camp . . .'

'Don't worry, they won't. They've got their portion, and an order has already gone out for your return . . .'

'Yes, but it is night, and there are hardly any trucks on the road. How can I come? . . .'

'Damn it! You must be here by eight in the morning.'

'I'll try, but I may be late . . .'

Sukhanov thought a moment.

'All right. I'll telephone the mine director at once to deliver you to Yagodny. Wait and be ready to go . . .'

I hung up. My friend was convulsed with laughter.

'Instead of bursting with laughter, you'd do better to think about feeding a man,' I said angrily. He roused himself to immediate action.

'Hey, professor!' he shouted to his orderly, 'get us another supper.'

I had time barely to eat and warm up when there was a knock at the door and a bearded sleigh-driver came in.

'Who is to be taken to Yagodny?'

'I am,' I said, rising and bidding my friend goodbye . . .

The mine director's sleigh stood waiting at the door. I climbed in, wrapped myself in the sheepskin coat lying there, and we started. It was not yet dawn when we arrived. Without going to the camp, I proceeded directly to the office which was steam heated, hoping to catch a nap before work. But my hopes were in vain. At the office I found the head book-keeper from the Taskan electric station, sleeping across three chairs. He woke when I entered and greeted me with joy, and then, having had enough rest, he demanded that we get down to business at once. And so we poured over the papers until work hours. When Sukhanov came, I reported that everything was in order and that the Taskan representative could go to the bank for money. My chief only shook his head.

'What a madcap you are, Petrov. Now what devil prompted you to crawl under the wire? Don't you know those scoundrels could have shot you in the best of form? And you have only a few more months to go . . . You are quite mad.'

And that was the end of the incident. There were no further repercussions. The camp officials, big and little, gritted their teeth, but after the reprimand they had received they did not dare to trouble me again, while I, on my part, tried to be prudent and keep out of trouble.

February came, the month when I was to be freed from camp. I was not certain of liberation, since politicals were often served up surprises like the extension of their term a few days before its expiration. I knew that the allocation department in Magadan had long ago requested a statement concerning my activities, both in our office and in camp. The report of the former was more important, and I knew that it was most favourable. The camp report – I was shown it secretly – was very brief and very dull, but contained nothing detrimental. In addition, my old acquaintance, Bazhenov – the head of the regional N.K.V.D. – was to submit his opinion of my character. What he wrote I do not know. I talked to my friends who worked in Magadan, asked them to do everything possible to facilitate the formalities of my release. Several days before the end of my term, I received a letter from one of them who wrote that my personal card was in the file of those to be freed from camp and that, by all indications, there would be no difficulties.

On the surface, the changes in my position would not be too great. I was to occupy officially the post of head of the Economic Planning Section in our department. My functions would be the same. The only difference was that I would move to the free settlement, a few feet away from the camp, and would receive 1,400 rubles a month instead of my present 80.

And yet I looked forward with a certain excitement to the approach of the crucial date. The future remained dark, insofar as I tried to imagine it outside the boundaries of 'my native Kolyma'. But looking back, I often wondered how a man could pass, relatively unharmed, through all the experiences I had endured. But if I were asked whether I regretted spending six years of my life in such inhuman conditions,

I would find it difficult to reply. Of course, all dreams of normal life, of education, all illusions native to youth in all times and epochs, were dispelled without a trace. But the years of prison and camp undoubtedly gave me something – though what, precisely, was still difficult to determine at the time. Perhaps the main thing I learned was the ability to clearly distinguish good from evil, truth from falsehood. And that was no small lesson.

The day finally came which rounded out exactly my six years in camp. Six years – 72 months, 312 weeks, 2,190 days . . . Was it much or little? . . .

Early in the morning I was called to the camp office. Following the established procedure, the office director asked me my name, the term of punishment, and the article of the Criminal Code under which I had been sentenced.

I replied to all the questions, and he checked them against the documents lying before him. There were no errors.

'Orders have come for your release from camp, in connection with the expiration of your term,' he said.

'Right, it's as it should be,' I replied.

'From the present day, from this hour, you are free.'

'I am happy to hear it.'

'Sign here that you have been informed to that effect.'

I signed.

'Do you have a photograph of yourself? Let me have it.'

He took the photograph from my hands, spread mucilage on its back and pasted it to the previously prepared certificate which confirmed my liberation from camp. He put a seal on it and handed it to me.

I thanked him and left the camp, never to return. A new life was beginning. But was it new? . . .

On the way from camp I stepped in to see a friend who owned a radio. The latest news was being broadcast: fierce battles were raging in Western Europe. A vague premonition flashed through my mind – the roar of cannon was too loud, too many bombs were bursting over the cities of Europe.

The day was clear and frosty. Nothing distinguished it from the day before. And I felt pretty much the same.

And yet, a new life was beginning. A life that was still to be realized.

Book Two

ESCAPE

Part I. Through Fighting Russia

---

1. EXTRAORDINARY BULLETIN

'T**wo spades,**' the chief engineer said as he arranged his hand.
'Three diamonds,' said Ivanov.
'Three spades,' said the chief clerk somewhat timidly.
'Pass,' said I, and the chief engineer announced, 'Four spades.'
Just as Ivanov led his ace of spades the loudspeaker hanging in the corner suddenly went silent. Until then it had been broadcasting a physical culture lesson from Moscow. A couple of seconds later, after the ace of spades had taken the trick, the voice of the announcer intoned loudly:

'Attention, comrades, attention!'
The voice was so unusual that we all looked up involuntarily.

'This is an extraordinary government bulletin. Attention, comrades! The Vice-Chairman of the Council of People's Commissars and the People's Commissar for Foreign Affairs, Comrade Molotov, is about to speak,' the announcer shouted, his voice growing progressively louder.

This was something new. Never in our lives had any of us heard an 'extraordinary bulletin'. I looked at my watch and realized that in Moscow it must be 7 a.m. What could have got Molotov out of bed so early?

While the announcer was repeating his preface for the third time we looked at each other silently. My heart was beginning to beat a little faster.

At last a muffled and somewhat stuttering voice began to speak. It was Molotov.

'Citizens of the Soviet Union! The Soviet Government and its head, Comrade Stalin, have instructed me to make the following announcement:

'At 4 a.m., without making any demands on the Soviet Union, and without declaration of war, German troops invaded our country, attacked our borders in many places, and subjected our cities to bombardment from their aircraft.'

The cards seemed to lower themselves to the table.

'The government calls upon you . . . to unite your ranks even more firmly around the glorious Bolshevik party, around our Soviet Government, around our great leader Comrade Stalin,'

Ivanov got up and turned off the loudspeaker. Then he went to the cabinet. We heard the clink of a glass and the gurgle of liquid. The smell of vodka filtered into the room.

The cards were forgotten. My guests sat quietly, not looking at each other, for ten minutes, and then left. Ivanov gripped my hand hard as we parted.

Left alone, I lit a cigarette and went to the window. Below, at the foot of the hill, stood the tents of the local concentration camp in crowded rows, surrounded by a double fence of barbed wire – the place which I had left only recently.

War! A chill went up my spine as I thought of the significance of this development. Who would win? Could it really be . . .? My eyes went involuntarily to a little picture hanging on the wall, of a man with moustache and a pipe in his hand. I remembered the words of a friend, a Socialist, who had died in a hunger strike two years before.

'The war will start any day now. My whole hope is that the dogs will attack one another. If the Germans hang Joe, well, our peoole will be able to breathe freer anyway.'

War! And the victims? How many would there be? What would happen to those still in the camp? As if in answer to my thought a detachment of guards appeared, marching with a quick step up the only street of the settlement. They disappeared into the gate of the camp, and almost immediately I saw two of them hauling something dark into the tower nearest to me. Looking at it hard, I managed to distinguish a machine gun.

The next days brought many troubles. In the first place several dozen people who had been freed from the Northern Goldmining Administration Camp earlier because their terms were finished were re-arrested by the local authorities of the N.K.V.D. and sent to a more remote camp. Kostya Ivanov and I, who worked in the administration, managed to escape this fate through our good relations with the High Command. Ivanov got his discharge pay quickly and left for Magadan.

There was a rumour that all prisoners of German descent had been collected from the various camps and taken to the Serpantinnaya execution camp to be shot.

Rations were cut sharply, and the camp regime was tightened up: prisoners went out to work only with a strong detail of guards.

In addition there were events of a more general character. All bank accounts and savings were frozen, and after work all the voluntary employees of the camp had to have military drill. However, nobody in the Kolyma District was subject to military service: Dalstroy, as a powerful 'trust' of the N.K.V.D. doing the most important job for the government – gold mining – was considered a militarized organization.

During one of the meetings of voluntary employees which former prisoners like me were permitted to attend the head of the political department said:

'Counter-revolution is not asleep in the camp. We have received reports from all camps that prisoners are petitioning to be sent to the front, because, they say, they want to defend the fatherland. Patriots, so to speak. It is evident that the enemies of our fatherland and state wish to be issued weapons and then go over to the Germans. Camp commanders have received orders to mete out severe punishment to all those who submit such petitions.'

But a carpenter working on the new building, a former artillery captain convicted after Tukhachevsky's plot, said, 'They don't believe us when we tell them we want to defend our country against the invader. But I know that our army hasn't recovered by a long shot from the purges of 1938; three-quarters of the commanding personnel was liquidated and the present regimental commanders hardly know how to sign their names. We are prisoners, that's true. But after all we are still Russians! Why do they deny us the right to die in battle against the enemies of Russia? The High Command itself doesn't believe all the accusations that were made against us.'

An order came from Magadan, signed by Nikishov: the plan for gold production was to be curtailed. No new gold fields were to be opened, and production was to be continued only in the fields already being worked. At the end of the gold washing in the areas under production, or earlier if possible, 10,000 men were to be transferred from our mining administration to the west where they would come under the jurisdiction of the road-building administration. The healthiest men were to be picked. Work in the lead-mining administration was to be intensified.

By the end of August groups of workmen were already being sent to the west, where through hills and swamps, in deserted and isolated country, a road was being built to the Indigirka River and, still farther, to Aldan. Land communications with the rest of Russia were being created.

News from the front was not comforting; the Soviet armies were retreating rapidly eastward. The Donets Basin was threatened, as was the northern Caucasus, where my mother, the person dearest to me in the whole world, lived. There was growing danger that I would be cut off from her. There were other reasons too which prompted me to go back home. They were foggy and indefinite, and even when I was alone I avoided thinking about them.

At the beginning of September when the first snow fell I took warm leave of the friends with whom I had gone through so much. In my pocket I had a complete set of documents and about 3,000 rubles which I had received in pay at my final discharge. The suitcase with my belongings was packed.

It was a moonlit night when I boarded a truck bound for Magadan to pick up provisions for the north. Shaking hands again with the friends who were seeing me off, I looked over the settlement, now white with snow, for the last time. The truck started up, gathered speed, and began to climb the pass.

2. MAGADAN

I WENT to Ivanov's apartment in Magadan where, since his arrival from the North some weeks before, he had been directing the construction of the new Dalstroy headquarters building. He had been trying without success to get permission to leave. I learned from him what a complicated business it was.

Nikishov, the head of Dalstroy, had received instructions from Beria not to admit any new personnel, either prisoners or voluntary employees, to the Kolyma. A large number of the latter had collected at Vladivostok, where they were sending desperate telegrams to Magadan; none of them wanted to go into military service and Dalstroy was their only hope of salvation.

At the same time departures from the Kolyma were also forbidden. A few members of the Komsomol who had decided to volunteer had left their posts several months before, receiving a complete discharge from Dalstroy. They were now living in the apartment next to Ivanov's, as they could not get permission to take passage on a ship. About a thousand former prisoners, almost exclusively from the 'socially close' category, who were not liable to a second arrest, had gathered in the Magadan transit camp. They were all waiting to be taken to Vladivostok and meanwhile were playing cards and organizing drinking bouts.

There wasn't much alcohol but just at this time a ship arrived with a large load of Soviet champagne, apparently as a result of a misunderstanding. Champagne was something like small beer to Kolyma throats, used to drinking spirits, but in the absence of the latter it was extremely popular.

Soon after my arrival in Magadan I was invited to dinner by a highly placed official from headquarters with whom I had established good relations a long time before. During dinner there was lively discussion of the rumour that Smolensk had been retaken by Soviet troops, but it was not known when or where the rumour had originated. Much later I learned that it had covered the whole country and that its source was party organizations, which had been instructed to raise the morale of the people by such devices.

When the guests had all gone I was left alone with my host, with whom I was able to speak frankly.

'Why did you come to Magadan?' he asked, leaning back in an armchair and exhaling a cloud of smoke.

'I want to go home, to my mother,' I answered.

'Do you want to go into the army?'

'Well, if the worst comes to the worst I can go into the army.'

'How many years did you serve out here? Five, six?' he asked.

'Six.'

'That's not enough, really, not enough,' he said unexpectedly.

I was silent. The conversation was taking too serious a turn.

'By staying here you will escape mobilization. We'll find you a suitable job. And when the war is over – then go with God.'

'But how will it end, Andrew Stepanovich?' I asked. It was his turn to be silent. Then, finishing most of the champagne in his glass, he said, 'It's hard to say right now. We have information that at the front and in the areas near the front there is complete disorganization and that the army doesn't want to fight. The Germans are advancing at the rate of 75 miles every twenty-four hours. The sudden entry of Japan into the war in the Far East is feared. We can't expect effective help from anywhere.'

'And then?'

'What do you mean, "then"?' he asked in an irritated voice. 'You're not a child who has to have everything explained.'

We were silent again. Then I said decisively, 'You may be right, but I still want to go, if it's at all possible. I want to get to where my mother lives, and after that we'll see. I shall ask you to help me arrange my departure.'

'Well, if you've decided . . . Come and see me in two days; I'll tell you what to do.'

In a few days I received a short note from him introducing me to the wife of the head of the personnel department. She turned out to be an amiable woman. No one else was in the apartment and we could talk freely.

'Yes, I know. Andrew Stepanovich has told me about you, but it's a difficult problem. I can tell you confidentially that almost all the Dalstroy ships have been taken away from us to bring cargoes from America, and all navigation will soon cease. My husband is waiting for permission to ship to Vladivostok at least some of the people waiting in Magadan more than three months. The lists have already been made up.'

'Can I hope that Ivanov and I will be included?'

'Wait, I'll try,' she said, and picked up the phone.

'Yes, it's me. How are you? Here's what. Two men will have to be included on the first priority list for shipment to Vladivostok – Petrov and Ivanov . . . They'll be in to see you . . . You're welcome . . . Yes, I'll wait.'

Then she told me whom to see in the personnel office.

'Do you have money?' she asked. I nodded.

'Give him some – well, about 500 rubles apiece – and he'll take care of everything. Only I warn you again, be careful in Vladivostok. They sort out former prisoners there: some go directly into labour battalions and are sent to the front, and some are sent back to camps, especially former political prisoners.'

I thanked her and left.

The next day Kostya and I went to see the man about whom the director's wife had told me. The money lay in prepared envelopes together with our documents. The official did not open them but told us to return in a week for our documents. When we came back at the appointed time everything was ready: we were included in the passenger list of the first transport.

The first transport was also the last: the steamer *Dalstroy* was making its last trip from Nagayevo, after which it was scheduled to sail to America for lend-lease supplies.

When we had finished all we had to do we went to the supply office to draw rations for the voyage. In the director's office where we had to go to get an order signed I overheard a conversation. A representative of the mining administration was speaking.

'For a month we haven't received any fat, sugar, or salt. Even the rations for the voluntary workers have had to be reduced to a minimum. I urgently request you to issue us at least the indispensable items, even if you can give us only half quantity!'

The director answered, 'Remember once and for all – and you can tell your fellow workers too – that the rations in all deficient products' – and which ones are not deficient, thought I – 'have been reduced by 90 per cent until the end of the war. Of course, if the war is over quickly . . .'

This ended their conversation. The director signed our requisitions. For a week's voyage we were to be issued ten pounds of bread and four pounds of herring. In addition we were to receive soup once a day on board ship. It occurred to me that this was exactly the same ration I had received on my trip to the Kolyma as a prisoner, but I did not mention it.

Finally the day came when several hundred of us ex-convicts, who were, according to the Constitution, full-fledged citizens of the Soviet Union, but who really had a status which differed little from that of actual convicts – were taken to Nagayevo, where they began to load us on the ship. The embarkation process started in the morning, but it was evening before the last lucky passenger was aboard. There was a control post at the gangplank where the numerous documents of each man were painstakingly examined. The moment we boarded the ship each man's scanty baggage was torn open and inspected and he himself subjected to a humiliating personal search. They were looking for gold.

From the top deck the aristocrats of Soviet society were looking down on us – voluntary employees of Dalstroy and officers of the N.K.V.D. They were assigned cabins. We were put in smelly, dimly lit holds.

It was almost dark when the gangplank was taken up. Most of the passengers remained below, but I went on deck. Ignoring the cold and wind, I stared at the darkening shore.

The engines started and the ship moved slowly away from the pier. The Kolyma was receding into the past . . .

Images of the recent and yet so distant past flashed through my mind. Almost six years of my life I had given to this God-forsaken region. I remembered people who had become animals under the influence of camp conditions, and perhaps for the first time I thought of them not with the feeling of the superiority of a survivor, as was customary on the Kolyma, but with real pity and sympathy. It is a terrible thing, this battle for existence in the camps. The chance of survival is so small. There are so many degraded and sinking people. Human tragedy is seen at each step in such limitless quantities that all human feelings are dulled and the capacity to pity and sympathize dies away. They say about any man who has survived a winter on the Kolyma that his 'eyes have been frozen off', that conscience and pity are dead in him.

With these thoughts, from somewhere in the depths of my soul, there rose up such a terrible, uncontrollable hatred for those who created this hell on earth that I felt afraid of myself. I looked up to where the gay, carefree officers of the N.K.V.D. were strolling in their warm overcoats and watching the dwindling shore. If looks could kill, they would immediately have ceased to exist.

Suddenly feeling chilled, I went down to the hold.

3. THE OPEN SEA

Toward morning the wind grew stronger. Almost no one from the hold ventured out on deck. The criminals sang mournful songs, sitting on the hard log shelves in their underwear. It was hot and stuffy. Opposite me one of these singers was intoning, squinting at the little light and swaying in time to the rolling of the ship. Behind him former (and future) thieves and bandits were playing cards and swearing. For them the trip across the 'Big Country' would be short. In Khabarovsk or maybe even in Vladivostok they would be caught stealing and sent back to camp . . .

A gong sounded, and some of the men went on deck for their soup with the dishes and kettles they had provided themselves with in Magadan. They had to juggle these containers to carry their miserable soup over the slippery frozen deck. Almost no one succeeded. With each lurch of the ship they would slide and fall, amid the laughter of the warmly dressed group of voluntary employees who were watching from the deck above.

From the cabins came the sound of a victrola. By the entrance to the passengers' quarters there hung a sign: 'Former prisoners strictly forbidden to enter.' However, it so happened that I once had occasion to go through this forbidden door. About halfway to Vladivostok the officials travelling with us decided to make up some sort of roster of ex-prisoners, and we were summoned to one of the cabins in alphabetical order.

Sprawling in an armchair at a table covered with papers was an N.K.V.D. official with an unbuttoned military shirt and a cap pushed back on his head. Beside him slouched another, apparently his assistant. There was a chair in front of the table.

I greeted them as I entered, but received no answer. I sat down. The man in the armchair looked up.

'Who allowed you to sit down?' he shouted suddenly, using the familiar 'thou'. I got up silently, feeling the blood rush to my face. It had been some time since I had been yelled at in this way. I was out of the habit. Probably he read something uncomplimentary to himself in my look.

'They've become sloppy and lax.'

He brought out some descriptive obscenities. 'They've begun to think they are free citizens,' he went on in a mocking tone. 'Just wait, you'll see what we do with you. . . . Last name?'

'Petrov.'

'First?'

'Vladimir.' He checked the list.

'What did you serve time for?'

'I was accused of anti-Soviet agitation. Article 58–10–11.'

'Accused . . .' he mimicked, again mocking, and looking at me maliciously. 'Of course you don't consider yourself guilty?'

'No, I don't.'

'I wonder why they released you. . . . How long did you serve?'

'Six years.'

'Only six years? That's not much. Let's have your documents.'

Silently I gave him a pile of papers. I felt my hands tremble and controlled myself with difficulty. He took the papers and began to write something on the sheets lying in front of him, with the help of his assistant.

'That's all. You may go. Next!'

'How about my documents?' I asked with sinking heart.

'You'll get them when you need them.'

Then I took out another paper, the letter signed by the director of the personnel section of Dalstroy which his wife had given me just before my departure. It contained a very substantial résumé of my work in Dalstroy and called for all possible co-operation to be given me. Looking it over, the official consulted his assistant in whispers and then handed back the documents without looking at me. I took them and left silently.

It turned out that all former political prisoners had their documents taken away, except for myself and Ivanov, who had a similar letter. What happened to those people I don't know.

The weather improved somewhat, although we were already on the ocean. Soon land appeared on the horizon to our right. It was Japan. We learned this because guards who had suddenly appeared began to chase everyone into the hold, letting them out only to eat and use the toilet, which had been established next to the galley where the soup was doled out.

Kostya and I were lying on our shelves and talking when we felt the ship's engines stop. A man came down the ladder and shouted 'Hurray, fellows! Our ship has been arrested by the Japanese!' There was a hum of voices and someone tried to go on deck, but we had been locked in the hold. The man who had brought the news was saying, 'We are in the Japanese Straits, and a cruiser is ahead of us and won't let us go any farther. Pack up your things, boys, we'll be on our way to a Japanese jail now!'

This joke seemed so amusing to everyone that an uncontrollable gaiety sprang up among the criminals. Each was at his wittiest. A few men were trying to force the hatch cover open.

'Hey, guard! Let us out to the latrine!' they shouted with curses. After ten minutes or so the guards began to let them out one by one. I decided to go too to see what was going on.

When it was my turn I went up on deck. The guards hurried me along. Sitting in the badly constructed roofless latrine, I managed to distinguish a new-looking Japanese cruiser signalling us with coloured flags. They were answering something from our bridge. A group of the 'command' stood around the signalman looking very worried.

I went below and told Kostya all I had seen. This business was more than interesting. The thought of the possibility of suddenly finding ourselves 'abroad' nearly drove us wild.

A day passed and we did not move. The Japanese wouldn't let us go. That night several former political prisoners – the ones whose documents had been confiscated earlier – were removed from the hold. Later it turned out they had been locked in a coal bin, where they almost suffocated. They were also beaten up.

The next day nobody was allowed on deck, in spite of the shouts and protests of those who were trying to go to the toilet. Three barrels were brought by the guards to serve as substitute. It was becoming difficult to breathe.

Also there was no soup.

Not till the next morning did the engines start again and we were allowed out of the hold. Going up on deck I saw the silhouette of the Japanese warship far astern, hazy in the approaching dawn. In the distance, on the north shore of the strait, winked the lights of some Japanese town.

The political prisoners returned from the coal bin. They had no opportunity to wash as the showers were only for the 'aristocracy'. They went silently to their places and even the discovery of the disappearance of their few possessions, which had been stolen by the criminals, did not call forth any external display of emotion. The atmosphere of a concentration camp, with no rights whatever for political prisoners, was preserved in full on the ship, although officially there were no prisoners among us.

About twenty-four hours later we again stopped in the open sea, though this time there was no apparent reason. We were no longer fed. The provisions had given out and the galley was closed.

We were not prevented from going on deck and Kostya and I spent all our time there, seated on our belongings.

The reason for the delay became clear at last when we saw a small launch approaching. We were waiting for the pilot. When the launch came alongside a man climbed up a ladder which had been lowered for him and took his place on the bridge. The launch turned west and we slowly followed it.

We went in a series of zigzags.

'A minefield!' Kostya decided. I agreed. We were still far from land; we could hardly distinguish it on the horizon, and there was no reason to be afraid of submerged rocks. The ship moved at a very low speed, accurately following every turn of the launch.

Another twenty-four hours passed before we drew near to shore. But this was not Vladivostok. It was a little settlement with a pier, which we were apparently unable to approach. Someone who had talked to a sailor told us we were in the Bay of Nakhodka, fifteen miles from Vladivostok, and that Nakhodka now contained the base section of Dalstroy, which had been transferred from Vladivostok. It was true: an extensive camp could be plainly seen, surrounded by a high barbed-wire fence with towers at the corners.

Hunger was beginning to torment us seriously.

We spent the night at anchor and in the morning the debarkation began.

4. THE FAR EAST AT WAR

KOSTYA and I were faced with a complicated problem in strategy. We had learned in the evening that the voluntary employees would be sent ashore first, and that then the former prisoners were to be taken to the Dalstroy 'allocation point' (inside the barbed wire), where they would be checked again. Those permitted to proceed farther would be issued free tickets from Khabarovsk on, but as far as Khabarovsk they would all be transported in freight cars under heavy guard. We had strong reason to fear that instead of to Khabarovsk we would be shipped to another concentration camp.

Before dawn we carried our belongings on deck, shivering with the early morning cold and looking toward the shore, from which a cutter and a barge were approaching. It was not hard to guess that the barge was to take the passengers ashore.

When the cutter pulled alongside and an officer of some sort had come aboard and gone up to see the captain, we lost no time in dragging our bags to the gangplank and asking a sailor from the cutter to lower them into the barge.

'I can't do that until I get the order,' he said.

'Listen, old man, what do you care? You can see that we are passengers,' Kostya said to him, 'and we want to get into the barge early so as not to be pushed around in the crowd when everyone starts disembarking.'

His voice was soothing, almost affectionate, and I noticed that while seeming to pat the sailor on the hand he shoved a rolled-up bill into it. The sailor at once dropped his strict manner.

'Well, all right, but quickly, so no one will see you.'

In an instant we were in the barge. We hid our things behind some canvas lying in the stern and made ourselves as small as possible behind the wheelhouse. We couldn't see the ship but we heard sounds up there: the whistles and shouts of the guards chasing the 'prisoners' into the hold.

An hour later the voluntary employees began to descend into the barge. They took places on the deck and paid no attention to us, apparently thinking us members of the crew. I kept scanning them anxiously, afraid that someone would recognize us, but luckily none of our 'friends' were among them.

Finally we began to move. As we slowly drew near the shore Kostya and I got up from our place of concealment.

The passengers were sitting on benches looking at the water fearfully, as there were no railings on the barge.

Suddenly there was a shout, 'Suitcase overboard! Stop! Stop!' We saw a small suitcase bobbing up and down in the water beside the barge, while two passengers, a man and a woman, continued to cry out. The others seemed indifferent.

Our old friend the sailor came up to them.

'What's the matter, citizens? Why all the shouting?'

'Our suitcase! Can't you see, that suitcase there, it's ours, please get it quickly. It has all our – documents – in it!' said the woman with a stammer.

'All right, I'll get it right away,' said the sailor, taking a long boat hook down from the wheelhouse. 'But what will you give me?' And he stopped.

'What? What'll I give you? I won't give you anything. It's your duty to see that everything is in order; you get paid for it. I'll tell the captain that you practise extortion,' shouted the man.

'Oh, so?' said the sailor coolly. 'Then get your suitcase yourself.' He crossed to the other side, boat hook in hand.

'Have you gone out of your mind?' the woman whispered fiercely to the man. 'That bag has . . .' I couldn't hear the rest. The man jumped up and yelled, 'Oh, you stupid fool! Sailor, come here! I'll give you 50 rubles, but for God's sake get that suitcase!'

The sailor came over silently, looked at the departing suitcase, and said calmly, 'It's too far away – can't reach it with a boat hook. You shouldn't have haggled with me.'

'Listen, comrade sailor, signal the cutter, make it go back. I'll pay for everything. And you'll get 200 rubles.'

'So that's the way it is?' The sailor was mildly surprised. 'Two hundred already . . . But I can't signal the cutter; there's only one man there and he's in the engine room. He wouldn't hear me anyway.'

Now both the man and the woman began begging the sailor to save the suitcase.

'Well, O.K. It's cold, but I can swim over and get it,' he offered. 'But that will cost you money.'

'Yes, yes, quickly! It's filling up and sinking. How much do you want?'

'One thousand rubles,' said the sailor without blinking an eye. The man almost shrieked.

'How much? A thousand? You're insane! Will you take 300?'

'No.'

'Well, 500 then?'

'If you still want to argue, swim over and get it yourself,' said the sailor in an irritated tone. 'I wouldn't get it for 3,000 now. Anyway, it's sinking.'

'Ai, it's sinking!' screamed the woman. 'You're an idiot!' she shouted at her husband. 'Sailor, quick, you'll get 2,000!'

'I wouldn't go for 5,000,' said the sailor with unruffled calm. 'It will sink anyway.' He stared at the suitcase, which was almost too small to see.

'Citizens, what is he doing to us?' The man turned to the others with tears in his voice. 'Half the money we earned on the Kolyma is in that suitcase! Help us! Make him dive in and get it!'

The crowd was silent. Several men in N.K.V.D. uniform snickered among themselves.

'You shouldn't have haggled so much,' said the sailor patronizingly, when the suitcase had disappeared under the water. 'You're too greedy.' And with another look out over the water he went into the wheelhouse.

The hubbub continued. If they had not been separated husband and wife would have started fighting over whose fault it was that their money was in the suitcase. The barge was already pulling up to the dock.

Perhaps the incident of the lost suitcase, which was being discussed excitedly by everyone, including the officials who met the barge at the dock, saved us some explanations when our papers were inspected. There was only a short dialogue.

'Hey, citizens, you're former prisoners,' said the official inspecting our passports. 'How did you happen to get into this barge?'

'By the personal order of the ship's commissar,' said Ivanov haughtily and unabashed. 'You can see that there are only two of us from a thousand former prisoners.'

This strange reasoning was unexpectedly convincing.

'That's right, there are only two of you. All right, go ahead.' Grabbing our things, we ran to the trucks which were standing near by.

The other passengers were already there. We climbed into the back of the last truck. Soon the Bay of Nakhodka and all the Dalstroy buildings disappeared around a bend in the road. Only a dozen or so Kolyma people were still with us. They were all voluntary employees.

As the sun rose we entered Vladivostok.

We felt violent pangs of hunger. It had been forty-eight hours since we had eaten anything, but we had forgotten that under the influence of all our worries. Now our stomachs began to contract painfully.

The trucks stopped at the railroad station. We checked our bags and went into the city, leaving our fellow travellers behind. It was early and the shops had not yet opened. While we were looking for a place to eat Kostya and I talked incessantly, experiencing our first moments of actual freedom. Everything connected with the Kolyma, with Dalstroy, and with the years we had spent in concentration camps was behind us.

We got something to eat in a small snack bar to take the edge off our hunger, and then we went for a walk.

Built on the slopes of several hills, Vladivostok is a picturesque city, with its streets running up and down. To the south we could see the port with dozens of ships. Farther out near the horizon we could make out an island, which even in the Kolyma we had heard no ordinary citizen was allowed to approach.

There were trenches along the streets in many places, and on the hillsides one could see machine-gun nests. The street lamps were painted dark blue. About half of the people who were beginning to appear in the streets were soldiers and sailors. There were almost no women or children in sight. Strangest of all, there were absolutely no Chinese, numbers of whom had always lived in Vladivostok. We found out later that all the Chinese in the city had been taken away the first week of the war. In general everyone was evacuated from the city who had no direct function in the port, the army, the navy, or the railroad.

All that morning our chief occupation was eating. We had breakfast in the famous Golden Horn, and Kostya, who was taller than I and had a prodigious appetite, ate all his own food and everything that I left. The two-day fast caused by the Japanese cruiser had caused a psychological hunger in us, and in one morning we ate more than in half the journey at sea.

In the course of our walk around town we bought ourselves two new, well-made suitcases. Contrary to our expectations, there turned out to be a fair amount of goods in the stores. We knew, of course, that Vladivostok, like other port cities which foreigners often visit, was in a special position in regard to supplies. But we had supposed the war would have caused a reduction.

The U.S.S.R. was divided into several 'zones' of supply. The first contained Moscow, Leningrad, Odessa, Novorossisk, and Vladivostok. These cities received (for Russia) many goods at low prices. One could buy sugar and even butter. Sometimes underwear and other items of clothing were available. Moreover, wages were higher than in the other zones.

The second zone contained the centres of industry, the big industrial cities, and the capitals of the union republics. Sugar and butter were harder to get there; the sale of clothes, shoes, and other goods was controlled more strictly and was handled in the main not by stores but by factories and organizations.

The third zone was a group of cities and regions contained in a special list confirmed by the government, which had a particular significance in the economy of the country. All one could get at a fixed price was bread and sometimes some sort of cereal or meat. Clothing and footwear were sold only to the best Stakhanovites of the factories and to the party aristocracy. Wages were a good deal lower than in the first two zones.

The rest of the U.S.S.R. was included in the fourth zone, and everything was proportionately worse there.

Thus in Vladivostok, in the first zone, we supplied ourselves with the essentials we had not been able to buy in Magadan. We had money. In the first place, we had received a fairly large sum as discharge pay; and in the second place, according to an old Kolyma custom, the friends of a former prisoner departing for Vladivostok take up a collection for him. About 5,000 rubles had been collected for Kostya and me, which wasn't bad.

We went to the station with our purchases and repacked our belongings in our new suitcases. Then after another long and unpleasant document check we bought our train tickets. We asked for passage to Moscow but they would sell us tickets only as far as Novosibirsk. Our express would leave in the morning.

We dined in the Cheliuskin, a restaurant well known to all naval men who have ever been to Vladivostok. To be more accurate, Kostya had dinner there. I couldn't. We had eaten so much that the sight of food was repulsive to me.

A drunk sat down at our table.

'Are you from the Kolyma?' he asked.

'Yes.'

'Very pleased to meet you. I'm Drozdov, a mechanic.'

We bent our heads to signify that we were pleased, too.

'I've been here three weeks. I'm from the Kolyma too. But they won't let anyone go back. So here I am, waiting. No more money; I've drunk it all up. Lend me 50 rubles.'

Kostya and I exchanged glances and I gave him the money. The mechanic beamed.

'Thank you. What about you? Are you going into the army?'

'No, right now we're going home.'

'That's bad. They'll draft you straight off. They're taking everyone.'

'Well, if they draft us, they draft us. You can't escape the army,' said Kostya. The mechanic laughed drunkenly and winked.

'Ha, ha! That's funny! "You can't escape the army." Why, only fools are going into the army. Why go into the army when the war will be over in three months? Only hoofs and horns are left of the army now.'

And the mechanic reeled back to his friends.

I looked around. The restaurant was packed. There were a lot of officers, but also many people in civilian clothes. A few women were laughing shrilly. Smoke filled the far corners like fog. On a stage at the side of the room a small orchestra was playing gypsy love songs and a gaunt woman with an emaciated face was singing. The air was heavy with the fumes of wine and vodka. At one table an argument started. Tablecloth and dishes clattered to the floor and the waiters fluttered around, trying to get control of the situation.

A young girl in a very décolleté dress approached and bending over us whispered:

'Do you need opium? I have some – Chinese . . .'

I shook my head and she went on to the next table.

Kostya had dozed off from too much food and wine. His head was nodding.

Three men in uniform appeared in the doorway. They walked through the room a few times looking for someone. Apparently finding him, they approached one of the tables and said something. A man in civilian clothes got up and followed them. Suddenly from the crowd an army officer shouted, 'Hey, you blueheads! What do you want here? Why aren't you in the army?'

I couldn't believe my ears. It had never occurred to me that one could talk like this to the N.K.V.D.

The men stopped and two of them came over to the soldier.

'Who are you? Show your papers!'

'Go to the devil's mother, will you?' the officer shouted, without getting up.

'Show your documents, comrade major!' ordered the N.K.V.D. man imperatively.

'Get out of my sight, do you hear?' The major raised his voice. At the other tables officers were beginning to rise. One of them, stepping between the major and the N.K.V.D. official, said, 'You'd better go.' The rest of the military were making threatening sounds. Seeing that their position was untenable, the 'blueheads' departed. The major's friends began to persuade him not to make any more trouble.

It was now midnight. Noticing some of the officers putting on their coats and getting their bags out of the cloakroom, I inquired if they were going to the station. When they said they were, I asked whether they would mind our joining them, since we were not acquainted with the town. I went back to our table to jerk the deeply sleeping Kostya awake.

It was very dark outside.

'Watch your step,' warned one of the officers, 'there are trenches all around here. Every morning they drag out the drunks who have fallen in during the night.'

The officers were also going west. In spite of the protests of the railroad men, we went out to look for our train. It was on a siding in the railroad yards not scheduled to leave for several hours. Having found our car and our places with the aid of pocket flashlights, we settled ourselves as comfortably as possible and went to sleep. In my sleep I heard the train approach the platform, the kerosene lamps being lighted, and the noise of people piling into the coach. At last we began to move. Through the window I saw that it was snowing, and it occurred to me that this was the third time I was seeing the first snow this year. The first was up in the far North the beginning of September, the second in Magadan the day we sailed.

Lying on the top shelf with Kostya still asleep across the aisle, I looked out of the window of the coach. Yesterday's snow covered the ground. There were no signs of habitation on either side of the track. Between the infrequent stations and settlements there was nothing, not the smallest village. At the stations a great many soldiers were waiting for troop trains. Only officers were on our train.

There was an inspection, not only of tickets but of documents, too. Everyone was thoroughly and minutely examined. We learned that something was not in order with the papers of one old man sitting below when the N.K.V.D. man announced, 'Collect your things; you will get off at the next stop.'

'Citizen commander, I have only three more stops to go. Here is my ticket; I'm a local resident. Here is my passport; please let me go on to my stop.'

'No, you will get off. You have no permission from the military commissar for the journey. Maybe you are a deserter.'

'Me a deserter? I'm sixty years old!'

'Enough talk! Get your things, at the double. Forward march!' The old man began to fuss around. Then he took his bag and went to the end of the coach. The inspector turned to me.

'Your papers!'

I handed him the whole batch. My documents were all in order – I had made certain of that in Magadan. Still he asked, 'When were you discharged from your camp?'

'Before the war.'

'Where are you going?'

'Home, and then into the army.'

He moved on, apparently satisfied.

Inspections of documents continued regularly during the whole trip, once and sometimes twice a day. Almost always someone was found with something suspicious either in his papers or in his baggage, which was also occasionally inspected. Or else the N.K.V.D. man just would take a dislike to a passenger's face. And always in such cases these people were taken off the train. What was done with them later we didn't know.

In our coach there was a lieutenant who was on his way to the front after serving in the Far East for three years. He told us that the object was first of all to catch escaped prisoners from the camps, and army deserters, whose number had grown immensely since the start of the war; but chiefly to make people 'feel that the Soviet regime was still powerful enough to be feared'.

He also told us that many soldiers and officers (at that time they were

still called Red Army men and commanders) had been sent from the
First and Second Far Eastern armies to the Moscow front, and that
these transfers were continuing. It was true that our 'express', which
travelled at an average speed of 12 miles an hour, was always being
held up at stations hours at a time to let long troop trains full of
soldiers through to the west. Troop trains scarcely halted at the
stations, for fear of desertions.

The general picture in the Far East, all the way to Irkutsk, was
encouraging. One could judge by the quantity of produce which,
according to old Russian custom, the local peasants brought to the
stations to sell. Since there were no diners on the train the passengers
bought what they needed during the long stops. The conductors had
quantities of food in their compartment. They said that further west,
beyond Irkutsk, the prices of everything were much higher. Apparently
they simply meant to do some speculating.

In Irkutsk we had to change trains, and Kostya and I were able to
spend the whole day in the city.

We had a proper dinner. We ate the famous Baikal fish called *ómul*
and bought a supply of vodka and liquor which we were told was
almost impossible to obtain farther west.

When our train had travelled several miles from Irkutsk a document
and baggage inspection of grandiose proportions was arranged for us at
a small station. N.K.V.D. inspectors took food away from those who
had too much; we were relieved of three bottles of vodka. The Far
East ended at this station and the guard was especially strong there,
oriented particularly towards travel from the west, so that refugees from
European Russia could not penetrate into this region where life was
still more or less normal. It was much easier to leave it, however, and
the five hours lost by the train during the inspection, it was said,
were a mere trifle compared to what the east-bound trains had to go
through.

The Far East had ended. Siberia was beginning.

5. LIFE ON THE RAILWAY

EVERYTHING after Irkutsk carried the imprint of war, everything that could be seen and heard along the great Trans-Siberian Line, with its countless long stops at stations of all sizes. Only numerous camps on both sides of the tracks remained as reminders of the prewar Siberian scene. The guard towers still stood at the corners of barbed-wire fences; wooden arches still held their coloured slogans, quoting from the pronouncements of the 'Father of Peoples'. One could still see groups of people dressed in grey, escorted by guards with ante-diluvian rifles. None of this had changed since my trip from Leningrad to the Kolyma six years before.

But something new had appeared. The crowds at each station were the most noticeable change, with their suitcases, bags, knotted bundles, or just packages. They seemed to be old residents of the stations. Men and women of all ages and little children were sleeping on blankets under benches, sitting on the dirty floors, crowding the lunch counters. Often it was impossible to force your way to the exit through the sitting, standing crowds of grimy people with a hungry glint in their eyes.

These were refugees evacuated by the government from the regions being given up to the advancing German armies. Except for two bowls of cloudy soup issued every day without charge at the station counters, these people were devoid of help from the authorities. They spent weeks in the filthy and almost unheated stations. Only much later were they allocated to collective farms by the local authorities or sent to factories and mines.

At each station, before the train had even stopped, little children in rags would run alongside the cars shouting, 'Bread, Uncle, a little piece of bread!' The station police would chase them off the platform.

After a long stop in Krasnoyarsk one of the passengers, a responsible official, judging from his well-fed look, told us:

'A girl came up to me at the station and asked me for something to eat. I told her I didn't have anything. She kept on begging and said that if I gave her something, she – do you understand? – in other words, she was ready for anything, absolutely anything. So I went back to the coach, got a loaf of bread and some fat, and gave them to her.'

The eyes of a lieutenant who was riding with us began to gleam. 'And then what?'

The passenger giggled in an embarrassed way.

'My, aren't you curious! I got what I wanted.'

The lieutenant jumped up without saying a word and hit the man twice with his fist. Then he wiped his hand on his shirt and sat down again. The other was speechless for a moment; then he shouted, 'How dare you? I'll call the N.K.V.D. and you'll see the inside of a jail!' He rushed out of the car.

The fellow was soon back with one of the N.K.V.D. men who always rode on each train. He was telling him something and showing him some papers. The N.K.V.D. man began to question us and everyone started talking at once. Only the lieutenant remained silent.

The N.K.V.D. man listened to us and then turned to the one the lieutenant had hit. 'Collect your things. Quick!'

'What? What's the matter?' The passenger looked as if he could not believe his ears.

'I'll show you what's the matter, you bastard,' the N.K.V.D. man yelled and struck him a tremendous blow on the head. 'The country is fighting the Germans while you enjoy your dirty little affairs. Let's go! Move fast!'

And he began to drive the man toward the end of the train, with shoves in the rear.

Another circumstance which showed that the nation was at war was the total disappearance of food at the stations. Cucumbers were the only things brought to the train by the peasant girls; if there happened to be anything else it was sold secretly at fantastic prices. Kostya and I had either eaten or given away our food supply and we were beginning to be sorry. Though we had money, it was often impossible to get food.

The stations between Krasnoyarsk and Novosibirsk were also overflowing with refugees, but of German descent. We quickly learned that these were all former citizens of the so-called Soviet Autonomous Republic of the Volga Germans.

The ancestors of these Germans were settled two hundred years ago on the left bank of the Volga, not far from Saratov. Only their language, an archaic German dialect, and a few customs remained from their German origin. These and their Protestant religion were the sole features which distinguished them from other Soviet citizens. They could speak Russian well and had their own Communist party, which was part of the All-Union Communist party. They also had the same Soviet administration, collective farms, and so forth as the rest of the country. Yet as soon as war started with Germany all 500,000 of them were 'resettled' to Siberia in a period of a few days. The whole 'operation' was carried out brilliantly. Strong units of the special troops of the N.K.V.D. were moved into the area of the former 'Republic', as well as the railroad personnel necessary for military transportation. In a week all the towns and villages of the 'Republic' were deserted. The people were given two or three hours to pack and were allowed to take along one or two small bags of food apiece. Everything else was left behind.

LIFE ON THE RAILWAY

While still in transit, all the men between sixteen and fifty-five were taken off the trains at small stations and sent to unknown destinations. Only the women, children, and old men arrived in the far reaches of Siberia and their situation was even worse than that of those refugees we had seen earlier along the way.

I lay on my shelf and tried to think why the government had acted this way toward its own subjects. They had had no contact with Germany for a very long time and they had little more reason for sympathizing with the enemy than all Soviet citizens had. Moreover, they lived a good 500 miles from the front. Yet they had been thrown off the land where their fathers, grandfathers, and great-grandfathers had been born; deprived of everything, and in fact condemned to slow extinction – all without having committed any crimes against the Soviet authorities. Their 'Republic' had ceased to exist. The very names of their towns and villages were immediately changed by order of the Supreme Soviet of the U.S.S.R., so that even the memory of the Germans on the Volga would vanish. The Constitution of the U.S.S.R. was amended to omit mention of this 'Republic'.

I tried to avoid getting off at the stations after this . . .

We got into Novosibirsk at night. The enormous new station was completely filled with evacuees, and for the first time we saw wounded returning to the front after convalescing.

Novosibirsk was the first lap of our journey. Here in the morning we would have to choose a new route and buy tickets. But meanwhile Kostya and I managed to find a place on the station floor and settled ourselves on our bags not far from a group of officers, deciding to spend the rest of the night there. It was impossible to think of sleep. We looked around us and talked over our impressions.

Our attention was soon attracted by the officers. They were talking loudly. One, a tall, thin captain, was saying, 'The Germans are occupying the Donets Basin, and our men are being bowled back and can't seem to hold on. The staffs are full of fools, or traitors. The commissars are being shot in the back. If things keep on this way, it won't be long before the war is over.'

This was very strange. Never in my life had I heard such criticism of the High Command.

Somebody we could not see said, 'The party men are getting the medals – the parasites. When it comes to battle they're sick and stay in the rear, but when it's medals they're out in front. We've shot two of them already in my outfit . . .'

A small lieutenant was talking, 'In our outfit someone shot the chief of the Special Section [the army N.K.V.D.] in the back of the head during a German barrage. After that they didn't appoint another. The regiment just had no Special Section.'

'Those are all trifles,' said the captain. 'The important thing is that we've been retreating for six months now without a let-up. Three five-year plans were spent getting the army ready, but our equipment isn't worth a damn. We're short of everything, and the soldiers are hungry in the trenches. The Germans have tanks and trucks; our men are always on foot. Rear headquarters spend their time drinking and fooling with girls, and evacuating themselves farther and farther from the front . . .'

The one we couldn't see interrupted the captain again. 'The commissar calls a meeting and shouts, "Let us die, comrades, for World Revolution, for the Communist party, and for Comrade Stalin!" And then one of the boys lets him have it in the back with a rifle butt, and he topples over. I guess something must have been damaged; he died the next day – for Stalin.'

I felt extremely uncomfortable. Kostya had been glancing around with a worried look for some time. He leaned over to me and whispered in my ear, 'We'd better get out of here. They'll grab them all for talking that way and send them to the Kolyma. And they'll grab us, too, for listening.'

I agreed and we moved to another place, as far away as possible, near a group of refugees.

As soon as it was light we went out into the city. We knew that Novosibirsk was crowded. Several ministries, a large number of trusts and other organizations, and a few theatres and institutes had been transferred here from Moscow. Though it was very early people swarmed on the streets, hurrying somewhere. Queues of several hundred each had formed in front of stores and restaurants. It took us about four hours to get breakfast, but the time was profitably spent in questioning the people around us about the local situation.

One talkative ex-resident of Moscow advised us not to try to go any farther west.

'Don't even think of it,' he told us. 'You won't get to Moscow in any case; they won't let you get beyond Kazan. There are only unheated freight trains from here on, and the temperature as you can see is 55° below. It would take you a month at least. Not only that, but sometimes they draft people right out of the trains, so you'll end up in the army instead of in Moscow.'

'But my family is in Moscow,' said Kostya, 'that's the only place I want to go.'

At least that's what he told the stranger. I knew that Kostya, with his ex-political prisoner's passport, could not legally, under threat of long imprisonment, go closer than 65 miles to Moscow.

'Forget about it,' the Muscovite said in a low voice. 'The Germans will take Moscow any day now and your family will find themselves "abroad". I'm a fool – I went away and left everything . . .'

His information was corroborated by others. Only troop trains were allowed through to the west, and only refugees and dismantled factory equipment were being shipped to the east. An engineer told us that he had been made to accompany the equipment of his factory.

'. . . I had to leave my family and give up my apartment. And for what? As soon as we got past the Ural Mountains there was an order to unload the equipment immediately. They wouldn't even let us do it at a station. We were taken to an open field a few miles away and had to dump all the machines into the snow. When you get farther west on any line you'll see the stuff lying around in the snow from Novosibirsk to the Urals. My advice to you is go south, to Tashkent. That's an easier trip. When you get to the Caspian you can cross over to Europe. That is, if the Germans haven't taken the other shore by that time.'

Kostya and I had already discussed this last alternative for our journey. Central Asia was better off than all the other parts of Russia, except possibly the Far East. And they still had passenger trains there.

And so, having considered all the circumstances, we decided to go to European Russia by way of Tashkent. Kostya gave up his hope of getting to Moscow and decided to accompany me to my destination, where we still had a chance of arriving before the Germans. We had no concrete plans for the future. Our friendship and mutual desire not to get into the army held us together. To die for Stalin and World Revolution was not what we wanted to do.

Novosibirsk had nothing to make us want to stay there. The city was so full of new residents that not the smallest corner could be found to live in. Many people who already had jobs were still living at the station.

However, it was almost impossible to leave the place. Half an hour before the departure of every train a couple of dozen tickets were sold to the public; and there was always a line of several hundred people at the ticket window. All the other tickets, according to the glorious Soviet tradition, were sold somewhere, in a place unknown to the public, to various 'responsible workers' making trips in connection with their duties, to officers, medal winners, and other representatives of the Soviet aristocracy. The ticket agents were said to do a fine business taking bribes from ordinary passengers; but when Kostya finally found himself at a ticket window after a thirty-hour wait and offered the cashier an extra 100 rubles if he would sell us two tickets to Tashkent, the cashier began to shout that he was being insulted and Kostya had to make himself scarce. Either 100 rubles was not enough (as the other passengers claimed) or the cashier was scared to take money from strangers.

We lived three days at the station. Every new train from Moscow enlarged the crowd. Only the wounded were found places somewhere in the city. All our attempts to get tickets were unsuccessful, and Kostya had caught cold from lying on the cold floor. We had to do something about our situation quickly.

Having chosen the most impressive documents from the pile we had bearing the big seal 'Dalstroy, N.K.V.D., U.S.S.R.,' I took my place in the queue leading to the station manager's office. Although it was 4 a.m. there were ten people ahead of me. Five hours later the office opened.

Carefully I placed five 100-ruble bills between the documents, and when it was my turn entered the office.

'What do you want? Make it quick!' said a man in military uniform who was sitting at the desk.

'My friend and I are on our way from Dalstroy to the Caucasus to join the army at our place of residence. We need two tickets to Krasnovodsk on the Caspian Sea,' I said immediately.

'That's impossible. There are no tickets for the public.'

I started to explain to him heatedly the circumstances leading to our arrival in Novosibirsk.

'Your papers!' he interrupted.

I handed him the batch I had prepared. He took the documents and looked through them hurriedly.

'All right. You'll get your tickets. But see that no one knows about it,' he said, returning the papers to me. He wrote out an incomprehensible message and added, 'Go to window 18. That's all. Next!'

I dashed out of the office overjoyed and ran to tell Kostya. Of course the money was gone. I had not even noticed him take it from among the papers.

At window 18, where tickets were usually sold to railroad personnel, we presented the station manager's message and were promptly sold tickets. There were no other people at the window.

That evening we were on our way south. There were a great many passengers. Normally, only as many people are allowed in a Soviet train as there are seats, and the seats are numbered. But railroad personnel must find some way to eat and live. The manager sells tickets, the ticket agents sell tickets, the train conductors sell tickets – without seat numbers; and the porters allow people into their cars for a sum of solid cash. As a result, there are at least twice as many passengers as seats.

But we had seats on benches, since our tickets were 'most correct'.

Through the windows we saw the endless steppes of Kazakhstan. The railroad was single track, so again we spent hours at the stations, letting military trains pass in both directions. The stories we had heard in Novosibirsk turned out to be true: at every station there were piles of machine tools, electric motors, and other equipment removed from European Russia. Part of it was packed in boxes but much had no covering at all. In some places equipment lay in the open steppe, by a railroad siding, covered by a thin layer of snow.

The passengers in our train were for the most part Moscow people who had been evacuated from the capital. They were all very pleased to be going south. They considered themselves extremely lucky. Only a few privileged people were allowed into Central Asia. Here, it was said, life was still good, almost prewar: you could buy anything and even find a room.

6. INTERLUDE IN ALMA ATA

KOSTYA's condition was steadily growing worse. As his Novosibirsk cold had turned into a serious case of flu with a high temperature and a great deal of coughing, we decided to leave the train at Alma Ata, the capital of Kazakhstan, which is one of the Central Asian Soviet republics. After a long explanation at the N.K.V.D. office in the railway station we were finally allowed into the city.

Alma Ata turned out to be a small and extremely attractive place. The part near the station had retained some of its ancient, exotic oriental qualities: narrow alleyways, single-story white houses with flat roofs, crowded small courtyards full of fruit trees, and impassable mud everywhere. There was no snow. Water gurgled in small irrigation ditches along the roadsides.

These ditches also ran along the city's principal streets, which were planted with tall poplars. The centre of the city was entirely new; three-quarters of Alma Ata was built after the Revolution. The houses were well constructed, and the Opera House, built in the Moorish style, was magnificent. The streets in the centre of the city were paved with asphalt. There were a lot of stores and a variety of goods was still available in them.

In other words, we were pleasantly surprised.

We went into a café and ordered ice cream, a luxury we had not seen for years. Kostya assured me that ice cream was good for the flu and he must have eaten at least a quart of it. It actually seemed to make him feel considerably better. Having wandered around the city and questioned several people about places to eat, we learned that there were only two large restaurants. We went to the one called the Kraikom Dining Room. It was excellent. There was a large hall with booths on the second floor, and a stage where an orchestra was playing 'The Blue Handkerchief'. The restaurant was crowded, but after about half an hour we were able to get places at a table. Since we had eaten very little the last two days on the train, we ordered a large dinner and a bottle of wine. Then we began to look around.

A pretty girl was singing sentimental popular songs on the stage. The guests were obviously not from these parts. Except for two policemen by the cloakroom, there were no natives of the Mongolian type in sight.

Never in my life anywhere in the U.S.S.R. had I seen people with so much money as in Alma Ata during the war. Some did not bother to keep track of their money at all and spent it recklessly. Once in a crowded streetcar someone's suitcase fell open and wads of large bills rolled out. I don't know how much money there was. The owner couldn't have retrieved more than half of it, but he didn't look the least bit upset. He must have lost tens if not hundreds of thousands of rubles.

In Alma Ata I had occasion to notice another phenomenon wholly strange to me: anti-Semitism. Where I had happened to be before the war, there was almost none of it. It was strictly forbidden by law. People were put in prison for terms of three to five years just for using the word 'kike' instead of 'Jew'. But this seldom happened. The 'Jewish question' didn't exist. So I was astonished when, on our second day in Alma Ata, a group of Moscow students came up to the restaurant table where we were sitting with two others.

One of them addressed me. 'Have you been sitting here long?'

'About an hour.' I shrugged my shoulders.

'And this man?' pointing to my neighbour.

'I don't know; he was here when we came,' I answered.

'Listen, friend, how long have you been here?' The student addressed the man directly.

'What business is it of yours?' asked the latter angrily, in a voice with a Jewish accent.

'Hey, I think you're a kike! It's our business because the likes of you sit here for days on end, while we have to wait an hour to get a table. Listen,' he said to a passing waiter, 'has this citizen eaten already?'

'Yes, he's eaten.'

'Well then, get the hell out of here,' the student shouted, 'or we'll throw you downstairs!'

'What right have you to talk so?' spluttered the man. 'I'll call the police!'

'The police, eh?' said a second student. 'Come on, boys, grab him under the arms, we'll show him the police!' And they seized him by the arms and legs and carried him out of the room. Another student took his place.

I sat there, not knowing what to think or say. The people at the neighbouring tables had listened to the scene but no one had interfered. Kostya and I were afraid to do anything, as we had not yet received permission from the police to reside in Alma Ata and our documents, in general, were doubtful ones. But still I got up, went to the door, and looked down. The man who had been thrown out was talking heatedly to a policeman who was not even listening. The students came back and at several tables places were made ready for them immediately.

I asked the one sitting with us, 'How can you make a scene like that? You can be put in jail for it.'

'There's a war on, and a lot of things can be done,' he answered. 'And these parasites should be destroyed. Why isn't he in the army?'

'Well, you don't seem to be in the army either,' I remarked.

'I can be called up any day, but even if he gets in, he'll be in the quartermasters or the medics. Stalin gave an order: no kikes are to be taken for soldiers. So they live here like kings. They stole a lot of money in Moscow during the panic and now they've become millionaires.'

The student was exaggerating when he talked about 'millionaires'. I had seen Jews on the streets of Alma Ata from Bessarabia and Poland. You could recognize them by their dress and speech. But they were destitute. One could tell from their looks that they didn't have even a few rubles for a meal, let alone millions.

Looking back now, I find it hard to explain these appearances of anti-Semitism. Usually the outbreaks ended in mere profanity and bad language, and there were very few fights. But the police took no measures whatsoever. This was absolutely new. I do not think that any Nazi influence was involved here. We all knew very little about the actual content of Nazi ideas; and in the Soviet Press there was not much mention of the anti-Semitic measures of Hitlerism. Perhaps the fact that more Jews than others were given permission to enter Central Asia was significant. Perhaps Stalin's order which the student had mentioned (and which was actually given) antagonized the soldiers who were sent to the front. Or the widespread opinion that the Jews had got hold of more money than anyone else in the Moscow panic may have been a factor. It was hard for us to judge.

We were very careful not to get mixed up in any such incidents, knowing that inspection of our papers would end badly for us.

We lived in Alma Ata illegally. The first evening of our stay there, after an unsuccessful attempt to find a room, we persuaded the door-man of a restaurant to take us in for a substantial sum. After the restaurant closed we went to the other end of town, on the edge of the native quarter, where the doorman lived. His house consisted of two rooms with a hallway. In one room with a separate entrance lived two girls who always had company. Drunken sounds and singing were audible all night.

With the doorman lived his wife and daughter and a Spanish girl, Teresa, who spoke Russian very badly, one of the group of Spanish youth who had been brought to Russia in 1939, after Franco's victory. The old doorman took me into his own bed. His wife and daughter slept together in the other. Kostya, being the sick one, was given a bed in the hallway, where Teresa slept on a trunk. In the succeeding days we tried to find another place to live, but it was hopeless. There were half a million people in the city whose normal population was 150,000. In addition to this, there was one advantage in living with the old man. He did not require us to go to the police for a residence permit. We knew that there was no chance of our getting permission to live in the capital of the Kazakh Republic. We remained in the old man's clay house, in spite of all its discomforts.

Kostya still had the flu. Unlike other sick people he did not stay in bed but wandered about town every day, developing a passion for strong applejack. He even started a romance with Teresa. In other words, he showed no desire to get well. But we could not continue our journey, because his temperature was always above normal and we could not risk his having a serious illness while travelling.

At the end of the year the Germans captured Rostov. In a few weeks the way home might be cut off. I was beginning to get seriously worried. I tried everything to force Kostya to make an effort to cure his everlasting flu so that we could be on our way west. But he did not listen to me, and he would disappear until late at night, returning thoroughly drunk. Something or other was bothering him and he was trying to drown it in drink and romantic adventures.

The New Year, 1942, was drawing close. We agreed to spend New Year's Eve together, in the small room of the old doorman. A light snow had fallen, but the weather was fine. In the morning we bought all the things we needed to celebrate the New Year. This was not easy. The food situation in Alma Ata was growing worse every day and prices had shot up in the three weeks that we had been there. In order to get pastry, which was sold only in the foyer of the Opera House, we went two nights running to see an opera in the Kazakh language. Kazakh operas alternated with Russian ones. This opera was so hard on one's senses, the music so wild to the European ear, that it was all we could do to sit through the first act. Then we would run out to the foyer, buy our pastry, and hurry out of the theatre.

However, the Russian opera was excellent in Alma Ata. All 2,000 seats were always sold out, and I had to reserve tickets a week in advance. But there were only 100 to 150 people in the audience on the nights that the Kazakh operas were presented, and most of them had free tickets. The Kazakhs themselves preferred the Russian operas.

Only a few hours were left until the New Year, but Kostya was still missing. Teresa and I had waited for him for a long time. He had promised to come at six, and it was already eight, and no Kostya. I decided to go out and look for him, trying to remember the places where he might be.

On a dark side street I finally ran into Kostya. He was waving his arms and muttering to himself. He scarcely recognized me. I grabbed him by the arm and dragged him to the nearest streetcar stop. Breathing heavily and staggering, he tried to tear himself from my grasp. His eyes moved around aimlessly and he continued to mumble. The heavy smell of vodka was everywhere.

At the car stop I sat him down on a bench, sat down opposite him, and kept my hands on him lightly. His eyes were completely senseless and he was smiling at something with an idiot's smile.

Suddenly, not saying a word, he hit me on the head with his heavy fist. I went down in the snow. When I got up he was still grinning senselessly, looking at me triumphantly. I was very angry, but the streetcar was approaching so I pushed him into it and got on myself.

When we got to our stop I had to tear Kostya away from the streetcar straps. He didn't want to get off. The conductor helped me. I shoved Kostya forward, and he staggered on, waving his hands weakly and showing a distinct tendency to fall into the nearest irrigation ditch.

When we got to a deserted spot I gave full vent to my irritation. My ear was still aching from his blow. I knocked him down with some difficulty, sat on his stomach, and began to hit him with a sort of evil joy. He tried to defend himself, giggling, but I was merciless and didn't care where I hit him. Then I rubbed his face with snow and put some down his neck. He tried to make himself as small as possible. After this I put him on his feet and led him home.

Teresa was horror-stricken. Of course there could be no question of a New Year celebration for Kostya. We undressed him and put him to bed.

The doorman's wife and daughter had gone out somewhere, and the old man had not yet returned from the restaurant, so Teresa and I greeted the New Year together. She was unhappy. Something in her had called forth memories of far-away Spain, which she had left three years ago. She recalled her native sunny Barcelona, battles with Franco's troops, and her last days in Spain. In her very broken Russian she told me about her arrival in Moscow.

'At first it was fun and fine. They greeted us with music and flowers. Then they gave us apartments and some of us went to the Crimea for a rest. After that there was nothing. We had to go into factories. The work was terribly hard. The director spotted me and gave me lighter work – but not for nothing.' She shook her head sadly. 'Then another factory, another director. They are all the same.'

She began to cry. In a mixture of Russian and Spanish she complained through her sobs about her fate – how hard it was for a lone girl to live in a foreign country.

'Why did I leave Spain? My mother is in Barcelona, and I had many friends there. Some of them are left. And now I'm in Russia, in Asia, among these nasty people. I'm almost a prostitute!'

Then she went to pieces completely. The shouts of our neighbours' drunken guests and Kostya's heroic snores did nothing to make her forget the thoughts that were torturing her. With great difficulty I managed to quiet her and persuade her to go to bed and forget her troubles on the eve of the New Year. She could scarcely understand me. I sat down beside her and stayed there, holding her tear-stained hand in mine, until she went to sleep.

The old man came home in a very gay state, and his wife and daughter showed up, too. The daughter had brought a boy friend with her, one of the local firemen. It was very late before we managed to get to sleep, finding ourselves places on the beds and on the floor.

Kostya was the last to wake up. He sat up in bed and inspected himself in the mirror for a long time. There were three large bruises on his face.

'Where did I get these, Vladimir, do you know?'

'I don't know, old man,' I answered. 'I met you last night very drunk and well decorated.'

'I don't remember a damned thing about where I was or what I did. I went to Zina's first.' Zina was another of his girl friends. 'I remember leaving her house. Then I went into a small restaurant. They were drinking something there. And that's all I remember. How can I show myself in the street with a face like this?'

'You can't,' I said quickly. 'The police would spot you at once and ask for your papers.'

'You're right. I'll have to stay home. My temperature is up again. I just took it. We've absolutely got to get a local residence permit. The old man has been pestering us about it and we might get into trouble any minute. Have you made any progress?'

I had tried to get a residence permit several times; but the police would only grant one if you had a certificate from the city soviet stating that you were allowed to stay in the city of Alma Ata. I could not get such a certificate in spite of the fact that the secretary of the city soviet, a nice young woman, treated me with extreme civility.

Kostya heard me out and then said, 'You're a fool and you don't know anything. That girl has designs on you. I was going to tell you that a week ago. Test it out. Go there tomorrow and tell her you have no place to live. You'll see, she'll give you a certificate.'

It turned out that he was right. The next time I went to the city soviet I took Tonya home from work and said, 'Tonya, what'll we do? Kostya and I have no place to live any more.'

She showed immediate interest. 'You mean you have no more money?'

'No, we've got money, but the landlord doesn't want to keep both of us any more.'

'He'll keep one of you?'

'He'll let one of us stay, but he demands a residence permit.'

Tonya squeezed my hand sympathetically and said, 'We'll have to think of something. I know. I can put one of you up temporarily at my place. I have two rooms and there are four of us – Mother, myself, and the two children. But we'll fit you in somehow. Let's go in and take a look.'

Tonya had two clean rooms, and two small children about four or five years old. They were locked in, as their grandmother was out working.

'Here, look, we can put one of you up here,' she said, pointing to two boxes standing in a corner. 'It won't cost much.'

We had dinner together and Tonya told me about herself.

'I had a husband. He was called up right away and was lost in the second month of the war. One of his friends wrote me that he was probably killed. So I live alone with the children. The work isn't bad. I can make out . . .'

Tonya was alluding to the material 'gratitude' of the countless people who wanted something from the city soviet.

'But still, it's dull.' And she was lost in thought.

I stroked her hand.

'Don't be sad, Tonya. You are still young. The war will be over and you'll live well again. Let's go to the theatre this evening. I have tickets.'

Tonya cheered up. On the way to the theatre we decided that I would move into her apartment and she would arrange for both Kostya and me to receive a letter from the city soviet to the police about residence permits.

'But only after you move in,' she added half seriously.

During the show I kept trying to find a way out of the situation. I knew what Tonya was driving at, but I didn't want to get caught in her matrimonial trap, although she was a nice girl and an attractive one. The thought of going west to my mother was still lodged firmly in my mind. Every delay was risky. At the same time, I did not want to leave Kostya and go on alone. That was extremely dangerous in those times. And Kostya was exaggerating his illness in order to stay in Alma Ata. The only thing to do was to stay too until I could get Kostya to leave.

It was late when Tonya and I got home after the theatre.

'Why should you go home now?' she said, not looking at me and speaking in a slightly trembling voice. 'Spend the night here, since you've already decided to live with me.' Her laugh was short and forced.

Everyone was asleep in the apartment. It was warm and quiet.

There was one thing more that I felt I should tell Tonya: who we were, where we were coming from, and what we had been. While I was telling her about the past years of my life I noticed that she answered me at rarer intervals. I did not know what she was thinking.

In the morning, when I was taking her to work, she stopped suddenly and said, 'Don't be angry with me. I'll get you a letter from the city soviet, but – we'll have to give up the idea of living together. I can't take the risk. I'm afraid for you, too. I'll see you tonight.'

We said goodbye and I went my way dejectedly. From one point of view it was a good way out. I hadn't deceived Tonya and I hadn't told her that I loved her (she probably would not have believed me anyway). And there would not be a false connection between two people who did not belong together. On the other hand Tonya's words had hurt me. I had considered our relationship, if we were to have one, as well as her attraction to me as something serious. But as soon as she had learned of my six years at forced labour as a political prisoner she had dropped me as something frightening and dangerous. I was no different from what I had been before I told her, but my accursed past had come between us. What if I had been in love with Tonya? How would her change of attitude have affected me then?

In the evening she avoided my eyes. She gave me the letter which she had promised us, and tried to talk of other things. Apparently she was even unhappier about it than I. I rose to leave several times but she wouldn't let me go, although she would not talk about our parting.

That night she cried several times.

When it began to grow light I got up and dressed quickly. Tonya woke up and called me over to her. She began to speak, holding my hands.

'I guess fate hasn't been kind to me. I knew that you wouldn't stay with me long; we are too different. But I couldn't help trying anyway. And now I've been punished. You would have left me anyway. I'm older than you are, and I've got two children. Why should you want to stay with me? You would have left, wouldn't you?' she kept asking, large tears flowing down her cheeks.

I stroked her head and didn't think of myself any more, but only that she was much more unhappy than I. She was hoping for something. For a moment she believed something.

'Perhaps we would have had to part. Tonya. They would have put me in the army. There's the war, after all.'

'Yes, the army,' she repeated, as if trying to reassure herself. 'But they don't take people like you. They are afraid to give them weapons. I heard about it at the city soviet. Oh, well – I just don't want you to think badly of me. I want you to understand me. I am a member of the party. I have a responsible job and a family. Sooner or later the N.K.V.D. would find out about your past. And then – then everything would be over anyway. No, it's impossible! And we can't see each other any more. Believe me, it will be harder for me than for you. But you know that anyway. And now, good-bye. Go.'

I walked along the streets of the city feeling miserable.

The next day I went to the passport desk of the district police and presented my letter and papers. I sat a long time waiting for a decision.

People kept passing me. The official to whom I had given my papers came out of the chief's office several times and looked at me strangely. There was a telephone conversation in the office and I was beginning to get worried. Then I was called in.

The chief received me standing, with my passport in his hand.

'You are Petrov?'

'Yes, I am.'

'Are these your papers?' He showed them to me.

'Yes, sir.' I took them hurriedly.

'How long did you spend in the camps?'

'Six years.'

'For counter-revolution?'

'Yes, sir.'

'Do you know that you are forbidden to enter a number of localities, among which are the capitals of union republics?'

'No, I didn't know that.'

'Well, now you do. Sit down and write.'

'What?'

'I'll tell you what to write. Do as I say and keep quiet.'

I sat down at the desk and took up a pen. The chief began to dictate:

'I, the undersigned, hereby attest that I am aware I do not have the right to live in a series of localities, as listed in Directive No. — of the Council of People's Commissars, of — date, among which are the capitals of all union and autonomous republics, the principal cities of districts and regions and within a radius of 65 miles of each of these; that I am forbidden to approach the national boundaries of the U.S.S.R. and all seacoasts closer than 130 miles. I am also aware that in the event of my violation of this directive of the Council of People's Commissars I am criminally liable under existing laws. I agree to leave the city of Alma Ata within twenty-four hours after 12 noon, 13th January 1942.'

'Write your address and sign it,' ordered the chief.

An hour later I was telling Kostya about it.

'What do you think we should do?' he asked.

'I'll go to Tashkent tomorrow, and on from there.'

'I don't think we should.'

'Why not?'

'I hear that on the other side of the Caspian all mobilized enterprises are run much more strictly than over here. As soon as we get to Baku they'll mobilize us.'

'Maybe so, but if we stay here they'll be certain to arrest us and send us back to camp.'

'Bunk! They haven't got any system any more. The city is jammed and the police won't touch us. Did you give our correct address?'

'Of course not. But it's not so hard to find us.'

'I don't agree. I've decided to stay and I advise you to do the same.'

'No, Kostya, I've got to go. The Germans are practically certain to start another drive in the spring and I won't get home.'

'Well, do as you like. Maybe there's some point in your going, but not me. My family is in Moscow, and if I go anywhere it will be there.'

'And they'll hand you right in. You know you can't enter Moscow.'

'To hell with the law!' Kostya was irritated. 'What do we have to be afraid of after the Kolyma?'

And so we parted. The next day I took the train to Tashkent. Kostya remained in Alma Ata. Six years later, in the United States, I learned that he got into the army after all, fought over an immense amount of territory, and had all sorts of adventures. After the war he deserted and he is now in Western Germany.

7. ACROSS THE CASPIAN SEA

ON reaching Tashkent in the evening I was told that our express would go no farther and we must change trains. The enormous square in front of the station was packed with thousands of men, women, and children, standing, sitting on their belongings, or milling about among stuffed burlap bags, huge bundles, and rickety trunks. They had been brought here on cattle trains from faraway European Russia and put off with no idea when or where they would go next. The station itself was empty, the tall windows of its spacious waiting rooms casting a bright light on the wet and shivering crowd.

I learned that I could not get the ticket to continue my journey until the next morning, and that to get it I would have to present, besides the other documents, a certificate that I had bathed in a public bath and that my clothes had been disinfected in Tashkent. I also learned that no one was allowed inside the station because of the expected arrival of an important official.

Since the prospect of sleeping on the square did not appeal to me, I checked my two bags and set out to find a room. The city was dark and gloomy. Although the front was far away all the street lights were out; only a small blue-tinted electric bulb flickered feebly here and there. I made several attempts to secure a room at one of the near-by hotels, but the complacent clerks answered my questions as though I had just escaped from a lunatic asylum, or else they didn't answer at all but turned their broad backs on me. As I wandered farther into the town, pondering my problems, a brilliant idea occurred to me. After a few inquiries and a few more darkened streets I found what I was looking for: a large door with the sign 'Public Bath'.

A number of men and women sat dozing along the walls of the large entrance hall. As I entered three men accosted me so suddenly that I stepped back. They pulled at my sleeves, all talking at once.

'Do you want a certificate?'

'Of disinfection?'

'Of having bathed?'

'Are you going west?'

It took me some minutes to grasp the fact that they were professional certificate procurers. For a small sum they would go through the governmental cleansing and disinfecting process for people who did not want to risk ruining their own clothes in the disinfection chamber. Looking the certificate procurers' clothes over carefully, I became convinced that it would be madness to risk my own: all their garments looked as if a great cow had chewed them thoroughly and for a long time.

I inquired what the friendly services of these representatives of a

312

hitherto unheard-of profession would cost me. It was ten rubles for my suit and five for myself. That seemed fair, and I gave my name to two of them who wrote it down carefully on a piece of paper and joyfully departed to wash and be disinfected. The third one remained with me.

'That's all,' I said, 'I don't need any duplicate certificates.'

'I take antityphus shots for anyone who needs a certificate of immunity to typhus. They won't let you past Ashkhabad without one. The shots are given right here. If you want one, I'll be glad to take it for you.'

It might be useful I thought, and I had no desire for an injection myself.

'How much?' I asked.

'Twenty-five rubles,' he said. Then, seeing my face lengthen perceptibly, he added zealously, 'But you must understand – this is an injection against typhus, it's not just giving your clothes to be disinfected. Look, I'll show you.' He bared his arms and his back. They were speckled with needle pricks.

'Yes, but you gain by all this, too,' I said. 'You've had over a hundred shots. That's enough to make you immune from typhus for life. I'll give you ten rubles.'

'Twenty.'

'Fifteen is my limit.'

'All right,' he agreed happily. And writing my name on a smudgy piece of paper, the typhus expert disappeared down a corridor.

I went to the ticket window, behind which a young girl was peacefully sleeping. Waking her up as gently as I could I asked her if private bathrooms were available.

'Yes,' she said. 'First class, three rubles an hour; second class, one and a half.'

'Can I rent one for the whole night?'

'For the whole night? Are you that dirty?' she asked incredulously.

'No, I just want to sleep there. There's a couch in the room, isn't there?'

'Yes, in a first-class room. But I don't know about letting it for the whole night. We never do that. This isn't a hotel, citizen.'

'But what's the difference?' I said. 'I'll pay for eight hours and everything will be in order.'

'Are you alone?' the girl asked with sudden suspicion. 'Two people as a rule are not allowed in one bathroom.'

She put an emphasis on 'as a rule'. I understood and set her mind at rest that I was alone.

But as I turned around with my eight tickets, I found that two young girls had got up from a bench while I was talking and now stood waiting.

'Pardon me,' one of them said in a low voice, 'did you get a private bathroom?'

'Yes.'

'Just for one person?'

'Just for one.'

'You don't want to get one for two?'

'No, thank you.'

'Excuse me,' said the girl almost in a whisper and moved back to her seat.

I thought for a moment and then went after her.

'Do you need money very badly?' I asked, touching her arm.

'Yes,' she whispered, not looking at me.

'How much?'

'One hundred rubles for a ticket to Novosibirsk.'

I quickly figured up how much money I had left. It seemed to be enough. Taking 100 rubles from my wallet, I handed them to the girl. She looked at me inquiringly.

'Shall I go with you?'

'No, thank you. I want to sleep.'

The disinfection specialist was the first to come back with a certificate. Then came the typhus pincushion, and last of all my representative at the public bath. I paid them all and went to my private bathroom where I took a good hot bath and went to sleep soundly on the soft couch.

It was barely dawn when I joined the throng which was besieging the ticket windows of the Tashkent railroad station. From all parts of the crowd there arose sighs and grunts from people who were being pushed and squeezed. After a while I felt someone's hand making its way into one of my pockets. I turned around and saw a young man next to me. He was looking into the distance with a vacuous expression on his face.

'Hey, friend! You've made a mistake. My money is in a different pocket.'

He looked at me quickly and the hand disappeared from my pocket. A few moments later there was a shout in the crowd, 'My money's gone! Police!'

Ploughing my way ruthlessly through the mob, I soon reached the window in spite of the clutching hands of my fellow citizens. I was too experienced to try to find the end of such a fan-shaped queue. Straining every muscle, I reached for the thick iron grill which protected the cashier from the frenzied crowd, gripped it tightly, and shoved a bunch of papers and money through it, yelling at the top of my lungs, 'To Krasnovodsk!'

A man in N.K.V.D. uniform sitting next to the cashier took my papers and began to look through them. I held my breath. Could something be missing? But everything seemed to be in order and in five minutes I had my ticket and my papers back. The only thing with-held was my change, 50 rubles, but I had expected this. It was a war-time levy, not provided for by law, which ticket agents all over Russia were imposing on travellers.

Before I had elbowed my way out of the building a loud voice behind me shouted, 'No more tickets! Clear out, citizens!'

I learned at the station that the train would not leave before noon, although it had been scheduled for the evening before.

Contrary to expectations, the train was not crowded, there were even empty seats, and the crowd in front of the ticket windows began to seem a figment of my imagination. There were four people in my compartment: two Red Army lieutenants, an engineer from a Moscow factory, and myself.

The lieutenants had been wounded at the front, had spent a month in the Tashkent military hospital, and were now returning to the front. The engineer had been evacuated from Moscow with the equipment from his plant, and was now on his way to look for his family who had been evacuated to Saratov by mistake. The plant equipment had been dumped along the road, because the train was confiscated by the military authorities and had to be unloaded immediately. The engineer had impressive documents from the Central Committee of the All-Union Communist Party, and he was able to buy tickets to any destination without trouble. He also had a good deal of money.

The train was considered a fast one, although it travelled at the usual wartime speed of 10 to 15 miles an hour. The lieutenants and the engineer decided to start a poker game. I was invited to join, but I refused. A man from another compartment came in; and the game started. I lay on the top shelf and watched it from there.

The game was for fairly high stakes. Some of the pots amounted to 1,000 rubles, and most of them were taken by the lieutenants. After a while I succumbed to temptation and sat in on the game. At first I lost, but then I got a streak of luck and won so steadily that presently the others refused to play. My winnings amounted to 4,000 rubles. We all talked it over and decided to spend the money together at the first chance.

The chance came the next day. When the train was approaching Ashkhabad, the capital of the Turkmen Republic, a rumour started that it would go no farther and we would have to change there. The rumour was confirmed and we soon found ourselves going out into the square in front of the Ashkhabad station. There was a fifteen-hour wait until the next train, and we decided to explore the town and rest somewhere until it was time to go to the station again.

Our exploration for the most part consisted in buying bottles of vodka and food to go with it. Then one of the lieutenants went out on reconnaissance and came back with the information that he had found an apartment where we could stay for 100 rubles until our train left. We set out, heavily laden with food and drink bought with my poker winnings.

The old woman and her two daughters who lived in the apartment greeted us pleasantly and quickly set a table for us. Soon an impressive battery of bottles was arrayed on it. A fire was started in the stove and the old woman began to cook supper with the food we had brought. She and her daughters were obviously very hungry, and we invited them to eat with us. One of the girls disappeared for a few minutes and came back with a friend, a pretty eighteen-year-old girl called Valya. We all sat down and the feast began.

I sat between one of the lieutenants and Valya. On the other side of Valya sat the other officer. We ate a lot but drank still more. The glass in front of me was never empty for a second. The lieutenant next to me kept filling it up. After a while I began to feel dizzy and tried to refuse to drink more; but Valya, who had been whispering in the ear of the lieutenant next to her, started persuading me to take another drink. Looking into her pretty dark blue eyes, I drank again and again until there came a moment when everything vanished and I sank into an abyss.

It was dark and quiet when I awoke. I was in bed. I began to feel my pockets with nervous movements. My wallet was gone.

What time was it? My train was leaving at 4 a.m. And my tickets? They were in the wallet! I jumped out of bed and put on the light. I checked my pockets again: no wallet, no watch. I went into the next room and turned on the light. From three beds the eyes of the old woman and her two daughters looked at me.

'Where is everybody?' I asked.

'They've gone to the station. One of the men said he would come back and wake you in time for the train.'

'They've taken my money. I've been robbed.'

'Good lord! That can't be. Maybe the officer that slept in the same bed with you, the blond one, took it along so you wouldn't lose it. He'll surely bring it back.'

Not at all reassured I hastened to the station. Remembering my two suitcases – the checks for them gone, too – I stopped at the baggage room, explained what had happened, described the suitcases, and asked the attendant to see if he still had them.

'I don't need to look,' he said. 'An officer came and got them about half an hour ago.'

I plunged into the crowd looking for the thieves and soon found the engineer.

'Where are the officers?' I cried.

'I lost sight of them a while ago. They disappeared all of a sudden. Why?'

I told him.

'I'll watch for them here,' he said, 'and you run to the N.K.V.D. and notify them.'

The N.K.V.D. officer on night duty interrupted me as soon as I opened my mouth. 'Who are you? Show me your papers.'

'My papers were stolen along with everything else. That's just what I'm trying to tell you!'

'I know nothing about that. Till I see your papers I can't be sure that you are not a deserter or a runaway from a concentration camp. I can't do anything for you without your papers.'

I went back to the waiting room. Naturally there were no lieutenants there. The train came in at last. I stood watching everyone who went through the entrance to the platform but it was no use. The engineer promised to look for the thieves at the terminal station in Krasnovodsk, but this was not very comforting.

It was already morning. I went to the N.K.V.D. again, but the man on the day shift was even more suspicious of me than the night man had been. He would not even talk to me and when I kept on trying to prove my statements he yelled, 'Shut up or I'll throw you in jail!'

I went back to the apartment where the ill-fated party had taken place. The old lady looked at me with frightened eyes and asked about the results of my search. She advised me to go and see the city prosecutor and also to apply to the Presidium of the Supreme Soviet of the Turkmen Republic.

One of the girls handed me my silver cigarette case. 'I found it on the floor,' she said. 'At least you've got something to sell.'

I sold the cigarette case in half an hour, at the first jeweller's shop I came to, for 100 rubles, and went to find the prosecutor.

The prosecutor's secretary was curt and official. 'File a written application and the prosecutor will examine it and give your case the required action,' he said.

I asked for a sheet of paper and wrote out my application. Then I went to the other side of the city, to the palace which housed the government. After a few hours' wait, I was received by a secretary who made an appointment for me to see the President of the Republic the next day.

I made one more try after leaving the palace. I went to the headquarters of the city police and spent the rest of the day trying to find an official who could help me. I never found one. Everyone I spoke to looked at me with suspicion, although I was well dressed, spoke politely, and could produce witnesses that I had been robbed. Finally an old and respectable policeman gave me some good advice, 'Better run along. I've heard people talking about you here. If you come again tomorrow, you'll be arrested.'

'But what can I do? I have a long way to go, no money, and still worse, no papers. If I travel without papers I may get sent to a concentration camp.'

'It may be worse for you if you stay here. Remember, Ashkhabad is only 15 miles from the border and there is a special regulation here: people without documents can't stay in the city more than a day. Take my advice and beat it.'

I decided to try my luck the next day anyway, when I would see the President of the Republic.

The President's reception room was not in the government palace but in a small building on one of the central streets of the city. I was surprised to find only four people in the waiting room – three natives and a Russian. I could not understand why there were so few people who wanted to see the President and why I had been granted an appointment with so little trouble, without even being asked for my papers. I was about to ask the Russian about this when the door opened and an attendant called my name.

I entered a long, modestly furnished room. At the far end of it, behind a large desk, sat a little old man with an unimpressive Mongolian face. His secretary stood next to him.

The President extended his hand across the table to greet me.

'Take a seat please. What can I do for you?'

I explained that I had been robbed and needed money and some sort of papers to get home. I promised to send the money back if it could be loaned to me.

The President listened intently, putting his hand to his ear and nodding sympathetically. When I finished he looked up at his secretary.

'What can we do to help this unfortunate young man?'

The secretary shook his head and said, 'We can't do anything to help you. For documents you should apply to the police, and as for money, you'll have to get it any way you can. The budget has not been approved yet and the Supreme Soviet of the Turkmen Republic has no money for unforeseen expenses.'

The President shook his head sadly.

'Yes, no money, no money at all. I'd be glad to help you, but we have nothing to help you with. And as for the papers, you'll have to get them from the N.K.V.D. They know all about papers; they'll give them to you.'

I explained that I had already been to the N.K.V.D. and to the police and that they had refused to issue me any documents at both places. I asked the President to write a short letter to the N.K.V.D., asking them to give me some papers. He shook his head again.

'No, we don't write anything here. I'm sorry.' And he extended his hand to me again.

I left the reception room. It was clear to me now why so few people came to the President of the Republic with their problems.

I had to do something and do it fast. I did not dare to begin to travel again without a passport or an equivalent document. A week's journey was still ahead of me and dozens of police check points at any one of which I could be put in jail simply and easily.

I started up the street in dismay and soon came to a handsome grey mansion separated from the street by a beautifully kept garden, surrounded by a tall iron fence with a gate and a sentry. The sign on the gate read: Central Committee of the Communist Party of Turkestan.

Here is the real power, I thought, and with an air of implacable determination I asked the sentry for a pass to see the First Secretary of the Central Committee. The sentry looked at me with surprise, and I told him my story.

'What tommyrot,' he said, shrugging his shoulders. But still he picked up the telephone and began to repeat what I had told him to someone. Hanging up the receiver, he shrugged his shoulders again and wrote out a pass for me. Then he pressed a buzzer and instructed a soldier who had appeared as if from nowhere to take me in.

I was led through endless corridors into a large, sumptuously furnished room filled with the pleasant fragrance of good brandy. Two men and two girls were seated comfortably in a couple of armchairs and a sofa.

I stopped at the door, not knowing whom to address. One of the men, sitting on the sofa, said, 'Well, let's have your story. I'm Ivanov, Secretary of the Central Committee.'

Trying my best to fit into the convivial tone of the company, I told the story of my misfortune once again, embellishing it with amusing details, both true and improvised. They all kept laughing gaily, evidently pleased with the tale.

'Well, brother, you certainly got yourself into a mess,' said Ivanov. 'Our N.K.V.D. men will put you behind barbed wire in no time.'

'That's just what I'm saying,' I hastened to agree. 'They'll put me there and I won't get out until the end of the war.'

'I don't really quite know how to help you,' said Ivanov. 'We don't give out documents to suspicious characters and if I send you to the police they'll arrest you. Well, I'll see.'

He went to a telephone and took up the receiver.

'This is Ivanov, Secretary of the Central Committee. Look here, a scrawny chap will come over to see you shortly. He's been robbed of all his money and papers. Give him some sort of a paper so he can get to his home town. What? Yes, I know him, not too well though.'

What? No, I won't write anything for him myself. You write it; that's what you're there for.' And he hung up.

'Now you go straight to the station, and they'll give you a paper. And don't hang around here long. You'll get in trouble. Leave tonight.'

'And what about money for the ticket?'

'Money?' Ivanov laughed loudly. 'You'll have to look for money somewhere else, brother. I haven't had enough for myself for a long time. And what do you need money for – can't you steal a ride?'

We parted in the friendliest possible way.

At the station the N.K.V.D. man on duty, the same one to whom I had applied the night I was robbed, issued me a paper, cursing softly. The paper stated that I had officially reported the loss of my passport and that this was to serve as a certificate of my identity for one week. As I left the room he murmured something to the effect that my sort should be in jail.

Although I had a little money from the sale of the cigarette case, I decided not to buy a ticket in order to save the money for future needs. When the Krasnovodsk train pulled in I ducked into a coach while the ticket inspector wasn't looking.

The two-day journey in the train was torture. The fact that I did not have a seat was not so bad; some of the passengers were kind enough to let me use their seats from time to time. But I couldn't sleep. As soon as I saw a group of inspectors come into a car (tickets and documents were checked at the same time) I would go to the other end of the train immediately. The inspectors were so slow that they never reached me. At the first stop I would get off the train and run to the end which had already been checked, and work my way back to my car. The passengers soon noticed that I always left the coach just before a check, and they began to take an interest in my case. Two wounded Red Army men found out that I had very little money and shared their food with me. When I was with them I could risk dozing off for a few minutes because they would always wake me when the inspectors appeared. In this way I finally got to Krasnovodsk.

I had neither the time nor the desire to look around the city. I learned that there was a ship in the harbour which was about to leave for Makhachkala, on the Caucasian side of the Caspian Sea. I also found out that before getting on the ship everyone had to go through an especially thorough documents check. You had to have a passport, a certificate from the army, permission from the military commissar to embark, a medical and disinfection certificate, and a ticket. I had none of these, and so it was hopeless to do anything legally. I would have to sneak aboard at all costs, because there was not to be another ship for two weeks.

It was getting dark when the ship started loading. I made two attempts to go aboard as a porter, offering to carry people's baggage for them, but each time the grim N.K.V.D. men on the gangplank chased me back into the crowd on the pier. The crowd got smaller and smaller, and I kept on trying to find some way of getting aboard without papers and without a ticket.

Soon it was completely dark, and almost no one was left on the pier. A strong, cold wind was blowing and I thought longingly of the warm coat which had been stolen along with the other things by those damned lieutenants. Lost in that sad thought, I stumbled over a cleat to which a hawser leading to the bow of the ship was attached. I caught my breath and, glancing quickly around, grabbed the rope and jumped off the pier. Going hand over hand as fast as I could, shaken by the wind and hearing the sounds of the black water under me, I finally reached the bow and clambered aboard with difficulty. I saw something whitish beside me. It was a gun, with a canvas cover over it. I got underneath the canvas and lay still, shaking like a leaf from the cold.

I don't know how much time passed before the ship's whistle gave two blasts and I began to hear the sound of the capstans pulling in the ropes. The old ship, trembling and rolling slightly, slipped into the night.

Feeling sure that I could not be thrown overboard, papers or no papers, I crawled out of my hideout and set out to explore the ship.

The vessel was old and decrepit but in my position I could not complain. I found my way to the steerage where it was warm, but seasickness was spreading among the passengers. There were no empty bunks. I wandered about the passageways of the rolling ship, hanging on to rails and banisters, until by chance I came across what seemed to be the officers' smoking room. It was empty, and letting the morrow take care of its own evils, I stretched out on a couch and went to sleep.

I woke up when a large wave hit the old ship so hard that I was knocked off the sofa. My head banged on an iron table attached to the floor next to it. When I had got my wits together and understood where I was, I scrambled back on the sofa and sat up. An elderly man in naval uniform sat on the other side of the table looking at me. In front of him was a bottle and some food on a spread-out newspaper.

'Had a fall?' he asked rather indifferently.

'It seems so,' I answered.

'Why aren't you in a cabin?'

'I don't have a cabin.'

'Why not?'

'Because I don't have a ticket,' I answered defiantly.

The man thought for a while, or perhaps just did not feel like talking.

'Do you play chess?' he asked, with no obvious connection with our previous conversation.

'Sure.'

He pointed to another chair at the table and drew a box of chessmen out of the drawer. The board had little holes in it, so that the rocking of the ship would not spill the men all over the floor. Silently he arranged the board and nodding his head at the remains of his breakfast asked, 'Hungry?'

I said I was. Holding a sandwich in one hand, I bravely moved the king's pawn with the other.

The seafaring man turned out to be an enthusiastic chess player. By the time the Caucasian shore could be seen through the misty dawn we had finished perhaps twenty games, each of us winning about an equal number. When it was fully light my partner got up and said, 'Thanks for the company. We'll tie up in an hour. Better think of a way to get ashore.' With that he walked out.

Even without his advice I had been thinking about this problem. It was a complicated one. I couldn't pull the same trick I had in Krasnovodsk because it was broad daylight. When the gangplank was lowered I saw that there were three men from the port security force at each end of it. I realized that I would have to face the music. I joined the crowd of passengers moving toward the gangplank.

'Your papers?' said a tall man in military uniform.

'I don't have any papers.'

'What? Hey, you on shore, take this man to the guardhouse!'

A policeman, holding a rifle on the ready, grabbed me by the sleeve as I stepped off the gangplank and led me off the pier. In a few minutes we reached the headquarters of the port security force. The policeman shoved me through a door with a sentry in front of it, not too politely, and said, 'Wait here.'

I found myself in a dimly lighted room where several people lay on the ground or squatted along the walls. At the end of the room, where there was more light, sat a man in uniform at a desk littered with papers.

Something had to be done. In a couple of hours I would be in jail, and there was no chance that I would be released. I stood by the door for a while, opened it slightly, closed it again, and then firmly approached the uniformed man at the desk. He raised his eyes.

'What do you want?'

'Where's the chief?'

'He's not here. What do you want him for?'

'I have information that the two thieves who robbed me are on board a ship which is due this morning from Krasnovodsk. I want to file an application for their arrest.'

'Well, you better hurry. The ship is already in and the chief is down there checking papers. You'd better get there in a hurry; the passengers are already coming ashore.'

I started for the door.

'Not there, you can't go out there. Use this door,' he shouted, pointing to a door behind him.

I left by way of the back door. Asking a passing worker how to get to the railroad station, I set off as fast as possible in the direction he showed me. There, I lost myself in the crowd which filled all the corridors and halls of the station as well as the square in front of it. These were people trying to get a passage either north to the Kuban or in the opposite direction to Tiflis.

I managed to get some rye bread and a glass of tea without sugar at the station restaurant, and then I mingled in the large crowd by the ticket windows, where it was dark enough so that the police could not find me in case they decided to look for the man who had arrived from Asia without any documents.

The train was more than twelve hours late, but the crowd waited patiently. About 10 p.m. the ticket window opened and the ticket agent shouted:

'The train from Tiflis is full and will take no more passengers. No tickets will be sold!'

That didn't matter to me. I had no money for a ticket. Pushing my way through the angrily muttering crowd, I went to another window where platform passes were being sold for only a ruble each. I bought one and rushed out on to the platform as soon as I heard the bell announcing the incoming train.

The train was on the first track. With a banging of teakettles passengers poured out of it to get hot water in the station. I concentrated my attention on the nearest car, at the entrance of which stood a woman porter, waving a lantern. The engine gave a whistle, signifying its imminent departure. The passengers were running back to the train, and I went with them.

'Where are you going, citizen? This isn't your car,' shouted the woman with the lantern.

'Never mind, I'll get to my car later.' I shouted. 'Can't you see I'm from the train? I haven't even got my coat on!' I paid no more attention to the woman and climbed into the coach.

The train was jammed with people. There was hardly room to stand. I managed to push my way into the middle of the car and crawled under a seat, with the consent of the passengers sitting there. Some of them expressed the fear that I would steal the belongings they had shoved under there, but I did my best to assure them that I had no such intention. When I was safely installed between their bags I stuck my head out from under the bench and said, 'One more thing, citizens! Do me a favour. Don't wake me up if the conductor comes for the tickets; I don't have one.'

They did wake me up, but not until morning. The train was slowing down. My journey was almost over.

8. HOME

A LITTLE railroad station in a small city in the south of Russia. There was nothing unusual about it except that this was the station of the city of my birth, from which, fifteen years before, I had set out for Moscow to begin my adult life.

I was careful not to enter through the passenger entrance, where they were checking tickets. I went to the end where freight cars were standing and found a small gate used by railroad employees.

It was early on a February morning, there was snow everywhere, and I felt chilly without a coat. A shaky old trolley came by. I got into the empty car with its ice-encrusted windows, bought a ticket, and went to the front platform where it was colder, but I could look out and see the city.

Nothing had changed in the fifteen years I had been away. Not one new house. The streets, except for a few of the central ones, were still paved with cobblestones and just as dirty as ever. The only new feature was that the store windows had been filled up with bricks in case of bombardment. And the trees which had been quite small when I had gone away were now so tall that their branches met above the street.

I got off the trolley and began to walk toward home. Everything was the same, but older and more ragged: houses begging for repairs, sagging fences, broken brick-paved paths. Even the holes in the paths seemed to be the same.

I passed few people. They had worried faces and were dressed more poorly than ever. No one paid any attention to my strange, coatless appearance. A sanitary barrel, on a cart pulled by an old horse clattered by me, spreading a very bad smell.

At last my street. Here is my gate and the yard where I played when I was very, very small. I enter the yard. How tiny it has become! That big tree by the house – I planted it myself once. And the house with the closed green shutters, covered with ice, grown rickety. Two unfamiliar dogs are barking.

My heart is beating fast. I knock on the shutter and go to the door. A minute passes, two minutes.

'Who's there?' says a voice that is so familiar.

'It's me, Vladimir. Open the door, Mother!'

I hear quick movements behind the door. It opens and I enter the house. My mother, almost fainting, hugs me and cries.

We go up two steps to the tiny kitchen, into the next room, and sit down together. We can't find the words we need.

'Why didn't you telegraph me that you were coming?' my mother said.

'I have very little money, Mother.'

'Why look, you haven't any wraps on! Where's your coat, and your things?'

'I haven't any. They're all gone.'

'How? Where? Oh, well, you can tell me later – Wait.' And she stared at me, her eyes wet with tears. She had changed terribly. At the age of fifty she already looked very old. Her face was crisscrossed with wrinkles and her hair was almost all grey. She seemed to be shorter – or perhaps it was I who had grown.

'You know, George was killed.' She pronounced the words with trembling lips and hugged me again. My heart contracted. My brother would be twenty-two now, but I remembered him as a happy seven-year-old boy.

'Somewhere between Kiev and Zhitomir, last summer. I wrote you. Didn't you get my letters?'

'No, I didn't get them.'

'How did that happen? And about your father?'

'I got one letter, from which I gathered—'

'Yes, he was arrested in the spring of '38. They didn't try him, but they gave him ten years in a concentration camp. They sent him to the Pechorsky camps in the northern Urals. There haven't been any letters – I don't know if he's still alive.'

'He may be, Mother. See, I'm all right.'

'You're the only one left to me, Vladimir. I blame your father for disowning you after your arrest. They called him to the N.K.V.D. office and told him to sign a paper that he was breaking all ties with his son as an enemy of the people. They threatened him and he signed. Three years later they took him anyway.'

'It's all right, Mother. This is the third time he's been imprisoned. With God's help, he'll live through it.'

'No, I doubt it. He was very sick when they took him.'

We were silent for a minute.

'And you, Mother, are you still working?'

'Of course, what else?' She was surprised. 'I teach in three schools at once. There are a lot of classes. We work in two shifts because half the schools have been taken over for hospitals. But what are we talking for? You need to wash up, and have something to eat!'

And she began to fuss around in the manner of all the mothers in the world who see their sons after a long separation.

My mother was making a show of energy; I could see that. She had been used to working for many years and that kept her going, although she had become a shadow of the mother I used to know. And as for grief, there was so much of it that it had disappeared somewhere in the depths of her being and did not show in her everyday existence. Otherwise it would have been impossible to live.

My brother's clothes fitted me fairly well, and I changed into them after taking a thorough bath in the kitchen.

My mother kept looking nervously at her watch.

'Is it time for school?' I asked.

'I've got to go, Vladimir. I can't be late. If you miss a class without a doctor's certificate they send you to court. You'd better get some sleep. I'll be home by evening.'

After she left I couldn't sleep. I went out for a walk. I met two old friends outside whom I remembered from early childhood, but there was no conversation. After greeting me and expressing their happiness that I was home again, they avoided looking in my eyes and quickly said good-bye, murmuring excuses.

I visited some relatives, my mother's brother and sister. They were genuinely glad to see me. My cousins had become grown-up girls; their brothers were in the army. And their life? It was the same as it had been fifteen years before, only a little drabber and a little harder. But the young girls did not feel this and tried to make the most of what they had. Both of them were members of the Komsomol; both were studying in the medical institute, where they were preparing to be wartime doctors. They both had admirers from among their childhood friends.

I tried not to tell them about what I had been through. It was plain that they both wanted and were afraid to hear how things actually were in the prisons and concentration camps. But probably they did not want to know very badly. I led the conversation to current affairs, the state of the city, and the evacuation which people were already whispering about, although the Germans were still far away, near Rostov.

I couldn't get rid of the feeling that I was a stranger among my own family, that I could not shake the accursed past in the Kolyma from my shoulders. Time must go by before I could return to my old life.

9. A 'WOLF'S TICKET'

I HAD to find work quickly. I could not continue to live off my mother. She earned a trifling salary and the price of everything was tremendously high. My first problem was to obtain documents; without them no one would even talk to me.

After a long wait the police gave me a certificate of lost passport. They instructed me to register immediately for the draft. The head of the local military commissariat questioned me. At the end he asked, 'Have you ever been sentenced by the Soviet authorities? If so, when and for what?'

'I have. I was sentenced by the Tribunal of the Leningrad Military District, in 1935, to six years' imprisonment for anti-Soviet propaganda,' I answered promptly.

The officer put down his pen and looked at me.

'So? Well, that complicates the situation in your case. Frankly, I wanted to send you directly to the front. We've got more demands for men than we can handle. But the fact that you were sentenced complicates matters. Do you want to go to the front?'

'In general, yes. Of course, I'd like to stay with my mother for a while, but if I'm needed, Comrade Commander—'

'See here, don't call me "comrade"; that isn't proper. Personally I don't care, but you might run into trouble if you do it in the future. Former prisoners are not our comrades. Say "citizen", that would be better. Understand?'

'Yes.'

'Wait a minute. I'll talk it over with – the proper authorities.'

The officer left by the side door. A minute later a man I didn't know opened the door, looked at me silently, and then closed the door again. The officer who had interviewed me returned.

'According to law, you are eligible for service only in construction battalions,' he said, handling me my card. 'But there are no requisitions at this time for such organizations. It's your good luck. When you are needed you'll be called. That's all.'

I left the office and in the corridor looked at my draft card. In the upper right-hand corner there was a zero. This was the category to which I had been assigned for political reasons. It meant I did not have the honour of defending my country with arms. It also meant I would be drafted into an auxiliary battalion where soldiers swell up from hunger, where only the worst equipment, often taken from corpses, is issued, and where more people perish from typhus than from enemy shells.

'Well, we'll see about that, dear comrades,' I thought as I left the commissariat building.

Immediately after this I began to look for work. In the first organization to which I applied there were ten vacancies, any one of which I could easily have filled. Many of the employees had recently been drafted. I was received cordially, and the director of the personnel office asked me to fill up a form.

I sat down at a table and filled up the first form. At the bottom of the sheet there was the question: 'Have you ever been sentenced by the Soviet authorities? If so, when and for what?'

I wrote the truth without hesitation. Sooner or later it would come out anyway. I handed the form to the director.

He read it, nodding his head approvingly until he got to the last question. He raised his eyebrows and looked at me.

'Is this true?'

'Yes.'

'We have no work for you here. We don't take counter-revolutionaries into our organization,' he said sharply.

The blood surged to my face.

'You have no reason to talk this way. In the first place you don't know under what circumstances I was arrested. In the second place, I have served out my term and have received all my rights as a citizen again.'

'All your rights?' He laughed sarcastically. 'You'd better save that story for your grandmother, my dear sir. I've told you: we have no work for you, now or in the future. Good-bye.'

I left and slammed the door. He jumped out after me.

'Hey, you! Be careful how you slam doors, or I'll send you right back where you came from!'

I kept on walking and did not turn around.

I spent almost a month visiting half of the offices in the city, and everywhere, with small variations, it was the same. People were needed everywhere and everyone wanted to hire me, but the desire disappeared the moment I spoke of my past.

One middle-aged engineer with whom I talked, said:

'We can't take you. Not because we don't want to. We have a great deal of work and no one to do it. Six more men were taken for the army yesterday. But we can't take you. The personnel department won't approve it. Their instructions are very specific on this point. You're outside the law. And the sooner you realize it the better it will be for you. You'll get fewer blows to your pride. There's only one place you can go – to a collective farm. Or you could get a job as an unskilled labourer working for the city, as a street sweeper for instance. You're not the first to be on this spot. We've had others. Remember, the Soviet Government never forgives anyone for anything!'

This I understood a long time before, and my sympathies for the

Soviet regime had not grown as a result. What should I do? Go to a collective farm where, after all the horses, cars, and tractors had been mobilized for war, all three were replaced by human beings? It's true that you could eat fairly well there – I had already investigated the subject. But you had to work fifteen hours a day under the watchful gaze of members of the party and Komsomols who had been sent to the farms especially to hurry up the work and oversee it.

And somehow I didn't want to be a street sweeper—

At last fortune smiled on me. Thanks to one of my father's friends who still had an important position, I was hired by the Industrial Bank as a junior inspector of construction. The director made me promise that I would never reveal my past.

'I'm risking a great deal, taking you. But we live under one God and none of us is insured against a fate such as you have suffered. Maybe something of the kind will happen to me some day. Then you can remember me!'

I had to do the work of two men, sometimes three. I did not complain. I was happy. I was used to work and I appreciated having such a job. It was no collective farm.

Summer was approaching, and heavy fighting was renewed along the entire front. The Germans were obviously trying to break through in the south, toward the Caucasus. But there was no change in our lives. Money for construction was still being granted by the central office of the bank, which had been evacuated from Moscow and was now somewhere in the Urals.

Yet a feeling of alarm pervaded the city. Highly placed officials, using various excuses, were sending their families away, to Tiflis or even to Central Asia. Party and Komsomol organizations were forming groups and training somewhere outside the city. Rations for the population suddenly increased. The contents of several big warehouses, which the railroads were unable to evacuate to the south, were given out to the populace.

In May all the offices and schools in the city were empty. Almost everyone had been sent to collective farms for work which was described as 'weeding'. A mere handful remained in the offices. In the city the periodical registration for the draft was taking place. I registered again myself, and two days later received instructions to report to the military commissariat for a medical examination, taking with me all the things a soldier needed on the march.

I went to the commissariat but without any belongings, so that I would have an excuse to return home and say good-bye.

In the commissariat I was led into a big room, told to undress, and take my place at the end of a line of naked men. The line was moving

330 THROUGH FIGHTING RUSSIA

quickly. On one side of the room there was a long table at which there were several army medics in white coats. Each man's card was located quickly. Each of the medics asked one question and noted the answer on the man's card.

'Have you had tuberculosis?'

'Have you had any venereal disease?'

'Have you any physical defects?'

'Any complaints?'

At the end of the table stood a man with a stethoscope. Poking his stethoscope into the chest of each naked man and examining him quickly, this doctor made the last mark on the card, which was then handed to the commissar, seated at a separate table. He would put his own mark on the card and say: 'Go to table 8,' or 'Go to table 6,' or 'Go to table 3.'

Table 3 was mentioned more than the others and this was where I was told to report.

A man with a roster sat there. He found my name immediately and said, 'Get dressed quickly, take all your things and go to room 20, the orderly room of the construction battalion. Ask for the first sergeant and give him your draft card. Next!'

I got dressed quickly, but I did not go to the construction battalion orderly room. Some time before I had decided that if they sent me to a line unit I would go, but not to a construction battalion. I was not that much of a fool!

I went down into the yard and toward the gate, on the other side of which there was a crowd of women who had come to say good-bye to their men. They kept asking the sentries for permission to see their husbands and sons. The sentries did not answer them. Sometimes they would shout something like 'Go away, aunties! You're not going to see anyone. This isn't a jail, it's the army! Scram!'

Someone tried to leave the commissariat through the gate. He was rudely pushed back.

'No one gets out! If you go in you can't come out!'

'But they've let me go. Look, I've got three fingers missing on this hand,' the man tried to explain.

'The hell with your hand. Get yourself a permit to leave from the commissar!'

The situation was bad. I stood in a dark doorway trying to figure out how to get out into the street. Suddenly some of the women tore past the sentries and entered the yard of the commissariat building. The rest began to push in after them. For a few moments there was complete chaos in the yard. The sentries shot their rifles into the air trying to restore order, and I managed to slip out into the street.

Back at the bank the director said to me, 'Did they really release you again?'

'Yes, for bad eyesight and a weak heart.'

'Amazing! Yesterday they drafted a neighbour of mine. He's got a terrible heart, is lame in both feet, and can't even see the door of the room he's in without glasses. You're pretty lucky.'

'Are you displeased?'

'Oh, on the contrary, I'm very happy about it. You know how much work there is.'

Strictly speaking, I was a deserter. My conscience did not trouble me. I was ready to go into the army proper, although there was very little that I wanted to defend. But to die from typhus and convict-like labour in a construction battalion was something else.

Two weeks later when there was another draft registration in the city, I reported as if nothing had happened. With great difficulty my card was finally located – filed among the cards of the men who had been sent to the front. Again I was threatened by the draft.

Then I decided on a doubtful step. I wrote a letter to Stalin in which I related my story, complained about the fact that I was not trusted and that they would not let me go into a line unit in the army, and requested that he intervene in my case.

I knew that the letter would go no farther than the local committee of the Communist party. But perhaps they would do something there when they had seen how patriotic I was.

The letter brought results in two days. I was summoned to see the chairman of the city soviet.

'Your profession?' he asked.

'Construction engineer,' I answered, without blinking an eye.

'Are you familiar with earthworks?'

'Perfectly.'

'As of today you are drafted by the city soviet. You will direct a section of the entrenchments that are being dug around the city. Report to the commissar.'

The commissar told me to come and see him the next morning.

In the morning about thirty of us, together with the commissar and two army officers, drove out beyond the city in two trucks. Our mission was explained to us. The city was to be surrounded by an anti-tank ditch five yards deep. A section of it was assigned to each of us. The shovels had already been delivered and were stacked in piles, waiting for the workmen to arrive.

The following morning about three thousand workers appeared at my section: city employees, schoolboys, high-school students, and others. I set them along the line which had been traced out the day before, picked out a few assistants, and the work began.

An army major appeared to show me where the other emplacements were to go: artillery, machine guns, mortars. We paced around the field together and he began to explain what was needed. When we reached a clump of bushes he said, 'Let's sit down and rest a while.'

He wiped his forehead. We began to smoke.

'When may the Germans be here?' I asked him.

'Probably in a week or so.'

'But we won't be able to finish all this work in a week!'

'Well, why don't you send a telegram to Hitler and tell him to wait until we do?' the major said angrily.

'Well, if it's the way you say,' I asked, after a silence. 'Why are we all here? What are we digging this ditch for?'

'So that the population will know that the government is here and that it's strong. If we slacken up on the reins, these locals will immediately begin shooting at everyone they don't like from around corners.'

'Well, what about the war? Do you think we'll lose it?'

'No, I don't. In order for the Red Army to win, all these peaceful citizens and the soldiers who desert to the enemy have got to have discipline in the areas just behind the front. We've got to shoot everyone who retreats on the spot.'

'Who's going to do the shooting?'

'We have enough experts at that sort of thing,' said the major, getting up. 'Go on digging your ditch, or if you don't want to, go on back to town. You're planning to evacuate?'

'So far, no.'

'So far? Well, you won't later either, I'm sure of it. You're all like that.'

He went across the field to his car, forgetting about the locations of the rest of the emplacements.

The commissar no longer appeared at our project. It was rumoured that he had already gone away. Only a few hundred people still came out to my section. The ditch was finished in several places, but there were still large untouched spaces between sections.

'That's all right,' an officer who had come out to see how the work was progressing told me, 'the Germans will go across the ditch anyway. They'll think the untouched parts are mined.'

I stopped going to this job because my mother fell ill. To safeguard her I also arranged to change my address and move in temporarily with a friend of mine, Nikolai Volkov, a military engineer who was engaged in dismantling the oil refinery and shipping the equipment south. Once I went to see the director of the bank I had worked in. He was sitting in his office with his secretary, almost buried in papers.

'It's good that you've come. You can give us a hand.'

'What do you want me to do?'

'Take all these papers downstairs to the furnace room. There's good fire there. Throw them all in the burner.'

Until late that evening we burned the files, covering years of the bank's activities. Finally only a few folders of current business were left.

'Well, that does it,' said the director with relief. 'Thanks for your help. Incidentally, can you use some money?'

'Naturally! There never was a time when I couldn't.'

'Here, take some!' He opened his briefcase which was stuffed with big bills and handed me a stack of them. 'Here's 5,000. Is that enough? I've already settled with the others.'

'Thanks, that's plenty,' I said. Five thousand rubles was a half year's salary for me.

'Are you evacuating or not?' asked the director.

'I haven't decided yet. I probably will.'

'You mean you probably won't. You'd be a fool if you did. Stay here, you'll get along with the Germans. But I'll give you an evacuation certificate anyway. You can get rations on it.'

Late that night, with money and a certificate that I was to accompany the bank's valuables to Tiflis, I returned to Nikolai's apartment.

Nikolai was indignant.

'It's a disgrace what's going on. Everyone who has anything to do with money is stealing hundreds of thousands of rubles. The banks are handing it out to directors and head book-keepers for the asking. Workers and employees get chicken feed: two months' pay. They're looting the warehouses of shoes, clothing, everything.'

This was actually true. The population of the city, which for so long had not seen good food or new clothes, had suddenly become rich. If you knew someone, or had evacuation certificates, you could get ham, preserves, butter, and other things which only the old folks remembered and which the young had never even seen because under the Soviet they benefited only a few privileged officials. People with packages and pails filled the streets, happy and smiling, loaded as they had not been for years.

Meanwhile the evacuation was proceeding very slowly. The important people had sent their families as far away as possible long before. Almost all the N.K.V.D. people had left, as well as a large part of the Communists and most of the city's Jewish families.

At home my mother was ecstatic as she showed me her booty for the day: several quarts of oil, a large jar of jam, some margarine, and a pair of shoes. The neighbours gave us a bag of flour in addition to all this. They had taken several right from the mill on a wheelbarrow.

The last evening of Soviet control over the city came. In the distance was the sound of cannonading. Groups of soldiers passed through the city. The streets were full of people; nobody wanted to stay home.

Suddenly there was a distant but very loud explosion. The sky in the south grew red.

'What is it?' we kept asking each other.

Explosions began to come from various parts of the town. People ran through the streets.

'They've blown up the station and the power plant!' someone yelled on the run.

'Fill up on water right away!' one of us shouted, dashing to the tap in the yard. Everyone disappeared to look for buckets. But it was too late; the water was not running any more.

'We'll have to clean out the well,' someone lamented. 'No water's been drawn from it for ten years; it's full of dirt.'

I went to the centre of town. It was almost light because of the fires. Suddenly there was a roar not far off and another building crumbled; it was the headquarters of the city committee of the party. People were chasing about and shouting. Someone was calling for help, saying that there were dead and injured in the near-by houses.

I had reached the outskirts of the city without noticing it. A mill was burning with a bright flame which lit up a crowd of hundreds, many of whom were running into the fire at the risk of their lives to get a bag of flour for their hungry children.

When I got home I found Nikolai, in uniform, packing some things in a bag.

'Where to?' I asked.

'I'm going east. The cars are gone and the railroad has been cut. So I'm going on foot.'

'Have you blown up your plant already?'

'Don't talk to me in that tone!' he snapped. 'I didn't blow up anything. Those God-damned N.K.V.D. men did all the blowing up. It's lucky we found a couple of the charges; at least half the plant is still standing.'

'What are you going for? Following the N.K.V.D.?'

'I've decided to go, Vladimir, and you shouldn't blame me for it any more than I blame you for staying.'

I was silent. He finished packing and we went out into the street together. The night sky was blazing. The sounds of artillery had obviously come much closer. Soldiers and officers were still running through the town. The local people were all on the street too.

'Come with me as far as the bridge,' Nikolai said. 'You won't sleep anyway.

'Don't be surprised that I'm leaving with the Soviets. There are a lot of reasons for it. In the first place I don't believe Germany will beat Russia. Sooner or later the Germans will lose the war and I don't want to tie myself to a lost cause. In the second place I believe – I'm absolutely convinced, do you hear – that after the war the air in Russia will become cleaner and we'll get our freedom. Please don't laugh. Stalin will give us our freedom whether he wants to or not. Don't forget that the people are armed now and if the Communists won't give them their freedom they'll take it themselves. And we'll have a new life.

'I'm not trying to convince you. I'd be very surprised if you decided to go with me. Your accounts with Stalin are too involved and you'll never make your peace with him. You are an enemy of the Soviet system. Forgive me, this is the first time I have talked to you frankly about this, but I know it. You are an irreconcilable foe of everything Soviet. That's why your place will always be among the enemies of Bolshevism.

'I'm no friend of Stalin's either, although I'm a Communist. But I hate the Germans more, and only Stalin has the power to organize a defence against our enemies. The Americans and the English will help him. They have a common enemy. And we'll win, I know it.'

At that moment flames suddenly shot up from a three-story building on the corner. There was a short, dull report. We took cover in a doorway from the flying bricks. Two minutes later we went on again.

'And you justify everything, forgive everything?' I asked.

'No. There will be a reckoning for everything. For the thousands and hundreds of thousands of innocent lives that have been destroyed, for these demolitions here – but not now. This isn't the time to settle the bill with Stalin. Today I support him, but after the war I will demand a reckoning as the price of my support.'

'The devils in the other world will give you a reckoning with hot coals,' I said, 'or you'll rot somewhere behind barbed wire. I've seen people who believed in fantasies before.'

'Well, what of it? If I rot, that means it's my fate to rot. But I've chosen my path and I'm going to stick to it.'

We continued to walk in silence. The city was behind us, lit up by dozens of fires. The road which led to the bridge was getting more and more jammed with people. Most of them were soldiers, but there were some civilians and even some women and children. Sometimes tanks and mechanized artillery drove through the crowd. At last the road was so packed that I suggested a detour along the river bank.

Climbing over several fences we reached the river. Loud noises and shouts were coming from the bridge. Apparently the crowd was enormous there.

A few shots rang out; we could see the flashes. They were mostly on the city side of the bridge. We went down to the bank and walked along the river. Something floated by, not far from us.

'Crushed,' Nikolai said, not looking at me, 'or shot while crossing.'

'Is that necessary too? To strengthen discipline?' I asked.

Nikolai did not answer. We were near the bridge now.

With a loud roar a streak of flame shot upward in the centre of the bridge. One span sagged toward the water. We could see the people on the bridge by the light of the flames. They were shouting and waving their arms.

'The bastards!' said Nikolai. 'They've blown up the bridge before all these people got across.'

'Well, how are you going to cross now? Swim?' I asked him.

He looked at me oddly and said, 'That's an idea. The water's warm and I'm not a bad swimmer, you know.'

He sat down and began to undress. Then he tied his clothes in a knot and gave me his bag.

'Take it if you want it; I won't need it.'

'I won't either; let it stay here. Well, goodbye, Nikolai. Maybe we'll see each other some day, but more likely we won't.'

'Goodbye, Vladimir. Try to understand me, just as I understand you!'

We embraced. Then he jumped into the water.

'Toss me my stuff!' he shouted. I threw him his clothes.

'Goodbye!' His head disappeared into the darkness.

I returned to my mother's house as fast as I could. She was waiting for me anxiously, wondering why I had been gone so long. I persuaded her to go to bed and went out in the street myself.

Dawn was coming. The sounds of rifle and machine-gun fire came from the north-east. The artillery had stopped. The streets were almost deserted.

Here and there a soldier was running toward the river. An armoured car rumbled past. I could hear the occasional whistle of a bullet, and I turned into an entry where a few people stood huddled against the door.

The sound of firing was very near.

Suddenly a light tank came into sight around the corner, with its top open, followed by a second and a third. Painted on the side of each was a black cross.

A motor cycle with two Germans on it drove up to us. One of them shouted, '*Wo ist die Brücke?*'

No one answered him, and the motor cycle roared off.

The Soviets were gone.

The German occupation was beginning.

Part II. Under German Occupation

10. THE FIRST DAYS

THE number of Germans who entered the city was amazingly small. Only on the central streets (perhaps because they alone were well paved) could automobiles, occasional tanks, and motor cycles be seen dashing back and forth. But still the townspeople were surprised at the mechanization of the German Army and compared it involuntarily with ours, which moved almost entirely on foot.

The Germans kept to themselves and paid little attention to the people who filled the streets. However, there were a few cases of soldiers taking watches away from passing civilians.

In general the population was well disposed toward the occupants and there was something of a holiday atmosphere. On the main street I met an acquaintance, a book-keeper from the restaurant trust. He had tears in his eyes.

'It's about time, Vladimir Nikolaevich,' he said, 'for the damned Soviet regime to end. How many years I've waited for this day!'

'Don't you think you're being a little hasty? We don't know what the German rule will be like yet,' I said.

'It makes no difference what it will be like. Can't you see, even the air has changed somehow! I can curse Stalin all I want and nobody makes me yell Heil Hitler either. You're young and you don't appreciate this. Wait a while and taste a bit of freedom!'

'But maybe it will be harder on us in other ways.'

'What other ways? Nonsense! Maybe there won't be much to eat, but we're used to that. We won't be thrown out of our houses either. The comrades left enough room in all the committee buildings. Of course a lot has been blown up and there are a few fires that haven't been put out yet, but that will take care of itself. Look at their soldiers – how well dressed they are! And they must stuff them with food!' He continued in raptures.

Looting persisted in the city. People were taking everything they did not have a chance to take earlier. They scurried around with packages, with full pails, with bags. The Germans did not interfere. I noticed one of them standing by a wrecked warehouse and photographing the crowd which had gathered in the street. A boy threw a roll of cloth out through a broken window. There was a scuffle, but no one was angry. Everyone seemed to be in an unusually good humour.

There was a distant explosion. A few minutes later someone ran by shouting, 'The city soviet has been blown up.'

I went to the centre of the city, but the German sentries were not letting anyone through to the scene of the explosion.

For two or three more days buildings which had been mined by the retreating Soviets kept blowing up. There were both delayed-action mines and booby traps which would explode if someone opened a door inside the building. Sometimes the Germans would blow up a building when their sappers found a mine they could not take out safely. There were a few victims, mostly from the local population.

The second day after the arrival of the Germans I almost became one of these victims. A friend and I were walking along one of the main streets and discussing everything that had happened, particularly the destruction of the mined buildings. We had almost reached the big, white military hospital, in front of which a few Germans were standing about. We knew that about two hundred wounded Red Army soldiers were in it – there had been just time enough to evacuate the officers. Suddenly there was a tremendous explosion and I was thrown to the ground. Flying stones filled the air. Everything grew dark with dust and smoke.

Feeling dizzy and rubbing the back of my head which ached considerably, I looked for my friend. He was unconscious and his face was bleeding. His cheek had been laid open. I lifted him up and looked around. The hospital was in ruins. Among the stones in front of it lay the crushed bodies of several Germans.

Cars drove up and the street was roped off. Some Germans came up to us and said something which I did not understand. One of them threw me a small package in which I found a bandage and some cotton. I tied up my friend's cheek as well as I could. Meanwhile the Germans had dug out their own dead and began to carry the bodies of the Red Army men from the hospital, laying them out on the pavement. It looked as if not a single Soviet soldier had survived the blast.

I took my friend home and went back to the centre of the town. In those days not only I but everyone in the city was in a sort of feverish condition. There had been a radical change of everything we had grown accustomed to throughout our lives, and it produced a nervous reaction. Everyone kept hurrying somewhere in a state of excitement, exchanging news and impressions.

I remember how astonished we were at one small incident on the first day of the occupation. Late in the evening, when no one would risk walking in the unlit streets, the people who lived around our yard had locked the gate and were sitting talking on the benches in the small garden.

Suddenly, a loud knock at the gate. We looked at each other.

'Who could it be? Germans? Looters?'

Several of us went to the gate.

'Who's there?'

There was an answer in German and the knocking resumed. We opened the gate. There was a young German soldier. He looked at us, entered the yard, and began to speak. I managed to make out that he was searching for one of our neighbours. The man whose name he pronounced came up to him.

The German took out a piece of paper and gave it to him. A candle was was produced and it turned out that this was a letter from Rostov, from the man's daughter, with whom the German was acquainted. She wrote everything was quiet in Rostov although much of the city was in ruins.

The soldier stood there uncertainly. But for us the tenseness was gone now. We took him to the end of the yard where supper, wine, and vodka were quickly laid out for him. At that time everyone had plenty to eat from the looted warehouses. The soldier made himself at home. He took off his cap and belt with its knife, unbuttoned his tunic, and even tried to say a few words in Russian.

An interpreter was found: an old German woman who had lived near us for thirty years. Everyone crowded around the unexpected guest, asking what would happen to us. One thing amazed us; how he could have dared to come to us alone, at night, unarmed, and even drink vodka, in a newly occupied city where theoretically every house could contain an ambush. After supper the German was unable to say a word. He was thoroughly drunk. Someone put him up for the night, giving up his own bed.

At the end of the second day the looting was over. German military policemen walked around with lists of some sort, checking them with maps of the city, which they had had printed liberally before its capture. On all warehouses, shops, and surviving factories they posted short but eloquent notices, 'These premises are under German control. Looters will be shot.'

However, they posted no guards. There was no need for them. Our people had been used to discipline since childhood, and everyone understood that in time of war if you were caught you would be shot on the spot with no one to appeal to.

At the same time, notices from the German kommandatura appeared announcing that the city was under martial law and civilians were forbidden on the streets from 10 p.m. until 6 a.m. All citizens were instructed to return to their jobs. The exchange rate was set at ten rubles to one Reichsmark. Lastly, it was stated that the Germans had come to liberate the Russian people from Bolshevism, and the population was urged to seize partisans and commissars and bring them to the kommandatura.

The notices were printed in Russian and German, headed by an unfamiliar sign: a black eagle with a swastika.

People crowded around the placards, read them, and went home discussing them.

One evening I went to see a friend, the elderly engineer Arsov. There were about twenty people at his house, all members of the city intelligentsia: doctors, lawyers, engineers, professors.

The lawyer Sorokin was talking.

'This morning Alexandrov and I were at the kommandatura. The Commandant received us. We offered him our services to organize life in the city. We gave him a list of the demolitions the Soviets made before leaving, but he had a completer one of his own. After a little talk the Commandant said he wanted to appoint me burgomaster. I told him I'd like to consult with my friends before deciding whether or not to accept. So I'd like you all to give me your opinions.'

Krichenko, the senior engineer of the destroyed power plant, said, 'Of course there are various ways of looking at the possibilities of co-operation with the Germans. In principle I am against it.'

'Maybe it's because you were a Communist?' said someone.

'No, it isn't,' said the engineer sharply. 'It's obvious in recent history that Communists can co-operate with Hitlerites very success-fully. But I consider myself a Russian, and the Germans are invaders. It's true that they say they have come as liberators, but we have still to be convinced.'

'Let's be practical,' Sorokin interrupted. 'Do you want to work in the future city government?'

'I am being practical. You're not the burgomaster yet and I'm not your subordinate. So please don't interrupt me.

'Comrades, I . . .'

'Comrades are all over with,' someone else broke in. 'We've become misters.'

Krichenko continued without looking around.

'. . . consider that we must work. In the city there are more than 100,000 people who have been left to their fate by the Bolsheviks. The power plant, the water system, and the railroad have been destroyed. There isn't one vehicle left that will run. In a couple of weeks the food that the population has managed to stock up will be gone and the situation will be catastrophic. I myself am going to the power plant tomorrow to do all I can to get it working as soon as possible.'

'I thank you,' said Sorokin majestically, writing something down in his notebook. 'Who else would like to express an opinion?'

Professor Vanin, the director of the city hospital, got up.

'At the moment there are about 500 people in the hospital without any food supply. Our drugs are almost gone. I shall continue to work.'

'The city will be divided into three districts. We need three district burgomasters,' said Sorokin. 'Who wants to have the jobs?'

Three volunteers were found.

'What is the situation in regard to the Jewish question?' someone asked.

'I asked the Commandant about that. He said the matter does not interest him, that along with the army there are S.S. units that are specialists on the Jewish question, but no S.S. units have arrived yet.'

'Didn't you ask what would happen to the Jews?'

'No, I didn't. But I don't think anything very pleasant will happen to them.'

Sorokin's friend, the lawyer Alexandrov, said, 'I guess we can consider that the basic framework of the future city government has been formed. Sorokin and I will report to the Commandant about it tomorrow. I ask you all to think about this and talk it over with people who feel they can be useful in this work, as well as to start thinking about how to solve the problems that are before us.'

People began to leave. Our host, Arsov, who had accepted the administration of the First District, turned to me.

'What do you think? Do you want to work with us?'

I shrugged my shoulders.

'I don't know what all this will involve and how it will turn out. Frankly, I would like to wait a bit and see.'

He started to try to convince me that we had no right to wait, that somebody had to take the responsibility of restoring the city to normal life, that the population, after all, was not to blame for the situation.

'You must understand, Vladimir Nikolaevich, that all of us who are able to do anything have a citizen's responsibility before our people. We can think about the moral side of co-operating with the Germans but we have no right to forget that no one is going to worry about the little people. The Germans have their own worries; they are fighting a war, and probably looting. The population has nothing. You know that as well as I do.

'The Bolsheviks blew up everything they could when they left. Did you know that tremendous charges were discovered in all the transformers in the city today? If they hadn't been found all the houses around would have been blown to hell as soon as the power plant started up again.

'And then after all, Vladimir Nikolaevich, we must begin to believe in something. We've been living for the last twenty-five years with no faith of any kind, without any hope for something better. You're young and you don't realize the horror of such a life. You have nothing to compare it to. I'm twice as old as you and I've seen a lot – a lot besides Soviet concentration camps. I'd like to believe that out of the blood and fire of war there's a new life starting for us, a better one than what went before, a freer one. Why should we be sorry if Hitler beats Stalin? What can we lose? The Germans won't conquer Russia, that's obvious to any child. Russia can swallow the whole of Germany and there will still be room left.

'You'll tell me, "Russian blood is being spilled, and the Germans are doing it." Believe me the Germans will never be able to kill as many people as Stalin has. And I am ready to close my eyes to the destruction of the Jews, terrible as that is. That is the point where the Germans go insane. But at least they leave the non-Jews alone.'

'What about the prisoners of war? You know how they are treated in the camp.'

'Yes, I know, the conditions are awful there – an appalling death rate after only a week and a half. But the U.S.S.R. stayed out of the international conference about prisoners of war and doesn't look out for them through the International Red Cross. If we work with the Germans, we'll be able to help them somehow. But if we just stand aside and condemn everything, no one will be better off. Think about it.'

I finally agreed to organize the clearing of the streets of all the debris which had littered them during the explosions, as well as to list the residential buildings which had been damaged. It was obvious that there would be no way of making any further repairs.

'Incidentally,' I asked, 'how is the city going to support the people on these jobs?'

'The Germans say they have captured some of the money in the State Bank. There is going to be a directive about paying all the cash which is still left in the various cash drawers about town into the city treasury. And then there will be taxes.'

'Who is going to be taxed and how?'

'Private trade and privately owned workshops are going to be permitted. The owners will have to buy licenses, and they'll pay the taxes. The food and goods left over from the looting will be sold. Also the Germans are supposed to put up some money.'

'What about police?'

'The German military police are to organize the police directly. The only thing I know is that some former officers of the Tsarist army are going to be in it, as well as some of the city's former Soviet policemen.'

'Well, we'll see how it goes,' I said getting up. 'Where is your office going to be?'

'We don't know yet. We're to look for a suitable place tomorrow. Come over in the morning.'

On the way home I pondered everything that had occurred, and the future. Something was troubling me. I had just consented to work for the city government, or, stated in official Soviet language, 'to collaborate with the enemy'. Had I done the right thing? I could not decide. I had some foggy, for the most part emotional, objections to it. I began to examine myself:

Whom are the Germans fighting against?

Against Russia.

Who are you?

I am a Russian. The Germans are my enemies.

Do you want to help your enemies?

No.

Whom do you want to help?

My own people, the people of my home town, deserted by the Soviets, invaded by the Germans.

Is it possible to help them without helping the Germans at the same time?

This was a difficult question. In order to help the people in the city it was necessary to take things from the Germans, even though these things had been seized by the Germans elsewhere. To take things from them was not necessarily helping them. But this answer did not seem convincing. I tried to approach the matter from another point of view:

Who is defending Russia today?

The people, and not very willingly.

Who is organizing this defence?

Stalin and the Bolsheviks.

Should you help Stalin in this?

For what purpose?

To chase out the invaders.

And in doing this, strengthen the Soviet regime?

Perhaps, but—

No! No, a thousand times!

Memories of the Kolyma swept over me; I rid myself of them with difficulty.

Stalin isn't defending Russia, he is defending himself and his power at the cost of enormous sacrifices on the part of the people. Moreover, the Germans are today the only power fighting against Bolshevism, the No. 1 enemy of my people. Therefore they are the single hope for our liberation from it.

Do you know what the occupation will bring with it?

No. But I don't believe it could be worse than before. Besides, I don't believe the Germans can conquer Russia.

But this was not entirely convincing either. At any rate Nikolai, who had swum across the river to join 'his own' a few days back, believed it complete nonsense: that after the war everything would become better.

There remained one more approach, a most logical one:

Do you have any means of existence?

No.

How are you going to live if you don't work?

I've got to work.

Do you know that *any* form of work in an area occupied by the enemy is considered aid to the enemy under Soviet law?

I know it.

Would you rather starve or break a Soviet law?

I laughed inwardly at the childishness of the question. Break a Soviet law? How can you avoid breaking it, even in a 'peaceful' non-war period? Where do all the millions of Soviet forced labourers come from? They must have broken some Soviet law.

But wasn't it enough that I, a man of military age, who had been convicted for counter-revolution, was not in the army and had not been evacuated? Wasn't this enough in itself for the 'comrades' to shoot me whenever they got the chance? Now I was really outside the law.

I was calm. There was no mistake. I would go to work.

11. THE SLIPPERY WAY

THE next day we found an empty building, abandoned by a trust, and set up our district government. At first there were ten of us, but by the end of the day there were more than enough people who wanted to do something to help.

My duties were not complicated. Every day people who lived in houses damaged by explosions or fires would come to my office. I was supposed to inspect the damage, determine the materials needed to repair it, and if the materials were available, to issue them. They had to do the repair work themselves. The workmen that I assembled were taken over by Burgomaster Sorokin to repair buildings occupied by the Germans.

I still had little contact with the Germans, although numbers of them had arrived. They were billeted in schools, office buildings, and, in part, in tents on the main square. Some of the officers moved into private apartments. In such cases the people who lived there would either double up or move elsewhere.

About a week after the beginning of my work I was summoned to the kommandatura to see a German lieutenant who spoke Russian. I had heard about this lieutenant, whose name was Lüttich. He was said to be making a lot of money issuing permits to enterprising businessmen to bring food into the city from the surrounding country-side.

The lieutenant was about fifty years old and he had three chins. He waved me into a chair without getting up.

'Sit down,' he said. 'Burgomaster Sorokin tells me that you organized the workmen who are repairing our buildings.'

'That is correct.'

'Well, will you please collect twenty or thirty more to fix up the N.K.V.D. building? Do you know where it is?'

'Yes.'

'It was somewhat damaged by fire, but not much. It must be repaired in a very short time.'

'I can find workers all right, but they have to be paid. The city government still doesn't have enough money.'

'For this job there will be money,' said the lieutenant, opening a drawer. 'Here's 1,000 marks. Write me a receipt. In two weeks bring me a list of your workmen and I'll pay them what's coming to them. That's all.'

I left, taking the money and a paper that Lüttich had prepared stating that I was charged with directing the repairs of No. 45 Lenin Street.

The next day, after assembling ten workmen, who promised to find more, and paying each of them 50 marks in advance, I set out for the former N.K.V.D. building. On the doors, which were not locked, there was the customary notice that all looters would be shot.

The building had been considerably damaged in the fire. Going from room to room, occasionally asking the help of one of my men to unlock a door, I wrote down in my notebook the extent of the damage and what materials would be needed to repair it.

It seemed strange the building had not been blown up. They had probably been in too much of a hurry. The drawers and closets were open and all the papers had been destroyed. Later I found an enormous pile of ashes in the furnace room. In one drawer I came across a revolver which I stuck in my belt.

Having inspected the upper floors, we went down the cellar. An ironclad door led into a long corridor from which others branched out to the right and left. There were doors along these corridors, also iron surfaced, with peepholes and slots to thrust food through. We went down the dark corridor. The workmen peered into the cells on both sides. All were empty, the doors were open, and only the heavy air of the unventilated cellar spoke of the unhappy life which people had led here.

At the end of one corridor there was still another door, but this one was locked. One of the men said, 'Let's open it and see what's inside.'

I was undecided. Lüttich had only referred to repairs in the office part of the building. But the workers had already begun to pick at the lock. In a few minutes the door was open. We saw a stairway leading downward into total darkness. A repulsive sweetish smell met our nostrils.

We looked at each other and I said, 'It's too dark there; we won't see anything anyway. Another time. Let's get to work.'

Upstairs the workmen began to knock out charred doors and floors. and I went over to the kommandatura, looking over my notes on the way.

'Did you inspect the building?' Lüttich asked me.

'Yes. A lot of work has to be done on it. If we can get money and materials we can repair it in a month.'

'That's too long. It's got to be done in two weeks.'

'Then we'll need more money. To do it in two weeks I'll need fifty workmen at 50 rubles each per day.'

'You're out of your mind!' Lüttich shouted. 'Fifty rubles! Don't you know the order that all wage rates will be the same as under the Soviets?'

'I know they got about 15 rubles under the Soviets but since then the price of food has gone up tremendously.'

'I don't care how much bread costs. I'll pay 15 rubles and you find the men!'

'No, on those terms I won't be able to get anyone. I'm sorry, but I'll have to refuse the job.'

'You can't do that. The city is under martial law and you'll be punished.'

I shrugged my shoulders.

'I'm ready to work myself. You can make me do that. But I can't force anyone else to do it. I'm not the police. And even if the police were around the workers would still run off.'

Lüttich began to curse in German and then talked to someone on the telephone.

'All right,' he said to me finally, 'how much money will you need?'

'About 4,000 marks.'

He leapt up from his chair, sat down again, and made another telephone call. Then he said, 'You'll get 4,000 marks but you get the materials yourself wherever you can.'

'But—' I tried to object.

'Don't argue with me!' Lüttich yelled. 'Take it wherever you want; I'll give you a requisition. In two weeks the building must be ready. You've received your advance on the money.'

'All right. It will be done. One more question: have you been there?'

'No, I sent a soldier over. Why do you ask?'

'There are cells downstairs. There was a prison there.'

'I know that. The N.K.V.D. is never without one. This is my second year in Russia.'

'Yes, but in addition to that there's a cellar.'

'A cellar? Did you go down there?'

'No, it was pitch dark.'

'That's interesting. I'll be there tomorrow morning at ten and we'll take a look.'

At exactly 10 a.m. Lüttich appeared with a soldier. I was waiting for him. They had a carbide light and a large flashlight. Taking two of the workmen we went downstairs, through the prison corridors to the stairway we had discovered the day before.

The air grew more suffocating as we descended. On a landing there were two cells. Their doors were locked and had no peepholes. Lüttich ordered the men to break them open. One of the cells was empty.

The second cell contained two corpses, a man and a woman. They were in an advanced state of decay. I felt nauseated and retreated to the stairs. Lüttich and the others followed me.

'How do you like that?' asked Lüttich. 'The interesting thing is we've been finding this sort of thing in every city we've occupied.'

I did not answer. We went to the bottom of the stairs. The soldier inspected all the corners of the cellar, his lamp held high over his head. We could see nothing, but the air was full of the stench of corpses.

'There must be bodies here,' said Lüttich. 'I know there must be. This is probably where they shot them.'

Suddenly one of the workers found a trapdoor and shouted to us about it. Lüttich raised it himself. I had to jump back. My head began to swim from the smell.

'See, I told you there must be bodies,' said Lüttich triumphantly. 'Your N.K.V.D. always shoots people when it's in a hurry to retreat. All right, now we can go.'

When we were upstairs he said, 'This will make good propaganda. I will give orders for those bodies to be pulled out of there. Good-bye.'

The next day, guarded by a few soldiers, about ten prisoners of war from the near-by camp arrived. They were made to carry the bodies from the cellar and lay them out on the sidewalk in view of the crowd which had assembled.

In all they found twenty-eight bodies. Some of them had their arms twisted behind them with wire. All of them had been shot in the back of the head. All had rotted considerably.

One of the workmen who kept running out to see what was going on told us:

'There were four women among the bodies, young ones, too. A woman in the crowd recognized her husband who had been arrested right after the beginning of the war; she fainted. Someone recognized a neighbour of his who was drafted a month ago. He just couldn't understand why he had been in the N.K.V.D. jail. And then a girl recognized her brother who had been sentenced to three years, before the war started, for speculation, I think. Nobody knew the others. Probably from the country, or newcomers to town.'

The bodies lay there for two days. Then the Germans themselves took them away somewhere.

We finished the work on time and Lüttich gave me the money to pay the men, swearing heavily as he did so. I was pleased. Until the last minute I had been afraid that he would not pay me and I would be in trouble with the men.

Lüttich came to inspect the repaired building in the company of an officer who wore black insignia on his uniform. On his cap, underneath the eagle with the swastika, he had a skull and two crossed bones. Burgomaster Sorokin appeared and kept talking to the officer in his broken German.

'Why are you underfoot so much? Don't bother me,' said the latter in perfect Russian.

Sorokin mumbled something and withdrew a few paces.

'He's the local burgomaster,' Lüttich explained.

'A-a,' grunted the latter noncommittally.

During the inspection the S.S. man (Lüttich identified him to me as such in a whisper) wrinkled his nose occasionally but said very little. I sensed that Lüttich was afraid of him.

'Do you think this building will be suitable?' Lüttich asked him.

'It doesn't matter. It's too big, but it doesn't matter,' said the S.S. man.

We went out. I asked Lüttich if I could go. He nodded and I started off in the direction of the public bath which had just begun to function again.

In the evening we had the periodical meeting of the district government. Arsov, the district burgomaster, said, 'A special S.S. unit has arrived in town. We have been instructed to compile a list of all Jews and also a list of the apartments of those Jews who have left the city. All Jewish property is to be under the control of the S.S. The Jews themselves are, too.'

'Will there be reprisals?' asked Likhachev, the head of our industrial section.

'Officially they told us in the kommandatura that the Jews will all be resettled to the Ukraine. But unofficially . . .'

'. . . they will be shot,' said Kondakov, the secretary of the district government.

Arsov looked at him uncertainly and then asked him to bring in the book of city-wide directives. When Kondakov had gone out, Arsov said to us in an undertone:

'I didn't want to talk about this in front of Kondakov, who approves of it. The thing is that the question of the Jewish rosters was brought up a week ago by the Commandant. Kikin, the burgomaster of the Third District, and I tried to protest from the very first, but Sorokin did not support us and the Commandant confirmed the order. Actually the rosters have been ready for a long time. We could have altered them if the police hadn't received a copy at the start – and the police are completely in the hands of the Germans. Day before yesterday there was another conference and we did not deliver rosters, making the excuse that they had to be checked. But today the Commandant began to raise hell and say he didn't want to get into trouble with the S.S. because of our sabotage, and that if the rosters weren't in by to-morrow each of us would become personally acquainted with that organization . . .

'So try to warn anyone you can. Do it carefully; the S.S. has a lot of agents around already and it will be bad for you if you get caught. We've managed to warn a few people already.'

Thanks to the night pass which the kommandatura had issued me, I was able to visit a dozen of my friends on a bicycle and ask them to tell all the Jews they knew to go into hiding. Many Jews had learned already and managed to leave their old apartments.

I went to see a girl I used to know at school, the daughter of a Jewish father and a Russian mother. She was married to a Russian.

The whole family was assembled there and had already decided on a course of action. The father was to flee to the south, through the thin front lines to the Soviets. He was ready for the road with a leather coat and a rucksack. A document had been forged for the daughter proving that he was her stepfather and that her real father had not been Jewish.

The atmosphere was so painful that I left for home very soon since, there was nothing I could do to help.

The German order was published the next day: all persons of Jewish ancestry were to gather in an appointed place within twenty-four hours, bringing their valuables with them.

When the German trucks, loaded with Jews, were slowly rolling down the street in front of our district government office, Kondakov called me over to the window. About thirty vehicles went by. I recognized an old music professor, a cellist, a tailor whom I had tried to persuade not to register, and two others.

I turned and went away from the window. Kondakov was saying loudly, 'This is the end of the Jewish lordship over us! The damned parasites have drunk enough of our blood!'

I couldn't stand any more.

'Especially your blood, Kondakov, isn't that right? It seems to me you were a member of the party and spent your whole life in soft spots in various city soviets.'

'Meaning exactly what?' said Kondakov challengingly.

'I mean that your kind are the ones who have been sucking the people's blood.'

Kondakov came over to me.

'You watch out, you might have to pay for those words!'

'Don't try to threaten me. Your comrade Communists threatened me so much that I've stopped being afraid of them.'

Someone was pulling at my sleeve. I turned and saw Arsov. He was trying to draw me into his office.

'You act as if you want to follow those kikes to where they are going,' Kondakov was saying with menace in his voice.

Arsov went on pulling at me. I found myself in his office.

'What's the matter with you? Are you out of your mind?' Arsov whispered. 'Don't you know that Kondakov is an S.S. agent?'

'I don't give a God damn whose agent he is,' I said loudly.

'No, please, I beg of you for your own good, be careful with him. He can mess things up for you. I didn't choose him for this job; he was sent me from the kommandatura.'

'What are you trying to make me do? I didn't stay here when the

Germans came in order to be afraid of Communists like Kondakov.
And I don't intend to let them scare me in the future. You should fire
him!'

'I can't. The city government and all the district governments have
such "representatives" from the Germans with instructions to watch us.
The city government is in a mess. The city is not being supplied
properly, and Sorokin and the whole administration bow and scrape
to the Germans. This isn't what we bargained for when we agreed
to work!' Arsov said bitterly.

'What about the power plant?' I asked, somewhat calmed down.

'It's going to start running next week but the city will get almost no
power at all; the plant is only partially fixed. The power will go to the
buildings occupied by the Germans. But the water system is going to
work again everywhere. At least the people won't have to go to the
river for water any more.'

'What did you say was wrong with the food supply?'
Arsov waved his hand.

'German patrols are taking food away from the peasants as usual, so
that only half of it gets to market in town. You know yourself what prices
are. They are talking about issuing ration cards, but there is nothing
to give out on them yet. Things are bad. The only thing is that they're
worse on the Soviet side.'

'Doesn't it seem to you that things look quite different now from
what you thought, when you were persuading me to go to work here?'

'Yes, and on a smaller scale we are just as much to blame for it as
the Germans are. If some decent people were in the city government
instead of this crowd of flannel-mouthed lawyers things might have
been different.'

'You mean, for instance, the liquidation of the Jews?'
Arsov bent his head.

'Yes, the Kultur bearers are not what we expected. They are about
as humane as our N.K.V.D. men. But all this is out of our hands and
doesn't change our responsibility toward the population of the city.
Since we took on this job we've got to do it properly. We've got to
fight for everything from the Germans – but instead of that Sorokin
crawls in front of them.'

'We've got to change the administration of the city government,' I
said, 'and put new people in. This is a troubled time and all kinds of
garbage like your Kondakov floats to the surface.'

'That's right. We must clean out the city government. But how?'

The next few evenings those of us who were dissatisfied with Sorokin
and his colleagues worked out strategy and tactics for our fight to
change the city administration. It was decided to lay the groundwork:
the individual members of our district government who had occasion

to deal with the Germans were to discredit Sorokin in their eyes in every possible way. After this we would inform the Commandant officially that a change in the city government was necessary. We decided to put up Likhachev, the head of our industial section, as our candidate for the post of burgomaster. He was a deeply religious person with a great deal of self-control, not too energetic but possessed of a sense of personal integrity which was rare in those times.

Krichenko, the head of the power plant, was chosen as his assistant, and I as his second assistant.

Shortly after this Arsov told me that the Commandant of the city had agreed to receive the three district burgomasters without Sorokin being present, and with them, six people from the district governments. We all went to the kommandatura.

At that time the Commandant was a Captain Schwarz, by profession an artist and musician from Dresden. He was a short man with a great deal of self-assurance, convinced that he understood the Russian problem perfectly. When all of us were seated around a table Captain Schwarz told us through a girl interpreter,

'Please, gentlemen, speak freely.'

In a short but eloquent speech Arsov outlined the problem. He told of the complete loss of authority by the burgomaster, and stated in the name of all of us that none of us would continue in our jobs unless the burgomaster and several of the other lawyers in the city government were removed from office.

Schwarz listened attentively, asked the interpreter to repeat sentences several times, and then said, 'All right. I'll think about it. Whom do you propose as burgomaster?'

Likhachev was named. The Commandant asked to see him privately 'in order to become acquainted', and told us that we would have his answer the next day.

The Commandant decided in our favour. Sorokin was told that he was relieved of his position, and Likhachev was appointed in his stead, with Krichenko and myself as his assistants.

That evening I told my mother what had happened. She did not seem pleased at my 'promotion'.

'You shouldn't have taken this position. I don't think the Germans will stay here long. Then the Soviets will come again, and what will become of you?'

'Well, Mother,' I said, 'it's a little late to think about that. No matter what I did under the Germans, even if I was just a street cleaner, my fate would be sealed. The devil himself seems to have tied my fate to them. I have no choice; I have to go where they go. There can be no return for me. If they retreat, we'll have to flee with them.'

My mother lowered her eyes and was silent a moment. Then she said, 'You, yes, but not I. I'm not going anywhere. And my fate and the fate of my brothers and sisters will depend on what you do now.'

I tried to point out to her that she could not stay in any case. But the conversation was too far from reality. The Germans had penetrated as far as Mount Elbrus and it was hard to visualize them in retreat. So my mother and I came to no agreement. I decided though to find myself a separate room again, so as not to compromise her.

A chance to do this turned up a few days later. Igor and Zina Gorsky, who had fled from besieged Leningrad a year and a half before, received a small house on the outskirts of the city from the kommandatura, because they had agreed to start an inn for German officers. Igor was the son of a childhood friend of my mother's. He offered to rent me one of the rooms in their house. Collecting my unimpressive baggage, I moved over there.

12. CITY FATHERS

AT the start there was a great deal to do in the city government. In the division of responsibilities finance, supply, and transportation were assigned to me. Krichenko was responsiblef or the economy and trade. Likhachev himself was to run the police (under direct German military police control) and the legal section.

Every morning we were supposed to appear at the kommandatura together with the three district burgomasters to discuss the problems which had arisen the day before. In addition to the Commandant we had dealings with Oberkriegsverwaltungsrat Albrecht, the specialist for civilian affairs.

There were numerous problems. The city food supply was a question which never left the agenda of our daily conferences. The situation was very serious. Malnutrition among the population threatened to become actual starvation. The German Wirtschaftskommando, which collected food from the farms, supplied only the German forces. The people had received ration cards on which they could get a pound of bad maize bread a day, and nothing more. A black market existed but the prices soared every day. Only the wealthiest could afford to buy there. These were the entrepreneurs who had appeared in such numbers: restaurant and theatre owners, shopkeepers, etc.

The Commandant sincerely tried to better the situation. He went out to the Wirtschaftskommando with us several times, although he had no control over its activities. These visits did not succeed in helping matters, however. Only when we were finally able to persuade the Germans to remove their guard details from the roads leading to the city and let traffic pass did the food supply increase and prices fall somewhat.

The city had its own transportation: a few dozen horses which had been assembled after the Soviet retreat. Some of these however had been appropriated by the new 'entrepreneurs'. It took a month of hard work to recover them and get permission for representatives of the city government to drive out to the villages where they could buy up food at low prices to give out on the ration cards. There was never enough hay for the horses; it was confiscated for the German Army. Once I presented a written report to Oberkriegsverwaltungsrat Albrecht stating that the horses would die if they did not receive more feed. The next day he returned the report to me with the notation: Refer to the city veterinarian.

The police constituted another problem. Almost every day we received complaints from the population about outrages committed by the police. Outright plundering, occasional rape, constant drunkenness in headquarters, beating up of detained persons, blackmail, and similar activities were typical.

The chief of police set the tone. He was an ex-Soviet officer who had endeared himself through bribery and other means, it was said, to the head of the German military police, who would not hear of his dismissal. All our recommendations to clean up the police brought no results. The outrages continued.

Once, however, I received an unexpected visit from a friend.

'Do you know who your chief of police is?' he asked me.

'Sure. Sharov. He's said to be an ex-major in the Red Army.'

'He's no major. Before the war he was head of the N.K.V.D. in Taganrog.'

'How do you know?'

'I have two friends who were evacuated from Taganrog. One of them saw this Sharov today. He recognized him immediately because he'd been in prison there. Only the name isn't Sharov, it's Fokin.'

I asked my friend to bring the two people from Taganrog around to see me the next day. Then I told Burgomaster Likhachev about it. We decided to gather all the information we could on Sharov-Fokin. We requested data about refugees from Taganrog from all the district governments. Then the Burgomaster's secretary was instructed to visit all the Taganrog people and show them Sharov's picture, to see if anyone would recognize him.

The results were excellent. Ten out of the thirty people asked recognized the photograph as Fokin. All this was compiled into a report.

'Let's go to the kommandatura,' said Likhachev.

'That's no use,' Krichenko said. 'The Commandant is wholly under the influence of his military police commander. We've got to go to the S.S.'

Half an hour later we arrived at the former N.K.V.D. building, now occupied by the S.S. After a long wait in the hallway we were taken to the same gloomy officer, Rauberg, who had come to inspect the building with Lüttich.

'What is it?' he asked.

Likhachev explained.

'Do you have proof?'

He was handed the folder with the statements of the Taganrog people.

'I'll look into it. Goodbye.'

A few days later the S.S. made wholesale arrests among the police. About thirty men were gathered up along with Fokin. There were rumours that some of them were shot. The Commandant asked us to name a new candidate for the post of chief of police. It was not an easy task. Only the police had any measure of real power and it was imperative to appoint a man of unquestionable honesty and integrity to the post. Unfortunately there were not many of these.

At the same time that they purged the police the S.S. arrested the assistant to the burgomaster of the Third District and two employees of the registration section. Nothing was known about their fate for a long time. Finally the Commandant announced that they had been shot for concealing Jews in their district.

Two men came into my office one day. One was tall, very solidly built, and limped heavily, supporting himself on a cane. The other, a short man with an intelligent face, was extremely pale and emaciated.

The first introduced himself as Chernov, a former officer in the White Army, and showed me an old picture of himself in uniform. On his chest, over the St. George ribbon, was a sword and crown-of-thorns insignia, which marked him as a participant in the once famous 'Ice Expedition' led by General Kornilov, who was killed on the banks of the Kuban in 1919.

The second, Kalinnikov, was a well-known professor of medicine in the city. My brother had once attended his lectures.

When they were seated the tall one began to tell their story.

'We didn't know each other before,' he said, 'although just before the Germans got here we were both in the local N.K.V.D. jail, charged with anti-Soviet activities. We knew nothing about the situation at the front because we had been in custody for more than six months and no news got through to us.

'Sometime toward the end of July we were wakened up and told to get dressed and leave our cells. When about thirty of us had assembled in the prison yard, a truck arrived and we were taken to the station under heavy guard. We managed to count more than twenty cars in the train standing there; they were all freight cars with small barred windows. There must have been at least five hundred prisoners loaded in later; there were more than sixty in our car.

'Almost half of them were citizens of foreign nations, arrested just after the war began. There were Greeks, Iranians, Turks, Germans, Bessarabian and Polish Jews; they had not been sent to Siberia earlier with the others because of transportation shortages. Almost none of them had been questioned by the N.K.V.D. and they were ignorant of the charges against them.

'The train left before dawn with a strong group of guards aboard. It made frequent stops and stood still for long periods. Day came, and then evening. At one of the stops there were shouts from several of the cars for food and water. Nobody had any rations. All we heard for answer was the cursing of the guards. People were weak from thirst in our car.

'Finally the train stopped in the middle of the open steppe. We could hear the thunder of artillery fire in the distance. The guards surrounded the train. After a few hours we sensed movement outside. Some of the car doors were being opened and there were shouts of "Everybody out of the train!"

'Our door was opened and we received the same orders. People began to step down on to the railroad bed. Suddenly at some signal the guards opened up with sub-machine guns and machine guns which were mounted on the car platforms. The prisoners began to rush around. Some fell and were covered with blood. Some tried to hide under the wheels; others climbed back into the cars.

'The firing continued. When the shouts outside had subsided, the guards came to the doors of the cars and began to shoot inside. The walls were pierced with hundreds of bullet holes. Sometimes they simply threw grenades through the open doors.

'We lay in our car; we hadn't had time to leave it when the shooting started. The bodies of some of the prisoners served as cover for us. Both of us were wounded. I was hit in the leg by six bullets. The professor got three in his arm and shoulder.

'Finally the shooting stopped and the guards disappeared. In spite of our pain we crawled to the car doors. Everything was quiet. So far as we could see nothing was moving in our car or around it. We managed to bind up each other's wounds.

'Another night passed. In the morning a few German light tanks came up to the train. The Germans inspected the entire train and found only fourteen people alive, all of them wounded. All the rest were dead.

'We were taken to a German field hospital and later to a recently occupied city. After we were better they let us go home. It turned out that the prison train was not able to get to its destination in the east. The railroad had been cut by the rapidly advancing Germans. So, according to instructions, the guards shot everyone.

'A few guards were caught by the Germans. They were hanged on the main square of the city where we were convalescing.'

I asked how I could be of assistance. Professor Kalinnikov said, 'After my arrest my wife and two small children were evicted from their apartment and settled in a barn outside the town. The apartment was taken by a Communist who is working here for your city government. He took over our belongings. I request that my apartment be returned to me. And then if possible I'd like to find some sort of work; I'm entirely without means.'

'Who is the Communist who took over your apartment?'

'Orlov. Here are the papers to back up my statements.'

He handed me his wife's passport where her former address was noted, together with an affidavit from the neighbours that the family had been forcibly evicted without the right to take along their furniture. I took the papers and called up the head of the district police station. I asked Kalinnikov to wait.

'And what can I do for you?' I asked my other visitor.

'The only thing I want is to fight the damned Communists,' he said, 'but apparently it's not time for that yet. So perhaps you could give me some sort of work here in the city government. I can settle my personal affairs myself.'

'Have you got any kind of papers?' I asked.

'There's not much that I managed to save. Here it is. And here is my autobiography.'

'All right. Come and see me tomorrow if it isn't too hard for you to walk,' I said. 'I'll try to find something suitable for you.'

As they were leaving they met the head of the police station just coming in. I told the latter what was needed. I knew him quite well and was able to talk frankly. He shook the professor's hand.

'I've heard about this already,' he said, 'both about your shooting and the apartment. I believe you have applied to the police about it.'

'Yes, I have,' said the professor somewhat drily, 'and without result.' While he was speaking the police officer handed me a hurriedly written slip of paper: 'Please ask the professor to leave the room.'

'Listen, Professor,' I said, 'could you please come back tomorrow morning? I can promise you that we'll do all we can.'

When he had gone the head of the police station said, 'Don't promise him too much. This Orlov·who grabbed Kalinnikov's apartment is now working for the S.S. And he's not the first Communist to do so. Three-quarters of the S.S. agents I know about are former party members.'

'Maybe the S.S. doesn't know it.'

'All those bastards know, believe me, although I haven't asked them about it.'

'Will you be able to prove that they belong to the party if you have to?'

'That would be easy. But don't get involved with Orlov, that's my advice to you.'

'Well, we'll see about that. But meanwhile, you hunt up an apartment in your district for Kalinnikov, in case I don't get anywhere. It's easier for you than for our housing office.'

'I'll try but it won't be simple.'

He left, and I called up Orlov and asked him to come over. When he came in he sat down immediately without waiting for an invitation.

'Orlov, are you aware that Kalinnikov has returned?'

'I am.'

'Do you know that you are living in his apartment?'

'I do.'

'Don't you think that you should find yourself another one now that the owner is back?'

'No, I don't. I'm quite comfortable where I am.'

'You don't think you can be removed from his apartment?'

'No, I don't.' His tone became more and more insolent.

'Why are you so sure?' I asked.

'Because—' He hesitated for a second. 'Well, it doesn't matter. Here, read this.' He thrust a piece of paper at me. It was a piece of S.S. stationery on which it was stated that Orlov was under the special protection of the local S.S. unit and it was forbidden to make trouble for him in any way. It was signed by Rauberg, the S.S. man who spoke perfect Russian.

'Are you satisfied?' he smirked.

'Absolutely. You may go. But one more thing. I think you had better find yourself some work elsewhere and leave the city government.'

'Are you discharing me?' he asked defiantly.

'No, just giving you advice.'

After he had gone I went to see Likhachev and told him what had happened. Likhachev got very excited.

'I don't believe the S.S. know who they are dealing with. We've got to go over and tell them right away,' he exclaimed.

I did not think much would come of this. If we had to tell this story it would be better to do it in the kommandatura where some of the officers were well disposed toward us and our affairs. But Likhachev insisted and asked me to go with him.

We had to wait an hour before Rauberg received us.

'What is it?' he asked.

'Petrov will tell you everything.'

I repeated the whole story.

'Well, what do you want?' he asked.

'In the first place I want Orlov discharged from the city government. We don't want anything to do with Communists. And then I want to evict him from the apartment and give it back to the man the Soviets tried to shoot.'

'You won't do either one of those things,' Rauberg cut me off.

'But why?' stammered the Burgomaster confusedly.

'Because I forbid it.'

'Excuse me, but I am responsible to the city Commandant and you have no right to forbid me . . .'

'Shut up!' Rauberg brought his fist down with a tremendous bang. 'If you talk to me like that I'll grind you into powder, you and your Commandant, too! Get out of here and if anything happens to Orlov I'll throw you both out of the city government and out of your apartments, too!'

As we left the former N.K.V.D. building Likhachev's lips were trembling. He mumbled indignantly, 'How dare he talk like that! We're going to the Commandant right away!'

The Commandant only shrugged his shoulders and said, 'The S.S. is not under my command and they have a lot more rights than I do. My advice to you is to remain on good terms with them and not argue with them. They can do anything they want.'

'But this is impossible!' exclaimed the Burgomaster. 'There must be some justice! To whom is this S.S. unit responsible?'

'To S.S. Reichsführer Heinrich Himmler,' answered the Commandant. 'Have you any more questions?'

Lickhachev frowned but said nothing.

'I have one,' I said. 'We've found a candidate for the post of police chief. He's a former officer in the White Army whom the Soviets tried to shoot along with Kalinnikov.'

'All right, send him around. I'll talk to him.'

'Well, are you still going to look for justice?' I asked Likhachev on the way back to our office.

'Please don't joke! This is beyond endurance!' he exclaimed. 'Why did we trade the Bolsheviks for the Germans? What have we gained? The Communists have penetrated everywhere and keep right on making trouble for the anti-Communists and those who have suffered from the Soviet regime! What's the difference between what we had and what we have now?'

'Difference? There is a difference. Under the Bolsheviks you wouldn't be burgomaster and I wouldn't be your assistant. We'd be in jail or dying from typhus in a construction battalion at the front. There's another difference. Now at least you dare express your indignation at injustice. Under the Bolsheviks you wouldn't have risked it. And there wouldn't be hundreds of shops and restaurants opening up for Russians and Germans who have money. On the other hand, hundreds of Jews would still be alive. . . . But now nobody stops you from cursing Stalin and the Soviet authorities.'

'Don't try to be amusing about all this,' said Likhachev sullenly. 'I am very dissatisfied. This isn't what we hoped for when the Germans came.'

'Well, what choice did you have? What do you expect?'

There was nothing else to say.

In the evening we had a conference in the office at which my suggestion to appoint Chernov chief of police, subject to the Commandant's approval, was confirmed. It was decided to give Kalinnikov the best accommodation we could and pay him 10,000 rubles out of the city treasury in compensation.

By this time about 5,000,000 rubles had accumulated in the treasury from various sources, mainly from taxes collected from the new merchants and manufacturers. In addition to this there was a fund of 3,000,000 which the Germans had 'contributed'. All payments made by the treasury had to be approved by Oberkriegsverwaltungsrat Albrecht. But we decided to pay out this 10,000 rubles at our own risk even if it were not approved. This was not an excessive sum. At that time a small family needed a minimum of 3,000 rubles a month to live.

Chernov was the first to appear at my office in the morning. I offered him the post of chief of police. He accepted and went off to see the Commandant. His appointment was confirmed on the same day and he began to act in his new capacity. He appointed several of his friends to various posts in the police, and a measure of order was restored.

Kalinnikov was offered the post of director of public health. With the help of the police, an apartment was found for him.

Time went by. The city was slowly being restored to normal.

Power and water were available everywhere. There were vegetables at the market, and some meat even made its appearance. Prices, however, kept rising. It seemed that the Germans had an interest in this. Some of them made a great deal of money selling supplies earmarked for the army from the warehouses.

Not until the autumn, four months after the coming of the Germans, was the city government able to issue food regularly to the population, on ration cards. The ration was not satisfactory: a pound and a half of low-grade bread daily per person and ten pounds of various grains per month. However, it was cheap and available to all.

The first day of the ration was one of celebration in our office. It had taken untold effort to squeeze a month's ration for the city from the Germans and the surrounding countryside. There was no knowing what it would take to keep it at that level.

Residents often came to the city government with their troubles. They complained about evictions and resettlements; about fuel, of which there was a shortage. The Germans were cutting down trees in the woods outside the city, as well as in the park, for their own use but were allowing almost none for the population. Coal was delivered only for the power plant.

We did all we could to help. It was not nearly enough, but the situation was not much worse in this respect than it had been before the Germans came. The thought that it was undoubtedly harder on the other side of the front seemed to console people.

It was quiet in the city. Robberies had stopped completely. There had been no partisans anywhere near since the beginning of the occupation. There still were none. The town was almost entirely isolated from the outside world. The daily paper, run by a professor of our Industrial Institute, discussed only local happenings. All outside news came through the kommandatura. Later, however, the Commandant presented the editors with a good radio set of Soviet make as a sign of his special approval and permitted them to listen to Soviet radio stations.

I acquired a personal enemy in the kommandatura in Lieutenant Lüttich. It happened in the following way.

One of the restaurant owners came to me and said: 'Please help me. My restaurant has the lowest prices in town. They are so low that even city government employees – who get the lowest salaries going – can eat there. I buy my food in the villages outside of town. Every time I make a buying trip I have to pay 2,000 or 3,000 rubles to Lüttich for a kommandatura pass. Yesterday he demanded 50,000. I just can't pay anything like that.'

'Try and bargain with him.'

'I tried but it's no use.'

'Well, then, close up the restaurant.'

'That's impossible. I've put all my own money into it and a lot I collected among my friends. Lüttich is ruining me.'

I promised that I would try to do something about it. Since this was far from being the first complaint of this sort, I assembled all the material and presented it to the Commandant the next time I saw him.

'Of course we could make trouble for Lüttich,' said the Commandant, 'but would all these people be willing to present their complaints in written form? And bear in mind that I can't promise that Lüttich would be transferred from here or lose his influence in city affairs.'

I thought about it. Of course no one would be willing to submit a written complaint.

'You'd better pay no attention to this,' continued the Commandant. 'After all Lüttich is a German. Lüttich is the victor; you are the vanquished. I think that everything is in order.'

The discussion ended on this note. However, the Commandant warned Lüttich about his conduct. The warning had little result except to make Lüttich furious at me. Later on this attitude of his had it consequences.

I developed another enemy in the person of Oberkriegsverwaltungsrat Albrecht. This was my fault. I was celebrating my birthday with a group of city government people. There was a knock at the door and the Commandant, the Oberkriegsverwaltungsrat, and Lüttich walked in, all somewhat drunk.

'You should have invited us,' said the Commandant. 'We may be Germans but we like to have a good time, too.'

There was nothing to do but find a place for them at the table. All of them drank more than they ate, with the exception of Lüttich.

At the end of the evening they could hardly stand up. We began to dance and sing. The Commandant sat at the table downing glass after glass of sour claret and saying, 'Why is there a war? Who needs a war? In Dresden I was an artist, I have a wife and children.' He took out some photographs. 'I like it in Russia. There are nice people in Russia. Better than in Germany now. When the war is over I'm going to live in Russia. I don't need Lebensraum. I'm an artist. I'm going to live in the Caucasus and paint pictures.' Drunken tears rolled down his fat cheeks.

Albrecht, on the other hand, was having a great time. He hugged every girl in sight and waltzed with them. Then suddenly he felt tired, sat down in a chair, and went to sleep. Everyone thought this was annoying. People were having a good time, but in the middle of the room there snored a fat German. Someone suggested putting him in the closet. I agreed immediately. We carefully picked up the Ober-kriegsverwaltungsrat and carried him into the closet, where we set him down on some pillows and closed the door. The fun went on.

At last, when the guests began to leave, we had the problem of getting the Germans home. They had no car. Of the three only Lüttich was on his feet. He agreed to undertake the task of assisting the others home, since he considered it unseemly for civilians to escort drunken Germans. Albrecht was carried out of the closet. He had stayed asleep and was feeling considerably better. We put his overcoat on him, fastened his pistol belt around him, thrust his cap on his head, and led him outside.

The Commandant did not want to put on his coat.

'I like it here. I don't want to go to Germany,' he muttered.

Lüttich tried to persuade him to go. We promised to get together for another party later. Finally we managed to put his coat on and get him outside. The Commandant saw the moon and the moonlit snow-covered street and refused to leave.

'I don't want to go,' he kept mumbling. 'I like it here.'

He was pushed out with difficulty, and Lüttich led his two colleagues off toward the kommandatura.

The next day he told Albrecht that he had been put in the closet when he was asleep. Albrecht was incensed and said to me the next time we met, 'This is an outrage. You had no right to do that. I am a German, I'm an officer, I'm your commander, and you put me in a closet in front of everybody. It shows a lack of respect. You are trying to destroy the authority of the German Army.'

I tried to justify myself to him, but Albrecht remained hostile to me.

Some time later I was almost shot.

During one of our conferences the district burgomasters complained that more and more people kept appearing with notes from Rauberg on S.S. stationery demanding that they be given jobs in the city government. Some happened to be young girls.

I said indiscreetly that the girls might have earned Rauberg's protection by performing some service for him.

The next day I was summoned to the S.S. Rauberg received me with a deep frown, pointed to a chair, and was silent for half a minute. Then he narrowed his eyes and began to speak.

'How do you feel? Are you bored with life?'

'I don't understand.'

He leapt to his feet and shouted, 'You don't understand, God damn you! I'll explain so you'll understand. Admit that you said things about me!'

'Who, me? I've said absolutely nothing . . .'

'Silence!' he thundered. 'I know everything that goes on in your office and the intrigues that you are spreading against the victorious German armies. I'll throw you all out, you Russian pigs! Do you think we stand on ceremony here? Admit what you said!'

'I don't understand, honestly I don't,' I said, feeling that things were going badly for me. Rauberg banged the desk with his fist, sat sat down, and hissed. 'Tell me what you said yesterday: that I fix my mistresses up with soft jobs in the city government.'

'I didn't say that. I said that the girls that you send to us have probably done some service for you.'

'O-o-oh, you bastard!' he yelled, biting his lower lip. His jerking hand unbuttoned the holster at his side and he pulled out his pistol. 'Don't lie to me! My information is from people that I trust absolutely! Admit it, you son of a bitch, or I'll kill you on the spot! Do you think that just because you are the assistant burgomaster nothing can happen to you? Don't you know that I shot the burgomaster of Taganrog with my own hand? Field Marshal Kleist himself came down to plead for him but I shot him anyway. Don't you all understand yet who we Germans are and what you are – Russian filth? How dare you talk about us? If I wish it all your girls will sleep with our soldiers and I'll send them all to work in your city government to replace the chatterers you have there now!'

It was obvious that Rauberg was beside himself and was perfectly capable of putting a bullet into my head at any moment. I had no illusions about my 'legal' position and I knew that he could kill me with no fear of punishment. Rauberg was shouting, '. . . do you think that it's the beginning of the end just because the German Army has had some bad luck at Stalingrad? You're wrong! Stalingrad will be taken and all its defenders will be hanged on the trees that are still standing! And I'll rub all of you here into dust!'

The telephone had been ringing for several minutes. Finally Rauberg noticed it and picked up the receiver.

'Who's speaking? . . . What? . . . Let them wait . . . I said let them wait! How many times do I have to tell you, damn you! . . . Yes . . . Oh, excuse me Herr Sturmbahnführer . . . All right . . . immediately.'

'Get out of here and remember what I told you,' he said, turning to me. 'One more little remark and I'll hang you on the market square.'

I stood up.

'I presume you will have no more cause for complaint because I am leaving the city government as from today. Appoint anyone you want in my place.'

'You'll stay in your job as long as you're ordered to! Get out.'

I left his office. Several S.S. men were standing in the corridor near the door. They had evidently been listening. One noncommissioned officer whispered to me as I was leaving the building, 'We called up on purpose. Rauberg goes off his head sometimes. We thought he was going to shoot you right there in his office.'

My mood was not a happy one. I cursed the Germans and the day I had gone to work for the city government. It would have been better to start a restaurant or just get a job as a waiter. And then I remembered: Stalingrad. What had happened in Stalingrad? There was nothing about it in our newspaper. I went to the newspaper office but they knew nothing there. The S.S. had confiscated their radio set a few days before.

I went to see an officer who had treated me well in the past, and told him what had happened in Rauberg's office.

'You were very careless,' he said. 'You don't understand the A B C's of our organization. Don't you realize that the S.S. can do absolutely anything? The commanding general of an army or a front can't give orders to Rauberg. Everybody hates the S.S. and everybody's afraid of them. They do what they like. Do you know who Rauberg is?'

'No.'

'He's a Volksdeutscher from Odessa. He had relatives in Germany in the Ministry of the Interior. He's made a career already, although he was a Communist for ten years before the war.'

'And do you consider this a normal state of affairs?'

'Normal?' he repeated with a shrug. 'No. But nothing can be done about it. The High Command of this front has written to Berlin about him and several others like him. The only answer they got was that it was none of their business.'

'Incidentally, what was it that Rauberg was saying about Stalingrad? What's happened there?'

'Things aren't good there. One army has been captured and a retreat has begun on that section of the front.'

'What's the situation on this part of the front?'

'So far we're standing firm, but it's possible we may have to pull back to the west somewhat here, too, in order to shorten the lines of communication.'

Back at the office I told Likhachev about everything. Then I handed him a written resignation and asked him to tell the Commandant.

'I'm going to quit, too,' Likhachev said unexpectedly. 'I've wanted to for a long time. Let's go to the Commandant.'

The Commandant did not give us an answer that day. Later he agreed in principle to our resignations but we were ordered to stay in our jobs until replacements could be found for us.

One day I happened to run into the girl whose father was a Jew and had been forced to flee at the beginning of the occupation. From her husband who was working in our office I knew that she had suffered some unpleasantnesses. We had dinner at my house and afterward I asked how things were going with her. She began to cry.

'Do you know what happened to me?' she sobbed.

'I've heard something about it. But I think that everything is settled now and you won't be bothered any more.' She raised her head and looked at me angrily.

'Settled? Do you know what it cost to settle it? Do you know that my husband has moved to another apartment?'

'No, I hadn't heard that; but please don't tell me if you don't want to. Don't get wrought up.'

'No, I want to tell you. A little while after the liquidation of the Jews I was ordered to report to the S.S. Someone had told them that I was half Jewish. First I was interrogated there. They made all sorts of measurements of my profile and decided that I was Jewish. They kept me for a day in one of the cells. Then they called me up for more questioning. There were two of them, both S.S. officers. They asked me more questions, took more measurements. Then – they ordered me to strip completely – do you understand? There were two of them . . .

'After that they gave me a certificate that I wasn't Jewish, but I had to go on meeting them. Once they didn't let me go home for three days. I couldn't conceal it any longer. My family has simply fallen apart. I can't take my child in my arms any more.

'Later I was given to some others. There were a lot of them, almost all S.S. men. One of them infected me, I don't know which one. I infected others. Syphilis, but so far, in concealed form. I think they are beginning to guess now. Do you know what can happen to me?'

'Yes.'

'Yes, there was an order: for infecting the heroic soldiers and officers of the Führer's army, death by firing squad. Right?'

'That's right.'

'I don't care now. My life is ruined; it's all over. I want to get revenge, but how? What can I do to those loathsome beasts? Infect them with venereal disease?'

'You've got to hide out for a while. The front is moving back. It's possible that this city will be retaken. Then you can find revenge any way you know how.'

We were silent, thinking of the same thing. Then she said, 'No, I can't stay here. Too many people know that I have lived with S.S. men. When the Reds come they'll shoot me anyway. There's no way out. I want to end it myself. And it's time; I'm too tired of life to want to go on. Look at me!'

It was true, it was hard to recognize her. She was only twenty-six but she looked thirty-five or more. Once she had been the best student in our school.

'Good-bye, Vladimir. If you get the chance, tell my husband that I'm not as much to blame as he thinks. Oh, I wanted to live so much! To go to Europe, to look at the world! And what happened? From the very beginning I had no choice. Either they would kill me or I would kill myself. I took a third path, a slippery one, but I can end it any time. I've got some poison with me. They'll never shoot me. But meanwhile—' her laugh was entirely without mirth, 'meanwhile I'll go out with my little officers and leave them a souvenir from me. Good-bye.'

I embraced her but she pushed me away.

'Don't kiss me. It's in a dangerous stage.'

I sat alone in the darkening room for a long time after she had left.

It was January and the news from the front became more alarming for the Germans every day. Their retreat was proceeding without panic but steadily. Restaurants and shops closed one after the other. People were streaming to the Ukraine with German passes.

My work at the city government ended, but not in the way I had expected. A restaurant keeper came to see me one day accompanied by his friend Kondakov, the secretary of the First District.

'We have come to contribute a small sum. Business is good.'

'How much and for whom?'

'Ten thousand rubles, in your discretion. You know whom to give it to.'

'All right, leave the money.'

They left the office. I took the money and went to Likhachev's office to tell him what had happened. He was just transferring his affairs to the new burgomaster.

'Submit a written report and put the money in the safe,' said the new burgomaster. 'I'll report it to the Commandant.' I followed his instructions.

Two days later I learned that the restaurant owner had filed a complaint to Lüttich about me saying that I extorted a 10,000 ruble bribe from him and had ruined him completely. Kondakov signed as a witness. Lüttich told the new Commandant (the old one had returned to Germany). The Commandant called the new burgomaster and ordered him to discharge me for bribery. The burgomaster, a friend of Lüttich, for diplomatic reasons did not consider it necessary to mention that the money was in his safe. Lüttich had told him that both the kommandatura and the S.S. were interested in getting rid of me with some sort of scandal. The only witness to my innocence, Likhachev, had already gone to the Ukraine and it was impossible for me to prove anything.

However, I did not try very hard. Under the circumstances it did not make much difference.

My discharge from the city government had only one harmful social effect, and this was impossible to correct. I had one function which I kept secret from absolutely everybody and which I could not hand over to my successor without calling down the most unfortunate consequences on my own head.

Shortly after the city was occupied by the Germans a camp for captured Red Army men was set up on the outskirts. There were several thousand prisoners there and the conditions in which they were kept were frightful. They lived in a barbed-wire stockade without shelter of any kind and they were literally tortured with hunger. The death rate was extremely high. I believe that three months after the camp was established several dozen men died every day. Throughout the summer and fall more prisoners continued to be brought to the camp from the front.

The stockade was always under heavy guard. The local people made many attempts to slip food through the wire to the prisoners but they were always chased away by the German soldiers on guard. Some on both sides of the wire were shot down for such attempts.

A few of the townspeople found relatives in the camp and kept coming to the city government office to ask us to intercede for these prisoners with the Germans and request their release. Likhachev made many trips to various German offices, pleading in every possible way, but it was useless. He always received a flat refusal.

One day one of my old schoolteachers came to me and told me that her son, one of my childhood friends, was a prisoner in the camp. She had come to ask my help in getting him released. After some thought I wrote a memorandum as follows: 'To the Prisoner-of-War

Camp Commandant. Request immediate release of prisoner-of-war Red Army lieutenant Alexei Alexeev.'

I typed out the memorandum on the burgomaster's stationery, stamped it with the official seal of the office, and signed as illegibly as possible. Then I explained to my friend's mother that there was very little hope of success, gave her the memorandum, and told her how to find the camp commandant.

To my astonishment she appeared the next day, radiant and excited, and told me that her son had been released on my note. I asked her to keep quiet about it and hide him somewhere as well as she could.

But apparently she could not keep the secret, because soon I began to receive similar requests. I knew that I risked being sent to the camp myself and I was very careful to whom I gave such letters, which had absolutely no legal basis. Several dozen people left the camp in this manner. The only explanation I could think of was that the camp commandant was somewhat feeble minded and was so impressed by documents and seals in the German language that it never occurred to him that they could be written by someone who had no right to do so. Even the smallest hint to the S.S. from some informer in our office would have been enough to get me into deep trouble.

On leaving the city government I regretted that I had not made wider use of my powers in this respect. I did not dare to tell anyone on the new burgomaster's staff about my method. It would have been reported to the Commandant immediately.

As my activities as a 'civil servant' ended, I decided that I would not get myself another job. I stopped going to the government offices. Only occasionally, in the evening, a few of my friends would gather at my place to discuss what was happening. Once in a while I would visit two German officers I knew in order to learn what was going on.

There was plenty to talk about. After the German defeat at Stalingrad the Caucasian front became unsteady and moved farther west. The retreat was slow but continuous. Refugees passed through our city in long lines. They were in a hurry to get away as far as possible. All night I could hear the creaking of wagon wheels and the shouts of the drivers under my window. People rode on horseback, on bulls, on cows, or just walked, having loaded their travelling bag on someone's cart.

All the German road blocks had been removed long before, and townspeople who had been out to the villages spread the word that practically no one was staying behind there. In some villages almost all the houses were deserted.

One day a peasant came in to see me. He had formerly delivered potatoes to city government employees, and now he had come to ask permission to spend the night in his wagon in the yard of the house I was staying in.

In the evening, over a glass of tea, he said, 'The whole population is on the move. Nobody wants to stay behind. A man who came through the front lines went through our village with his wife and child. He told us that as soon as the Soviets take over anywhere they grab all the men from fifteen to sixty-five for the army and confiscate all the livestock and food. And if a burgomaster or a policeman or anyone who worked during the German occupation happens to fall into their hands, they hang him on a tree or a lamp-post, right in the street.'

'Where do you intend to go now?' I asked.

'It doesn't matter where. Right now I'm headed for the Ukraine; they say the Germans will hold on there. It's best not to think too far ahead.'

'Do you think the Germans are going to win the war?'

'Who can tell? There was a German noncom down our way who said they would make a deal with the Americans soon and both would fight the Soviets together. Maybe they'll win.'

'Have you got anyone on the other side?'

'Yes, I have two sons in the army. Well, with God's help they'll come out all right and I'll see them after the war.'

'Maybe you'd better stay. You must be fifty years old, at least.'

'Fifty-eight. That doesn't matter. The Soviets take people like me. They have special punishment battalions for us. They send them out ahead over the minefields that the Germans leave behind, and the army follows. The ones that get through without blowing up are sent out again and again. They don't arm them; they give them orders to take guns from the Germans.'

Among the German officers the mood was also pessimistic. One was quite definite about it.

'It was clear to those of us who had the capacity to think,' he said, 'that this war was lost in 1941 when we failed to take Moscow. And then the Führer made a fatal mistake when he appointed Rosenberg, a well-known Russian hater, to run the occupied territories. Around here you haven't met our civilian occupation authorities. When you get to the Ukraine you'll see for yourself.

'The wisest thing for us would be to end the war now; but we've cut off the path to an armistice ourselves. The French, the Poles, and the Serbs will never make peace with us, although things are still quiet inside those countries. Peace with America is impossible because of the Führer's point of view on the Jewish question – that's probably their most serious quarrel with us. You know, in the army a lot of us don't approve of the Jewish policy. That leaves England and Russia. But in England there are a bunch of Germanophobes in power, although they should be more interested than anyone else in keeping a strong Reich. And as for the U.S.S.R., it would be easiest of all to make peace with it, but we know that Stalin can't be trusted. He'll make peace and then attack us in the rear as soon as he can.'

'What do you think is going to happen to our city?' I asked. The officer shrugged his shoulders.

'It will probably be given up soon. I've heard that the front is going to be stabilized quite a way to the west of here, on the lower Kuban. There's no serious defence being planned for this area, although the Soviet Army on our part of the front is not very powerful. The retreat here is being planned for reasons of general strategy. I advise you to leave as soon as possible.'

'But where? You say you've lost the war . . .'

'Where? To the west, to the Ukraine, and later, to Germany. There you can get lost in a mass of people in the same plight as yourself. After the war is over, you can figure out for yourself what to do.'

'I think you are being too pessimistic.'

'Perhaps I am, but I'm not the only one who thinks this way, although it's better not to say so openly. I hope you understand that what has been said is between us.'

I was deep in thought as I left him. It was time to make some decision: the front was only fifty miles to the east. Of course there was just one thing to do and that was to go west. But my mother stubbornly refused to go with me and I could not find the strength to leave her.

'You must understand, Vladimir,' she kept saying, 'I'm more than fifty years old and very sick. I've lived here all my life. Everything I know is here. All my relatives are here. Where should I go?'

'But Mother,' I tried to convince her, 'the Bolsheviks won't forgive you for the fact that I worked for the Germans. They'll persecute you, they'll send you to Siberia.'

'That doesn't matter. It will happen if it's my fate. If I have to die I won't regret it. To live as I've lived all this time, the last twenty years, just isn't worth it, Vladimir. I have only one little hope left, that maybe your brother George is still alive somewhere, that the news of his death was a mistake. Maybe he'll come back when the war is over. But you go ahead. You have no choice. You haven't had a choice for a long time, my dear son.'

Tears were running down her cheeks.

She was right. There was no choice for me. It would be, to say the least, stupid to let myself fall into the hands of the returning 'liberators'. I began to plan my departure.

It was time I left. The city government had gone already, almost to the last man. The government building had burned down one night under suspicious circumstances. The story was repeated everywhere that it had been done to cover up all traces of the burgomasters' division of the treasury among themselves. I don't know how much truth there was in this.

The restaurants, the stores, and the workshops were closing one after the other. The city was becoming more and more deserted every hour. Sometimes at night the sound of artillery fire could be heard in the distance.

Though my mother remained for the time being in our old apartment, I found a deserted house in a near-by village and transferred her belongings to it. Of course this transfer of residence did not make things entirely safe, but it was generally considered to be especially important to be in hiding during the first days.

13. FLIGHT

THE railroad had already been cut by advance units of the Red Army somewhere to the north of the city, and only one escape route remained open: directly west along the Kuban River. One could go on military vehicles, by horse, or on foot.

A small group of us assembled for the journey. There was the Gorsky family, from whom I had rented my room for the last few months, and two tradesmen who had owned several small shops and had liquidated their affairs. The tradesmen had supplied transportation: six horses and three carts. I had supplied 'legal protection' in the shape of various German documents from the kommandatura, and I was considered to be generally in charge of the expedition.

We had already loaded two of the carts in our yard when our tradesmen arrived and announced that they had changed their minds. They had decided to go into hiding near the city.

We had to get under way without them, although neither Igor Gorsky nor his wife nor his mother-in-law nor I had ever had anything to do with horses—and the tradesmen had generously presented us with four horses and two carts.

I spent the last evening with my mother, to whom I gave most of the money that I had left and all the things I didn't need for the long journey.

It was late when we said goodbye.

I walked the whole length of the city through the badly lit streets. Everywhere it was quiet except for the central streets, where the wagons of the refugees crawled on in unending files, sometimes held up by military police who were letting truck convoys through. Occasional flashes appeared on the eastern horizon but almost no sounds of explosions could be heard.

At the Gorskys' house everything was in a mess. Almost all our things had already been loaded on the carts and we had to sleep wherever we could find a place. In the yard the horses were peacefully chewing their oats with a crunching sound, snorting slightly, and shuffling their legs. Igor, a flashlight in his hand, was stuffing a few small bundles under the cover of a cart.

It was not yet dawn when we harnessed the horses and drove out of the yard, dressed as warmly as possible. Igor's little five-year-old daughter Nina sat next to me. Igor with his wife and mother-in-law rode in the other cart.

The streets were almost empty. Not quite certain which street ran into the road we wanted, we set out for the western limits of the city.

The carts rumbled over the cobblestones. There was no point in hurrying the horses; if they should quicken their pace the carts would shake terribly. I felt unsure of myself in the role of coachman, but I tried not to make it evident that the horses, strictly speaking, were going as they liked and that it cost me tremendous efforts to make them turn corners when necessary.

It was already light when we reached the outskirts, but the streets were as deserted as before. In the last block I noticed an enormous puddle ahead, covered with a thin coating of ice. Doubt gripped me. I tried to stop the horses but without success. At a measured pace they entered the puddle and I was horrified to see the water come up to their knees. The cart followed the horses. There was a short splash – and we stopped. The wheels were entirely under water.

Having made a couple of unsuccessful attempts to pull the cart out of the water, the horses settled down calmly and answered all my shouts and whip with irritated movements of their tails.

Igor came up and after a short discussion we decided to unhitch the horses and try to get out of the puddle in reverse. After getting soaked, I managed to lead the horses out on to dry land, but when I had hooked the traces to the rear axle and tried to make them pull in the other direction, they would not strain a muscle.

We tried hitching the second team to the cart but the results were the same. Passers-by shouted advice to us, but it was about as useful as a bank is to a dead man.

We unloaded the cart, which had been sinking deeper and deeper into the thick mud. Even the horses were incapable of pulling it out.

Meanwhile the sun had passed its zenith. We made a meal from the supplies we had brought along, and tried to decide what to do. It was becoming obvious to us that inasmuch as we had not even managed to leave the city, a journey of hundreds of miles through strange country with horses would be something of a problem. However, be that as it might, we had to get out of the puddle, and I set out to find help in the city.

I was lucky. In about half an hour I came across a German truck taking on a load at a military warehouse. I explained my predicament as well as I could and asked for assistance. Finally, after a prolonged parley, the Germans agreed. They drove over to the scene of our tragedy and with no trouble at all pulled the wagon on to dry land with a rope.

Evening was approaching and we decided not to go any farther that day. In addition, under the influence of our painful experience, our desire to continue the trip with horses had evaporated.

'I'd rather stay with the Bolsheviks; let them send me to Siberia, let them hang me, but I'm not going anywhere in these wagons,' said Igor's wife, Zina. Igor muttered something darkly. I kept quiet.

We hitched up the horses and went home, stopping in at my mother's on the way to tell her about our unfortunate start.

In the morning there was a renewed discussion of the problem. Zina wanted to stay. Her mother thought that we had better go. Igor was neutral. His brother, who had decided earlier to stay, advanced arguments in favour of remaining.

I left the others to decide what they were going to do, having told them that I was departing under any and all circumstances, and went downtown.

Just after turning into the main street I came upon the body of a man who had been hanged. It swung back and forth slightly in the wind, the feet about a foot off the ground. The passers-by looked furtively and hurried on. I stopped.

It was the body of a man twenty-five years old. He was badly dressed. There was a wooden shield on his breast with an inscription in Russian: 'I looted.'

A few blocks farther, on the boulevard, there were two more. Their signs said: 'I incited people to destroy Germans.' At the marketplace there were three more bodies, but these had apparently been shot first and then hanged. They were labelled looters. One of them was a woman.

I went to one of the district police stations, the head of which I knew very well. It was empty. All the police had left two days before.

I went to military police headquarters. Luckily I ran into a lieutenant whom I knew there. He was surprised to see me and somewhat suspicious.

'Are you still here? Why haven't you gone? The whole city government left a long time ago. You're not planning to stay by any chance, are you?'

'No, I'm not planning to stay. I've had too much to do with you and your countrymen to risk my neck. But my friends and I have no means of leaving.' And I told him about our unsuccessful attempt to navigate the puddle.

'I think I may be able to help you,' he said. 'One of our units is leaving tonight and they'll be able to take you in one of their vehicles. How many of you are there?'

'Five.'

'All right. I'll write you out a note to that effect.'

'Thank you very much.'

'Leave everything. Get away tonight with the column I told you about. Here's the note. The front line units will be in town tomorrow; the field headquarters is already here. And a couple of days after that it will be too late. Goodbye.'

I managed to locate the unit which was leaving that night for the Kuban, and with the help of the lieutenant's note persuaded them to take us along. Then I hurried home, where Igor and Zina, having overcome their misgivings, were sorting out their belongings again, leaving out all inessentials. I explained where they had to go to be taken into the convoy, and then rushed over to my mother's. On the way I noticed columns of smoke in several places. The Germans were burning something.

My mother was already settled in her new home, with her sister and a friend. They occupied two rooms in a deserted house, in an area where no one knew them. My mother was overjoyed to hear that I had found a way to leave. I tried again, for the last time, to persuade her to come with me. She shook her head:

'Let's not talk about it, Vladimir. It's decided. I'm staying no matter what awaits me in the future. Goodbye, my darling. My heart tells me that you and I will never see each other again. I won't live long, and you can never return. I don't believe in any changes after the war. Don't you believe in them either. If the way is ever open to you to come back, seek out my grave and say a prayer over it. . . .'

That night we left the city, which was partly illuminated by the light of fires and occasional flashes from the artillery battery firing on the high bank of the river.

There were about twenty trucks in the convoy. A corporal was in charge. There were very few soldiers. It was cold and damp, and we tried in vain to get warm, huddled together in the corner of the canvas-topped truck.

When we arrived at the convoy's destination, a small Cossack village on the left bank of the Kuban, we had to climb out of our truck and try to find another. We spent all day by the side of the road, seated on a pile of suitcases and bundles, trying to flag down passing trucks, but we had no luck. Then we set out to look for shelter for the night in one of the small houses along the road. This was not an easy task. Soldiers were billeted everywhere, and there were many other refugees like ourselves. Finally a Cossack who was about to leave the next day himself permitted us to spend the night on the floor of his kitchen. We were busy until late at night carrying our baggage in. Zina stood guard, Igor and I carried the bags, while little Nina and her grandmother stayed in the house. After this we decided to leave some more things behind, and pack the others more compactly so the process of moving would not be so difficult in the future.

In the morning we resumed our vigil by the side of the road. After a few hours' wait we managed to stop a German truck. The driver, for a bottle of wine, agreed to take us a few dozen miles farther.

We spent that night in someone's hayloft where we almost froze, and in the morning went back to the road.

After three days of this type of travelling we reached a Cossack

village by the name of Varenikovskaya, where we were ordered off
our truck by military police who announced that we could go no
farther on military vehicles; they were to cross the Straits of Kerch
at a different point from the civilian refugees. We had another 50
miles to get to the straits and no idea what to do.

Varenikovskaya was overflowing with refugees and we had to spend
the night by the road in a repulsive mixture of rain and snow. Only
Nina and her grandmother were allowed to stay under the roof of a
near-by stable.

Igor and I found a German headquarters where, it was rumoured,
passes were issued to cross the straits on the ferry. As the corporal
was filling the pass up for us a German general walked into the room.
I asked him for help in getting to the crossing and requested that we be
given some food, since our supplies were running out and it was impossible to buy anything.

The general heard me out silently. Then he told the corporal to
write out two memoranda, one to the Verpflegungstelle telling them to
issue us ten food rations, and another to instruct a lieutenant, who was
taking some wagonloads of Russian volunteers for the German Army
to the crossing, to take us with him.

We returned to our 'camp' in triumph. We were equipped with a
great morale builder: ten soldier's rations, each consisting of two pounds
of bread, two cans of meat, a few cigarettes, and small quantities of
butter and jam.

It was not hard to locate the lieutenant who was supposed to take
us with him. He turned out to be a quiet young man, the son of an
Austrian bishop. He immediately turned one of his six wagons over to
us. Our countrymen, the volunteers, obeyed his orders with a certain
amount of grumbling, and the team of horses that they hitched up to
our wagon was definitely the worst in the column. When we finally
began to move Igor and I did not dare sit in the wagon because it was
evident that our team could never hope to pull such a load. On the
upgrades we had to help the horses by pushing.

We travelled on back roads which our guide, one of the volunteers,
apparently considered to be the shortest route. There was a certain
advantage in this, however, because we spent the nights comfortably
in tiny settlements, being the only transients there. We were able to
get milk for the little girl, sometimes even bread.

Our wagon was on the tail end of the train. Little Nina rode up in
front with Lieutenant Georg. Whenever we got too far behind he
would stop the column and wait for us.

The idyll ended when we reached the straits, after several days on the
road.

At the crossing there was real chaos. Tens of thousands of carts and
wagons were crowded in a dense pack along the shore. And as for

people, there must have been at least a hundred thousand. Two ferries were running back and forth to the Crimean shore, and the people without horses were given priority. Hundreds of unhitched horses wandered through the human mass looking for hay or straw.

We decided to go on without horses, especially as ours were too weak to be of any value. We unhitched them, spreading out all the remaining feed in the wagon so that they could reach it, and took our place in the enormous line waiting for the ferry.

Every type of person was in the crowd. Old men, young men, women, children, members of the intelligentsia, peasants, Cossacks, and even workers. Some were very hungry; others had large supplies of food with them. Some had piles of baggage, others small bundles or nothing at all. A steady roar of thousands of voices arose from the mob. People were shouting, moving about, sitting or lying on bundles of straw.

The cold March night came on. A few people tried to light fires, but others protested; they were afraid of bombing by Soviet planes. We were told that a week before our arrival a few bombs had been dropped on this spot, and afterwards the crowd had been strafed with machine-gun fire at low altitude. More than two thousand had been killed. This happened by daylight, and the pilots could not help but see that there wasn't a single German soldier at the ferry landing.

At the end of the next day our turn to board the ferry finally came. Flocks of seagulls circled over the water and followed the ferry. When a wide strip of water had appeared between us and the Caucasian shore, I suddenly felt that still another period of my life had moved into the past. . . .

On the other shore everyone coming off the ferry was immediately loaded into trucks and taken to the railroad station. This operation was being run by Germans dressed in uniforms of an unpleasant yellow colour that I had not seen before. I was told it was that of the German civilian administration, the organization directed by Rosenberg and by Reichskommissar-for-the-Ukraine Koch. In the Caucasus, in the regions near the front, we had had only military administration.

On the road to the station we passed through the city of Kerch, or to be more accurate, through what used to be the city of Kerch. There was nothing left of it but piles of ruins, the result of heavy fighting a year before.

At the station we received a little bread and soup and were directed into a broken-down freight car which was dirty, cold, and not exactly cosy. The Germans were rough and rude with the refugees, not much better than the N.K.V.D. with prisoners.

When the cars were packed full the train started up. We huddled together for warmth, but it did not help much. We were seated on the few bags we had left; two had been lost during the crossing.

The train moved slowly, stopping often. The ruined stations were crowded with Germans, local residents, and refugees. There was snow everywhere, and people stamped their feet and rubbed their hands and ears to keep warm.

Our car did not get any warmer and little Nina was so cold that she began to cry. We had already left the Crimea and had stopped at Melitopol when we decided to leave the refugee train.

Long experience had taught us that the worst route to travel over was the one taken by everyone. Since we knew a little German and were equipped with various German documents, we had a chance to make our way independently.

The Melitopol station, which we finally persuaded two German sentries to let us enter, was full of soldiers. There was very little light, and so much smoke that the few electric bulbs were scarcely visible. By one wall stood a line of soldiers and officers who were being doled out coffee and soup by girls with little red crosses on their caps.

Igor and I got into line too, and we received five portions of coffee and soup in our kettles, which made us all feel stronger. I noticed that many soldiers were going into another room and coming out with bundles of rations like the ones we had received at Varenikovskaya by order of the general.

My mouth watered at the sight of all the sausage, Swiss cheese, boxes of Norwegian sardines and other wonders. I gathered up my courage, took out the general's note and the pass we had received when we left, and presented them to the sleepy corporal sitting at the ration table. He did not even read them. Having seen the stamp which showed that we had already received rations four days before, he placed his own stamp on the note and gave me a ticket good for five four-day rations. With this ticket I received so many wonderful things that I could hardly carry them all at once.

My friends greeted me enthusiastically and we immediately began to eat.

From this day on I drew regular rations at every Verpflegungstelle upon presentation of my precedent-hallowed document. None of the clerks bothered to read the well-stamped paper. They merely sought out the last date and issued me rations for the next period.

My conscience did not trouble me a bit. I don't know how else we would have existed all this time. We had very little money, and the food which the Germans issued to refugees at so-called 'evacuation points' was insufficient and very bad. We travelled in freight trains as before but got out at stations very often to rest and get warm.

In Zaporozhe we found ourselves on a flatcar in a train bound for Dnepropetrovsk. The planks were strewn with hay and the hay was covered with snow; we burrowed into it as deep as possible to get away from the biting cold wind.

The train made many long stops and finally halted completely. I climbed out of the hay and saw that we were in an open field. Jumping off the car I ran to the engine to find out what was the matter. The German engineer told me that a few miles ahead a Soviet tank column had broken through and captured the next station, Sinelnikovo. In addition to the refugees there were two German soldiers and a fireman aboard the train. They conferred with the engineer and decided to go back to Zaporozhe.

Just as the train began to move backward I noticed a flash of fire very close, behind a group of buildings. Then there was the report of a gun, a second, and a third one. From somewhere in the direction of Sinelnikovo came answering reports. A shell whirred overhead and burst not far from the train, which began to increase speed.

We got back to Zaporozhe in the morning, utterly frozen. While the others slept in the station Zina and I found out that it was possible to get to Kiev only by travelling on the other side of the Dnieper, passing over the famous Dneprostroy Dam. We received a paper from the local kommandatura with instructions to the military police to take us to the next station. After a long wait of several hours at a cross road to which we dragged all our things, we climbed into a truck that the military police stopped for us.

The Dneprostroy Dam had been so well blown up by the retreating Soviets in 1941 that the Germans had only been able to set two turbines going again. As we crossed it we breathed a sigh of relief. Once again we had escaped our countrymen advancing into the Ukraine.

On the other side of the Dnieper we had to take one more train to get to Kiev. Since leaving our native city we had changed our means of transportation twenty-five times.

14. A FREE ENTERPRISE

IN Kiev we moved into an 'evacuation point', a large school building which had been hurriedly converted into a dormitory. We were assigned to a former classroom that contained only twenty people. The building had a dining hall where once a day we were given some murky water which was called soup. Without the German soldiers' rations which I kept on drawing at the Kiev station, we would have had a hard time of it.

We ate part of the rations and sold the rest in the market. We had little money and the future was very unclear. Having learned that the wages paid around town were extremely small and didn't cover a quarter of one's living costs, we began to give serious thought to the problem of earning a living. I had a few skills for which there was no use; Igor was a mechanical engineer, but he could not find a suitable job either.

Finally an old friend of Igor's advised us to become smugglers. It must be pointed out that before I left home I had obtained a document from the kommandatura listing my destination as Lvov, which had become part of the Ukraine at the time of the Soviet-German agreement of 1939. After the Germans occupied the Ukraine Lvov became part of the 'governor-generalship', as Poland was known. Between the Ukraine and the governor-generalship there was a border, guarded by the Germans, but some goods got through to Kiev from the west, and it was said that the people who brought them made a lot of money.

We decided to deal in cheap jewellers' goods, which a friend of Igor's sold at the market. Jewellery was generally unavailable under the Soviets and was in great demand. We sold a few of our belongings, gathered all our money together, and Igor departed for Lvov. The main problem for him was now to get back. The pass was good only in one direction.

I was seeing Kiev for the first time, but it was not necessary to have been there before to realize how devastated this one of Russia's most beautiful cities was. The entire centre had been mined by the retreating Red Army. Explosions and fires had continued for a week after the Germans took over the city. As a result five or six of the central streets lay in ruins their entire length.

This barbarous annihilation was incomprehensible, inasmuch as most of the industrial points, the factories and plants of Kiev, were not damaged.

One quickly came to understand the relationship which existed between the Germans and the local population. Everywhere in the Ukraine the Germans felt that they were masters. The Ukraine was ruled from Rovno by Reichskomissar Koch through innumerable Stadtkomissariats in the cities and Gebietskomissars in the villages. Everywhere the Germans were frankly and systematically despoiling the population. They immediately understood the value of the Soviet collective farm system when it came to collecting taxes from an entire village at once. In the cities there was a rationing system, but the rations were very small. The Germans did not allow a free market and regularly confiscated the food that peasants tried to bring to town.

All the best buildings in Kiev were occupied by Germans. Restaurants, hotels, and theatres were decorated with the sign 'Nur für Deutsche'. Even special latrines 'For Germans only' were built in all the railroad stations of the Ukraine.

We happened to arrive in Kiev during a relatively quiet period, but one could still see remains of signs ordering the shooting of hostages: for one German killed in the street, up to 300 peaceful citizens in the surrounding houses would be shot. All Kievans vividly remembered the destruction of several tens of thousands of Jews in a deep ravine outside the city.

One local resident who had recently made his way back from the countryside told us:

'Outside of the big cities there's no life at all. The Bolsheviks left their agents everywhere behind them – the partisans. Although they knew what reprisals would follow every time a German was killed, they began a reign of terror. The partisans shoot one blameless German soldier; the Germans shoot 100 innocent citizens. Then some relatives of the dead shoot another couple of German soldiers, and so it goes.

'As a result an open hatred exists between the population and the Germans. Yet when the Germans entered the Ukraine, they were usually greeted with flowers and with bread and salt – genuinely greeted.'

A priest from a small town not far from Kiev told us:

'In our area three villages were burnt to the ground and the population annihilated by the Germans. And why? The partisans again. A group of Communists and military N.K.V.D. people who were left behind for partisan activities in 1941 recently began to be active. They burst into one village and hanged the Gebietskomissar and the elder that he had appointed. In two days there was nothing left of the village but smoking ruins. In another village two soldiers and a policeman were killed during a partisan attack. That village was destroyed by Germans, too. A few people survived and they joined the partisans. Now the partisans movement keeps growing. Trains get derailed, German warehouses are robbed, and the local people also; Germans are hanged. And who are the main sufferers from all this activity? The peaceful citizens. The partisans hang just one German, and a whole village is rubbed off the face of the earth, hundreds of old men, women, and children are killed.'

In the Ukraine there was no trace of the comparatively free inter-course between the population and the Germans that I had seen in the northern Caucasus. It was clear that here the Germans were merely occupiers and could claim no missionary-liberator role.

When we began to try to find an apartment, I made frequent visits to the local city government and became very well acquainted with the head of the housing section, a man of real culture and refinement. Under the Soviets he had been a professor in the local university; he had co-operated with the Germans by conviction.

'What is the general policy of the Germans here?' I asked.

'It's very primitive. They simply milk the Ukraine as much as they can. All enterprises are in German hands, mostly run by private individuals who know how to make money. I don't know on what basis Ukrainian factories are given to these rotten German business-men; probably for services rendered to their Führer. The Germans control everything. They've kept all the state and collective farms intact, and it's no exaggeration to say that today the whole of Germany is being fed by the Ukraine. At any rate all our grain, butter, and meat are being shipped west.'

'How does the population exist?'

'What do they care about the population? They live somehow; they're hungry but they stay alive. This region is very rich. Nowhere in the world is there such soil as we have in the Ukraine. The hatred of the people for the Germans is an absolute fact. It's too late now to patch up relations, even if the Germans should suddenly decide to make things better. The gulf between us is too great.'

'Do you know whether it's possible to go to Europe?'

'Right now it's very easy. So many people have been taken into the army in Germany that they have a great man-power shortage. Until recently the Germans asked people from fifteen to forty-five years old to go there voluntarily, but now they're shipping people out by force. Sometimes they simply grab young people off the streets and put them on a train. There haven't been any such incidents in Kiev yet but I'm sure there will be.'

'May I ask you a personal question?' He nodded. 'All the time we have been talking you haven't said a good word about the Germans; you criticize their activities and find no mitigating factors in their behaviour. How is it then that you keep on working in the city govern-ment? I know you'll be blamed by the Communists and those with them, but I'm not referring to them now. I want to know what your own thoughts are about it?'

'That question is a very easy one to answer. The life of this place of 600,000 depends to some degree on the city government. While I remain in my position I can be sure that mistreatment of people will be held to a minimum; I consider myself an honest man. Don't think that the Stadtkomissar is unaware of my attitude toward the Germans. They've been able to organize a good spy service. But I execute all his orders and don't send him any requests that the Germans cannot, or will not, which is the same thing, comply with. If I'm removed some Volksdeutsche will be appointed in my place. He'll try to be more Catholic than the Pope. He won't have any interest in the fate of Kiev and its citizens, and he'll spend his time licking the boots of the German administration. So I stay here, although, believe me, it would be much more pleasant and restful to quit.'

He advised me to find some job in a hurry in order to avoid being caught by the police and shipped to Germany because I was unemployed.

I decided to apply for work to the office of the stadtkomissariat which had to do with small city enterprises.

I was received by a fat, jovial German in a yellow uniform whose name was Schwarz. I told him about my past and spread out all my papers including the German ones for him to see. He called his secretary over.

'We must find some sort of work for this gentleman.'

Meanwhile Igor had returned from Lvov. We had been worried about his long absence, and there had been reason to worry: he had almost been detained by the police with all the goods which he had bought. Only after a great deal of trouble had he managed to get permission to return to the Ukraine.

He brought two suitcases full of cheap jewellery with him: glass beads, brass earrings and necklaces, brooches, etc. His friend the tradesman looked at the goods and offered to buy the whole lot at once, without even bothering to inspect each item separately. He offered us 100,000 karbovanetses.* However, this was not an excessive sum of money. A pound of butter at the market cost 600 karbovanetses at that time, and a three-pound loaf of bread 200. But for us it was a good deal and the profit was almost 100 per cent.

We held a meeting and decided that I should prepare to leave immediately for Lvov before the money had been spent. The prospect did not appeal to me at all. Since childhood I had felt an aversion to commerce and this had been strengthened by my Soviet upbringing. But we had to live, and I set out with the same document that Igor had used. Zina went with me. We could both speak German. We spent the night at the Lvov station and took a train for southern Galicia where, according to information we had, the goods we needed could be obtained at a lower price.

*Ukrainian equivalent of rubles.

Looking out of the window of the car, we marvelled at the cleanliness of the little stations we passed and the neatness of the carefully cultivated fields. The town we went to, Stryj, was very clean and light, a place such as we had never seen in Russia.

We completed part of our business the first evening and decided to spend the night again at the station in order not to make the acquaintance of the police. To stay in the city one had to register at the police station. Leaving Zina guarding the baggage, I made another trip to an address we had been given to arrange for the purchase of a couple of hundred cheap ornaments.

It was dark on the way back to the station. Only an occasional street light broke the gloom. The streets were almost deserted. I walked on, depending on my memory to find the way. Across my path, which I thought was the correct one, there was a small gate. It was open and two men stood by it smoking and talking in low tones. For some reason I did not ask them how to get to the station, although in the light of one of the cigarettes, which had suddenly flared up, they looked like policemen.

They did not stop me. A block or two later I noticed that the doors of most of the houses were open and I could see people inside engaged in ordinary household activities. There were a number of people in the street, too, they were not going anywhere, merely standing around in groups talking, or walking back and forth singly.

Farther on, the street was blocked off with a wooden fence. I turned back, walked a block, ran into another fence, and turned back again. In confusion I said in German to the first man I passed, 'Can you please tell me how to get to the railroad station?'

He looked at me in surprise. 'The station? You can't go to the station even if you have a pass. It's too late.'

'Pass? Why should I need a pass to go to the station?'

'Don't you live here?'

'No, I just arrived in town today.'

'Do you know where you are?'

'No, I don't.'

'You're in the ghetto,' said the man, and something in his voice broke. I felt goosepimples on my back. It was not exactly a feeling of fear. I had nothing to be afraid of; they wouldn't keep me in the ghetto. But knowing the position of Jews under the Germans I was overwhelmed by the tragedy of these people. I had the sensation of being in the society of living dead men. That is what in fact they were.

The man understood what was going on in my mind. In a quiet, somewhat sorrowful voice he said, 'I don't think you have anything to fear. Come with me; I'll take you to the gate. Perhaps they'll let you through in spite of the late hour.'

He led me to the same gate through which I had entered. Two men in uniform stood there as before. They were internal ghetto policemen. My companion explained to them that I had accidentally entered while the gate was still open – before 10 p.m. – and that I had to get to the station to catch a train. He added the last on his own.

The policeman answered that he had no right to open the gate at night, that strict discipline had to be maintained at all times, because the least violation would have consequences for all the inmates, who were linked in mutual responsibility. I might be noticed leaving after the curfew, so he could not risk letting me out.

I was somewhat at a loss. In the first place Zina waiting for me at the station might think that something terrible had happened to me if I did not appear. Secondly, the tense feeling which had come over me when I first found out where I was was still with me, and in addition the prospect of spending the night on the street did not appeal to me.

'Is there any way of letting my companion know where I am?' I asked the policeman. 'She is waiting for me at the station.'

'We can try,' he said. 'We have a telephone here and some friends at the station who can try to find her. What's her name?'

I wrote Zina's name on a sheet of paper from my notebook. The policeman handed it to his silent companion who disappeared into the nearest doorway with it.

'About a place for you to spend the night,' said the policeman, 'I don't know what advice to give you. We have no hotels here.'

'I'll try to fix you up,' said the man who had brought me to the gate. 'If you wish, you can stay in my house. We're crowded, it's true, but we have a spare bed. My brother, who is not with us any more, used to sleep in it . . .'

I thanked him and accepted the invitation after a moment of hesitation. I couldn't explain the reason for my hesitation or say that it distressed me to be in the company of these rejected and doomed people. While the other policeman was still telephoning I told them the reason for my coming to Stryj, who I was, and where I came from. My guide and host-to-be told me that his name was Rosenberg (like the famous Minister's, he added with a wry smile), that he was a tailor by profession, and that if I wanted he would try to help me purchase the goods for which I had come.

The second policeman returned and said that Zina had been located at the station and told not to worry, that I would return in the morning. Rosenberg and I said good night to the policeman and went back into the ghetto.

'Here is my apartment,' he said, letting me into a small, dimly lit room. 'These are my wife and children.'

As I entered a young woman with completely grey hair got up from behind a table, and two children, a boy and a girl about four or five years old, crawled off their chairs and froze, staring at me. The woman looked at Rosenberg, and speaking in dialect he explained in a few words how I had come there.

Pleasantly, but without smiling, she asked me to take off my coat and sit down at the table.

'We've had supper already,' she said, 'but I'll prepare something for you, although we haven't much to offer.'

I was not hungry but I was afraid to offend her by refusing, so I asked her for a cup of tea; or better, just hot water, I added hurriedly, noticing that she looked at her husband in confusion when I mentioned the word 'tea'.

'That's fine,' said Rosenberg. 'Now you sit here and I'll go and find out about the purchases you want to make. Tell me again exactly what you want.'

I felt very awkward making use of his services, but he obviously wanted to do something badly and I told him that I needed cheap earrings and brooches. He put on his hat and went out.

Mrs. Rosenberg heated up a teakettle on a small stove, kindling the fire with shavings. She explained that they had a very good electric teakettle but that in the ghetto it was forbidden to use electric heaters of any kind. With the cup of water appeared a small jar of jam which I did not touch, seeing with what longing the little girl was looking at it.

The mother apologized that she could not converse with me since she did not speak German. I answered that we could speak Ukrainian which I understood sufficiently. She began to talk about things in general, about the front which was moving west, and remarked that the worse the Germans fared in the war the worse it was for the Jews.

'But why?' I asked.

'Because when they have to retreat anywhere, they never leave a single Jew alive behind them,' she said bitterly.

I kept quiet. What could I say? After a while I asked her if they had any chance to leave the ghetto. She shook her head.

'Sometimes rich and single people manage to get away from it, although generally the ones who remain are made to pay for it. But people like us, with children—' she pointed to the boy and girl who had climbed up into their chairs again and were showing me their books. 'It's hopeless.'

Rosenberg returned with two elderly Jews. He was in a fairly gay mood, although it seemed to me then and later that his gaiety was artificial, that he forced it in order to cheer the people around him. One of the men with him wore on his coat the large yellow six-pointed star with the word 'Jude' in black.

'Well, all your business is in order now,' said Rosenberg. 'My friends Schreibmann and Valkevich will help you.'

Schreibmann had a little suitcase with him, from which he took out his goods and spread them on the table. He had brought several dozen brass earrings studded with coloured glass, and some brooches.

Rosenberg's wife began to put the children to bed, and we talked in low tones. I looked over the ornaments; they were all suitable. I asked the price. Schreibmann quoted a price which was so low that I was amazed.

'Isn't that too cheap?' I asked. 'Usually I pay a great deal more for things like this and I don't want to cheat you.'

Schreibmann gave a wry laugh.

'Don't be surprised. Jews are disliked because they always sell cheaper than others. And besides, I don't feel like making a lot of money any more. I don't need much now.'

'But it's still too cheap. I'll make a much bigger profit than usual on your goods, and there's no reason to charge such a low price.'

'I told you the price,' said Schreibmann, 'and you can pay that. But if you like, give something to Rosenberg who introduced us.'

'Please, please!' Rosenberg protested, 'I really don't need anything.'

'Yes, you do, Rosenberg,' said Schreibmann firmly. 'You know that as well as I do. You have children.'

'Well, we can discuss that later. But here is Valkevich. His goods are not here; they're in town·at a friend's house, and if you wish he'll write you a note and you can choose what you need there tomorrow.'

Valkevich, the one with the star on his coat, merely nodded.

'All right,' I said, 'please do that. I'll take everything that's here, naturally.' We counted up the ornaments and I paid Schreibmann. Meanwhile Valkevich wrote out a note and handed it to me saying, 'Here it is. The price of everything you pick out there should be more or less the same as for these things.' He pointed at the table. 'But they'll charge you more. You know nowadays even one's best friends don't do anything gratis.'

'And what about the money. Shall I give part of it to you now?'

'Young man, you don't know how to do business. How can you give me any money when you haven't even seen the goods you are to buy, and when it might turn out that there are no goods at all there? You can pay in full there, and they'll give me what's coming to me.'

The agreement was concluded. Schreibmann and Valkevich left.

The children were already in bed, and another bed had been prepared for me off to the side.

'You'd better go to bed now, it's twelve o'clock,' said Rosenberg. 'My wife and I will turn in later; we always stay up late. She's going over to visit a neighbour now.'

Mrs. Rosenberg wished me good night and went out. At once all vivacity drained out of Rosenberg's face. Silently he went over to the children's bed, looked at them for a moment, and then turned to me.

'I can understand a great deal,' he began. 'I can understand

Germans hating Jews and considering them subhuman, and destroying them. Perhaps there were Jews in Germany who used to make
trouble for Germans; I can understand that, too, although I can't
believe that all German Jews were bad. Let them do what they want
with me, although I have never in my whole life done harm to anyone.
My father and my grandfather were tailors, and I myself have been
working since I was a child. Let them destroy me because there may
have been other Jews who made trouble for non-Jews. But my children!
How are they to blame?'

He was quiet for a minute and then continued:

'You are from Russia. I know that life has been hard there, but at
least it doesn't matter there whether you are a Jew or not; it's hard for
everybody. But here – horrible times! My wife and I have resigned
ourselves to everything long ago. I lost my brother; my wife her whole
family. In what way are we better than they? But I can't bear to think
about the children. If I had any hope that they could live, even with
people who don't love them, I would hang myself tomorrow so as not
to trouble the Germans. As I died I would think that my children
would grow up and find a little piece of happiness for themselves in the
world. That's all that I would need.'

'Isn't there any way of settling the children with some family
outside the ghetto?' I asked. Rosenberg looked at me, his eyes narrow.

'There's a possibility, why not? But I don't have the million zlotys
I would need to pay people to take them. I don't have 100,000; I don't
even have 10,000. My former friends don't want to recognize me when
I walk down the street with a yellow star on my chest. Who wants my
children besides myself?' He pronounced the words with such deep
feeling that I felt shivers up and down my spine.

There was silence. Rosenberg sat down at the table and covered his
face with his hands. When he took them away there was a guilty and
embarrassed half smile on his face.

'Please forgive me for what I've said. I shouldn't have said all that.
What have Jewish woes to do with you? You must have troubles enough
of your own. Please go to bed; it's getting late. I'll go and get my wife.
She's waiting for me to call her.'

He left the room and I undressed and got into the bed that had been
prepared for me. I could not sleep, and as I lay with my eyes closed I
heard the Rosenbergs come in, put out the light, and go to bed.

Perhaps for the first time the tragedy of the fate of the Jews rose
before me in its full horror. What were the ghettos of medieval times,
the 'pale of settlement', and other restrictions on the Jews in tsarist
Russia, or even the pogroms, in comparison with their present fate?

Sleep did not come. The bed upon which one who had so recently
been killed had slept burned me. Only toward morning did I doze off
for half an hour. When I opened my eyes and saw that it was light

outside, I began to dress quickly. Trying not to make any noise, I took a piece of paper which was lying on the table and wrote a few words of thanks to Rosenberg, putting a couple of hundred marks under the paper.

As I was leaving the house I bumped into Rosenberg, who was just coming in. He had risen earlier than I.

'Good morning,' he said. 'I hope you managed to get a little sleep.'

'Yes, thank you,' I answered. 'And now it is time I went to the station.'

'You haven't forgotten Valkevich's note? Don't fail to see those people. Come, I'll walk with you to the gate.'

We walked through the narrow streets, past still-sleeping houses, on the walls of which were signs in Hebrew and six-pointed stars of David. The gate was already open and the same policeman who had been on duty the evening before greeted us.

I said goodbye to Rosenberg and went to the station. Zina was waiting for me. We had something to eat and then set out to finish up our affairs. We were through at noon, and having no trouble getting a permit from the local German kommandatura to return to Kiev, we started back the same day.

The trip back was uneventful; the profits were bigger than any of us had imagined; but I wasn't myself for a long time afterward.

Life went on, and we had to begin to think about the next trip to Poland. Prices were going up in Kiev. The future became more indefinite every day, and money began to acquire more and more importance. We did not dare to make another trip with the old pass. Every time the police on the border had studied it with growing suspicion. And so I went to the stadtkomissariat to see Schwarz. The fat, jovial German in yellow uniform to whom I had reported when I first came to Kiev. He knew all my past and had studied all my papers.

I told him about our predicament frankly and asked him to send me to Poland, ostensibly on official business, and to issue me the necessary papers. Equally frankly I informed him that he, too, would profit from our enterprise.

He found the last idea very pleasant and without much pondering ordered his secretary to prepare the papers.

I noticed right away that something unusual was happening in the stadtkomissariat that day. Germans were moving from office to office and whispering together excitedly.

As he gave me the papers Schwarz cursed softly under his breath, but not at me. I ventured to ask him what had occurred.

'I'll tell you what's happened! Those damned Italians have betrayed Germany!' he thundered.

'How?'

'Badoglio and that old bastard the King arranged a coup d'état, arrested the Duce, and made a truce with the Americans and English.'

'What's going to happen now?' I asked.

'How should I know?' Schwarz shrugged his shoulders. 'Let the Führer's head ache over it. What did he have to tie himself to those cowards for? A long time ago some French general said, "If Italy is against us, we'll need four divisions in reserve; if she is neutral, we'll need eight; and if she is with us, we'll need at least twelve." And he was right, that Frenchman.'

'Can the change in Italy have an effect on the eastern front?'

'It's had an effect already.' He began to swear again. 'A whole Italian army corps has gone over to the enemy. The rest are being disarmed in a hurry and sent to camps in Germany.'

I said goodbye to Schwarz and left. There was a lot to think about.

Only I could go to Poland with the papers I had received from Schwarz. As soon as we had collected the necessary funds I set out for Kraków. The place charmed me completely. A small ancient city on the Vistula, with churches, palaces, and a castle on the hill where Frank, the Governor-General, resided, Kraków was the best of the cities I had seen thus far. The clean narrow streets of the centre and the wide avenues of the outer ring lined with tall, thick trees; the somewhat old-fashioned citizens, the open carriages with courteous if expensive drivers, the lack of wartime damage – all this was most unusual and extremely attractive.

With this background the atmosphere of the German occupation contrasted vividly. There was frank, undisguised hatred between the Germans and the Poles. The city was full of signs reading 'Out of bounds to Poles'. They were everywhere, in hotels, restaurants, and stores. There was only one other sign in evidence – 'For Germans only' – and this was a match for the first.

The trolleys in Kraków were divided in the middle by a rope. Only Germans were allowed to enter by the front platform; the Poles used the rear one. Usually there were but two or three Germans in the front half; often it was completely empty. In the rear people were packed like herrings in a barrel. Only Poles had to pay for their rides.

There was no fraternizing whatsoever between the Germans and the population, except for unavoidable contacts between occupiers and occupied. I never saw a Polish girl walking with a German soldier, or any German in the company of Poles.

A Polish tradesman with whom I had dealings said, 'There can be no talk of any normal relations with the Germans. That is impossible. Poland was a free, independent, democratic state. No one was hungry; no one was in need. There was a certain amount of friction with Byelorussians and Ukrainians, but nothing serious. In the provinces where there were non-Polish populations there were no special restrictions for them. It is natural that Polish was the official language, since the Poles were the ruling nationality. But before the law everyone was equal.

'And so the Germans, in alliance with the Soviet Union, grabbed Poland. Many cities were ruined; the paw of the occupier descended on all Polish property. They took away the freedom we had had in Poland; they took away everything. Why? Poland didn't threaten anybody and didn't constitute a danger to any nation. She was just a sweet fruit ready to be picked. Now we are insulted everywhere we go. They treat us like beings of a lower order. A lot of people have been killed, and not only Jews or Poles married to Jews.

'How can we possibly make our peace with the Germans? Poland is the victim of the Great Powers, and the people of Poland will never agree to the inevitability or the right of any coercive foreign regime.'

'But what can you hope for,' I asked him, 'squeezed in as you are between Germany and the U.S.S.R.? Under present conditions Poland will inevitably be the prey of one or the other.'

'At the moment, yes. But I'm certain that England and America will crush Germany and the U.S.S.R., too, whom they are now so friendly with. That's the only way we will get our former freedom back. Otherwise Poland is lost, no matter how the war comes out.'

There was nothing to be said against this. He was right. The Poles, who had really lost everything as a result of the war and the occupation, had every reason to hate the invaders. But what about the Russians? What had the Russian people lost in the parts of their country which had been occupied? Freedom? They did not have it to lose. Economic well-being? They did not have that either. Moreover, during the war nobody had any doubt that, no matter how hard life was under the Germans, it was easier than 'on the other side', where people worked almost twenty hours a day, hungry and exhausted; where millions were mobilized into an army whose generals looked upon their soldiers as cannon fodder.

Undoubtedly it was easier to perish 'over there'. Under the Germans at least there was a chance to survive.

My trips to Poland went on for some time. I went to Kraków a few more times, visited ruined Warsaw and several other places. Every time I noticed the relations between the population and the Germans becoming tenser. In some places troop trains were derailed. Fortified guard points were erected along the railroads, and day and night you could see Germans standing guard behind their earthworks and barbed wire.

The Kiev newspaper reported that in the near-by town of Vinnitsa, an enormous cemetery of mass graves had been found. Each grave contained piles of bodies. They were people who had been shot by the N.K.V.D. during the purges of 1937-38. There were some who said that these were bodies of Jews shot by the Germans, but soon live witnesses appeared who had seen the pits dug.

One day I met on the street a doctor friend who had just come from Vinnitsa. He completely agreed with the official story.

'They are wrong around here when they blame the Germans for this thing,' he said. 'That is secret Soviet propaganda at work. Most of the bodies are of residents of Vinnitsa and thereabouts, and there never were many Jews there. They were shot long before the war, during the purge which Yezhov directed in 1937. A lot of people who are still alive have recognized relatives among the bodies. The graves were found in the city park which was opened to the public before the war started. Before that it was surrounded by a high fence and the N.K.V.D. would let no one in.'

'Wouldn't bodies have changed in five years so that they couldn't be recognized?'

'Sometimes they could be told by their teeth or by their hair. Often papers were found on them.'

'Were a lot of them dug up?'

'They've uncovered about 5,000 bodies so far, but undoubtedly there are more; they are still excavating.'

'But why aren't the Germans using the case for propaganda as they did the Katyn Forest massacre?'

'The devil only knows why. Probably because they don't care now. They'll have to let the Ukraine go soon and there's no use spreading any more propaganda.'

Meanwhile events did not wait. The situation in Kiev, too, was tense; Soviet troops were approaching the Dnieper above and below it. The day came when we had to leave the city.

Without much trouble I got passes from the Stadtkomissariat for our entire group to go to Poland. The group now included Sasha, a friend of my school days, and formerly a talented engineer, whom we had met in Kiev, and who was living with us. Our belongings were all packed; some of them were to be left behind. We abandoned our apartment and moved to the station where, after a wait of three days, we got places on a flat car in a train going to Lvov.

Our departure was not a problem because no large part of the population was fleeing to the west. In general the picture was totally different from the one I had observed in the northern Caucasus. The people who were fleeing from Kiev had been connected with the Germans in some way – working in the city government, the police, or in some office – or else their children had been shipped to Germany involuntarily for forced labour. There were quite a lot of the latter; the Germans had taken over five million young men and girls from the Ukraine. Sometimes their parents decided to follow them, sure that otherwise they would lose their children forever.

In addition to these categories, the Volksdeutsche were naturally going, as well as the refugees who had arrived in Kiev earlier from cities farther east.

However, the masses of the population remained to wait for the Soviets, and the reason for this undoubtedly was their firm hatred of the Germans.

I saw no hangings in the streets of Kiev, although there were rumours that the Germans were catching and shooting Communists whom they hadn't touched before. It is a strange but undeniable fact that the Germans everywhere willingly hired Communists. They considered them more experienced in administrative work and more capable than the others. So far as I know, these Communists who found themselves the 'favourites' of the Germans never betrayed the confidence which was placed in them.

And so in all only a few tens of thousands of people were leaving Kiev; but the Germans were employing all means of transportation to take grain, cattle, manganese, and other goods they needed out of the Ukraine. All roads were thronged and traffic moved in only one direction. Seated on our flat car we could see two trains ahead of us and two behind. A hundred metres apart, we all crawled south-west.

In Kazatin we were supposed to turn toward Shepetovka, but there was such a jam there that our train continued to Zhmerinka, in order to proceed toward Proskurov and Lvov from there. This turned our thoughts toward a new route.

The territory between the Dniester and the Bug, which was called Transnistria during the war, was occupied not by the Germans but by the Rumanians. It was known everywhere that life in Transnistria was incomparably better than anywhere else in occupied territory in Europe. A large part of the products which appeared on the Kiev black market came from beyond the Bug.

Earlier we had made attempts to move to Odessa; partly because my father's sister and her daughter lived there, but the Rumanians absolutely refused to let any refugees from the Caucasus or the Ukraine into their territory. Even Germans were not allowed to go there except on especially important missions. The border guard was very real and effective.

Chance had helped us. Zhmerinka was on Transnistrian territory. Of course the station was guarded and no one was allowed in the city, but we could try . . .

An argument began on our flat car. Igor and Zina were for continu-

ing on to Lvov, since they considered that our choice had already been
made and there was no point in making side trips. Sasha and I were
for going to Transnistria. We were united by an unexpressed desire to
remain on our native soil as long as possible and put off real emigration till sometime in the future.

The argument would not settle itself, and we decided to draw lots.
The lot fell on Transnistria.

When our train stopped that night in the midst of several others at
the freight station in Zhmerinka, we carefully lifted our things off the
car and made our way to the outskirts of the town, ducking under
several railroad cars. It was so dark that no guard spotted us, while
the other passengers decided that we were moving to another car of
the same train; we had kept our plan strictly secret.

When our baggage was piled next to the wall of a dilapidated little
tavern, Sasha stayed with Nina and her grandmother, while Igor,
Zina, and I wandered through the dark and dirty streets knocking at
doors and asking to be allowed to spend the night. Before very long
we found exactly what we needed – a whole hayloft, full of fresh and
fragrant hay – and moved everything in. It was good to sleep there.

15. IN TRANSNISTRIA

IN Russia Zhmerinka had always been a synonym for a very small and very dirty city. We were convinced of the fairness of this reputation the next morning.

After the night's rain we had to walk around the streets with great care; not one was paved. The town was built on hills and on the down slopes we had to hang on to each other or to fences. It was not clear where the street ended and where the pavement began. Everything was covered with a thick layer of sticky clay. Probably it had looked the same thirty, and a hundred, years before.

But there was something in Zhmerinka which distinguished it from all the other towns of Russia and the Ukraine under German occupation: an abundance of food in the market. Naturally no sanitary or hygienic standards could be applied to this market; the dirt was just as thick as everywhere else. But the food was out of all proportion to the population of Zhmerinka. There was fat, so rare in the Ukraine. There was butter, bacon, vegetable oil, meat – which we had almost forgotten existed: pork, chicken, goose – and many other things that made our eyes pop.

Moreover, it was all inexpensive. We bought a lot more than we needed, enough for a week; our greediness got the better of us.

According to the plan we had worked out the evening before, I was to start for Odessa immediately. The Governor of Transnistria, Professor Alexianu, resided there, and I was to get official permission for our group to enter our particular 'promised land'.

By-passing the station, for lack of this document as yet, I went right to the tracks and had no difficulty getting on a train whose cars were marked 'Zhmerinka to Odessa'. After a while the train started. The conductor went through checking the tickets. Having none, I offered him double the price, saying that I had almost missed the train and had no time to buy a ticket. He was completely satisfied, either by my explanation or by the money. Naturally he did not give me a receipt for it.

A little while later the conductor came through a second time, shouting, 'Get your papers ready; military police check!'

Two bewhiskered Rumanians entered the car and began to look over everyone's travel permits. When they got to me I somewhat hesitatingly handed them my permission to go to Poland. It was in German and decorated with a large swastika stamp.

The pass was good for Poland, and I was on my way to Rumania, but the police were satisfied for the simple reason that they did not know German and apparently had respect for the swastika. Having turned the pass around a few times, one of the policemen handed it back to me and saluted. I nodded at him patronizingly and turned away.

A few hours later I got out at the Odessa station, entered one of the waiting droshkies, and gave the man my aunt's address.

I had never seen my aunt, although I had corresponded with her from time to time. She was not at her apartment, so I went to a small shop which was pointed out to me, and there, standing behind the counter, I immediately recognized Aunt Shura by her resemblance to my father.

'What can I do for you?' she asked.

'These two cakes please,' I said.

'Anything else?'

'Yes. I'm looking for an aunt who doesn't know her own nephew. Can you help me?'

She looked at me thoughtfully, started to speak, and then suddenly ran around the counter and hugged me.

After a few minutes of happy and disconnected conversation, she darted out into the street, called a little girl, and said to me, 'Well, let's go home. There won't be many more customers today, it's too late. The neighbour's daughter takes care of things for me when I have to leave the shop.'

As we left she filled a basket full of goods from the shelves – fruit, pastry, meat, and so forth.

Later we were seated at a table covered with a clean cloth and loaded with good things, telling each other our stories by turn.

'Well, as you see,' said Aunt Shura, 'I have become a shopkeeper in my old age. Before the Rumanians came I was a schoolteacher. Then half the schools were shut down and I was without a job. I thought a great deal, and then, getting together as much money as I could, I opened a store.'

'Does it pay?'

'Well, in a way. I can't save any money, but I have enough to eat and I help my daughter Tamara out.'

'Tamara is married?'

Aunt Shura sighed.

'Don't talk about it! He's not a bad fellow, but a German, a Volksdeutsche. Don't get the idea that this marriage is a concession to the spirit of the times; they were married three years before the war. But he's always sick and he's a person who's completely unadapted to life. So I have to support them.'

'You're wonderful, Aunt Shura.'

'Well, I have to do a little hustling. I get up at 4 a.m. and go to the market to buy food for the store, while I can still get it first hand and cheap. I open the store at 7, and stay there almost without a break until evening. Now what about your plans?'

'I'm in Transnistria illegally. The first thing I have to do is get permission to live here. I'm not alone; there's a group of friends with me, five people. Can you suggest anything?'

'Of course. I have friends in the city government and in the governor's office. We can go there tomorrow morning.'

'And your store?'

'I'll take care of that. Someone will take my place for a while.'

It took three days to get the permission we needed. During this time I got to know Odessa. It was an amazing place.

The Rumanians captured Odessa in the very beginning of the war, after a short siege during which the city was seriously damaged by bombing and artillery. During the evacuation by sea several ships full of refugees were sunk. From the Nikolaevsky Boulevard you could still see their masts and funnels in the harbour.

Odessa and the territory between the Dniester and the Bug rivers was given to the Rumanians 'to administer', according to a preliminary agreement between Hitler and Antonescu, and after the war Transnistria was to be joined to Rumania in compensation for her participation in the war and for the loss of Transylvania to Hungary.

Having seized this territory the Rumanians began to organize it in earnest and with a view to a long tenure. The railroads were repaired quickly. Reconstruction was started on the buildings in Odessa which could be restored to use. The demolished power station reopened, the streetcars started running, and hundreds of stores opened, as well as workshops where essential articles were manufactured.

Unlike the Germans, who regarded the Russian territory they occupied as an area to loot and strip and the Russians as a people designed by fate to be slaves of the German race, the Rumanians immediately introduced an entirely different order in Transnistria.

The first, and perhaps the most important thing they did was to grant everyone complete freedom of private initiative in trade and commerce. The taxes which were to be collected from the peasants were set at reasonable rates. The population was able to use the railroads for all types of shipments.

This does not mean that the Rumanians did not despoil the country. They removed a great many things to Rumania: equipment from large plants, food, luxurious furniture from the houses of the Soviet aristocracy; but at the same time they gave great freedom to the Russian population, which not only helped to heal the scars of war but also produced a well-being unknown under the prewar Soviet regime.

Some schools were open in Odessa (under the Germans schools were very rarely opened), and the university was functioning, which would have been unthinkable under German occupation.

Four newspapers were published in the city in Russian, and various other periodicals made their appearance. There were performances every day in the magnificent Opera House, and in addition some theatres and a few moving picture houses were open.

The several city markets were overflowing with food at attractive prices, especially compared with the rest of occupied Russia. Nonedible goods were expensive. These were mostly second-hand articles or contraband smuggled from Rumania. But absolutely everything was available.

On the principal streets there were fine restaurants and pastry shops. Hotels functioned, not only for Rumanians but for Russians as well, whereas beyond the borders of Transnistria I had never seen a hotel which wasn't occupied exclusively by Germans.

The very behaviour of the Rumanians was different. They did not look like conquerors. Most of the civilian Rumanians were residents of Bessarabia who knew Russian and loved Russia, though not Soviet Russia. When in 1940, after an agreement with Hitler, the Soviet forces 'united' Bessarabia with Russia, the population experienced the same woes as the people of eastern Poland. Everyone was robbed; thousands were sent to Siberian concentration camps, and the ones who survived developed a wholehearted hatred of the Soviet regime.

However, the Bessarabians did not lose contact with real Russian culture, valued it, and treated Russian intellectuals with great respect.

It was not hard to deal with the Rumanians. Any favourable decision and privilege could be obtained. It was merely necessary to give the proper officials bribes of sufficient size. Money settled everything.

It sounded like a joke when Aunt Shura told me about the time the Rumanian military warehouses in Odessa had been robbed. The culprits were caught red-handed at the market, selling strips of parachute silk. They were tried by a military court and two of them were sentenced to death. Their friends collected something like 5,000 marks and gave it to the military prosecutor. The next day the condemned men were freed.

This potency of money was something new to me. In the Soviet Union before the war money did not have this power. Bribery was punished by imprisonment, and both givers and takers were sentenced. Every offer of money was looked upon as a provocation and it was rare that anyone dared to take it.

Under German administration it was rare to find a German who was willing to break a general rule against bribes. There were such cases but they were unusual. In general I came to the conclusion that the famous German honesty was not a fairy tale.

In Transnistria, under wartime conditions, the possibility for Russians to avoid unpleasantnesses by paying bribes was definitely an advantage. After all, the appetite of the Rumanians was a fairly modest one. When the Office of Public Safety held up permission for me and my friends to move to Odessa, I merely asked the captain in charge, 'How much?' He looked at the ceiling and answered with a shrug, 'One hundred marks.' I was surprised. You could buy a pair of geese or six pounds of good salami at the market for 100 marks.

Upon receiving the permission I lost no time getting back to Zhmerinka, and a few days later we returned to Odessa in full force.

Without much trouble we found a six-roomed apartment. From the warehouses of the city government we received some old furniture, almost free of charge. We were in no great hurry to find new work. The money we had saved in Kiev allowed us not to worry about this immediately upon arrival. Still, a month later Igor went to work as an engineer at the power station for 1,000 marks a month. This might have been enough for a small family without pretensions, but there were six of us. My friend Sasha found a job as a watchman in a store. He was paid 400 marks there; this was about enough for one person.

I found a few friends in Odessa, refugees from the northern Caucasus; among them were some of my fellow workers in the city government at home. All of them had arrived before me, usually illegally, having paid large bribes at the border. They either had jobs or were opening shops. Sorokin, our first burgomaster, was there, working in a candy factory. His successor had started a profitable second-hand store. A group of our entrepreneurs had opened a large restaurant with gambling . . .

Once, walking along the street, I passed a sign which said 'Recruiting Post for Russian Volunteers.' My curiosity led me in, and I immediately ran into a friend, head of one of the police stations in my home town. We went to the nearest restaurant together and began to talk.

'You've probably heard about the Russian volunteers for the German Army,' he said. 'Until recently there were not many of them, and most of them were on the north-eastern part of the front. They are grouped in battalions which are part of German regiments: a battalion of Russians, and two or three of Germans.'

'Who is in command of them?' I asked.

'Within the battalion they have their own Russian officers. Above that, naturally, all Germans. But there is also a general political command, under General Vlasov.'

'Vlasov? The name sounds familiar.'

'It probably is. He was one of the principal directors of the defence of Moscow in 1941, and an organizer of the Soviet counteradvance. At the beginning of the war he commanded the best motorized corps in the Red Army. In 1942 he was captured by the Germans near Leningrad and later began to organize Russian anti-Bolshevik forces on this side.'

'What forces is he organizing?'

'Mostly prisoners of war. In the first year of the war the Germans captured about 5,000,000 Russian soldiers and officers. Or perhaps it's more accurate to say that they surrendered. Vlasov is forming his Russian Army of Liberation from these prisoners. Of course, it's not an army yet – merely separate units in the German Army – but they've promised him to collect it into one force and put it into action on the eastern front.'

'Are a lot of people volunteering?'

'Yes, a good many. Not all of them of course for idealistic reasons. The conditions of prisoner-of-war camps are frightful. Maybe half of them have already starved to death. The Germans treat our soldiers like animals. Stalin has proclaimed all prisoners of war outside the law and doesn't help them at all, and the U.S.S.R. is not a member of the International Red Cross. So some of them are volunteering. At least they get fed and have a good chance of surviving.'

'Where are they using these units?'

'Mostly in the rear areas, as railroad guards, and against the Communist partisans. Very rarely at the front.'

'Are you recruiting for them?'

'Not now. We've received orders to recruit for the Russian Corps in Serbia. It consists of old emigrants, White Guards. It's commanded by General Steiffon and is operating against Tito's bands in the Balkans.'

'Is the recruiting successful here?'

'Well, not too much so – ten or fifteen men a week. Life is good in Odessa, so there aren't many people who want to go and fight. The ones who volunteer are usually those who for some reason have to get out of Odessa quickly. For instance, criminal elements, thieves, sometimes bandits, or simply homeless refugees.'

'Do you think they'll thank you for that type of volunteers?' I asked him. He waved his hand.

'I don't give a damn. I'm not looking for any medals for this work. My job is to take everyone who is willing and send them to Belgrade. Usually about half of them desert on the way, but that's outside of my responsibility. Recently we recruited some Cossacks here for Chernov – do you remember our police chief? He's a colonel now and very much respected by the Germans. Well, out of the two hundred we sent him only eight got there. The rest ran off in Poland somewhere.'

'Where did you find Cossacks in Odessa?'

'Hell, that's just a name. Actually it doesn't make any difference. The units which Chernov is forming are called Cossack units. They say that Chernov is having his complications with the Germans now, but I don't believe it.'

'You've got a soft job here.'

'I have to make my money on the side. They don't pay me anything here. But our men who accompany the volunteers bring contraband from Poland, Rumania, and even Serbia.'We have passes to cross borders.'

A thought flashed through my head. 'Listen, I don't want to volunteer for any army, but if there's a chance of my making a trip to Poland I would be very grateful.'

'Certainly; nothing could be easier. It's a little hard to get there now. The front passed the Dnieper a long time ago and the only remaining railroad, through Proskurov, is under fire sometimes. But if you want to risk it, I can arrange it for you.'

Losing no time, we went to his office, and he wrote out passes for Igor and me to go to Poland.

We left on New Year's Eve. We were supposed to 'accompany' three volunteers, but they announced to us at the start that they were perfectly capable of finding the way themselves, and it was obvious that they did not intend to go into any army.

We celebrated the New Year in the Zhmerinka station, which was full of Germans. By all appearances the front was very close. For a moment we were undecided whether to go on to Poland or turn back.

Just at midnight there was so much firing that it almost seemed like a Soviet attack. But it was only the Germans welcoming the New Year, 1944, and perhaps saying goodbye to Russia – they were all being shipped to the west.

We reached Kraków without adventure. We were in a hurry to get back and every hour was valuable. For this reason, we decided not to look for profitable goods but simply to buy gold, which cost much more in Odessa than in Poland. I found my old Polish acquaintances, with whom I had done business before. They were full of optimism.. The Germans were obviously being defeated and they were hoping for a speedy liberation of Poland.

When I told them not to be in too much of a hurry to celebrate, because the arrival of the Soviet 'liberators' did not mean a great change for the better, my warnings were received sceptically. I reminded them of the experience of Lvov and other cities which had been under Soviet occupation from 1939 to 1941, but they answered that times had changed, that the Americans and English would not allow the Poles to suffer.

I did not argue, but changed the subject to business. I needed gold, in coins.

'We have Swiss francs, 20-franc pieces.'

'How much?'

'Fourteen hundred marks.'

That was on the expensive side, but there was still a point in taking them. We could make a 30 per cent profit in Odessa.

The return journey was a long one. We tried to go by way of southern Galicia and Chernovitsy but were detained and sent back; no civilian traffic was allowed there. In Lvov we changed to a troop train with reinforcements on its way to the front, and finally reached Odessa after three days of very difficult travelling.

The situation at the front had had its effect on the money exchange. Our trip was very worth while. We received twice what we had paid for the gold. But prices everywhere had risen greatly, and the question of making money promptly arose again.

Looking back on that time, I am surprised to what a degree most of us who had broken forever with the Soviet regime and chosen the road of exile avoided thinking beyond the immediate future. Like the proverbial ostrich we tried not to notice the catastrophic position of the Germans at the front. Many comforted themselves with the idea that everything would still change, that international diplomacy would lead to an agreement for a united front against Stalin, or that the Germans would gather new strength and begin to advance again – although there was absolutely no basis for such beliefs.

However, around the time of our return from Kraków a few far-sighted tradesmen were beginning to liquidate their affairs and provide themselves with passes to go to Rumania. But these were individual cases. The city as a whole went on living, having a good time, going to the theatre and the movies, and no special feeling of alarm was noticeable. Perhaps, to a certain extent, there was a half-hidden nervousness and a desire to 'live like a man' before the coming of difficult times in the future.

Whatever the causes were, I fell under the influence of the general mood, and in January, two months before the Red Army took Odessa, a tiny jewellery and trinket shop had its opening on the main street. Igor, Zina, and I took turns working behind the counter. Every evening we put our entire stock into two big suitcases and carried it home, as a precaution against robbery. After supper we added up the profits of the day.

The profits were not great but they covered our everyday expenses, so that we did not have to touch our 'capital'. Prices everywhere continued to mount, but for us with our shop this was not frightening; our profits rose proportionately.

One of the commercial curiosities of that troubled time was the value of gold. From the sale of the coins we brought from Kraków we made a profit of 10,000 marks. If we had held the coins until it was time to leave Odessa two months later, we would have made 100,000 marks, because in the last days the people who were remaining in the city were buying up gold and unloading their marks, which were losing all value in the area.

It was not until the middle of March that we emerged from our commercial hypnosis and realized that the Red Army was approaching Tiraspol, that land communications with Rumania had actually been cut off, and that it was high time for us to flee. However, this turned out to be a very complicated operation. As soon as we began trying to arrange it we learned that the Rumanians were not letting anyone into Rumania, with the exception, naturally, of those who could pay astronomical bribes. There was only one answer to all the requests and pleas of those to whom the Soviet return meant the gallows: 'Rumania is a little country; we can't take anybody.'

At the doors of the Rumanian kommandaturas, military police stations, and other installations there were dramatic scenes, as desperate people seeking a means of escape were unceremoniously kicked out of the offices. Suicides occurred; people opened their veins in the streets in the middle of crowds.

After a few tries which were fated from the beginning to fail, I went to see the friend who worked in the recruiting office for Russian volunteers.

'We are helpless while the Rumanian authorities are still in the city,' he said. 'The Rumanians are a despicable nation. They hate the Germans and those of us who are fleeing with them. As soon as they stop being afraid of the Germans they'll betray and sell out everybody. We must wait until the Germans take over Odessa; they are not far from here now. Everything will be simpler then.'

The city was changing before our eyes. Stores were closing one after another. Their owners were either going to Rumania, having paid fat bribes for passes, or hiding their stocks in preparation for the arrival of the Red Army. Occupation money kept falling in value and we managed to sell the entire stock of our shop, even the worst items, very profitably. Finally our shop closed too.

When Tiraspol was taken the Rumanians gave up Odessa and handed it over to the Germans. This had no effect on the life of the city, which was visibly dying. The university closed down. Only one paper had been published for quite a while. It was becoming harder and harder to buy food at the market.

Sasha came in as we were packing.

'You're leaving?' he asked.

'Naturally we're leaving, but we don't know exactly how yet. What do you plan to do?'

'I'm staying. And please don't start all over again telling me the complications I may run into if I stay. I've thought it all over and decided.'

'You lucky fellow,' I said. 'What have you decided, if it isn't a secret?'

'I won't be an emigrant. And I won't be a slave of the Germans in

Germany. I'm ready for anything. I don't care if they shoot me or send me to the front in a punishment battalion. My whole life has been spent in Russia and it's going to end here.'

'Well, Sasha, if you've decided you've decided; we won't discuss it any more. I'm going west, to Europe, because I still have confidence and believe that I can make a real life for myself by emigrating. And furthermore, I'm sure there will come a day when I, too, will return home.'

The days went by. The Red Army was already breaking through to the Carpathians, but no possibility of departure had as yet turned up for us. The Germans had made some sort of agreement with the Rumanians and refused to help Russians leave the country. We were beginning to regret very seriously that we had fallen into this mouse trap and not gone straight on to Germany six months before.

One night there was a loud knock at our door. It was Aunt Shura.

'Get ready quickly,' she said. 'Tonight all the Volksdeutsche are being taken out. Tamara and her husband are going and they are taking me, too. They are loading barges at the docks. We are all ready, and you'd better hurry. They're not checking papers and anyone who wants to can go. There's plenty of room.' And she sped out.

We began to pack as fast as we could. The power station was not working and it was dark, but luckily we had candles. In about an hour all our bundles and suitcases were ready and carried downstairs, where we loaded them into a handcart that we bought from the janitor.

We hurried to the harbour through the dark streets. Little Nina, who could not understand why she had been awakened, was crying.

The streets were deserted. The only people we met were German patrols or people bound for the harbour. There were flashes in the north-eastern sky, but we could not hear the guns.

The port was badly lit and a large crowd was there. We had trouble elbowing our way to the gangways. It was a strange sight. It looked as if people who had come to the port were beginning to have doubts whether to leave. Many who had already climbed into the barges would suddenly start to carry their things ashore again.

It was quiet. There were almost no Germans around. Occasionally people standing on the shore would shout something to the ones in the barges. Here and there relatives and friends were parting.

We quickly loaded our belongings into a barge and stowed them in one of the holds. The confusion was gradually diminishing. I went up on deck and stood on the side of the barge nearest the shore, away from the others.

My mind was almost blank. The worries and alarms of the last few days made it hard to concentrate on anything. But strange sensations seized me at this last moment.

In a narrow line along the shore I could make out Odessa. Beyond it lay the limitless country which had once been called Russia, where the people talked my native language, where there were many places that I knew, and where many dear and close to me still remained.

There, not so far from me, was the roar of guns, and people were dying. Russian people. They were fighting against the enemy who had invaded their country and were defeating him and driving him out of Russia. They were saving their country and, at the same time, the fearful regime which had tortured and oppressed Russia for almost thirty years. At this turn of history, by an extreme concentration of his false propaganda, Stalin had managed to fool the people again and convince them that the concepts 'Soviet regime' and 'fatherland' were synonyms.

There was another way, which I had chosen, but which was unacceptable to many. There was no third way. The stamp of inevitability and compulsion lay on those who were fighting over there and on those who were about to leave their country on this barge. Over there they were fighting to strengthen and re-establish the regime, hating it and wishing its fall but seeing no way to bring this about. Many heads were full of foggy hopes for improvement in the future.

We were fleeing Russia because we saw that Stalin's regime was strengthening itself in the process of beating the Germans. For us the thought of a return to life as it was before the war was impossible – the endless official hypocrisy of government propaganda, sucking out the last of life's juices with Stalin five-year plans. For the many who knew the vengefulness of the Soviet regime staying behind was equivalent to suicide. At best they could expect a slow death in a concentration camp; at worst a noose around their necks on one of Odessa's squares.

We were choosing a road into the unknown, the foreign, and, obviously, the unfriendly. A tiny bit of freedom was left to us; the freedom to choose our way. We had decided to go and we were going. And each one of us, consciously or instinctively, grasped at this bit of freedom as he parted with his country.

The gangplanks were taken away and the engine of the tug began to work. Odessa with its blinking, covered light bulbs began to sink into the gloom – the last piece of our own land. There would be no return. I bade an unspoken goodbye to my country where everything that had been part of my life, both good and bad, remained.

Part III. Europe

16. RUMANIA, VANISHING EDEN

THE night was cold. The general mood was a grim one. As the sun rose we docked at the small port of Ackerman. There we were met by Germans who were to take care of the seven big barges full of Volksdeutsche. The Rumanian officials watched our debarkation but took no part in it.

All of us, in the course of several hours, were taken to a movie house, in front of which smoke was already rising from two field kitchens; the people who had arrived before us were wandering around armed with spoons and dishes.

Having piled our baggage in the foyer of the theatre and eaten some German rations, Igor, Zina, and I went out into the streets, leaving Nina and her grandmother to guard our belongings as usual. We found a small square, where we seated ourselves on a bench and began to discuss our situation. It could be summed up as follows:

We had left Russia and were now in Rumania.

We did not know Rumanian, except for a couple of hundred words.

All our resources were in German marks, which the Rumanians did not want to change into their lei. The official rate of exchange was one to sixty, but on the black market, as we had learned immediately, marks did not bring more than 10 per cent of their nominal value.

We had no official right to live in Rumania. We were there thanks only to the Germans, and we would have to take our cue from them whether we wanted to or not.

To go on with the Volksdeutsche shipment was highly undesirable. Safe in my pocket I had a paper which I had received from the German kommandatura of Odessa stating that we had permission to proceed to the Austrian town of Graz. Why had I named Graz, when I had been asked where I wanted to go, I don't know. I did not want to go to Germany proper, and the story that I had relatives in Graz seemed to slip from my lips. The lieutenant who was questioning me said, 'This is very pleasant; I'm from Graz too. What street do your relatives live in?'

'On Adolf Hitler Platz,' I said, looking him straight in the eye and only blushing slightly. I still don't know whether there was a square named for Adolf Hitler in Graz, but the lieutenant did not say anything more and wrote out the document.

Now, looking back on this incident after a span of years, I think that perhaps it was not an accident that I named Graz as my destination. If so, a happy one. It happened that at that time my future wife was there. I did not know her or have the slightest inkling of her existence at the time. But that's the way it happened.

It meant that I would have to part with my dear Aunt Shura and her daughter, who were tied to the Volksdeutsche by Tamara's marriage and did not want to leave their chance countrymen. Yet I had to set out to find the local German kommandatura. It was located in a small house and was in complete chaos. The commandant, a fat captain and two corporals, his assistants, had just arrived that morning. They were busy carrying boxes of papers into their new offices under the contemptuous glances of passing Rumanians. Pulling out a packet of all kinds of papers, I explained to the commandant that we needed one more document, which would enable us to travel through Rumania without risk of being stopped by the local police.

'Are you sure that I have the right to issue such a document?' he asked me.

'Of course! A document issued by a German Army commandant on Rumanian territory will be binding on the local authorities.'

'But what do I have to write in it?'

I began to explain, but he interrupted me.

'I see that you know more about being a commandant than I do. This is the first time I've been appointed to the job. So write out whatever is necessary yourself – I don't even have a typewriter – and bring it to me; I'll sign it.'

In order to take full advantage of this arrangement, I found a lawyer's office where they were willing to let me use a typewriter and typed out a *Marschbefehl* in language which was forceful but not enough so to arouse the commandant's suspicions. He signed it almost without looking and stamped it. After leaving his office I hesitated for a while and then went back to the same typewriter and added on the top of the document 'Wehrmachtsgefolge. Reisst in zivil'. This meant that I was in some way connected with the German Army without actually being military, and that I was travelling in civilian clothes. The reason for this was very simple, and we reaped its benefits immediately: in a couple of hours Igor and I were dragging a bag full of German rations home from the port. From then on we no longer had to worry about the food problem as long as we were travelling in German-occupied Europe.

It was becoming obvious that we had nothing more to do in Ackerman; that the Dniester River, which separated us from Russia, was not an effective barrier to the advancing Red Army; and that it was best for us to exit as soon as possible – first to Bucharest. After that we would see.

Railroad communications were restricted to one line only. The other, through Kishinev, was already under fire from advance Soviet units. There was not much time left.

Having moved to the station, we took our places on the platform in the evening, although the train would not leave until the next morning. This was necessary because there was an enormous crowd there, mostly composed of local Bessarabian residents, and there was not much chance of our finding a place on the train. We bought tickets, however. Unlike the Germans, the Rumanians did not give up their railroad profits, in spite of the war.

On the third day of this journey we pulled into the North Station in Bucharest and climbed out of the train, vastly relieved to feel solid ground under our feet. We checked our baggage and before long found a decent and inexpensive hotel which was willing to rent one big room to us all.

After a little rest and sleep we went out to explore the city. The impression it made on us was stupendous. We walked around, staring at everything, and couldn't believe our eyes.

The wonderful wide, clean streets, lined with big, good-looking houses, the endless chain of opulent store windows, the well-dressed people on the streets, all this was new and did not resemble Poland or Odessa or anything we had seen in Russia before the war.

The same idea came to all of us at once: we had to buy what we needed and clothe ourselves properly; all of us, in spite of the relatively good life we had led in Odessa, looked like tramps by European standards. Having found, without any special difficulty, one of the places where illegal money changing took place, we changed German marks into Rumanian lei and began to occupy ourselves purchasing clothes.

I did not buy very much, but my capital nevertheless was reduced by about one-third. However, a new suitcase had made its appearance in my life, filled with new underwear, a spare suit, a new felt hat, and a pair of shoes. Since we intended to go on to Germany, we also purchased some articles which we thought could not be had there: principally a large amount of toilet soap, bacon, and cigarettes. These proved to be a wise acquisition, and later on we thanked our fate for the chance which had thrown us into a country where such treasures were available.

By the time we had finished shopping amid the opulence of Rumania, my companions, and especially the ladies, had become stubborn and categorically announced that they preferred remaining in blessed Rumania to going to the National Socialist Reich. Many other Russians who had fled to Bucharest from Odessa came to the same decision, especially those with a little money. I had to spend hours trying to convince my friends that after a while all the local blessings would go to the devil, because the Soviets would take Rumania in the near future and the same 'paradise' we had recently quitted would be created here.

Not many agreed with me, but I finally managed to convince the members of our little group by telling them straight out that I was going under all circumstances and without delay. If they wanted to, they could stay without me.

The day that we finally decided to leave was the day of the first bombing of Bucharest by American planes. This was the first, but, unfortunately, not the last American bombardment that we were to witness. It produced a deep impression on us, and still more on the Rumanians. The station and the railroad yards were the target, but many bombs fell in the centre of the city. When we climbed out of our cellar the streets we had recently admired for their smart look were blocked with ruins.

We ran to the station where all our baggage was stored. It only vaguely resembled the place we had arrived at a few days before. More than half of it had been smashed to bits, including the baggage checkroom. Excavations had already begun, however, and to our joy it turned out that the corner of the room where our baggage was stored had come through with the least damage. We did not even bother to go back to the hotel. We crowded into a truck and went to a small station beyond the city, where communications were still intact, thus managing to get away before a mass of people began to flee the capital.

We reached Timisoara, near the Serbian border, where we had to change trains.

At a small border post the Rumanian border officials took us all off the train on the excuse that we did not have entrance or exit visas for Rumania. We were put in the station under the guard of a sentry. The officials told us that we would be sent back to the Timisoara jail until 'the matter was cleared up'. The German military documents which we possessed were declared invalid by the border guard officer. We expected the most unfortunate consequences and the night that we spent on the border was one of the least cheerful in quite a while, although we had become more or less accustomed to unpleasant experiences.

The danger was a very real one. From time to time Rumanian soldiers came into the room in which we were sitting, forcing us, unknown to their officer, to open our baggage for a 'search' and trying to steal things. There was no possibility of resisting and many of our belongings later turned out to be missing.

In the morning I went out on to the station platform. A train from Timisoara, carrying a full load of Germans, had just come in. While it was being checked I went up to a German major who was pacing up and down the platform and explained our situation, asking his help. He was interested and indignant over what I had to say. He was particularly angry that the Rumanians did not respect the German military documents I had with me.

Beckoning to me to accompany him, he strode into the office of the commander of the Rumanian border guard detachment and began to raise a row.

'How dare you act like hooligans, you scoundrels!' he yelled. 'So you won't obey the German Army any more! You're a bunch of bastards and not allies; you're cowards and traitors!'

The Rumanian officer, who had jumped up at the German's first words, stood at attention with his palms flat against the seams of his trousers, trying to stammer out an answer in broken German.

'Silence!' the major shouted. 'You will release these people immediately and put them on this train or I'll have your post shot to cinders!'

Several other Germans had appeared at the door, attracted by the shouting. They were whispering among themselves, obviously sympathetic with the major.

The Rumanian was forced to capitulate. He called three soldiers and ordered them to load our baggage on the train and release us. The German major, already climbing back into his car, continued to curse and wave the revolver which he had pulled out during their one-sided conversation.

The train was half empty and we had very comfortable accommodation. It was bound for Serbia.

A Serbian conductor came into the train. He sold us Serbian tickets and at the same time changed our remaining Rumanian lei into Serbian dinars at a piratical rate.

The 'independent state' of Rumania was behind us. We were entering what used to be Yugoslavia, now occupied by the Germans.

17. EXCELLENCIES AND GENERALS

WHILE still in Odessa I had learned the address of the Russian centre in Serbia, which had sent volunteers to the Russian corps being formed by the Germans. We knew that since the Revolution a large number of White Russian emigrants had settled in Serbia.

Being sure that it would not be difficult to get to Germany, we were in no hurry. We got off the train at the Belgrade station, hired a hand-cart for our luggage, and set out for the Russian House, an address which our porter knew.

After a long hike we reached Queen Natalia Street in which this house was situated. Its high porch was full of people, who were observing our small procession with interest. I could imagine that it was not without a certain amount of colour. The porter was pulling the cart over the cobblestones; Igor and I were pushing it from behind and catching the suitcases which kept falling off when the cart bumped on the uneven street. Behind us walked the old lady holding Nina, who was inspecting this new strange city with interest. Zina brought up the rear, pulling along on a string a puppy which we had recently adopted. We stopped at the driveway to the house. Since nobody made a move to come down to us, Zina and I ascended to the porch. The people divided silently to let us through. I turned to the doorman.

'Is this the Russian House?' I asked. It was a superfluous question. A sign clearly announced the fact in large letters.

'That's right. What can I do for you?'

'I would like to see one of the directors.'

'Which one?'

'Unfortunately I don't know anyone here. Anyone; it doesn't matter.'

The doorman turned to a little old man with a trembling chin who did not in the least resemble a director of anything.

'Your Excellency, please talk to this gentleman,' he said.

The old form of address sounded strange to my ears. His Excellency came over and gave me a questioning glance. Struck with doubt as to his position in the house, I asked him, 'Are you in charge of the Russian House?'

'No, not I. The general is receiving no one today. May I help you?'

'Perhaps you can. We have just arrived from Russia and have got to find a place to stay. Perhaps you could advise us where we can find accommodation.'

'Oh, that's quite complicated. Wait out here; I'll see what I can find out inside.'

He disappeared. I looked down and saw that the cart was still

412

there, loaded with baggage. The puppy was yapping beside it, and Igor was rolling a cigarette. I joined him. Zina, her mother, and daughter had disappeared. Igor's attempt to start a conversation with the people staring down at us from the porch didn't take. After a few minutes Zina reappeared.

'I think things are going to be all right,' she said. 'The fact that Mama is both the daughter and the widow of tsarist generals is going to help us. She's found some sort of acquaintances already. We'll probably get fixed up here. The Russian House covers a whole block; it's the building of the old Russian Imperial Embassy in Belgrade. They can't fail to find a place for us.' With that she disappeared again.

An hour passed and I went up to the porch again, elbowing my way through the growing crowd. The old man with whom I had talked before tried to conceal himself from me but I caught him.

'Listen, Your Excellency, why are you making us wait? Have you received any answer from the management about us?'

'No. We won't be able to settle anything today. Today is Sunday and we don't receive visitors. The general said that he will consider the question tomorrow and then decide what we can do for you.'

'Can't I see the general himself?' I asked.

The little old man looked frightened.

'Please! Please! That's impossible. Nothing can be done until tomorrow.'

Things were taking an unpleasant turn. I went out to look for Zina and her mother and found them in conversation with some local ladies of obviously aristocratic origin. French words and sometimes whole sentences kept appearing in their speech. I called Zina aside.

'Well, are you getting any results here? It's growing dark and we're still out on the street. I hate to think what we'll have to pay the porter, too.'

'No, nothing yet, but they are all very nice. As soon as they found out that I was a general's daughter and that Mama is not only the widow but the daughter of a general, they became very cordial.'

'Has any one of the nice ladies invited us to spend the night?' I probed.

'Really! How could they, after such a short acquaintance?'

'Well, in that case, here's what we'll do. Finish up your conversations. Igor and I will go and look out for a hotel right away. If you want to go on with your chats that's your business, but I don't intend to spend the night in the street.'

I left Zina without listening to her explanations. Having explained to the porter that we had to find a hotel, we set out with him. Our women did not catch up with us until a quarter of an hour later. They nagged at us a long time for being so impatient.

We went to five or six hotels. Some were 'Nur für Deutsche'; others were full. Finally near the station we found a large hotel where for a big bribe we managed to get a room for the five of us and the dog.

While the others were hauling the baggage up to the fourth floor I had time to go to the station and draw a *Marschverpfiegung* for my 'troops'. It was quite dark when we began to eat. That evening, for lack of other food, the puppy ate excellent soldiers' sausage, of which we were all extremely fond ourselves.

The next days passed in making contacts at the Russian House. Igor objected to going there at all, but Zina and her mother, as persons of aristocratic antecedents, broke the ice of the local society and finally managed to reach the general himself.

Actually, upon closer acquaintance, the general turned out not to be as haughty as we had originally thought. When he realized that we were not penniless refugees looking for charity he became quite pleasant and after we had offered him some German rations a few times (in spite of his generalcy, he had to procure his food on the black market) he even came to feel a certain bias in our favour.

We inspected the Russian House. It was a very large institution which occupied a city block opposite the royal palace. It consisted of several buildings and a complete plant: supply rooms, kitchens, and dining halls.

The Russian House had become the refuge of a great many White emigrants. Thousands of them had resided in Serbia before the war. Since then some of them had gone to Germany and some had entered the Russian Corps which had been created to fight against Tito's Yugoslav partisans. The rest had gathered in Belgrade; the countryside was becoming too disturbed for those who lived there.

In general the Russians in Serbia found themselves in a difficult situation. For twenty-five years they had benefited from the hospitality of the Serbian people and government, enjoying almost the same rights as the native population. Then the war started. Serbia was occupied by the Germans. The White monarchist *émigrés*, counting on Germany's ultimate victory, offered their services to the Germans, including actual military help. After long bargaining the Germans decided to form a Russian corps, announcing that it would be sent to the Soviet front to fight against the Bolsheviks. Several thousand volunteers assembled. Former colonels enlisted as privates. A Russian general of German extraction was put in command.

However, the Germans changed their plans unexpectedly. The corps, which was subordinate to the German commander in Serbia, was sent to fight against the partisans, who by that time were succeeding in poisoning the life of the occupying forces. It is true that the corps was used only in the fight against Tito; it absolutely refused to take part in any action against Mikhailovich. But even Tito at that time was popular enough in Yugoslavia, where everyone unanimously hated the Germans. As a result the Russian volunteers, dressed as they were in German Army overcoats – and later all Russians in Yugoslavia – began to be hated as enemies by the Yugoslavs.

The Russian House, under the command of General Kramer, was the refuge of the nonmilitary part of the emigration, but Kramer was also under the orders of the German commander, who helped the Russian colony by supplying it with a certain amount of food (naturally taken from the local population) and money. The money belonged to the Russian House. It consisted of proceeds from the sale of valuables brought from Russia after the Civil War – the contents of the former Petersburg 'Lombard'.* The Yugoslav Government had previously handled these valuables. Now the Germans had laid their hands on them and gave Kramer only enough for his current needs.

The dining room 'for the poor' in the Russian House was terrible. Former Russian aristocrats, for the most part over the age of sixty-five, ate their modest, bad-smelling dinner, and spent hours discussing the most humdrum things in the most refined language.

The Russian House had its own high school, a good military and historical museum, and, most important, a wonderful library of 200,000 books – the biggest Russian library outside the borders of Russia.

No matter how far removed from us in spirit were these countrymen of ours who had left Russia twenty-five years before, one could not fail to respect them for the persistence with which they had preserved their national identity during their exile. In Belgrade and the provinces the Russians had done a great deal after the first World War to develop Serbia, but they had hardly mixed with the local population. Their children studied in Russian schools and in one of the two Russian cadet corps. Most of the marriages among the younger generation took place within their own Russian circle.

The possibility of living among countrymen was very attractive to Zina and her mother. Again they began to say that it was not worth going on to Germany, that it was more comfortable in Belgrade and much more fun. But in this case Igor was firmly allied with me. Being a modest and somewhat shy person, he could not stand all these ex-'excellencies', and in addition he was eager to settle somewhere for good and begin to work. To find work in Serbia was out of the question. Even the Serbs had difficulty in finding it.

It was decided to leave soon after Easter. We attended the solemn midnight mass at the Russian House church. All the former officers wore their old uniforms. The orders of the Russian Empire sparkled on their chests. The ladies were dressed in their most magnificent finery.

In the morning we went for a walk, leaving the puppy at the hotel. We decided to get some lunch at the Russian restaurant, but it turned

* A bank specializing in loans with valuables as collateral.

out to be closed. Just as we reached the door the city's air-raid sirens began to sound. This was the first air raid in Serbia since the very beginning of the German occupation. The streets emptied. Anti-aircraft fire began. We heard the hum of approaching aircraft. We decided not to stand in the doorway of the closed restaurant and so crossed the street to a shop on the other side, which was open. Suddenly bombs began to rain from the sky with their own peculiar whistle. We withdrew into the depths of the store. There was a tremendous roar followed by the tinkling of broken glass. The street had suddenly become black as night. The building shook, fruit flying off the shelves everywhere. Igor was thrown to one side.

The bomb explosions began to sound farther away. Fifteen minutes later it became lighter. I looked out in the street and saw that there was only a pile of ruins where the Russian restaurant had stood.

The all clear sounded, and we raced back to the hotel. It was in one piece, but two houses near by were on fire. Not a window-pane in the hotel was unbroken. The door to our room lay in the corridor. We found our puppy, scared half to death, huddled between two wine barrels in the cellar.

Obviously we weren't too lucky. The American bombings, here as in Bucharest, were beginning a week after our arrival. The United States Air Force seemed to be following us around Europe.

The city had suffered fairly severe damage, more than from the first (and only) German air raid at the beginning of Germany's war with Yugoslavia. A row of large houses in the centre of town had been demolished and one of the bridges across the river had been damaged, but cars could still cross to the other side.

We decided to continue our journey, and as soon as possible. General Kramer agreed to issue us documents which stated that we belonged to the White emigration. We had heard that former Soviet citizens had a harder time in Germany than most others.

A couple of days later we received official visas from the German envoy to Nedich's government and departed for Budapest and Vienna.

We took with us dim memories of Serbia as a half-starved country, of an alien Russian colony, and of burning buildings in Belgrade after the air raid. Standing in the corridor of our railroad car and looking out at 'allied' Hungary, I remembered a conversation I had had with an intelligent Serb in a Belgrade restaurant.

I was sitting at a table reading a Russian book, waiting for the waiter to bring me my meal. The man sitting next to me addressed me in almost perfect Russian.

'Excuse me; you've just recently arrived in Serbia, haven't you?' he said.

'Yes, I just got here from Russia a few days ago.'

'May I ask if you plan to enlist in the Russian Corps?'

'Definitely no. I don't want to fight, particularly in the German Army, and especially under the present circumstances.'

'Yes, you're quite right!' The respectable-looking Serb seemed to come to life. 'I can't understand the local White Russians. They've lived here for years, taken advantage of our hospitality, and now they are helping to destroy our patriots!'

'So you thoroughly dislike the Germans?' I asked.

The Serb flushed.

'Everybody hates them. Who asked them to come here? What are they doing here? We lived quietly and well before and didn't threaten anybody. But then these —— occupiers came. However, it won't be long now before they go back home and Yugoslavia will be free again. The Russians will come from the east, the King will return, Mikhailovich will form a government, and everything will be fine again.'

'But aren't you afraid that the Russians will establish the same system here as they have in the U.S.S.R. – nationalize everything, and introduce the collective farm system?'

'Oh, no! You don't know our people! We are a liberty-loving folk. We're great individualists, with a strong sense of private property. The Soviet system would not do for us at all. If you take away land from our peasant, he will immediately rise against the regime. He'll kill and burn until he gets his way. Tito has sold out to Moscow, but we have Mikhailovich, and all of our sympathies are with him.'

I did not try to argue with him. I did not try to prove to him that the Russian people love freedom too, that the Russian peasant also wants his own land, and that in spite of all that, the Soviet regime does what it wants with Russia. I let him keep his hopes . . .

18. INTRODUCTION TO VIENNA

EVERYTHING turned out very stupidly. It was rather cool in the train, and I kept the wallet containing our money and documents in my coat pocket in order to be able to get at them quickly whenever there was an inspection. When we got to the South Station in Vienna and began to carry our belongings to the baggage checkroom, I took off my coat and left it with Nina, who was guarding our bags on the platform.

As I was walking through the waiting room I accidentally bumped into a tall military figure in a black S.S. uniform, hitting the side of his jaw with my head in an extraordinarily clumsy way. I don't remember whether I slipped or whether he got in my way, but the fact remains that the collision took place. The S.S. man was apparently a very nervous person. Without listening to my apologies he began to shout loudly, studding his almost incomprehensible tirade (I think it was in the Thuringian dialect) with many barely comprehensible curses.

He grabbed me by the arm and started to drag me somewhere, out of the crowd that had surrounded us. I could understand his irritation, because I could judge the force of our collision by the pain in my own head. But when he pushed me into a small, dark room in the station and locked the door, any sympathy I might have had for him disappeared immediately and completely.

I wanted to smoke but my cigarettes were in my overcoat, and this made me realize that I had no documents with me at all.

It's all right, I thought. While Igor and his family are still at the station it will be easy to find them. I have nothing to fear. I have come to Vienna with a perfectly good visa and the rest of my papers are in order.

However, when I noticed that it was entirely dark outside, and I began to feel strong pangs of hunger, I became worried. I knocked on the door a few times but there was no sign from outside. Then I began to hammer at it. Finally I heard a voice say, 'What's the matter?'

'I want to see the commandant.'

'It's too late; he isn't here. You'll see him tomorrow.'

'I have to get my papers from my friends.'

'You can get them tomorrow.'

'But my friends will leave the station . . .'

'Tomorrow.'

'I want to eat.'

'Tomorrow, damn it! I told you tomorrow; now shut up!'

Further conversation was useless. I tried to sleep, seated on a chair in the corner. After a while I succeeded.

Grey dawn appeared at the window. I was awakened by spasms of hunger and began to beat at the door again. Another voice, without opening the door, said it was too early.

'I've been without food long enough,' I yelled. 'Can't you give me something to eat?'

'We don't feed anyone here. You'll get fed in jail. You'll be taken there when the commandant comes.'

This was highly unpleasant. I asked the man to inform the commandant of my desire to be allowed to talk to him as soon as possible, and began to pace up and down the room.

About two hours later a tall military policeman led me to the commandant's office.

'What's the matter? Why are you here?' said the commandant.

I explained to him what had happened. He shrugged his shoulders.

'I don't know anything about it. No complaints have been filed with me by any S.S. men. Who are you and what are you doing at the station?'

I explained that I had just come from Serbia, and before that from Russia, and that I had to find my friends.

'What friends? Where are your papers? Let's see them.'

I explained to him again that my papers were in my coat, that my coat was with Nina, and that Nina, alone, or with her parents, was waiting for me now, somewhere around the station. The commandant grimaced as he listened to me. Then he began to shout, sitting up straighter and straighter as his voice grew louder, 'Who are you trying to fool? What Nina? What parents? Obviously you've escaped from a camp. Damn you anyway; they've brought all of you here from all sides and now we Germans can't live in peace any more on account of you. I'm sending you back to camp right away. Corporal!'

The corporal appeared and handed me over to a private, without listening to my protestations. The soldier took me by the sleeve and we went out into the square and took a trolley.

'Where are you taking me?' I asked. We were standing on the platform of the trolley.

'To camp,' the soldier answered. 'But I don't know why they are sending you there.'

'I don't know myself. The only thing I'm guilty of is that I accidentally hit an S.S. man in the face.'

'Hey, that's interesting. Tell me about it.'

I related what had happened. He looked thoughtful.

'Did they ask you where you were from and what your name was?'

'I told the commandant where I was from, but I wasn't asked what my name was. Why?'

'Well, I'm supposed to take you to a very bad camp.'

'Why are you taking me there then?'

'Because I'm a soldier and I have my orders.'

At this point I began to try to convince him that he would be an even better soldier if he let me go, and that after all it was the S.S. man's fault that he had crashed into me.

'The hell with the S.S. man; he got what was coming to him. But I have to give the commandant a receipt from the camp proving that they accepted you.'

'Isn't there some camp that's better and closer?' I asked in a low tone. He looked at me thoughtfully, 'Maybe that's a way out. I can always say I took you there by mistake. And probably the commandant won't bother to check on it. All right. Let's get out here and take another streetcar.'

Presently we arrived at a group of wooden barracks, surrounded by barbed wire, with two soldiers on guard at the entrance. My 'escort' went into the small orderly room and came out a few minutes later holding a piece of paper.

'You stay here. Good luck to you. Goodbye,' he said.

A man in civilian clothes, probably a Pole judging from the few words he exchanged with another man that we passed, led me to one of the barracks. It was equipped with two decks of wooden shelves and smelled of bedbugs. There was almost no one there. I lay down on the mattressless, blanketless cot which was pointed out to me, and tried to sleep.

It was dark when I was awakened by the sound of many voices. Again I felt the pangs of acute hunger. This was the second day without food. I struck up a conversation with the people in the barracks, who turned out to be Ukrainian workers deported to Germany a year before. They told me where the mess hall was and I hurried over.

The dark and filthy dining hall was crowded with people trying to get to a large pot from which a brown liquid was being doled out. When I received my share I asked about bread but was told that bread was given out only once a day, in the morning, and that one had to work somewhere to be eligible for it. However, bread was also available if I had money.

I had some money sewed into my trousers; the money for our immediate expenses was in my overcoat pocket, somewhere with Nina. I rushed to the latrine, ripped the lining from part of my trousers, and got out 100 marks. I gave them to the man who had offered to sell me bread. He looked the bills over and said, 'That money is no good here. Those are occupation marks, not German; they aren't worth as much. If you want I'll give you 25 real marks for that.'

'All right, but hurry up,' I said, tortured with hunger. He gave me 25 German marks for my 100, and for 5 of my new marks I received two pounds of bread.

Feeling a little stronger, I went back to the barracks. In conversation with my fellow prisoners I learned that all of them worked in a big factory not far from camp, and that this camp was considered a very bad one, one of the worst in Vienna.

Some sort of camp official entered the barracks shouting, 'Any newcomers here?'

I did not make a sound. There were no other new men in the barracks. After the official had left, the man next to me asked, 'Don't you want to register? Don't forget that you won't get any bread unless you work.'

'Bread is only of secondary interest to me. Tell me, do they send you to work under guard?'

'No, but they check on attendance at the factory. If anyone is absent, they inform the camp, and he is docked a month's pay and gets a smaller bread ration.'

'What kind of pay do you get?'

'Up to 20 marks a month.'

This was more than modest, and I thought that I could well do without it.

'When do you go to work?' I asked my neighbour.

'At 6.30 a.m. Work starts at 7. At noon we have a break for lunch, which is brought from the camp. From one o'clock we keep on working until 6.30. That's a total of ten and a half hours. By 7 p.m. we are back in camp.'

'Do they let you go to town?'

'Yes, on Sundays. But you have to have this badge on your chest.' He showed me a jacket on which there was a piece of white cloth with the word OST printed on it in blue.

'What does that mean?' I asked.

'It means we are Ostarbeiter, workers brought in from the east. If you want, I can give you a badge like that; I have several of them. That way you won't have to go to the camp office.'

'Thank you, I wish you would give me one.'

I pinned the OST badge to my jacket with a safety pin.

'Tell me,' I said, 'will they assign me a bed?'

'Yes, but you'll have to register first.'

I decided to sleep on the boards.

The next morning I got up with all the others and washed at a tap outside the barracks. I shaved with a razor borrowed from one of my neighbours and went out to work with the others.

I looked around, trying to print the locality on my memory. I wrote down the names of the streets we passed in my notebook. When we got near the factory gates I separated myself from the column and began to walk along the pavement alone. Nobody paid any special attention to me. Apparently here every man was responsible only for his own actions.

After walking a few paces, I took the prominent OST badge off my

jacket and entered a small tobacco shop. They refused to sell me any
cigarettes without a ration card, so I bought a map of Vienna and
went on walking.

I stopped at a small square to sit down on a bench and study the
city plan. I was quite far from the centre of the city. My problem was
to locate my friends. It was not easy to do. I didn't dare go back to
the station for fear of meeting the commandant or the S.S. man. Without any concrete plans, I located a streetcar line and took a car going
toward the centre. Getting off at the last stop, I found myself at the
Ring, on Schwarzenberg-Platz. I entered a small café and asked for a
cup of coffee and a telephone book, in which I looked up the address
of the Russian Club. Then, for a small consideration, I was given the
privilege of using the telephone. I began to call up every hotel in the
city, one by one, asking each one whether my friends might be among
the guests. This pastime took all the morning. Everywhere I got the
same answer: nobody by that description had checked in recently.

After that I began to explore the city. Vienna appealed to me greatly.
The houses were attractive. The wide streets were clean, orderly, and
had many trees. The people were dressed neatly, in a somewhat old-
fashioned manner. Not many uniforms were in evidence. I noticed
how well groomed even the dogs were. Men as well as women walked
with them on leashes.

All the cafés were full and I was amazed how many people of working
age did not seem to be working. One might think that it was peacetime,
that Germany was not losing her conquered territories, and if it had
not been for occasional wounded soldiers it would have been easy to
forget about the war altogether.

I bought a paper and went into a café. The news from the front was
not good for the Germans. Fighting was in progress in the Carpathians,
on Rumanian territory, in Poland, in the Balkans, and in Italy. I went
on calling up hotels, but still without success.

Hunger began to bother me again. My attempts to have dinner at a
restaurant were not very successful. With the exception of some sort
of potato paste and coffee, everything was sold on ration cards, of
which I had none.

I set out for the Russian Club. On the door of the club there were
two notices. The first announced that the club was open only once a
week, from 7 p.m. to 11. That day was five days off. The second sign
declared that this was a club for the OLD emigration. The word
'OLD' was underlined twice.

It was already late and I hurried back toward camp. I was on time.
Just as I reached the gates of the factory the workers began coming out.
Pinning on my OST badge, I mingled with the crowd.

The next day I continued my search. It was hard to imagine that anything had happened to my friends. We all had excellent documents and enough money. All of us spoke German, and Vienna seemed too peaceful a city to contain many unforeseen unpleasant occurrences.

I was afraid to go to the police for information without my own documents in my possession. The incident at the station had made me extremely cautious. But the camp was not an alluring place. I had no desire to stay there with the other Ostarbeiter.

On the third day, sitting in a small café on Schwarzenberg-Platz after my 'dinner', I began to talk to the proprietor, a fat Viennese with light blond hair, resembling an albino's. I asked him cautiously where foreigners arriving in the city usually stayed. He brought the telephone book over and crossed out a large number of hotels where foreigners could not stay. He advised me to pronounce the names of the people I was looking for with great clarity.

Once again I sat down with the telephone and after an hour and a half of endless conversations I received an answer from a small hotel not far from the Prater which made my heart leap with joy, 'Yes, they are here. They checked in two days ago.'

I was certain that I had called up this hotel earlier, but I did not want to lose any time speculating about it. I set out for the other end of the city, having asked the proprietor of the restaurant for directions how to get there.

The hotel bore the proud name of Europa, but was a small building, three stories high, probably about 200 years old, located on a narrow side street.

The desk clerk told me what room to go to. Once again I was with my friends! They had all been terribly frightened at my long absence. For two days they had kept watch at the station, hoping that I would appear. They could not imagine what had happened to me. It never entered their heads to look for me in the station kommandatura, but this was probably a good thing. The commandant might have remembered the whole incident and decided to make sure that I was really in the punitive camp.

The Gorskys were living in the hotel illegally. They had not as yet registered with the police, and as a result they had to pay exactly twice the normal rate for their room. I arranged with the clerk to live in the same room, for a little additional rent.

Igor told me that on the black market, at the Prater, he had been offered half the face value for his occupation marks. Although this was more than I had received at the camp, it was still not enough. A number of problems now faced us. We had to change our money into real Reichmarks, get ration cards, register with the police, and settle the question of work. The law required all foreigners (as Igor had already learned) to work wherever the Arbeitsamt ordered them to.

This was a very unappealing prospect. Neither of us wanted to work ten hours a day for the Germans in some factory and receive only trifles for pay.

I solved our money-changing problem the next day. I went to several banks where occupation marks were being changed, but only in limited quantities, 50 marks a person. I noticed that the tellers made no record of the transaction, and therefore I assumed that there was no check or control on the money-changing process. In a small savings bank on the Prater I made friends with the teller, a middle-aged Viennese who turned out to have a fierce hatred for all Germans from Germany.

I met him after he was through at his office, and the slab of bacon and two pieces of Rumanian soap that I gave him enabled us to find a common language fairly quickly. As a result he changed all our marks into real ones at the normal rate, one to one, reserving for himself a small commission of 2 per cent.

A solution was also found for the ration card problem. I learned that foreigners arriving in Vienna could draw ration cards for a month without going to work. Naturally this privilege was not extended to the Ostarbeiter. Since Zina had a paper which certified that she was an invalid (this was a fiction she had bought in Kiev for a small price) and since her mother was over sixty, we only had to worry about ration cards for Igor and me.

It was not long before Igor got a job, through the Arbeitsamt, as a draftsman at a radio factory, at 300 marks a month. I temporarily remained in the ranks of the unemployed, buying ration cards on the black market. Igor's factory gave him a small room in a camp, about five feet by ten, but this camp did not in the least resemble the one where I had spent my first days in Vienna. It was for certain foreign workers – Frenchmen, Dutchmen, and Greeks, whose working conditions were a great deal better than those of the Ostarbeiter. Since there was obviously no space for me in Igor's room, I rented an inexpensive furnished room. The old landlady was frightened when she first found out that I was a Russian. In her opinion all Russians were barbarians whose sole nourishment was derived from the flesh of babes in arms. However, with the help of the all-powerful bacon and soap, I managed to get on the good side of her fairly rapidly.

We told the police that we were White emigrants from Serbia. They pretended to believe us and registered us as such. But in order to get passports it was necessary to go to the Gestapo and present our genuine documents.

The elderly, one-legged Gestapo Kriminalrat studied our pile of papers carefully for a long time, shaking his head slowly. Finally he said, 'You are not foreigner visitors at all; you are just plain, ordinary Ostarbeiter, and you'll have to live in camp. Only Russians who left

Russia before 1939 and have documents to prove it are considered foreigners.'

'But wait,' I objected. 'We are not Ostarbeiter. We came to Vienna of our own free will; nobody forced us to leave Russia . . .'

'Don't talk nonsense,' said the Kriminalrat, but not angrily. 'Nobody forced any of your countrymen to go to Germany; every last one of them has come here of his own free will.'

'Yes, yes, that's right, I'm sorry,' I hastened to agree. 'But we were travelling by individual decision and we even received official visas from the German Minister in Belgrade.'

'Visas, visas,' the old man mumbled, 'I don't give a damn about visas. The devil knows what I'm going to do with you.'

He began to study our documents again. At that moment Zina's head appeared around my shoulder. She gave me a sign with her eyes to move aside. Then she placed a small package on the Kriminalrat's lap. My heart stood still. I was sure it was more of that soap and bacon from Bucharest, and I waited for an explosion. I went over to the wall and began to inspect a map of Vienna with great interest.

'What's this?' asked the old man severely.

Zina said something in a low voice. The intonations of her voice were very seductive and convincing. I heard the rustle of wrapping paper and the old man's soft coughing.

'All right,' he said, 'what the hell? Leave all your papers here and come back in a week.'

We thanked him and left. I scolded Zina for slipping a bribe to such an important official, trying to explain that it might have ended in a catastrophe, but she merely laughed.

A week later we were told that we could apply officially for a passport, and a month after that we all received brand new passports enabling us to live in Germany with no great risk of ending up behind barbed wire. Our 'citizenship' was described as 'unsettled, formerly U.S.S.R.'

Thank God, I thought, for that word 'formerly'.

The time went by. We got to know Vienna fairly well and we became very fond of the city. We had enough to eat, especially in the first days when it was still possible to draw our famous Marschverpflegung at the railroad station. Later when we had become too well known at these soldiers' ration points, we were forced to give up this source of supply with a heavy heart.

The local police questioned me several times as to the reason I was not working. I made various excuses, but I felt that my freedom would soon be over and that I would have to go to work in some factory. This is what would have happened if it had not been for a lucky break.

We had become acquainted with several of the White Russians living in the city. One was a very pleasant young count who was working in the local propaganda department. Being fluent in several European languages he was employed in translating articles for the German-controlled Balkan press. He had good connections, and when I told him about my difficulties in finding a decent job he said:

'That's easy. I can fix you up. Are you registered in the Arbeitsamt? No? Well, go and register, but tell them you are a journalist by profession and that the propaganda section has requested you to work for them.'

'But I don't want to work in the propaganda department!'

'Don't worry, you won't. Just tell them that so they'll call me up and I can confirm it.'

'But won't they send me to some other place?'

'No. Journalists, writers, artists, and actors, as members of free professions, are not subject to the labour mobilization. I'm well acquainted with these laws. But to avoid trouble you must have some sort of work certificate, and I'll get one for you.'

Everything worked out smoothly. I reported myself as a professional journalist with great aplomb and haughtiness. They did not even bother to check on the telephone and issued me a paper stating that I was to work for Count Reder. He in turn procured for me a document which stated that I was 'affiliated with the propaganda department'. On the basis of this paper I began to draw regular ration cards, and the police duly noted in my passport that I was a journalist by profession.

Only one other problem remained: money. Our capital was melting away; Igor's pay was small. Of course the prices of rationed food were low, and there was almost enough to live on in the rations. In this respect the Germans were extremely efficient. The size of the rations was much smaller than in the Soviet Union, but there 95 per cent of the food rations were never given out to the population, which received only bread. In Vienna all the food which was announced at the beginning of the month was either distributed or replaced by an item of equal food value. Of course, it may be pointed out that most of this food was taken from Russia by the Germans. Still the fact remains that when Russia was in possession of all her food we saw very little of it; we had to come all the way to Germany to get it.

During the summer our little group began to make some real money at last. Having studied the situation, we decided there was a good market for cheap jewellery here. We found brass and various stones of all possible colours in Vienna shops and began to spend our evenings in the manufacture of earrings and necklaces. Viennese Fräuleins, who had been starved for such ornaments ever since the government had forbidden the manufacture of luxury goods, purchased our trinkets willingly. Later we made contacts with several stores, which bought our products in large quantities and sold them out in the villages.

We earned from 1,500 to 2,000 marks a month and were able to buy clothes gradually, as well as to supplement our diet on the black market. Of course we ran some risk of getting into trouble with the authorities because of our illegal activities, but the Germans had not been able to institute a real control over the country. The black market was forbidden, but in the Vienna amusement park on the Prater a large crowd of black marketeers would gather every Sunday. Most of them were foreigners, Ostarbeiter included, but one could often see local citizens trying to barter a few cigarettes or a little bacon for bread and ration cards. In the big camps, especially in the Greek ones, there was a real bazaar on Sundays. You could buy good suits, new shoes, and many other things which were not available in Vienna's stores. There were occasional police raids but not many people were caught. Specially placed sentries usually managed to signal the approach of the police and people had a chance to run off.

Meanwhile, events were moving in the world. When the news of the Allied landings in Normandy and the subsequent defeats of the Germans in France came through, it became obvious that the end of the war was not far off. The only chance for German success would have been the use of the mysterious and terrible weapon which Goebbels and other German leaders mentioned many times. But only orthodox Nazis believed it should be used. Most people thought that such a weapon would call forth retaliations on a vast scale in the form of even greater bombardment of German cities by British and American aviation.

Secret weapon or not, Germany was not being spared. We had air-raid alarms every day, but the planes usually flew on farther to bomb Berlin and the industrial targets of the western and central provinces. Austria and Czechoslovakia, so far, were not bombed as much. There had not been a single raid on Vienna. Of the other Austrian cities, Graz, Linz, Krems, and Wiener Neustadt were hit the hardest.

At the end of the summer General Kramer and the entire staff of the Russian House in Belgrade came to Vienna. The only things they managed to bring with them were the famous Petersburg treasure and a few items from their museum. Everything else, including the enormous library, fell into the hands of Tito and the troops of the Red Army which took the city. A small number of White emigrants who either could not or would not flee to Germany stayed in Belgrade. Reports of merciless treatment of all those who helped the Germans in any way, and of the relatives of the men in General Steiffon's Russian

Corps, which was retreating into Croatia, came through the front lines
to us in Vienna.

Our Belgrade friends arrived in Vienna very different from what
they had been at home. They were no longer in the least uppity. The
general himself, his wife, and several friends moved into a large hotel
in the centre of Vienna. In the evenings a Russian company would
gather there, play bridge, and talk over the latest news, which was
becoming less and less favourable to the Germans.

In this hotel I met several famous White generals, heroes of the Civil
War in Russia. Some of them wore Russian uniforms; others were in
civilian clothes. They were inactive and spent their time on their
personal affairs, although they did occasionally see various highly
placed Germans.

By this time the Russians, under German sponsorship of course, had
created several military commands. In northern Italy was Ataman
Damanov's Cossack group, fighting against the partisans of the
Italian resistance movement. In Croatia, in addition to General
Steiffon's Russian Corps, the First Cossack Division of the German
General Pandwitz was stationed, operating against Tito. In addition,
various national legions were included in the German Army: Georgian,
Kalmuk, and Tartar. Finally there was the Ukrainian S.S. Division,
made up of volunteers from Galicia.

All these forces were connected with their national centres in
Germany, which were inimical to each other and all hostile to
General Vlasov. This German policy was formulated under the direct
supervision of Rosenberg, Minister of the Eastern Provinces (although
there were no longer any eastern provinces), who was trying to split
the Russian anti-Bolshevik forces as much as possible. Why he wanted
to do this no one could figure out. Such a policy might have made some
sense at the time of the German victories in the east, when the dismem-
berment of Russia was part of the German plan, but it was senseless in
1944 when the Third Reich was on the brink of destruction.

Many people condemned the attitude of the Germans toward the
Russian anti-Bolshevik movement on the grounds that if the Germans
had immediately taken steps to create a free Russia, they could have
acquired a loyal and powerful ally for themselves in the east and the
outcome of the war would have been quite different. I did not agree
with them: the Germans and a free Russia, liberated by them, were
two irreconcilable things. In order to do that they would have had to
stop being Germans.

19. AMERICAN BOMBS

THE people of Vienna had begun to be convinced that the Anglo-Americans had decided to spare the city in their flights over the Reich, but they were to be disappointed.

On September 10 I left my house and headed toward the Gorskys' apartment. On the way there was an air-raid alarm, and all walking on the streets stopped. Thinking that this was just another one of the daily alarms we had when American planes from Italy flew over Vienna, I paid no attention and continued on my way.

Anti-aircraft guns began to fire from their emplacements at the top of the tall iron and concrete bunkers which had been built in various parts of the city during the summer. Their firing grew more intense. In the bright blue sky I could see the high-flying bombers with puffs of flak around them. There were a lot of them. Shrapnel from the flak shells began to rain on the street, and I decided to take cover in the doorway of a house.

A moment later the bombing began. The bombs fell with wild screams; the air shook with explosions. I quickly went into the house and down to the cellar. Several Austrians were huddled in the far corner, only occasionally saying anything to each other. The whole cellar trembled. An old man kept sucking on a bottle.

A bomb whistled down and burst somewhere very close. The lights went out. The roar of the plane engines was on top of us. One of the women began to have hysterics and the children started to cry. Suddenly there was a huge crash. The house shook. Dust filled the cellar, along with a few bricks which clattered down from somewhere. Almost simultaneously I heard the distant crackle of burning wood and smelled gas.

The whistle of bombs and the sound of their explosions could still be heard, but it was receding into the distance. Covering my mouth with a handkerchief, I began to make my way slowly along the cellar wall. In one corner there was a little daylight. It came from a partially blocked window and a small ventilator. I began to clear away the bricks and other debris, scratching my hands badly in my haste. The old man came over and handed me a crowbar with trembling hands. Blood was trickling down his face, mixed with dirt.

Finally I cleared a small passageway. When my face reached the ground level a wave of intense heat hit it; the house was on fire. With great difficulty I forced myself through the window and outside. Then I helped the old man crawl out. He kept calling the others who had been in the cellar with us but we could hear no answers. At that moment a few other people came up and began to widen the hole. I went on my way.

The streets along which I had passed so many times were un-recognizable. In many places there was nothing left but rubble. A few buildings were on fire. The all clear sounded and people poured out into the street.

The house which contained the 'camp' where my friends were living had not been damaged. Nobody was home. Looking in the mirror in their room, I noticed for the first time that I had a big abrasion on my forehead and that I was covered with dirt. After cleaning up a bit I set out for my own place.

The area where I lived was roped off by the police. After checking my documents and convincing themselves that I really lived there, they let me through.

From a distance I could see that only memories remained of the house where my room had been. All three floors had been demolished. Only a corner of the first was still standing. Apparently one bomb had made a direct hit on the house and another right in front of it. Two streetcar rails, bent by the explosion, had climbed into the window of my room.

Crawling up the rails, I managed to get inside. The ceiling had not collapsed, but everything was covered with bricks, dust, and junk. I started to try to retrieve what I could of my belongings. My suitcase, with some things in it, was under the bed, unharmed. I made a bundle of everything else in a blanket, all mixed up with dirt, and clambered back to the street with difficulty. I saw the old landlady in the crowd which had gathered there. She was sitting on a broken chair looking around with wandering eyes, her hands folded in her lap. She did not even recognize me.

It was already quite dark when I got back to the Gorskys' place. They were horrified to see me in such shape and began to ask what had happened. I was so tired that I threw my things down in the corridor, crawled under the bed where Nina and her grandmother slept, and was asleep in an instant.

In the morning I hurried back to the part of town where I had lived to get a certificate that I had been bombed out. With this certificate you could buy certain items of clothing in the stores, but, more im-portant, it made it easier to find a new apartment.

There were apartments available in Vienna, but they were controlled by an inspector in the Rathaus, a repulsive sort and a Nazi to the mar-row of his bones. Whenever I talked to him the desire to smash his face in rose in me. My conversations with him always went something like this:

'What do you want in Vienna anyway? Who invited you to come here?'

'I was brought here by your countrymen,' I would lie.

'Oh? And why would they want to bring you here?'

'I don't know; you'll have to ask them.'

'You are, perhaps, the only Russian in Vienna?'

'You know that I am not.'

'And where do they live, the rest of the Russian pigs?'

'Where they were put, in camp.'

'And why can't you live in camp? In what way are you better than the others?'

'I'm not better than the others, but I happen to have the right to live outside of camp.'

'Oh, you have the right! Well, all right, so live outside of camp. What do you want of me?'

'I want an apartment, as I've told you several times.'

'I don't have any apartments for people like you. There are apartments in Vienna only for Germans, and not for all the garbage that has been blown in here recently. Your allies, the Americans and British, are bombing the Germans, and it would be funny if I gave apartments to Russians while Germans had to sleep under the open sky.'

'In other words you don't want to give me an apartment?'

'So you've finally figured that out!' the inspector would say. I would get up and leave.

Such conversations had taken place several times. Finally I realized that I could get nowhere with him and started to look around for other means of getting what I wanted. I found a way. Having penetrated to the office of the secretary of the burgomaster of Vienna, I obtained, with the help of more of that bacon and soap from Rumania, a written order that a 'category 3' apartment should be assigned to me. A 'category 3' apartment was one with serious deficiencies, one which Germans often refused.

Grumbling and cursing, my old friend the inspector wrote me out a paper by which I obtained a damp and neglected apartment in a small side street near Schwarzenberg-Platz. The Gorskys and I moved there the next day. They had decided to give up their crowded little room in camp. Our apartment consisted of two rooms with a kitchen, but the best thing about it was that there we were our own bosses and did not have to take orders or kow-tow to anyone.

We saw only the people we wanted to see. A few friends from Russia used to drop in, mostly Ostarbeiter, formerly doctors and engineers. General Kramer and his friends also were regular visitors. We spent the long evenings manufacturing our trinkets or playing endless rubbers of bridge.

Vienna was bombed often, but the centre of the city was seldom hit; the bombers concentrated on the industrial suburbs. A few camps were hit, and there were casualties. There were not enough good bunkers and shelters to go around, and foreigners frequently were not allowed into them, though they would fight for entrance.

Once the police held me up on the street and made me help clean up bombed buildings, along with a group of others. There had been such press gangs around before, but I had always managed to elude them successfully. This time I was not able to do so right away.

We were taken to the area which had been hit on the previous evening, handed shovels, and instructed which parts we were supposed to clean up. Policemen stood near to make sure that we worked.

The work was dull, boring, and obviously useless. To do what they wanted not a few dozen but a few thousand people were needed, so there was no point in trying to work hard.

Suddenly another policeman ran up and whispered to our guard. We were ordered to disperse. Not understanding the reason but very happy, I ducked through a hole in the wall and, jumping from one pile of debris to another, reached the street. I heard whistles all around.

Unexpectedly I came across a group of about ten men in Red Army overcoats digging in a fairly deep hole. A group of Germans stood watching them at a respectful distance. I realized that these were Russian prisoners of war digging out an unexploded bomb. An unpleasant chill ran up my spine and I hurried away from the place.

I paused for a moment in the next street. The same policemen who had caught me earlier were standing by the wall of a half-ruined building, blocking the street and detaining anyone who tried to pass. I changed my direction and had not yet reached the corner when there was a deafening roar. I turned around. On the place where the policemen and the group of detained civilians had stood there was a column of dust. The wall had collapsed from the concussion of the bomb's explosion and buried them under it.

There was plenty in Vienna under almost daily bombardment to amaze those of us who had come from the Soviet Union. Everything that could be repaired was repaired right away, efficiently and with no particular fuss. Streetcar traffic very rarely stopped; there were merely occasional changes in the routing. Factories continued to operate, although the effectiveness of the work was diminishing: there was serious impairment of railroad communications, causing lack of raw materials, coal, and various parts which had to be brought from a distance. But the food supply for this city of millions continued to be adequate. The unharmed streets were cleaned every morning and retained an illusion of peaceful living.

As usual, in an unchanging ritual, the honourable citizens of 'the second Paris' took their bearded dogs out for a walk; they crowded around the doors of streetcars in the same way, allowing others to go first in exaggerated politeness. The innumerable cafés of the city were still full from morning until night, except during air raids.

One Viennese, whom I met in a night club, said:

'Why should it surprise you? We have nothing to fear. We didn't start the war and we won't lose it. We lived quietly and peacefully before the Anschluss and we'll live the same way after the war. Vienna will be full of tourists from all parts of the world and life will be light and gay again. You are surprised at our calmness, but I assure you it is to our credit. If we began to react to Herr Goebbels' hysteria, it would not make it easier for him and life would be more unpleasant for us. Nobody can save the Reich now, and Austria has already contributed too much to the adventures of the last few years.'

'But what are you Austrians doing to free Austria from the Germans?' I asked. He shrugged.

'Why should we do anything? Isn't there enough blood already? There are a lot of people here who have come from Germany. They are not all bad people, and it isn't worth it to complicate the situation by individual or mass killing of such people. When the time comes, they'll get out themselves. Take the case of Warsaw. The Red Army was already on the other side of the river. Stalin incited an uprising among the Polish nationalists underground in the city and then sat back and laughed while the Nazis destroyed both the city and the nationalists. Hitler's a fool. If he had surrendered Warsaw to the Soviet along with the underground army of General Bor, it would have been a major victory for Germany, because your Stalin would have lost his peace and quiet and your N.K.V.D. would have had a lot of work to do. The Poles are a hotheaded people. We are calmer here.'

'I agree with you. In general, if Hitler had arranged to leave organized anti-Communist groups of local citizens in the cities which he surrendered to the Red Army, the results might not have been bad.'

'Perhaps, but maybe not,' my philosopher-companion answered. 'This way, many of these people will have a chance to get under American or British authority, while if they stayed behind they would be eliminated sooner or later. But enough of these sad subjects! How do you like that girl over there, the one in the yellow dress? Isn't she cute?' He stuck an old-fashioned monocle in his right eye.

Apparently his opinions were shared by most of Vienna's citizens. Their protests against the Nazis went no further than an occasional sign chalked on a wall: 'Down with the brown dog Hitler,' 'Hang Goebbels,' 'Long live free Austria without Nazis,' 'Hurry up and lose the war.' These signs, which often appeared near streetcar stops where a lot of people always gathered, often lasted for a suspiciously long time, sometimes for three or four days. Everyone pretended not to notice them, but I saw eyes furtively reading them with obvious pleasure. The faces of these Austrians, as they were reading, would express the thought, 'Look how brave we are!'

20. UNDER ST. ANDREW'S FLAG

AFTER the eastern front had been broken through at the Vistula, while the Red Army was besieging Budapest and all Germany was trembling under the daily raids of Anglo-American aircraft, an event occurred which had an important effect on the lives of the many millions of Russians in Germany.

The Russian language papers announced, and it was confirmed by the German Press, that a congress of anti-Bolshevik Russians had met in Prague, which had elected a Committee for the Liberation of the Peoples of Russia, headed by General Vlasov. This committee had published a manifesto with a short political programme. The High Command of the Wehrmacht had agreed to the formation of Russian divisions under Russian command from the volunteers in the German Army. The chairman of the committee, General Vlasov, was appointed commander of the unified Russian troops. The Russian Army of Liberation had been promised its own uniform, distinct from the German, and was to have its own flag, of St. Andrew:* the diagonal blue St. Andrew's cross on a white field.

The strangest thing about all this was that this event, which had taken place on the eve of the total defeat of the Reich, called forth the greatest enthusiasm among the Russian population of Germany. This population was large: about 5,000,000 Ostarbeiter; at least 2,000,000 prisoners of war – all who had survived in the camps of the 5,000,000 prisoners taken since the beginning of the war; and at least 1,000,000 like me who had left Russia of their own free will to escape the advancing Red Army and Comrade Stalin's N.K.V.D. This is a total of at least 8,000,000 at a conservative estimate.

Of course by no means all of these were declaredly anti-Bolshevik. Most of them were passive, realizing the inevitability of Soviet victory in the war. Many of them were trying to get home and hated the Germans and everything connected with them. In the Ostarbeiter and prisoner-of-war camps pro-Soviet elements were spreading intensive propaganda, scaring the others with quick retaliation or promising amnesty and developing fantasies about the 'evolution of the Soviet regime', thereby carving themselves out future careers.

But there were many Russians who were being pushed into a trap with no way out. These could look forward only to very doubtful patronage by the Soviet Union's Western allies after the defeat of Germany. It was among them that the formation of the Committee for the Liberation of the Peoples of Russia called forth indefinite but lively hopes. It seemed to them that the formation of a strong organization supported by its own national army could put the Russian anti-

* The flag of the old Imperial Russian Navy.

Bolshevik cause in Germany on its feet and increase their own chances of salvation.

In addition, many of them thought that even in this unfortunate moment the appearance on the eastern front of General Vlasov's Russian divisions would bring results, that the Red Army would begin to fall apart and would stop fighting against a Germany which was no longer dangerous to Russia, and the whole war might end differently.

Every evening now our apartment was crowded with people talking over the news. We tried to persuade General Kramer to join Vlasov and create a political mission from the committee in Vienna. The general waved his hands and said he would be happy to serve the people but that in all honour he could not offer his services to Vlasov, he must wait until he was invited to join, and so forth.

Apparently events in Prague and Berlin were moving slowly, because after the first reports there was a lengthy silence. The papers said nothing more.

Desiring to become more closely acquainted with what was going on, I asked Count Reder, the head of the office where I was supposedly employed as a journalist, to issue me a paper which would enable me to go to Berlin. At the beginning of winter I set out for the capital of the Reich.

The trip was an uncomfortable one. All the windowpanes of the train were broken, and the wind and snow blew in on those who were unlucky enough to be seated by windows which had not yet been boarded up. The walls of the cars were shot through in places, the result of strafing by Allied fighter planes. Naturally the train was not heated.

During the day when air raids started the train would either stop in an open field or try to get through the next station without stopping. From Prague on, the stations were jammed with people – refugees from eastern Germany running from the Red Army. The picture was the same as in the Ukraine when the great German retreat started, except perhaps that there was more order and the refugees were better cared for by the local authorities.

We reached Berlin at night. I managed to locate a small hotel near the Anhalt station. I had a map of Berlin but I found I had to orient myself. The city was already largely destroyed and many streets were only ruins. But still life went on. The transit system, S-Bahn and U-Bahn, ran quickly and efficiently even during air raids, except in the section of the city actually under bombardment. The streets were crowded. One heard many foreign languages – French, Polish, Italian, Russian.

At noon on my first day in Berlin I found my way to Dahlem, the residential suburb where Vlasov's staff was quartered in several small houses. I had no definite plan. I wanted to see what kind of people were running the movement, what shape it was in, and what prospects it had for the future.

The first house I entered was the office of the organizational section of the committee, which was headed by Major General Malyshkin. People passed from room to room, consulted together, wrote things. There were a few uniforms but the majority were civilians. I sat down and watched. I felt a distinct pleasure in being in the atmosphere of a Russian office after such a long time.

A spectacled man stopped on his way to another room and said, 'Are you waiting for someone?' I got up.

'No one in particular. I've just come from Vienna.'

'From Vienna? Very good. Has a mission from the committee been organized there yet?'

'Not yet, but it may be soon.'

'Are you going to take part in it?'

'That I don't know yet. I came here to look around and decide.'

'Do you want to talk to someone?

'With pleasure, but I don't know with whom.'

'If you can wait, the general will receive you in an hour.'

An hour later I was sitting in a chair in the general's office. He had a simple, typically Russian face with intelligent, light grey eyes, and was wearing a German general's uniform without the swastika.

'I've been told that you've come from Vienna. Tell me something about yourself,' said the general.

I told him as concisely as possible who I was, how I came to be abroad, and what I was doing.

'You probably want to ask me about something. Please feel free to do so,' he said.

'Could you clarify the objectives of the committee for me?'

'Certainly. The committee was created for the unification of anti-Bolshevik Russian forces in Germany. You've read the manifesto. Our practical problems are as follows: To create a united Russian political centre; to give all possible material and legal aid to Ostarbeiter and prisoners of war in camps; to create a Russian army of liberation; to propagandize our ideas abroad and in Russia.'

I interrupted him.

'With your permission I should like to find out what the relationship of the committee is with the existing national centres: the Byelorussian, Ukrainian, and others.'

'That's a hard question. We have invited them to unite with us. But some of those people are very nationalistic and anti-Russian. They are encouraged by Rosenberg's East Ministry and at present there is no chance of full union. We are creating parallel national sections within the committee and I am sure that most of the people who at present cling to rival organizations will come over to us.'

'As I understand it, Rosenberg is against Vlasov and the committee. Who supports you in the German Government?'

'Himmler, and to a certain extent, Goebbels.'

'What does Hitler think of it?'

'If anything, he's probably opposed to it. He hasn't said anything about Vlasov and he won't. But Himmler and Goebbels have a lot of independent power at the present time and their support will be decisive. Hitler won't interfere.'

'What is the army's attitude?'

'The army has been resisting the movement and continues to do so. Keitel does not want to surrender the Russian military units now under his command to Vlasov. But he'll have to obey Himmler's order.'

'What can be done to make things easier for our prisoners of war and workers?'

'We've been promised that the Ostarbeiter are going to have equal rights and rations with other foreigners. Himmler has issued a categorical order forbidding Russians being punished or beaten. The OST insignia that they all had to wear earlier have been abolished.'

'How have these orders been carried out in practice?'

'Not too well. Nobody has any real check on what the local German authorities do in their area. But if the committee develops branches in various places, this will be easier.'

'What about the formation of the army?'

'As I have already said, the German High Command is obstructing us in every way. But the work goes on. The first division of the R.O.A. is now being formed. Recruiting in prisoner-of-war camps is continuing.'

'Successfully?'

'Not too successfully. You see, I am being completely frank with you. You understand that the moment is not a propitious one and the position on the front is bad. However, people are still coming to us, people who are strongly anti-Bolshevik.'

'You spoke of spreading propaganda in Russia. How are you going to do that?'

'The situation is good as far as that's concerned. More than any of our other objectives that coincides with German plans. Millions of leaflets are being printed and dropped behind the Red Army's lines. We also have the radio at our disposal and we publish three newspapers.'

'Do you believe in the final success of this whole enterprise?' I asked. The general thought for a moment and then said:

'It's hard to say. But there's no way out of our position. One way or another, Germany has lost the war. There's an agreement between Stalin and his allies to return to Russia all Russians who left there after 1939. If we are scattered and disunited they'll catch us all, send us home, and destroy us. If we can create an army, even five divisions, say, and gather all non-military anti-Bolshevik Russians under its protection, our situation can change radically. We'll have some bargaining power with the Allies. Finally, if all our plans are realized and the R.O.A. is strong and is sent to the eastern front, who knows? Maybe the situation will change there, too.'

'Why haven't the Germans allowed Russian units on the eastern front so far?'

'In the first place they are afraid that there will be desertions to the other side. There's no basis at all for that fear. Secondly, they are afraid of the opposite, that there will be desertions from the Red Army to us, and the R.O.A. will become too strong and the anti-German temper in its ranks will grow, thereby playing into the hands of the enemy. And then the German leaders have not been able to agree among themselves on the problem of the committee.'

'Do you think that any agreement can be made with the Western Allies before the end of the war?'

'I'm sorry, but I cannot answer that question. Everything that has to do with that is a secret. You can be certain, however, that everything possible will be done to save the Russians here.'

'Thank you. Now everything is more or less clear in my mind.'

'Well, what have you decided? Will you take part in organizing a branch of the committee in Vienna?'

'With what function?'

'Purely political. Propaganda, aid to Ostarbeiter and prisoners of war, information, liaison with the committee.'

'I can't tell you definitely about myself yet. But I'll try to help you in general. Who is being considered to head the branch in Vienna?'

'Nobody as yet. Can you recommend anyone?'

'There is a General Kramer there. He was a general in the White Army and lived in Belgrade before the war. He's not bad, but he has a large entourage.'

'Well, every White general has an entourage like that. We have to accept that. In any case, we'll look into it. Meanwhile, give the matter some thought. A representative of the committee will go to Vienna soon to prepare the ground in high German circles. Leave your address in the office. I'd like you to talk to some of the people there. Try to collect more people from the Soviet Union and fewer from among the Whites . . .'

I took leave of him.

I stayed in Berlin another three days, wandering from one little house in Dahlem to another. My general impression was favourable. Most of the people were young, sincere, and firm anti-Bolsheviks. It was obvious that they were going about their jobs with great intensity, in spite of opposition from the Germans.

I observed all this, thinking: it's late, too late. If all this had started even a year ago, the chances for success would have been much greater.

I saw Vlasov too, while I was cooling my heels in the office of his assistant, Lieutenant-General Zhilenkov. An enormous man, in a general's overcoat with no insignia of rank, a Russian tricolour badge in his cap, and wearing glasses, he immediately filled the small reception room with his person. I noticed expressions of great respect, mixed with great admiration, on the faces of everyone present.

Stopping for a moment at a desk, he asked in a ringing bass voice, 'Well, how are things, gentlemen? Are the Germans surrendering?'

'It's bad, Andrei Andreevich, they're still holding out,' said General Zhilenkov's adjutant.

'*Nichevo*, that's all right. We'll break their sides in for them. Fight hard. What we're doing is right. If we can only fix the Germans, we'll have no trouble taking care of the Bolsheviks!'

He disappeared into the office, talking as he went.

At that time and later I met various people from Vlasov's movement. Many of them were intelligent, personable, serious minded, and well acquainted with conditions; in some of them I sensed a fanatical desire to take part in the fight against the Bolsheviks.

Vlasov himself was probably not distinguished by a particularly sharp or deep mind. He often said the wrong thing or more than was necessary. But he possessed something which the others did not: great personal charm and an inner power which set him off from the people surrounding him and made him the perfectly logical choice for the leadership of the whole movement. It was said that his influence on the mass of the soldiers was almost unlimited and that whenever he spoke invisible threads of mutual understanding stretched between him and every member of his audience. One could feel that he was a man of the people who had not lost his spiritual connection with the people. He fully shared the life of his comrades in arms.

I think that Vlasov's anti-Bolshevism was an organic feeling rather than a theoretically thought-out political position. He had many of the characteristics of a Soviet leader, of the career military commander that he had been all of his adult life. His attitude toward White emigrants was always somewhat suspicious; he could not stand monarchists, but from political considerations he controlled himself and they often left him enchanted by his courtesy and kindness.

That is what happened to General Kramer. Upon my return to Vienna I convinced him that he should go to Berlin to talk to Vlasov about organizing a branch of the committee in Vienna. He went, together with his old friend General T., a famous hero of the White movement, and returned a week later fully convinced of everything the committee stood for. He had received full authorization for organizaiontal activities in the territory of former Austria.

On the way back from Berlin I witnessed a terrible event: the bombing of Dresden. The air-raid warning caught us in an open field. The train stopped about 12 miles from Dresden. There was nowhere to run and hide, so most of the passengers, myself included, left the train and took cover in a small clump of trees.

The sky was clear and everything was plainly visible. The mass of planes closed in on the city from several directions and unloaded their bombs. The ground trembled and there were blasts in the air from the distant explosions. Probably a great many incendiary bombs were dropped, because we could see columns of smoke and flame appear over the city in several places. The raid did not last long but it was horribly effective.

When the planes had gone we returned to the train, thinking that everything was calm now, although we were afraid that the railroad had been cut and we would not be able to proceed beyond Dresden.

The train did not start. No all-clear siren had been heard. The horizon was covered with smoke. Suddenly we heard again the awful roar of hundreds of planes overhead, flying at a great height. We raced back to the woods, and just in time. Two bombs fell, one hitting the tail end of our train and smashing several cars.

Dresden was again the target. The bombing of the burning city went on for another half hour. I think that this time the bombs were bigger.

At last everything was quiet. The bombers had gone for good.

There was a lot of activity at the end of the train. People were dragging the killed and wounded out of the wrecked coaches. The bodies were left in the field; two of the cars which had not been hit were cleared for the wounded. The unhurt passengers crowded into the remaining cars with some difficulty and the train started.

A few miles from Dresden it stopped again. The tracks ahead had been ripped up by bombs. Since I had no baggage, I started to walk toward the city. The closer I got the more horrified I was at the results of the raid. Apparently everything had been bombed, without distinction. There never were any large plants or much production of war matériel in Dresden, and this, the first raid of the war on the city, I thought, might just as well be the last. Everything that had not been flattened was burning.

Even Germans who had seen a good deal of the war felt lost. An old captain, walking beside me, was saying to someone, 'This was a terrible raid! There were several hundred thousand refugees from eastern Germany in Dresden; they were living in the streets and squares because the houses were so crowded. The damned Americans, look at the way they make war! What do they want? To have nothing left of Germany? Do they want the Red flag to fly over the ruins of our Fatherland? They'll win the war, but they don't know yet how much they will have lost!'

I had to walk all the way around the city; railroad traffic was re-sumed only at the second station beyond Dresden. I must have tramped about 10 miles and felt completely worn out.

A few days later a committee member, Yurii Zherebkov, arrived from Berlin: He was the head of Vlasov's section for foreign relations. I had heard a lot about him while I was in Berlin. He was from the old emigration but was still young and had recently come from France, where before the war he had been a dancer in a night club or something of the sort. After the occupation he had developed some shady relation-ship with the German authorities, and to everyone's surprise, he was suddenly appointed the head of the Russian emigration in France, in his own way a small Führer, as Kramer had been in Serbia. After the Allied invasion of Normandy he fled to Germany, and by Himmler's personal orders was included in the committee when it was formed in Prague. Everyone regarded him with suspicion. It was generally said that Vlasov had often tried to get rid of him, suspecting him correctly of being a German agent, but so far this had proved impossible. The Germans were very suspicious of Vlasov and limited his activities whenever possible. They had reason to believe he had definite anti-German leanings.

However, when Zherebkov came in to see us late one evening and I had talked with him for a while, he did not make a bad impression on me. There was no doubt that he was intelligent. He spoke French and German perfectly, was well bred and reserved. There was also no doubt that his connections with the Germans were excellent, because on the very next day he was received in personal audience by the Reichsleiter of Vienna, Baldur von Schirach.

I did not consider that good relations with the Germans were necessarily against him. Obviously, without the Germans Vlasov's whole enterprise was doomed to failure, even in the scope in which it was conceived. However, it was a repellent thought that in a Russian national movement there was a Russian who was hand in glove with potential enemies of that movement.

Zherebkov left a couple of days later, having received permission from the local authorities for the formation of an affiliate of the com-mittee in Vienna.

Kramer, in his new role as the committee's chief plenipotentiary, asked me to take part in the work in whatever capacity attracted me most. I had nothing to lose, and at that time it seemed that some results might perhaps be achieved. Therefore I assumed the functions of a general organizer: the recruiting of personnel and assignment of duties to them, as well as the organization of aid for Russian workers and prisoners of war in German camps.

There was a lot to think about. By the end of my first month's work in the movement I was convinced nothing could be expected from the Germans but promises and perhaps good intentions. Very few of them actually had our interests at heart or tried to help us in our work by their own desire.

One of these few was a certain Klug, an inspector in the Vienna propaganda department. Klug turned out to be a good fellow, and whenever I needed German support I always went to him and always found him willing to help. If some camp commandant had to be punished for cruelty to the workers, or some camp kitchen had to be investigated for theft of food, or a maid had to be rescued from her sadistic German mistress, I invariably asked Klug for assistance and he always did what he could. I think he believed in the success of the Vlasov committee more than I did, and like us he butted his head against the hard wall of German routine, trying to achieve a change of attitude toward the 'people from the east'.

Sometimes, however, even he despaired, and then he would say, 'Our Führer, of course, is a great man, but he is surrounded by fanatics and idiots. If he doesn't get rid of them we shall lose the war!'

'I'm afraid that you've lost it no matter what happens,' I would say.

'Oh, no. You're not acquainted with the facts. A terrible new weapon has been invented which can change the whole course of the war. It will be used any day now; soon, you'll see.'

'It's too late. Soon your enemies will be fighting on German soil and then your new secret weapon will destroy Germans along with Allied troops.'

Klug would breathe heavily and shake his head.

But he did not give up, and worked a great deal, sometimes spending all night at the office. In particular, his efforts made it possible for General Kramer to move from a small hotel room to the building of the old Soviet Embassy to Austria. These new offices greatly enhanced our prestige in the eyes of the German authorities. The place was full from morning till night. More and more people who needed protection from the Germans and material and legal aid came to us. The staff spent days and days visiting camps, trying with all their strength to make life easier for the prisoners of war and the Ostarbeiter.

Yet I was becoming increasingly disappointed in my job. I spent more and more evenings at home instead of in various camps. I felt that with the situation at the fronts so increasingly unfavourable to the Germans, more and more people were turning away from us. No mass support was being created for the movement, and it was becoming less and less certain that it was necessary. What was there for the masses to support? What did the Vlasov committee want from people? Volunteers for the R.O.A.? But it was quite plain that to enter the R.O.A. on the eve of the death of the Third Reich was madness. We had information that Vlasov had had a great deal of trouble pulling

R.O.A. units out of the army to organize the R.O.A.'s single division, and had only recently started on the second one. The German High Command was obstinate in its refusal to release Russian soldiers from the front.

Under such conditions, why were contacts needed among the mass of the Russian workers and soldiers in the camps? We could not help them substantially; there was no doubt about that. We could do very little to make their lives easier at the moment, but we could compromise them badly in case of a Soviet occupation.

I decided to go to Karlsbad where Vlasov and the committee had moved from Berlin, to talk to the people there and present to them my proposals for future policies of the committee. These proposals were based on the assumption of Germany's defeat in the very near future. I advised the union of the R.O.A. with the Cossack regiments in northern Italy, the occupation of a small amount of territory on the Austro-Italian frontier, and the evacuation there of all who wanted to flee from the Red Army and the revenge of the advancing 'liberators'. Through friends I had connections with the Cossack staff in Italy, and I knew that it would support this plan. In addition, conversations were being held with commanders of various German units who expressed a willingness to come under Vlasov's command and share his fate.

Of course, even should my plan be realized it did not mean that all of us would be saved. However, it seemed to me that it created conditions which would make it possible for us to bargain with the Allies independently of the Germans.

I also suggested that, in case it was impossible to implement this plan, R.O.A. units should be demobilized immediately, secret arms and ammunition supply points created, and the officers and soldiers should be converted to civilian status to allow them to scatter through Germany and await a better time, retaining the wherewithal to fight again.

In general it was obvious to me that now, in February, 1945, we could count only on our own powers and had to be ready for the cry to arise at any moment, 'Save yourself as best you can!' Of course, while the Germans were still willing to give us things and make concessions, it was imperative to get the maximum benefits out of them. But we had to be ready to grab what we could for ourselves in the approaching chaos.

Armed with all the necessary documents, signed by Kramer, I set out for Karlsbad. This journey was much more complicated than my previous one to Berlin. American planes hovered almost constantly over central Germany during the day. In Passau, Regensburg, and Eger my train was caught in air raids and I had to scurry to station bunkers.

This made the sight of Karlsbad, when I finally emerged from the train there, a great contrast to what I had seen during the trip. A peaceful, very colourful town, it was situated in a narrow valley, with a river flowing through the middle of the town. There were no signs of bombing and there was not a single anti-aircraft battery on the surrounding heights. The place contained no military headquarters or industry. It was full of wounded, and numerous hospitals, converted from prewar hotels, with big red crosses on their roofs, served as shields and protected Karlsbad from raids.

I had business with General Zhilenkov, head of the propaganda section and, as it was said, Vlasov's right-hand man. Another big department under the committee was the civilian section, also directed by a former Soviet general by the name of Zarudny. A third ex-Soviet general was Malyshkin, whom I had met in Berlin, and a fourth was Trukhin, Vlasov's chief of staff. The two latter were the most admirable personalities in the management of the committee. Both were intelligent and undoubtedly sincere in their anti-Bolshevik ideas, and in spite of the confused situation prevailing at the time they both retained their clarity of mind and purity of purpose.

I visited General Malyshkin in his room.

'For God's sake tell me frankly, Vassily Feodorovich,' I asked him, 'what you are still hoping for? For help from the British and Americans?'

He shook his head.

'Personally, I have no hopes at all,' he said in a dull voice. 'There were supposed to be conversations with them in Switzerland. Zherebkov was supposed to attend to that, but I'm sure he never got beyond Himmler's office. But even if the Allies should make us promises of some kind, there would be no use hoping that they would keep them. Stalin has them where he wants them.'

'Well, what then?' I probed. 'What can be done? Couldn't we organize a local defence? Couldn't we collect the troops we do have, pull away from the Germans, and capitulate independently?'

'Nonsense. What could two or three divisions do? If we resist, they'll bomb us until there's nothing left. If we surrender, they'll hand us over to Stalin.'

'How about getting to Spain or Switzerland?'

'It's too late for Spain now. That should have been done at the end of last summer. If we do it now we'll lose three-quarters of our personnel. And it would be impossible to take the civilians along on such an expedition. Switzerland is out: they would hand us over.'

'If that's the case there's only one thing left for us: everyone for himself. If we can't help the people we have no right to keep them in the R.O.A. We've got to give them the chance to save themselves individually. Give them money, clothing, documents, and disband them. An R.O.A. uniform will mean the firing squad for certain if they fall into the hands of the N.K.V.D.'

Malyshkin waved his hand.

'I know all that; I've known for a long time. Maybe disbanding our men would be the correct decision. But it's too late now. The machine has been wound up and it's working now on its own power and it will continue to work until it's destroyed along with Germany. Well, there won't be long to wait. Already it's almost impossible to get to Berlin from here. The fronts are closing in from both sides. Vlasov and Zhilenkov still believe they can make a deal with the Americans. I don't believe in anything any more.'

'What would you say to the R.O.A. turning against the Germans and fighting them?'

'That would be low and dishonourable. We're not Rumanians or Hungarians. We're Russians. Maybe the Germans have fooled us and broken their promises. That leaves our hands free for independent action. But they at least trust us. And we won't stab them in the back. We're not Communists!'

'Well, what's left?'

'For us, the gallows probably. But you and your friends, you're free to make your own decision. You've got to try and save yourself. Can I help you in any way?'

'Thank you, I don't know. Perhaps you could give me another appointment. I want to leave Kramer as soon as possible.'

'His Excellency is getting on your nerves? I understand. What sort of a paper do you need?'

'Appoint me the committee's representative, a fictitious one of course, somewhere near the Italian border. I'll take care of the rest myself.'

'All right, I'll tell Levitsky. Anything else?'

'I don't think so. Goodbye, Vassily Feodorovich. I'm really no less pessimistic than you, but still I want to wish you and all of those with you the best of luck. I hope you'll be able to save yourselves. Perhaps we'll meet again.'

He shook his head.

'If everything crashes and they begin to destroy our soldiers and officers, we won't have the right to save our own necks. Neither Vlasov nor Trukhin nor Zhilenkov will try to save themselves. There are situations when everyone must perish together.'

'Yes, like a captain going down with his ship . . .'

'Yes, like a captain. Many mistakes have been made but blood washes away a great deal. In our efforts there was a spark of something great and clean, and that must be preserved for the future. Good-bye.'

I left him with a heavy heart.

The next day, having obtained an order from Malyshkin's office appointing me the committee's representative in Klagenfurt, in southern Austria, I took leave of all my new friends. In the lobby I ran into Vlasov. He recognized me and said, 'I'm going to Berlin right away.

I'm going to try to do everything possible and impossible. Tell them in Vienna not to lose heart. Not everything is lost yet. Goodbye.'

He left the hotel, followed by Zhilenkov and two S.S. men. A minute later his car disappeared around the bend.

In his trail, I set out for the station myself.

This time I went by way of Prague, where I had to change trains. I took a walk around this amazing city, untouched by bombs or war, perhaps the only such under German rule.

When I got back to Vienna, however, I learned from the newspapers that even Prague had been raided shortly after I had left.

21. THE CRASH

THE situation in Vienna had become noticeably tense while I was away. The Soviet front was fast approaching the borders of Austria. Hungary had been completely occupied already, as well as about half of Slovakia and all but a portion of Croatia next to the border. At the same time it seemed as if the Americans and British were slowing up; in Italy they had not reached the Po and in Germany they had not yet entered Bavaria.

General Kramer was entirely indifferent to the fact that I was leaving. He went to Karlsbad shortly after my return. While I was transferring my affairs to my friend Nikolai Ayrov, the latter and I managed to do a series of good deeds, which consisted mainly of giving out documents to all who wanted them, enabling them to leave Vienna in a westerly direction. Without such papers it was impossible to get passage on the railroads. Some time earlier I had equipped myself with a duplicate of our Vienna office seal, and now, when people who wanted to flee found themselves up against the stone wall of the bureaucracy introduced by Kramer and his Belgrade adjutants, I was able to help them 'through the back door'.

In addition to this we developed a means of obtaining papers for those who wanted to go to Italy, since the documents issued by our office were not valid there. We got them through a Volksdeutsche from Russia working in the Vienna section of the East Ministry, an extremely pleasant man who loved Russia and things Russian. All the time I was in Vienna this man, Flescher by name, ran this office, and I know that very few Russians were ever refused a request which it was within Flescher's power to grant.

He helped Ostarbeiter, prisoners of war, and emigrants whenever they got into trouble. He wrote admonitory letters to camps whose inmates were treated particularly badly. He arranged for passports, apartments, and even financial relief. All this was done with no desire for gain on his part, although at times people made a lot of money through his help. He knew that some of the people who came to him with requests were fooling him and using him for their own ends, but when he was told about it he would answer, 'What difference does it make? Suppose someone does get something out of me. It's all the better for him, and none the worse for me.'

When I asked for passes to Italy for several people, he said, after thinking a while, 'You see, strictly speaking I have no right to do that and could even be punished for issuing such passes. But considering that the days of the Third Reich are numbered, I'll do it, and I'll keep on doing it in the future.'

Kramer returned from Karlsbad with the announcement that Vlasov had authorized him and his friend General T. to form a 'separate corps' of the R.O.A. with headquarters in Salzburg, and that the Vienna section of the committee must move there immediately. A thorough mess resulted. After an unsuccessful attempt to get a few railroad coaches for themselves, their families, and baggage, the staff stopped appearing in the office, each one searching for some means to get himself out of Vienna. Kramer bought himself a car (where the money came from, no one knew), and his aides tore all over the city searching for gasoline, offering gold, German marks, and American dollars for it.

One morning I went to the office and found it deserted. The rooms were unlocked, the desks stood with open drawers containing all sorts of papers, records of the staff, and lists of volunteers recruited for the R.O.A. in Vienna.

I locked the door and left, returning after lunch with Nikolai Ayrov, and we spent the afternoon burning papers in front of the building, right on the street. Not a policeman appeared.

Vienna continued to be bombed occasionally, but we had noticed a long time ago that the anti-aircraft batteries had stopped trying to defend the city. Everyone said that there was not enough ammunition, that it had all been taken somewhere, either to the Tyrol or to southern Bavaria, where a last ditch defence was being planned and Hitler was supposedly sending the best units of what was left of the German Army and the eagles of the Hitler Youth.

During this period there was one terrible raid on Vienna during which the centre of the city suffered, including many historic buildings – the Cathedral of St. Stephen, the Parliament, the Opera House, the Municipal Theatre, the Rathaus, and others. This raid was pointless and unnecessary; everything was crumbling without help from the bombers.

Most of my friends had already gone west, some to Salzburg, others to Innsbruck in the Tyrol, some to the Italian border. Some, counting on the swift arrival of the Americans, had set out for Munich.

I kept delaying my departure. Leaving the Gorskys to arrange for our transportation, I spent my time with Flescher, visiting the Russian workers' camps around Vienna, making sure for myself that none of the camp commanders were preventing the workers from leaving town if they wanted to. Von Schirach had given orders to that effect, but sometimes the commandant would make deals with the management of the factories which were still operating, and hold up the workers.

The workers who left were supposed to be issued a week's rations and 50 marks.

I expected that few of the Russian workers who had been brought to Germany by force would want to flee to the west. Their only crime in the eyes of the Soviet authorities was that they had observed the different and better life led by the Germans and could compare it with life at home to the disadvantage of the latter. They had a good chance of leniency upon their return to the U.S.S.R. Their life in Germany had not been much better than that of the prisoners of war. Pro-Soviet agents had been energetically at work among them for a long time, threatening them with dire consequences if they tried to escape and were caught. Most of the Russian workers knew no German and had no means of any kind.

Nevertheless, there were still thousands who wanted to go west. What did they want? What were they looking for? Probably many of them could not have explained it. But as the 'liberators' drew near, the old fear and hatred of the Soviet regime, unforgotten through the years of the war, began to arise again in the mass of workers, feelings that were more organic than conscious. And many of them fled.

Flescher said that in many of the camps where the Nazi commandants had tried to keep the workers there had been killings and beatings. In one camp the commandant was hanged, two others were knifed, still another was lynched by a mob. Such killings had taken place before, in protest against the cruelty of the camp administration or the guards, but the Germans had seldom been able to find the guilty ones. Now such incidents were happening more and more often.

We were still not ready to leave Vienna. A group of about fifteen of us had gathered, and since the trains were no longer running we had to find some other means of transportation. We collected some money, and Zina and Igor, together with our friend Nikolai Ayrov, who was the leader of a similar group, bought two wagons. One had two horses, the other only one. Our group drew the single horse. It was big and strong and bore the original name of Fritz, but it was lame in one hind leg. This time, unlike that far-off occasion in the northern Caucasus, we were not afraid to travel with a horse. We had in our group a former colonel in the White Army and a Cossack captain, both of whom were excellent horsemen.

We took the wagon to the outskirts of Vienna, on the left bank of the Danube, to the captain's house. From an Austrian I bought a small radio, to help orient us as to the position on the fronts. The Austrian papers no longer printed correct information, and the Austrians themselves almost never listened to foreign broadcasts although they had every opportunity to do so.

'It's strictly forbidden,' said my acquaintance when I would ask them to pick up the London B.B.C. 'We cannot break the law.'

The front was now about 30 miles away. All sorts of errands distracted me, and I had not yet assembled the necessary documents for the journey. To ensure that everyone would eat on the way we had to have military documents. After a great deal of trouble I managed to get a few blank *Marschbefehl* forms. I had the necessary seal, and it was easy to sign the name of the proper official. Klug, my friend in the propaganda department, who had stayed behind, the last in his office, to burn files, issued me a document stating that I was to escort a vital convoy of goods and people to Italy. In this document I was a captain . . .

Since I was a captain I had to acquire a uniform. This I did not succeed in doing, so I had to be satisfied with a military shirt with Cossack shoulder straps which a friend supplied me. In civilian trousers and shoes and without a cap, my military appearance was doubtful. However, a small pistol peeped bravely out from behind my belt.

Nikolai Ayrov did not wait for us but left three days ahead of us with his group. We agreed to meet him in Salzburg. We had decided against the direct route to the Italian border through Klagenfurt, because of reports that advance units of the Red Army had penetrated as far as Wiener Neustadt, which was on the way. There were two other possible routes: directly west to St. Pölten, or, if the worst came to the worst, north-west along the left bank of the Danube.

Everyone was impatient to leave, but we lost another day thanks to Flescher. Although I had said good-bye to him the day before, Flescher arrived in the morning and asked me to accompany him on a visit to a prisoner-of-war camp east of Vienna.

As we were approaching the camp, moving slowly through the flood of refugees from the east, we could hear the sound of artillery fire. The front was quite near, but there were few German soldiers around and the only army vehicles we saw were moving west, away from the front.

The camp turned out to be a group of dirty barracks surrounded by barbed wire. There were two guards at the gate, but they let us through without a word. A crowd of men were moving about in front of the barracks, dressed in olive-drab Soviet military overcoats with the letters S.U. painted on their backs in black. A grey-haired prisoner approached us and introduced himself as the camp elder.

'Call the men together,' said Flescher. 'I want to speak to them.'

'Everybody's here,' said the spokesman. 'All you have to do is shout.'

'Wait a minute,' said Flescher. 'How many men have you got here?'

'A little less than 2,000.'

'What's their attitude toward the possible arrival of the Red Army?'

'I'll be damned if I can figure it out,' shrugged the elder. 'Of course, a lot of them would like to run for it, and our guards have said that they will let anyone out who wants to go, but they can't make up their minds. Where can you go without documents and without money? And in the last few weeks the Soviet propagandists have achieved results. They promise that Stalin will forgive everybody. They hanged two men last night who were trying to persuade everyone to leave camp. See, the bodies are still there.' He pointed to two motionless forms by the barbed wire.

'All right, make the men be quiet. I'll talk to them,' said Flescher.

The elder began to shout, 'Quiet, quiet everybody! Listen! We're going to get the latest news. Bring a table, quick!'

A table appeared from somewhere and Flescher got up on it, handing me his thick briefcase. When the men had gathered around him and become reasonably quiet, he began:

'Listen, soldiers! Germany has lost the war. Surrender is possible any day now. Units of the Red Army may be here tonight. There won't be any resistance until Vienna. You are free to do as you like. Those of you who want to can stay here and wait for the Russians. Or you can start moving toward them. Or those of you who want to can go west to the places the Americans and English will occupy . . .'

At this point everyone started shouting at once. I could distinguish a few of the phrases:

'Who is he, what does he want?'

'Down with the Fascist agitator!'

'Let's get him!'

'Quiet, let's listen to him!'

'Shut up, you bastards!'

'Down with the Communists!'

The elder and a few men that he called over gathered around us. I began to be somewhat frightened. If anything happened, it would be impossible to get away. I glanced back at the gate and saw the two guards looking with curiosity at the boiling mob. Flescher stood on the table, very pale, waiting for a chance to speak. After a short time he took advantage of a break in the noise to continue.

'I beg you hear me out! Nobody's trying to force anyone to go anywhere. But nobody should try to interfere with anyone either. I cannot do very much for those who want to go west. I can only issue group documents, one for every group of fifty men, to go to Munich, and 50 marks for each man. You'll also get some rations . . .'

The shouting began again. Under pressure from the crowd the table began to shake, but Flescher kept his balance. 'Those of you who want to go west,' he shouted over the noise, 'leave the camp one by one. You'll get your money as you come out. There will be a document for each group.'

He jumped down off the table, and just in time. A piece of metal, hurled by somebody in the crowd, flew over the table and hit someone on the head.

Surrounded by several prisoners, we reached the gate safely.

The guards let us through with obvious unwillingness. I think it would have amused them more to watch us being lynched in there.

There were about six prisoners with us, headed by the elder. Flescher turned to the guards.

'Hold your guns ready. Let them out one at a time. If there's any kind of disorder, fire in the air.'

'And who might you be?' one of the guards asked suddenly. 'You'd better go and find Hitler and save him, and leave these people alone. They want to go home, and where are you herding them to?'

Flescher grew still paler. 'Silence, dog! It's none of your business. Do what you're ordered to!'

The guard backed up, holding his submachine gun pointed at Flescher. The latter suddenly whipped out a revolver and fired. The guard, wounded in the arm, dropped his weapon. At that moment the camp elder knocked the other guard's gun out of his hands. Flescher nodded approvingly.

'Take the weapons yourselves and maintain order. Nobody who wants to go is to be held up. Is that clear?'

'Quite clear, Comrade Commander!' a few voices answered simultaneously. A crowd had collected near the gate and was watching us through the barbed wire. Flescher took some *Marschbefehl* forms out of his briefcase and handed them to me.

'Write their names down on the other side.'

'Let them out one by one,' he added, turning toward the spokesman. The gate was opened. There was a moment of confusion. Nobody came out. The roar of many voices hung over the camp. Then the first men began to come.

'Name?' Flescher asked.

'Andreev, Ivan,' said the first. I wrote it down. Flescher drew a bill out of an envelope full of money and gave it to him, showing him where to stand. They began to issue in a steady stream. When fifty men had collected and elected a group leader, Flescher gave him a document with a roster on the back and commanded: 'Group, attention! You're free! To the west, forward march!'

The second, third, and fourth groups were collected and sent off. Most of them came through the gate empty-handed, but some had small bundles of belongings. The noise in camp did not diminish. There were shouts of 'Bastards, traitors to the fatherland! Fascists!' and other answering shouts, 'Spies! God-damned N.K.V.D. swine! You didn't get away with it, you sons of bitches!'

The two prisoners standing at the gate with submachine guns shouted, 'Don't crowd, men! Get in line. You'll get to America, don't push! Hey, you there, no fighting! Hey!' And they would fire into the air whenever serious fights started. A tall, gaunt prisoner, who had relieved another on the submachine gun, shot a man through the wire.

'Hey, what are you doing?' Flescher dashed at him.

'That's the worst one of all, Comrade Commander,' the man with the gun answered calmly. 'He's been making up lists for a long time to give to the N.K.V.D. if they came. A dog deserves a dog's death. They'll all thank me for it. Listen, see, it's quieter already. More men are coming out.'

He was right. Things went more smoothly. When the camp was half empty Flescher handed the blank forms and the money to the elder.

'You fix the rest up yourself. There will be enough money. There was 100,000 marks when we started. All the passes are signed. Good luck!'

The elder shook hands with us warmly.

'Thanks for coming. We didn't know what to do. Some of the men were talking about hanging themselves before the "liberators" come, God damn them . . .'

In the car I asked Flescher where he had got so much money, and all the passes. He shrugged his shoulders.

'I took the money out of the bank,' he said. 'It's all that was left in the East Ministry account. Rosenberg won't need it any more. I have some more money at home. I got the blank forms from a regimental commander that I know, a very good man.'

'When are you going to leave Vienna?'

'I don't know. I'm going to stay here till the last moment, while I can still do something. What about you?'

'I've been meaning to leave for the last three days. Everything's ready.'

'Have you got a car?'

'A car? Hell no. One horse and a wagon for fifteen people. We'll walk.'

'Why didn't you tell me before? I could have found you one. But it's too late today. And tomorrow, who knows what will happen? Which road are you taking?'

'I don't know, probably west to St. Pölten. Why?'

'Don't go that way. Vienna is being by-passed on the south and the Reds might get to St. Pölten ahead of you. Go along the left bank.'

'All right, if you say so.' I got out of his car at my house and shook hands with him warmly. 'Maybe we'll meet again; I hope so. Good-bye.'

'I doubt it,' said Flescher. 'There will be a mess now. If you can, get out of Germany and Austria. Things won't be good here . . .'

His car pulled away and disappeared around the corner.

There was a note from Zina on the table in my room, 'Everything is ready for us to leave. Come to the captain's immediately. We're starting tonight, can't wait any longer. Dinner's in the kitchen. Bring the radio. Zina.'

I was a bit annoyed at the categorical tone of the note. After all, I was the leader of the expedition and had all the necessary documents in my pocket. But after I had tuned the radio in to the B.B.C. and laid the dinner out on the table, I felt considerably better. They couldn't leave without me, anyway.

After eating I rested a little. The radio announced that northern Germany had been cut off from the south, that Berlin was almost surrounded, that American troops had entered Bavaria, that the fall of Vienna was expected in a couple of days . . .

It was growing dark fast. I took the radio under my arm, said good-bye to the janitor, asking him not to disturb the papers in my apartment before the Reds came – there was a lot of anti-Soviet literature there – and left the house.

The streets were empty. I could have taken one of the rare evening trolleys, but I preferred to walk the length of the city. I felt no fatigue at all, though the day had been a hard one.

I came out into the Ring by Schwarzenberg-Platz, reached the ruined Opera House, and turned into the narrow streets of the First District. Here and there I passed wrecked buildings. The pavements in some places were blocked with debris, which for several days now no one had tried to clear away. There was very little light. Only an occasional blue bulb partially disclosed the extent of the damage.

Poor beautiful Vienna! What will happen to you when you come into the possession of my countrymen? Almost as if in answer to my thoughts the distant hum of airplane engines came to my ears. There was no air-raid alarm. The anti-aircraft batteries had been silent for several days. In the distance I could hear the reports of exploding bombs.

Crossing a canal, I walked along the Prater. Thoughts ran through my mind at random. I had come to know so many streets and attractive places in Vienna. For some reason I thought of our walks in the Vienna woods and the small restaurant on a hill where we had had dinner when we happened on it by accident as we wandered through the thick growth of trees. Then I remembered swimming off a boat in the Danube and how I had almost drowned while making for an island with little Nina on my shoulders. I remembered the 'giant wheel' and the 'Lilliputian train' on the Prater, and then a moving-picture with the Italian tenor Beniamino Gigli.

Halfway over the big Franz-Josef Bridge I stopped and looked at the Danube. If it flowed in the opposite direction, I thought, it would be red with blood. A few miles downstream the Red Army was crossing to the left bank.

The suburbs were beginning. I increased my pace, finding my way with difficulty through this unfamiliar section where there were no street lights on at all.

It was midnight by the time I found the captain's house. Everyone was there, but no one except little Nina was asleep. The wagon, heaped high, stood in the gateway. Fritz was chewing his oats in a detached way in the yard. I had a distinct sensation that something was missing from this picture. Then I realized what it was. Our puppy, a big dog now, was not there. Some months earlier, having nothing to feed it, we had to give it away to a friendly German who worked as a guard at the airport.

We crowded into a small room. I told them the latest news and explained that we would have to move along the left bank to Krems, where we might cross to the other side if the situation permitted. This seriously lengthened the journey to Salzburg, but we had no choice. The risk of falling into the hands of the 'comrades' was too great.

Everybody decided to try to get some sleep before the hard day ahead. I went outside and stretched out on the wagon on top of the baggage. I still had no desire to sleep.

Another period of my life has ended, I thought. Again I've got to run for it. Where? How far will I have to go this time? Where will the end be? When can I stop being a fugitive and become a normal human being? I was confused. I tried to ask myself whether I had made any mistakes during the year I had lived in the Reich, but I put aside my own questions. What meaning could they have, especially now? In any case tomorrow's flight had been determined by events that happened long before. Where? In the Ukraine? In the Caucasus? In Soviet concentration camps? The devil himself couldn't answer that question. Well, my conscience was clear at least in one respect: I had never caused any hurt to the people I met during my wanderings. Perhaps if anything I had done more good than was expected in those troubled and self-serving times. And what about the political question? From a 'general' point of view, how did my conduct in the past year appear? At this point I experienced a complete loss of interest in this process of self-analysis. I noticed the sky in the east begin to grow light and at the same time became conscious of the dull echoes of artillery fire in the same direction.

Jumping off the wagon, I yelled as loudly as I could, 'Everybody up! Time to get off!'

22. WESTWARD

OUR group consisted of six men, seven women, and two children, one of whom was fifteen years old. This was a girl, Nadya, the daughter of the old book-keeper, Ivan Ivanovich. The other child was our Nina, who was now eight.

There were two genuine military men in the group, the Cossack captain and the retired colonel, Michael Petrovich. I could hardly be considered military, in spite of my Cossack shirt with the big, un-Germanic-looking shoulder straps and the revolver in my belt. Of the women, two were over sixty-five: Zina's mother, and the Cossack captain's mother-in-law, a grumpy old woman with an unpleasant character.

Someone always led Fritz. At first it was the colonel and the Cossack captain, but later the others began to take their turn, including Igor and me. The wagon was heavily laden and Fritz had a hard time of it in spite of the good road. For this reason no one was allowed to ride save on the level stretches. Usually everybody walked, stringing out before and behind Fritz for half a mile.

The Cossack captain had by far the most baggage, and I turned out to have the least. I made a remark to the captain about the amount of junk he was taking along, but he replied that he hoped to get another horse along the way, although how he was going to 'get' one he did not explain.

We left Vienna before sunrise and skirting the suburbs, where small groups of people were erecting barricades under police supervision, we took the Krems road, deserted at that hour.

Fritz strained with all his might. He was a good Austrian horse, used to hard work. We had bought him for one pound sterling in gold, the coin having been obtained from Ivan Ivanovich, who hoarded money. In all fairness I must say that he charged us only three-quarters of the black market rate for the coin.

By about eight o'clock a lot of people had appeared on the road. Refugees who had been spending the night at various places along the way were now setting out again. We passed some of them; others passed us. There were almost no cars. About half the travellers were journeying as we were, on foot with their baggage on a wagon. The other half had no need of a wagon because they had taken nothing with them. There were a few who rode in comparative comfort, seated on wagons. These were Germans, probably Bauerführer and other officials, who were too intimately tied up with the Hitler regime to risk staying behind.

It was a colourful crowd. There were many foreign workers, among them Russians and Ukrainians, and others of more intellectual background, speaking Polish, Serbian, Bulgarian, and Russian. For some reason I thought of the numerous Ministers who had fled from the countries allied to Hitler, Rumania, Hungary, and Bulgaria, as well as from the pro-Nazi movements in Yugoslavia. I had met many of them in the Hotel Imperial in Vienna: Horia Sima, Salaczi, the grey-bearded Tsankov, Nedich. One day the Croatian Ante Pavelich had appeared there and disappeared the next. Where were they now? Probably already in Salzburg, in Innsbruck, in Switzerland, while their countrymen were measuring the highways of Austria with their feet.

My thoughts turned to Vlasov. The last reports were that the two divisions of the R.O.A. were moving to Prague from Ulm in Württemberg. What for? No one knew. In the last communiqué of the German command was a report that 'an R.O.A. unit under the command of Colonel Sakharov was thrown into action on the Oder front . . . the operation was a great success and the enemy was thrown back', and 'a large number of deserters from the Red Army went over to the R.O.A. ranks during the action'. Had it really happened that way? In any case, it no longer had any significance. The last cards in the great game had been laid on the table a long time ago, and there was nothing left but for Hitler to pay his losses. It was true that he himself did not admit defeat, and on the radio he and Goebbels still spoke of victory and of the terrible secret weapon which was to ensure it; but now even the most fanatic of Hitler's followers did not take this sort of statement seriously.

By evening we reached a small town on the banks of the Danube, having walked 20 miles during the day. We tried several dozen houses before we found one where we were allowed to spend the night in the kitchen. The attitude of the Germans toward us had improved in these last weeks of the Reich's existence. Many of them were probably brooding on the swift justice which would come to them as members of the super-race.

I got the whole group up very early, and while Fritz was being harnessed I managed to run downtown for some supplies. In the Verpflegungstelle nobody expressed the slightest doubt of my right to draw military rations. My documents were in order, and no one seemed surprised at my costume. Some men dressed entirely in civilian clothes seemed to be drawing rations there.

The second day was like the first. The same crowd was on the road, headed west as before. We passed several columns of Russian prisoners of war. They were moving without guards at route step, without baggage of any kind, and seemed to be in a gay mood. I talked to some of them. They were part of a group which had come a long way, from somewhere near Breslau.

'We just keep walking, friend, while our strength holds out,' said an elderly soldier, wearing worn-out boots and no hat. 'We've been on the road for three weeks now. We've been through Slovakia and Bohemia, and now we're footing it through Austria.'

'Where are you headed?' I asked him.

'God alone knows. Somebody said Munich. They say the Americans will be there soon. That's why we're going there.'

'Want to go to America, eh, Pop?'

'Might go there, too, why not? People live in America, too,' he laughed. 'Only, my boots are ripped. I'm afraid they won't last all the way to America. Our boys, the younger ones, have promised me a new pair. They say they'll take them off some farmer around here. They're rich here, they have a lot of everything!'

'Where's your home, Pop?'

'It's a long way from here, my dear friend, on the Volga. It will soon be four years since I left home. Two years at the front and two as a prisoner.'

'Was it hard?'

'Hard, son, very hard. A lot of us have been buried in that time. When we defended Moscow in '41 a lot of the boys got it there, an awful lot. The Germans destroy a division, but Marshal Zhukov, may God give him health, sends in another one to take its place. They destroy it; he sends still another. Sometimes a division throws the Germans back only 200 paces and gets used up, but Marshal Zhukov, he's a man of character, he advances again. Most of those divisions were Siberian. That's where they found their graves.'

'Still, Moscow was saved,' I remarked.

'That's right, we saved it, can't say anything against that,' the old man agreed heartily. 'They did right. But they say that a million of our boys died there, the best and the youngest. Maybe Moscow shouldn't have been defended at all, if it cost so many lives. It's such a pity. They say that under the Tsar, when the French were marching on Moscow, the generals were careful with the soldiers and saved the army by letting Moscow go. Of course, there's a lot more people in Russia now. A million more or less, what's the difference?'

'Maybe so,' I said. 'But the ones that have to die don't like it now any more than they did then; it will always make a difference to them.'

'That's right, son. A man has only one life. Sometimes it's a lousy one, but it's still a life. God damn that Moscow anyway!' he shouted quite unexpectedly.

'How's that?'

'All the misery is coming from Moscow now. In the whole war they couldn't find a single bomb to knock off Stalin, may the devils eat him and all his filth!'

'Why do you think that would do any good?' I asked him.

'As if everyone doesn't think so! You think that way yourself. How

can anyone think differently? Look, the war is over. Every man goes
back to his own home, the French, the English, they'll all go home,
I'm sure. And we, as if forsaken by God, have to run somewhere, God
knows where. Why? Look what I have lost if I go to America or somewhere. My old woman is at home; I've got three sons in the army, maybe one of them is still alive. I've got a daughter, grandchildren. But
I'm going. I'm going because although I'm fifty-five I don't want to
die. I spent five years in a concentration camp, son, I was sent there as
a kulak. I had two cows and two horses, so they called me a kulak. I
finished my term before the war, but they wouldn't let me go home.
They settled me in Kazakhstan and ordered me to work in a mine.
What kind of a miner am I when I spent my whole life, and my father
and grandfather before me, ploughing the soil? Let the others believe
what they want, but I know. The damned Bolsheviks will never forgive
us háving been prisoners of the Germans. And I believe that there was
an order to consider all prisoners of war traitors to the fatherland. Has
anybody ever heard of such a thing before?'

He walked beside me without looking at me. Two other younger
prisoners who had been listening to our talk were also silent. Then one
of them said, 'No, there won't be any salvation for us, not in that
Munich and not in America. Because Stalin has acquired great power;
he commands in America too. They'll give us back to him, I feel it in
my heart.'

The other nodded. 'That's right,' he said. 'We should find a place
here somewhere, before Munich, where we can stay. Go to work for
some farmer and hang on here. Let's look around, Vanka, before it's
too late. Let's walk another three days to get farther away from the
"comrades" and then leave the column. Yesterday there were forty
men missing already.'

The prisoners in front stopped for a rest. I said good-bye to my
companions, giving them all the tobacco I had in my pocket and
wishing them luck.

We passed the ruins of Krems. It began to rain. It took us several
hours to find shelter, in the barn of a farm. We were wet to the bone.
While the others were changing and trying to dry themselves out over
a small iron stove, I went to the house with my radio and asked permission to plug it in. Having tuned in to an English station, I soon heard
the latest news: Germany was cut in two. The last resistance was
concentrated on the Oder. Vienna was surrounded. Soviet troops had
reachéd the Danube west of the city. I questioned the owner of the
house, who said that he had heard firing on the other side of the river
during the night, and it was not known whether the Germans or the
Russians were there at the moment.

When the rain had stopped and we set out once more, I kept looking
at thé other bank of the river, thinking that maybe there, a half mile

away, were our countrymen, and no worse fate could happen to us than to fall into their hands.

We conferred as we walked. I reported the latest news and the Cossack captain became very excited.

'If that's the case, we've got to find a new road, somewhere north. If the Reds are on the other bank they can cross with no trouble at all and then we're kaput.'

Michael Petrovich, the retired colonel, agreed with him.

'I know this region. In about three miles there's a detour through the mountains. The road isn't so hard, and we'll make better time there because there won't be a crowd. We won't get back to the river until Linz.'

We decided to take the mountain road. In a little while the colonel was proven right: the road divided and we took the right fork. There was no crowd, but our Fritz's task became a great deal harder. We all had to help him on the steep inclines. We decided to spend the night in a small village beyond a military airport.

While we were having supper I said to the captain, 'It's a tough road and the horse is using up its last strength. You promised to find another one. If you don't, we'll never get to Salzburg.'

'All right,' he said. 'I'll take some money and go look for one. There are a lot of horses here in the village, and some of the refugees may be willing to sell.' He set off on his errand.

We lay down on the floor in a row and went to sleep. A roar overhead and a knock at the door waked me. Jumping up, I opened the door and saw the captain.

'Get up, get up!' he shouted. 'American planes, they're going to bomb the airfield. Hurry up! I've hitched up the horses.'

'What, did you find one?' asked Michael Petrovich incredulously.

'Yes, I bought one, a good one. It'll be easy going from now on. Hurry up!'

Everyone was fully awake and on his feet. We trooped out of the yard, the captain leading the horses. The hum of the engines became stronger.

The bombing started just after we had cleared the village. The bombs fell whistling and exploded with deafening roars. The air was in movement all around us.

We had put all the women on the wagon and had to jog to keep up with it. The road ran downhill.

We slackened our pace only half an hour later. The horses were breathing heavily. From the top of the next hill we looked back. Something was burning. It was the village where we had spent the night.

Dawn broke. We decided not to rest until noon. The women took turns sleeping on the wagon, which the two horses now had little trouble in pulling.

It was a bright day. At noon we rested by the side of the road in a quiet spot. A few refugees passed by, but not many. A soldier in uniform came up to us. He was pushing a bicycle with a baby carriage attached to it. He hesitated a minute and then said, 'Excuse me, please. Could you give me something to eat? I haven't eaten for twenty-four hours. I have a child here . . .'

Zina gave him some bread and a piece of meat. He thanked us, and going to the baby carriage took out a little girl, not more than six months old. Then he took a cup, put some water in it, and began to mash up the bread with a spoon. Zina offered him a little sugar and some canned milk. The Austrian was immensely pleased.

'Oh, thank you, thank you very much.' he kept saying. 'Maybe my little girl will live through the trip. I'm going to the Tyrol with her; we have relatives there.'

I went up to the carriage. The baby's face was terribly pale and drawn. She was crying in a thin little voice. Her skin was transparent, her bright blue eyes wide open. I thought to myself that she would never make it to the Tyrol. Having fed her, the soldier gulped the meat and the rest of the bread.

'I'm from Krems,' he told us. 'My wife was killed in the bombing four days ago. Everything we had was destroyed except the bicycle and the baby carriage. They're all I have now.' He got up, put the baby back in the carriage, and began to wheel his bicycle on up the hill.

A few minutes later we started on ourselves.

Night caught us on a particularly desolate and lonely part of the road. There had been no trace of a house for several miles. We were forced to spend the night under the open sky. It was cold; a thick fog wrapped us around, and we all slept badly. The old book-keeper, who had been coughing for the last two days, had finally come down with a bad cold, and we had to put him on the wagon. His daughter Nadya was worried that he might not be able to continue the journey, and begged us not to abandon them on the road. I comforted her and told her that none of us had any intention of doing that.

I was walking with her about 100 paces behind the wagon when suddenly there were cries up ahead. I quickened my pace. The wagon stood in the middle of the road and two Austrians were arguing hotly about something with the Cossack captain. Coming closer, I gathered that the Austrians considered the horse which the captain had bought that night near the airfield as their own.

'He stole it from us,' cried one of them, a tall stout man, 'this scoundrel in officer's uniform!' He made for the horse and began to unhitch it. His companion helped him. The captain tried to prevent them, protesting that the horse had been bought and paid for. He was having a hard time proving it, since he knew hardly three dozen words of German and possessed no papers of any kind on the deal. I broke into the conversation, but the Austrians refused to listen and became more furious every minute. Suddenly I became so angry myself that I almost lost my self-control. I whipped out my small revolver and fired a shot into the air, yelling for the men to get away from the horse immediately. But they turned out to be no cowards. The tall one pulled a revolver twice as big as mine out of his pocket. The captain got frightened and began trying to persuade me to calm down and let them have the horse.

'What do you mean, give it back, damn you?' I yelled at the captain. 'Did you buy it or didn't you?'

'I did buy it, for 3,000 marks,' he answered.

'From whom?'

'I didn't ask the man's name. What do you expect, anyway?'

'Did you get any kind of receipt?'

'No.'

The Austrians were looking at us with curiosity. One of them kept on unhitching the horse.

'Can you prove the horse is yours?' I asked the captain.

'It's mine, I bought it, damn it! But we can't defend it against these bastards and we'll have to give it up.'

'Listen, I'm telling you for the last time, if that horse is yours, we'll find some way of keeping it. There are soldiers passing by all the time and they'll help us. I'll go for help right away. But if the horse is not yours, they'll have the right to hang you on the nearest tree for horse stealing! Is that clear?'

'Well, the hell with them! Let my money and my horse go! Let them take their damned horse!'

I had no more doubts as to the ownership of the horse.

When the Austrians had taken the horse and gone, roundly cursing us all, I said to the captain, 'Tonight we'll be out on the big road by the Danube again, and you'll have to find some new arrangements for yourself. Fritz can't pull a load like this.'

That is what was done. When we got to the shore road again we took half of poor Fritz's load off the wagon and left the captain, his wife, and his mother-in-law to find new means of transportation. The captain promptly went into a tavern, bought himself a handcart, sold most of his cargo, and continued on foot. His wife kept screaming at him and his mother-in-law even offered to use her fists on him.

We did not see them again. Everyone supported my decision and was indignant at the captain's conduct.

Before long we reached Linz and crossed to the right bank of the Danube. Keeping in touch with the war situation on the radio, we knew that the Soviet troops had been held up soon after taking Vienna and were no longer a direct threat to us. At Linz we split up. Zina, her mother, her daughter, and I boarded the train for Salzburg, taking some of the baggage with us. The others, under the leadership of Michael Petrovich and Igor, set out for Salzburg the old way, with the wagon carrying a much lighter load.

The train was packed with soldiers, and we had a hard time finding places. For the first time I heard German soldiers and officers damning Hitler and the war. But even now there were still some who defended the Third Reich. One of them, a wounded soldier apparently, who was covered with decorations including the Ritterkreuz on his neck, was silent for a long time while the others tore into the German leadership, and then suddenly became hysterical.

'Shut up, you cowards and bastards! The Fatherland is dying because of you! The Führer led you from one victory to another. You stuffed yourselves, you drank, you raped, and sent bales of your loot back to your brides! You were happy and you always shouted "Heil Hitler!" And now when our country is perishing, thanks to the treachery of our allies and some of our generals, you yell, no, you hiss, that the Führer has led us to a dead end, that we're all finished; you surrender to the Americans after the first shot, and you still have the nerve to wear military uniforms! I've always said and will say to the end of my days, "Heil Hitler!" ' The man trembled all over as he poured this out. Nobody answered him.

In a low voice I began to talk to the infantry captain sitting next to me. He turned out to have been born in Latvia and had been through the whole Russian campaign. We changed to Russian so that the hysterical soldier opposite us would not understand what we said.

'Let heroes like that one criticize us,' the captain said, 'but after all we should admit our failure some time, if only at the end of the war. Of course there was a time when we all felt ourselves to be heroes, when the whole of Europe from the Atlantic Ocean to the Volga belonged to us. But that time is gone, and no power in the world, no secret weapon, can change the situation. It's too late. There's nothing left for us to do except surrender. The diplomats in Berlin have always been bad. There hasn't been an outstanding figure there since Bismarck. The only diplomacy they know there is the diplomacy of the fist. It's our fault that we missed the moment when a separate peace could have been made with the Anglo-Americans.'

'But wasn't such a peace offered and refused?'

'Yes, because it was offered not by diplomats but by corporals. They are not all idiots in London and Washington. Churchill at least understands that the victory in this war belongs exclusively to Stalin. Sooner or later after the war he'll take over all of Europe. A separate peace was impossible, that's true, but at least he might have organized our defeat. We might have made it easy for the British to take Greece by invasion, we might have handed the Balkans and Poland to them and prevented your countrymen from coming into Germany. We might have saved our country from their revenge, but none of this did we do.'

'I don't think anything like that would have been possible,' I answered. 'In the Allied agreements it must have been decided who would occupy the Balkans and who would get what part of Germany. England couldn't have broken those agreements.'

'Bunk. Churchill is a realistic politician and saving Europe from Communist seizure means more to him than any piece of paper. But it's all useless now. We've lost the war with a bang, and now we've got to get ready to pay off. The surrender will come any day now and then it will be every man for himself. I would fix myself up, but this uniform makes it hard.'

'That's no problem, it seems to me. Your uniform isn't glued to you. You should be able to get rid of it.'

'That's not so easy. Right now the military police are being very energetic about rounding up deserters, although nobody can understand why.'

A thought flashed through my head.

'Would you like to change clothes? It happens that I need a uniform.'

'Why do you need a uniform, for God's sake?' The captain was very surprised.

'I'm on my way to Italy, with military documents but no uniform. They might hold me up on the border. I have about a dozen friends with me whom I have to get into Italy. A uniform would come in very handy.'

'Can you give me any kind of Russian documents?' the captain asked. 'I can speak Russian fluently, as you can see.'

'As many as you want. I've got all the necessary equipment, typewriter, forms, seals.'

'Fine, we'll get it all done in Salzburg.'

Leaving Zina and her family at the Salzburg station, I went with the captain, although Zina was afraid that this might be a trick and tried to persuade me not to. The captain took me to a friend's apartment, and there we promptly changed clothes. I gave him a certificate on the forms of the committee's branch in Vienna, so that the Germans would not take him for a deserter.

'Well, now I'm an Ostarbeiter,' said the captain, shaking hands with me. 'I'm going to murder the German language and await my liberators from the east.'

On the outskirts of Salzburg the three women and I found the barracks at which we were supposed to meet the others. We left our baggage there and went to town to have dinner. Then we began to look for General Kramer's headquarters. The first thing we saw when we found it was two R.O.A. sentries at the door. They refused to let the women through, but my captain's uniform stood me in good stead.

With a bold step I entered the building which housed the offices, and in the very first room I met one of Kramer's friends and helpers, Colonel Zolotov. His eyes popped when he saw me.

'What you? We were all sure that you had stayed in Vienna to greet the Soviets. And in uniform too! So you decided to run for it after all.'

'I came here to see the general and find out how things are going with you.'

I took a few steps toward the door on which there was the sign 'Chief of Staff of the Separate Corps of the R.O.A.' The colonel jumped up and tried to bar my way. I dodged him and walked into the office. Kramer was sitting at a desk in full general's uniform, talking to an aide. Upon seeing me he raised his eyebrows very high.

'Hello! I'm glad to see you. Have you been here long?'

'I haven't been here long and I'm not staying. I'm just passing through. I came in to say hello.'

'Wait, wait!' The general jumped up. 'You're in uniform! And a captain at that! That's amazing! What kind of a masquerade is this, anyway?'

'Oh, General, is there any point in noticing such trifles? In these times everyone amuses himself as he can. I, for instance, love masquerades. You probably love farces. How are things with the corps? Have you recruited a lot of soldiers?'

Kramer frowned. 'Everything here is going excellently, excellently! It's possible that in a month's time our corps will go into action. And where are you bound, if it isn't a secret?'

'It is a secret, General, a deep secret. I'm on a special mission from the High Command of the German Army. At present I'm on my way to Geneva, and then to other places. I'm sorry, but I have no right to discuss the details.'

The general was obviously in doubt whether to believe me or not. Apparently he considered me capable of anything. In any case he adopted a friendly tone and began to tell me about his personal affairs, avoiding the subject of the corps of which he was chief of staff.

After half an hour's conversation we said goodbye. In the corridor I bumped into Nikolai Ayrov, who had left Vienna a couple of days before we had. He was in civilian clothes and cursing loudly. Taking his arm, I left the building with him.

'Aren't you in uniform yet?' I asked. 'How come? I'm sure they could find a suitable job for you here around the headquarters.'

'The hell with all of them!' he said. 'They've started a side show here! The staff gets bigger every day; they salute and call each other "excellency". But in the corps itself there are only 100 officers – all White emigrants from Serbia – and two soldiers. You saw them standing at the gate. The commander, a friend of our Kramer, sits in his hotel lobby all day and receives callers. He's smart and sly. He's in civilian clothes. He says he hasn't accepted command of the corps yet, that he's waiting for instructions from Vlasov.'

'What do you mean to do now?' I asked him.

'We're going to Munich in about three days. Here it's still dangerous, the Soviets may still get here. Kramer has a car ready for him at the back door day and night. What about you?'

'I'm going to Italy. And my advice to you is to come with us. It will be better there when everything goes to hell.'

'No, I'm not going to Italy. Our friends the Cossacks have distinguished themselves so much there fighting the partisans that every Russian will have to avoid Italy for a long time to come. The partisans will be in charge long after the end of the war. They'll take care of all the Cossacks, and it wouldn't be too good for us, either. It's better to go west.'

'No, the south is better. With Italy considered allied to the Americans and British there won't be an occupation there and life will be easier than in other places,' I insisted. The conversation led to nothing; each of us stuck to his own opinion. We set out for our barracks, near which was the wagon belonging to Ayrov's group.

On the evening of the next day Fritz arrived together with Michael Petrovich and the others. Lying on the floor on straw pallets, we discussed the next part of our journey. Suddenly I became aware that Ayrov's propaganda had taken effect on the members of my group. All of them voted to join with the other group and set out for Munich in a solid front, with two wagons. Zina was a particularly vehement defender of this point of view.

'In times like these,' she reasoned, 'it's particularly important to be among one's friends, among one's own people. In Munich there will be about 50 of us, all of whom know each other well and will always be willing to help each other. That's the most important thing of all.'

Igor observed strict neutrality. He was willing to go in either direction, finding reasons for and against each of the alternatives. The argument went on and on until it was midnight.

Tired of repeating my reasons, I announced decisively, 'Fine. Go to Munich. I'm going to Italy as I said before. And I'm going tomorrow, because I want to have as much time as possible to get south out of the northern regions where the Cossacks have been operating. The Americans have already reached the Po Valley. I'll have to hurry.'

'Well, go ahead, and we'll go to Munich,' said Zina. 'We'll all be together and you'll be all alone.'

'I'm not standing in your way; the sooner the better,' said I, having the last word and pulling the blanket over my head.

Upon waking up in the morning I collected my small amount of baggage and threw out a few things that I could do without. After breakfast I began to take leave of my friends. However, they had apparently talked things over among themselves and changed their minds again, because after a weak attempt to persuade me not to part company with the others Igor suddenly said, 'The hell with it, we're going to Italy with you. We've got a good little group, better than any. We've travelled through the whole of Russia and half of Europe together; this is no time to part company.'

Zina was silent. Michael Petrovich and two others were still for going to Bavaria with Ayrov. Our group now consisted of seven, the Gorsky family, Ivan Ivanovich and Nadya, and myself. We decided to leave Fritz with Michael Petrovich, since our road lay across the mountains, where there was still snow and the going would be rough. In addition, there was no point in travelling with a horse when the trains were still running. We were not passionate lovers of hiking.

There were many reasons why we had to hurry. The bombings were still going on and railroad communications might be cut at any time. Therefore, after a farewell dinner and saying goodbye to those who preferred to remain in Germany, we took our things to the station and left for the south that same evening.

I think that those who stayed were very uncertain as to the correctness of their decision, inwardly agreeing with many of my arguments. I had no doubts at all. I was sure that the road I had chosen was the best of those that remained to us.

EPILOGUE

THERE WAS SOMETHING symbolic in our crossing into Italy. German uniforms were everywhere but officers and men knew that the game was up and displayed little of the self-confidence we had become so accustomed to in the last three years. The once invincible army was streaming north along winding mountain roads and nobody questioned us, strange as our troop must have looked, hitchhiking our way southwards. The World of the German was disintegrating before our eyes. Not being part of it, we could observe the collapse with detachment.

During our brief sojourn in Trento, which we reached after a few amusing and even risky episodes, we passed under the Allied rule as a small British unit occupied the city without firing a shot. Having resumed our journey, this time as refugees from the Nazis, we eventually reached Genoa. Everything we encountered was unfamiliar but the adjustment to life in this dazzlingly colorful, enchanting country was accomplished with no difficulty at all.

I grew to love Italy, which I came to know well in the next two years, traversing it in every direction as I made my living by petty smuggling and blackmarket operations just sufficient to permit me to live outside the refugee camps. There was little money, sometimes none at all, but that did not matter in the least. Life was easy and independent and full of small adventures, nonetheless exciting because they were small.

As normality began to take hold, beggars like myself started looking across the ocean for an opportunity to start a new life. By the will of fortune I came to America but could have landed in Australia or Brazil just as well. With the arrival in New York yet another page of my life opened.

The great charm of life in the United States was in my feeling that I was no longer a foreigner, a feeling I had never had before, even in Russia. As I grew wise in the ways of this country, I learned that this feeling was not quite well-founded, that although all Americans were equal, some were more equal than the others. This discovery did not depress me. In the sea of conformity there was plenty of diversity to satisfy my requirements as I continued to follow my own path, jealously guarding the most prized possession man can have, his independence. For it is in the clashes with one's environment rather than in a happy dissolution in it that excitement of living is found, and that ideas and interests and truly worthwhile associations most fruitfully develop.

Yet colorful as my life has been, I am not going to describe it because an effort at remembering the past takes something away from the present. And those who enjoy living today would not want to part with any of it.

DATE			